LISTENING TO MOVIES

LISTENING TO MOVIES

■ ■ ■

The Film Lover's Guide to Film Music

FRED KARLIN

Foreword by Leonard Maltin

SCHIRMER BOOKS
An Imprint of Macmillan Publishing Company
New York

Maxwell Macmillan Canada
Toronto

Maxwell Macmillan International
New York   Oxford   Singapore   Sydney

Schirmer Books
An Imprint of Macmillan Publishing Company
866 Third Avenue
New York, NY 10022

Maxwell Macmillan Canada, Inc.
1200 Eglinton Avenue East, Suite 200
Don Mills, Ontario M3C 3N1

Macmillan Publishing Company is part of the Maxwell Communication Group of Companies.

Library of Congress Catalog Card Number: 93–14304

Printed in the United States of America

printing number
1   2   3   4   5   6   7   8   9   10

Library of Congress Cataloging-in-Publication Data
Karlin, Fred.
    Listening to movies : the film lover's guide to film music / Fred
Karlin.
       p. cm.
    Includes bibliographical references and index.
    ISBN 0-02-873315-0
    1. Motion picture music—History and criticism.   I. Title.
ML2075.K37   1994   93–14304
781.5′42—dc20   CIP
                                                                      MN

The paper used in this publication meets the minimum requirements of American National Standard for Information Sciences—Permanence of Paper for Printed Library Materials. ANSI Z39.48-1984. ∞™

To Ray Wright—my friend, teacher,
and colleague

RAYBURN WRIGHT (1922–1990)

In 1970 Ray gave up an active life as a conductor/
arranger and film composer in New York City to teach
at the Eastman School of Music. He became head of
the Jazz Studies and Contemporary Media program,
and co-chair of the Conducting and Ensembles Department. Through his willingness to share his experience
and knowledge, he has influenced many composers and
film music students over the years, creating a legacy we
will never forget.
Photo credit: Louis Ouzer

Contents

Foreword by Leonard Maltin   *ix*

Preface   *xi*

Acknowledgments   *xiii*

PART ONE   HOW IT'S DONE

Chapter One ■ Planning the Score   3

Chapter Two ■ Composing the Music   17

Chapter Three ■ Recording and Mixing   42

PART TWO   THE MUSIC

Chapter Four ■ What to Listen For   67

Chapter Five ■ Evaluating a Score   85

Chapter Six ■ A Closer Look at Eight Films   92

Chapter Seven ■ Reviews   145

Chapter Eight ■ The Silents and Other Special Films   154

PART THREE   HOLLYWOOD

Chapter Nine ■ The Studio System   175

Chapter Ten ■ Freelancing   196

PART FOUR   SHOW BUSINESS

Chapter Eleven ■ The Oscars   207

Chapter Twelve ■ Songs and Soundtrack Records   221

PART FIVE   A SHORT CHRONOLOGY

Chapter Thirteen ■ Decade by Decade   237

PART SIX   PERSONAL PROFILES

Chapter Fourteen ■ How They Get Started   249

Chapter Fifteen ■ The Composers and Their Credits   257

Appendix A ■ *Academy Award Original Score Nominees and Winners*   *312*

Appendix B ■ *Soundtrack Shops and Vendors*   *320*

Filmography   *323*

A Selective Annotated Bibliography   *377*

End Notes   *389*

Index   *405*

Foreword

I would never call myself an expert on movie music, though I've always been a fan. Having read Fred Karlin's book, however, I now understand more about the process—and the significance—of film composing than I ever dreamt I might.

Most educated film buffs probably know that a film score must be precisely timed; many of us have heard that scores are composed under a great deal of pressure. It isn't hard to extrapolate from stories of artists in other media that inspiration is the single biggest challenge in creating a score.

Listening to Movies, however, amplifies and clarifies each of those points, and dozens more. By drawing on first-hand experiences of working composers, past and present, Karlin strips away layers of theoretical pomp and gets down to basics. At first, his list of categories and subcategories may seem clinical, but in fact, they define and identify every facet of this formidable field, and enable even a layman-reader like me to follow along without a moment of confusion.

I learned many things from this book, large and small: that Spock's theme in the original "Star Trek" series was played on a bass guitar (and played, it turns out, by one of my favorite jazz musicians, Barney Kessel) . . . that the great Erich Wolfgang Korngold never used a stopwatch, but relied on instinct (and luck) to time his scores . . . that some composers were notorious procrastinators, while Franz Waxman once managed to score three

pictures at the same time, dividing his day into separate thirds!

Having the opportunity to examine eight notable film scores in detail is especially rewarding—even for an amateur like me. I've always loved Korngold's music for *The Adventures of Robin Hood,* but I've never had a chance to analyze it, cue by cue, until now. (I also never realized, until Karlin points it out, that Warner Bros. emphasized this majestic score in its final sound mix, so sound effects never drowned it out.)

What impresses me the most about *Listening to Movies* is its extraordinary range, embracing everything from scores for silent films to the show-biz aspects of composing in Hollywood. Many film buffs, and music enthusiasts, will no doubt turn to it as a reference work as well, thanks to several useful indices.

Film music was never meant to stand on its own, but to serve instead as part of a greater whole. In recent years, that definition has been bent, even broken, as movie scores have come into their own in recordings and even concert performances. It has also been the subject of a number of scholarly and informative books. Fred Karlin's contribution to the field certainly ranks as one of the best, and to my way of thinking, one of the most thorough on a subject many of us cherish, but few of us really know.

Leonard Maltin

Preface

It is almost impossible to make movies without music. Movies need the cement of music. I've never seen a movie better without it. Music is as important as the photography.
—*Bernard Herrmann, composer*

I have written *Listening to Movies: The Film Lover's Guide to Film Music* with the hope of illuminating the world of film music in Hollywood and offering some suggestions for understanding music in movies. There are no technical prerequisites for enjoying film music or reading this book—you don't have to read music, play an instrument, or have any previous knowledge of music. Just the everyday experience of watching films in theaters and on television and videotapes is enough. Most of us come to this study well prepared with a lifetime of viewing and listening experience. The more you really listen, the more you will hear, and this book can guide your understanding of what to listen for. This book won't teach you how to score a motion picture, of course, but I hope it will give you a greater understanding and appreciation of your favorite films and soundtracks. Although I have limited my discussion to music in theatrical motion pictures, the same principles outlined here can and should be applied to the music heard in television films.

I am also hopeful that everyone who enjoys films and film music will appreciate the wide range of musical styles and attitudes used in film scoring now and in the past. There is no one style of score that is exemplary, but there are exemplary scores for *specific* films. *Jaws* could have been scored in different ways, as it surely would have been if ten scores had been created by ten composers selected throughout film music history. But the score that John Williams created was without question exemplary in the way it works for that film. Although I have found the symphonic scores from the thirties through the eighties to be particularly useful in drawing attention to the various elements of film

scoring, I am equally interested in dramatic electronic scores like Giorgio Moroder's *Midnight Express* (1978), jazz scores like Johnny Mandel's *I Want to Live!* (1958), and contemporary scores like Thomas Newman's *The Player* (1992).

I have freely interrelated comments made throughout the history of film music in order to create ongoing dialogues between generations. As you will see, many things haven't changed for composers over the years. Constants include intense time pressures, the quest for excellence, and the desire for improved communication with filmmakers. The scores of many composers are referenced throughout the book, with films from the thirties juxtaposed to those released decades later. Eight films are examined in greater detail in Chapter 6.

I have excluded any detailed discussion of musicals and songs, which are the sole subject of many other books. For the reader wishing to explore this aspect of music in films, there is a separate "Musicals" listing in the Bibliography. Similarly, it is well beyond the scope and length of this book to include a separate study of foreign films, although many composers from around the world will be found herein, including French composers Georges Delerue and Maurice Jarre; Italian composers Nino Rota and Ennio Morricone; and many British composers, including John Barry, John Addison, and Richard Rodney Bennett. Many other non-American composers and a sampling of their credits are listed in Chapter 15.

I have drawn on the words of composers, filmmakers, creative artists, and technicians who have collaborated throughout the history of films. Included are excerpts from the 49 new interviews I conducted specifically for this book. I am deeply indebted to the following interviewees for their significant contribution: Gillian Anderson, Buddy Baker, Bill Boston, Paul Brickman, Matthias Büdinger, Jon Burlingame, Allen Cohen, Bill Conti, Sandy De Crescent, Randy Edelman, Danny Elfman, Bobby

Fernandez, Terri Fricon, Arthur Hamilton, John Hammell, Grover Helsley, James Newton Howard, Dick Hyman, Mark Isham, Ralph Ives, Michael Kamen, Louis and Annette Kaufman, David Kraft, Richard Kraft, Miles Kreuger, Randall D. Larson, Clifford McCarty, Greig McRitchie, David Newman, Randy Newman, Thomas Newman, Marni Nixon, Rachel Portman, David Raksin, Nick Redman, Mike Rubin, Marc Shaiman, Steven C. Smith, Herbert Spencer, Armin Steiner, Ford A. Thaxton, Tony Thomas, Robert Townson, Shirley Walker, Kenneth Wannberg, John Waxman, Glenn Wooddell, and Hans Zimmer.

I have also utilized oral history interviews from the American Film Institute, from Yale University, and from Southern Methodist University. Most of these were taken by Irene Kahn Atkins during the 1970s. Other illuminating first-person accounts used in this book include those by Miklós Rózsa, Dimitri Tiomkin, and Henry Mancini in their autobiographies; by Bernard Herrmann in Stephen C. Smith's biography; by Jerry Goldsmith, Hans J. Salter, and others in Tony Thomas' two excellent books on film music; and interviews found in several journals including *Film Music Notes, Films in Review,* Elmer Bernstein's *Film Music Notebook,* and the ongoing quarterly film music magazine *Soundtrack!,* published by Luc Van de Ven (which is required reading for anyone interested in keeping current on the world of film music). I am especially grateful that this documentation exists, and that there is a growing interest in continuing the fine work in this area.

F. K.

Acknowledgments

To the greatest extent possible, the story of film music in Hollywood is told here through the words of those who have been there. Some of the composers quoted herein have already been inducted into a hypothetical hall of fame by virtue of their contributions to the history and legacy of film music, while others continue to develop their own personal voices with each new film they score. The points of view of journalists, authors, music editors, agents, record executives, and others are represented here as well, for film music also is the heart of their daily existence. These men and women have been cited in the Preface, and I extend my heartfelt gratitude to them here as well.

MUSIC

Most people never have the opportunity to see the handwritten manuscript of film composers and orchestrators. My grateful appreciation to the motion picture studios and their music publishing companies who gave their permission to reprint short excerpts from their scores. Thanks to ABC Distribution Company, a division of Capital Cities/ABC Video Enterprises; Columbia Pictures; Famous Music Corporation; Sidney Herman; Al Kohn; Jay Morganstern; Rebecca Olshanski; Paramount Pictures; Raul Perez; Jack Rosner; June Shelley; Sony Pictures Entertainment; Georgett Studnicka; Warner Bros.; Warner/Chappell Music, Inc.; and Keith Zajic.

Thanks also to the many people at university archives, music libraries, and music preparation services who were so very helpful in making the original music available for my use: Leith Adams; Charles Bell; Bob Bornstein; Emile Charlap; Columbia Pictures Music Library; James D'Arc; Bob Dolan (Valle Music); Danny Franklin; Joel Franklin; Danny Gould; Joe Hench; Lisa Janacua; JoAnn Kane; Suzie Katayama; Stuart Ng; Vic Sagerquist; Martin Silver; Don Tharp; and Jim White.

PHOTOGRAPHS

My special thanks to the studios and their representatives who granted permission to reprint stills from their films: Columbia Pictures; Kathy Lendech; Larry McCallister; Metro Goldwyn Mayer; Paramount Pictures; Joan Pierce; Terry Saevig; Judith Singer; Turner Entertainment Co.; and Warner Bros., all of whom made it possible to illustrate this book with appropriate and enlivening photographs.

Thanks also to many others who helped with the photographs and examples: Academy of Motion Picture Arts and Sciences (hereafter abbreviated AMPAS); Leith Adams; American Museum of the Moving Image; American Society of Composers, Authors, and Publishers (hereafter abbreviated as ASCAP); Bob Badami for his spotting notes; Bill and Dick Bernstein for their timing notes preparation; Albert K. Bender (Max Steiner Memorial Society); Eddie Brandt's Saturday Matinee (in North Hollywood, Calif.); Broadcast Music, Inc. (hereafter abbreviated as BMI); Lester Cohen; Ned Comstock; Kim Dankner; the Larry Edmonds Bookstore (in Hollywood); Camille Fielding; Peter Figen; Terry Geesken; John Hammell; Christopher Husted; Lauren Issoa; Michael Kochman; Ernst W. Korngold; David Kraft; Michael McGehee; Eleanor J. Mish; Tina Morrow; Museum of Modern Art/Film Stills Archives; Martha Ragland; Thomas Newman; Louis Ouzer; Paramount Pictures; Jamie Richardson; Mike Rubin; Warren Sherk; Karen Sherry; Steven C. Smith; Tony Thomas; University of California at Santa Barbara; USC Special Collections; Luc Van de Ven (*Soundtrack!*); Paul Van

Hooff; Marc Wanamaker; John Waxman; Bob Witkowski; and Doris Wright.

Thanks also to Nina Rota for permission to use the photograph of her father, Nino Rota. A special thanks to Gay Wallin and Alexander Courage, who took and preserved so many historically valuable shots; Wayne McCall, who made copies for me as I collected my materials, and reshot the color photos in black and white; and Keith Puccinelli, who created the streamer graphic for a flip-page illustration that will some day be brought to life.

RESEARCH

Many authors, interviewers, and copyright holders gave me their permission to reprint excerpts of their works in this book, and to them I am especially grateful. Others helped me gather the data contained in Chapter 15, "The Composers and Their Credits." Thanks to the American Film Institute and its Louis B. Mayer Library; AMPAS; Gillian Anderson (Music Division, Library of Congress); ASCAP; Rudy Behlmer; Lyn Benjamin and the Kraft-Benjamin Agency; Phil Berk; Elmer Bernstein; BMI; Bill Boston; Lance Bowling; Todd Brabec; Wayne Burgos and the Carol Faith Agency; Ned Comstock; Carol Cullen; *Daily Variety*; Ronald L. Davis; James Doody; June Edgerton; Pam Euwing and the Robert Light Agency; A. Edward Ezor; Leland Faust; Janice Fournier; Ellis Freedman; Stephen M. Fry; Craig Stuart Garfinkle; David Gershenson and Helen T. Gershenson; Charles Goldring; the Gorfaine-Schwartz Agency; William Hamilton; *The Hollywood Reporter*; JASRAC; Marvel Jensen; Carl Johnson; Jo Kelly; Nancy Knutsen; Kristine Krueger; Randall D. Larson; Robin Little; Linda Livingston; Leonard Maltin (for his *Movie and Video Guide*); Lawrence B. Marks and Associates; Brian May; Clifford McCarty; Pat McLaughlin and the Shukat Company; Linda Harris Mehr; Rod Merl; Stan Milander, Cathy Schleussner, Jeff Kaufman, and the Milander

Schleussner Kaufman Agency; Annie Morgan; D. Brent Nelson; Annemarie North; CG O'Connor; Paramount Pictures; Jeannie Pool; Derek Power Co.; André Previn; Vivian Perlus; David Raksin; Jamie Richardson; Doreen Ringer; Miklós Rózsa; Donna Ryan and the Ryan Co.; Sandra M. Saka; Warren Sherk; Daniel Selznick and Selznick Properties, Ltd.; Steven C. Smith; Society for the Preservation of Film Music; George Stevens, Jr.; Patrick Stockstill; Tony Thomas; Luc Van de Ven (*Soundtrack!*); Toru Watanabe; Ridge Walker; John Williams (film music journalist); Glenn Wooddell; and Fred Zinnemann.

Thanks also to Lucas Kendall (*Film Score Monthly*) who made available to me all of his research lists of shops, record companies, and dealers, portions of which are reprinted herein.

VIDEOCASSETTES AND CDs

Thanks very much to Bruce Kimmell and Bay Cities Records; Ed and Gary Suchow, George Curtin, Sherlyn Perkins, and Jack Ward, at Captain Video (Montecito, Calif.); Grover Helsley; Al Lutz and BMG Classics Distribution; Robert Townson and Varèse Sarabande Records; and Brendan and Martha Searls at Video Schmideo (Santa Barbara, Calif.) for helping out with invaluable research materials.

READERS

Thanks to Bob Axelrod (Schirmer Books), who read the manuscript in its earliest stages and offered understanding and support, and to John Milligan and Shelly Lowenkopf who also read the manuscript early on and offered valuable suggestions.

Thanks also to the three reviewers who responded quickly and helpfully to our request for comments on the work in progress. My special thanks to Clifford McCarty, who corrected credits errors and offered his extensive knowledge whenever needed. My loving thanks to my wife, Megan, who went over the final manuscript page by page, and applied her writing expertise and eye for detail so helpfully in her quest for clarity. And a very special thanks to Jonathan Wiener, my editor at Schirmer Books, who offered so many valuable suggestions in shaping and polishing the final draft; and to Maribeth Anderson Payne, then Editor-in-Chief at Schirmer Books, who asked me to write a general interest book about film music.

Finally, many thanks to Leonard Maltin for contributing his enthusiastic Foreword.

PART ONE

HOW IT'S DONE

■ ■ ■

Planning the Score

■ ■ ■

I agonized for over a month, looking for an approach to Logan's Run
[1976]. Once I found it, the music took off like a racehorse.
                                        Jerry Goldsmith, composer

THE SCRIPT: STARTING EARLY

Typically, the composer is asked to read a script
prior to the first meeting. The filmmakers have
been working on their project for a year or two, and
can usually recite the important dialogue as they
watch the film. Although filmmakers often hire a
composer before or during the filming, most of the
time the composer comes onto the project during
the editing. So the script helps familiarize him with
the film.

Some composers like to read the script before
and during the time they compose. "I always ask
for the script," Alex North said in 1988. "For me,
ideas are often triggered by a phrase or line in the

script." In the late thirties and forties, Erich
Wolfgang Korngold would begin composing his
themes while the film was shooting, using the script
as his guide. He thought of the script as if it were
the libretto for an opera, and the Korngold scores
for epic action films like *The Adventures of Robin
Hood* (1938) and *The Sea Hawk* (1940) are very
operatic.

More recently, however, composers have been
nearly unanimous in their concern that they will
make serious misjudgments if they actually begin to
write music solely on the basis of the script. The
problem? A script simply is not the film—it's just a
suggestion of what the film might be. Composer
John Barry says, "You can have preliminary ideas
from the screenplay, but it's the film that actually

counts in the end. . . . The fabric of the picture—the way a movie looks—dictates a lot to you. I love seeing the movie—that's when you make the real decisions."

Working from the script can be especially tricky with regard to pacing. "It can get you in trouble sometimes," says David Shire. "The one thing you *don't* get from the script is the rhythm of the picture; the way it flows and what its momentum is. And that's one of the major things that music precisely should relate to and look into."

Difficulties notwithstanding, some directors like to bring the composer in before production begins. Director Paul Brickman asked Thomas Newman to score *Men Don't Leave* (1990) well before he began filming, hoping to be motivated by the music. Brickman wanted a real two-way connection between his film and the music. "The creation of the music and the instrumentation was going to dictate what I was going to do visually." Director Peter Weir also likes to work that way, and asked Maurice Jarre (with a soft J, rhymes with far) to compose themes for *The Mosquito Coast* (1986) so he could use Jarre's music on the set while he shot the film. Although those themes weren't used in Jarre's final score, they were helpful in establishing the film's atmosphere.

Even though most composers don't like to compose based on a script, they do like to be brought in as early as possible. According to Jarre, "If you have read the script, even if the director and producer make changes, there is still the basic idea. You have the time to think about the film, and if it is a period piece or a picture involving ethnic music, there is plenty of time to do your own research."

SCREENINGS

Occasionally the composer is invited to watch dailies (the footage from the previous day's filming). Since every take selected by the director is screened at the dailies, this can be very tedious. First you see the master shot, which is a long shot with all the action in the scene. Then you see various medium-range and close-up versions of the same scene shot from different angles. Consequently you may find yourself listening to the same two-minute conversation for interminable lengths of time, depending on how much footage the director shot and how much of it he or she wants to have available for editing.

As helpful as it can be for composers to get an early start, watching dailies is generally counterproductive. Dailies dull the composer's emotional response to the edited version of the film by dissipating his first reaction. Without exception, that first reaction is extremely important, because the composer's response during the first screening is a reliable guide to the film's emotional content. This first reaction provides the best gauge as to whether a film is delivering the emotions it promises. Because of this, the rough cut is an ideal time for a composer's first screening. At that stage the film tells the story from beginning to end with most of the elements in place. Final sound effects are still to come; special visual effects will still have to be added (in fact, sometimes the effects are so complicated and take so long to create that the composer doesn't see these until after he has recorded the score); and naturally, more polishing, trimming, and editorial manipulation will be done, but at this point it's possible to watch the film from beginning to end and monitor the entire emotional experience. Later on, after viewing the film many times and studying each sequence, the composer will inevitably be immune to these emotional reactions.

EDITING THE FILM

Bringing a composer in early may actually influence the final editing of the film a bit, depending on the flexibility of the director. It is very typical for a composer to see a music-dependent scene in rough cut and feel it is just the right length only to find the director has cut the scene in half by the time the editing is finished. Then, when temporary music is added, the director may realize that he has shortened the scene too much.

This happens because music needs time to develop, and invariably makes a scene seem shorter. Leaving enough time for the music to make its point can heighten the effectiveness of the film. Even more subtle adjustments for the music can help a composer, especially if a particular emotional moment, or possibly the end of a sequence, is slightly too short. Hans Zimmer scored *A League of Their Own* (1992) for Penny Marshall. "With Penny, there are certain things where I'm going, 'Just give me two more frames here, because that'll just make that a little neater for me.'" Two frames is barely perceptible—a figure of speech. But two *feet* (1⅓ seconds) often makes a difference.

Once the composer and the sound effects team are working with the film, it's not always practical to make even the smallest adjustment, as an editorial change affects not only the composer's timings, but all the editors working on the film—the film editor, as many as a dozen sound effects editors, and the music editors. "It's difficult for everybody," Zimmer adds. "The sound department says, 'Now we've got to change 72 [sound-effects] tracks!' But the whole point is, we are all trying to make the film as good as possible." In reality, changes are often made until the day the scene is scored, and sometimes after that as well.

When Bernard Herrmann worked with Orson Welles on his score for *Citizen Kane* (1941), Welles was willing to reverse the usual directorial priorities to accommodate the music. "The film was so unusual technically that it afforded me many unique opportunities for musical experiment," Herrmann said. "It abounded in montages, which were long enough to permit me to compose complete musical numbers, rather than mere cues to fit them. Mr. Welles was extremely cooperative in this respect, and in many cases cut his film to suit these complete numbers, rather than doing what is ordinarily done—cut the music to suit the film. In the scenes of Kane's newspaper activities, I was able to write a

Orson Welles and Bernard Herrmann at the RKO Studios in 1940 during the scoring of *Citizen Kane* (1941).
Photo courtesy of The Museum of Modern Art/Film Stills Archive (N.Y.)

kind of miniature ballet suite, the various photographic montages being presented in the form of complete little dance numbers of the 1890s, including gallops, polkas, hornpipes, schottisches, etc. . . ."

ROLE MODELS

What's lacking most now is intelligence in approach. . . . The composer isn't usually the person who determines what style of score it's going to be. I think they [listen to possible role models], decide what the score is going to be like, hire a composer who writes like that, and ask him to write something similar.

Richard Kraft, composers' agent

Selecting a piece of music as a role model can be the most effective way for a filmmaker to make his ideas clear. It's a very specific way to communicate. Any music can be used as a role model, depending on the director's taste and musical interpretation of his film.

Here are some examples of music that filmmakers and film composers have actually used as role models:

Classical Music

- *The Planets* (Gustav Holst) for *Star Wars* (John Williams, 1977)
- *Romantic Symphony* (Howard Hanson) for *E.T.* (John Williams, 1982)
- *The Firebird Suite* (Igor Stravinsky) for *Deal of the Century* (Arthur B. Rubinstein, 1983)
- *Salome,* "Dance of the Seven Veils" (Richard Strauss) for *Sunset Boulevard,* Gloria Swanson descending the staircase (Franz Waxman, 1950)
- *Music for Eighteen Musicians* (Steve Reich) for *Risky Business* (Tangerine Dream, 1983)
- *Carmina Burana* (Carl Orff) for many film scores.

Film Music

- *North by Northwest* (Bernard Herrmann) and *First Blood* (Jerry Goldsmith) for *Back to the Future* (Alan Silvestri, 1985)
- *Outland, Alien,* and *Coma* (Jerry Goldsmith) for *Psycho II* (Jerry Goldsmith, 1983)
- *Conan the Barbarian* (Basil Poledouris) for *Total Recall* (Jerry Goldsmith, 1990)
- *Clan of the Cave Bear* (Alan Silvestri) for *Bat 21* (Christopher Young, 1988)
- *Rain Man* (Hans Zimmer) for many film scores
- *Star Wars, Return of the Jedi, The Empire Strikes Back* (John Williams) for many film scores.

Musical *styles* can become role models—traditional southern blues, for example, for the film *Crossroads*

(1986). The styles of classical composers are often used as role models. Elmer Bernstein used Mendelssohn and Elgar as role models for *Trading Places* (1983), and Johnny Mandel used Bach for *Deathtrap* (1982). Pop music and various song styles have had a big influence also.

The composers in the thirties, forties, and fifties drew on familiar classical styles both out of a high regard for the powerful emotional influence these styles would have on the audience and also because in many cases it was the most natural music for them to write. This is still done today. "I try to find a good parallel in a classical piece or a classical style," says Carl Davis, describing his work method, "then I go on my own way. But I always like to have a classical reference. It's almost become my trademark."

When George Lucas met with John Williams to discuss the music for *Star Wars* (1977), his original idea had been to use classical music by Dvořák and Liszt on the final soundtrack. In describing what he was looking for, he also referred to some of the classic film scores, like Max Steiner's *Charge of the Light Brigade* (1936). They agreed on the intention of the music, but Williams was able to convince Lucas that original music would better serve the purpose, and allow for specific thematic development tied into the film's characters. "George made it clear to me that things like direction, speed, and pace were very important, and I took it from there," Williams remembers.

There are times, as in the case of *Star Wars,* when role models can be an extremely effective creative stimulus. Director Billy Wilder used a role model for the famous staircase scene in *Sunset Boulevard* (1950). "All the time we were rehearsing," he said, "we played a recording of Richard Strauss' *Salome,* especially the 'Dance of the Seven Veils,' when Swanson descended the stairs into her final madness. When it came to the actual scoring, I told [Franz] Waxman to give me something just as good or better! That didn't rattle him at all. He did nobly."

TEMP TRACKS

We live now in a film world of preconceived ideas.... If a composer can interpret these ideas in a satisfactory way he's OK, but he may often have better ideas of his own.

John Scott, composer

[The problem is] guys are just cloning the temp scores.

Ford A. Thaxton,
soundtrack record producer

Temp tracks can be really dangerous.
Paul Brickman, director

Director Billy Wilder asked Franz Waxman to use Richard Strauss' "Dance of the Seven Veils" from *Salome* as a role model for his scoring of Gloria Swanson's descent down the staircase at the end of *Sunset Boulevard* (1950).
Photo courtesy of Paramount Pictures
Copyright © 1950, 1992 by Paramount Pictures. All Rights Reserved.

Sometime during the editing process, the musical role models may be mixed onto the soundtrack of the edited film. Since they are considered to be temporary, they are called "temp tracks." A particular scene or sequence may be "temp'd" ("tracked") or more often, the entire film will have a "temp track" consisting of many pieces of music.

Creating temp tracks from role models sounds like a good idea—the director finds pieces of music that appeal to her and also seem to express musically what she feels her film is all about, and then she temp-tracks her film with that music. When the composer sees the film he knows exactly what the director is looking for and what she expects from the music. It seems like this would make for perfect communication. Sometimes it does and sometimes it doesn't. If those role models become the director's predetermined, very specific blueprint for the final score, it can be the kiss of death for originality. Many times the director *expects* the composer to replace his temp track with music that is virtually the same. In these cases, the composer may find himself imitating the temp track to satisfy the director. Creatively, this is stifling.

Like many composers, Randy Edelman has seen this happen. "Every film is temp scored. So I *use*

the temp score. You want to know where they're at. The temp scores are so involved and so intricate, and people spend so much time and money on them now. Of course, they don't want *that*. But they want it to sound *just like* that. And if they have a hot cue in there, boy, you'd better come up with something that sounds like it. If I'm not close to the temp, or I think they're going in the wrong direction, then I tell them. But generally, you've got a good idea where they're going. If they start out with a big religious piece, I'm going to give them a big religious piece."

Even when the temp track isn't exactly imitated, the score will often become generic if the overall sound of the temp track is duplicated too closely. In other words, it won't really be tailored to the specific film, but rather to a certain *type* of film or story. Television scores for one-hour action series are often generic, for example. These scores are interchangeable to a great extent. The score from one episode could easily be used for another episode, or even another series. In features, the score for one Western often sounds as if it could just as effectively accompany another Western.

Realistically, temp tracks themselves can't be very fresh because they are compiled from existing music, and most often from recent high-profile film scores. Composers' agent Richard Kraft has noticed this generic effect countless times in motion pictures. "Half of the equation is 'What are you going to do?' and the other half is *how* you do it. But the '*What* are you going to do?' seems to have gone out the window, and the temp score tends to be a bunch of clichéd ideas put together by a music editor. You're doing a thriller, so you go to the record store and buy a bunch of 'thriller' movie scores. The process of deciding 'What are we going to do in *this* movie?' is gone."

Not every film is unique or original, nor can every film score be one-of-a-kind. "But what's so boring is—they're the same records," Kraft observes. "I mean, everyone owns the same records. . . . They're all on CD, *and* they're using *film* music. I mean, they should be going to something else. I've had cases where composers have done scores based on a temp track, and the temp track was a score *they* had written. So they're now doing a watered-down version of themselves. And it's pointless. At least *Rain Man* [1988] didn't sound like the ten movies that preceded it. It sounded like the ten movies that *followed* it."

I'll listen to the temp music once with the director, just to get an overall feel for what he's looking for . . . but I won't listen to it again. I tend to not go to previews or advance screenings, anything with the temp music. I don't want to hear it.

Danny Elfman, composer

I've changed my attitude over the years, about pre-tracking pictures. It's good to see where a director's going, what's right and what's wrong.

Jerry Goldsmith, composer

Since temp music is one of the director's strongest, clearest ways to communicate, it's usually unwise for a composer to ignore it. But as we have seen, temp tracks can really inhibit original ideas. There are times when ignoring the temp track can be the best solution. Maurice Jarre had difficulty finding his main theme for *Doctor Zhivago* (1965). "David [Lean] did use a temp track for *Doctor Zhivago*. He fell in love with a supposedly old Russian folk song, a very nice piece of music. When I viewed the rushes, he said that he wanted this theme to be incorporated into the score. However, when MGM tried to clarify the copyright situation, it turned out not to be a traditional folk tune, but an original piece of music for which MGM could not get worldwide clearance; so they did not want the theme used.

"When I heard about this decision, I had to start to write something completely new with only a few weeks to go to the recording sessions. Up until then, I had been relaxed because I knew that I was going to use this folk song as the main theme. So when writing a new theme, subconsciously or not, I tried to go around this melody that I had heard so many times before to get the same kind of feel and phrasing.

"Every time I presented a new theme to David, he rejected it and said that I could do better. I wrote four different themes in this time, but none of them was quite right. By this stage, I was not only getting depressed, but also panicking because time was running out. Then, one Friday, David told me to stop work, to stop thinking about the film or the music and go away for the weekend to the beach or mountains, to clear my brain and start afresh on the following Monday. So I did this, which was very hard because of the pressure and with the days running out. Anyway, Monday arrived and I realized that the stupidity was this temporary track. I should try to write something totally different, and I wrote a kind of waltz. After those two days of clearing the brain, in one hour on Monday morning I had found 'Lara's Theme,' which was the opposite of the original temp track."

Most composers like to be flexible in their use of temp tracks. Obviously their creative response can have a considerable effect on the final score. More often than not, though, if the composer remains open to the director's temp, he can benefit greatly, as Jerry Goldsmith has discovered. "I find an intelligent composer will let a director's temp track speak for itself. For example, I just finished *The 'burbs* [1989] with [director] Joe Dante, who temp-tracked the film himself. I must say I got the idea for the whole musical approach from what Joe had tracked. At first I thought he was completely coming from left field, but after studying it, I realized he was dead-on. It was a direction I doubt I'd have taken if I hadn't received that input."

SPOTTING

The hardest thing in scoring is to know when to start and when to stop.

Max Steiner, composer

When the editing is finished, the resultant film is called a "fine cut" and is said to be "locked." At this point the composer, director, producer, film editor, and music editor meet to decide on the placement of music; they "spot" the film. This is called a "spotting session." In those cases where the film continues to be edited almost up to the first day of recording, the film will be spotted at some point near the end of the editing process or when time runs out.

Most composers see the film several times prior to spotting, often on videotape. This allows the composer to get to know the film scene by scene and take notes on possible placement of the music before discussing it with the filmmakers. Bronislau Kaper's work method was typical. "Before I have

any meetings with the director or the producer, I like to run the movie three or four times myself, because if I don't, I'm at a tremendous disadvantage versus people who lived with the movie, who saw every foot 50 times. And they talk about it like clairvoyants. And I talk about it like a man. So I have to know the movie quite well."

Films used to be spotted in a small screening room, with the film projected on a screen. Although it still may be done this way, more often the film is spotted in an editing room, using a flatbed editing machine. The flatbed shows the picture on a small attached screen, and can run several units of magnetic sound film in sync with the picture—dialogue, or dialogue and temp music. Everybody gathers around the machine, which is usually operated by the film editor. Either the projector or the flatbed machine can be stopped and run back and forth as necessary.

It can take as little as three or four hours to spot a film (especially a movie made for television), or as long as two or more days. A full day is not unusual. During this time, whenever a decision is made, the music editor will write down the exact place where music starts. There is a counter on the flatbed (or beneath the screen in a projection room) which indicates how many feet and frames (16 to the foot) any frame is from the beginning of the reel. The music editor makes all her notes based on the footage counter readings (which may be in feet and frames, minutes and seconds, or both). She indicates where the music starts and stops, and notes any important requests the director may make (such as, "I'd like a change in the music on the cut to the shot of the ocean"). At the end of the session, these notes are typed out and become the spotting notes.

There are two goals during a spotting session. The first and most immediate is to determine exactly where the music will start and stop throughout the film. The second is to discuss the function of the music as it pertains to specific scenes, and even specific moments within a scene. Sometimes the music's function is obvious—to amplify the shock and establish terror as the title monster is revealed in *Alien* (1979), for example. But determin-

```
"EDWARD SCISSORHANDS"    MUSIC SPOTTING NOTES    8/7/90


1M1    MAIN TITLE    SCORE    4:30

      Main title/Old Lady tells story/Camera moves up to
house/Edward looks down on the neighborhood below.  Music starts
with yet to be shot main title sequence and continues as the Old
Lady prepares to put the little girl to bed.  The camera slowly
moves out the  window and over the snow covered tract homes up to
the house on the hill as the Old Lady starts to tell the story of
Edward Scissorhands.  The music should give a sense of transition
and that the story is beginning as the picture dissolves to
Edward's POV of the tract without snow and should be out with the
cut to the houses.

1M2    TOM JONES SOURCE    PRERECORD    1:10

      Possible Tom Jones source music for Joyce.

1M3    ORGAN I SOURCE    :45

      Peg skips Esmarelda's house/Esmarelda plays her organ/Peg
decides to try the house on the hill.  Esmarelda's organ music
starts on the exterior of her house as Peg decides to skip this
address.  Music continues through the interior angle of Esmarelda
playing and the cut back to Peg as she returns to her car.  Music
segues to 1M4 around the shot of the house reflected in her rear
view mirror.

1M4/2M0 CASTLE ON THE HILL    SCORE    6:00

      Peg decides to try the house on the hill/Peg drives to
the house/Enters the garden/goes into the house and
upstairs/finds Edward.  Music segues from the source organ around
the cut to the house's reflection in Peg's rear view mirror.
Music plays as she drives to the house, discovers the topiary
gardens, enters the house and meets Edward.  Music is out when
Edward thrusts his scissors forward.  Notes and comments: We
talked about this cue being in three parts. 1. Driving section-
should be creepy scary with weight but understated. 2. Garden
section-creepy magical. 3. Interior-wonderment but still scary.
When she is in the garden look to catch the movement in the
window.  Remember that Peg's reactions are triggered by scissors
sounds and that these sounds will be spread out throughout the
interior.

2M1    BEAUTIFUL NEW WORLD    SCORE    :50

      Peg and Edward drive through the neighborhood to Peg's.
Peg has befriended Edward and offers to take him to her house.
Music starts on or prelaps cut to Edward and Peg driving.  Music
plays from Edward's POV, his wonderment at this new world as he
and Peg drive.  This is the flip side of 1M2.  Music is out on
the cut to Marge as she calls Helen.
```

The first page of music editor Bob Badami's spotting notes for *Edward Scissorhands* (1990), directed by Tim Burton and scored by Danny Elfman. Badami, who has worked with Elfman on a number of his films, took detailed notes during the spotting sessions and included significant comments about mood, specific moments to hit with music, and notes about the sound effects.

ing the spotting and function aren't always that straightforward. Should there be music over the main titles of *Psycho* (1960), and if so, how should it make the audience feel? What point of view should it establish? Should it suggest things to come? When Vera Miles slowly climbs the stairs, should there be music, or would silence be more suspenseful? If there is music, should it suggest something terrible is about to happen, perhaps building to a strong, accented chord? Or should the music suggest the eerie feeling of the house in a more atmospheric, subliminal way? Questions like these are frequently discussed in spotting sessions.

As we have seen, if the film has been very elaborately temp-tracked, many of the spotting decisions may already have been made by the time the composer joins the filmmakers for the actual spotting session. A lot depends on the director. John Williams points out that *Jaws* (1975) was "strictly spotted by Spielberg, indicating exactly where the music should come; directors such as De Palma and Hitchcock, however, gave [me] loose instructions on such matters."

If many of these decisions have not yet been made, spotting can be (and often is) collaborative, with everybody sharing their ideas. In such circumstances it can be a very stimulating experience, especially when a group decision is creatively satisfying.

No matter how the placement of music is determined, all composers agree on the significance of spotting. Max Steiner, whose score for *King Kong* in 1933 suggested the future potential of dramatic scoring, believed that selecting the location of the music was not only the most difficult thing to do, but the most important. "Music can slow up an action that should not be slowed up and quicken a scene that shouldn't be [quickened]. Knowing the difference is what makes a film composer."

Perhaps the most important questions raised are: Why should we have music there? What is the function of the music at that point? Composer Jerry Fielding had fine criteria for deciding whether or not to recommend music for a particular scene: "If the film is working, if it's doing what you want it

to do, then stay the hell out! There's no need to put music in a picture unless you have some reason to say something or you feel the need for underlining or emphasizing, de-emphasizing or weighing, or making it more pretty or decompressing or letting down or piling up or doing what the film is failing to do, or can't do on its own."

This pretty much sums up the possible reasons for putting music in a scene. The least defensible reason filmmakers sometimes offer is the one that composers find most disconcerting: "The scene's a little weak," the director says candidly. "We'd better put some music in there." Dimitri Tiomkin, who was one of the most outspoken of all composers, blessed with a good sense of humor, complained good-naturedly about this in 1961. "Every time a producer or director realizes he has shot a lousy scene, he decides to put in some music. . . . Frankly, I don't like to put music over horse chases and during gunfights, but sometimes they're so lousy I have to."

The best reason to score a scene is that music will add another dimension to the elements already in the film. In describing the spotting process for *Vertigo* (1958), Bernard Herrmann said, "The whole recognition scene, for example, is eight minutes of cinema without dialogue or sound effects—just music and picture. I remember Hitchcock said to me, 'Well, music will do better than words there.'"

Nothing is as loud in films as silence.
Bronislau Kaper, composer

Silence can make a very strong statement in a film; using it properly can be emotionally powerful. If music ends suddenly, the resulting silence has the effect of accenting the next moment in the drama. In fact, stopping the music abruptly is frequently done to emphasize the pull of a trigger, the impact of a knife, or some other equally dramatic action or revelation.

When music fades out to silence, it can create nervewracking tension in suspenseful situations. Conversely, if the music plays for too long a period of time, it becomes a part of the ambience of the film itself and can easily be taken for granted, even nullifying any emotional response. "I was watching *I Confess* {1953, scored by Dimitri Tiomkin, directed by Hitchcock} on television." says Jerry Goldsmith. "I could not *believe* the music—it started and it didn't stop. I know about those early Warner Bros. pictures—the music quantity was dictated by Jack Warner, because Hitchcock's use of music is quite intelligent, but this just went on and on and on. . . . It was totally meaningless.

"Economy is a strong factor in my own theories about scoring. I feel less is better than more. Music should be used only when it is really necessary. However, that was not the guiding force in the pioneering days in Hollywood scoring, partly because the old films lacked reality and were steeped in fantasy—and as Jack Warner said, 'fantasy needs music'—and partly because studio heads like Jack Warner loved to have their pictures afloat in music. The reason so many of Max Steiner's scores are long is that Warner demanded they be that way. Steiner often argued that the pictures would be better with less music, but he was overruled."

The theory that less is more is favored by some directors, but others feel they need more than may be necessary. Randy Newman, who scored *Awakenings* (1990), believes a more economical approach to the music would have been more powerful. "I was somewhat unhappy with how much music {director} Penny Marshall wanted in that picture. In my opinion, she was tugging at the heartstrings, expecting music to do things that it shouldn't be asked to do. And not saving it for spots where—boom—it'll get you, you know. I would have had 12, 15 minutes less in that picture. And I think it's the best score I ever did. I liked the music I wrote, even the 12 to 15 minutes I would have cut. But I think it would have helped the picture to have less."

Film editor Paul Hirsch was amazed at Bernard Herrmann's notion of where to bring music in while they were spotting *Sisters* (1973). "My idea had been to reflect {a sense of anticipation} in the music; there would be this growing tension building

to a crescendo. But Benny said, 'No. Watch—this is what I want to do.' We reran the scene and I asked, 'You bring in the music here?' He said, 'No, not yet—not yet.' We played the whole scene through, and suddenly when she cuts him, he said, *'That's* when I start the music.' Instead of playing the whole buildup, he let that play silent; then, at the release, where you might have ended the music, he started it. I later noticed he did the same thing in the famous crop-duster scene in *North by Northwest.* He was brilliant in his sense of how silence was an effect also."

Spotting is a developed skill, requiring practice and an innate sense of drama. Whatever the reason for spotting music in a particular sequence, many composers will tell you that it depends on what feels right. Goldsmith says, "I work completely emotionally. I cannot intellectualize about the role of music in film. I decide if it should be there purely by my emotions."

COMMUNICATING WITH THE DIRECTOR

I think that the director ought to make the movie. I think that the musician is an extension of the director.

Robert Aldrich, director

In general, I "yes" everybody, and then I go and write what I want.

Dimitri Tiomkin, composer

If the director isn't pleased, music doesn't stay on the soundtrack. Not only must the score serve the film—it must also satisfy the director. Consequently it is crucial that the composer understand the director's vision and musical preferences. Discussions regarding many dramatic elements—including subtle shifts of mood and so on—are important for the composer and director throughout the scoring process.

Here are some typical creative questions that arise time after time:

- What is the overall dramatic tone of the film, and consequently the score—dark, subdued, witty, macabre, whimsical, haunting, driving, menacing?
- What approach or combination of musical approaches would create an ideal musical style for this particular film? Are there any relevant role models—romantic symphonic, blues, rock-and-roll, electronic, contemporary keyboards and drum machine pop, jazz, Aaron Copland Americana, John Williams space-epic, Jerry Goldsmith supernatural?
- What is the most appropriate instrumentation for the film—big symphonic orchestra, electronic keyboards-guitars-percussion, chamber group, jazz combo?
- How involved in the drama should the music be? Should it be restrained, or emotional and full-blown?
- Should it be treated as a genre or nongenre score—for example, if a Western, does it need a traditional orchestral score, a small folk ensemble featuring fiddle and harmonica, or perhaps an electronic score?
- Should it be an instrumental score, a song score, or an instrumental score with songs? With exceptions, this decision is almost always made by the filmmakers and music supervisor.

These are all extremely important issues, both for the director and for the composer. Even though the director may already have arrived at the answers to many of these questions by the time the composer is on the job, give-and-take is still ideal; just as the composer wants to know—in fact, *should* know—what the director wants, the director can benefit greatly from listening to the composer's ideas. Composers get a lot of insight from discussing questions like these with filmmakers.

Directors have varying levels of musical involvement. James Horner, who has scored such diverse films as *Star Trek II* (1982) and *Star Trek III* (1984), *An American Tail* (1986), and *Glory* (1989), has seen a lot of different attitudes. "There are all types: those who don't want to discuss music at all and rely on you completely, those who pull examples out of opera that they think are going to help you, those who think they know much more than they actually do know, and those who are very quiet and know a lot more than they let on. I've met filmmakers who literally don't want to discuss music at all, and filmmakers who are demanding and exacting to the point where you never want to work for them again because they can't relinquish control at all—filmmakers who would write the music themselves if they could."

Perhaps the most successful of the director-composer collaborations since the mid-seventies has been that of Steven Spielberg and John Williams. Their first project together was Spielberg's *Sugarland Express* (1974). As Tony Crawley reports in *The Steven Spielberg Story,* Williams said to Spielberg, "You're going to hurt the movie if you want me to do [a score like Aaron Copland's] *The Red Pony* or *The Appalachian Spring.* It's a very simple story. The music should be soft. Just a few violins. A small orchestra. Maybe . . . a harmonica."

Spielberg was disheartened. "I'd really wanted 80 instruments. And Stravinsky conducting! Johnny talked me out of that concept and got me to believe the score should be gentle. Almost cradle-like. And so we began a very prosperous relationship, I think, for both of us. We're major collaborators on all my films."

Williams agrees. "We're temperamentally well suited to each other, but in Steven's case, that's not very hard because he's a very good general."

Spielberg worked in close collaboration with Jerry Goldsmith on *Poltergeist* (1982), Goldsmith's first project with him. "Anything I did was not of my own volition," says Goldsmith. "It was a joint effort in that we both agreed what we were trying to do with the music for the picture. We wanted a childlike theme for the little girl; Spielberg felt that much of the action in the closet should have a quasi-religious atmosphere to it. There was something definitely nonhuman about it, yet it was not evil all the way. It was discussing specifics like that which resulted in our approach."

I look at a director always as a secret code that has to be cracked.

Danny Elfman, *composer*

We all talk about the same thing: emotions.

Philippe Sarde, *composer*

Some directors are more talkative about the music than others. It may seem surprising, but too *little* communication can be as unnerving as too much. While working on his score for *Pretty Woman* (1990), James Newton Howard says, "I didn't have a lot of dialogue with the director, Garry Marshall, and I was never quite sure I was doing what he wanted me to do, and that's important to me." At times like that, the composer usually encourages the director by asking questions about things like the dramatic tone of the piece, which character's point of view to play, and the internal emotional qualities of a scene.

If too little discussion can make a composer nervous, confusing terminology is much worse. The stories are legion, and the following is typical. "I remember a few years ago when I was working on a bad picture with a bad director," Richard Rodney Bennett recalled in 1976. "He kept telling me in one certain section he wanted a 'funky flamenco feeling,' and I simply didn't know what he was talking about, and I did this section four different ways. He wouldn't tell me what he wanted and I didn't know what 'funky flamenco' meant because both of . . . [these words] to me mean something very precise."

This kind of miscommunication can quickly lead to a creative impasse, at which point all a composer can do is encourage the director to react to specific pieces of music. But in the area of verbal communication, there are more effective ways. The ideal solution in most cases is to use the language of the filmmaker, and talk in dramatic terms. That's how Goldsmith described his dialogue with

Spielberg on *Poltergeist,* and this kind of dialogue seems to work best for everybody. As Maurice Jarre explains, "I prefer directors who tell me things like 'It should feel very romantic,' or 'Very soft sound.' That is easier to understand, rather than directors who make comparisons with classical pieces, so they can go too far and request . . . an oboe solo when they really mean a clarinet or bassoon solo. Some directors are very insecure and don't really know what they want, so we can mess about for weeks trying different instruments, and finally it ends up with the director not trusting the composer."

David Raksin, whose classic scores include *Laura* (1944), *The Bad and the Beautiful* (1952), and *Force of Evil* (1948), has found that simple musical or emotional expressions can be helpful. "When you're trying to make clear to a composer what it is that you think you need in the way of music, at least have the courage to say, 'I want it loud,' 'I want it soft,' 'I want it fast,' 'I want it slow'; 'It should be tense here, It should be relaxed here'—whatever. And composers also need to be able to talk in those terms, to talk to filmmakers in their own dramatic terms about what's going on. To ask whether they want the composer to go with what they see in the picture or whether there is something underlying the action, because sometimes it's not simply that we do not see what is underneath the surface—sometimes it just *isn't there.*"

Here's an example of how effective a clear dramatic description can be. When Lee Holdridge worked with director Ron Howard on *Splash* (1984), their dialogue got him started in the right direction. "Ron said something to me that really echoed in my mind. He said, 'Don't make the underwater scary. Make it a very safe place to be.' Very simple. That set me off on a certain road, and that helped lead me to that beautiful love theme."

Avoiding confusing abstraction without being misleadingly specific is ideal, then. Directors like temp tracks because they are specific, but it is clear that they can be too specific. For the composer, as Danny Elfman emphasizes, "The critical thing is, am I thinking what the director is thinking? . . . The hardest part of being a film composer is not writing the score, it's climbing inside the director's head and seeing the movie through his eyes and yet still giving it your own identity."

Never at a loss for words, the legendary producer David O. Selznick always made his wishes known, often in very simple terms. Shortly after Dimitri Tiomkin had screened *Duel in the Sun* (1946), he received a memo describing the nature of the various themes he wanted to hear before the score was recorded: "Sentimental love," "Old memories," "Jealousy," "Flirtation," "Conflict," "Orgiastic."

A few meaningful words can make a big difference. "When I was scoring *Mr. Mom*," (1983), says Lee Holdridge, "the director, Stan Dragoti, said, 'Children's symphonic music.' I looked at him and I said, 'You mean like *Peter and the Wolf?*' and he said, 'That's it.' I immediately understood that you use the orchestra with a light touch."

Alfred Hitchcock planned his scenes in great detail before shooting. He also prepared detailed music notes for the composer and music department, and sound notes for the sound effects people. His music notes for *Vertigo* were typical of his style. For example, in the scene set in Midge's apartment, he asked for "something that is unobtrusive and yet unpopular enough to get on Scottie's nerves, who perhaps is not a devotee of classical music. There has been a suggestion that we play the Bach Concerto No. 1, which I am open-minded about—perhaps Mr. Herrmann may have some ideas. On no account should the music be unfamiliar. If we use classical music, the composer should be recognizable to those who know classical music."

As specific as he was, Hitchcock expected his wishes to be taken seriously. Bernard Herrmann, however, followed his own sensibilities. When he saw powerful dramatic values in the edited version of *Psycho*, he realized it could be a special film. "Hitchcock . . . felt it didn't come off," Herrmann recalled. "He wanted to cut it down to an hour television show and get rid of it. I had an idea of what one could do with the film, so I said, 'Why don't you go away for your Christmas holidays, and when you come back we'll record the score and see what

you think. . . . ?' 'Well,' he said, 'do what you like, but only one thing I ask of you: please write nothing for the murder in the shower. That must be without music.'"

Fortunately, Herrmann believed music was essential for the shower scene. When Hitchcock heard the cue, he agreed, and the music Herrmann wrote and recorded for the *Psycho* shower scene became one of the most famous and imitated moments in the history of film music.

Basically, directors do best with a straightforward discussion of the dramatic and emotional content of their film. When Fred Zinnemann was considering the music for *Five Days One Summer* (1982), which Elmer Bernstein scored, he wrote some music notes to express his thoughts. It is not necessary to have seen the movie to see how a fine director thinks about music for his film.

1. . . . The music should add to the interior dimension of the film. And . . . it should mainly reflect Kate's point of view and the changes of mood and tensions.

2. The first part should be mainly joyful, even exuberant, reflecting Kate's and Douglas's happiness at being together. Obviously there have to be darker undertones as required by the content of the scenes in the first part.

3. The brief music for the main title should hopefully be very sparsely scored—perhaps only one or two instruments?

4. The overall mood of the film changes rather dramatically from the point when Johann has seen the boot in the glacier.

5. I would like to emphasize the silence of the snowy mountains.

6. It is important to maintain the three moments of absolute silence: the old woman in the village when she realizes what Johann is telling her; then, the first time that the face of the dead man is uncovered. Finally, the body falling after having been hit by the rocks.

In these notes, Zinnemann addresses the questions of the function of the music, tone and dramatic shifts of tone, point of view, the use of silence, and the use of instrumental color. These are among the most vital issues the composer and director face when considering the best musical choices for a film. Zinnemann's notes still allowed Bernstein considerable creative latitude.

Ideally, a composer will have the opportunity to make a creative contribution. If he feels that he is simply being required to do what the director asks without an honest dialogue—a kind of painting-by-the-numbers approach—he may lose the ability to contribute much to the film. And that state of mind can absolutely kill the creative impulse, encouraging the composer to function as a musical secretary.

This is a difficult problem to resolve. Working with a particularly strong director simply emphasizes the problem, as Gerald Fried discovered.

"Both [Stanley] Kubrick and [Robert] Aldrich are very strong, opinionated people. I found that I had to be careful in my choices. Not just musical and dramatic considerations—I had to figure out what *they* would interpret as musical and dramatic considerations . . . I found it a little bit intimidating, even though if I were to make a movie I would probably insist on the same prerogatives to have my composer reflect *my* tastes."

In the early days of motion picture production, the producers (along with the music executives) often made the music decisions. In television films, the producer remains a major factor in the decision-making process. Since the sixties, though, motion pictures have been dominated by the directors. Although you cannot know how much these filmmakers have shaped the score you are hearing, you can be sure that the film's soundtrack will reflect their musical and dramatic preferences.

Composing the Music

■ ■ ■

I've heard some say the music just writes itself, but I'm skeptical. My guess is, creative people are reluctant to admit they suffer in the process of creation. But I see suffering as an inescapable part of the experience.

Jerry Goldsmith, composer

FUNCTION

The task at hand is to serve the film.
Jerry Fielding, composer

The biggest problem is to make the initial decision about the musical evaluation of the picture. You have to decide what the music must do.
Elmer Bernstein, composer

The composer defines the function of the music in the film throughout the creation of the score. By the time the score is finished, he will have answered many questions: What is the music supposed to do for the film? In what way can it best support the

drama? In what way can it personalize the characters and the theme of the story, thereby becoming specifically identified with that particular film?

No matter what the film or its subject matter, decisions relating to function are critical. One of the most important functions of the music is to express and clarify the basic dramatic theme of the film. Billy Wilder's *The Lost Weekend* (1945) is a good case in point. When the film was previewed, a temp score had been used that was totally inappropriate for this story of alcoholism. Miklós Rózsa, who composed the score, explains what happened.

"The opening shots of the New York skyline had some jazzy xylophonic Gershwinesque music (in the Hollywood musical vernacular, New York means Gershwin), and when Ray Milland was fishing for the whiskey bottle, the audience roared with laughter. As soon as they began to realize the film was actually a stark drama about alcoholism, many started to leave. No applause was forthcoming at the end. Next day the studio was full of gloom, and there was talk of shelving the whole picture.

"I tried to explain to [producer] Charles Brackett that the music was to blame, since it led the audience to expect a comedy. He was very depressed and not totally convinced, but he told me to go ahead and do what I felt was right. Much to the discomfort of the musical director [Louis Lipstone], I wrote an intense, impassioned, and dramatic score in which the weird sound of the theremin [an early electronic instrument sounding similar to a soprano vocal without words] became the official 'voice' of dipsomania."

With Rózsa's score in place, *The Lost Weekend* won the Academy Award as Best Picture; Ray Milland won an Oscar, as did Billy Wilder for his direction, and Rózsa was nominated for Best Score.

When the exact concept and tone of a film is not obvious, defining the music's function can be difficult. At his first screening of *Die Hard* (1988), composer Michael Kamen was unsure about the film's emotional impact. "The film had a very sure direction by John McTiernan, but it just seemed very emotionless. I was struggling to put some emotional context into the score.... When I see people dying, I react emotionally to it. I don't celebrate that....

"At the end of the day, it's curious—Bruce [Willis] got a lot of music, [Alan] Rickman takes very little music. I just put a drone under him, and he's as bad as he needs to be."

CONCEPT

An appropriate concept for a film score will function properly within the dramatic context of the film, but will also have an overall point of view. Basically, this point of view is the *idea* that becomes

the basis for the score. The idea determines the way in which the score functions in the film, shaping the orchestration, melody, harmony, and rhythm. Rózsa's story about *The Lost Weekend* tells us that he redefined the function of the music which was reflected in the temp track, and created a score that emphasized the dramatic theme of the film—the nightmare of alcoholism. This became the concept of his score.

RoboCop (1987), set in the near future, is about a dead cop turned into a cyborg. Composer Basil Poledouris says that the director, Paul Verhoeven, "Wanted to have a large score.... On the other hand, he also wanted me to communicate some of the ideas that he had about man versus machine. That suggested to me using electronic music, although I knew we would end up using an orchestra. Basically, each represented the two realities—the electronic being the machine, and the orchestra being the human aspect of the film. There are places where they merge, and that's when his consciousness is starting to resurface, [as he remembers] what his life had been...."

John Barry recalls that director Sidney Pollack wanted the score for *Out of Africa* (1985) to emphasize the dramatic theme—the love story between the characters played by Robert Redford and Meryl Streep. "The focus of the movie was essentially on the characters," says Barry, "and that's exactly the way we went with it."

So the expression of the dramatic theme of a film can be the basis for the score's concept. As we have seen, one or more musical styles can also define the concept. Other musical elements used in developing the concept include orchestration and instrumental colors, ethnic or geographic influences, the characters, and historic/period influences.

Orchestration

The shaping of the score's concept may start with the orchestration—perhaps a decision to use a large orchestra rather than a chamber group, or an electronic instrumentation. It would then include a decision as to *how* a big orchestra would be used—the style of the music, for instance, or the level of its involvement with the drama. John Williams discussed this with George Lucas in order to arrive at a concept for *Star Wars* (1977).

"It was George Lucas' concept to use classical music, and he said we'll use this or that piece. And I said, 'Let's try the following thing—I think it should be classical-music-sounding, in the fully dressed symphonic kind of cloth, if you like, but that if we do our own music, original music, we can then take the themes and reshape them and put them in a major key, minor key, fast, slow, up, down, inverted, attenuated, and crushed, and all the permutations that you can put a scene and a musical conception through, that you wouldn't be able to tastefully do if you had taken a Beethoven symphony and scored it with that.'"

The search for a concept is often talked through by the director and composer. In the case of *Star Wars,* Williams says, "I think the idea really was collaborative. Lucas had some idea of what it should be and I brought my own ideas to it and together we worked out an approach that worked to whatever extent it may have.

"What was intentional was just the idea of trying to produce a beautifully set symphonic sound that struck late-nineteenth-century emotional and maybe even intellectual chords in some way with the listener, so that the music, the emotional part of the soundtrack, was very familiar in the sense that its ethos is familiar for many . . . wrapping the whole thing into this warm package. The kind of thing that [Erich Wolfgang] Korngold, in fact, did so beautifully. He brought the Vienna Opera House to the American West. And in an odd way, in a similar way, it worked, I think."

With or without a full symphony orchestra, composers sometimes use a specific instrument to represent a particular character, and this shapes the concept. Michael Kamen and Eric Clapton did that with their score for *Lethal Weapon* (1987). "We have two main characters," says Kamen. "They both have specific themes, and specific colors. So the Mel Gibson character is played by Eric Clapton on gui-

tar, and the Danny Glover character is played by David Sanborn on alto sax. And that never varies, that becomes formulaic."

Kamen points out that the use of these colors was mutually arrived at by himself, film editor Stuart Baird, director Dick Donner, and producer Joel Silver. This concept has continued through the sequels, *Lethal Weapon 2* (1988) and *Lethal Weapon 3* (1992).

Ethnic and Geographical Influences

Ethnic instruments, scales, and rhythms can become the basis for the concept. Anton Karas' use of a solo zither to evoke post-World War II Vienna on the soundtrack of *The Third Man* (1949) is a classic example of this. Since Karas used a specific solo instrument to characterize the location, this concept also relies on orchestration. This kind of overlapping of musical elements and ideas is not unusual in film music.

Some other examples of scores using ethnic and geographical materials for their concept include *Stand and Deliver* (contemporary Los Angeles Latino; Craig Safan, 1987); *Under Fire* (Nicaragua; Jerry Goldsmith, 1983); *Old Gringo* (Mexico; Lee Holdridge, 1989); *The Mission* (late-eighteenth-century Brazil; Ennio Morricone, 1986). Some of the older classic film scores incorporated ethnic and geographical influences also—scores like *El Cid* (1961), in which Miklós Rózsa utilized melodies and scales from medieval Spain.

In *Lethal Weapon,* Michael Kamen balanced his good-guy music described above with a different approach for the bad guys. "Although I had a theme for Riggs and I had a theme for Murtaugh, I didn't have any music or any clue as to how to deal with the bad guys. And it was Joel who suggested to me that all of the bad guys in the movie had probably been in Vietnam, they had probably been together in a commando unit, and they had all gotten corrupted together. And he suggested that I use a vaguely Oriental motif, which worked out."

Characters

Not only is this is a good example of the use of ethnic materials in developing the concept, but it also illustrates how the concept can evolve from the characters themselves. Very often the concept comes directly from the characters and their personalities. In the case of the original "Star Trek" television series, Gerald Fried remembers writing Spock's theme ". . . for an instrument that couldn't possibly be romantic, a bass guitar, down in the low register, with no resonance. It just klunks out the theme, but nevertheless I told Barney Kessel, a jazz guitar player who performed the theme, to play as expressively and as warmly as possible. I thought the tension between trying to play *espressivo* and the impossibility of doing it would be the kind of thing that would be appropriate for Spock." So Fried's concept was to characterize Spock through the use of orchestration.

When David Newman worked with director Norman Jewison on *Other People's Money* (1991), they discussed a musical concept that would grow from the main character, played by Danny DeVito. "Jewison focused on this guy's obsession with money," Newman explains. "And so we figured out that this thing [about money, suggested by the music] is running in his head all the time. He's also motivated by his own moral sense—he's very moral in his own way. He's very consistent in what he believes and doesn't believe." Newman's main theme for DeVito attempts to express these qualities—delineating a person who is aggressive, self-righteous, and overbearing.

Historic and Period Influences

Again there is often an overlapping of several elements when historic influences are incorporated into a score. In Lee Holdridge's score for *Old Gringo* (1989), for instance, not only are various aspects of Mexican music used, but the Mexican musical materials are also *historically appropriate* to the 1913 revolution of Pancho Villa, at a time when brass bands were prevalent.

Composers must always decide to what degree the historic period in which the story takes place should influence the score. There are scores that immediately evoke the period—Nino Rota's score for *Romeo and Juliet* (1968), for example, and Patrick Williams' forties-sounding score for the World War II story *Swing Shift* (1984).

Sometimes, though, the most conspicuous musical influence of the period is heard coming through radios and played by bands and dance bands ("source music") rather than in the score itself. At other times, a composer may choose to ignore the historical period in developing a concept, or to let the historical music influence a more contemporary musical approach. Alex North says that in *Spartacus* (1960), "I wanted to write music that would interpret the past in terms of the present. Which isn't to say I didn't look backwards in certain respects, but always I was looking for things that would fit into a contemporary frame of musical thought—as, for instance in the sequence where the slave army trains and prepares for battle . . . [in which] I used a strange $\frac{5}{8}$-meter early Greek style still unfamiliar today." Because this rhythmic pulse is so unusual, it tends to sound "modern," even though it is historically appropriate for the film's period setting.

RESEARCH

It's not a case of using the music per se, it's a matter of letting it seep into the recesses of your mind so that when you sit down to write, the subconscious is permeated with the sound and the style of that music.

Alex North, composer

Whenever a film composer finds himself working in a specific style of music, whether historical, ethnic, or pop, he may end up doing some research. This can be as simple as buying a couple of CDs and getting the flavor and idiomatic details of the mambos from the fifties. Or it can be as complex as studying the authentic native music of a particular region of a country.

Miklós Rózsa was very interested in the historical research that he was able to do as preparation for scoring historical epics—films like *El Cid* (1961), for instance. In fact, he spent considerable time in Spain doing research about medieval Spanish music for that project. His account detailing his preparation for *El Cid* is typical of his fastidious attention to historical detail: "There was research to do, because I knew nothing of Spanish music of the Middle Ages. . . . I spent a month in intense study of the music of the period. I also studied the Spanish folk songs. . . . With these two widely differing sources to draw upon, I was ready to compose the music. As always, I attempted to absorb these raw materials and translate them into my own musical language."

Similarly, he went back to original source material when it came time to score *Ivanhoe*. He described his research method in *Film Music Notes* in 1952.

I wanted to create again a score which sounds and is stylistically authentic. I found a somewhat similar situation in musical matters between twelfth-century England and first-century Rome. As Roman music was largely influenced by the Greek, so came the music of the Saxons under the influence of the invading Normans. It is a well-known fact that people on a lower level of civilization readily absorb the culture of the invaders or neighboring countries which have a higher civilization, as a subconscious expression of their longing for the higher level of life which usually goes with higher civilization. The sources of Saxon music are extremely few and far between, but there is a large amount of music from the twelfth century available, of the French troubadours and trouvères, who brought their music with the invading Normans to England. The various themes of *Ivanhoe* are partly based on original sources and are partly my own.

Rózsa did a great deal of research in preparing to score *Quo Vadis* (1951), the first of his historical epics. He explains how he went about it in his autobiography, *Double Life*.

It is not easy to know exactly what music the Romans played on their instruments, since none of their written music survives. But several examples from Greek monuments and tombstones have been deciphered by scholars, and as Greek civilization dominated Rome so completely in the fields of religion, architecture, literature, and drama, it seemed reasonable to employ these Greek sources as a basis for my music. Nero's song is an authentic Greek melody, and every piece of source music is based on something from the period. Sometimes a short fragment was enough to serve as a point of departure.

By the time he composed the music for *Ben-Hur* (1959), his score for *Quo Vadis* had become *the* role model for films in this genre, and he was able to use his earlier score as a stylistic prototype.

André Previn, who was at MGM with Rózsa, observes, "In order to keep himself interested, Miklós did an amazing (and probably unnecessary) amount of research for each of his projects, and so he was a real expert in biblical instruments, plainsong, Gregorian chant, and the like. He was, in other words, a scholar."

British composer Malcolm Arnold sometimes traveled to an appropriate location to prepare for his composing assignments. "On *Island in the Sun* [1957] I studied West Indian music on the Island of Grenada, and . . . *Nine Hours to Rama* [1963] . . . necessitated going to India, where I worked with Indian musicians."

Most composers, though, stay at home. "I have a vast library of all kinds of music," says John Scott, "from Oriental to primitive, Indian chants, Eskimo chants, a lot of South American music." Scott, a British composer who divides his time between England and the United States, finds this archival approach works fine. Henry Mancini has collected a large library of similar materials which he refers to when necessary.

TIMINGS

If the picture inspires me, I don't even have to measure or count the seconds or feet. If I am really inspired, I simply have luck.
　　　　　　　　　　　Erich Wolfgang Korngold, composer

It is not necessary to do calculations with feet and frames, seconds and microseconds to understand how film composers work with timings. Even the composers don't spend a lot of time working out mathematical calculations anymore. They all have VCRs in their studios, set up near their pianos or (more likely) electronic keyboards, and they write music to a videotape copy of the film—not that the timings are any less important now, but computers and timings on the videotape copies of the film make it easier. Fitting the music to the film still requires split-second accuracy, but the process is relatively painless. Here's how it works.

The videotape has a digital time code and corresponding audio sync pulse that is recorded on one channel of the videotape, and visually displayed on the top or bottom of the screen. It looks like this:

3:01:32:04

The first number on the left is usually the number of the reel, so while reel one is playing, the first number would read 1, and reel two would read 2. The second number represents the minutes into the reel, the third number the seconds, and the fourth number the frames (or fractions of a second). So wherever the videotape is stopped, if it's in the pause mode, you can read those numbers and know, to the frame, exactly where you are in the film. In the above example, the film is 1 minute, 32 seconds, and 4 frames into reel three. Since these numbers move along in real time

like a digital clock, you can see the seconds pass by as you watch the film. This time code is called SMPTE (pronounced "*simp*tee"). The acronym comes from the Society of Motion Picture and Television Engineers, who adopted this standardized sync pulse.

After the spotting session, the music editor prepares timings sheets for each cue (each separate piece of music) in the film. These timing notes usually are calculated to hundredths of a second, and indicate every cut, all the dialogue (including the pauses at the ending of phrases), and all the significant action: people moving, a cat meowing, doors slamming—everything.

Typically the music editor also works with a videotape. The timings sheets he creates often have two columns of numbers. One indicates the real time from the beginning of the cue, so the first frame of the cue is shown as :00 seconds. The second column uses the cumulative timings displayed on the screen, so if the cue starts at 1 minute, 32 seconds, and 4 frames into the reel, then that is the number in the adjoining column. In this way, the composer always knows exactly where everything happens in each cue and each moment's relationship to the entire film.

Many younger composers now work very much the way Erich Wolfgang Korngold did back in the late thirties, relying heavily on instinct. According to his son George, the composer never even used timing notes (although all his colleagues did). And he didn't like using a stopwatch. So he simply went into a projection room and ran the film reel by reel, cue by cue, time after time, playing the piano and composing his score while watching the picture.

That's what many composers do now, except that they are at home, studying a videotape. It's really very much the way the early silent movie pianists worked when they improvised on the spot (see Chapter 8). Now, the existence of the SMPTE time code makes the actual synchronization much easier for the many composers who write with the aid of a computer. SMPTE revolutionized the process of film scoring.

TIMING NOTES   PAGE 1

TITLE: DRUGSTORE COWBOY

DATE: 5-20-89

CUE: 4M3   SCORE   START: 04:01:14:02

THE HEX. BOB IS LIVID. NADINE HAS BROUGHT A CURSE ON THE HOUSEHOLD BY
ASKING BOB ABOUT GETTING A DOG. RICK, TAKEN ABACK, ASKS BOB IF THERE ARE
ANY OTHER TENDER SUBJECTS TO AVOID. "AS A MATTER OF FACT, THERE ARE," BOB
TELLS HIM. "AND WE MIGHT AS WELL DISCUSS THEM RIGHT NOW, BEING AS HOW
WE'RE SHUT DOWN FOR THIRTY DAYS." HE LEANS FORWARD FOR EMPHASIS, AND TELL
THEM: "HATS."

01:14:02	:00.00		MUSIC STARTS A BEAT AFTER LINE AS BOB SINKS INTO A COSMIC REVERIE.
01:14:24	:00.73		WITH A SHRUG OF HIS HAND, BOB: "OKAY..."
01:15:14	:01.40		HE CONTS: "...HATS."
01:16:19	:02.57		BOB GESTURES AND DIANNE SHAKES HER HEAD AS BOB CONTS: "IF I EVER SEE A HAT ON A BED IN THIS HOUSE..."
01:18:26	:04.80		PAUSE.
01:20:03	:06.04		BOB TRIES TO CONVEY THE ENORMITY OF IT -- HE CONTS: "MAN, LIKE YOU'LL NEVER SEE ME AGAIN."
01:22:14	:08.41		WAVING HIS ARM, HE CONTS: "...I'M GONE."
01:23:26	:09.81		DIANNE AGREES: "THAT MAKES TWO OF US."
01:24:29	:10.91		END LINE.
01:26:25	:12.78	CUT	ANGLE ON RICK AND NADINE ON ARMCHAIR.
01:27:10	:13.28		NADINE'S AMAZED: "WHY A HAT?"
01:28:25	:14.78	CUT	DIANNE AND BOB, AS BOB COMES BACK: "I GUESS THAT'S JUST THE WAY IT IS, SWEETIE."
01:30:17	:16.52	CUT	RICK AND NADINE. THEY'RE SILENT.
01:32:07	:18.18	CUT	CLOSE BOB. HE'S WARMING UP: "...AND THERE'S MIRRORS."
01:33:05	:19.12	CUT	MED CLOSE DIANNE. SHE SHAKES HER HEAD IN DEJECTED AGREEMENT.

The first page of timing notes for Cue 4M3 (the third cue in reel four) for *Drugstore Cowboy*
(1989). Music editor Bill Bernstein (no relation to Elmer) wrote these timing notes for Elliot
Goldenthal, who scored this story about a junkie.

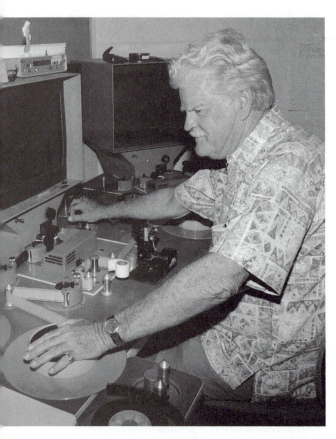

Music editor Dan Carlin works at a flatbed editing machine, taking timings and checking sync. The white film by his hand is blank stock used as filler when there is no sound on the unit. This blank film is referred to as "leader" or "slug"; sometimes old, unused footage from other films is used as leader. *Photo: Gay Wallin*

Sophisticated computer programs called "sequencers" make it possible for computers to store information about the notes, dynamics, and other nuances that composers play on their electronic keyboards. By means of the SMPTE signal, the computer can be set to start the music wherever desired, either exactly as performed while watching the videotape, or at any other moment. Then, when the video is played, the SMPTE signal will cause the music program to lock in and play back the music in perfect sync with the videotape. Since the place-

ment of the music can be shifted at will, this system offers easily accessed flexibility plus absolute accuracy. A talent for math, although helpful, is no longer a prerequisite for film composing. There are computer programs that can make any necessary calculations and tempo adjustments. There are no more worries about hitting the precise moment the building explodes in *Lethal Weapon 3*—everything can be hit dead-on with relative ease.

Composers frequently use a steady tempo as their frame of reference for a section of the score. This tempo can be generated by the sequencer and sounds like the click of a metronome. When a composer uses the sound of this computer-generated click as a tempo guide, she can start by writing the music at the tempo she thinks is most compatible with the dramatic needs and rhythm of the scene, and then speed up or slow down the music as necessary to refine the sync. A lot of cues are written just this way.

Danny Elfman scored *Batman* (1989) and *Batman Returns* (1992), films which required a particularly close synchronization between the dramatic action and the music. "Everybody kept asking, how did you make all these things hit in just the right place," says Elfman, "and I said, you know, it was really ridiculously easy. I would look at it and I would start to get a feel for the editor's tempo, and then I would just start writing out the bars and I would be amazed at how many of the hit points I was looking for were falling [into place at that tempo]. I wouldn't even have to do that many odd-number bars to catch up."

These methods are not revolutionary; only the technology itself is new. But everybody has benefited from it. Music editor Ken Johnson says, "Because of the computer, it now takes an hour to do bar breakdowns that used to take a half a day or more."

In the thirties, before music editors as such even existed, a "music supervisor" went into a projection room and timed each cue with a stopwatch. Today it's inconceivable to consider taking timings in that laborious way, especially because of the inevitable inaccuracy of the system. "We would always have to adjust on the scoring stage," music editor John Hammell remembers. This practice prevailed, however, until the mid-forties when footage counters were added to the Moviolas (editing machines), at which point music editors began taking accurate timings from the Moviola.

TIME PRESSURES

You know, people bitch about not being given enough time, but panic is a great inspiration.
Michael Kamen, composer

Keep in mind that all of this is taking place within a very short period of time. True, the research, conceptualizing, and even theme writing may begin well before the picture is locked and turned over to the composer to score. But as Kamen says about these schedules, "The best of them still leaves me breathless."

To work under intense time pressure requires tremendous concentration and endurance. Franz Waxman's son John remembers the time in the mid-fifties when his father had three simultaneous deadlines. "He'd get up in the morning and work on a contemporary jazz score for *Crime in the Streets* until breakfast, take a break and work on a Kirk Douglas Western called *The Indian Fighter* until lunch, and then from lunch till dinner work on *The Spirit of St. Louis,* the Lindbergh film. He'd segment the work so he wouldn't go totally nuts."

How bad can it get if you're only working on one film at a time? Well, on *Robin Hood: Prince of Thieves* (1991), Kamen didn't even *get* the film until 3½ weeks before his delivery date. The score contained 2 hours and 11 minutes of music.

"As far as I know, nearly everybody who could orchestrate in L.A. was visiting me and taking pieces of paper away. I also had people helping me with take-downs [transcribing previously written, recorded, or sequenced music] and people helping me rework cues for different sections of the score. Then, unbelievably, while I'm working on this film with two weeks to go, they're still cutting the damn thing. They switched reel one and reel two, and I had written a *symphony* for reel one. I had to rescore it. We brought people up here with dulcimers at four in the morning. Everything that could happen happened."

Randy Newman, who balances his film scoring with performing and recording his songs, hopes things will improve some day. "I get more time than most people get. I've demanded it. Still, they cut me. One was eight weeks, one was nine. But the first thing the agent asks for me is ten weeks. That's what it should be. . . . I wish they would just give people more time, and things would be better. I can't imagine anyone having a family and doing six pictures a year."

PROCRASTINATION

You would think that in this line of work procrastinating would be out of the question—that the pressure of deadlines would be a sure cure. It often is, yet several composers have had reputations for getting incredibly behind schedule, and then having to finish everything during the last few days before the scoring sessions.

Hugo Friedhofer had that reputation. Ironically, when he orchestrated for Max Steiner, he found that Steiner himself seemed to procrastinate. "Max always seemed to suffer a great deal more than he actually did, you know. Everything became a big problem and it was largely histrionics, because I think Max wrote rapidly and fairly easily, but strangely enough, Max always dramatized everything that he did. . . . Say we ran [the movie] on a Thursday; he said, 'You should have something by Monday,' and on Monday I would get this tearful, pathetic call from him saying, 'Puppsy, I must have eaten something—I have food poisoning—I can't get 'anything off the ground,' and I would say 'OK Max, take it easy, whenever you're ready,' so he would, two or three days later, come with a heap of sketches."

Jerry Fielding occasionally got so involved in compositional details that he lost sight of the schedule. Greig McRitchie orchestrated many of his scores. "He was the only guy I ever saw who would write out the percussion exactly, with staccato marks on the snare drum parts, on his sketch. Incredible. And he was one of the first guys to ever break up the rhythms, you know—$\frac{5}{8}$, $\frac{3}{8}$. That's what takes forever.

"I remember *Straw Dogs* [1971]. The rape scene—he must have taken two weeks. And I used to say, 'Jerry, what are you doing?' He was involved with tone rows in those days [sequences of the 12 notes of the chromatic scale, formulated from a system of composition developed by Arnold Schoenberg]. I said, 'Why are you experimenting with this right in the middle of a picture, Jerry?' But he used to do that. Then, at the last minute, he'd call me in, and Lennie Niehaus, and he'd just throw stuff at us—just timing sheets and the themes—and say, 'Here, *you* guys figure it out.'" Ironically, on those occasions when Fielding got behind, it was because of his determined preoccupation to continue growing and exploring fresh musical possibilities for film scoring.

THEMES

I believe in strong themes which are easily recognizable, and which can be repeated and variated according to the film's needs. But the variations must be expressive and not complicated.

          Franz Waxman, composer

Getting the theme is always the struggle. . . .

          Jerry Goldsmith, composer

Usually the themes come first—the musical material that will become the basis for the score. Although a theme is often a fully developed melody, it can be shorter, or even not completely developed. If it's much shorter, only a few notes, it is called a "motif," or "motive." These themes and motifs not only spring from the concept of the score, but also help to clarify the concept and make it come to life.

The most famous motif in film music history is the short "shark" motif John Williams wrote for *Jaws* (1975). It has become part of the popular culture, and almost part of the language. If you sing it—*Da*-da, *Da*-da, *Da*-da, *Da*-da—everybody knows what you mean: things are getting scary. The most famous motif in television music history is the opening phrase of "Twilight Zone."

These motifs are perfect for their projects, and are now inseparable in our minds from their dramatic sources. Everybody agrees that this oneness of drama and music is ideal, but it's difficult to explain exactly how this inevitable material is created. Certainly, working from a well-defined concept can help. Not everybody thinks conceptually, though, and many times the thematic material comes first, and then actually establishes, or in fact *becomes,* the concept.

Most composers begin a score by getting deeply involved in the film itself. Mysterious as the process may seem, the best film music really comes from the films. The more you become emotionally connected with the film, the more likely it is that the themes will evolve naturally from the drama. John Morris explains how elusive the actual creative process is: "I don't know how I write for film. All I know is that I memorize the movie first and get to know its heartbeat. Then the process begins, all of it unconscious. I find the hidden tempo in a chase sequence which even the editor himself didn't know was there. I find the themes for the picture, and if I haven't provided the right ones, all the doors remain firmly closed, and refuse to open. It's that simple."

When a composer has become deeply involved in the film, it is easy to recognize that the doors have opened. "At some point on every project, I suddenly get this incredible sense of excitement, this complete inner assurance that what I'm doing is right," says Rachel Portman, whose credits include *Used People* (1992) and *The Joy Luck Club* (1993). "It can be something very small, like a four-note melodic chain or a movement from one chord to another, that you suddenly know is going to be the heart of the music, the language and the syntax for the entire film."

David Raksin agrees. "It's mostly instinctive. It's what somebody once called the 'ah-hah' effect. In other words, you're doing it, and all of a sudden it sounds right to you. . . . The reason they talk about the theme for *Laura* [1944] is because it is what is described as 'haunting.' And the reason is, it has some relationship, not so much to the girl as to the feeling which is behind her.

"Every so often you get a picture which gives you nothing at all, and then you're struggling, you're using your so-called professionalism." When that happens, it's very difficult to connect with the film—there is simply nothing there with which to connect.

The search for the perfect theme has its hazards. Ira Newborn, who has scored a number of John Hughes films, has frequently been asked to write a new piece of material similar to a role model such as the original "Dragnet" television theme or the opening theme in Richard Strauss' "Also sprach Zarathustra" (the music used by Stanley Kubrick in *2001: A Space Odyssey*). He writes his new (original) material, then often hears from worried studio legal departments—they become concerned that they might be sued for plagiarism.

In fact, when a theme sounds just right, it may be a little too inevitable. Composers are always worrying about whether their latest terrific theme has already been somebody else's terrific theme. "Like, one time, I came in to MGM," says Raksin, "and Broni Kaper, who was a very smart guy, said to me, 'Have you written your thematic material?' I said, 'I just came up with the main theme.' 'Play it for me.' I played it for him. He said, 'You're going to have to change a couple of notes.' I said, 'Really? Why?'

He said, 'Because it sounds like Franz Waxman.' 'Waxman! No!' So I went and I changed the notes, and I said, 'Is that it?' and he said, 'Yes, that's great. Now it's different.' It was just a matter of a few notes."

COMPOSING

I try to add to the film something that wasn't there before.

> *Richard Rodney Bennett, composer*

I try for emotional penetration—not for complementing the action. To me, the important thing about music in film is statement.

> *Jerry Goldsmith, composer*

As a rule, film scores evolve bit by bit; through repeated viewings of the film and the sequences to be scored, through trial and error, through the interaction with the filmmakers, and through the constant discovery and development of appropriate music. Though it is difficult to explain, film composers learn to trust the process. It works. Jerry Goldsmith, since the sixties one of the most respected and prolific film composers, relies on the creative evolution of his scores but confesses that it's never effortless. "Everything I do takes a tremendous amount of feeling my way around dark corners, like a blind man in a curved tunnel. When I was a student I had to fight discouragement because I was unbelievably slow. Over the years I've developed technique, but I still haven't found an easy way to be a composer."

At first, anxiety can build up, and composers have to deal with this added pressure. With all his experience and successes, Alfred Newman suffered like everyone else. "I think that's just part of the job," his son, David Newman, says. "My father would sit there and just stare at a blank page, like all of us have. It's scary getting or not getting the jobs, and then it's scary doing them."

Max Steiner's hobby was model ships. Seated at his piano in this mid-thirties photo, Steiner pioneered the use of music in films with his scores for *Cimarron* (1930) and *King Kong* (1933). When he was with RKO Pictures between 1929 and 1935, Steiner composed music for approximately 68 films, (many simply Main and End Titles), and co-composed and music-directed dozens of others. At Warner Bros., his credits for 1941 alone include 39 films, which is undoubtedly why he kept his ships so conveniently located.
Photo courtesy of the Academy of Motion Picture Arts and Sciences

Most composers take time at the beginning of the process to familiarize their subconscious with the film and its needs. But after a while, no one waits for inspiration. As French composer Georges Delerue said, "In reality you have to force yourself, you have to concentrate on things like a sportsman [athlete] does. That's when the ideas arrive."

Laurence Rosenthal, who composed the score for *The Miracle Worker* (1962) and has faced tight schedules on television miniseries like *Peter the Great* (1986), explains that no matter what happens, the music must be written. "Almost every composer has his moments of more or less high inspiration, and also moments when he simply relies on his craft to do a decent, professional piece of work."

If there's a secret formula, it's emotional involvement and persistence. Composing a film score requires tremendous discipline. As Rosenthal suggests, a mastery of the craft helps. Goldsmith shares this practical attitude. "We like to think it is all art, but let's face it, we have to rely on craft a lot of times. I mean, this is not like sitting in the ivory tower waiting to be struck by great inspiration. We have deadlines all the time, and you sit down at nine in the morning at the piano to start working and you know you have to produce so much music that day and you have to keep on that schedule for the next five or six weeks because you know you have to record this music at the end of that time. You've just got to do it. But I've learned over the years, the craft sometimes inspires inspiration, rather than the other way around."

If a cue is particularly difficult to get a handle on, getting away from the project helps. In that sense, scoring a film is like any other creative endeavor. "Sometimes, when I'm working, and I'm having trouble with a sequence, I'll go for a drive," says Raksin. "When my mind's diverted, new ideas or combinations often emerge."

Composers have different work habits. While some go off to separate studios or offices to do their writing, most have a studio at home. Some try to maintain more or less regular daytime working hours, but this is a civilized life-style few can enjoy. Ernest Gold works that way, though.

"I'm usually up by 5:00 or 5:30 when I work on a picture score, and after some breakfast, before even getting dressed, I go directly to my studio and start work and I work until about 10:00 or 10:30, then I take a little break to get dressed.... Then I will stop for lunch very briefly, and work some more. Then usually around 4:00 in the afternoon, by that time I'm getting pretty tired and drawn out. . . . If possible, I try not to work past 5:00 in the afternoon. I'm essentially what I call jokingly a 9 to 5 composer."

John Williams often composes in his studio at Universal. "In my own case," Williams says, "I work at the piano. I don't use synthesizers or electronic equipment and all that stuff. My musical education is such that it predates all of that, and although I know a little bit about it, I haven't developed the skills. I use the piano, that's my old friend in music. And I probably use it more for writing than any composition teacher would tell you is a good idea, but that's been my practice always. So part of my process is tactile. It's in the hands, that certainly is true. But as the score develops and as I know the material more and more, and get towards the end of the film, I use it less and less, as the music sort of begins to take over, and I become less oriented toward the keyboard. . . .

"I work very hard and I work long hours and I am not all that quick, although people seem to think I am, because when I am working on a film, I may have to produce a lot of music. But, I'm patient with it. . . . Some films are easier than others. The material comes more quickly. I think it always helps to love the film which you are doing and that's a very rare experience, although I have certainly been lucky in my life with films."

Working at home can be difficult, with all the obvious distractions. Like Johann Sebastian Bach in his day, some composers relish being in the middle of things. Bernard Herrmann was that way. But many need a more isolated environment. Orchestrator Greig McRitchie, who has worked on scores by many composers, including Alfred Newman, James Horner, Jerry Fielding, and John Barry, finds he needs long stretches of quiet to concentrate successfully. "If my wife comes in and says, 'I don't want to bother you, but—'I say, 'You've already bothered me. Forget it. I'm off for an hour.' Because I've got to imagine the orchestra in my head, you know." Just the distractions related to the film itself can be disruptive—a call from the producer about the budget, the music editor calling up about

John Williams plays one of his complete seven-staff sketches as he works on a score. Although Williams uses the piano while he composes, more and more film composers are using electronic keyboards and computers to compose in order to take advantage of digital technology.
Photo: Alexander Courage

a change in the length of a scene in reel three, the orchestra contractor calling to discuss which clarinet player to hire.

Whatever happens, concentration is crucial. "I block *everything* out when I do a picture," says Randy Newman. "I don't go to appointments, or dentists. . . . I don't answer the phone. I don't do anything else. I hate talking, even to the people involved in the picture (except for the music editor)."

Most composers put a film score together bit by bit, filling in the missing pieces like a jigsaw puzzle. But Bernard Herrmann appears to have had the ultimate work method. "It seems almost incomprehensible," says Elmer Bernstein with admiration, "but he would start with the first piece of music in the film and write a prologue or overture—then he'd just write straight through the film, from beginning to end, in ink, on score paper."

DEMONSTRATING THE SCORE

Maybe John Williams doesn't have to [demonstrate the score], but anyone else has to do it or they won't be able to work.

Randy Edelman, composer

I couldn't have someone show up on the [scoring] stage and say, "We talked about it, and here it is."

Paul Brickman, director

Although some composers much prefer that the director *not* be too specific, we have seen that most directors have moved away from the use of language as the sole method of communication. Hearing the composer's music for a scene and responding to it is a much more specific way to work, and of course, it gives the director much greater potential for input and control.

Randy Edelman, whose scores include *Ghostbusters II* (1989) and *Dragon: The Bruce Lee Story* (1993), feels that demonstrating the music for the director has become absolutely mandatory. And not just themes, but the *whole score,* cue by cue. No longer does the composer sit at the piano pounding out rhapsodic arpeggios. The composer performs and/or programs a complete electronic simulation of the score. The director and producer can make comments and give the composer suggestions or requests for changes, which are sometimes immediately demonstrated by the composer.

Before the evolution of this technology, playing themes and cues on the piano was common at least as far back as the forties. Demonstrating the score on piano has its drawbacks. For one thing, this method assumes that the director can imagine what the composer's pianistic performance will sound like when played by the orchestra. Hearing the piano sketch and translating that into the sound of an imaginary orchestra is a difficult skill, requiring experience and strong musical instincts. Second, not all film composers are brilliant (or even capable) pianists, although almost all play the instrument well enough to use it as a composing aid. While it's easy to visualize accomplished pianists like Dave Grusin, John Williams, or André Previn giving a convincing pianistic performance of a score, what about composers who are trumpet players, like Quincy Jones, Ennio Morricone, John Barry, and Neal Hefti? Johnny Mandel's instrument is trombone (he played in the Count Basie band, in fact). Michael Kamen and Gerald Fried played oboe before they began composing for films. "I can't play piano worth anything," Danny Elfman admits, describing one of his piano demonstrations, "and I had to play everything on the piano. I put on this big presentation [for the filmmakers]. . . . I don't think I've ever sweat more in my life, 'cause I'm pounding these things out, making mistakes all over the place. But I was able to convey the *spirit* of the thing, if not perfect performances."

Unsatisfactory piano demonstrations have undoubtedly led to the rejection of many worthy cues. Even the finest musician can be confused by an inept performance. David Raksin plays clarinet, saxophone, and "composer's piano." His theme for *The Bad and the Beautiful* (1952) is a great melody, ideally suited for sax or strings. One day, he says, having just composed the theme, "I was trying to write it down, when all of a sudden the door flew open and in barged André [Previn] and Jeff [Alexander]. And André said, 'What the hell is that you're working on? I heard you tinkling away.' I said, 'It's a theme I'm going to use in *The Bad and the Beautiful*. . . .'

"At their request, I played the piece. André and Jeff looked at each other, and they looked at me, and André said, 'Lunch!' That was his comment! I went on despite this, and composed the score. André came on the stage when I was recording it, and he was in a great state of excitement over the theme; and he said, 'You've got to give me a copy of that tune. I must record it. It's just sensational. . . .' And I said, 'Why, you louse! You were the first to hear it, you and Jeff, and you said it was nowhere!' And André said, 'The way you play, who can tell?' And he was right."

SAMPLING

With rare exceptions, things are much different now. The electronic demonstrations Randy Edelman referred to have become commonplace. During the mid-eighties, the rapid evolution of electronic keyboards was stimulated by the expanding computer technology in general, and the development of MIDI (*mih*-dee) in particular. This acronym stands for Musical Instrument Digital Interface. It's simply a way of connecting two or more computer-oriented devices so they can send musical information back and forth.

Amazingly, when MIDI was developed, instrument manufacturers from all over the world got together and actually agreed on a set of standards for this new interface. They weren't sure, but they thought there might be enough potential to warrant standardizing the entire MIDI technology so that any machine made by any company could connect to any other machine or machines. Complete compatibility was their goal. The results: a certifiable technological revolution. *Everyone* was interested. The greater the interest, the more sales, so more money was available for further expanding the technology. Meanwhile, the equipment quickly became more and more affordable.

One of the resultant miracles of this electronic fantasia is sampling. If you think sampling is something rappers do, you're absolutely right. It's the same technology with a much different application. There are machines called "samplers" that will digitally record any sound. Basically, if you record a flute note into a sampler, you can play it back through the use of any controller connected to the sampler (or sample playback module) with a MIDI cable. The controller is usually a keyboard, but can be another activating device, such as a specially prepared MIDI guitar controller. Rappers sample segments of previously recorded songs in much the same way, by recording the CD digital signal directly into the sampler and then integrating it into the music by playing it back at will.

Without getting into the details of exactly how

this is done, state-of-the-art sampling can make the sound of that flute available to anyone who has the equipment to play it back. Since the sampled sound is a digital rendering of an acoustic flute, it sounds more or less like an acoustic flute. The better the flute performance, and the better the sampling technique and equipment, the more realistic the sampled flute will sound. With the use of proper sampling techniques, the flute sound can be heard on any note (within its assigned range) activated by the controller. Play a trill on the keyboard controller—hear a flute trill.

Every instrument of the orchestra has been sampled by various manufacturers, including groups of instruments such as a large violin section, four trumpets, and so on. Frogs, jet planes, stadium crowd applause—any sound can be sampled. A number of different companies make these samplers, all of which function as playback machines for sounds compatible with the specific machine in question. And there are sample playback machines available which don't sample new sounds but will play back preprogrammed sounds stored in the internal memory of the machine. Ferris Bueller used a sampler to play toilet flushes and other realistic sounds over the telephone to the school principal in a scene in *Ferris Bueller's Day Off* (1986).

So for a few thousand dollars, anyone in the world has an orchestra to fool around with, and for somewhat more, an even better sounding sampled orchestra. The Rolls-Royce of them all, the Synclavier, was several hundred thousand dollars for the basic stripped-down model, which was available with numerous irresistible (but costly) options until the manufacturer went out of business in 1992.

Incidentally, you needn't possess the keyboard virtuosity of Vladimir Horowitz to sound relatively brilliant with this equipment. Once the notes, accents, dynamics, and other performance characteristics are in the computer, you can make any corrections you want, just like fixing mistakes on a word processing program. Played a wrong note in bar 10? No problem. Just delete it, or change it to the correct note. Want the whole thing up a half step? Easy. It can be done in one command. Best of

A computer, electronic keyboards, a videocassette monitor, recording machines, special electronic effects, a recording console, and speakers surround composer Thomas Newman. Like many of his colleagues, Newman composes (and sometimes records) in his home studio.

all, if the music is too fast to perform with a limited keyboard technique, just slow the tempo down to a comfortable pace, then speed it up again to play it back. Or "step" it in, note by note. Imagine how intrigued directors are upon entering this musical futureworld.

WORKING TOGETHER

Some of the people who share a concern about the negative manifestations of this work process are neither composers nor directors, but film music aficionados—astute longtime observers of the soundtrack scene. While recognizing the value of the technology, composers' agent Richard Kraft worries about the consequences. "The good side of it [being able to dummy up cues on a synthesizer] is that the director can have input when it's

meaningful—not when there are 90 musicians waiting. The down side is, the director feels compelled to comment on things that are often not significant. They get so caught up in, 'Can we change this sound?' It's not their field of expertise, and yet [by being so involved] they're forced to have an opinion."

> *You just wonder how far [a director auditioning every cue] can go. And it hurts to be rejected, even though you realize it's part of the process.*
> *Thomas Newman, composer*

Some directors want more of an involvement with the composing process than the usual procedure allows. In a departure from the short time schedules of most scoring situations, director Paul Brickman had Thomas Newman work on the score of *Men Don't Leave* (1990) for months, trying out various ideas and themes. Although working this way can be exhilarating, it can be unnerving for the composer and frustrating for the director. Yet Newman and Brickman endorse the process and find it productive, and they both describe their working relationship as excellent. Here are excerpts from their comments about their experiences on Brickman's *Men Don't Leave.*

> *Brickman:* I like to explore. You can always go in and pick off-the-shelf solutions. And they could be fine. Audiences could go with it. But I think it's our responsibility to try to push things a little bit, and see where we *can* go. And that takes time, because there's a lot of rejection involved.
> *Newman:* I made attempts before shooting at colorizing things, giving him ambient textures. As much as that interested Paul, I learned that he was more interested in melody and theme.
> *Brickman:* Anything that came to mind, I thought should be explored. Even if you don't use it, it tells you where you don't want to go. Or, it might give you an indication, in a very small way, of . . . a certain direction.

Newman: The difficulty of that whole process, though, is how much do you trust someone to keep rejecting your ideas and still believe in you, and still believe that eventually you'll get the right idea? So as much as you can say, "Well, OK, let's just experiment," there's still a certain amount of pressure on a composer who wants to do a good job.

You want to give directors options, though. In the end, it's probably to your advantage, because if they don't like something, they're not going to like it. *Nothing's* going to make them like it.

Brickman: One direction you were going that I was trying to pull you away from was your sense that the film initially was more threatening—the music was scarier.

Newman: Yeah, except I think that was your interpretation of the ideas. I didn't think I found the music as scary as you did.

Brickman: You scared the hell out of me.

Newman: Paul was always very clear. Of any director I've ever worked with, the sense of where he was going was always clear to him. Sometimes it was less clear to me, but when it came down to making choices, he always made the right ones. And in fact, I disagreed with some of the things he did in the dub, and I remember a day when I was kind of upset by that, and then I saw the movie and I thought, man, he made great choices.

Newman emphasizes that a great deal depends on the director if this give-and-take is to work. "If the relationship is good, and there's a certain amount of respect, then I think that it's utterly fine. If you're in a situation with someone who's just a power freak, then it's really unpleasant." If the director is simply in love with the process itself, and takes advantage of his own power to manipulate the music through the composer, "then even if you go through the process of showing them everything, it doesn't matter. They want to hear everything, but then they don't trust the fact that they've heard it and accepted it, and accepting means nothing now. Then they're asking, 'Why does it sound different now than it sounded then?' and that's a bad situation."

Many times a filmmaker will give a great deal of direction to the composer, becoming an active creative partner in the development of the concept and the dramatic approach of the score, and then relax and become less involved after the basic concept is set. This kind of relationship seems to work very well. Marc Shaiman received similar guidance from director Rob Reiner when he composed his first dramatic film score, for Reiner's *Misery* (1990).

"Rob is very sure about what he wants," Shaiman says. "Although my ego is huge and I have no trouble fighting with someone about something I feel strongly about, it was nice to have someone who was saying, 'Can you make this like that?', 'Can you make this like this? I only want this to be like this. . . .' He came by once, he came by the second time, then . . . it was like, 'Oh, I don't need to come by. I'll just come by next week.'"

It isn't always that comfortable. When Shaiman worked on *The Addams Family* (1991), differences of opinion developed. "As a composer, and a human being, that's the hardest part," Shaiman says. "You're trying to please the director, you're trying to please the producer, and you're trying to please yourself."

The resultant tension can be brutal. "My solution was to collapse and be brought to the hospital—I'm not kidding. There *was* no solution. Luckily, the producer and director and I actually really liked each other a lot. We were really friends through moments of whining and bickering. But . . . I am only who I am, I can only write what I can write, and eventually it gets down to—'Well, guys, this is how I see this cue; this is how I write; and there's no time left. This is it.'"

ORCHESTRATION

Orchestration is without doubt one of the most important elements of music in motion pictures.
                                        Bronislau Kaper, composer

I believe that the foremost principle of good scoring for motion pictures is the color of orchestrations. The melody is only secondary.

Franz Waxman, *composer*

As we have seen, the basic concept of a score can develop from instrumental colors. In *Up the Down Staircase* (1967), my themes came directly from the instruments, not the other way around. Five recorders (vertical wooden flutelike instruments dating back to the Middle Ages) were used as one-fourth of the 20-piece orchestra (with no strings). The main theme developed conceptually from the principal character in the film, a high school teacher (Sandy Dennis) coming to work for the first time to a tough neighborhood in New York City. The use of the recorders as primary instruments was suggested by her personality (nonassertive and wispy) and background (medieval literature). Significantly, the theme, with its interweaving lines and independent accompaniment, was especially suitable for this recorder ensemble, perhaps more so than for any other instrument or group of instruments. The theme would not have evolved as it did had it been conceived for saxophones, strings, or even modern orchestral flutes. Even the harmony accompanying the theme suggested the Renaissance harmonies usually associated with recorders.

The specific sound of a particular instrument or group of instruments can characterize or represent a major dramatic element. Consider the dramatic power of the unaccompanied trumpet solo at the beginning of Italian composer Nino Rota's score for *The Godfather* (1972). Composers in the late sixties and seventies, including Lalo Schifrin, Quincy Jones, and Jerry Fielding, were particularly apt to create an instrumental texture that could unify a score. "What I try to create by way of getting attention is a certain sound," Fielding said. "Most people can recognize a sound, even though subconsciously. Think, for example, of what Rózsa did with the theremin in *Spellbound* [1945; see Chapter 6]. It was at that time a new and unique sound, and it immediately summarized the psychotic condition of the hero. That sound not only told the audience

something potent about what they were watching, but signaled that something strange and exciting was likely to happen."

The specific color doesn't have to be as exotic as the otherworldly soprano-like theremin to be effective. Franz Waxman felt instrumental choices were a primary consideration in his scores, even within the standard symphonic orchestra used for the scores of the forties and fifties. "There are instances in which the mood of a scene will be accomplished by underscoring it with a single instrument. The tone color alone of the instrument will determine the acquired mood. In *Pride of the Marines* [1945], in the scene in which John Garfield walks alone through Pennsylvania Station, as the camera booms high, giving the vast space of the terminal and the awful sense of loneliness of the man, going to war without a soul to bid him farewell, I used a solo trumpet. There is nothing as sad or as lonely as the sound of a trumpet, and it was right for that scene. That one single instrument colored the mood. . . . Looking at a scene or a sequence, I may see a horn or I may see massed violins. . . ."

During the years of the studio system, the availability of staff orchestras led to a standard orchestrational approach for the vast number of film scores of the thirties through the mid-fifties. Many of the Max Steiner and Alfred Newman scores of those years, for example, feature a basic string color that establishes the sound for the majority of the picture, with little variety. This was much less so of the Waxman, Rózsa, and Herrmann scores, as these composers used the full range of orchestral coloration more often.

Selection of the type of orchestra, solo colors, and orchestration can be as important as the choice of melodic and harmonic materials. The pioneer in this area of orchestral variety was Bernard Herrmann, who began experimenting with small, unusual ensembles during his radio years at CBS in New York City in the thirties. Herrmann always orchestrated his own scores, and throughout his career he continued to personalize his orchestrations. Although his orchestral flexibility didn't seem to have much impact on the standard practices in Hollywood, he was convinced of its virtues. "Since the middle of the eighteenth century, the symphony orchestra has always been an agreed body of men performing a repertoire of music. But since a film score is only written for one performance, I could never see the logic in making a rule of the standard symphony orchestra. A film score can be made up of different fantastic groupings of instruments, as I've done throughout my entire career."

His score for *Citizen Kane* (1941) demonstrates this philosophy. "Many sections were written for odd instrumental combinations which avoided the conventional orchestral sound. I had sufficient time to orchestrate all of the music and to conduct it and think about it. Twelve weeks were devoted to the score as against the usual six weeks or even less given to other pictures of this length and importance."

Herrmann also realized the power of recording technology in emphasizing the sound of the instruments. "The motion picture sound track is an exquisitely sensitive medium. With skillful engineering, a simple bass flute solo, the pulsing of a bass drum, or the sound of muted horns can often be far more effective than half-a-hundred musicians playing away." This awareness allowed him to take full advantage of the dramatic power of orchestration.

Though he did use symphonic orchestration during the forties for *The Magnificent Ambersons* (1942), *The Ghost and Mrs. Muir* (1947), and other films, his more adventurous orchestrations never really influenced the Hollywood mainstream. When Alex North arrived in Hollywood in 1951 to record his scores for *A Streetcar Named Desire* and *Death of a Salesman,* he surprised the recording musicians and executives by orchestrating for smaller, more personal instrumental combinations. As he was not part of the studio system at that time, it didn't occur to him to consider using the entire staff orchestra simply because they were available.

To compose and to orchestrate are parts of a single moment. Whoever writes music for films without orchestrating each segment is nothing but a dilettante.

Ennio Morricone, composer

Those people who feel that composers should do their own orchestrations should have been at Universal [in the forties]. There simply was no time for such luxuries.

Hans J. Salter, composer

Don't let anyone mistake these gentlemen's unquestioning music habits as hack work; any examination of their scores would prove the most enviable, sophisticated knowledge of what makes an orchestra sound.

André Previn, composer
(re: the MGM orchestrators in the fifties)

There are some film composers who do their own orchestrating. In television, for instance, though the schedules are horrendous, the budgets rarely cover the expense of orchestration, so the composers tend to orchestrate their own scores. If time were no consideration, many composers would enjoy orchestrating their own music for features. As far back as 1945, though, Miklós Rózsa said, "When a film score has to be completed in a few short weeks, this is physically impossible." Since this is still true, the music a composer writes for feature films is typically orchestrated by one or more orchestrators.

In 1937, Dimitri Tiomkin had nine orchestrators working with him on his score for *Lost Horizon.* What did they do, and how did they do it? According to orchestrator Bernhard Kaun, who worked with Tiomkin on the picture, "Since he was a pianist, one had to rethink his ideas in an orchestral way. I did this in the few numbers that I did for him. He would give his pianistic sketches to a good arranger who would make the best of it. But it was still Tiomkin's music."

As a rule, composers make elaborate sketches on music paper containing from three to as many as ten or more staves. Ideally, all the basic musical materials should be on these sketches—melody, rhythms, harmony, counterlines as needed, as well as orchestrational indications—"brass" next to a group of accented chords, "French horns" for a counterline, "violin harmonics" for a high sustained note.

In reality, not all sketches are that complete.

Some sketches are far less detailed than others, both in their attention to the actual compositional ingredients, and also with regard to the composer's orchestrational intentions. Since orchestrators are conscious of the potential impact on future job opportunities of unwise indiscretion, they rarely say much on the record about how much they actually add to a composer's music.

The greater the detail on the sketch, the less there is for the orchestrator to contribute to the actual orchestration. When the sketch is less than complete, however, that doesn't necessarily mean that the composer doesn't know what he wants, nor does it mean that he can't make his wishes known to the orchestrator. "There was a wonderful musician named Frederick Hollander—a brilliant pianist, but he didn't know anything about an orchestra," explains Arthur Morton. "He used to say, 'You're the orchestrator, do what you want.' I replied, 'Freddie, I could orchestrate this 12 different ways. Please play it for me.' Well, Freddie had wonderful hands—he played beautifully. I heard him play through the score and immediately I knew what he wanted. Then I would say, 'That's a clarinet there,' and he would say, 'Of course!' ... You try to get your ears in tune with the composer's."

Orchestrator Maurice De Packh, whose orchestrations include those for Alex North's *Streetcar Named Desire* (1951), *Death of a Salesman* (1951), and *Viva Zapata!* (1952), described the sketches of several of the composers of the day. His comments illustrate the ways in which an orchestrator works with a film composer.

Alfred Newman's sketches are what I would call very sparse. They are only the skeleton of the music, but when he turns them over to an arranger he accompanies them with very full verbal explanations and many illustrations at the piano. Hugo Friedhofer's sketches are quite complete usually, although he might occasionally give you a sketch with a comment like, "Give this an outdoor, woodwindy, Sibelius kind of color." Roy Webb's sketches are somewhat like piano music. Adolph Deutsch's are complete and detailed. But the most meticulous sketches of all are David Raksin's; sometimes they are so detailed that I wonder why he doesn't orchestrate while he composes.

De Packh then goes on to describe what he sees as the orchestrator's role.

Every arranger [orchestrator] is expected to make certain adjustments in the interest of balance between the sections of the orchestra. They may have to strengthen the violin line with the flute playing an octave higher, for instance. . . .

The orchestrator ought to know the picture as well as the composer does. They are really collaborators, and the best results are obtained when they understand one another's thoughts and feelings about music in general, not just a particular sequence being scored. If I were working for a composer of, say, very classical tastes, I certainly wouldn't orchestrate his music in the style of Richard Strauss.

Over the years, orchestrators have been relied upon to accommodate any style of music and any period of music history. "All of us were expected to be total chameleons," says André Previn, describing his years at MGM during the fifties. "'I want this to sound like. . . .' Fill in the name of your preference: Ravel, Tchaikovsky, Strauss, Count Basie, a Broadway pit; that was an instruction we all heard many times during working hours, and we were expected to nod submissively, go away, and produce the musical goods."

Orchestrators fill in and elaborate on any details not on the composer's sketches. Often, but not always, this is because of the typical time crunches. For example, Leo Shuken orchestrated a lot of Victor Young's music. "Victor Young would fill up anywhere from two to five lines full of notes," Shuken said, "but he indicated no orchestral colors, which I liked, because it gave me a chance to be an orchestrator in the best sense." As Paramount Pictures music editor/executive Bill Stinson remembered it, "Young had a couple of orchestrators who knew his style and they really were his sound. You would turn lead lines over to them and tell them to score the picture, then he'd come in and conduct it."

The nature of the music has a lot to do with the orchestrator's opportunity to bring something of his own to the score. "In a score like *Hawaii* [1966] or a score like *The Magnificent Seven* [1960], which is quite straightforward in terms of tutti, conventional orchestral symphonic writing, orchestrators have contributed a great deal, I would say," says Elmer Bernstein, composer of these scores. "On the other hand, in terms of pictures where the sound is still much more transparent—take a score like *To Kill a Mockingbird* [1962] or *The Birdman of Alcatraz* [1962]—there were orchestrators on those pictures, but the orchestrators in those instances were much more like secretaries. I mean, I wouldn't say that the orchestrators contributed in any way to those types of scores."

Often composers establish close personal and artistic ties with orchestrators. Arthur Morton began orchestrating Jerry Goldsmith's music in 1962: "[Arthur Morton is] my closest friend. We first met in 1960. Because of the time needed to transfer what I've written to the full orchestra . . . I will write the music out in 9 staves, and he will transfer it onto 24 or 30 [staves], whatever . . . [is needed for the particular orchestra]. He's a comrade, and someone to listen to me. He knows how I think so well, he's like a psychiatrist who comes and discusses the problems with me."

Greig McRitchie has worked with many film composers since the early 1960s. He feels part of his contribution is personal. "You make the job of the composer easier. I act as a court jester a lot of times. I'll make jokes, take the pressure off of him that way, which helps an awful lot, I think. Give him confidence—some of the guys lose confidence. And I'll say, 'Oh, we'll make it, don't worry about it.'

He finds out what the composer wants, and then does whatever is needed. "James Horner, for instance, is great with the strings. He'd write maybe five or six different violin lines, all intertwined.

And he'd write maybe two bars, and then say, 'Now, go ahead, you continue.' Which is a great way to save time. But you have to trust your orchestrator."

Randy Edelman faxes his sketches to McRitchie. "But I miss the personal contact," McRitchie laments. "He sends me an audiotape of the music—that's very helpful. . . . And he writes out the sketch."

Jack Eskew has orchestrated many of Bill Conti's scores, including *Rocky V* (1990), *The Karate Kid II* (1986), and *Broadcast News* (1987). "We sit down and go over every sketch and discuss what this ought to be and what that ought to be, and at the end of this [talk] session the page is full of the notes that we've made. I'll add some of the chord parts, but melodically I never add a note. I'll never say that I do that much for Bill—his music is pretty easy to orchestrate. He has a very logical hand. The interpretation is completely Bill. We don't have a partnership. I just assist Bill in those areas that he needs assistance."

Herb Spencer orchestrated all of John Williams' scores from 1974 until 1990. Beginning as a contract arranger for Fox in 1935, he orchestrated such diverse films as *Alexander's Ragtime Band* (1938, Alfred Newman), *Forever Amber* (1947, David Raksin), *Cleopatra* (1963, Alex North), *Hello, Dolly!* (1969, Lionel Newman), *M*A*S*H* (1970, Johnny Mandel), and *The Way We Were* (1973, Marvin Hamlisch).

Spencer described what it's like to work with Williams: "John generally makes a very good sketch. If you look at it carefully, all the information is there, but sometimes there are suggestions back and forth. 'Why don't we do—?' He might buy that and say, 'Yes, let's do it that way.' He always plays it for me exactly in tempo. He's a good enough piano player that he doesn't stumble through it. The tempo and the intention of the sound—everything is right there."

Williams knows exactly what he wants and how to get it—but as McRitchie points out, "Some people need more help than others. I won't work with the guys who are hummers. . . ."

Bars 9 through 16 of Jerry Goldsmith's sketch for the Main Title of *Star Trek—The Motion Picture* (1979). The first two staves are indicated for woodwinds, the next two for brass, the final three for strings, plus a line at the bottom for percussion. The first page indicates that the cue is written for a $13\frac{4}{}$ click in $\frac{6}{8}$ meter, with no sharps or flats in the key signature.

Star Trek—The Motion Picture (*Jerry Goldsmith*)

Copyright © 1979 by Ensign Music Corporation

Arthur Morton's orchestration of Jerry Goldsmith's Main Title for *Star Trek—The Motion Picture* (bars 9 through 12). Morton orchestrated the sketch shown above. Goldsmith's theme for the movie was used as the theme for the television series "Star Trek: The Next Generation."

Star Trek—The Motion Picture (*Jerry Goldsmith*)

Copyright © 1979 by Ensign Music Corporation

Hummers? "For years I'd heard about the 'hummers of Hollywood,'" says Michael Kamen, who lives in England, "the guys who can't write music and get great orchestrators to help them out. I never knew how to use an orchestrator—I just felt it was easier to do it all myself. Hiring an orchestrator seemed like a cop-out. Then I got to Hollywood for *Lethal Weapon* and was told how normal it is for a composer to use one. I discovered it *was* possible to sit down with somebody and explain what I want. These guys color a score like pros. They make really fine touches that I wouldn't even think of.

"After all, does it matter if Michelangelo was the guy who actually chipped off the last flake of marble on David's ass?"

By far the most persuasive argument for working with an orchestrator, though, is the time factor, a benefit that John Barry appreciates. "The most important thing is composing the right music; it's spending the time you have getting the composition correct with the movie. I can do a sketch on maybe a three-minute cue in one day. We call them sketches, but actually, they're so comprehensive. The orchestrator then really puts that into a full score for the copyist, but he doesn't add any musical content. I can write flutes, woodwinds, octaves, or whatever, then he writes all that out, so that's three days' labor I don't have to bother with, and I can be getting on with the next thing. The orchestration for the music is a strange process—it's a lot of work, but it's not a lot of creative work—it's just the nuts and bolts of what you wish to do."

Composers who come to Hollywood from New York, England, or other parts of the world are usually concerned about using an orchestrator. They often have gotten into the habit of orchestrating their own music, and are reluctant to give up any control over their work. French composer Georges Delerue continued to do his own orchestrating when he moved to Los Angeles, and felt that a composer's individuality was endangered if he gave up that prerogative. "What bothers me a bit about certain American composers that are really remarkable is that they may sound a bit alike. Which is not sur-

prising if you realize that they use the same orchestrators. You can count the good American film composers on the fingers of your two hands— that's not a criticism, it goes for France, too—but there are not many good orchestrators, either. So they're always the same orchestrators who are being asked, and there resides the danger of things becoming a bit stereotyped."

This never concerned Aaron Copland, universally recognized as one of the finest American composers. When pressed by a colleague to defend his use of an orchestrator for *The Red Pony* (1949), he had a quick rebuttal. "Look at this and answer me the following: If I dictate a letter and it is typed for me, who actually wrote the letter, me or my secretary?" As André Previn points out, "It's a valid point, but only if the composer's sketch, or short score, is as complete as Copland's obviously was."

Once orchestrated, the full scores are sent to a librarian, who supervises the extraction of all the instrumental parts and prepares a complete set of instrument "books," one for each instrument in the recording orchestra for each session: Trumpet 1, Trumpet 2, Trumpet 3, Trombone 1, and so on. If the budget allows, the scores and instrumental parts are proofread to correct possible errors as well. During these weeks, incidentally, the orchestra contractor has been tracking the projected expenses to be sure the music production costs won't excede the budget established by the music department or production company. She coordinates and supervises all the logistics of the sessions, including such things as booking the scoring stage (studio), renting any special instruments, arranging for the instrumentalists to bring all instruments indicated in the scores, and many other details.

The composer will have created a score ranging from 30 to 45 minutes in duration, up to 2 hours or more. Ideally, the score will be consistent in its concept. A well-crafted score will have enough variety to be interesting, yet enough repetition and development of basic melodies, motifs, and other musical material to be structurally sound. It will synchronize perfectly with the picture when conducted and performed as intended. It will serve all the emotional and other dramatic needs of the film. And now the music will be recorded on the scoring stage by a hand-picked freelance studio orchestra which has been called together by the contractor with the supervision and/or approval of the composer, or, in the case of scores recorded outside the United States, possibly by an existing orchestra like the London Symphony Orchestra (LSO). But the collaboration between the filmmakers and the composer continues on the scoring stage, and then onto the dubbing stage for the final mix.

Recording and Mixing

■ ■ ■

I like working with musicians. . . . That's the best part of being a film composer, to go out on a stage with 70 or 90 musicians. . . . That I dearly love.

Basil Poledouris, composer

PRERECORDING

It's amazing how the close-up of hands establishes the fact that the man is really playing. And if you believe the first few bars, from there on, they believe everything.

Bronislau Kaper, composer

Before the film is even shot, there may be music to compose, orchestrate, and record. On-screen instrumental (and vocal) performances are rarely shot with the final sound and photography done simultaneously. These performances are almost invariably recorded before they are photographed (that is, they are prerecorded), which means that when you see

music being performed in a film, chances are the musicians on camera are faking it.

If you're watching a performance of Louis Armstrong in *Hello Dolly!* (1969), Armstrong is simply pretending to play the trumpet on camera—he has already prerecorded his own trumpet part. If you're watching Richard Dreyfuss rip off a dazzling cloudburst of notes in *The Competition* (a 1980 film about a group of skilled pianists competing for top honors), you're simply watching him fake it brilliantly, while listening to an expert performance prerecorded by a pro.

Instrumental and vocal dubbing were well-kept secrets during the thirties, forties, and fifties. José Iturbi was a very popular artist, but Columbia Pictures did not reveal to the public that Iturbi played

the piano solos for Cornel Wilde in the Chopin biography *A Song to Remember* (1944). Similarly,
Artur Rubinstein played piano while Katharine
Hepburn faked it as Clara Schumann in the 1947
film *Song of Love*. It would have been good press
for the studios to publicize the use of these popular
artists, and yet as late as the mid-fifties the studios
were still misrepresenting these facts to the public.

The studios reasoned that the public wouldn't
find the performance believable if they knew that
the actor wasn't actually playing the instrument or
singing the song. At MGM, Harold Gellman was
responsible for teaching Elizabeth Taylor enough
piano technique so she could fake it in *Rhapsody*
(1954). When he wanted to publicize his work
with her, the studio legal department refused him
permission to do so. Music editor Ralph Ives was at
MGM at the time (his wide-ranging credits include
Quo Vadis [1951], *The Bad and the Beautiful*
[1952], *On the Town* [1949], and *The Godfather*
[1972]). As Gellman told Ives, "Their comment
was, 'It would destroy the image that the studio
was trying to preserve.'"

Maintaining the illusion can be complicated.
Most actors cannot learn to fake convincingly
enough when the director wants close-ups on their
hands as they race up and down the keyboard. An
accomplished pianist's hands are usually substituted
for the close-ups. While André Previn was at
MGM, says Miklós Rózsa, "We discovered that
André's hands looked on camera much more like
Barbara Stanwyck's than those of the lady pianist
hired for the film, so . . . the hands you see playing
the piano music in *The Other Love* [1947] are actually André's."

There are few technical problems in shooting
these close-ups when only the hands (and sometimes the arms) are shot. During the editing the
close-ups are integrated into the medium and long-
shots of the performance, creating the illusion that
the actor is really peforming. But there are times
when the director wants to show the pianist's hands
and then, in the same shot, pull back to show the
actor's body. This is a much more difficult illusion,
and making it work can require a backbreaking ef-

fort. Bronislau Kaper, who was an excellent pianist,
became Conrad Veidt's hands in *A Woman's Face*,
George Cukor's 1941 film in which Joan Crawford
plays a woman who has plastic surgery. "Conrad
Veidt was sitting at the piano," Kaper recounts.
"First of all, he showed his hands. Now, when they
showed his hands, those were my hands. I was
squatting behind him with my hands at both sides
of his body, so that you could see I had a jacket to
match his jacket, and shirt, cuffs, cufflinks, everything exactly. Only the hands were a little different.
And I was playing. Then gradually the camera

Claudio Arrau, the renowned Chilean pianist, performed the
piano solos for Elizabeth Taylor's character in the 1954 MGM
motion picture *Rhapsody*. John Green and Bronislau Kaper
were co-music directors for the film's score. Green is conducting Rachmaninoff's Piano Concerto No. 2.
Photo courtesy of Marc Wanamaker/Bison Archives

Erich Wolfgang Korngold reviews a portion of his score for the Warner Bros. film *Deception* (1946) for co-stars Paul Henreid and Bette Davis. During the filming, considerable care was taken to create the illusion that Henreid was actually playing the cello.

Photo courtesy of Ernst W. Korngold

pulled back, and then you saw him, but without the hands. It's a very simple trick. . . . I must tell you, the difficulty was not to do it, but to disappear suddenly, because . . . [otherwise], in a long shot, I would be sitting there behind the guy."

Regardless of the musical style, the difficulties are the same. One of the worst problems occurs when the actor fakes it so poorly that everybody can tell immediately that he isn't playing the music. It *must* look absolutely convincing or reality takes a holiday. That was a problem for composer-pianist Dick Hyman while he was working on *Scott Joplin* (1977, directed by Jeremy Kagen). He prerecorded all the piano solos in the usual way only to learn that Billy Dee Williams, who played the role of Joplin, hadn't been coached on how to fake performing to Hyman's prerecordings convincingly.

"It turned out he had not any idea whatsoever

of how to play a keyboard," says Hyman. "So his fingers looked extremely wrong for whatever it was he thought he was miming. In some places, therefore, we had to rerecord the piano. He had tried to mime what I had prerecorded, and then I had to rerecord more or less the way that he had done it, which was excruciatingly difficult, trying to figure out what could be done musically that would go with his fingers. In some cases we were able to cut away altogether from the hands."

Whatever is done with piano can be done with any other instrument, including strings. Erich Wolfgang Korngold wrote a cello concerto for Paul Henreid's character to play in *Deception* (1946, with Bette Davis and Claude Rains). The following excerpt is from an article by Jack Hiemenz that appeared in the *Village Voice* in January 1976.

> One can only marvel at how totally *professional* Henreid looks during his cello-playing scenes. It turns out that Warners took great pains to ensure that look of authenticity. For long shots, the man you see performing is actually a double. For medium shots, you are seeing the real Henreid, who's been coached by a professional cellist. In the sustained close-ups, though, Warners pulled a sneaky. What you are really seeing is not what your eyes are telling you; actually, you're watching Paul Henreid backed up by *two* cellists, who are invisible except for their arms, which protrude through false sleeves—and it is they, not our distinguished actor, who are doing the actual playing.

The following year, Warner Bros. followed with *Humoresque* (1947), the story of an ambitious violinist. "John Garfield . . . had to be photographed playing the violin, simulating the technique of the left hand fingering and the right hand bowing it," Oscar Levant wrote in *The Memoirs of an Amnesiac.* "They had great difficulty with this scene. They couldn't arrive at a modus operandi until finally, in close shots, they had two violinists crouched out of camera range; one did the fingerwork and the other the bowing. The violin was attached to Garfield's neck. The real playing was prerecorded by the great

Isaac Stern, and I accompanied him on the piano. After a couple of takes, I suggested, 'Why don't the five of us make a concert tour?'"

It was easy to joke about this charade—it must have looked ridiculous while they were shooting, but it's the image on-screen that counts. Specialists are usually assigned to productions during the filming just to be sure that whenever scenes like these are shot, everything looks right and is perfectly in sync with the music.

SYNCHRONIZATION

In order for all this effort to pay off, the music must be exactly in sync with the film with one-hundred-percent accuracy. This would be easy if the score were initially recorded directly onto the film itself. However, it is not. It's either recorded on analog or digital audiotape, or on 35mm film stock that has been coated with the same surface as audiotape (called "mag stripe" or "full coat"), or on both simultaneously. Until the recorded music is prepared by the music editor for the final mix and subsequently dubbed into the picture, it isn't physically in sync.

There are two ways that sound is locked into sync with the picture. Usually the music is transferred to 35mm sound film and edited onto a music reel at the correct starting point. Since it's on film, these music units can be shifted as little as one frame in order to assure perfect sync. In some cases, however, the music is recorded on (or transferred to) a multitrack tape recorder (perhaps a 32- or 48-track digital machine). That recorder is locked to the projector by using a sync pulse such as SMPTE.

With either method, if the score has been timed accurately and the music is performed exactly as timed throughout—bar for bar, beat for beat—the recorded score will play exactly in sync, and will be able to be locked in later with the picture.

Music editor Abby Treloggen builds the music unit for a reel, syncing up the cues to the picture and dialogue track. For overlapping cues that segue, there might be two or more units for a reel (an A unit, a B unit, and so on).
Photo: Gay Wallin

The traditional way to fit the music to the film during scoring is to record the music while watching the picture projected onto a large screen or a television monitor on the scoring stage. Several conducting aids are used to help achieve a well-synchronized peformance:

1. *Clicks.* They can be generated by a small device called a "digital metronome," or by a computer. Either one can be set to any desired tempo, and will generate a clicking sound that functions as a time-keeper, or metronome. When this method is used, the conductor (and usually the entire orchestra) wears headphones and performs to the tempo of the click. It's most common to record an entire cue to click, although the clicks can be dropped or intro-

duced at any time. They may be used to set the initial tempo for a bar or two before the first downbeat and then dropped out as the music begins. If they are going to be used to record, they are frequently used also as a guide when rehearsing the orchestra. This way, by the time the orchestra is ready to record, sync will already have been checked by the music editor during a rehearsal with the film.

Clicks are most often used for recording rhythmic music at fast tempos, music using any kind of rhythm section (that is, any combination of drums, bass, keyboards, and guitars playing a steady tempo), and music designed to accent minute details in the action (cartoon animation is always recorded to click). Some conductors, however, record their entire score to click. Although this method may sacrifice a degree of musical expression because of the inflexible tempo, it is a very efficient and fast method and good sync is guaranteed.

Dimitri Tiomkin claimed he introduced the use of a click track in his scoring of *Alice in Wonderland* in 1933. Max Steiner used clicks frequently, even for romantic scenes, and he, too, claimed to have used them first. Others credited with "inventing" the click track include Scott Bradley, Oliver Wallace, Carl Stalling, and music editors Steve Csillag ("*Chill*-ogg") and Charlie Dunworth. In reality, all these men contributed to the evolution of the technique.

2. *Streamers.* Streamers are three-, four-, or five-foot lines that appear to move across the screen diagonally from left to right. When they get to the extreme right-hand side of the screen, they serve as a sync point for the conductor. A three-foot streamer takes two seconds to move across the screen.

The music editor prepares the film sequences to be recorded, scribing the streamers onto the film dupe used for scoring. There are always streamers to designate the beginning and end of each cue. If the orchestra is recording to click on the cue, there is a streamer to let the music editor know when to start the clicks. They can be used anywhere else during the cue; typically the conductor selects these spots

and indicates them on the score, but the music editor may add any he feels might be helpful.

When recording to videotape, the music editor uses one of the several available computer programs to place the streamers electronically on the videotape. The effect is the same.

3. *Punches.* The music editor can take a small paper punch and actually punch a hole in any frame. It takes punches on two or three consecutive frames to create a clearly visible effect. This effect is like a quick flash of light and is used as a warning device at any time during a scene. In the early days a red grease pencil was used instead of a punch.

4. *The Newman System.* Back in the thirties, music editor Charlie Dunworth developed the Newman System for Alfred as a visual guide while he was conducting. Dunworth would punch every other frame of film for 18 or 20 frames. The punches cause a flash of light on the screen, which can be seen even if you are not looking directly at the screen. This effect is perfect for keeping the music in sync with the picture because you can read the score and still see the flashes of light without looking up.

When music editor George Adams worked with Alfred Newman, he noticed that Newman didn't sync up with all the flashes. It wasn't necessary, since the flashes were used to provide guidance for the conductor and not necessarily a strict tempo. This gave Newman a lot of flexibility with the tempos, yet he could always return to the tempo of the flashes when he wished in order to hit an upcoming streamer perfectly.

5. *Large sweep-second clock.* Every scoring stage has one, mounted on the edge of or near the conductor's stand. (Digital clocks are not used for conducting because you don't get a feel for the flow or forward motion of time.) The music editor starts the clock from :00 every time the orchestra begins to rehearse or record a cue, and this allows the conductor to check the timings on his score so he can come to the downbeat of the next bar at exactly the right time.

6. *Dialogue.* The conductor can hear dialogue track in her headset as a conducting aid. Although

very few conductors do this, it's an excellent device for keeping track of the scene timing-wise without even looking at the film.

Almost everybody uses one or more of these conducting aids, but Korngold and Herrmann preferred to rely upon their intimate knowledge of the footage coupled with an innate sense of timing. Music editor Len Engel, who had worked with Herrmann, admired his amazing skill. "He hardly used any cue marks on a film. When I first started working with him I found this hard to believe—how could he catch cues with nothing on the screen? No click tracks, nothing." This is very unusual, but it can be done by an intuitive and skilled conductor.

There are several technical steps that are taken to further ensure successful synchronization of the score. Many scores are recorded on 35mm magnetic (mag) film stock, which, since it is film, has sprockets and is therefore sprocket-driven, on a machine actually locked to the motion picture projector. Also, music recorded onto analog and digital tape always has some sort of sync pulse recorded onto one track of the tape so it can be "resolved" during playback. The process of resolution simply causes the playback tape machine to go at exactly the same speed as the machine on which the music was originally recorded.

In a recording session, we did everything simultaneously. The voices and the orchestra and all the sound effects.

Ralph Ives, music editor
(re: Fleischer Animation Studios, 1934)

In the early days of sound, technology was much less sophisticated—so much so that recording the score was astonishingly difficult. As late as 1934 everything was recorded simultaneously at the Fleischer Animation Studios in New York City—music, actors' voices for the cartoon characters, and sound effects. Music editor Ralph Ives was just beginning his apprenticeship then.

"We had two long tables . . . and these were where all the sound effects were placed, and two mics, one for each of the sound effects tables. They had pots and pans and all different kinds of things, depending on what sounds were needed for the picture.

"It was an incredible thing. The orchestra sat near the right side facing the screen, the singers and actors on the left side facing the screen. On the left edge of the screen I had mechanically animated a 'bouncing ball' by punching holes in the film to set the tempo for sync, but there was also a conductor who followed the screen. They did a solid reel, which in most of their cartoons ran seven or eight

Equipment on or near a scoring stage podium includes a headset (one-ear only in this photograph, although some conductors use the normal double set), a large sweep-second clock (typically operated by the music editor using a remote control), a Urei Digital Metronome, which is the black rectangular object beneath the clock (another is usually found at the music editor's table as well), and a microphone enabling the conductor to be heard in the recording booth. The computer to the right of the podium (typically placed at the music editor's table) can be used by the music editor to add or change streamers, punches, and preprogrammed click tracks. The full orchestral score is in front of the clock.
Photo: Gay Wallin

minutes. So they'd start at the top and go all the way through.

"They recorded on wax discs, I'd say about two or three feet in diameter. This is pre-acetate—very hard wax, about four inches thick. They could only play it back once—that was the only chance we had to check the recording. When they were through with that take, they had some kind of a lathe to shave that layer off so they could start again. The master was the optical negative that they made simultaneously.

"They had several rehearsals, and when they thought they had everything ready, they would go for a take. They'd spend one day doing a short. They'd print up two, sometimes three takes, from which I would intercut the best parts. So actually, with one recording session, they ended up with a complete dub of their reel."

From about 1929 to 1932 or 1933 they worked this way in Hollywood also, recording on giant records, something like 36 to 48 inches across. "The records were tremendous," says John Hammell, who joined Paramount as a music editor a few years later. "They were mounted on the back of the projection machine, locked right into the projector."

Irvin Talbot conducted the Paramount scores at that time, and it was very difficult. "He used to tell me he'd be scoring a whole reel on record," says Hammell, "and then, say, down on the end of the reel, Clara Bow would be doing a dance. A big production routine. And he'd have to swing into that, nonstop. They had no way of stopping that record, so if he *did* make a mistake, he'd have to go back and do the whole damn *scene* over."

Synchronizing the score to a film was not any easier in 1935. After visiting the scoring stage during the recording of the famous factory sequence in Charlie Chaplin's *Modern Times,* Sidney Skolsky, columnist for the *Chicago Tribune,* wrote about his experience.

The orchestra starts rehearsing the music for the factory sequence in which Chaplin revolts against being a slave of the machinery, throws the place into confusion, and does a wild dance. The music is as difficult as the scene. Every note must be on time with the film; and the music is not loud and brazen, as expected of factory sounds. The orchestra rehearses those few bars again . . . again . . . again. It is almost an hour later. And just those few bars rehearsed. Yesterday they worked from 9:00 in the morning until 4:00 the next morning, and about half a reel [five minutes] was completely scored. It costs Chaplin on the average of a thousand dollars an hour to score this flicker. Now, after several hours of rehearsing, Newman and Chaplin agree they will try to record this scene.

RECORDING

In the recording of film music for motion pictures, it is possible to achieve total perfection of performance. Don't settle for anything less!

Alfred Newman, composer

[Because the director has already heard an electronic version of the music] when I show up with the orchestra . . . the directors know exactly what's coming up, only it sounds better. It's fun and games, and it's an absolute ball.

Randy Edelman, composer

Every composer agrees that the climax of the entire process of scoring a film takes place on the scoring stage. Hearing your music performed by some of the world's greatest musicians is an absolutely unparalleled experience. The music will almost certainly be well recorded, using state-of-the-art technology, and no listening experience compares to that provided by the playback monitors of a well-equipped control booth. This is also the time when the score is fine-tuned by the performances of the conductor and orchestra, and by the sound of the recording itself.

There is a large support group of people working on a scoring session, all contributing to make

Jerry Goldsmith conducts his score for *Legend* (1986) in London. Due to an executive decision by Universal to attempt to appeal in the States to a considerably younger audience than originally intended, his score was released with the film abroad but not in the U.S., where it was replaced with a "younger" sound.

Photo: Alexander Courage

things go well. The following are usually on the stage itself:

- *The conductor* (most frequently, but not always, the composer)
- *The musicians* (anywhere from 1 to 110)
- *The music editor,* who runs the click machine and the clock; "slates" (that is, verbally numbers and identifies) the takes and makes notes accordingly; monitors the performances for sync and quality, often reading the scores to do so; and may discuss dramatic points with the composer
- *The librarian,* who distributes the music for each instrument and is available to make corrections and changes on the instrumental parts, if necessary

- *The orchestra contractor,* who has booked the musicians for the sessions; makes any necessary last-minute adjustments (for example, replacing a missing player, which is rare but does happen); calls a rental service for a newly requested instrument; supervises orchestra deportment; and keeps track of all business matters relating to the session (hours worked, instruments played, and so on)
- *The stage manager,* who sits near the music editor and acts as a liaison between the scoring stage and the recording crew (in other rooms)

The recording booth (control room) crew includes:

- *The recording engineer* (mixer), who is responsible for recording the music, and is in charge of all details, both technical and artistic, pertinent to that end (number of mics, type and model of mic, mic placement, which instruments are recorded on which tracks, and so on)
- *The orchestrator* or other *booth representative,* who works closely with the mixer, informing him about upcoming solos and other textural details, and communicates with the conductor through a talk-back mic that is fed into the conductor's headset
- *The music supervisor,* who acts as a liaison between the filmmakers and the composer, as necessary. Not all films have a music supervisor; in some cases, the music supervisor may act as booth representative.
- *The recordist,* who operates the recording machines in the booth

The rest of the technical support group includes:

- *The projectionist* or *videotape operator*
- *The dialogue operator,* who sets up the 35mm dialogue track for each cue if the session is being scored to film (as opposed to videotape)

Armin Steiner makes an adjustment on the recording console on the 20th Century Fox Scoring Stage. Steiner's classical music roots plus his years as a pop and rock and roll recording mixer give him the kind of broad-based background especially helpful for a film scoring mixer.
Photo: Lester Cohen, courtesy of ASCAP

■ *The recording crew,* which includes one or more people (usually set up in an adjoining area to the booth and stage) who are responsible for the operation of all recording machines not in the booth itself. These machines typically include the 35mm mag machines.

Once engaged, one of the first things the composer does is to book a scoring stage for the required dates. This is usually done as far in advance as possible, partly because every composer has his favorite recording mixers and recording stages, and partly because, amazing as it sounds, there aren't always enough stages available if a particular week gets busy.

Recording motion picture music is both an art and a science. Doing it well involves a solid knowl-

edge of microphones and their qualities, a background in the science of acoustics, an intimate familiarity with the history of recording, and an in-depth understanding of the latest technology. Above all, the goal, as with any good recording, is to create just the right sound for each score.

The composer's booth representative is often an extension of his sensibilities and tastes. When an orchestrator is involved, he often provides that service. "I'm always on the scoring stage," says Greig McRitchie. "With Basil {Poledouris} I'll make suggestions for changes on the stage. I don't let the orchestra know what I'm saying. I talk to him only {the orchestra doesn't hear me}, from the booth. He hears me on his headset. I'll say, 'Basil, let's put that on piccolos (or flutes).' Or, 'Why don't you call a ten? I think we ought to fill in a certain part for the horns.'"

Prior to recording the most important input the composer offers the mixer is a description of the music and the desired effect. Armin Steiner (no relation to Max Steiner), a freelance mixer who for many years was the music recording engineer at Fox, likes to have as much communication with the composer as possible before the sessions. "With most of the composers I work with, I would like to have a one-to-one discussion, to find out what's on their mind, how do they approach this thing, so I know how I can best serve them. When Lionel Newman was alive {and head of music at Fox}, God bless him, at least I knew about every picture that I did at Fox. I ran the pictures with him, I knew the texture of everything that I was going to do. We had meetings and everything. I don't see the films anymore, but I do know the instrumentation of the orchestra, hopefully a week or two before. And they do talk to me ahead of time, as much as possible. If it's an orchestral score, they will tell you that this texture is like Prokofiev or this texture is like Tchaikovsky.

"When I did *Home Alone* {1990} with John Williams, for instance, he said, 'Well, this must be Prokofiev's Classical Symphony in style.' So I knew pretty much what he was going for."

Changes

There isn't one score I've done that ended up being recorded exactly the way I originally wrote it. You have to listen to the director's suggestions, be able to make changes (even on the recording stage) and, hopefully, remain constantly creative.
                                        Jerry Goldsmith, composer

When we get to the session, I'm very demanding. . . .
                                        John Schlesinger, director

When you're recording, that's where you learn the most, because you see what works and what doesn't work, and then you have to deal with all that. I find that really fun and interesting.
                                        David Newman, composer

John Williams and director George Miller discuss a cue during the composer's scoring sessions for *The Witches of Eastwick* (1987) on the Fox Scoring Stage. Working together while the music is being recorded helps to ensure a unified point of view about the music and its relationship to the drama. Changes can be (and often are) made on the scoring stage with the hope of improving the dramatic effectiveness of a scene or cue, and better expressing the director's vision of his film.
Photo: David Kraft

It should be no surprise to hear that changes are often made during the scoring sessions. After all, it's the last chance for the composer to fix a misjudgment in orchestration by omitting an instrument, changing an instrument's register, or even adding an instrument or a whole section of the orchestra to a passage.

If the composer has done mock-up sampled versions of the cues, then the chances are there will be few if any changes on the stage. In those cases, both the composer and the filmmakers have had the opportunity to preview everything with picture and to make changes prior to the live scoring sessions.

Hans Zimmer works that way with Ridley Scott, for instance, and consequently doesn't see much of him on the scoring stage. "He doesn't really turn up at any of my orchestra sessions, because he says he's heard it all, and it can only get better. It's totally cut and dried at that point." In general, Randy Edelman has found this to be true, too, of the filmmakers with whom he has worked.

Working without the benefit of hearing the score before recording, however, creates a much more open-ended dialogue between the director and composer when they are on the scoring stage. John Schlesinger, often cited by composers as a director with a keen sense of musicality, says, "Although I can't compose, I know when the score is too thick or when it wants putting into a different kind of sound or use of a woodwind, or we don't want strings or we want more strings or we want a solo violin or whatever." So he gets very involved in these decisions during the recording process.

You have to be very quick on your feet when changes are requested, and some composers are more responsive to this pressure than others. At times things can get extremely hectic, with the director running out onto the scoring stage every few minutes to have a discussion with the composer. The director may know precisely what he wants and be asking for it, but this also may be a sign that the director is simply very unsure of his picture.

If the film has been recut without notifying the composer, changes are made during the recording session whenever possible. In the old days, "If you fooled around with a scene after Max Steiner, the top man at the time, had scored it, there was hell to pay," says director Robert Wise, who edited *Citizen Kane* for Orson Welles in 1941. "Orson didn't pay much attention to that. Bernie [Herrmann] had the timings, and Orson made some changes in a scene [in *Citizen Kane*]. I tried to say this would be very difficult when we got to scoring, but Orson wouldn't hear it. Well, we got to the scoring stage with the new timings, but Bernie wasn't upset; he said, 'Okay, we can cut this bar here, and I'll pull this together. . . .' and he very facilely and quickly adjusted his music, with great judgment, to fit the changes. I had worked with a lot of music directors before, like Max [Steiner] and Roy Webb, and they wouldn't hear of a change in their music. I was so impressed with Bernie—that he didn't bat an eyelash."

Bobby Fernandez, head music mixer at Warner Bros., says that last-minute changes are still made. "I've seen it happen where a composer has written stuff only to come on the scoring stage, rehearse to picture, and find out that nothing fits because the picture's been cut and no one bothered to tell him. If it's a quick change, you can do it right there. If it's gonna take some time, then it's 'let's move on to something else and we'll tackle it in the morning.'"

Performance

These players were genuinely amazing. It was a daily exhibition of the highest technical proficiency, and no one who witnessed it will ever forget it or disclaim it.

André Previn, composer
(re: the MGM orchestra in the fifties)

A lot of the time, you'll go in and just play whole notes of unchallenging music, then you turn the page and there's a solo that'll put you on edge.
Dick Nash, studio trombonist

Once the session begins, the procedure is pretty much the same on all sessions. Remember, the mu-

sicians have never seen this music before, so the first time through they are sight reading.

At MGM in the fifties, according to André Previn, "They would casually glance at the parts on their stands, the ink still wet, and would proceed to play with the same expert disdain a professional parking lot attendant uses to back a new convertible into a tight space."

Although the studio musicians were astonishingly efficient when Previn began his tenure at MGM in 1948, studio musicians have become much more versatile since then, primarily because of the increasing diversity of musical styles used in scoring films. One of the most important reasons for rehearsal time is not to perfect the performance of the *notes,* but to refine the appropriate style of performance for the score. Contemporary studio musicians are extremely flexible stylistically, but in 1951, when Miklós Rózsa was recording *Quo Vadis* with the Royal Philharmonic in London, he found their stylistic approach especially satisfying by comparison with Hollywood. "The Hollywood studio orchestras," he observed, "consist of excellent musicians, but there is no style whatsoever—or, at least, a Hollywood style inappropriate to the lean and hungry music I had contrived for early Rome. But to be fair, when Hollywood studio musicians were engaged, it was on the basis of their ability to play popular music and jazz. Hollywood demanded a particular expertise for her musicals which was totally unsuited to symphonic music. It took my orchestras a long time to realize that for me they had to play differently. When we first recorded *The Thief of Bagdad* [1940] the concertmaster played his solos with the most nauseating vibrato and glissandos. I complained, and he said, 'Oh, it's the gypsy in me!' To which I replied, 'No, my friend, it's the MGM in you.'"

The pressure on contemporary studio musicians is extreme, and those who are successful in this profession are able to function brilliantly and with great consistency under the toughest circumstances. As keyboardist Randy Waldman points out, the unspoken subtext is always there—"the pressure of knowing you always have to play perfectly. You're sitting in a studio with anywhere from 30 to 100 musicians, and you can't make a mistake because every one of them is looking at you, expecting you to be perfect every time."

Each cue is rehearsed one or more times without projecting the film. Typically, the cues are from 30 seconds to 5 minutes long. But a cue can be as short as 5 or 10 seconds. (This is rare in feature films, but listen to the John Morris scores for Mel Brooks' *Young Frankenstein* [1974] and others for many examples of this device used where needed.) Or a cue can be as long as 8 or 9 minutes (also rare, but James Horner, for one, is inclined toward long cues, which you can hear exemplified in his *Star Trek II* [1982] and *Star Trek III* [1984] scores).

When the music for a sequence gets to be too long or too complex to be performed comfortably in one take, the cue can be broken down into several shorter ones, each overlapping the next so that they will ultimately sound like one continuous cue.

Conducting

Alfred Newman was one of the composers . . . who impressed me the most. He was a genuine conductor and interpreter of music; he brought things to other people's scores that the composers themselves didn't seem to be able to.

John Williams, composer

Some great maestro might tell you that motion picture conducting is easy. Let him try it.

Dimitri Tiomkin, composer

Film conductors have their own personal styles for working with the musicians. Dimitri Tiomkin could be informal—one of the gang. He spoke to the musicians as partners. "I am no Prokofiev, I am no Tchaikovsky," he would say to the orchestra with his thick Russian accent. "But what I write is good for what I write for. So please, boys, help me."

One way or another, efficiency is definitely a cornerstone of the best conductors, who know that simple, direct explanations are a must. "There is a famous story about a composer who conducted his own music and was very nervous," Bronislau Kaper recounts. "He talks to a bassoon player, and he says, 'You know, this moment here, when the bassoon comes, it took me a long time. I wasn't sure, should I put the bass clarinet or should I put the bassoon. But the character—you feel here like something is happening in the world. And the whole world starts dancing, and you feel like you're seeing little girls in light dresses, and they're all kind of floating in the sky. You understand? With wings.' And the bassoon player said to him, 'Do you want it *forte* or *piano?*'"

By all accounts, Alfred Newman was the most illustrious and admired film music conductor during the forties and fifties. He had a personal style

When keyboardists such as Mike Lang arrive at a scoring session, their computer, electronic keyboards, and sound processing racks are already set up by their assistants. Although early synthesizers were sometimes used on scoring stages during the seventies, their prevalence has increased tremendously since 1985, as rapidly evolving technology has made their use more and more practical and effective in orchestral recording situations.
Photo: Peter Figen

that everyone responded to. Though he was loved by all, he tolerated no unprofessional conduct by anyone while he was working. "He was tough; he had to be," recalls Ken Darby. "After he'd been out here just a short time, he was rehearsing the musi-

By the time Dimitri Tiomkin scored King Vidor's *Duel in the Sun* (1946) he had reluctantly resigned himself to conducting his own scores. During his first years of film scoring he had preferred that others conduct for him. His score for *Lost Horizon* (1937) was conducted by Max Steiner, and other studio music directors conducted for him during his early years in Hollywood. In time he realized that he would have more control over the sound of his music if he conducted, personally shaping the tone color and dynamic shading of the orchestral performance. In the nineties, some of the more recently active composers prefer to let more experienced and technically proficient conductors shape their music while they supervise the scoring sessions from the recording booth.
Photo courtesy of Marc Wanamaker/Bison Archives

When Alfred Newman arrived in Hollywood, he had already established himself as an outstanding conductor on Broadway. His desire for perfection earned him the admiration and loyalty of the musicians in his orchestras.
Photo courtesy of ASCAP

cians over at Goldwyn Studios when two men came over by the soundstage and began talking loudly over the music. Alfred put down his baton, stopped the orchestra, and said, 'Those men either get off the stage or I do.' Everybody hushed up, and then Samuel Goldwyn and Louie Mayer left the soundstage without a fuss and Pappy—everyone who knew him either called him 'Pap' or 'Pappy'—resumed."

Violinist Louis Kaufman was Newman's concertmaster (first-chair violinist) for years. "Alfred Newman was a dictator of everything that went on," says Kaufman, "and he would tolerate no nonsense. He insisted upon absolute discipline. But it paid off."

Greig McRitchie did some of the orchestrations for Alfred Newman for *How the West Was Won* (1962) and had the opportunity to watch him work. "Newman had a great camaraderie with the orchestra. He made great friends with the good guys in the band. He knew them well, and they really performed for him. And he took his time. I think he recorded three minutes a day. Of course, today they'd throw you off the stage [if you recorded so little music in a day]! Today it's three minutes an hour. He might rehearse all morning, and then record all afternoon. He was a terrific conductor."

After rehearsing without film, the film is then projected, typically for one or more additional rehearsals to picture. Then, during the takes, the stage lights dim, leaving an overhead spotlight on the podium. The musicians have a small light on each music stand.

On a typical big-budget film, the orchestra might record 5 to 10 minutes in a 3-hour session. Particularly tough music may take longer, and easy cues will often go faster. The 3-hour sessions, by the way, are timed just like a psychiatrist's hour—50 minutes to the hour. In accordance with union regulations, when the musicians take a "ten," they are breaking for the remaining 10 minutes of the hour.

Paul Talkington (orchestra coordinator), director Paul Verhoeven, and composer Basil Poledouris listen to a playback during the recording of Poledouris' score for *Flesh and Blood* (1985; released on video as *The Rose and the Sword*). Playbacks require intense concentration. Otherwise, an error or an unwanted noise may go undetected until it is too late to rerecord the cue.
Photo: David Kraft

Playbacks

If there is time, the composer and conductor join the mixer, music editor, and filmmakers in the booth for playbacks of good takes. They all study the recorded version of the cue for possible improvements of the music, the recording sound and balance, and the dramatic sync and effectiveness. Changes may be discussed, and if they are, the conductor gives notes to the orchestra prior to another take.

Like all mixers, Bobby Fernandez has a surprising reason for listening to playbacks. "I like to play back to make sure that everything is on tape. Because I've had cases (not many, thank God) where I thought something was recorded—and you have to rely on your assistant who's in the next room moni-

toring the takes—only to find out that it's *not on tape*. So what do you do then?"

Filmmakers often think the music sounds too loud when they hear it in the booth, but that can be because during the recording it is monitored at dangerously loud levels. Fernandez realizes the psychological effect of hearing the music so loud against the film, and counteracts that effect during the playbacks, but judging the final effect of a cue in the context of the film can be difficult even when it is played back at a softer level. "We've had cases where we'll play it back against dialogue, and the director will say the music *itself* [as opposed to the volume] is too loud for the scene, and we'll say, 'Let's play it back again,' and we'll turn the music down a little, and they'll say, 'No, that's all right— it's OK.'"

On a choice (or "print") take, the music is played back once without dialogue to be sure everything is just right. Then, if time permits, it may be played back again with dialogue. When he mixes the cue, Fernandez, like Steiner, Danny Wallin, John Richards, and the other top mixers, is careful to get an evenly balanced mix for soft cues that will be played under dialogue. "If you have a dialogue scene and you mix the piano up where it sounds beautiful on the scoring stage, all of a sudden your strings are gone when you get that piano down so it clears the dialogue. So you have to mix it so it *sounds* like an equal level for all the instruments when you play it back at a very low volume."

DUBBING

A film composer's immortality stretches all the way from the recording stage to the dubbing room.
Erich Wolfgang Korngold, composer

"Keep that God-damned music down" was a popular battle cry [in the forties and fifties]. I had to speak up for myself, because nobody else did.
Hans J. Salter, composer

Many a composer's heart is broken in the dubbing room.

Henry Mancini, composer

The dubbing sessions are the final mixing sessions during which the dialogue, music, and sound effects are recorded together onto one composite track (Dolby Stereo, six-track, mono, or whatever format). Every dubbing session tries for the perfect blend of these three elements.

Perfection is rarely absolute—there are too many conflicting opinions. There is a lot of give-and-take among dialogue, music, and sound effects during the mix, and the composer, music mixer, and music editor may not be satisfied with the balance. As a music recording engineer and dubbing mixer, Grover Helsley has watched this dubbing-room interplay over the years. "Behind those three elements are a lot of people, each one of them with

an idea, from their point of view, of what the mix should be. The director or producer, whoever is in charge on the dubbing stage, has to almost be a referee and make a decision. Those are not always decisions I or you or the effects people or whoever might agree with, but in his opinion that is the best compromise, if you will, for the film.

"So often, inexperienced film composers don't understand that you're *not* going to hear every single note. There are just some things that are going to have to go by the wayside in order to enhance the film. Ultimately that's what we're doing—be it effects, dialogue, or music, we're enhancing the film and telling the story. That's the number one thing, the story. We're not doing an album, we're not doing a concert, and some things just have to go away. Too many people in all three areas don't always understand that."

The dubbing stage is really a theater, varying in size from a small screening room to a fairly large one. They all contain basically the same equipment: a large screen at the front of the room, with a counter at the bottom indicating the exact footage from the start of the reel ("footage counter"); an extremely long mixing console (the "board"); long rows of quarter-inch inputs (a "patch bay") used to route sound and effects signals from one source to another, with dozens of short patch cords curling in midair from one spot to another; and racks of sound manipulation devices ("effects") stacked one above another in racks here and there near the console. A ping-pong table is fairly standard equipment, along with a putting iron and several magazines that predate stereo. Fresh donuts and bagels are optional, and coffee brewed to keep the faint of heart alert is always close by.

The rerecording mixers will be working with dozens of tracks in all. Traditionally, these tracks are all on 35mm mag, with up to three discrete tracks per unit of magnetic film. The recording/playback machines used to play these units, called dummies, are set up in another room in the building.

The music tracks can get complicated. Bill Stinson was the music editor on *White Christmas* (1954). "The tambourine scene, the interlocutors at the end and all that, I cut that. Now, there were taps, there were hand claps, tambourines, vocals, and every one of those things had to go on a different track. You can have eleven, twelve, fifteen music tracks for a musical sequence. You can have a chorus, maybe you have Bing's vocal [Bing Crosby], Rosemary Clooney's vocal . . . plus the orchestra track. It's all synchronized, it's all sprocket-driven. It's a fascinating thing, really." In cases of extremely complex sound jobs, there may be as many as one hundred different tracks; in fact, the "76 Trombones" marching band sequence in *The Music Man* (1962) required nearly that many.

The key term is "sprocket-driven." During the dubbing process, all these machines are locked into the picture, and all the dummies are locked together in sync. The machine operator can disengage them from the picture, and can unlock any individual dummy if necessary, but as long as they remain locked, when one moves, they all move, either backward or forward. They can be driven up to 10 or 12 times normal running speed for fast forward and fast reverse, always in sync.

> *No, no, no! Louder! I can still hear the music!*
> *Sam Zimbalist, producer*
> *(spoken to the dialogue and effects mixers while dubbing* Quo Vadis, *1961)*

> *It was actually quite spectacular at one point, until they added a million cows.*
> *Marc Shaiman, composer*
> *(re: one of his cues in* City Slickers, *1991)*

As a rule, the director comes into this facility as the leader and ultimate authority. Athough he may not be present for some of the more technical finessing that can take hours (and sometimes days), he is there when it counts the most, and his word is final.

Directors have different styles on the dubbing stage. Some have carefully preplanned an approach to the soundtrack, working closely with both the composer and the sound-effects team. George Lucas took this approach on *Star Wars* (1977), an extraordinary sound job.

Like most Hollywood dubbing facilities, the machine room for Dubbing Stage A at the Disney Studios can accommodate dozens of sound units, each built onto thousand-foot reels (up to 10 or 11 minutes of film). Music, sound effects, and dialogue units are all played back in sync on these interlocking machines.
Photo: Gay Wallin

Alfred Hitchcock made copious notes for the music and sound departments. The following excerpts from his notes for *The Man Who Knew Too Much*, dated October 5, 1955, reveal how specifically he thought about the use of music in his films.

Reel III

In the marketplace, of course, we get the general sounds from the various drumbeats and we should particularly hear both the fast music of the dancers and in the distance the music of the acrobats at the same time. And the teller of tales should be an equal blending of this. But each time we move backwards and forwards we should let whatever music we are closest to dominate the scene. Naturally, there will be other distant sounds as well, including traffic.

Reel VIII

After Jimmy [Stewart] and Doris [Day] walk across the street toward the chapel we should hear the faint choral music which comes from inside, which increases as they get nearer and nearer to it.

Reel IX

The choir singing should remain as is, and make sure when Jimmy and Doris sing that his voice is pretty much the same volume as the rest of the singing. Or rather, I should say, the rest of the singing should be brought up to maintain the same level throughout. It is only when Doris sings that it should be brought up to the rest so it directs attention to her.

Reel XI

In this reel, of course, the main sound will remain exactly as the existing music track from beginning to end. It will be noted that we have taken dramatic license to preserve the same volume of sound whether we are in the hall, the lobby, or the corridor, and this should remain so in order not to disturb the music unity of the cantata. . . .

Reel XII

As soon as we are in the embassy, I think we should have no atmospheric sounds at all because here we are going to rely upon the background music to dramatize this whole scene at the embassy between the Draytons and the ambassador.

When it finally gets down to the volume of the music in the dub, however, Miklós Rózsa voices a common complaint among film composers: "Sometimes the music almost disappears, and more times than not its effectiveness is greatly diminished. Instead of allowing the music to merge with the action for an augmented effect, the engineers, at the command of the producers and directors, submerge the music, apparently because they feel it might distract attention. This could not be the case if the music is aptly composed for the picture."

This familiar refrain has been heard over and over again throughout the entire history of film music. In recent times, what you hear on the soundtrack is a reflection of the director's taste and his preferences for achieving dramatic emphasis. Does he mix the sound effects to be bigger than life, so that they actually dominate the soundtrack in action films like *Terminator II* (1991)? Or does he favor the music, as Kevin Costner did in *Dances With Wolves* (1990) and Michael Mann did at times in *The Last of the Mohicans* (1992)?

Producers are not always present on the dubbing stage steadily for days and weeks on end. They tend to come and go, checking the progress and commenting on playbacks of dubbed reels.

In the old days, there was so much ongoing production at the studios that the producers often didn't go to dubbing at all. John Hammell says that, at Paramount in the forties, "They were all so busy with grinding out these pictures that they didn't have any time to go to a dubbing session. God, to get Hal Wallis to come up to that stage and hear something was a federal job.

"The editor ran his dubbing sessions. Toward the end of his career he would come up and listen to the finished reels. In the beginning he didn't." At that time the producer (and especially strong ones like Wallis) had the power to make all creative decisions, yet Wallis chose to delegate his authority when it came to dubbing.

David O. Selznick was one of the strongest-minded producers in the history of Hollywood, and one of the most creative, involved in every phase of his productions. In his search for perfection, he began to compare the effect of music on his films' soundtracks with that of the other studios, and especially those produced by Warner Bros., which was a very music-oriented studio in those days.

In that regard, he wrote this memo to Ray Klune in 1941:

For some time now I have been noticing that there is something about the recording of the music in Warner Brothers pictures that makes the music infinitely more effective than in our own, and in fact in the pictures of any other studio. I don't know whether it is the choice of instruments, and the manner of orchestrating, or whether it is the recording or the dubbing. But in any case, there is a richness to the music, and a volume to it, without the slightest loss to dialogue, that is not characteristic of other studios' scores.

I wish you could study just what it is that they do.

DOS

Basically, Warner Bros.' secret was to dub the music louder.

Composers often go to dubbing, but not always. And they frequently come and go much as the producers do, checking out completed reels, and coming in when called to discuss a problem or a change.

These days they are typically welcome at the dub, and many directors not only want them there, but insist. It wasn't always so. Composer Hans J. Salter points out the situation as it was when he was scoring films in the forties and fifties. "We must not forget that, in the order of importance, music was at the very bottom of the heap. It probably still is. Sound effects were always favored over music. It took a gradual education of the producers until they began to realize that in certain scenes the emotional impact of the music did more for their picture than the static sound effects. It was a constant hassle, and once I was even 'asked' to stay away from the dubbing room so they could finish their picture without any interference."

Salter was lucky that he was only kept away from the dub once. There was a time when most of the composers were told not to go to dubbing at all. This was a common practice at Paramount. Commenting in 1961 about Hollywood in general, Dimitri Tiomkin said, "Do you know that 95 percent of composers are not permitted in the dubbing room? Look what they've done to me. I'm known as the loudest composer in America . . . me, who loves *pianissimo*! Believe me, audiences are getting sick of high-fidelity sound."

It's hard to believe that Tiomkin complained that his music was being dubbed too *loud,* but that approach to dubbing was the fashion for a while.

It's not usually a composer's chief complaint, but it can be an artistic problem.

Film editors play an important role throughout the dubbing sessions. They know the film better than anyone except the director, and they often have a clearer recall of details regarding alternate readings of a scene or a dialogue track, and so on. They usually have supervised the looping of replacement lines by the actors recorded after shooting to provide a clearer, cleaner, or dramatically better reading of a line or even a whole scene.

They are often appointed by the director to run certain stages of the dub, including the supervision of technical areas. If for any reason the director is unavailable, the editor usually takes over. There are many times when a director would prefer to let the supervising editor run the dubbing sessions, so he can come in fresh and hear what they've done.

The dialogue always wins. You have to hear and understand the story.
    Grover Helsley, music recording engineer

In Hollywood, three mixers work together to dub a film. One mixes the dialogue, one the music, and one the sound effects. (In New York City, one mixer does it all.) Each mixer sits at his assigned portion of the mixing console (or "board") and controls the sound quality and volume levels of his tracks.

Dialogue mixers are considered the head mixers. Although mixers all think of themselves as members of a team, the dialogue mixers are the captains. This tradition undoubtedly comes from the fact that the dialogue is considered the most important of the three sound elements.

Jack Warner loved music, and as we have seen, the dubbing at Warner Bros. was often sympathetic to the score. At MGM, though, things were different.

"MGM had a fetish about understanding the dialogue," says Bronislau Kaper, who was a staff composer there from the mid-thirties through the early fifties. "I didn't like MGM dubbing. It was so cautious. Everybody was afraid that somebody

Rerecording mixers Anna Behlmer (sound effects, whose credits include *The Babe, L.A. Story, Awakenings,* and *Kindergarten
Cop*), Danny Wallin (music, also a scoring stage recording engineer for hundreds of films, including *The Way We Were, Out
of Africa, Star Trek II, The Wild Bunch, Woodstock,* and *Camelot*), and Richard Portman (dialogue, whose credits include
The Godfather, Funny Lady, The Deer Hunter, Nashville, and
Young Frankenstein) shown in 1992, dubbing a film in Studio
2 at Todd-AO Glen Glenn Studios in Hollywood.
Photo: Gay Wallin

would come into the projection room and say, 'I
can't understand.' Even deaf people. Yes! We had a
producer called Al Lewin, a director, writer, intellectual. . . . He was the most intelligent man at
MGM. Now, he couldn't hear. He had a hearing
aid. I did a picture with him, *Saadia* [1953], and
he was arguing with me about the sound of the
music in the dubbing room. So finally, I hated to

say it, but I got aggravated, and I said, 'You know,
for a fellow who doesn't hear well, you're a little
too positive about sound.' But he didn't hear what
I said! . . .

"It is an old MGM tradition, when you have a
band right in front of you on the screen, and there
are three people at the table, and the band is blast-
ing, and you hear it loud—and one of the guests
would say, 'Waiter!' Right away they dub the music
so you know he said, 'Waiter!' and suddenly the
music becomes like from another *city.* Not from another room, another *city,* and it doesn't sound like a
band anymore."

Reminiscing about the emphasis on the dialogue track to the exclusion of the score, David
Raksin says, "They sit there and are horrified at the
possibility that some inconsequential word might be
drowned out. And all of a sudden music starts
going down the drain; it loses its sound; it loses its
power; it loses its vitality; and they're constantly
suppressing it."

> *If there was thunder, if it was just background
> thunder, it meant nothing. Music took precedence. If
> it was thunder that struck a building, something
> that was important to the plot, to me that took
> precedence.*
>
> Joseph Gershenson,
> *music director at Universal, in the 1950s*

Sound effects mixers are provided with so many individual tracks that they usually have to predub
their effects, mixing various elements onto new
composite tracks. For instance, they'll take all the
footsteps, perhaps, and combine them onto one
track; or they'll combine a number of different
tracks containing car sounds, tire squeals, clunks,
and bangs onto one or more new tracks so they are
easier to control as a unit. The down side of this
absolutely necessary procedure is that the balance
within each new composite track is now locked in
and very difficult to change. This can create problems, but the effects mixer can always put up the
originals for a particular moment and work with

them (in conjunction with the new track, if he so wishes).

Sound effects are often mixed so loud that they become music's chief adversary on the dubbing stage. First of all, the soundtrack can take a very loud level of sound effects during a dynamic car chase without apparent distortion. To compete, the music will often go into distortion and have to be reduced in level to become distortion-free. Second, directors often place a great deal of faith in the emotional effectiveness of big, powerful, and impressive effects. It depends on the film, but very often this faith is misplaced. Most of the time, even the best sound effects won't speak with the emotional impact provided by a good piece of music.

Still, sound effects specialists are as proud of their creations as composers are of theirs, and they fight for their space. When Rózsa worked on *El Cid* (1961), "Again and again the sound effects expert tried to persuade the director to take out the music that interfered with her precious clicks and booms. I argued that without the music the excitement was missing. But at the premiere a nasty shock awaited me: scene after scene was musicless. In one scene the music just stopped in mid-bar, presumably so the clinking of a sword could be better heard. I was so angry that I canceled a publicity tour I had agreed to undertake; I could not talk about music which nobody was going to hear."

Music director Joseph Gershenson took a practical approach at Universal. He felt that the story points were most important, and always adjusted his judgment to the dramatic situation. "When it was a question of music or sound effects, I would fight for the music. Dialogue, of course, had the preference, in my opinion. . . . And when I thought the music was too loud, I'd say so. If it was too soft, I'd say so. And I didn't win 'em all, one way or another."

Armin Steiner sees a growing tendency among directors to emphasize the effects beyond the point of reality or reason. "I can be very surprised at a film I've recorded when it's dubbed very badly—when so much time and effort has been spent on the music, and when I find that the director dubs it

so far down that it really doesn't do it justice. My biggest gripe today is that the sound effects have taken over beyond life—they're bigger than life. And I think that when they get to be bigger than life, the music suffers so badly. . . ."

Composers want to be able to say a lot [musically]. And in the end, they just can't. Because there's so much information being given that's not musical, that they're just a part of the whole.

Thomas Newman, composer

Music mixers have two primary responsibilities: first, to make the music they are given sound as good as possible, and second, to mix that music into the composite soundtrack with the maximum emotional power and finesse.

A music mixer uses a number of technical tricks to make it sound as good as it possibly can, including equalization (the emphasis and de-emphasis of selected registers and pitches in the tracks), reverberation (echo, like the sound added to your voice when you perform "Singin' in the Rain" in the shower), delay (which at its most pronounced causes a repeated version of a phrase as in the trumpet solos in *Patton* [1970]), and stereo placement of the individual tracks he has been given.

The music is often mixed onto three or six stereo tracks on the scoring stage during the scoring session. It goes onto magnetic film stock and the music editor prepares his units from these scoring-stage mixes.

Composers like to control their mixes as much as possible, so many times the music is recorded on a multitrack tape machine (either analog or digital), and then, in a separate mixing session, "mixed down" to a small number of tracks that will be transferred and prepared for dubbing by the music editor. Henry Mancini, for example, has always mixed down from multitrack.

When the composer has done some electronic prerecording himself, those tracks are often kept separate from any orchestra tracks added later. Randy Edelman always works this way. He sends his own three-track version of the score, fully orchestrated electronically, and also the acoustic orchestral version of the same music on another three-track. Everything is balanced, and the dubbing mixer can use however much of each version he wishes. "And it doesn't matter what kind of movie, what kind of score I do, that is what I do. I end up with three tracks of orchestra and three tracks of me, and (on some scores) a rhythm section."

This system works well for Edelman, in part because his communication with the directors is so good. "In most cases, the director has been at the studio with me, and it's already mixed. Alan Parker was there every minute with me when I mixed the score for *Come See the Paradise* [1990], so I didn't go to his dubbing, because I didn't have to. They know all the music—there're no surprises at all. If they come up here to my studio and don't like a cue, I won't go to sleep until I change the cue."

A few directors like to have even more control of the music than the usual three to six tracks offer. When Thomas Newman was mixing down his score for *Men Don't Leave* (1990) for Paul Brickman, he was asked by Brickman to bring it in to dubbing on as many tracks as possible, which turned out to be eighteen separate tracks. This is a lot of tracks to deal with in dubbing, but Brickman feels it's worth the extra time necessitated by working this way.

Brickman explains his point of view. "What can drive a lot of people crazy is, one, I do get involved in the smallest details. And two, I like a lot of options. So if something's not happening, I can shift gears. . . . You find things, and you surprise yourself. You can find something right there, even from a goof, that you didn't know existed. Because you've got the effects tracks going, and all that stuff, and you don't know where you're going to wind up."

When the dub is completed, the entire film is screened, often in another theater, if possible, so there is a fresh perspective on the sound as a whole. The overall effect may be disappointing. Bobby Fernandez was called in to remix the entire score for *Radio Flyer* (1992) after the first dub wasn't as effective as the filmmakers had expected.

"I was under the impression that they wanted to make it real big—it was a huge score. From the beginning, when I sat down and listened to the original dub, there were a lot of things that were missing. Half the score just wasn't making it up to the screen. So I rebalanced against dialogue and effects. I went in there and EQ'd [equalized] it, and brought it out, and I gave it a little more air and life, and we did the *entire* show again.

"So then we all sat back, and we looked at it. And then the supervising editor stood up at the end and said, 'The music is too big.' I said, 'Well, that was the whole purpose of me being here.' While we were doing it, everybody loved it. But when we sat back and listened to it all, then, yeah, OK, maybe it was just too *much* music. So we just went back in and lowered everything. It was a computer-automated board, so all my mixes were saved. It was just a matter of dropping everything about two or three db [decibels] and then it was fine."

MORE CHANGES

Changes after the preview are often painful, although fortunately I have not suffered any particularly smarting musical losses.
    Erich Wolfgang Korngold, composer

I have bad times with directors. Always we have big fights. They want me to change. I disagree. Then come terrible arguments. . . .
    Dimitri Tiomkin, composer

Films are often previewed for the first time *before* an original score is written. Temp tracks are used, and the film is previewed to get audience reaction, and then editing continues prior to scoring. There are also cases where the film is scored first, and then previewed.

After the film is scored, more changes can take place once the film previews again. "On one recent film," says orchestra contractor Sandy De Crescent, "We finished scoring in August. In December I get a call from Hans Zimmer: 'We have to go back in. They reshot the ending.' I thought it was a joke. I really thought he was kidding."

What made Zimmer's call so amazing to De Crescent was that they had already recorded six or seven endings for the film by then. "That sort of thing goes on a lot—more than people realize. There's an awful lot of that in so many scores."

Zimmer was no less amazed than De Crescent. "We ended up with ending number 26," Zimmer adds. "We previewed *19* endings. In Torrance. And we got notes back saying, 'Well, we preferred the ending last week.' How big is Torrance? There are 400 people in the cinema, 19 times 400—how many people is that? That is the population of Torrance. So after a while you run out of people. So everybody in Torrance has seen that one. I don't think that is the right way to go." Although a slight exaggeration, the point is well taken.

Music editors can perform minor miracles. With an excellent music editor to help guide the technical process and to make any actual music edits necessary, the composer may be able to make the required changes without even rescoring the revised sections of the film. This is certainly the best possible way to execute the changes that often must be made after the first public screenings, or previews. But the music editor has to have a fine innate musicality or the results can be devastating. "You can imagine how surprised I was," says Miklós Rózsa about an early score, "to hear a composition of mine after the sound cutter, in order to fit the music to the new length of the scene, had cut out every second bar. The effect was indeed astonishing."

The composer should be involved in these changes right up to the release date of the picture. In 1952, though, David Raksin suffered a lot on *Carrie.* "There was a final sequence, nearly seven minutes long, and almost without dialogue. I knew that Willie Wyler, the director, was going to shorten it; so, since we were working on an impossible time schedule, I asked him to spare me the necessity of

composing more music than we would actually use. He said he couldn't cut the sequence until he saw it with the music. So I wrote the sequence—it inspired some of the best music I have ever composed—and there was joy all over the place. Then they cut the sequence down to something like 56 seconds, and with that they destroyed the music. I was away, trying to recuperate, when they made the final cuts, and they did not permit me to assist with the editing of the music track. . . ."

In a 1961 memo to producer Henry Weinstein, David O. Selznick sums up the attitude of many filmmakers. In referring to Bernard Herrmann's score for *Tender Is the Night,* he says:

> As to Bernie Herrmann, you are quite correct in your statement that I had and still have enormous respect for him as being very considerably talented . . . .
>
> *Of course* Bernie Herrmann should be heard before any underscoring is taken out; but . . . musicians notoriously hear only their music, which is as it should be; but it is the *producer's* function, assuming there is a producer, to decide when the underscoring is damaging to the total effect, either because it is the wrong music, or because of any one of a dozen other reasons, including perhaps that it should not be in at all. You also have not yet learned, as believe me you will, not to judge music by what it sounds like separately, on the scoring stage or in the projection room. You are not releasing a score; you are releasing a *picture.* And if the audience is even conscious of the score, it defeats its own purpose—except when used to disguise bad or inadequate scenes, precisely as an architect uses vines to cover bad design. . . .

All composers would agree with Selznick when he says, "You are not releasing a score; you are releasing a *picture.*" And if any should forget from time to time, it is without question the filmmaker's obligation to utilize the music for the greater good of the film itself. Nevertheless, the ideal goal is to encourage the greatest empowerment of the score so that it can fulfill its function within and for the benefit of the film.

Scores, or sections or scores, are sometimes thrown out completely, and replaced by another score. The replacement scores are usually done by a different composer. "I think the first big one was *A Place in the Sun*" (1951), says John Hammell, who was a music editor at Paramount at the time. "It created a *riot* at Paramount. When you want to throw a score out—*impossible!* In those days they never blamed the music [for picture problems], which so often happens now." *Sun* is the first one Hammell remembers where one third of the score was replaced by new material by other composers.

George Stevens, one of the most musically involved filmmakers in the business at that time, was the director. However, as involved as he was, he preferred to let the composer record his score as he wished before he would offer any comments. As Hammell remembers, Stevens said, "I want him to do one hundred percent of what he visualized, and then we'll talk about it later.' He'd come to the scoring sessions and sit in the back there, but never say a word.

"When there was trouble on *Place in the Sun*, Stevens didn't like one major scene. He was a brilliant director, but hard to get along with. The scene was the tremendous close-up scene of Elizabeth Taylor and Montgomery Clift outside, dancing, and he didn't like it and he called Waxman and said, 'I want to change this, Franz. It just doesn't work.' Franz called his agent and he came back and said to George, 'No, I don't change my music.'"

John Waxman, Franz's son, explains that Stevens felt the dramatic emphasis was not what he had in mind. "He realized that what Father had written was a subtle score that told the audience Montgomery Clift did in fact murder Shelley Winters so he could have Elizabeth Taylor. Stevens wanted this point left up in the air for the audience to decide. . . ."

Hammell was a first-hand observer at the time. "What Stevens did was, he got five or six of the major scenes that he really wasn't happy about, but didn't mention those to Franz. Franz had a wonderful theme, and he loved that. So we kept a lot of those scenes. But for other major scenes, like the rowboat scene, he brought in Daniele Amfitheatrof for those. He did the rowboat scene, he did the scene where she goes to the post office to get the letters, and Loon Lake. Amfitheatrof was a great talent." Amfitheatrof's music was used for about 25% of the score, including the most exposed dramatic cues mentioned by Hammell.

"And for all of the tender scenes," Hammell continues, "the more romantic scenes, he got Victor Young, and Victor did those." Stevens used Victor Young's music for another 10% of the score—not really that much, but the total contribution of these composers (and several short cues by others) was significant.

Since then, replacing cues (and sometimes, entire scores) has become commonplace. Although Waxman was one of Hollywood's finest composers, he didn't have the contractual authority to insist that his music remain in the film. Most active Hollywood composers (even the most prestigious) have had one or more scores entirely replaced.

PART TWO

■ ■ ■

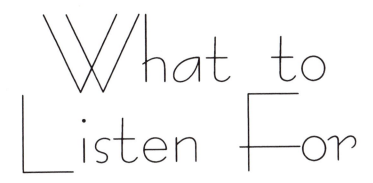

What to Listen For

■ ■ ■

Music is so important to the filmgoing experience that I think that if people understood what the impact of music is in a film, they would appreciate it more, and they would make more of an effort to listen.

Jon Burlingame, syndicated television columnist

It's just impossible to hear the music—'cause you're listening to the dialogue, which is why you're watching the movie in the first place.

Agnes Goodmanson, moviegoer

LISTENING

Many people can identify with Agnes Goodman-son's problem—they simply can't listen to the music while they're watching the film. And if you don't train yourself to listen, you may continue to find it difficult, if not impossible, to really *hear* the music. It's easy to miss the entrances of the music. When you are swept up in the drama, the music will often sneak in well before you realize it is there. Even after you begin to listen specifically for those moments when the music first enters a scene, it may take you a while to acquire the knack to hear it.

It will help if you understand the role of the music in a movie. Then you can begin to look at the film and the music from the composer's point of view. The composer must decide what the music's role is going to be both in the film as a whole and in each individual cue. The composer asks, Why is the music there, what should it say, and how should it be said? The key to effective listening is to be able to answer those questions as you watch the movie. At first it's not easy, but if you want to hear more, it's the only way.

There are two basic categories of music you will hear on soundtracks.

Source music is the music coming from a source on- or off-screen. Sources might include a car radio, a television set, a jukebox, a stereo system, a marching band, a dance band, and so on. Any of these sources might be seen or unseen; other examples of unseen sources would include a saxophone player practicing in a nearby apartment, or a stereo in a teenager's bedroom. Director John Hughes uses unseen music sources in films about young teenagers, including *Sixteen Candles* (1984) and *Pretty in Pink* (1986). He doesn't always feel he must show the audience exactly where the music is coming from—it is often implied. Since radio and records are such an important part of a teenager's life, it's not necessary to include a shot of a stereo system in the scene to establish the source visually. When source music isn't actually performed on screen, it is typically recorded after production of the film (that is, during postproduction).

On-screen source music can be recorded live during the shooting of the scene, in which case it is called "production track." Or it can be recorded prior to filming the sequence, in which case, as discussed above (see Chapter 3), the performers mimic playing instruments and singing vocals that have already been prerecorded.

Except for simple unaccompanied vocals like lullabies and "Happy Birthday," and an occasional church or gospel choir peformance (like the one in *The Color Purple*), the on-screen source music will often have been prerecorded in films dating from about 1935 on. But visually performed source music (like marching bands and dance bands, for example) may also have been recorded (or rerecorded) after the shooting and editing. All of the dance band music for *That's Life!* (1986), for example, was postrecorded by Henry Mancini after Blake Edwards had shot the film, even though there is a long party sequence at the end of the film during which the guests dance to an on-screen dance band.

Almost all on-screen songs are prerecorded. A notorious exception involves the songs for *At Long Last Love*, Peter Bogdanovich's 1975 musical with Cole Porter songs, starring Cybill Shepherd and Burt Reynolds. Bogdanovich insisted that the songs be performed live, just as they had been during the Hollywood films made in the early thirties. Neither Lionel Newman, then head of the music department at Fox, nor any other messenger of reason

could convince him of the fact that the development of prerecording techniques in the thirties represented a tremendous *improvement* in motion picture technique.

Often, filmmakers obtain the rights to use existing recordings on the soundtrack (frequently for sky-high fees), usually for some kind of source music. The on-screen parade scene in *Ferris Bueller's Day Off* (1986) uses the song "Twist and Shout," featuring Matthew Broderick (as Bueller) lip-syncing to the original recording. This effective scene was well integrated into the episodic storyline, but more often the nonfilmic motive for licensing these songs and performances is to assist in marketing the film's soundtrack album.

Original recordings have been mimicked in many films when master recordings were unavailable or too expensive (as is the case with Elvis Presley, Frank Sinatra, rock groups from the fifties and sixties, and many other artists). Rob Reiner and Marc Shaiman decided not to imitate Sinatra singing "It Had To Be You" on the soundtrack of *When Harry Met Sally . . .* (1989), but rather to go for the Sinatra feel. Harry Connick, Jr., with Shaiman's arrangement, did that very successfully.

The *score,* also called "underscoring" or the "background score," is all music on the soundtrack except that which is coming from a source on- or off-screen. The term "score" also refers to the entire body of music on the soundtrack, but if somebody says, "I wrote the score" for that film, they may be excluding the songs on the soundtrack, and they may not have composed all the source music.

An *original score* is music composed specifically for a film. Sometimes even original scores are supplemented with pre-existing music. For example, Oliver Stone used Samuel Barber's *Adagio for Strings* along with Georges Delerue's original music on the soundtrack of *Platoon* (1986). Composers do not refer to the music on the soundtracks of *The Exorcist* (1973) and *2001: A Space Odyssey* (1968) as scores, however, since these films contain no original music, but simply compilations of excerpts from pre-existing music.

Adaptation refers to pre-existing music that has

been arranged, orchestrated, and in many cases changed, extended, abbreviated, or developed by the adaptor (who then gets an "Adapted by" credit on the screen). The Scott Joplin rags used in *The Sting* (1973) were adapted by Marvin Hamlisch. Songs from *Fiddler on the Roof* (1971) were adapted (by John Williams) for the underscoring, as is the case with most musicals. The credit for *Sister Act* (1992), starring Whoopi Goldberg, reads "Original Music and Adaptation by Marc Shaiman."

SOURCE MUSIC

Source music can be well used to give the flavor of a particular period in time—the roaring twenties in which Gatsby lived, for instance, or the flavor of the early sixties when the high school students graduated in *American Graffiti* (1973). As Hugo Friedhofer said, "One certainly couldn't score a film like *American Graffiti* with a Korngold score. That was a picture that called for source music, as did *The Great Gatsby* (1974), and both films were adroitly scored in that fashion."

Source music can be effectively integrated into the dramatic underscoring, giving the score extra musical continuity. *Casablanca*'s screenplay called for "As Time Goes By" to be used as source music, played on screen by Sam (Dooley Wilson) at the piano in Rick's Café. Steiner then incorporated that theme as an integral part of his score to achieve additional unity and emotional power. In *Dark Passage* (1947), a bizarre example of the film noir genre, Bogart plays an escaped convict who has plastic surgery and hides out with the help of Lauren Bacall. The pop song "Too Marvelous for Words" is used instrumentally as phonograph source music several times, creating a link between the two of them. Then, as they say goodbye after his operation, and again later in the film, Franz Waxman uses this melody as an important theme in his score.

Dramatic films often have a great deal of source music in addition to the underscoring. In Alfred Newman's score for *All About Eve* (1950), as Rudy Behlmer points out, "Almost half of the score is source music: that is, music being played by the pianist during the party, by an off-screen group at the Stork Club, music coming from Lloyd's car radio." This music helps to define the glamor of the theatrical world and the people who are in the theater, and also establishes the reality of their time and place.

Many films of the seventies, eighties, and nineties are loaded with source music, which gives a certain hard-edged reality to the scenes in which it is used. The source music is usually balanced by a great deal of underscoring as well. Some films, like *Saturday Night Fever* (1977), *Footloose* (1984), *Flashdance* (1983), *Dirty Dancing* (1987), and *The Mambo Kings* (1992), feature dancing and emphasize record-oriented source music as an important part of the plot. *Fame* (1980) is an excellent example of a film that relies almost exclusively on various kinds of source music, including music for students practicing, dancing, and performing. From time to time the source music functions as underscoring, and it is extraordinarily well integrated into the texture and drama of the film.

STYLE

Quite often, a film composer must accept a musical language which is not up to date. The result depends on . . . how the composer is able to assimilate himself in the passage—interpreting a classical technique and language in his own particular style.
                                        Ennio Morricone, composer

I attempted to treat the familiar old forms in a modern way, so as to be consistent with the general musical style of the picture.
                                        Bernard Herrmann, composer
                                                (re: Citizen Kane)

You take pictures like New Jack City *[1991],* Boyz N the Hood *[1991]—those are contempo-*

rary pictures that speak of the times. And obviously those scores will date the picture.

Bobby Fernandez,
music recording engineer

You can begin to analyze the style of a score by considering all the familiar styles of music as your basic vocabulary. Jazz (*The Hot Spot*), Classical (*The Accidental Tourist*), Country (*Coal Miner's Daughter*), Blues (*Into the Night*)—these terms are very general in nature, but they're a good start.

If you can be more specific, that's even better. For example, Alex North's score for *Spartacus* (1960) could be called "symphonic," yet it is more contemporary sounding than Alfred Newman's romantic symphonic score for *Wuthering Heights* (1939). Give it whatever label you like, "contemporary symphonic" or "modern symphonic" or whatever—anything to distinguish it from other symphonic styles. It also seems appropriate for the Roman period drama it plays, so perhaps it could be called "modern Roman-symphonic."

Miklós Rózsa's scores for *Quo Vadis* (1951) and *Ben-Hur* (1959) also seem appropriately Roman. Nobody living today has heard the music of ancient Rome—it hasn't survived. But Rózsa's music for these films, based on his research of music from ancient Greece, now sounds Roman to us. Subconsciously these scores have become part of our musical background, evoking ancient Rome. We get a lot of our historical musical information from Hollywood, which is why it's so difficult for composers to break away from the established conventions. These conventions now *sound* authentic. Watch *Ben-Hur* and listen to Rózsa's historically evocative score—both the marching music for the soldiers and the quiet music underscoring the dialogue scenes.

The labels by themselves aren't important, but because it is the nature of film music to blend styles of music together, this can be a helpful way to think about the resultant musical style of a score. If you're telling a friend about John Barry's score for *Body Heat* (1981), you could say that it features a very smooth, sensual saxophone solo, accompanied by a lush orchestral sound.

Composers find that deciding on just the right style to use for a film score is not always easy. "You have to look at a film and say, 'Well, this is what its style is,'" says Basil Poledouris. "There has to be a stylistic consistency between all the elements of the film."

When Rózsa was working on the Van Gogh bio-pic *Lust for Life* (1956), starring Kirk Douglas, he asked himself what sort of music Van Gogh would have known. "He was a post-impressionist, but post-impressionism in music comes much later than Van Gogh's death at the end of the nineteenth century; pictorial trends are always between 25 and 40 years ahead. The music he himself knew would have been that of the eighties—Wagner, Liszt, César Franck—but I felt that mid-nineteenth-century romanticism had little in common with his work. Somehow I had to evolve a suitable style in terms of my own music. It had to be somewhat impressionistic, somewhat pointillistic, somewhat post-romantic and brightly, even startlingly, colorful—much like the tenor of his paintings."

The elements in a film that can affect the score's style include:

- *Ethnic*: Is there an ethnic aspect of the film, as in *Gandhi* or *Medicine Man*?
- *Historical*: Is there a period setting, as in *Dangerous Liaisons* or *The Babe*?
- *Geographical*: Are there locations that might influence the score, as in *Around the World in 80 Days*?
- *Genre*: Is the film a classic genre film—like the Western *Silverado*, for instance—which may have a strong influence on the score's style?

CONCEPT

As we have seen, the above aspects of a film may help to suggest an overall concept for the score. In the case of *Gandhi*, Richard Attenborough's 1982 biographical drama about the great Indian leader, the basic concept was to use the totally authentic Indian sitar-and-tabla music of Ravi Shankar, and also the Western orchestral scoring of George Fenton, and to combine those two elements when appropriate. Ennio Morricone used a similar approach in *City of Joy* (1992), the story of an American doctor (Patrick Swayze) who gets stranded in India and reluctantly helps out a needy clinic.

Remember that *the style/styles of the music* can define the concept, and often do. In his groundbreaking score for *Streetcar Named Desire* (1951), Alex North points out, "Jazz, ragtime, or blues runs throughout . . . and establishes the atmosphere of New Orleans. Blanche arriving at Elysian Fields, the shabby street where her sister lives, is surrounded by the sounds of the street and the strident music of the cheap cafés. Later, when Blanche and Mitch are dancing in a café near the waterfront, there is a wonderful spell of ragtime by the band. In encounters with her brother-in-law, Stanley, the mocking and insinuating blues solos—clarinet, saxophone, or muted trumpet—serve as constant dramatic contrast to Blanche's gentility."

North's concept involved not only the styles of jazz, ragtime, and blues, but also blending and contrasting those sounds with a conventional orchestra, so that the source music coming from the café becomes at times the score, and at other times is replaced by the orchestra. "The music was related to the characters at all times and not the action," North said.

Another example of a stylistic concept is Victor Young's score for *The Quiet Man,* the 1952 film directed by John Ford. Ford liked to use folk themes in his films, and this became the concept for Young's score. According to Scott Wilkinson's review at that time in *Film Music Notes,* "Victor Young's score for *The Quiet Man* is for the most part extremely well done. His handling of the orchestra and use of musical material gains the maximum of effect with the minimum of means, achieving a simplicity in the music and orchestra that fits the simplicity of the film. The Irish folk themes as well as the folklike quality of Mr.

Young's melodic line are treated with sensitivity. There is a particularly good use of group singing injected from time to time."

Wilkinson goes on to point out that Young changes his style here and there, and consequently devastates his concept. "The whole musical atmosphere suddenly changes at the introduction of a romantic note—where Mary Kate is seen herding her sheep, for example, and in the scene where she realizes her love for Sean. Here, Mr. Young takes on a lush, lush style that is the most commonly used writing for the situation and is quite inconsistent with his previous handling of the folkish type of story."

If a score establishes a clear concept or style, and then suddenly changes without a powerful and convincing dramatic reason, the music loses credibility in much the same way as an actor's performance would suffer if he suddenly changed from an Irish brogue to a Brooklyn accent in the middle of a film. Look for conceptual consistency in a score just as you would in measuring the quality of the film itself.

The characters in the story are perhaps the most typical motivation for melodies and other musical material, often defining the concept. Bronislau Kaper considered the title character of *Auntie Mame* (1958) in working out his approach to the score for this sophisticated comedy about an offbeat, fun-loving woman and her nephew. "What interested me about Auntie Mame," says Bronislau Kaper, "was not so much the fact that she was funny, but that she had a great soul. She acts frivolously and theatrically, but underneath it is her great love and compassion for people. This is what I tried to capture, the fact that she has suffered in life, but hasn't been crushed by it. With Mame, the first temptation was to comment on her gay, vivacious manner, but that would have been a mistake because Roz Russell conveyed all that magnificently—visually and spiritually. When something is effective on the screen, there is no need to add to it with obvious music. To have scored Mame comically would have cheapened the film."

Listen for *the use of specific instruments* as a key

conceptual element. The sax in *Body Heat* became part of John Barry's concept, and is a good example of a solo instrument defining and unifying a score.

Listen also for *ethnic influences*. Is there any Italian influence in the score for a film about a romantic affair in Rome or a three-generation Mafia family?

Determining the appropriate amount of ethnic "accent" can be difficult. When planning his score for *The North Star* (1943), Aaron Copland wanted to achieve the proper balance between ethnic and nonethnic elements. "Since the picture takes place in Russia, there was from the beginning the problem as to how 'Russian' the music ought to be. It was something of the same problem Shostakovitch would have had if he had been asked to supply a score for a movie which was set in the United States.... In general, guided by the fact that American actors were performing without attempting Russian accents, I determined on using a style that would merely suggest, without overemphasizing, the Russian element."

To achieve just the right quality for this "accent," composers frequently research authentic historical or ethnic music. But often the authentic ethnic sounds are too stark, and may be inappropriate to play the drama. The authentic music often has to be adapted significantly for contemporary ears. Many composers have had experiences similar to David Raksin's, early in his career. "After I had been working at Twentieth [Century-Fox] for a while, [music head Louis] Silvers asked me to come up with something for a scene in a picture called *Suez* (1938). As I recall, it was a sequence in which Tyrone Power and his intrepid comrades find themselves in an African village, so whatever I devised would have to work with the ambient sound effects. The following day I brought in some old recordings that would have delighted the 78 rpm soul of a dedicated researcher; I had remembered that many years ago an expedition led by Armand Denis and Leila Roosevelt had recorded the music of some African tribes in the Belgian Congo. Lou listened; in fact, he gave the music his full partial attention,

after which he stared at me with his baleful approximation of paternal incredulity. 'Are you *nuts?*' he asked. 'All that goddam drumming—it sounds like Duke Ellington!'. . . . So I had to invent some ersatz 'native' music, and Silvers was so pleased . . . that the next time they needed help in a crowded schedule he called upon me again."

MELODY

I believe *in melody. Maybe there are places where you don't want it, but I don't know where they'd be.*

Randy Newman, composer

I've noticed that despite all the sophistication of our times, the greatest device of all remains the simple, straightforward melody. Using it in a sparse and simple way is still the best way.

Jerry Goldsmith, composer

In Western music, melody has traditionally been the life-force of musical expression. Accordingly, in film music, for decades almost all scores were based on one or more themes that recurred throughout the picture. Although atmospheric instrumental color has become the primary musical element in certain types of contemporary scoring, most experienced composers still rely on melody as the backbone of their scores.

In order to work properly, as Elmer Bernstein says, "The melody must be an absolute extension of what is taking place on the screen." This "absolute extension" happens when the melodies reflect the context of the film through some of the elements that delineate the concept—ethnic, historical, geographic, characterization, orchestration, or style. Like Jerry Goldsmith and Randy Newman, Bernstein believes that melody unifies a score. "I've always been really partial to linear writing. I think [the] line is really the spine of music, personally."

Max Steiner took this idea even further, believing that every character should have a theme. Like many others, he endorsed the use of leitmotifs—that is, individual motifs or themes for different characters and situations. Most composers find shorter melodies—the motifs—very helpful. "The leitmotif technique is common in film scoring," said Franz Waxman, "that is, the attaching of themes to characters and then varying them as the situations change, and I have found this very practical in writing film music. It is an aid to composition and an aid to listening. Motifs should be characteristically brief, with sharp profiles. If they are easily recognizable, they permit repetition in varying forms and textures, and they help musical continuity. . . ."

As these motifs and melodies in a score are repeated and developed, they build up strong associative value and can become more and more effective through the course of the film. By the final reel of *E.T.* (1982), John Williams has established emotional connections through his themes for E.T. and the other characters. This adds tremendous emotional power to the music as they say goodbye.

The plot, the characters, or the style of the film may preclude a melodic score. But even films that could take a melodic approach are not always scored with the emphasis on melodies. This is because not all composers agree that melody is important or even desirable. Jerry Fielding, for instance, said, "For myself, I try to make . . . [the score] something that is not necessarily melodic. Opinions vary on this, but I don't advocate the leitmotive method in film scoring because I don't think audiences, other than those who are musically disposed, can retain melodies on short acquaintance."

Though Bernard Herrmann used motifs frequently, he is not known for using these motifs in a way that is distinctly related to specific characters or situations. He did employ this technique in *Citizen Kane*, though. "Although I am not a great believer in the technique of the leitmotive for motion picture music, the nature of this film demanded some leitmotives in linking together the various time juxtapositions. The most important motif—that of Kane's power—is given out in the very first two bars heard. The second motif, which should give away the secret of 'Rosebud' to anyone who listens carefully, is also stated right at the beginning of the picture. It occurs after the sudden going out of the light, and precedes Kane's statement of 'Rosebud.' These two motifs are the most important in the entire picture, and they occur throughout the film in many phases and in many orchestrations. The motif of power becomes a vigorous piece of ragtime. It is transformed into a hornpipe polka. It becomes the very last part of the finale, likewise with 'Rosebud.' It personifies Kane's nostalgic return to his youth and is used to portray the best part of his nature. Only one other motif of importance is derived from the tune, 'Oh, Mr. Kane,' a theme used in a satiric sense."

You can see how important these motifs were in structuring his entire score. The profiles of specific scores in Chapter 6 will help you to listen for these motifs in scores such as Franz Waxman's *The Spirit of St. Louis* (1957) and Bernard Herrmann's *North by Northwest* (1959).

Scores are so chintzy now. You used to get five or six good themes in a picture. Now, if you get one, you're grateful.
        Richard Kraft, composers' agent (1991)

Creating great themes is a special talent. "The ability to write melody is such a rare commodity," says Randy Newman. "You don't realize it until you look at some of this stuff by some of the most highly thought of people. I guarantee you that there aren't 10 people doing pictures who can write a tune. And some of those can't *score* a picture. It's awfully tough."

Henry Mancini, who is best known for his melodic scores and song themes, agrees. "Overall, Victor Young was my hero. I've gone down his path. Victor was a melody writer—you always came away from his pictures with something, musically—which isn't true of many other movie composers. He had the gift of melody, which, strangely, many composers lack."

TEMPO AND PULSE

To me, tempo is of prime importance. It could be a deciding factor in whether a scene works or not.
                                    Henry Mancini, composer

Even though Mancini is a thematic writer with the highest regard for melody, he places a great emphasis on rhythmic pulse, or tempo. This is not a contradiction—these two elements are very compatible and can work together in support of the drama. Music can move a film along, pushing it in a forward direction and generating the sense that something is going to happen. Elmer Bernstein's score for *The Magnificent Seven* (1960) is a definitive example of this collaboration of melody and rhythmic thrust, giving the first half of the film a drive and sense of momentum that the visuals and drama lack. As the seven men ride to the Mexican village they have been hired to protect, their horses move along at a lethargic walk while the score surges ahead powerfully. The theme itself (which has become inseparable from its rhythmic accompaniment in our minds) is one of the most well known in all film music. Both the melody and its accompaniment provide this effective musical propulsion. (See Chapter 6 for a closer look at this score.)

Film historian Steven C. Smith, author of the 1991 Bernard Herrmann biography *A Heart at Fire's Center*, agrees that forward motion and rhythmic thrust in a score is very important. "I think . . . every good film score contributes to that sense of a forward direction—the implication that the film is going somewhere." This doesn't mean that the music has to be particularly rhythmic in order to achieve this. Even slow, sustained pieces can project this feeling of pulling you forward (consider John Williams' slow theme for *Close Encounters of the Third Kind*, 1977, discussed in Chapter 6).

Edited film usually has an inherent pace and tempo of its own. "I look at film, and I can generally hear the tempo that works for that piece of film," says Danny Elfman. "Especially in early cuts of a movie, editors do have an internal rhythm.

And once you lock into that, it becomes very natural. The earlier cuts are more pure rhythmically. And then they start to look at individual cut by individual cut . . . and they're starting to get more microscopic and anal. And they're not any longer looking at the entire scene. This doesn't always happen, but I think it's very common. I can't say that very often what they end up with cutting-wise isn't better—it's just less musical."

The action also can have a clearly defined tempo. When silent movie organist Gaylord Carter was accompanying Laurel and Hardy films, he discovered that they seemed to be working to a steady tempo. "I've got a {silent} picture called *That's My Wife*," Carter explains. "They're having a fight in the living room and throwing things, and they're punching each other and kicking. If I can find a certain tempo, I can catch every one of those things. . . . And that happens on many occasions with them: you'll discover that they're operating to a beat, to a certain rhythmic pattern."

Watch a film while listening primarily to the tempo and rhythmic drive of the score. Here are some suggested films: *The Magnificent Seven* (1960, Bernstein), *Star Wars* (1977, Williams), *Planet of the Apes* (1968, Goldsmith), *Objective, Burma!* (1945, Waxman), and *Batman* (1989, Elfman).

HARMONY

Even the harmony can grow out of the film and its characters. In *Driving Miss Daisy* (1989), Hans Zimmer chose a nostalgic, thirties/forties feel with a clarinet solo playing the main theme. Although the film chronicles the relationship between Daisy (Jessica Tandy) and her chauffeur (Morgan Freeman) beginning in 1948 and continuing until 1973, Zimmer's musical concept suggests the roots of Daisy's racial attitudes, which have a long history prior to the late forties. The Southern-sounding harmony, an essential aspect of his concept, is appropriate to that expanded time frame (as is the theme itself) and is well connected to Daisy and her environment.

Zimmer took an entirely different harmonic approach in *Rain Man* (1988), Barry Levinson's film starring Tom Cruise as a materialistic car salesman (Charlie Babbitt) who learns that he has an older brother who is autistic (Raymond, played by Dustin Hoffman). In this film, the director and composer did not want a sentimental orchestral sound for the score, and the more contemporary harmonies played by Zimmer's keyboard textures help to establish an objective, nonemotional musical approach throughout much of the film.

In general, harmony is a more subtle musical element than melody or rhythm, and as such may be more difficult to distinguish. But it's definitely not necessary to understand or even recognize the harmonic language of the film score to feel it and appreciate it.

ORCHESTRATION

All of the big studios had big orchestras under contract. And they had to utilize them. So the composer was forced to write more expansively and extensively than he might have liked.

Hugo Friedhofer, composer

The day will come when the film without electronic music will be as out of date as the silents.

Ivor Darreg, journalist (1946)

Instrumental color, the final musical element, is even more significant in film scores than it is in concert music. At the right place in the film, the sound of a single muted French horn can play a dramatic moment as tellingly as a full orchestra. Changing the instrumental color at a particular moment in the drama can do as much to emphasize a dramatic point as any of the other elements.

As we have seen, until the late fifties, just the existence of the 45- to 50-piece contract orchestras tended to encourage a sameness of orchestration. "Warners always had a big orchestra, and I think it was a mistake," says Kaper. "I think that the change of the sound of the orchestra, intimacy and the contrast, are very important." Hugo Friedhofer, who orchestrated many of Korngold's and Steiner's scores, among others, agreed with Kaper. "Many times there were instances when a composer who would have preferred to use an intimate form of expression was thwarted. . . ."

Of all the composers scoring films in those days, Herrmann displayed the most individualistic use of orchestration, using the ideal instrumentation for each score. And, as Steven C. Smith points out, he used the instrumental colors so well. "I think one reason that he's had such an influence on those composers who followed him is his really imaginative use of the orchestra, as a psychological tool, in the fantasy and horror films. He moved away from the somewhat generic sound that was employed by a number of composers, and that gave his music greater identity. I think a lot of people could identify a Herrmann score after a few bars, while it might take them a little longer with some other composers."

FORM AND DEVELOPMENT

Musically, it was necessary to make each of the three fights with the sharks top what had gone before. Each had to represent a new mood.

Dimitri Tiomkin, composer
(re: The Old Man and the Sea, 1958)

In Citizen Kane . . . *the montage showing the passage of years and the waning affection was expressed in the form of a theme and variations. The very style of the montage practically dictated this form.*

Bernard Herrmann, composer

The form of the film always dictates the form of the music. If the big love scenes take place in reel five and reel ten, then that's where the love theme is likely to play. The structure of the film automatically puts the chase music where the chases are, and the psychological cues develop in a natural way where the scenes with internal conflict and revelation take place.

On repeated viewings, you may be able to notice the repetition of certain musical materials here and there throughout a score. Listen for the similarities in usage (are the three love scenes all scored with the same theme?) and disparities (is the melody used for the love scene in reel three now being used during the chase sequence?).

Listen to the material used for the end scene of the film (not the end credits). This music often represents the most basic dramatic statement of the film itself, and recalling this music can be helpful when reviewing a film.

Writing the melody is the easy part. . . . But then, it's what you do with it. That's the skill, that's the art, that's what makes a great film score.
Danny Elfman, composer

One of the greatest examples of musical development in the history of Western music is the first movement of Beethoven's Fifth Symphony. It begins with a famous four-note motif, which Beethoven then repeats down one scale step. Composers are fond of pointing out that anyone could have written those four notes, but no one else could have written the identical extended work he developed from that motif.

Richard Kraft, an agent representing film composers, has noticed a disturbing trend in many of the scores of the nineties: there often is *no* development of the musical material whatsoever. "You hear the Main Title and you go, 'This is going to be an interesting score,' and then you realize you've heard it all. It's just a color, and they either don't have the vocabulary to know how to expand on it, or they're not interested in doing it."

There is nothing mysterious about the tech-
niques used to expand and develop a score's musical materials—they come from the same basic musical elements already discussed: melody, rhythm, harmony, and orchestration.

Changing any one of these four elements will bring about a considerable change in the effect of the basic material. A simple example of this is a change of the instrumental color which plays the theme, perhaps a solo oboe assigned to the melody previously played by the cellos. In a compositional sense, this is not, strictly speaking, a development of the original material, since in this hypothetical example everything about the music itself has remained the same—only the *orchestral color* has changed. In film scoring, however, this can be a significant change in the musical and dramatic effect, and in fact appear to be a real compositional *development* of the basic materials.

Here are a few of the ways that musical material is manipulated by composers:

- The same melody is repeated, but accompanied with different harmony.
- The rhythm of the melody is changed, keeping the pitches the same.
- The statement of the melody begins on a different note of the scale, and then follows the same or a similar contour as the original melody. Harmony is adjusted and developed as necessary.
- The direction of the melody is reversed.

    As an example of this, take the first four notes of Beethoven's Fifth and sing the last one *up* from the other three, instead of down.

Try singing the first four notes of Beethoven's Fifth a few times. Now substitute the *rhythm* of the beginning of "Silent Night," but keep on singing Beethoven's *notes*. When you've got that, try the same thing with the beginning of "Joy to the World." Each rhythmic change has a significant affect on Beethoven's motif.

Beethoven's real mastery, though, is not the manipulation of the basic four notes, but the expanding music he weaves from the shape of those notes, connecting them and creating much longer musical lines that have their own absolute integrity. He also develops the harmony as all this is happening, which gives the music a strong sense of forward motion and power.

For composers, musical development is not an art easily learned, and it can be a demanding effort. "Writing a melody for somebody—that's the fun," says Danny Elfman. "How many ways you can twist and turn that melody is the skill and the work. By far, that's 90 percent of the job, in my book."

When he was first called in to score *Dick Tracy* (1990), he says, "I worked up about 20 minutes of thematic material and played it for [director] Warren [Beatty]. And it was a real simple thing—yes or no. Yes, you've got the job, and if so, you start work tomorrow. If you don't like what I did, forget it. In six days I worked up every thematic piece of material in the movie. There was no character unscored.

"So I worked up the entire thematic material for a major film in a week. And then spent seven days a week, fourteen hours a day, writing it down. That's the *work*—it's what you do with it."

SPOTTING

My basic approach to film scoring has always been the same. I ask myself, What did the director want to tell the audience with this scene? Where does the picture need help? Where can it carry itself without any help?

Hans J. Salter, composer

There are several important factors to consider when listening to the spotting.

■ How much music is there in the picture?
■ Where is it used? How is silence used?
■ Exactly where does it enter? What is the dramatic motivation for each cue?

■ Is it used to play the scenes that have an important dramatic or psychological text or subtext? Does it sometimes seem to be used as filler, just to keep scenes from seeming too empty?
■ How does it enter—does it sneak in softly, or enter loudly, with an accent?
■ How does it end? What is the dramatic motivation for stopping he music?

The overuse of music in films of the forties and fifties was a convention that tended to diminish the effectiveness of the music when its use was justifiable and necessary. When Celeste Hautbois was writing for *Film Music Notes* in the forties, she voiced a complaint which is still relevant today: "If the picture runs for 2 hours and 17 minutes, why does the music have to run for 2 hours and 17 minutes, too?" In reviewing Max Steiner's score for *Saratoga Trunk* (1945), she went on to say, "This score should have been diminished by two-thirds. . . . One feels sorry that there is so much mediocre stuff [in this score] to outweigh the good. . . ."

Aaron Copland, whose scores for films like *Of Mice and Men* (1939), *Our Town* (1940), *The Red Pony* (1949), and *The Heiress* (1949) are highly acclaimed, agreed with Hautbois. In 1949, he said, "Personally, I like to make use of music's power sparingly, saving it for absolutely essential points. A composer knows how to play with silences, knows that to take music out can at times be more effective than any use of it might be."

Alfred Hitchcock made masterful use of silence. But silence, to be effective, must be preceded by sound. "You've seen people in danger?" he asked. "People at some high point of tension? Let's do a scene: we're sitting in this room talking when suddenly a burglar enters and points a gun at us. We freeze. We don't move or breathe. Certainly we don't talk. At any dramatic moment such as this there comes a hush. When the danger is over, everyone starts talking. It's a release. So, in a psychological mystery, there are appropriate intervals at which I want the music stopped—with a hush!

Well, if we didn't have the music in the picture in the first place, we couldn't stop it for the effect."

When sound effects become a story point, they usually become predominant. *Earthquake* (1974, John Williams) is a good example of this. With effects as powerful as an earthquake, the flow from music to effects can be so seamless it's deceiving. "I have received many compliments for the earthquake music in *San Francisco* (1936) and the earthquake music in *Green Dolphin Street* (1947), except that there was no music in either sequence, only sound effects," Bronislau Kaper admitted. "There was a wild storm and flood sequence in *The Wild North* (1952), and people have told me how well I scored it. Again, there was no music. The trick is simply that I led up to those sequences with music and then dropped it for the sounds to take over, and picked up again with music after the sounds died down."

This aural illusion is not unusual. "I have, for example, been complimented on my music for the stag hunt in *Tom Jones*,"(1963), says John Addison. "Actually, there was no music until the hunt was over!" The famous chariot race in *Ben-Hur* is unscored—sound effects provide all of the dramatic tension on the soundtrack.

PLAYING THE DRAMA

Film music, even more than other music, must engage your heart. It's unabashedly, shamelessly gushy, and that suits me fine.
　　　　　　　　　　　　　Michael Kamen, composer

I believe in going with it, expressing emotion. Let's have emotional response—what are they afraid of?
　　　　　　　　　　　　　Elmer Bernstein, composer

I'm evaluating the [emotional] role I want music to play at any given point. Is it going to suddenly be over-the-top here? Or am I being real sneaky here? Or what am I doing?
　　　　　　　　　　　　　Shirley Walker, composer

One of the primary questions a film composer must answer is, How emotionally involved should the music be? Many of the classic film scores played to the hilt the emotional quality of the films they supported. During the sixties and much of the seventies, both filmmakers and composers tended to hold back, letting the emotions on the screen speak for themselves without amplification from the score. Most scores were emotionally cool. Johnny Mandel's score for *The Sandpiper* (1965, with Richard Burton and Elizabeth Taylor) is a good example of this, and is especially interesting musically because of the ingratiating theme Mandel used as the primary musical material (with Paul Francis Webster's words, it became "The Shadow of Your Smile"). A traditional approach would have been much less restrained, but not necessarily more effective for that specific film released in the mid-sixties.

During the sixties and seventies there were some exceptions to a less emotionally involved approach to playing the drama. Many, but not all, Westerns made during those years were scored orchestrally because the big outdoor sound that had been established in the forties and fifties generally was accepted by the filmmakers as being appropriate for that genre. The new genre of disaster film that John Williams scored, which included *The Poseidon Adventure* in 1972 and *The Towering Inferno* in 1974, was perfect for dynamic orchestral scoring. This genre—the jeopardy film—culminated in 1975's *Jaws*, but even those three big symphonic scores by Williams didn't bring about a tidal wave of emotional film scoring. It took the impact of *Star Wars*, released in 1977, to accomplish that, and since then, it again has become acceptable in the mainstream of filmmaking to allow the music have its own symphonic emotional voice.

In looking at a film, the prevailing question will be, What amount of emotional support does this *particular* film need? All the issues of musical style, concept, orchestration, and melodic emphasis are relevant, but the degree of emotional involvement is also a vital decision. The style used to express emotion should be tailored to the film also, of course. John Williams' orchestral style for *Star*

Wars wouldn't be compatible with director Robert Mulligan's films *Clara's Heart* (1988, Dave Grusin) or *The Man in the Moon* (1991, James Newton Howard). Because of this, the scores for these films aren't as emotionally obvious as, say, James Newton Howard's score for *The Prince of Tides* (1991). Often, of course, the extent of the score's emotional involvement in the drama is a reflection of directorial tastes.

Some composers really enjoy being as emotionally in-your-face as possible. "I tend to walk on a film with big toes," says Michael Kamen. "I have a difficult time tucking my music back. My inclination is to say, 'Hey! Look what I can do!' I'm not Mr. Subtle. Why would I be asked to make music and not want it heard?" But it isn't just a question of being heard. Kamen was referring not simply to loudness and bigness, but also to the emotional content of his music.

HITTING THE ACTION

The style I write, when it comes to action, is very, very cue-y. And especially movies like Batman Returns *[1992].*

Danny Elfman, composer

You know, in the beginning of "Raiders III" [Indiana Jones and the Last Crusade, 1989], the unbelievable things that Johnny Williams caught. He's really moving, and a guy smiles on the train and he'll catch it. Virtuoso thing, that opening.

Randy Newman, composer

Yes, I overdo it sometimes.

Max Steiner, composer
(re: hitting the action)

Whenever the music accents a specific moment in a film, it is hitting (or catching) the action. Cartoon scoring does this all the time—in fact, to such an extent that this type of musical-dramatic sync is called "Mickey-Mousing," after the star of the same name.

Max Steiner developed this style of dramatic scoring very early in his career, frequently emphasizing each action on the screen and each shift in emotion. Steiner explained why his music so often hit the action. "When a scene is weak—for example, if an actor raises his eyebrow in shock and looks like the very devil, my music helps get that shock idea across. In a Western, I catch everything. . . ."

There's no evidence to support his implication that he reserved this device exclusively for those moments where the drama was weak. "*The Informer* [1935] won me my first Oscar," he said. "John Ford also won for direction, and Victor McLaglen for his performance. When this picture was being made, our executive producer was not very happy about it and asked me, 'Who wants to see a picture that's always in fog?' The background was the trouble in Dublin in the early 1920s between the British and the Irish republicans.

"There was a sequence toward the end of the picture in which McLaglen is in a cell and water is dripping on him. This is just before he escapes and is killed. I had a certain music effect I wanted to use for this. I wanted to catch each of these drops musically. The property man and I worked for days trying to regulate the water tank so it dripped in tempo and so I could accompany it. This took a good deal of time and thought, because a dripping faucet doesn't always drip in the same rhythm. We finally mastered it, and I believe it was one of the things that won me the award. People were fascinated trying to figure out how we managed to catch every drop."

This is a perfect description of hitting the action. In spite of the Oscar for *The Informer*, though, not everybody endorsed this technique. In a memo to Katherine Brown on August 30, 1937, David O. Selznick, who had been working with Steiner, expressed his disagreements with him:

. . . The root of our decision to get a divorce . . . was my objection to what I term "Mickey Mouse" scoring: an interpretation of each line of dialogue and each movement musically, so that the score tells with music exactly what is being done by the actors on the screen. It has long been my contention that this is ridiculous and that the purpose of a score is to unobtrusively help the mood of each scene without the audience being even aware that they are listening to music. . . .

Some movies are more receptive to this kind of musical treatment than others. The Batman films, coming as they do from the exaggeration of comic books, are compatible with this approach, and Danny Elfman hits a lot of the dramatic moments in the action-oriented sequences. He points out that it is tough work, filled with detail. "There's no way to skirt over the stuff, there's no way to do it an easy way. And you know what? Even using the same major theme [in the sequel] and doing a 150-bar piece of music doesn't make it any easier at all. All you know is, OK, I'm using this melody, but, my God—I've still got to find the 97 hit points, and weave it around them. It doesn't take one second less than before."

Albert Glasser, who scored *The Amazing Colossal Man* in 1957, used every device he could think of to hit the action, often illustrating the story with various instruments and orchestral effects. He explained his scoring concept for that film to Randall Larson:

I wanted a very heavy, deep monstrous sound from all the basses. Whoever I had on the bottom—string bass, the tuba, trombones, low French horns, and so on—all of them would play almost in harmony, following his [the Amazing Colossal Man's] footbeats, but changing notes—up and down, back and forth, slowly, always in tempo. You can't go too fast or you'll make him walk too fast, it'd feel funny; you can't go too slow or you'll fall asleep. You more or less try to follow his rhythm, his tempo. On top of that, if things were happening, if his hand comes out and he pushes a house down, you catch it with cues [hitting the action], and all the brass flies up in the air in a shreiking sound, with dis-

sonance. Plus your simple crashes, your gongs, anything that would make a lot of noise and would augment what he's doing and make sense.

If somebody gets hurt, if he's chasing a little baby who's screaming, you have all the violins, way up, tearing your heart out, so the message that the violins say to the audience is, 'Look out! He's going to kill the baby!' You frighten them any way you can, as long as it makes sense. . . . If things are going to happen in a terrible way, you build up; the sound gets louder and louder and louder, heavier and heavier; you come up and up and up and it's about to burst; if nothing happens, you go down a little bit.

This type of scoring is clearly very specific, very illustrative, and much too on-the-nose for most contemporary films. Nevertheless, many composers, including John Williams, Michael Kamen, Elmer Bernstein, James Horner, Jerry Goldsmith, and many others who don't hit all the action, definitely *play the drama* when the film calls for it. "I love the way Max Steiner scored his films," says Elfman. "I just love the way he caught everything. And it went right with the imagery. And it just flowed right from emotion to emotion, and I just love that."

One of the things Steiner was able to do with this technique was to bring momentary emphasis to an emotional instant in the drama. I can recall hearing this approach dozens of times in theaters, and marveling at the music's ability to quickly catch you up in an emotional moment, only to let you go again as soon as that moment had passed. How *did* he do that, I would ask. Harold Browne describes such a moment in his 1952 *Film Music Notes* review of *The Miracle of Our Lady of Fatima*.

Steiner has a way of getting behind the action on the screen with a well chosen burst of sound which calls no attention to itself, falls as quickly as it rises, yet effects an intensity where none otherwise would exist. The film itself is powerless to produce much excitement in a scene where children play with a ram, yet the music makes it a small event. Thus, if the larger outlines of drama are accomplished by writer and director, the smaller undulations are almost entirely the work of the composer.

PLAYING THROUGH THE ACTION

The opposite of hitting the action is playing through the action. When the music is playing through the action, it is hitting nothing specifically, ignoring subtle and even not-so-subtle shifts of emotion. In Marvin Hamlisch's adaptation score for *The Sting* (1973), when he plays a Joplin rag like "The Entertainer" straight through a scene as the plot develops, he's playing through the action.

The idea behind this approach is to lay down one specific mood, sound, or atmospheric coloration, and let that be the underscoring for the entire sequence. Sometimes the scoring is cool and subdued (as in Mandel's score for *The Sandpiper*), but the music doesn't have to be passive. Jan Hammer's scores for the "Miami Vice" television series played through the action, ignoring many of the specific dramatic moments in the process, but the music was full of energy and set up a valid and relevant contemporary musical frame for the scenes.

In its purest form, this approach is very effective when it uses a particularly identifiable style of music. Good examples are *Deliverance,* with its use of bluegrass banjos, and *Going in Style* (1979), in which Michael Small used a vaudeville/dixieland jazz approach. In *The Fortune* (1975, David Shire) and *Dirty Rotten Scoundrels* (1988, Miles Goodman), each score uses a different style of jazz and jazz violin (the Joe Venuti–Eddie Lang jazz of the twenties, and the Stephane Grappelli jazz of the thirties).

The dialogue between those who favored hitting the action as Steiner did, and those who preferred to play through the action, continued into the forties. Isabel Morse Jones, music editor of the *Los Angeles Times,* commented on this disparity of opinions in May of 1945 in an article in *Film Music Notes.*

This leitmotive music, long used by the music men from the theater ranks, is giving place to mood music, atmosphere, and overall scoring which the experienced Max Steiner of Warner Bros. calls "symphony music." Erich Korngold of the same studio is addicted to it as well. Steiner was the first to point out the music closely synchronized with action, such as he writes, as "Mickey Mouse" music.

There has been progress through friction in film-music circles the past year. The theater men, arrangers, technical experts of the "Mickey Mouse" school are still the favorites of the producers who are a little apprehensive about the symphonists, the mood-music writers and the new musical resources advocated by Hanns Eisler and his 12-tone scale from Schoenberg.

PHRASING THE DRAMA

Should music be synchronized with the action? Yes and no.

Miklós Rózsa, composer

The most effective course in between these two extremes is to phrase the drama, hitting certain moments that seem to require greater emphasis (either subtlely or more aggressively) and playing through others while sustaining the overall emotional tone of the scene. For films that don't have the bigger-than-life sweep of *The Adventures of Robin Hood* (Korngold, 1938) and *The Empire Strikes Back* (Williams, 1980), this is often the most satisfying approach. It can work with epics as well, though, as it does during full-orchestra cues in *The Last of the Mohicans* (1992, Trevor Jones and Randy Edelman). In *Mohicans,* this approach is used effectively during some of the action sequences, in which the music plays *against* the action, underscoring the emotional impact of the film rather than illustrating the fighting.

Watch a scene that has music. Turn off the sound and notice where each new dramatic element enters—shifts in emotion, a new action, or dramatic emphasis. Not all scenes can be looked at in this oversimplified way, but this is frequently a very successful technique for getting inside a scene, and can make it easier to hear the relationship of the music to the drama. Once the scene is phrased dramatically like this, it is easier to hear the musical techniques that a composer uses to help delineate the drama. These include adding, subtracting, or otherwise changing any one or more of the four basic musical elements. Variations might be:

- *Melody*: A change of thematic material, or a new phrase or variation of the melody.
- *Rhythm*: A change of the rhythmic pulse through the use of additional motion (or by speeding up).
  A change of the rhythmic pulse through the use of less motion (or by slowing down).
- *Harmony*: Changing the key of the music, or the pitch level of the lead instrument(s).
- *Orchestration*: A change in the instrumental color that is playing a melody. For instance, at a key point in the drama, a guitar might replace an oboe without breaking the flow of the melody.

Shirley Walker lets the film direct these variations. "I never just change the music because musically we've been a little bit stagnant for eight measures or something. If there's nothing that's happening in the picture to warrant anything changing, I'll stay there for 20 measures."

David Raksin, who has taught film scoring to composers since the mid-fifties (first at USC, and later at UCLA as well) explains that there can be a natural, unforced flow to the music, within which certain dramatic points are emphasized, either through the above-mentioned means, or with a shift in dynamics (from loud to soft, or soft to loud).

This is what he did so well in his score for *Laura* (1944).

"You do not try to force the structure of the film into a musical form, but you try to define what the form of the scene is and see if you can match it with musical ideas—where you make the contours of the music work with what's happening in the film. Now, this isn't just simple cueing—in other words, it's not just waiting around for something on the screen and hitting it over the head with a meat cleaver, but it is a kind of a flow in which the music appears to be doing what music would be doing naturally, and yet it hits all the cues and all the significant places. For instance, what might be most important could be just a glance from one person to another, or a reaction. . . ."

PLAYING THE PSYCHOLOGICAL SUBTEXT

The function of music is not to illustrate but to complete the psychological effect.
Miklós Rózsa, composer

Herrmann was the master of giving a whole emotional subtext to the characters. That is what makes the film work.
Brian De Palma, director
(re: Obsession, 1976)

I really do think that under ideal circumstances the music should be a character.
Elmer Bernstein, composer

Raksin takes a very psychological approach to film scoring. His score to *Laura* was unusual in its execution of that point of view. But he was not alone. The following year (1945) Miklós Rózsa scored a film in which the subject itself was the psychological problems of the leading character (Gregory Peck), befriended by psychiatrist Ingrid Bergman. (See Chapter 6 for more about this film.)

In general, Rózsa, like Raksin, leaned more toward phrasing the drama and playing the underlying emotional subtext. The score, he says, "Should adopt the tempo, rhythm, and the mood of the scene and form a homogeneous unity with it. It should be synchronized more with the dramatic content than with the actual pictures, movements, and irregular happenings. This technique, which is itself comic, works very well with cartoons or broadly comic scenes, in which the humorous element must be enhanced and expressed by the music. But I don't think it has any place in the scoring of human drama or everyday life. . . ."

Film music can make its greatest contribution when it's inside the characters' heads. When a person stares out into the ocean or takes a lonely walk on the beach, her mind filled with unspoken thoughts, the music can reveal the internal drama. In a novel, the author might take a page or two to describe what the character is thinking, but in film, even when the character reveals his thoughts through the use of a voice-over, as William Holden does in *Sunset Boulevard,* it's the music that supports and amplifies his state of mind. This psychological dimension can be music's greatest contribution to the film experience.

In essence, music can tell you what's *really* happening, even if it's not on the screen. In *A Heart at Fire's Center,* Steven C. Smith mentions the conversation conductor-record producer Charles Gerhardt overheard between Bernard Herrmann and Geneviève Bujold, the star of Brian De Palma's *Obsession* (1976).

"As she spoke to Benny in a heavy French accent, I could tell he was about to get the hanky out. She told him of all the trouble she'd had with Cliff Robertson because he spent all his time in makeup and didn't make their love scenes meaningful. She said, 'Mr. Herrmann, he wouldn't make love to me—but you made love to me with your music.' And Benny started to cry. He would tell that story over and over at dinner, and start crying again every time."

Max Steiner had an even more demanding challenge: humanizing the emotions of the giant ape, King Kong. Raksin uses *King Kong* (1933) in his

film music classes as an example of psychological scoring.

"*Kong* is fascinating from the standpoint of what little Maxie manages to do in the moments where the music has to be 'anthropomorphic'—to generate sympathy for the great ape. When he develops emotions which we think 'human.' . . . There are places where Kong feels pity, he feels love, he feels frustration. I mean, a 'relationship' with a girl who is the size of your forefinger (if you happen to be a fifty-foot ape) is not exactly practical. So, especially in the end of the picture, which is still a very beautiful place, Steiner's music makes a great deal of difference."

When the acting is perfect, there still may be a lot left unsaid. Consider the scene in *Psycho* (1960) in which Janet Leigh drives off with the money. "What you actually saw was a very good-looking girl driving a car," says Herrmann. "She could have been driving it to the supermarket, to her mother-in-law's; she could have been just going for a ride before going back to work.

"Hitch said to me, 'Well, we'll put in voices occasionally from her mind—that they're missing the money now. . . .' I said, 'That's all right, but that still doesn't make it terrible.' That's when we both agreed to bring back the music we'd related to the opening of the film, which again tells the audience, who don't know something terrible is going to happen to the girl, that it's *got* to."

If the music fails to connect with the psychological underpinnings of the drama, it may not contribute meaningfully to the film. Ennio Morricone, who created the scores for all of Sergio Leone's "spaghetti Westerns" (as well as scores for films like *The Untouchables* [1987] and *The Mission* [1986]), sums up music's responsibility in this regard. "Music in a film with certain artistic value should tell the things that are not told in the film's dialogue, and therefore underline the psychological and subpsychological aspects, the characters, the relationships between the characters, the core relations between different situations and persons. You could say, the things which one doesn't say with dialogue or that aren't explicit in the chronological story and the action—these things should draw out the music." (See Chapter 6 for more about *The Untouchables* [1987].)

HOW TO LISTEN

I don't know who started this theory of the best film music being that which you don't notice, but it isn't true.

Henry Mancini, composer

The above facets of film music are all important, and your awareness of these will greatly increase your appreciation of the art and craft involved. To practice listening to film scores, watch a film of your choice more than once. Style is of no consequence in selecting a film to study. Neither is the release date of the film. Start with some sort of dramatic film rather than a comedy, however—anything from Chuck Norris martial arts films to *Now, Voyager* (Max Steiner, 1942) and *The Godfather* (Nino Rota, 1972).

Selecting a film that has an original soundtrack album available is a good idea. First, get the album and listen to the score until it's familiar to you. Check to be sure the score is on the album, and not just songs. Then, when you're thoroughly familiar with the music, rent the videotape.

It's going to be a lot more difficult to hear the entire score on the film's soundtrack. You won't be able to notice all the elements we have been discussing on the first run-through, so don't try. Instead, concentrate on just one element. If you miss something, stop the tape and listen to that section again.

Identify the concept during the first run-through. Is there a strong idea behind the music? If you want to study a film with a strong concept score, I suggest Dave Grusin's *The Milagro Beanfield War* (1988), starring Robert Redford. The setting is New Mexico, and the score incorporates folk music with a Mexican-sounding folk flavor. Listen

for the integration of the concertina (which sounds like an accordion and is first heard in the Main Title music). This concept established a close identification with the characters in the film and is easy to follow. Studying a film with a score that doesn't have a strong concept is all right, but pay attention to the overall style of the music in any event.

On the second running, listen for the amount of emotional involvement the score projects. Does it seem to be fully supporting the important emotional moments in the drama? Does it feel intense and passionate? Does it play a wide range of emotions? It's not that tough to answer these questions in the context of the film, because the drama itself will help point you toward the answers. There is a tremendous difference in approach between a death scene played by an introspective acoustic guitar and flute, and a death scene played soulfully by a large symphony orchestra.

During this running, you also may be able to think about the function of the music in the film. What is the music doing there in the first place? What aspect of the drama is it playing? Is it hitting a lot of the action? If so, you'll hear it emphasize key moments in the action.

On the third running, concentrate only on the melodies and motifs. If there is a Main Title cue, one or more of the main themes will most likely (though not always) occur there. This is true of *Milagro*. Notice where each theme is used, and how the themes are adapted to the different dramatic needs of the film as the score develops.

Finally, watch the film once more without concentrating on any one element. Try to judge for yourself how successful you think the score is, and how well it serves the needs of the film. By this time you will know the score well, and have a good sense of how it works in the film.

If you repeat this procedure with a half dozen films, combining the observations suggested above into each run-through, you will sharpen your awareness and ability to listen considerably. (See Chapter 6 for a more detailed application of these principles to eight representative films.)

Evaluating a Score

■ ■ ■

What I find sad is the number of missed opportunities. Because when you see a great film score, your jaw just drops. . . . Film scores could be so powerful, and they tend not to be.

Richard Kraft, composers' agent

Throughout the film industry, people say, "It works," or, "It doesn't work." If necessary, a reason may be given. A director might say to an editor, "It doesn't work—it's moving too slowly." Or, to a composer, "It doesn't work—it needs more energy." With or without a reason, though, the reaction always comes first, then the explanation.

Audiences respond the same way. If credibility is missing, the audience might laugh in the middle of a moment the director intended to be serious. At that point, the film isn't working. Miklós Rózsa's story about temp tracks for *The Lost Weekend*

(1945) shows what can happen if the music is inappropriate for the dramatic intention of the film.

Film scores must work. The great ones rise well beyond this necessity. Basically, there are two vital aspects of any score: it must completely and fully serve the film, and it must complement and amplify the emotional text and subtext of the film. These are basic qualities, but other factors, such as sincerity, musical independence, form and development, thematic strength, and overall originality are also important in evaluating any film score. Let's consider these qualities individually.

THE SCORE MUST SERVE THE FILM

Even if you don't particularly like the music, you can recognize its effectiveness in the movie.
Thomas Newman, composer

In order to truly serve a film, the score must reflect the film's dramatic theme(s), its characters, its rhythms and textures, and most important, its dramatic requirements.

Some films are more receptive to music than others. To serve the film properly, the spotting of the music, and the score, should reflect this. *Lawrence of Arabia* (1962) needed a much more dramatic and full-blown musical statement than *All the President's Men,* director Alan Pakula's 1976 film about the Watergate break-in and investigation. Pakula's treatment of *Washington Post* reporters Woodward and Bernstein's pursuit of the truth was very reportorial, like a docudrama. Emphasizing a you-are-there sense of reality, the film didn't need much music, and what there is functions primarily to support the tension and connect several scenes. Pakula never considered using a great deal of music, and ended up with only 12 or so minutes of David Shire's score. On the other hand, the music for *Lawrence* had a much more important function and much more space in which to exist and flourish. The same could be said of the Sergio Leone Westerns, the James Bond films, the *Star Trek* series, the *Star Wars* trilogy, and *Spellbound.* In every case, an outstanding score must satisfy the specific requirements of the film.

Getting inside the film and its texture is crucial. Cary S. Brokaw, Chairman and Chief Executive Officer of Avenue Pictures, and Robert Altman, director of *The Player,* sent a note to Academy Music Branch members in 1992 directing their attention to Thomas Newman's score for their film. In it, they wisely emphasized this point when they said, "In combining very distinct elements of drama, suspense, and comedy, *The Player* was an exceptionally complicated picture to score. This may be difficult to appreciate because Tom's score is so rich and assured. It is a score that seamlessly blends with the very character of the film. In our view this is the ultimate goal of any score."

EMOTIONAL STRENGTH

The scores I like—they moved me.
Randy Newman, composer

After learning everything you can about any art, the ultimate skill is to be able to forget about all that knowledge and simply enjoy the experience, just as you did when you were a child going to the Saturday matinees. The finer films make this easy as they draw you into their world. The more flawed a film is, the more difficult it is to suspend disbelief. Regardless of the quality of the film, though, professionals are usually able to simultaneously react emotionally and intellectually.

There are no precise rules dictating the emotional requirements of the music. Some scores will be basically restrained, others more aggressive. Some will be sparse in texture, others full and rich. In a really good score, though, the emotional *tone* will be undeniably appropriate for the film it supports.

Composers, like audiences, have their favorite emotional approach for the music. Some like a strong, emotionally involved score. Others, like Shirley Walker, prefer a more subtle application. "I'm not an advocate of music-in-your-face in film scoring," says Walker. "I love a score that sneaks up on you, and all of a sudden you realize that—oh, my gosh, I'm in a music cue. Where did this get started? And then it keeps you in the story, and then, all of a sudden it's not there anymore. How did it sneak away? Of course, even within the context of a score like that, there will be certain places where the music purposefully is sticking right out there, and pushing at you in a definite way."

SINCERITY

I find that I can spot when somebody's really comfortable doing a film, and it's really their sort of film, and then they really do a great job—that's when I find it's my favorite score.

Mark Isham, composer

There are times when a score fails to be convincing, no matter how much the music may pretend to have great emotional values by doing all the right things technically. Soundtrack record producer Ford A. Thaxton has studied film scores for many years. "You can watch some films and you just know the composer believed it . . . and you can tell when someone was just phoning it in. Marc Shaiman did *The Addams Family* [1991]. . . . The music may not be the greatest music that's ever been written, but there's this romance between Morticia and Gomez, and he gets the right feel there that these two people are deeply, deeply in love. And that's when you can really tell that composers care." Playing their relationship as comedic would not have worked. Even though it's a humorous fantasy, you must believe the characters within their own world.

A score is not successful if the music seems to be grafted onto the body of the film without any real connection to it dramatically. *Ladyhawke* (1985) has such a score. The film is a romantic fantasy directed by Richard Donner and set in the Middle Ages. Shortly after the movie begins, the music shifts abruptly and without reason from a traditional approach to generic rock-and-roll. If conceived properly, rock elements could be integrated into a score for a period film like *Ladyhawke,* but the music on this soundtrack just doesn't connect with the film.

Songs are often used with an eye to their business and promotional values, rather than their dramatic ones. As such, they may feel alien to the film. The Simon and Garfunkel songs in *The Graduate* (1967), an admirable usage of songs in films, are unquestionably in the best interests of the film itself. However, the inspired integration of songs in films is rare. Jerry Goldsmith speaks for the great majority of composers when he says, "What I object to is the forcing of pop music in scores for blatantly commercial reasons. It ignores the real function of scoring, which is to support the film's impact on the mind and the emotions of the audience."

MUSICAL INDEPENDENCE

It was always my endeavor to write music that made sense as music and, within the flow of the music, to accentuate certain things in the film.

Hans J. Salter, composer

I tried hard to write real music for the film, not just cues.

Michael Kamen, composer
(re: The Adventures of Baron
Von Munchhausen, *1989*)

The *popular* success of composers like Henry Mancini and John Williams is due to the fact that so much of their film music is enjoyable outside the context of the films. But musical independence cannot really be considered one of the most important gauges for evaluating a film score. Some outstanding scores may be difficult at best to listen to away from the film. Judged solely on the basis of their effectiveness out of context, the score for *New Jack City* (1991), with its authoritative rap songs, and Sergei Prokofiev's score for *Alexander Nevsky* (1938), one of the most illustrious symphonic works composed for a film, might be considered good examples of particular styles of music. But these scores would be excellent *film scores* only if they satisfied all the criteria for a great score.

Historically, composers have disagreed on whether they should try to create a score that can stand alone, away from the context of the film. Some feel that such independence is an absolute test of the quality of the score. In 1944, noted English composer Arthur Bliss wrote, "The person watching the film is already in an emotionally responsive condition and will tend to invest the music with wonderful qualities that it doesn't really possess. My argument is that in the last resort, film music should be judged solely as music—that is to say, by the ears alone, and the question of its value depends on whether it can stand up to this test."

Many times, however, a color or musical effect will say as much as a more complete musical idea, and may, in fact, be the most appropriate and effective way to score a scene, or even an entire picture. Thomas Newman's score for *The Player* (1992) is based almost entirely on passages of nonmelodic music and musical effects, yet it is a fascinating example of the use of music to enrich and add pyschological texture and tension to the existing dramatic elements.

Scores that *ignore* the inherent structure of a film have less potential for satisfying all of the needs of the film. Then, too, an outstanding film *score* isn't just 30 or 40 unrelated cues strung together over the course of a two-hour film. As Thaxton says, "Anyone can sit down, and with a limited technical knowledge, write a good, bombastic chase. But to make a score have a beginning, a middle, and an end, I think can unify a picture. And you enhance what's there."

MELODY

I think, really, beautiful melodies are the bottom line.

Armin Steiner, music recording engineer

FORM AND DEVELOPMENT

Of course, there should be a structure, an architecture to any score. It's not a piece here and a piece there. It has to be thought out. You can't approach each cue as a separate piece of music.

Jerry Goldsmith, composer

Since the film dictates the *form* of the musical composition, then it stands to reason that some films are going to allow for and support a much stronger formal organization of materials. Take two scores composed by James Newton Howard in 1991—*Grand Canyon,* and *The Man in the Moon. Grand Canyon* is, by design and execution, a very episodic film, because the story interweaves events in the lives of a number of different people. Although he created an excellent and supportive score for that film, Robert Mulligan's *Man in the Moon,* by its very nature, allowed Howard to create a more consistent musical vocabulary, and offered greater opportunities to develop and recapitulate the musical material.

"Most of my favorite scores are the thematic ones," says author Randall D. Larson, "because I like what the themes do, how they interact. Though I'm wild about a lot of Herrmann stuff which is nonthematic."

Melodic or nonmelodic? Each type of score may be necessary, depending on the needs of the film. Though great melodies go in and out of fashion in film scoring, they are at the heart of most great music. "I want melody," says Armin Steiner. "I want a lovely theme, I want it to be well orchestrated, and I want to be somehow inspired by the musical composition. I realize there's a place for 'effect' music—music that's done strictly for effect. If you're doing a horror film, you're doing something that requires that, and I perfectly well understand that, and in fact I have fun doing those things—but I love something that I can really get my teeth into as a piece of music, and something that has a very well constructed motif and is very well-constructed as a whole. And something which grabs you, something which has that hook. That I think is something that John Williams has always done, and many other composers."

ORIGINALITY

I look for originality in a score, more than anything else.

> *Grover Helsley, music recording engineer*

Originality can be one of the most highly valued virtues of a film score—not for its own sake, but because of the excitement a unique approach can bring to a film. A score needn't be particularly original to be considered truly outstanding; genre scores often fall into this category, using a musical approach and language already well defined by tradition. But originality is of major interest to film composers, and to many filmmakers. Composers hope to create scores as unique and personal as Elmer Bernstein's *To Kill a Mockingbird* (1962) and Henry Mancini's *The Pink Panther* (1964), but they also worry about more negative matters like the use of clichés, the possibility of repeating themselves, and the embarassment of inadvertently borrowing a few bars (or more) of someone else's music.

The majority of films released in a given year are not particularly original. They belong to one genre or another, or they are a new twist on last year's success story. The scores that go with them may be no more original than the films they accompany. "Scores can be effective without being particularly unique," says director Paul Brickman. "For my own work, I think I look for people who have something to say musically that no one else can say. I look for that in scripts that I read, and I think the same thing holds true for me with composers."

Composers' agent Richard Kraft and his brother, journalist David Kraft, emphasize the importance of originality in film scoring. "I'm not one of these people who says, 'Boy, it was great when Steiner and Rózsa and [Alfred] Newman were there, and that was the only way to score a movie,'" says Richard. "For what those guys were writing, it was great. But there's got to be more than one way to score a movie, and movies are a lot more varied now, and so I'm not one of these, 'Oh, in the good old days . . .' guys. My favorite period was the early sixties, where you had a great combination of things—new filmmakers, for example, who were also very talented. A lot of these guys came from directing cult television in New York, and came out here and made great movies. And the composers were a new batch of composers—they all were really smart and well trained. But they had no desire to emulate Rózsa. [The era that gave us the innovative scores of] Elmer [Bernstein] and Jerry Goldsmith—that was a great period.

"The subtle differences between Waxman or [Alfred] Newman—it's something a buff would know. But they all scored movies the same way. And so I'm not yearning for that. But I am yearning for that feeling when you saw the Sergio Leone/Morricone things for the first time and said: What the hell—what's going on! You think—what temp track could have led to that? Nothing."

The Krafts have suggested an excellent test for originality. Next time you see a movie, ask yourself what temp track could have led to that score.

Clichés

The reason technical devices become clichés is that they have proved successful over and over again.

> *John Addison, composer*

We try to do the unexpected, something that's not cliché. Sometimes you can do it, sometimes you can't.

> *Henry Mancini, composer*

On the other hand, where music is concerned, a conscious effort to do something "new" does not necessarily make it valid.

> *Alfred Newman, composer*

In the forties and fifties, overused musical devices were an everyday affair. In 1953, Jeffrey Embler reviewed Vlad's score for *Leonardo da Vinci* in the February "Sound Track" column of *Films in Review*. He said, in part:

Nearly every film-music cliché known to man is contained in this score. Rolling sixteenths signified wheels; vibraharp notes accompanied water; tremolo strings accompanied air-travel shots; flutes accompanied birds; the clip-clop of the xylophone was the clip-clop of walking horses; brasses represented moving horses, lions, etc.

Later in the same column, he continues his list of clichés.

In Hollywood it has become customary to assign definite musical themes to a film's leading characters. When the heroine enters, the violins soar into prominence. The presence of a small child calls for a few bars of music-box simulation. This sort of tired routine has, after many years, become inept and colorless.

1953 must have been a big year for clichés, because in the March issue, Gordon Hendricks, also writing in the "Sound Track" column, complained about the overuse of strings.

I think film composers ought to do something about "sweet" string accompaniments for sentiment on the screen. "Sweet" strings are used for everything from love between a man and woman to the feeling of a boy for his dog and an aviator for his plane. It is also used to accompany manifestations of conscience and patriotism, scenes of home and mother and childhood, and almost everything except outright hate, lust, or fear.

Some composers—North, Friedhofer, Rósza, Waxman, Tiomkin—have sometimes used interesting, unobvious music to accompany sentiment. It can be done. But few film composers shake loose from the easy, lazy cliché.

Even a simple transfer from a treble string to a lower string—a cello, for instance—would help a great deal. Or a less anticipatable melody in a violin. Or interesting rhythmic variations in a violin. Or other instruments solo. This was done in *The Red Badge of Courage* [1951] by MGM's [Bronislau] Kaper, where a banjo was used; by [Hugo] Friedhofer in *The Outcasts of Poker Flat*

[1952] where a woodwind was used; by [Dimitri] Tiomkin in *High Noon* [1952], where a human voice was used solo with an economical accompaniment; by [Franz] Waxman in *A Place in the Sun* [1951], where a "blue" reed [sax] was used beautifully to underline the wan relationship between George and his girl. . . .

Composers from Beethoven to Sibelius have used full orchestral textures to express tenderness. All we ask for is subtlety, and we have heard enough subtlety on sound tracks to know it is possible. We also know that subtlety pays off. [Waxman's] *Sunset Boulevard* [1950] and *A Place in the Sun* are cases in point. *High Noon*'s score seems to be heading for an Academy Award after a tremendous amount of critical acclaim and box office support.

Ironically, one of the biggest obstacles in the path of freshness is the rapidity with which a new idea turns into a cliché through imitation. In 1966, Alfred Newman said, "Today, it seems to me, if a gifted director creates a successful motion picture with a certain type of score, be it jazz, rock-and-roll, electronic, or for that matter, a zither solo, the formula is quickly plagiarized by others. Then the market is soon overrun by carbon copies of carbon copies!" This observation still continues to be true.

Self-plagiarism

If you think you've heard that theme before, it may very well be that you have. Max Steiner's obituary, printed in the December 29, 1971, issue of *Daily Variety,* addresses this issue:

Like all prolific composers, Steiner often repeated himself. The famous "Tara Theme" from David O. Selznick's "Gone With the Wind," for example, is a subtle reworking of a theme from a John Garfield crime meller, "They Made Me a Criminal," on which he was working the same year. And that theme he had in turn used a year or two before. No matter, because for those who appreciated Steiner's music, there was never enough." [©Daily Variety Ltd. Reprinted by permission.]

Self-plagiarism certainly isn't uncommon in any form of musical composition. Another film music example is Alfred Newman's use of the first part of his score for *These Three* (1936) in his score for *The Razor's Edge* (1946). Steven C. Smith has noticed Bernard Herrmann's use of his own earlier material: "Throughout his film career, in fact, Herrmann would reuse themes (or more often thematic fragments) in new works, either weaving them through fresh orchestration into a new entity or retaining them largely intact. The practice was far from unprecedented: Berlioz was particularly fond of reviving early works' themes and movements in later compositions. Yet Herrmann's reputation in later years would suffer from accusations of self-plagiarism, some of it justified: in the mid-1960s, as his life reached a crisis point, Herrmann seemed unable at times to compose new, fresh music."

Franz Waxman basically summed up many of the problems that have tended to influence film music over the years when he said, "We movie composers work mostly under pressure. We work for an industry and we do not work alone. We are dependent upon dozens of other individuals and vice versa. All of these factors have to be taken into consideration when evaluating a film score."

Though this is all true, I suggest that you *do not* consider any of this in evaluating film scores. As important as it is to get a good feeling for the work of film composers, and for the environment in which they work, the score on the soundtrack is the score, and should be judged as such. Respond to a work as it is, not as it might have been. The great acting performances left on the proverbial cutting room floor are legion. It is absolute fact that many great (and untold not-so-great) cues and scores have never made it past the dubbing stage, but you cannot evaluate what isn't on the soundtrack.

GOOD FILMS, BAD FILMS

Good music can improve a fine film, but it can never make a bad film good. We composers are not magicians. We write music.
                              Henry Mancini, composer

No music has ever saved a bad picture, but a lot of good pictures have saved a lot of bad music.
                              Jerry Goldsmith, composer

I know it is often said that music, no matter how good, cannot save a bad picture, but I think most of those who say it never worked at Universal in my day.
                              Hans J. Salter, composer

If the picture is good, the score stands a better chance of being good.
                              Max Steiner, composer

There is one extenuating circumstance to be considered, and that is the film itself. Just as certain films are inherently more receptive to music than others, certain films are simply better than others. Better films may inspire better scores. If the characters have more depth and complexity, if there is a deeper level of sincere emotion, the music flows more naturally as it is being composed. Nevertheless, as Jerry Goldsmith has pointed out, there are also plenty of average scores in excellent films.

Although David Raksin feels that the overall quality of a film typically affects the quality of a score, he feels this can be overcome. "I've done very good scores in lousy movies. *Forever Amber* [1947] was not much of a picture, but it's got a very, very unusual score." As Korngold said in 1935, "There have been some ordinary, program pictures which are forgotten after three months, but which will be long remembered by musicians as containing some rare musical writing."

When you have sharpened your listening skills, the above criteria will provide you with a very effective way to evaluate film scores. The next chapter takes a closer look at some specific films.

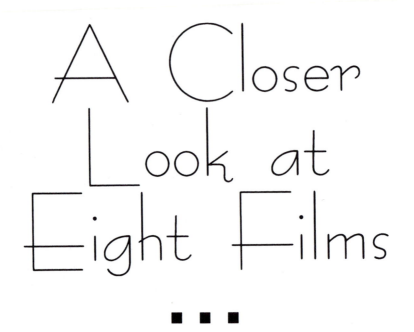

A Closer Look at Eight Films

The eight films discussed in this chapter appear in chronological order and offer a variety of stories and genres. Although no comedies are included, comedies can be viewed with the same focus and critical criteria as dramas. John Williams' score for *Home Alone 2* (1992) is constructed with the same architectural integrity he would bring to a dramatic film, but you will discover some scores for comedies that appear to be an anthology of unrelated cues. Whereas the score for a dramatic film would suffer without the buildup of emotional associations that comes from the repetition and development of musical material, this factor seems less important in contemporary comedies. By their very structure, these comedies often require a less unified compositional approach than dramas, and are more likely to include a variety of songs from sources other than the composer.

It's a good idea to see a movie first before you study a film and its score with the help of this chapter. Even if you've already seen a film one or more times, it helps to watch it again and notice your emotional reaction to both the drama and the score. Then you will find it beneficial to study the breakdown of elements discussed below: the style and concept, the spotting, the themes, how the music phrases the drama, the use of source music, and the tempo and pulse of the score.

It is especially important to realize that not all scores are easily heard and described in terms of thematic usage. Some scores are based on short motifs and rhythmic figures that are developed and interwoven throughout the score; some are even less thematic, relying primarily on instrumental textures and ambience for their effectiveness. Although the spotting notes and thematic identification that follow may improve your ability to discover and to listen to the various themes that are the basis of a score, it is unwise to become overly preoccupied with identifying various themes while watching a film. While the themes and their accompanying harmonies, rhythms, and instrumental colors definitely set the tone and style of a score, other issues are more significant in understanding how effectively a score is serving its film: How is the drama spotted? Is the music phrasing the drama or playing through? What is the overall concept of the score, and how does that concept illuminate the film? What is the tone of the score? Does the score's tone increase the clarity of the drama and intensify its power, or is it inappropriate? Apply the approach to listening to film music suggested in Chapters 4 and 5.

The spotting notes for each film reflect the music as it is in the release print, not as it was originally spotted. Occasionally the names given to the individual motifs and themes are taken from the cue sheets, but in most cases they have been made up for purposes of easy identification. Cue titles also are used for identification purposes; sometimes the composer or music editor gives each cue a title, but many of the titles have been added to help identify the moment in the film played by the cues.

Robin Hood (Errol Flynn) duels Sir Guy of Gisbourne (Basil Rathbone) to the death in *The Adventures of Robin Hood* (1938), accompanied by Erich Wolfgang Korngold's definitive action/adventure score (cue #35 in the spotting notes below). Korngold scored other swashbucklers and romantic historical epics, including *Captain Blood* (1935) and *The Sea Hawk* (1940), both starring Flynn and directed by Michael Curtiz.
Photo courtesy of the Academy of Motion Pictures Arts and Sciences
© *1938 Turner Entertainment Co.*
All Rights Reserved.

The Adventures of Robin Hood 1938 Music by Erich Wolfgang Korngold.
Orchestrated by Hugo Friedhofer and Milan Roder. Directed by Michael Curtiz, William Keighley. Errol Flynn, Olivia de Havilland, Basil Rathbone, Claude Rains.

Erich Wolfgang Korngold had won an Oscar in 1937 for his score for *Anthony Adverse,* and was in Vienna, preparing for the premiere of his fifth (and last) opera, *Die Kathrin,* when Warner Bros. cabled him requesting that he score *The Adventures of Robin Hood*. After some trepidation (discussed in detail in Chapter 9), he began his work on the score in mid-February 1938. His son, George Korngold, remembered that it was not an easy project for him. "My father was on the verge of stopping several times. I shall never forget his anguished protestations of 'I just can't do it,' which I overheard in the middle of the night through my bedroom wall. He was suffering, and at the same time producing one of his finest scores, the score which won him his second Academy Award." Korngold's score has proven to be the quintessential romantic epic score, timeless and universally affecting.

SYNOPSIS

In 1191, when King Richard the Lion-Heart (Ian Hunter) left England to fight in the Crusades, he gave his reign to his trusted friend Longchamps, whom he knew would be benevolent. However, Richard's evil brother, Prince John (Claude Rains), usurped the power of the throne. When it was learned that Richard had been captured, Prince John, with the aid of Sir Guy of Gisbourne (Basil Rathbone), became even more oppressive to the poor Saxons, brutally enforcing excessive taxation and scheming to kill Richard and take over the throne. In defiance of Prince John's treachery, Sir Robin of Locksley, commonly known as Robin Hood (Errol Flynn), gathered together a band of rebels. Under his leadership they robbed the rich and distributed this stolen money to the poor. Robin Hood was eventually captured and sentenced to hang. With the help of Lady Marian (a ward of the King's, played by Olivia de Havilland, who has grown to admire Robin Hood) and Robin Hood's band of followers, Robin Hood escaped the gallows and foiled the plot to assassinate King Richard.

STYLE AND CONCEPT

Korngold's musical style for romantic action films like *Robin Hood* and *The Sea Hawk* has served as a role model for big-scale symphonically orchestrated romantic-action films from the late thirties through *Star Wars* (1977) and beyond. Distinguishing elements in his score for *Robin Hood* include the utilization of the full instrumental resources of a large orchestra, the interweaving and development of a number of themes initially identified with a particular character or situation, the rich harmonic language of the late nineteenth century, and an involvement with the drama which is generally considered operatic in nature because of its close con-

nection with the action at all times. Korngold's own role models may have included Richard Strauss.

In dubbing, the Warner Bros. mixing crew favored the music more than the sound effects, allowing the full impact of Korngold's score to be heard and felt.

SPOTTING

The Adventures of Robin Hood is 102 minutes long and contains approximately 72:56 of score. This is a lot of music—72 percent of the film is scored—but the score does not at all feel excessive. Rather, the spotting sounds appropriate for the film.

There are no titles indicated on the original scores. The titles below are not those on the cue sheet; they have been added to help suggest the scenes being scored. The cue numbers don't conform to those listed on the cue sheet.

#1. Main Title (1:31) Music starts on the fade-in to the Warner Bros. logo, and goes out just before a man reads, "News has come from Vienna."

#2. Richard Seized (:10) Music starts after the man says, ". . . will make further public pronouncement tomorrow," and fades out as Sir Guy says to Prince John, "They're even more worried . . ."

#3. Tax the Poor (1:43) Music starts as Sir Guy and Prince John toast and Sir Guy says, "Tomorrow, your Highness," and fades out under Sir Guy saying to the miller, "What's your name?"

#4. Robin Hood Confronts Sir Guy (1:10) Music starts as Sir Guy lifts his arm to kill the miller, and fades out as the miller says, "Thanks, good master."

#5. Nottingham Castle (2:00) Music starts on the fade-in of a card explaining Nottingham Castle, and fades out as

Prince John says, "You're a very wise young woman."

#6. Robin Hood Enters Nottingham Castle (:58) Music starts after, "Open the door!" and goes out just after Robin throws a deer on the dinner table.

#7. Escape From Nottingham Castle (4:20) Music starts as an arrow hits Robin Hood's chair, plays through the fight and chase, and goes out just before Robin says, "Up you go. Quick!"

#8. "Pass the Word" (:25) Music starts as one of Robin Hood's men rides off after Robin says, "Off you go and good luck," and fades out as Prince John says, "Have it proclaimed in every village. . . ."

#9. Robin Hood Meets Little John (1:06) Music starts during the black after Sir Guy says, "I'll have him dangling in a week," plays Robin Hood meeting Little John, and fades out as Little John says, "When I brush this fly off, I'll give you a dusting for good measure."

#10. Robin Hood Fights Little John (1:23) Music starts after Robin Hood says, "Wait—I'll get myself a staff," and fades out as Robin and Little John laugh.

#11. Little John Joins Robin Hood (1:22) Music starts immediately following cue #10 (sounding like a segue) on the cut after Robin Hood and Little John are laughing, and fades out under Robin Hood saying, "I called you here as freeborn Englishmen . . ."

#12. The Pledge (1:50) Music starts after Robin Hood says, "Then kneel, and swear this oath," and fades out as one of the Sir Guy's men says, "Five men dead—murdered . . ."

#13. Robin Hood Sees Friar Tuck (1:40) Music starts as an arrow strikes the table in front of Sir Guy, and goes out as Friar Tuck wakes up.

#14. Friar Tuck Fights Robin Hood (1:38) Music starts after Friar Tuck says, "I'll not—I'm happy here," as Robin Hood slaps him with his sword and says, "You will!" and fades out as Friar Tuck says, "By our lady, you're the fairest swordsman I ever met."

#15. Friar Tuck Joins Robin Hood (:46) Music starts after Robin Hood says to Friar Tuck, ". . . boar's head, casks of ale . . ." and goes out as the men laugh after Will says, ". . . he looks like three of us."

#16. Robin Hood Attacks Sir Guy (4:29) Music starts during the black before the fade-in to Robin Hood's men preparing to fight in the forest, plays the ambush, and goes out after Robin Hood swings down from a tree, just before he says, "Welcome to Sherwood, my lady."

#17. Robin Hood Talks to Lady Marian (1:18) Music starts as the men begin moving out after Robin Hood says, "Well—let's away!" and segues to cue #18 on the dissolve to the feast.

#18. The Feast (1:24) Music segues from cue #17 on the dissolve to the feast, and goes out abruptly just before the announcement, "To the tables, everybody, and stuff yourselves."

#19. The Feast (Part 2) (1:18) Music starts on the dissolve to a continuation of the celebration just after cue #18, and goes out abruptly after Robin Hood jumps up on a table and says, "Hey! Friends!"

#20. Lady Marian (5:13) Music starts as the treasure is revealed as Robin Hood says, ". . . and there it is . . ." plays through Marian and Robin talking, and goes out on the fade to black as Marian rides away.

#21. Tournament (1:12) Music starts on the fade-in to the herald trumpeters playing a fanfare, and goes out with the trumpets playing before the herald says, "By order of . . ."

#22. **Tournament** (Part 2) (1:12) Music starts on the long shot of the tournament after the herald says, "The winning team will meet all comers," and goes out as Prince John finishes saying to Marian, "You'll find it much more interesting later on."

#23. **Fanfare** (:05) Music starts almost immediately after cue #22, on the cut to the herald trumpeters, and goes out just before a herald says, "The winning team . . ."

#24. **Tournament** (Part 3) (3:54) Music starts after Robin Hood taps a soldier on the helmet prior to participating in the archery contest, and goes out as Robin, having won the contest, bows in front of Prince John.

#25. **Robin Hood Captured** (:48) Music starts as Robin Hood moves to escape after Sir Guy says, "Arrest this man," and goes out abruptly as Sir Guy hits Robin.

#26. **Robin Hood Convicted** (:42) Music starts after Sir Guy says, "Take him away," and fades out as Sir Guy reads Robin's conviction charges.

#27. **Robin Hood Sentenced** (1:36) Music starts on the cut to Robin Hood after Sir Guy has sentenced him and waved at the guards to take him away, and fades out as Bess says, ". . . and I won't deny it."

#28. **Robin Hood Escapes** (4:28) Music starts on the dissolve to the gallows after Marian says to Robin's men, "Listen to me," and goes out on the fade-out to black as they ride off.

#29. **Robin Hood Visits Marian** (5:53) Music starts immediately following cue #28 on the fade-in, plays the scene between Robin and Marian, and goes out on the shot of meat being removed from a skewer.

#30. **Marian Caught** (:56) Music starts after Sir Guy says, "Escort Lady Marian to the Great Hall," and fades out under Marian speaking at the court of execution.

#31. **Robin Hood Meets King Richard** (3:58) Music starts on the dissolve to the forest after Much leaves Bess, plays Robin Hood meeting King Richard, and fades out as Much explains that Richard is in England.

#32. **King Richard Reveals His Identity** (:49) Music starts after Robin Hood says, "Where is he?" and King Richard says, "Here," and fades out as Robin says, "If we're going to save her and your throne, we've got to act now."

#33. **Procession** (3:06) Music starts during the black before the fade-in to the procession after Robin Hood says, "Suppose we visit him at his abbey tonight and persuade him to suggest a way," and goes out just before the cut to the herald trumpets playing a fanfare.

#34. **Fanfare** (:06) Music starts on the cut to the herald trumpets, and segues to cue #35 after the fanfare as the procession continues.

#35. **Robin Hood Kills Sir Guy** (5:10) Music segues from cue #34 as the procession continues, and goes out on the cut to Sir Guy dead on the ground.

#36. **Victory** (1:17) Music starts immediately following cue #35, as the men run up the stairs, and fades out as Richard says, "Yes—my brother."

#37. **End Scene** (1:32) Music starts just after Richard says, "What about you, Robin?" and segues to cue #38 at the end of the film.

#38. **End Titles** (:28) Music segues from cue #37 on the beginning of the End Titles, and goes out at the end of the End Titles.

The opening bars of Korngold's End Title cue for *The Adventures of Robin Hood* (1938) features "Robin Hood's theme." On his orchestration, Hugo Friedhofer indicates that the Warner Bros. string section had 16 violins, 4 violas, 4 cellos, and contrabass to record this cue—a small number of strings for a symphonic sound, although many television movies are scored with a section this size or smaller.

The Adventures of Robin Hood (Erich Wolfgang Korngold)
© *1938 WARNER BROS. INC. (Renewed) All Rights Reserved. Used By Permission.*

THEMES

There are at least eight principal themes in the score for *Robin Hood,* and Korngold weaves them in and out of the drama to build up a strong associative value. "Robin Hood's theme" is first heard in the Main Title; "King Richard's theme" is first heard over the cards explaining the background of the story; "Little John's theme" can be heard clearly in cue #10; "Friar Tuck's theme" is first heard in cue #13 as Robin Hood sees the Friar and takes his food; a "romantic theme," used during the feast sequence, is first heard under Robin's dialogue with Lady Marian in cue #17; the "love theme" used for Robin Hood and Marian can be clearly heard in cue #20 as they talk after visiting with the poor people; a "poor people theme" is first heard at the beginning of cue #3; and an "England" theme, expressing a respect and love for England, is first used at the beginning of cue #5.

"Robin Hood's theme" is used often. Other significant uses include cue #6; cue #8, as the people pass the word about the meeting; cue #11, after the fight with Little John; cue #14, played by the bassoon at the beginning of the cue; cue #16, as Robin's men prepare the forest; cue #17, at the beginning of the feast; the beginning of cue #18; the beginning of cue #24; and the End Titles. Cue #32 uses a minor version for the procession sequence.

Other significant uses of "King Richard's theme" include the beginning of cue #12 as Robin Hood pledges to fight; cue #20, as Robin and Marian talk at the table after his men declare that the money should go to help King Richard; cue #29, under the dialogue between Robin Hood and Marian; cue #31, as Richard travels on the road to meet Robin Hood; and cue #32, as Richard reveals his identity.

Other significant uses of "Little John's theme" include the second half of cue #14, as Friar Tuck and Robin Hood fight; and the end section of cue #16, during Robin Hood's attack of Sir Guy.

Other significant uses of the "romantic theme" include cue #18, after the sheriff is shown the clothes he must wear; and cue #19, as Robin Hood and Marian eat.

The "love theme" can be heard clearly in cue #29 after Bess leaves, as Robin and Marian kiss for the first time.

Other significant uses of the "poor people theme" include cue #12, on the card explaining Prince John's deadly ways; cue #20, as Robin shows Marian the poor people; the beginning of cue #27, after the sentencing; and the beginning of cue #30.

Other significant uses of the "England theme" include the last part of cue #20, as Marian and Robin talk after they see the poor people; and the last part of cue #29, as Robin and Marian talk.

PLAYING THE DRAMA

Korngold's score precisely phrases the drama and action of *Robin Hood* throughout the film. This close attention to the details of dramatic phrasing is actually a stylistic aspect of the score, and yet the music Korngold has written often has a very free musical feeling within the confines of the drama. You can notice this characteristic in many other film scores, including the other examples in this chapter. Korngold did this very well, and his score for *Robin Hood* is a masterful example of natural, flowing music written within the restraints of tight dramatic phrasing.

Cue #16 is a particularly good example of Korngold's phrasing the drama. As you watch this cue, listen for the shifts in musical material and emphasis as the film cuts back and forth between Robin Hood's men and Sir Guy prior to the attack.

SOURCE MUSIC

The source music in this score has been carefully integrated into the dramatic scoring itself, so that the few moments of visual on-screen source music are treated as a part of the score rather than as a separate element. To see how this works, watch the end of cue #1, on the pan across the drummer. His visual drumbeats have been incorporated into the symphonic scoring, which is timed to synchronize with the on-screen instrumentalist so that it appears as though he might be playing with the orchestra at that moment. This is a technique sometimes used in documentaries when it is desirable to continue the score rather than segue to the production sound of a native playing a flute or a rural southerner playing the banjo.

When Will plays the lute during cue #10 as Robin Hood fights with Little John, Korngold again uses the orchestra to represent an on-screen instrument, this time synchronizing with Will's on-screen lute-playing. Most of the on-screen herald trumpet fanfares are similarly scored from within the orchestra. The short independent cues #24 and #33 are scored with the same fanfare instrumentation so that all the on-screen trumpeting sounds alike.

TEMPO AND PULSE

Korngold's score drives the film forward with the spirit of adventure rather than the darker feeling that tension would contribute. This is an extremely effective approach for an action/adventure film like *Robin Hood,* very much in keeping with the overall tone of the film and of Errol Flynn's performance as Robin Hood. John Williams' scores for the *Star Wars* trilogy and the *Indiana Jones* trilogy achieve a similar tone and attitude.

Dark Victory   1939
Music by Max Steiner.
Orchestrated by Hugo Friedhofer. Directed by Edmund Goulding. Bette Davis, George Brent, Humphrey Bogart, Geraldine Fitzgerald.

Max Steiner scored eighteen of Bette Davis' popular films, including *Jezebel* (1938), *The Old Maid* (1939), *The Letter* (1940), and *Now, Voyager*

When Judy (Bette Davis) realizes she is going blind and will die soon (cue #20 in the spotting notes below), she comforts her grief-stricken friend. Max Steiner's music for the ending scenes of *Dark Victory* (1939) plays both the overall sadness of Judy's death and also her inner poise and courage as she faces the inevitable.
Photo courtesy of the Academy of Motion Pictures Arts and Sciences
© *1939 Turner Entertainment Co.*
All Rights Reserved.

(1942). Looking back on those years, Davis said of Steiner, "Max understood more about drama than any of us."

SYNOPSIS

When Judith/Judy (Bette Davis), a self-centered young society woman, becomes ill, she sees noted brain surgeon Dr. Steele (George Brent). He discovers she has a brain tumor, but doesn't disclose his findings. He operates, and in the process of following up his treatment he falls in love. When she accidentally learns she doesn't have long to live, she breaks off their engagement, thinking that he is acting out of sympathy. After several months of self-pity and superficiality, she reconciles with Dr. Steele, they get married and move to Vermont, where she faces her future with love and courage.

STYLE AND CONCEPT

Steiner's score for *Dark Victory* is thematic and emotional, with themes that express both the tragic circumstances of the story and the heroine's ultimate courage.

SPOTTING

Dark Victory is 106 minutes long and contains approximately 40:40 of score and 16:15 of source music. Considering the amount of music in many of the Steiner-scored Warner Bros. films, this is not a long score. Film music historian Clifford McCarty points out that the Max Steiner Society discovered in Steiner's possession recordings of cues for *Dark Victory* not used in the film, suggesting that the original spotting session probably called for a longer score.

For purposes of clarity, the following cue titles are mine and not those indicated on the cue sheet.

#1. **Logo and Main Title** (:55)

#2. **Judy and Challenger** (1:50) Music starts as Michael (Humphrey Bogart) goes to get her horse, and fades out after Judy (Bette Davis) and the horse fall.

#3. **Judy Falls Down Stairs** (2:25) Music starts at the beginning of the next scene as Ann (Geraldine Fitzgerald) enters, and goes out at the fade-out after Judy falls down the stairs.

#4. **Judy Sees Dr. Steele** (1:29) Music starts after Judy says to Dr. Steele (George Brent), "I'm sorry to have wasted so much of your time," and fades out as she takes his hand.

#5. **"We've Got to Operate"** (2:45) Music starts after the visiting consultant doctor says, "Dr. Steele will talk to you," and goes out in the hospital as Judy says, "Everything's pretty awful."

#6. **Judy in the Hospital** (1:36) Music starts after Judy says, "It is a distasteful subject, isn't it?" and goes out on the fade-out of the scene.

#7. **After the Operation** (:57) Music starts as Dr. Steele begins to open the door to Judy's hospital room, and goes out at the fade-out of the scene.

#8. **Judy Comes Home** (:30) Music starts right after the last cue, during the black before the fade-in, and segues to cue #8A.

#8A **Dance Orchestra Radio Source—"They Say"** (Edward Heyman, Paul Mann, Stephen Weiss; 3:04) Music segues from cue #8, and goes out as Judy and Dr. Steele sit on the couch at the party.

#9. **Dance Orchestra Radio Source #2 "All My Love"** (Bud Green, Wayne King, Alfred Deitzel; 2:34) Music starts a few seconds after cue #8A, as Judy and Dr. Steele begin to talk, and segues to cue #9A as Ann and Dr. Steele walk out onto the patio.

#9A Talk on the Patio (3:44) Music segues from cue #9 as Ann and Dr. Steele walk out onto the patio, and goes out as the scene fades to black after Ann, Dr. Steele, and Judy enter the house.

#10. "Don't You Know I'm in Love with You" (2:17) Music starts after Judy learns Ann has been to see Dr. Steele and goes out as the scene fades to black while Dr. Steele and Judy hug.

#11. Prognosis Negative (1:52) Music starts as Judy sees her medical file on Dr. Steele's desk, and segues to cue #11A on the dissolve to the restaurant.

#11A. Live Restaurant Source—"Wiener Blut" (Strauss; 3:31) Music segues from cue #11A on the dissolve to the restaurant, and goes out at the end of the restaurant scene.

#11B Live Night Club Source—"Oh Give Me Time for Tenderness" (Elsie Janis, Edmund Goulding; :27) Music starts on the dissolve to the nightclub immediately following the last scene, and goes out to a natural ending.

#12. Live Night Club Source #2—"Oh Give Me Time for Tenderness" (1:09) Music starts after the vocalist says, "'Time for Tenderness,' Malcolm," and goes out to a natural ending on the fade-out to black.

#13. "Parade Formation" (George Webster; 1:27) Music starts on the fade-in to the horse show, and segues to cue #14 on the optical wipe to the party.

#14. "March" (Howard Jackson; :19) Music segues from cue #13 on the wipe to the party, segues to "Cakewalk" (Howard Jackson; :30), and goes out during the dialogue at the bar.

#15. "Hail to the Winner" (Perry; 2:15)

Music starts immediately following cue #14, during the dialogue at the bar, and goes out on the optical wipe to the stable.

#16. Visual Radio Source—"Oh Give Me Time for Tenderness" (:16) Dance band music starts in progress after Michael turns on the radio, and goes out in progress as Judy turns it off.

#17. Judy and Michael in the Stable (2:55) Music starts on Judy after Michael says, "What good's ridin' and fightin' these days? What do they getcha?" and fades out as Ann enters Judy's bedroom.

#18. Judy and Ann in the Bedroom (1:17) Music starts a few seconds after cue #17 (#17 and #18 sound like one cue with a short pause), after Judy says, "Ann, you should be asleep," and goes out on the wipe to Dr. Steele and Alec (Ronald Reagan).

#19. Apology, Marriage, and Vermont (5:02) Music starts after Dr. Steele says, "Shall I make one?" and Judy answers, "No—no, thank you," and fades out under Judy saying, "Your lunch, Doctor."

#20. Judy Loses Her Sight (4:52) Music starts in the garden after Judy says, "It's funny, I can still feel the sun on my hands," and fades out as Dr. Steele says, "Why, I might even be acclaimed. I might even get our picture in the paper."

#21. "Our Victory Over the Dark" (8:02) Music starts after Judy says, ". . . and I'll wait home as a proper wife should—Darling," and continues to the end of the film, segueing to cue #22 at the start of the End Titles. This sequence was recorded as several shorter cues designed to overlap smoothly to sound like one continuous cue.

#22. End Titles (:26) Music segues from cue #21 on the start of the End Titles, and goes out on the black.

The opening bars of Max Steiner's Main Title for *Dark Victory* (1939) are a statement of "Judy's theme." Although Steiner's score favors the sound of strings, the entire orchestra is playing on this cue. Hugo Friedhofer, who orchestrated the score, added this note to Steiner at the bottom of the final page of the Main Title: "Maxie—It's nice work—if you live! 4:52 A.M."

Dark Victory (Max Steiner)

THEMES

There are four principal themes: "Judy's theme," first heard in the Main Title; the "illness theme," first suggested in cue #2 as Judy suffers a headache after ordering Michael to get the horse, and developed further in cue #5 as Dr. Steele talks to Judy about her symptoms; "Dr. Steele's theme," first heard near the end of cue #5 and heard at full length as Dr. Steele and Judy talk at the beginning of cue #19; and the "Dark Victory theme," first heard in cue #6 as Judy (in her hospital bed) talks with Dr. Steele and Ann.

Other significant uses of "Judy's theme" include cue #8, played full over the shots of Dr. Steele writing his journal and reading Judy's letter. Except for some short suggestions of this thematic material, this theme is not used significantly for the remainder of the film.

Other significant uses of the "illness theme" include cue #3, as Judy describes seeing two barriers as she was riding, and again as she tells Ann that she walked into a dog leash; near the beginning of cue #4, as she throws her gloves down in Dr. Steele's office; and during cue #11, as Judy asks, "What does prognosis mean?" to the end of this scene. After this cue, the "illness theme" is not used significantly for the remainder of the film, although the chromatic motif appears as secondary material.

Other significant uses of "Dr. Steele's theme" include the end of cue #6, after Judy says to Steele, "They're rather nice hands—good, strong hands," to the end of the scene; in cue #19, after Steele says, "Will you marry me?"; in cue #20, after Judy realizes she is going blind and will die soon, as Dr. Steele comes down the stairs, reads the telegram, and plans the trip to New York City; the beginning of cue #21 through Steele leaving in his car; and again after Judy says to Ann, "I'm the lucky one," through Judy saying, "I must go in now," and cue #22 (the End Titles). This theme functions as a bonding theme between Judy and Steele, and also as a statement of courage and inner strength for

Judy, and is therefore used more and more significantly during the last few reels of the film.

Other significant uses of the "Dark Victory theme" include the beginning of cue #7 (played initially by the harp); as the dialogue begins on the patio in cue #9A, and set as a waltz as Judy comes out on the patio and says, "What's the idea?"; cue #10, after Judy says, "Don't you know I'm in love with you?"; the beginning of cue #11; cue #17, as Judy says, "I just can't go on this way," through the dissolve to Judy walking up the stairs; cue #18, as Judy says to Ann, "I was saved"; cue #19, from Judy saying, "May I take back every rotten thing . . ."; cue #20, as Judy hugs Ann, who is sobbing (ending as Dr. Steele calls down from the second floor window), and again after Ann says, "Can you see anything? Can you see me?" to the end of the scene; and cue #21, after Dr. Steele leaves as Judy leans on a pillar and then walks to her bedroom, and again as the housekeeper enters her bedroom. This is the main theme of Steiner's score, and is used throughout the film.

PLAYING THE DRAMA

Steiner uses both the "Dr. Steele" theme and the "Dark Victory" theme to play the last twenty minutes or so of the picture, alternating between the two. Listen to cues #19, #20, and #21 to hear how this is done. In cue #19, he uses "Dr. Steele's theme," the "Dark Victory theme," and then "Dr. Steele's theme" again. In cue #20 he begins with the "Dark Victory theme," segues to "Dr. Steele's theme," and then reverts back to the "Dark Victory theme." In cue #21 he reverses the sequence again, beginning with "Dr. Steele's theme," then the "Dark Victory theme," then back to "Dr. Steele's theme," and then once again to the "Dark Victory theme." In all three cues each theme is given enough time to play fully and compassionately without interruption before moving on to the next theme.

Within this thematic context, he plays both the visual and the emotional drama as it unfolds. Early in the film he uses music very specifically to emphasize dramatic points in the dialogue. A good example of this occurs near the beginning of cue #3, just after Judy says to her friend Ann, "That colt didn't throw me—I threw him." The accent in the music is a stylistic characteristic of Steiner's, and is used here to highlight the potential seriousness of Judy's problem. The remainder of the cue continues to play this shift in tone. Later in the same cue, a heavier accent plays Judy's reaction after the housekeeper announces, "Dr. Parsons is here," and Judy's off-camera fall down the stairs is suggested by a series of heavy accents.

In cue #5 listen to the way the music stops after Judy says, "The sentence," to expose Dr. Steele's comment, "We've got to operate." The silence emphasizes this announcement after which the cue continues.

Dr. Peterson (Ingrid Bergman) probes the failed memory of "Dr. Edwardes" (Gregory Peck) after they realize he is suffering from amnesia. Miklós Rózsa's score for *Spellbound* (1945) uses the theremin to play Edwardes' tormented point of view. *Copyright 1945 CAPITAL CITIES/ABC, INC.*

SOURCE MUSIC

Hear how the dance band source music at the party (cue #9) segues smoothly into scoring based on the "Dark Victory" theme as Dr. Steele and Ann walk out onto the patio. In cue #11, the score segues into visual source music (a Strauss waltz played by an on-screen chamber group) at the restaurant.

TEMPO AND PULSE

Most of the *Dark Victory* score is slow, smooth-flowing music, without much feeling of pulse. However, Steiner takes advantage of those few moments where it is possible to lighten up the orchestral texture and interject a brighter tempo. These moments occur when Judy rides in cue #2; as Ann returns home from Dr. Steele's office in cue #10 (continuing as a waltz with increasing tension until Steele enters); and the middle of cue #19 from the fade-in to Vermont through the kitchen scene and Judy's walk to Steele's laboratory. Although this music may sound old-fashioned to you, scoring these moments with motion is a timeless approach.

Spellbound 1945
Music by Miklós Rózsa.
Directed by Alfred Hitchcock. Ingrid Bergman, Gregory Peck, Leo G. Carroll.

Alfred Hitchock recommended Miklós Rózsa to *Spellbound* producer David O. Selznick on the basis of his score for Billy Wilder's *Double Indemnity* (1944). According to Rózsa, Hitchcock asked for "a big, sweeping love theme for Ingrid Bergman and Gregory Peck, and a 'new sound' for the paranoia which formed the subject of the picture."

SYNOPSIS

The staff members of Green Manors, a "mental institution," are waiting for the arrival of their new chief of staff, the distinguished Dr. Edwardes (Gregory Peck), whom nobody, including present chief of staff Dr. Murchison (Leo G. Carroll) has met. Edwardes is immediately attracted to Dr. Peterson (Ingrid Bergman), but shows unusual signs of anxiety while staring at the fork marks Peterson makes on a tablecloth and, later, the lines on her bathrobe. After collapsing during surgery, he admits to Peterson that he is suffering from amnesia and believes he has killed the missing Edwardes and taken his place. They visit her friend and mentor Dr. Brullof (Michael Chekhov), and Edwardes recounts a dream which leads them to the ski slopes where the real Dr. Edwardes died. When the police find the real Dr. Edwardes with a bullet in his body, Edwardes (Peck) is arrested for murder. Then Peterson realizes who murdered the real Dr. Edwardes.

STYLE AND CONCEPT

The music is thematic in the Romantic tradition. Chromaticism is used to suggest the psychological aspect of the story—that is, Rózsa often uses notes and chords that are foreign to the key he is writing in, which creates a "strange" or "exotic" feeling. To further accentuate the psychological factors, Rózsa uses the unusual, ethereal instrumental color of the theremin, an early electronic instrument sounding somewhat like a soprano voice. This instrument is used at key moments to emphasize and heighten the effect of Dr. Edwardes' psychological disturbance. The overall orchestration of the score is straightforward and symphonic, relying heavily on the strings.

The use of the theremin for psychological

drama became a role model Rózsa himself emulated in *The Lost Weekend* (1945) and *The Red House* (1947). These scores, along with David Raksin's 1944 score for *Laura,* established the power of music to get inside a character's head. Rózsa's score for *Spellbound* won the Academy Award.

SPOTTING

Spellbound is 111 minutes long, and contains approximately 61 minutes of music. Although there are some very long music sequences which combine a series of overlapping cues, the score isn't nonstop. Still, as in many forties films, there is heavy use of music under dialogue throughout—not just in the scenes where it is used to suggest unusual psychological states of mind and reaction—so that viewers of this film today may consider that the music is overused. In the first lunchroom scene (cue #2), for example, music is spotted at the moment Dr. Edwardes sees Dr. Peterson to suggest an immediate attraction between the two. This scene probably would not be spotted this way in a more contemporary film because the immediate entrance of music would make their first meeting seem unreal and probably corny (even if the scene was meant to show that they were immediately attracted to each other). In cue #3, on the other hand, when the film has already established a rapport between Edwardes and Peterson, playing their relationship at this point helps to establish their growing attraction to each other; adding music also plays the warmer aspects of Peterson's personality.

The cue titles used to identify the cues are mine. Some of the cue numbers listed below are a composite of several shorter cues strung together to create the effect of one longer cue. The cue sheet actually lists 116 music titles, often as short as :10–:15, because it breaks down many cues into separate titles to identify the themes as they are used.

Famous surrealist artist Salvidor Dali designed the dream sequences. In this dream, Dr. Edwardes sits at a gambling table (cue #13 in the spotting notes below). These images are particularly compatible and effective with Rózsa's psychological approach to his score.
Copyright 1945 CAPITAL CITIES/ABC, INC.
Photo courtesy of the Museum of Modern Art/Film Stills Archive (N.Y.)

#1. **Main Title** (2:00) Music starts on the written "crawl" explaining psychoanalysis, and goes out on the dissolve to Dr. Peterson (Ingrid Bergman).

> *There is no music after the Main Title until the scene in the lunchroom. This is so because the intervening scenes are exposition, and at this stage of the film, score would serve no function. Playing the moment when the female patient bites the male attendant, for instance, would be superficial because it is a relatively*

insignificant story point depicting a routine event at the clinic. It is interesting to note that this scene was originally spotted as a cue, but was dropped.

#2. **Lunch Room** (1:40) Music sneaks in as Dr. Edwardes (Peck) sees Peterson off-screen. The music pauses abruptly just after Edwardes says, "I take it the supply of linen in this institution is inexhaustible," thereby highlighting the surprised reaction of the staff.

#3. **Afternoon Walk** (1:35) Music starts on the dissolve to the countryside, and goes out on the dissolve to the dining room.

#4. **Dr. Peterson Learns Edwardes Is an Amnesiac** (14:00) This extremely long music cue begins on the dissolve to Peterson in bed after she has spoken to the staff in the dining room, and fades out on the dissolve to the close-up of the real Dr. Edwardes' nurse.

#5. **Dr. Peterson Reads Note** (:30) Music starts as Dr. Murchison (Carroll) sees Edwardes' note on the floor, and goes out on the dissolve to the fireside.

#6. **Dance Band Radio Source** (:04) Music starts from an on-screen radio after the radio announcer says, "We will now resume our regularly scheduled programming," and goes out on the cut to the next scene.

#7. **Dr. Peterson to the Hotel** (1:05) Music starts on the dissolve to Peterson hurrying down the hotel corridor to Edwardes' room, and goes out on the dissolve to Edwardes lying on the bed as Peterson says, "Try remembering."

#8. **They Are Discovered and Leave Hotel** (2:05) Music starts with an accent for emphasis after Peterson says, "That must mean only one thing—that your name was not in Dr. Edwardes' files" as she sees his scarred arm, and goes out on the dissolve to the railroad station.

#9. Edwardes Buys the Tickets (2:15) Music sneaks in as they turn to get their tickets after he says, "I'll try," and goes out as they walk down the stairs to the trains.

#10. Train to Rochester (1:15) Music starts after Peterson says, "What did you do in Rome? Think," and goes out on the dissolve to the exterior of Dr. Bruloff's house.

#11. Dr. Bruloff's Bedroom/Razor Scene (9:20) This is another long music cue created from overlapping several shorter cues. Music starts on the dissolve to the bedroom, and continues until Dr. Bruloff says, "Good morning."

#12. Dialogue with Dr. Bruloff (3:35) Music starts on the shot of Peterson (back to camera) after Bruloff says, "The doctor told me not to smoke in the morning, but I'm too excited," and goes out as Edwardes wakes up and says, "Who are you?"

#13. The Dream (9:30) Music starts as Edwardes begins to describe his dream, pauses briefly at the end of the dream, and then continues as he sees the snow. The sound effects of the train wipe out the music. This cue segues into cue #14.

#14. The Ski Slope (2:20) Music starts on the fade-in to the slope, and segues to cue #15 as they fall to the ground.

#15. Dialogue at the Lodge (2:20) Music starts on the dissolve to the telegram, and goes out as the police enter.

#16. Prison Montage/Dialogue with Dr. Bruloff (2:50) Music starts with an accent after, "I'm afraid a bullet was found in the body," and goes out as Dr. Murchison enters the office.

#17. Dr. Peterson Knows (1:40) Music starts after Dr. Murchison walks away, as Peterson realizes that Murchison has admitted knowing the real Dr. Edwardes, and goes out as she opens the door to

Murchison's office and he says, "Come in."

#18. Dr. Peterson Confronts Dr. Murchison (2:55) After Peterson has analyzed Edwardes' dream, music starts just after Murchison says, "The weapon is now in my hand," as he takes his revolver from his desk drawer, and goes out on the dissolve to Edwardes, Peterson, and Dr. Bruloff.

#19. End Scene (:30) Music starts as Edwardes gives their tickets to the railroad man, and goes out at the end of the film.

THEMES

Spellbound is a very melodic score, with a "love theme" (including a "B" section that is often used as a separate theme), a "dementia theme," a "danger theme" with several motifs, and a more neutral theme. The "neutral theme" is a relationship theme for Edwardes and Peterson when they are less committed. There are also other motifs that recur throughout. Rózsa says that when he left the theater after the first preview with temp music, "I immediately jotted down the love theme—it came to me, as it were, straight from the picture." He points out that this love theme, although not his favorite, became his most recorded theme.

Three of the themes are played over the Main Title: first, the "dementia theme" on the "Spellbound" card, played by the theremin; then the "love theme" throughout the remainder of the title sequence; and finally, the "neutral theme," which begins over the written foreword explaining psychoanalysis. All three themes begin on the same note, and the "neutral theme" shares the same first three notes with the "love theme," which adds continuity to the score.

Significant uses of the "dementia theme" include Edwardes' reaction to the fork marks on the tablecloth at lunch in cue #2; in cue #4, his

This page from the conductor's score for *Spellbound* (1945) begins 21 seconds into Miklós Rózsa's Main Title, and includes two of the principal themes: the "dementia" theme, which begins on the "Spellbound" card, and the first bars of the "love theme" which follows. You can hear the theremin playing the "dementia theme."

Courtesy of the Harry Ransom Humanities Research Center
The University of Texas at Austin
Copyright © 1945 CAPITAL CITIES/ABC, INC.

reaction to the lines on Peterson's robe and the dialogue that follows, and again on his reaction in surgery and the dialogue that follows until his collapse; as Edwardes stands in front of the ticket window, through most of the cue #9; Edwardes' dialogue on the train (most of cue #10); in cue #11, after he sees the dark lines on the bedspread, again as he becomes agitated by the white sink, chair, and bathtub, and again as Dr. Bruloff talks to him from behind his desk and then gets the milk; and in cue #13, as Edwardes sees the snow and through the interpretation of the dream.

Significant uses of the "love theme" include Peterson and Edwardes' walk through the countryside in cue #3; in cue #4, beginning with the shot of the light under the doors as she walks at night, again as they move toward an embrace (leading to the symbolism of the opening doors), and finally as he writes the note to Peterson saying he loves her and is leaving; in cue #5, on the close-up of his note as she reads it; in cue #7, in the hotel room after she says, "I couldn't bear it without you"; in cue #11, as she looks in the bedroom mirror, and again after he collapses; and in cue #12, as she says, "I couldn't feel this way . . ." while Edwardes sleeps on the couch.

Significant uses of the "neutral theme" include the moment when Edwardes and Peterson meet in cue #2; as she takes the book off the shelf, and again as she admits to Edwardes she didn't come to discuss the book in cue #4 ; the beginning of the bedroom scene in cue #11; the beginning of the dialogue scene with Dr. Bruloff in cue #12 (with new harmony) and again as she hugs him at the end of the cue; and the beginning of cue #15, as Edwardes remembers his past.

Significant uses of the "danger theme" include cue #4, when Edwardes is in bed after his collapse in surgery, later in the cue as Peterson compares signatures, then under the dialogue in which he discusses amnesia with Peterson, and again as he mentions the initials "J.B."; cue #5, as

Dr. Murchison picks up Edwardes' note and hands it to Peterson; cue #8, after she says, "Your hand was burned," and continuing for most of the cue; in cue #11, during the razor scene, as Edwardes walks away from Peterson and slowly goes downstairs; in cue #13, as Edwardes insists that he turn himself in (from "You can't undo a murder"), and again as Peterson cuts the meat on her dinner plate; in cue #15, after Edwardes says, "I saw him plunge"; and cue #17, in which the thematic material is developed.

PLAYING THE DRAMA

The score is very emotionally involved in the film, playing every dramatic nuance. Throughout the film, Rózsa phrases his music so that dramatic shifts in emotional emphasis are accompanied by appropriate changes in the music. The appropriate theme is used to reflect the drama, and the music flows freely from one theme to another as the story develops. The themes themselves are developed (as an example, listen to the score after the statement of the "love theme" from the beginning of the sequence in which Dr. Peterson gets out of bed until she sees the light under the door).

Strong accents (sometimes referred to as "stingers") are used for emphasis. This technique, if exaggerated, often seems dated today. Examples include:

Cue #4
on the cut to Peterson's robe
on the reaction of Dr. Murchison after
    Edwardes collapses in surgery
on the shot of the two different signatures of
    Anthony Edwardes
on the close-up of Peterson after Edwardes says,
    "I killed him"

Cue #8

just after the hotel room door buzzer rings

on the close-up of the newspaper with her picture

Cue #9

as he sinks down on the railroad ticket counter

on the cop as they walk away from the ticket window

Cue #11

as Edwardes sees the dark lines on the bedspread

as he collapses

Cue #13

as the cop brings in the photos

Cue #16

the opening chord, in response to, "I'm afraid a bullet was found in the body"

after "The case is one of murder"

The score is frequently used for varying degrees of dramatic emphasis through the use of dynamics and texture. An excellent example of this is near the end of cue #18, as the revolver slowly turns toward the camera. There is an extra dramatic emphasis in the music as the revolver moves past the halfway point to aim directly at the camera, achieved by increasing the volume of the music (not the dubbing) and adding more low-register instruments to the texture. By waiting until this final move, Rózsa helps to maintain the level of suspense as long as possible before we realize what may be happening.

Rózsa plays a "red herring" (false alarm) as Peterson sees Dr. Bruloff collapsed in his easy chair near the end of cue #11, establishing accented tension through her walk over to him, until he wakes up, at which point we know he is all right and the musical tension is released.

In the forties, the studios required big, upbeat endings like cue #19, regardless of the subject matter and the dramatic resolution of the film.

SOURCE MUSIC

There is one very short source cue, a forties-style dance band (contemporary to the film's setting) which plays from an on-screen radio after the announcer says, "We now resume our regular programming."

TEMPO AND PULSE

The "love theme" and "dementia theme" are *legato,* flowing pieces which pull forward rather than drive. The "danger theme," however, is much more rhythmic, and acts as an emotional alarm, functioning to imply danger.

Sometimes the score continues to be full and urgent at moments when there is a pause in the physical action on-screen, giving the film forward momentum. While Peterson waits outside Edwardes' bedroom door, having seen light coming from under the door, the music continues playing her strong feelings even as she stands there uncertain about going in, which drives the drama forward.

During cue #11, as Edwardes takes the shaving cream and razor, the rhythmic pulse become explicit and insistant, creating a great deal of tension.

During the ski slope scene (cue #14) a strong rhythmic figure begins as they are halfway down the slope, and continues through the end of the cue, adding both urgency and tension.

The Spirit of St. Louis   1957
Music by Franz Waxman.
Orchestrated by Leonid Raab. Directed by Billy Wilder. James Stewart, Patricia Smith, Murray Hamilton.

Franz Waxman composed the music for *The Spirit of St. Louis* late in his film career, at the age of 50. Music plays an extremely important role in this film because so much of the story takes place during Charles Lindbergh's solo flight from New York to Paris, so that the possibilities for dialogue and visually interesting action are limited except for the flashbacks.

SYNOPSIS

In 1927, Charles Lindbergh (James Stewart) completed the first flight across the Atlantic. Adapted from Lindbergh's autobiography, the film begins the night before this historic flight and uses a number of flashbacks woven throughout the story of the flight itself to fill in details of Lindbergh's early career as a pilot in an air circus and as an airmail pilot working out of Chicago, and the building of the "Spirit of St. Louis" airplane.

STYLE AND CONCEPT

The style is symphonic, with a rich harmonic language and much more use of the full range of colors in the orchestra than Max Steiner's score for *Dark Victory.* The outdoor sequences, the large portions of film accompanied by the drone of an airplane, and the heroic nature of the flight allowed Waxman to use the brass and winds forcefully when called for without overpowering the drama.

SPOTTING

The Spirit of St. Louis is 138 minutes long and contains approximately 74:15 of score plus 5:48 of source music. Since music is accompanying the narrative, and is, in fact, often functioning in a narrative way as it details and supplements Lindbergh's

Charles Lindbergh (James Stewart) studies the map during his famous trans-Atlantic flight from New York to Paris in 1927. Franz Waxman wrote his score for *The Spirit of St. Louis* (1957) late in his career, and it is one of his best.
Photo courtesy of the Academy of Motion Picture Arts and Sciences
© 1957 Leland Hayward Productions, Inc.
and Billy Wilder Productions, Inc.
Renewed 1985 Warner Bros. Inc.
All Rights Reserved.

recollections and mood swings, *Spirit* does not seem to be overspotted. For an example of how long stretches of scored drama work, watch the section of the film from cue #27 through cue #30, a total of 22:15 of continuous scoring.

The titles listed below are those indicated on the cue sheet. Some of the following cues are indicated as two separate cues on the cue sheet. Additional descriptive titles have been added in brackets as necessary for clarification. The cue sheet credits cues #19, #25, #26, and #27 to Roy Webb and Ray Heindorf. These cues replaced Waxman's original scoring when changes were required after the movie previewed (a typical procedure at that time).

During the New York–Paris flight, Lindbergh remembers his days as a flyer in an air circus (cue #22 in the spotting notes below).

© 1957 Leland Hayward Productions, Inc. and Billy Wilder Productions, Inc. Renewed 1985 Warner Bros. Inc. All Rights Reserved.

#1. **The Spirit of St. Louis Theme {Main Title}** (2:04) Music starts as the first title appears during the main titles, and fades out on the dissolve to the "Garden City Hotel" sign. This cue is indicated as cues #1 through #4 on the cue sheet, which lists the uses of "La Marseillaise." According to Royal S. Brown in his liner notes for the Varèse Sarabande VSD-5212 CD of the original score, this was added to this revised version of the Main Title by Roy Webb and Ray Heindorf.

#2. **"Rio Rita" {Radio Source Music}** (Joseph McCarthy, Harry Tierney; 1:40) Music starts as Brent Mahoney sits out-side Lindbergh's hotel room, and goes out on the cut to the airport.

#3. **Peoria Airfield** (:32) Music starts on the dissolve to a windsock, and fades out as an airplane taxies toward the camera.

#4. **Forced Landing** (:32) Music starts as Lindbergh takes off and Burt, the airport supervisor, says, "What!" and goes out on the cut of the motor failing.

#5. **"Baby Face" {Radio Source Music}** (Benny Davis, Harry Akst; 1:58) Music starts in progress on the cut to the diner, and goes out in progress as the waiter turns off the radio.

#6. **The Spirit of St. Louis Theme {The Spirit}** (:15) Music starts on the banker as Major Lambert says, "The same kind of spirit . . ." and fades out under another of the assembled businessmen saying, "Wouldn't a three-engine plane be safer?"

#7. **The Spirit of St. Louis Theme {The Spirit, Part II}** (:15) Music starts on the cut to the notepad as the banker underlines "Spirit" after Lindbergh says, "I'd take the 200 miles any day," and fades out under Lindbergh saying, "I'm used to it—"

#8. **The Spirit of St. Louis Theme {Naming the Plane}** (:45) Music starts on the cut to the notepad as the banker circles the word "Spirit," and segues to cue #9 on the dissolve to the New York City street.

#9. **New York Street** (:20) Music segues from cue #8 on the dissolve to the street, and fades out on the dissolve to Lindbergh entering the office.

#10. **Off to San Diego** (:57) Music starts as Lindbergh moves to get on the train, and fades out as he slowly enters the Ryan factory.

#11. **Building the Ryan** (5:45) Music starts on the dissolve to Lindbergh and Don, the designer, working on plans of the plane, and fades out on the dissolve to gas pouring into the tank of the finished plane.

#12. Test Flight (1:10) Music starts as the plane takes off, and fades out on the dissolve to Lindbergh talking to the Ryan company staff.

#13. The Spirit of St. Louis Theme [After the Photos] (1:10) Music starts after the photos are taken of Lindbergh and the Ryan employees, and goes out as the "Spirit of St. Louis" comes to a stop and the the motor shuts off.

#14. St. Christopher (:37) Music starts as Lindbergh takes the St. Christopher medal from his nightstand, and fades out on the dissolve to Father Hussman taking a flying lesson.

#15. St. Christopher/Hotel Room (2:07) Music starts as the Father finishes saying, "How come I never see you around the church?" and fades out on the dissolve to Lindbergh coming downstairs the morning of the flight.

#16. Rolling Out/The Spirit of St. Louis Theme (5:10) Music starts on the dissolve to the hangar after the shot of Lindbergh considering the weather problem, and fades out under, "She's all topped off—425 gallons."

#17. Cape Cod (4:48) Music starts after the plane clears the trees, and fades out as Lindbergh says to the fly, "There's still plenty of land ahead—Nova Scotia, Newfoundland."

#18. Recollections/Nova Scotia (5:25) Music starts a few seconds after cue #17 on the dissolve to Lindbergh dozing, and fades out to the dissolve to Lindbergh on a motorcycle as he says, "I had her for about a year and a half, and then drove her down to Georgia. Traded her in on an airplane."

#19. Contact (Roy Webb, Ray Heindorf; 1:10) Music starts as the young Lindbergh rolls his first plane down the air-

strip, and ends abruptly as the motorcycle goes down.

#20. Solo Flight (:22) Music starts as Lindbergh's plane begins to take off over the barn, and ends with an accident on the dissolve back to Lindbergh on the flight to Paris.

#21. St. John's/The Spirit of St. Louis Theme (5:50) Music starts immediately after cue #20, on Lindbergh flying to Paris, and fades out under Lindbergh saying off-screen, "All right, folks, who wants to be the first one up there?"

#22. Barnstorming/The Spirit of St. Louis Theme (1:02) Music starts after the crowd laughing on the dissolve to the plane flying upside down, and fades out as the two planes land.

#23. "The Spirit of Independence" [Band Source Music] (Abe Holzmann; 1:35) Music starts on the dissolve to the flying circus, and fades out in progress on the dissolve to the exterior night shot of the flight to Paris.

#24. Iceberg (2:10) Music starts a few seconds later under Lindbergh's voice-over, and segues to cue #25 on the dissolve to the airstrip military inspection.

#25. March Comic (Roy Webb, Ray Heindorf; 1:36) Music segues in progress from cue #24 on the dissolve to the military inspection, and stops abruptly just before the officer says to Lindbergh, "You can't set that thing down here."

#26. Old Plane (Roy Webb, Ray Heindorf; :40) Music starts on the cut to Lindbergh's old plane collapsing, and fades out as he says to the officer, ". . . You have a little something on your nose."

#27. Comic Agitato (Roy Webb, Ray Heindorf; :35) Music starts a few seconds after cue #26, on the cut to Lindbergh chasing his plane, and segues to cue #28 on the dissolve to the close-up of Lindbergh flying to Paris.

#28. Asleep/The Spirit of St. Louis Theme/Asleep (11:40) Music segues from cue #27 on the dissolve to Lindbergh flying to Paris, and segues to cue #29 on the dissolve to the rear shot of the plane flying after Lindbergh wakes up.

#29. Fishing Boats/Ireland (6:35) Music segues from cue #28 on the dissolve to the rear shot of the plane, and segues to cue #30 on the dissolve to the map after the shot of the plane flying over a castle. The music pauses as Lindbergh yells down, "Which way to Ireland?"

#30. Plymouth/Fifty-eight Minutes (3:25) Music segues from cue #29 on the dissolve to the map, and goes out as he suddenly stops drinking from his canteen.

#31. Le Bourget (5:50) Music starts on the cut to the altimeter after the motor starts up again, and fades out under the crowd cheering. Notice the pause in the music to highlight Lindbergh saying, "Oh, God, help me" as he begins to land the plane.

#32. The Spirit of St. Louis Theme [Plane in Hangar] (:44) Music starts on the dissolve to the plane in the hangar, and fades out as Lindbergh stops by the plane.

#33. The Spirit of St. Louis Theme [Plane in Hangar, Part II] (:35) Music starts a few seconds after cue #2, on the cut back to Lindbergh after the shot of the crowd in the hangar, and segues to a band playing "Stars and Stripes Forever" on the dissolve to the parade.

#34. "Stars and Stripes Forever" [Visual Band Source Music] (John Philip Sousa; :35) Music segues in progress from cue #33 on the dissolve to the parade, and goes out on the fade to black at the end of the film. For copyright reasons, in prints released outside the United States, "Stars and Stripes Forever" was replaced with Abe Holzmann's "The Spirit of Independence."

#35. The Spirit of St. Louis Theme [The End] (:10)

THEMES

Waxman's score for *The Spirit of St. Louis* is based on two main themes, both stated in the Main Title. The first, "introductory theme," is a heroic series of two-note upward leaps of a fifth, an idea that sometimes functions independently as a two-note motif. The second, considered the "main theme" from *The Spirit of St. Louis,* is a flowing, soaring melody that gives the sense of being airborne when set in the orchestra.

The "introductory theme" can be heard clearly over the written explanation of the Lindbergh story at the beginning of the film. Other significant uses include cues #6 and #7, as Lindbergh discusses his proposed flight to Paris; cue #8, as the plane is named; cue #30, which uses both the two-note motif and also the entire theme based on that motif; and cue #31, as Lindbergh reads his map while he looks for the Paris airport.

The "main theme" is played during the Main Titles. Other significant uses include cue #12; cue #13; cue #17, on the successful take-off; cue #18, when he flies over Nova Scotia; cue #28, at the end, with the motif also; cue #29, as he realizes he's over Ireland; cue #30, as he eats a sandwich; and cue #31, as he sees Paris, after he says, "There it is!"

A separate theme representing the St. Christopher medal is introduced in cue #14; recapitulated in cue #15; and returns during cue #30 as Lindbergh holds the medal.

The French anthem "La Marseillaise" is also integrated into the score several times, including cue #1, cue #17, after the take-off, and cue #30.

The opening bars of Franz Waxman's Main Title Sketch for *The Spirit of St. Louis* (1957) indicate a unison orchestral statement of the "introductory theme." During the course of his score, Waxman uses the first two notes as a motif, and the next four notes as another motif (developed from the first one).

The Spirit of St. Louis (Franz Waxman)
© 1957 WARNER BROS. INC. (Renewed)
All Rights Reserved. Used By Permission.

In general, Waxman's score flows easily and effectively between these well-integrated melodic elements and less organic musical material that goes with the drama moment by moment.

PLAYING THE DRAMA

The music is an indispensable element in *The Spirit of St. Louis,* pulling the scenes along, getting inside Lindbergh's mind as he reminisces, and dramatizing his struggle to stay awake during his long trip over the Atlantic. Sometimes illustrative and always empathetic, Waxman's score enriches and heightens the storytelling as film music should. He phrases the drama as necessary, yet has created music that stands alone.

The sound effects frequently take over the soundtrack, becoming more prominent than the music. Cue #28 offers a good example of this, but there is give-and-take throughout the film, with the music sometimes rising above the sound of the airplane when the drama demands more music.

SOURCE MUSIC

There is very little source music in the film. The two radio cues near the beginning (cues # 2 and #5) help to establish the period by using the musical style and songs of the times. The band music in cue #23 during the air show suggests that a live band is playing, and the parade music used for cue #34 at the end of the film is supposed to be played by the live band that is seen briefly on screen.

TEMPO AND PULSE

Waxman's music has a great deal of energy when required, and his score for *The Spirit of St. Louis*

always feels like it is moving forward. At some point an executive decision was made to use several cues by Roy Webb and Ray Heindorf (see the spotting notes) which are clearly meant to add whatever upbeat tempo and comedic attitude is possible (cues #25, #26, and #27) during the flashback section of the film when the young Lindbergh has landed his old plane on a military base. Even the titles given to these cues ("Comic Agitato" and "March Comic") indicate this intention.

North by Northwest 1959
Music by Bernard Herrmann.
Directed by Alfred Hitchcock. Cary Grant, Eva Marie Saint, James Mason.

Bernard Herrmann's scores may seem to be more difficult to understand because they are less obviously melodic than Max Steiner's and Victor Young's. As involved as Waxman and Rózsa could be in developing their musical materials, they typically framed their scores around strong, lyrical themes. In this regard it is helpful to think of the thematic material from Herrmann's score for *North by Northwest* in terms of short pieces of musical material and motifs rather than longer melodies. The Main Title offers a good example of this. By extending these short ideas through repetition and development, Herrman creates a strong sense of thematic unity.

SYNOPSIS

Advertising executive Roger Thornhill (Cary Grant) is mistaken for a man named George Kaplan, and accused of being a spy by Lester Townsend (James

Mason). Townsend interrogates him, and then tries to have him killed. Thornhill then attempts to discover who George Kaplan is and why Townsend and his people are trying to kill him. Along the way he meets Eve (Eva Marie Saint) on a train, who, it turns out, is involved in Thornhill's pursuit. The film concludes with an extended chase sequence that ends on top of Mount Rushmore.

STYLE AND CONCEPT

In his scores for the Hitchcock movies, including *The Man Who Knew Too Much* (1956), *The Wrong Man* (1957), *Vertigo* (1958), *North by Northwest* (1959), and *Psycho* (1960), Herrmann created a sound and style that were uniquely his own. His scores for these and other similar films have become role models for countless film scores over the years. His score for *Cape Fear* (1962) was adapted by Elmer Bernstein for the 1991 remake of the film directed by Martin Scorcese.

SPOTTING

North by Northwest is 136 minutes. The score is approximately 48:47 long, plus 4:54 of instrumental source music. This is not a particularly long score, but then, both Hitchcock and Herrmann are known for their ability to use silence and sound effects with dramatic effect. Although music does play most of the action sequences, the famous crop-dusting scene is played without music. The score in that scene doesn't enter until the plane crashes into the truck.

The cue titles listed below are those indicated on the cue sheet, sometimes supplemented with additional bracketed titles for clarification.

The *North by Northwest* (1959) action sequence on Mount Rushmore is one of the most memorable and effective chases in motion picture history. Bernard Herrmann's dynamic music greatly contributes to its success. Listen for the "action theme," first heard in the Main Title.
Photo courtesy of the Academy of Motion Picture Arts and Sciences
© 1959 Turner Entertainment Co.
All Rights Reserved.

#1. Overture [Logo and Main Title] (2:13) Music starts on the fade in of the MGM Lion logo, and goes out as the elevator door opens.

#2. "It's a Most Unusual Day" [Hotel Lobby Source] (Jimmy McHugh, Harold Adamson; :18) Music starts in progress on the cut to the hotel lobby as

Thornhill (Cary Grant) goes to his lunch meeting, and goes out as he speaks to the head waiter.

#3. Kidnapped (2:12) Music starts after one of the kidnappers says, "Let's go," and fades out as Thornhill and one of the men enter the house.

#4. The Door (:39) Music starts after the library door is closed, and fades out as Lester Townsend (James Mason) enters and closes the door.

#5. Cheers (:42) Music starts after Leonard (Martin Landau) says, "Cheers," and fades out as the car door closes.

#6. "I've Grown Accustomed to Your Face" (Frederick Lowe, Alan J. Lerner; :06) Thornhill, now drunk, sings a few bars as they settle him in the car.

#7. & #8. The Wild Ride & Car Crash (2:45) Music starts on the two-shot of Thornhill and one of Townsend's men as the car begins to move, and fades out into the dissolve to the police station. (This cue is listed as two overlapping cues on the cue sheet.)

#9. The Return (:25) Music starts on the dissolve to the car after the court scene, and fades out under the dialogue with Townsend's housekeeper.

#10. Two Dollars (:43) Music starts after Thornhill's mother says, "Pay the two dollars," and fades out as they get out of the cab.

#11. "Rosalie" [Hotel Lobby Source #2] (Cole Porter; :18) Music starts in progress on the cut to the lobby, and goes out as Thornhill talks on the house phone.

#12. "In the Still of the Night" [Hotel Lobby Source #3] (Cole Porter; :45) Music starts just after cue #11 ends, and fades out in progress on the dissolve to Thornhill and his mother in the hotel corridor.

#13. The Elevator (:45) Music starts as Thornhill picks up a piece of paper off of the desk, and ends abruptly just before his mother says, "You gentlemen aren't really trying to kill my son, are you?"

#14. The U.N. (:58) Music starts as the cab moves after Thornhill says, "I don't know—just keep moving," and fades out as Thornhill says, "Where will I find Mr. Lester Townsend?"

#15. Information Desk (:45) Music starts after the woman at the information desk says, "One moment, please," and fades out as Thornhill says, "Please page Mr. Lester Townsend."

#16. The Knife (:43) Music starts just after the real Townsend gasps, and fades out on the dissolve to the newspaper.

#17. Fashion Show [Dining Car Source] (André Previn; 3:33) Music starts on the cut to the dining car, and fades out as Eve Kendall (Eva Marie Saint) says, ". . . and I don't particularly like the book I've started."

#18., #19, & #20. Interlude, Song from North by Northwest, & Interlude [The Dining Car] (1:18) Music starts after Eve says, "You know what I mean?" as Thornhill says, "Let me think," and fades out as Eve says, "Drawing Room E." (This is dubbed as one continuous cue, although it is identified as three different pieces on the cue sheet.)

#21. Detectives (:21) Music starts just after Eve says, ". . . I just saw two policemen get out of a car as we pulled into the station. They weren't smiling," and fades out on the cut to Eve in her compartment lying down, reading.

#22. Song from North by Northwest [Thornhill and Kendall in Compartment] (2:56) Music starts on the cut to Thornhill and Eve after the train exterior, and fades out as the porter enters the compartment.

#23. & #24. Duo & Song from North by Northwest [After the Porter Leaves] (1:10) Music starts as Thornhill hears the door close behind the porter off-screen, and fades out on the close up of Eve before the cut to the porter.

#25. & #26. Song from North by Northwest & The Station [Arrive in Chicago] (:52) Music starts after Thornhill says, "You're the smartest girl I ever spent the night with on a train," and fades out on the cut to Thornhill shaving in the men's room.

#27. The Phone Booth (1:14) Music starts on the second shot of Eve in the phone booth, and fades out as Eve says, "What took you so long?"

#28. Song from North by Northwest and Eve Says Goodbye] (:45) Music starts after Eve says, "Got your watch set for Central Time?" and he replies, "Yes, I did that, thanks," and goes out on the dissolve to the country road.

#29. The Crash (1:05) Music starts on the plane crashing into the truck, and fades out on the dissolve to the police looking at the pickup truck Thornhill has borrowed.

#30. Song from North by Northwest [Thornhill Finds Eve] (:52) Music starts on Eve as she opens the hotel room door, and goes out under Thornhill saying, "The meeting with Kaplan?"

#31. Song from North by Northwest ["I Want You To Do a Favor for Me"] (:54) Music starts on the cut to Thornhill after Eve says, "I want you to do a favor for me," and goes out under her saying, ". . . that you let the hotel valet do something with this suit first."

#32. The Question (:43) Music starts after Thornhill says, "Ever kill anyone?" and fades out under Thornhill starting the shower.

#33. "Singin' in the Rain" [Off-screen whistling] (Nacio Herb Brown, Arthur Freed; :30) Whistling starts just after Thornhill turns on the shower off-screen, and goes out on the cut to Thornhill opening the bathroom door.

#34. The Pad and Pencil (1:00) Music starts on the above cut of Thornhill opening the bathroom door, continues through the cut to the auction at :39, and fades out under the auctioneer saying, "Four-fifty is bid for the pair."

#35. The Auction (1:05) Music starts on Eve after Thornhill says, "Goodnight, sweetheart, don't think it wasn't nice," and fades out under Thornhill saying, "Fifteen hundred."

#36. The Police (:24) Music starts as two policemen take Thornhill from the auction, after Thornhill says to one of Townsend's men, "Sorry, old man—keep trying," and fades out under Thornhill saying, "I want to thank you gentlemen for saving my life."

#37. The Airport (:58) Music starts on the dissolve to the airport after the cop driving the police car says, "You oughta be ashamed of yourself," and fades out as "the Professor" (the government man, played by Leo G. Carroll) and Thornhill walk to the plane.

#38. The Cafeteria (1:10) Music starts as Thornhill moves away from the view of Mount Rushmore after the Professor says, "My blessings on you both," and fades out under Townsend saying, "Good afternoon, Mr. Kaplan."

#39. The Shooting (1:08) Music starts after Eve fires the second shot at Thornhill, and goes out as the Professor opens the back of his car and says to Thornhill, "Mr. Thornhill."

#40. Song from North by Northwest [Thornhill and Eve Meet in Woods] (1:20) Music starts after Thornhill says to Eve, "Well, I may go back to hating you—it was more fun," and fades out under Thornhill saying, "Wait a minute. What didn't you tell me?"

#41. Flight (:17) Music starts as Eve turns to run to her car after the Professor says, "I'm afraid we're already doing that," and fades out on the dissolve to Thornhill's hospital room with the radio announcer explaining the shooting of Kaplan.

#42. The Ledge (1:10) Music starts as the Professor leaves the hospital room, after he says, "See you in a few minutes," and fades out under the blond woman in bed saying, "Stop," and Thornhill saying, "Excuse me."

#43. The House (3:13) Music starts a few seconds after the end of cue #42, just before the dissolve to the street, and goes out as Thornhill climbs to the top of the beam near a window, and Townsend says, "There's nothing to worry about."

#44. The Balcony (:42) Music starts as the light from Eve's window catches Thornhill's attention after Townsend and Leonard have walked out of sight, and fades out as Leonard looks out the window.

#45. The Match Box (1:57) Music starts on the cut to Thornhill after Townsend says, "This matter is best disposed of from a great height—over water," and goes out on the cut to Thornhill standing in a recessed area overlooking the living room.

#46. The Message (:54) Music starts as Leonard throws Thornhill's matchbook onto the coffee table, and goes out as Thornhill says, "Darling . . ."

#47. The TV (:37) Music starts as Townsend and Eve leave and the door closes off-screen, and fades out as the housekeeper says to Thornhill, "Stay where you are."

#48. The Airplane (:57) Music starts shortly after cue #47 ends, on the shot of Townsend, Eve, and Leonard walking toward the plane, and goes out on the off-screen gun shots.

Music is continuous from the beginning of cue #49 through the end of the movie, although Herrmann scored this last 6:55 of the film with several overlapping cues. The following breakdown of cues is based on the cue sheet timings, not the scores.

#49. The Gates (:45) Music starts after Eve jumps into the car Thornhill is driving and they pull away, and segues to cue #50, on the cut to the top of the monument.

#50. The Stone Faces (1:07) Music segues from cue #49, on the cut to the top of the monument (starting with a strong orchestral accent), and segues to cue #51, on the shot looking up at one of the stone faces.

#51. The Ridge (1:30) Music segues from cue #50, on the shot looking up at one of the stone faces (this cue includes the dialogue scene between Thornhill and Eve), and segues to cue #52, as Townsend's man falls.

#52. On the Rocks (1:55) Music segues from cue #51, as Townsend's man falls, and segues to cue #53, on the cut to the two-shot of Townsend's man with a knife fighting with Thornhill.

#53. The Cliff (1:25) Music segues from cue #52, on the cut to Townsend's man fighting with Thornhill, and segues to cue #54, as Thornhill helps Eve up from the cliff.

#54. Finale (:15) Music segues from cue #53, as Thornhill helps Eve up from the cliff, saying, "Here—reach—now," and segues to cue #54, in the interior of the train, after the first full-volume phrase of the theme.

#55. Song from North by Northwest [End Scene] (:15) Music segues from cue #54, in the interior of the train, and goes out to black at the end of the movie.

THEMES

There are several themes and motifs Herrmann uses to unify his score for *North by Northwest*.

The most lyrical theme is the "love theme" (identified as "Song from North by Northwest" on the cue sheet), a recurrent theme used for Thornhill and Eve. The "love theme" is first heard briefly on the train in the dining car at the end of the conversation between Thornhill and Eve (cue #19); a longer version is played in cue #22, in Eve's compartment later that night. Many other uses of this theme follow, including cue #28 (as they say goodbye in the train station); cue #30; and cue #40. (Refer to the spotting notes above for a more complete list.)

There is an "action theme" stated in cue #1; again in cue #7, as the drunk Thornhill tries to control his car; the second half of cue #16, beginning on the high shot outside the United Nations; and several other places, including cue #52, as Townsend's man falls during the ending sequence on Mount Rushmore, and elsewhere, as they run along the monument.

There is an important "tension motif" used to a considerable extent in cues #34, #35, #36, #37 (with accented horns at the top), and #42. It would be a good idea to listen to one or two of these cues several times to memorize this motif, as this will help you to hear the many other uses and permutations of this material throughout the score.

A "dark unison motif" can be heard first in cues #9 and #13, played by the strings with little accompaniment. This material returns again later in the score, including during the cafeteria scene (cue #38).

Herrmann plays the romance between Roger Thornhill (Cary Grant) and Eve Kendall (Eva Marie Saint) with a recurring love theme. You can hear it during the train sequence pictured above (in cues # 23 and #24).

PLAYING THE DRAMA

Although Herrmann hits a number of key dramatic accents in this score, he tends to play through the drama in a number of cues, setting the tone without making specific reference in his score to the action. The Main Title music is used this way as well, setting the stage for the drama to unfold, and promising an exciting theatrical experience. The function of the action music for Thornhill's drunken ride (cues #7 and #8) is to play the excitement and potential danger of the ride, rather than to hit any of the action or make any kind of character statement.

Some examples of hitting the action in this score include several moments in cue #3, including the opening note of the cue, which emphasizes the seriousness of the situation. Again, the score accents Thornhill's attempt to open the car door en route. The rest of the cue is generally dark and straightforward. Cue #4 includes a slight crescendo/accent as we see a closeup of a mailing label with Lester Townsend's name and address. Just after this moment, the orchestral color changes to high strings as Thornhill looks out the window and sees men talking.

Most of the cues that use the "love theme" begin with the theme in the first bar, with no lead-in or preparation. The approach to playing the relationship between Thornhill and Eve is on-the-nose rather than more subtle. However, Herrmann sometimes starts the theme at a specific dramatic moment within a cue for emphasis. In cue #22, Herrmann begins the "love theme" conspicuously just after the long kiss (played by the violins) and then again after Eve says, ". . . Make women who don't know you fall in love with you."

plays the beginning of Thornhill's scene with Eve, adds a little atmosphere. It is spotted to fade out where it does so that Herrmann's score can begin a few seconds later.

Hitchcock enjoys having fun during his suspense movies; Thornhill whistles a few bars of "Singin' in the Rain" while he pretends to take a shower (cue #33).

TEMPO AND PULSE

Many of the cues have a rhythmic pulse, including the motivic material used in cues #34, #35, and #36. This adds a sense of urgency to the moment, and ultimately gives the entire score a sense of forward motion and drive.

Music doesn't need to be loud to establish rhythmic motion and a steady pulse. Listen to cue #43, as Thornhill approaches the house, to see how Herrmann is able to keep the rhythmic motion going even though the orchestra is playing softly. Cue #44 is played softly also, with a short rhythmic figure in the strings contrasting with the smoother lines of the woodwinds. Cue #45 introduces new material, still softly (though richly) in the orchestra. In all three cues, although the music itself is played softly, the cues are dubbed at a loud enough level to be very present and full sounding.

SOURCE MUSIC

The hotel lobby source music is arranged for solo violin, harp, and piano, to give the impression that these three musicians are playing in person somewhere in or near the lobby. The use of four pop standards for the hotel (cues # 2, #6, #8, and #12) adds an authentic quality to these moments, creating a credibility which is more difficult to achieve with the use of unrecognizable tunes.

The dining car source music (#17), which

The Magnificent Seven   1960
Music by Elmer Bernstein.
Orchestrated by Jack Hayes and Leo Shuken. Directed by John Sturges. Yul Brynner, Steve McQueen, Eli Wallach, Horst Buchholz, James Coburn, Charles Bronson, Robert Vaughn, Brad Dexter.

By the time of the release of *The Magnificent Seven* in 1960, there was already a rich legacy of film scores for Westerns. *Stagecoach* was one of the early Hollywood successes (1939; music by Richard Hageman, W. Franke Harling, John Leipold, Leo Shuken, and additional music by Gerard Carbonara). John Ford wanted to use some authentic American folk tunes, and music director Boris Morros selected a number of tunes, including "Shall We Gather at the River," "Gentle Annie," "The Union Forever," "She's More to Be Pitied Than Censured," "Bury Me Not on the Lone Prairie," and Stephen Foster's "Jeannie with the Light Brown Hair." In *Behind the Scenes,* Rudy Behlmer points out Ford's affinity with this music. "Ford always had live music played on the set while lighting and rehearsing. This was a throwback to the silent era, when music was provided off-camera to get the players into the proper mood for the upcoming scene. Over the years Danny Borzage (brother of director Frank Borzage) regularly played Ford's favorite nostalgic and sentimental tunes on his accordion for the entire company, whether on location or in the studio. His playing was sometimes augmented by that of other musicians, to make up a trio or quartet. Often some of the tunes played formed the basis of the score for a Ford film, such as 'Red River Valley' in *The Grapes of Wrath* (1940), 'Harbor Lights' in *The Long Voyage Home* (1940), and 'Bury Me Not on the Lone Prairie' in *Stagecoach*."

In the years following the release of *Stagecoach,* many of the high-profile composers of the forties and fifties contributed scores for Westerns. Dimitri Tiomkin scored many, including *The Westerner* (1940), *Duel in the Sun* (1946), *Red River* (1948), *High Noon* (1952), and *Rio Bravo* (1959). Following the creative approach of *Stagecoach,* he emphasized both the big orchestral sound associated with Westerns and also the use of folk tunes and folk instruments such as guitar and harmonica. Alfred Newman's Westerns include *Drums Along the Mohawk* (1939), *Broken Arrow* (1950), and *The Gunfighter* (1950). Shortly after the release of *The Magnificent Seven,* Newman scored the epic *How the West Was Won* (1962, directed by John Ford).

The main theme of *The Magnificent Seven* (1960) plays the heroic aspect of the seven men—the good guys. This theme is clearly stated in the Main Title.
© *1960 United Artists Pictures, Inc.*

Max Steiner (who had scored *Cimarron* in 1930 and *Dodge City* in 1939) composed the music for *Virginia City* (1940), *They Died with Their Boots On* (1942), and *The Hanging Tree* (1959), among others. Victor Young's Westerns include *Shane* (1953) and *Johnny Guitar* (1954). Miklós Rózsa scored *Tribute to a Bad Man* in 1956, Bernard Herrmann scored the frontier story *The Kentuckian* (1955), and Franz Waxman scored *The Indian Fighter* (1955) and the remake of *Cimarron,* which was released the same year as *The Magnificent Seven.*

Another film, released in 1958, became a classic role model for music for Westerns. Jerome Moross composed the music for *The Big Country,* often cited as a favorite score of many film music lovers. Among Moross' influences was music created not for film but for the ballet. "Of course, [Aaron] Copland's influence on film music is immeasurable," says André Previn. "His ballets *Appalachian Spring* [1944], *Billy the Kid* [1938], and *Rodeo* [1942] have left an ineradicable impression on a whole generation of composers, and I doubt whether any film composer faced with pictures of the Great American Outdoors, or any Western story, has been able to withstand the lure of trying to imitate some aspects of Copland's peculiar and personal harmony. Just as Elgar seems to spell 'England' to the minds of most listeners, Copland *is* the American sound."

Since the release of *The Magnificent Seven*, Elmer Bernstein's music for this film has been frequently cited as the quintessential score for a classic Western. It is thematic and rhythmically powerful, helping greatly to push the drama forward.

SYNOPSIS

The Magnificent Seven is adapted from Akira Kurosawa's classic 1954 film *The Seven Samurai* (which is set in sixteenth-century Japan). In the American version, a small Mexican village is being brutalized by bandits, and the villagers hire seven men to protect them. The selection and gathering together of the seven men is part of the drama, which climaxes in a confrontation between the seven and the bandits.

STYLE AND CONCEPT

Bernstein blends a folk-tune approach with a more orchestral/symphonic style and sound. Guitars (both picked and strummed) are used now and then throughout the score, sometimes subdued in the background, and sometimes more exposed. Rhythmic drive is among the most significant of the musical elements in this score, and perhaps contributes more to the film than any other aspect of the score.

SPOTTING

The Magnificent Seven is 126 minutes long and contains approximately 79:46 of score plus 3:07 of source music; two-thirds of the film is scored. This is a long score, but appropriate for the genre and the film. Although much of the action is scored, look for the duel between James Coburn (Britt) and the challenging townsman, played without music until Britt's knife strikes the townsman, at which point cue #9 begins.

In dubbing, cue #37 was shortened; you can hear it go out seemingly arbitrarily as Vin is shooting in the middle of the street. Although there may appear to be no dramatic motivation for the music to go out at this point, there are often other reasons to consider, including the increased dramatic impact of the sound effects when the music ends and a balance of emphasis between the music and sound effects.

The titles listed below (sometimes whimsical) are those indicated on the cue sheet.

#1. **Main Title** (1:53) Music starts on the fade in of the main titles, and segues to cue #2, on the dissolve to the bandits.

#2. **Calvera** (1:50) Music segues from cue #1, on the dissolve to the bandits, and fades out under Calvera (Eli Wallach) saying, "I can't tell you what a pleasure it is to see a village like this."

#3. **Council** (3:06) Music starts after Calvera says, "I'll be back—enough," and fades out on the dissolve to the village wise man after a villager says, "We'll ask the old man—he'll know."

#4. **Quest** (:57) Music starts on the dissolve to the three men riding into town after the old man says, "Then learn—or die," and fades out to the mortician saying, "Hey—I've been waiting for you."

#5. **Strange Funeral** (4:17) Music starts after Chris (Yul Brynner) says, "Oh, hell—if that's all that's holding things up, I'll drive the rig," builds to an abrupt pause before one of the protesters says, "Hold it—hold it right there," pauses again as the protester says, "Turn that rig around and get it down the hill," and is shot, and then fades out under the salesman announcing, "Boys, the drinks are on me."

#6. After the Brawl Is Over (2:46) Music starts as the crowd of townspeople cheer, plays the ride back to town, the dialogue between the salesman and Chris, and the dialogue between Vin (Steve McQueen) and Chris, and fades out after Chris hears a knock on his door.

#7. Vin's Luck (:55) Music starts on the dissolve to Vin riding at night after Harry (Brad Dexter) says to Chris, "Never mind—I'm in. Dirty dog," plays into the saloon scene (very softly as piano source music), and goes out just as Chris says to the waiter, "The cowpoke who just walked in."

#8. And Then There Were Two (:45) Music starts on the cut to Chris after Vin says, "How many you got?" and fades out as O'Reilly (Charles Bronson) chops wood.

#9. Britt (:52) Music starts after Chris says, "Where can I reach you?" and O'Reilly answers, "Right here," and fades out after the townsman says, "I'm talkin' to you. Look at me."

#10. Duel (1:22) Music starts as the knife hits the townsman, segues to saloon guitar-flute source music at :46, and goes out abruptly as Chico (Horst Buchholz) enters the saloon.

#11. Chico's Bravado (1:20) Music starts after Chico sinks down on the bar, plays Chris and Vin going to Chris' room, and goes out as the door swings open, revealing Lee (Robert Vaughn).

#12. The Journey (4:33) Music starts after Lee says, "There's a dry wash south of town. Pick me up there," and fades out on the ride into town as a villager yells, "Come out and make them welcome before we die of shame."

#13. Chico's Speech (1:43) Music starts on the cut to some of the villagers after one of them yells, "Who sounded the alarm?" and Chico answers, "I did," and segues to cue #14, on the dissolve to the villagers dancing after Chris says, "Now we are seven."

#14. Fiesta [Visual Source Music] (1:08) Music segues from cue #13, on the dissolve to the dancing, and ends abruptly as a villager tells them to stop the music.

#15. Stalking (1:14) Music segues from cue #14, on the cut to the long shot of Britt (James Coburn) and Lee moving on foot along the trail, and segues to cue #16, on the cut back to the fiesta.

#16. Meanwhile Back at the [Visual Source Music] (:32) Music segues from cue #15, on the cut to the fiesta, and segues abruptly (in progress) to cue #17, on the cut back to Britt.

#17. Small Suspense (:12) Music segues from cue #16, on the cut back to Britt, and segues to cue #18, on the cut back to the fiesta.

#18. Drum Improv [Visual Source Music] (:09) Music segues from cue #17, on the cut back to the fiesta, and segues to cue #19, on the cut to Chico.

#19. Worst Shot (2:55) Music segues from cue #18, on the cut to Chico, plays through Chris' talk to the villagers and the shooting lesson, and fades out under one of the villagers saying, "If Calvera does not come now, after all of this."

#20. Toro (3:16) Music starts after Harry says, "More work, less talk, huh," plays Chico and the bull, and Chico finding the woman, and goes out as his horse stops and he says, "Look what I found."

#21. Petra's Declaration (1:40) Music

starts just after the cut to Vin as he watches Chico and Petra ride off and says, "Gently, boy—gently," plays the dinner scene, and segues to cue #22, on the dissolve to the gun training.

#22. **Training** (1:32) Music segues from cue #21, on the dissolve to the training, and fades out as the old man says, "Buenos tardes."

#23. **Calvera's Return** (2:30) Music starts on the cut to Calvera's men after Vin says, "If, brother, if," and segues to cue #24, under Calvera's dialogue with Chris.

#24. **In the Trap** (3:07) Music segues from cue #23, under Calvera's dialogue with Chris, and goes out as the shooting begins.

#25. **Calvera Routed** (1:44) Music starts on the cut to Calvera's men riding out of town, and segues to cue #26, on the dissolve to the villagers celebrating.

#26. **Celebration [Source Music to Score]** (1:18) Music starts on the dissolve to the villagers celebrating, and goes out as the shooting begins again.

#27. **Ambush** (3:07) Music starts as Chico's hat is shot off, plays through the kids' dialogue with O'Reilly, and fades out under the villager asking, "Do your—hands sweat before a fight?"

#28. **Petra's Declaration** (1:44) Music starts as Vin smiles after he says, "Not for a long, long time," and fades out to a villager saying, "They got them—they got them all," as Chris and others return.

#29. **Quiet Moment** (:41) Music starts after the villager says, "Now, let's get out there on duty," and fades out to Chico saying, "That was—that was the greatest—"

#30. **Enemy Camp** (1:50) Music starts as Chico leaves after Chris says, "I'll write a song for you myself," plays through

Calvera's dialogue with his men, and builds to an abrupt ending before a villager says, "It's all right. You're all right. You had a dream."

#31. **Lee's Problem** (2:15) Music starts shortly after cue #30, after Lee says, "You feel it—then you wait . . ." and fades out on the cut to Harry and the villagers at the table.

#32. **Argument** (1:15) Music starts on Chris after he says, "Who's for going on and who's for giving up? I want to know now," and fades out under Vin saying, "I'm not saying we bit off more than we can chew . . ."

#33. **I Can't Give You Anything But** (2:14) Music starts after Chris says, "We'll lower the odds," and segues to cue #34, on the dissolve to the men riding.

#34. **Surprise** (2:04) Music segues from cue #33, on the dissolve to the men riding, and goes out before Calvera says, "You'll be dead, all of you. Like that . . ."

#35. **Defeat** (3:36) Music starts as Chris nods in agreement after Calvera says, "Only a crazy man makes the same mistake twice," and fades out as O'Reilly spanks one of the boys after the boy says, "Our fathers are cowards."

#36. **Crossroads** (4:44) Music starts on the cut to the seven men after Calvera says, "Adios," plays through their dialogue about going back into town to fight, and goes out with the first shot.

#37. **Calvera Routed** (:55) Music starts a few seconds after cue #36 ends, on the cut to Chris running, and goes out as Vin is shooting in the middle of the street.

#38. **Harry's Mistake** (2:44) Music starts as Harry is shot, and segues to cue #39, after Lee is shot.

#39. **Calvera Killed** (3:28) Music segues from cue #38, on the cut after Lee is shot, and segues to cue #40, on the dissolve to the villagers plowing.

#40. **Finale** (3:24) Music segues from cue #39, on the dissolve to the villagers plowing, and goes out to black at the end of the film.

#41. **End Titles** (1:16) [The end titles and cast of characters have been omitted from the commercially available videotape.]

THEMES

Elmer Bernstein points out that his score contains two principal themes: The "Magnificent Seven" theme, first heard in cue #1 (Main Title), and "Calvera's theme," heard first in cue #2 as we see Calvera and his men riding. "They had very, very specific functions," says Bernstein. "The general theme that people came to know was meant to be a general heroic theme for the seven. And there was a clear theme for the bad guys—very clearly delineated." The "Magnificent Seven" theme also includes a short theme/motif which functions as an introduction and interlude to the main theme but also stands on its own. This is first heard at the beginning of cue #1. There are also several themes with a Mexican/Spanish flavor which are used for the villagers and the relationship between Chico and Petra. "Subsequently, there were some more minor themes," Bernstein adds, "but they were secondary."

Other significant uses of the "Magnificent Seven" theme include cue #1; cue #6, played very softly in the trumpets under the dialogue between Chris and Vin; cue #8, as Vin and Chris ride; cue #10, played softly after Britt kills the challenging townsman, which serves to tie Britt and Chris together; cue #12, on the first dissolve to the ride as the men start their journey to the Mexican village; cue #34, on the ride to and from Calvera's camp; cue #35, used in a slow version under the dialogue between Chris and Vin; and cue #40, as they ride off. There is an interesting use of this

Bernstein created another theme for the outlaws—Calvera (Eli Wallach) and his gang—heard first in cue #2 as they ride to the small Mexican village.

theme at the beginning of cue #36, with a new musical setting.

You will hear the "Introduction" motif often; listen to cue #6—it plays several times near the beginning of the cue, and again after the men are back in town. As another example, it plays in the middle of cue #20, as Chico chases the young woman. Even the repeated-note rhythmic figuration first heard in cue #1 is treated as thematic material by Bernstein.

Other significant uses of "Calvera's theme" include cue #2, as we see Calvera and his men riding; cue #3, at the beginning and again as they ride off; cue #23, on Calvera's men near the beginning of the cue; cue #30, under Calvera's dialogue with his men; cue #34, during the last half of the cue as the seven are surrounded by Calvera's men;

and cue #38—a strong version during the last half as the villagers are freed and join the fight.

Some cues that include significant uses of the Mexican thematic materials include cue #3, played as the villagers discuss the need to "do something"; cue #4; cue #25, as Chris looks around, and later as the villagers realize what they've done; cue #27, played under the dialogue between O'Reilly and the three boys; cue #28; cue #33, for Chico and Petra; cue #39, as O'Reilly dies; and cue #40, played under the dialogue with the old man, the scene with Chico and Petra, and the three boys at O'Reilly's grave.

As important as the bold statement of themes and motifs can be in any film score, the manner in which these elements are manipulated and developed can be significant as well. The effective and artistic development of these thematic materials is a measure of the finesse and excellence of any score. The eight film scores represented in this chapter all offer clear examples of this quality. To study how Bernstein develops his thematic material in *The Magnificent Seven,* listen to cue #24, in which motifs from both "Calvera's theme" and the "Magnificent Seven" theme are interwoven. The beginning of cue #5 is fine example of Bernstein's development of the opening two notes of his main theme.

:00	Dissolve to the seven men riding ["Magnificent Seven" theme at :10]
:23	Men get off horses
:37	Men sneak up to Calvera's camp
:56	Dialogue
1:16	Dissolve to the men riding back to town
1:27	Men get off horses
1:38	Door opens suddenly, revealing Calvera's men ["Calvera's theme" at 1:43]
2:04	Music out before Calvera says, "You'll be dead, all of you. Like that . . ."

Phrasing the drama with the music is effective because the music is able to underline and emphasize the dramatic elements, but good film scoring also avoids emphasizing insignificant moments. Notice, for instance, that the score near the end of cue #20 does not hit the cut to the villagers digging a ditch, even though this cut changes the location of the action from Chico back to the town. Because the action at this point concerns Chico finding the young woman, the music stays with that moment and continues that image right through the cut of the villagers. The film then cuts back smoothly to Chico riding toward town with the same feel in the music.

PLAYING THE DRAMA

The score for *The Magnificent Seven* phrases the drama throughout. Important dramatic shifts of emphasis are hit, including cuts or dissolves to the seven or Calvera's men riding purposefully. A study of almost any cue will illustrate this technique of film scoring very clearly. In cue #12, for instance, the "Magnificent Seven" theme hits hard on the dissolve to the men riding after they pick up Chico.

Cue #34 is an example this scoring technique. Check the following outline of the dramatic sequence as you listen.

SOURCE MUSIC

There are a number of cues in which the score functions as though it is source music, playing through the drama with guitars and flutes as though there are several villagers playing quietly off screen.

Bernstein segues smoothly from score to source. In cue #7, for example, the score changes to off-screen piano for the saloon. Reversing the process, he also goes from source music to score, as in cue #26. The celebration sequence is scored with source music played by the villagers, which then segues to orchestral score near the end of the scene.

TEMPO AND PULSE

The rhythmic drive of Bernstein's main themes and overall dramatic approach to this score is largely responsible for its success as a film score and as a theme that has become a standard in the repertoire of American music. During the early reels of the film, it is often Bernstein's score that pushes the film forward and gives it momentum. Watch especially cue #12 to see how this works. In this cue, the men are riding slowly toward the Mexican village while the powerful music adds an urgency not on the screen.

Close Encounters of the Third Kind   1977
Music by John Williams.
Orchestrated by Herbert Spencer. Directed by Steven Spielberg. Richard Dreyfuss, Francois Truffaut, Teri Garr, Melinda Dillon, Cary Guffey, Bob Balaban.

Unlike most films, *Close Encounters* required the composition of one of the main themes prior to shooting, as the short motif used to communicate with the aliens was incorporated into the film's footage. John Williams tried over 250 different five-note motifs before arriving at the one used as the "communication" motif for the spaceship. Williams initially leaned more toward a seven-note motif, but Spielberg was concerned that the longer motif might sound too much like a melody, or at least the beginning of a melody rather than the unfinished sound of a short motif.

SYNOPSIS

Under the guidance of Claude Lacombe (Francois Truffaut) a select group of scientists and military personnel has been researching UFOs and other related phenomena around the world. They discover an airplane that has been missing since World War

In *Close Encounters of the Third Kind* (1977), when Roy (Richard Dreyfuss) and Jillian (Melinda Dillon) are obsessed with the inexplicable image of a mysterious mountain, John Williams uses a theme that represents not only the mountain but also the spiritual empowerment of the close encounter. As an example, listen to #46, beginning on the cut to the scientists after the exchange of hand signals.
Copyright © 1977 Columbia Pictures Industries, Inc. All Rights Reserved.

II, and a crowd in India that is chanting a five-note tune they claim to have heard coming from the sky. In Ohio, Roy Neary (Richard Dreyfuss) is called out to troubleshoot when his town suffers a local power outage. When he sights UFOs, he is overwhelmed by the experience and brings back his wife Ronnie (Teri Garr) and two sons, hoping they will see the spaceships. He returns to the same spot the following night, and sees a small boy, Barry (Cary Guffey), and his mother, Jillian (Melissa Dillon), whom he met at the previous night's sighting. Barry disappears during the arrival of a UFO at Jillian and Barry's house. Increasingly obsessed with their vision of an unusually shaped mountain, Roy and Jillian each drive to a secluded area of Wyoming when they see the exact image of this mountain on a television newscast announcing that the Army is evacuating everyone anywhere near the mountain due to a poisonous gas leak. When they meet again near the site, they are apprehended by the Army, but escape up the mountain. The mother ship lands, returning many servicemen thought to be missing in action, and also Barry, who is reunited with his mother. Roy is chosen by the space visitors to join them on their ship.

STYLE AND CONCEPT

John Williams' score utilizes elements from several musical sources, including impressionism (hinting at Ravel), romanticism, 12-tone devices, tonal clusters (groups of notes in close proximity), aleatoric sections (where the instrumentalists have some freedom within given parameters), and the motivic influences of Bernard Herrmann's film music in scores like *Psycho* and *North by Northwest*. Scored for large symphony orchestra, his score supports both the action and the idea of the film.

As is often the case with full-scale orchestral film scores, the concept is based largely on the style of the music, and the method of working with the thematic elements. One of the key conceptual elements in this score is built into the screenplay itself—that is, the "communication motif," which is integrated into the plot and also the score. Another central idea in this score is the deliberate contrast between the dissonant symphonic statements used to create suspense and tension—underlining our natural fear of the unknown—and the more flowing, ethereal, yet romantic moments which reflect the irresistible attraction of a close encounter of the third kind.

Close Encounters was released in 1977, the same year as Williams' first definitive epic space score, *Star Wars*. Both were nominated for Academy Awards; *Star Wars* won the Oscar. With these two

works, Williams established the musical language that would be used for this genre of film for years to come. In addition to the above-listed influences for *Close Encounters, Star Wars* had its own role models, including Holst's "The Planets" (1916) and the epic action/adventure film scores of Korngold. Nevertheless, in film music, the measure of originality frequently depends upon the creation of a fresh combination of previously established musical elements and styles, and that is so in this case. There was, in fact, relatively little symphonic film scoring at all in the seventies, except for Williams' own scores to the earlier *Poseidon Adventure* (1972), *The Towering Inferno* (1974), and *Jaws* (1975). The decade did include other symphonic scores, although they were decidely in the minority. Jerry Goldsmith's outstanding symphonic scores included *Patton* (1970), *The Wind and the Lion* (1975), *The Omen* (1976), and *Islands in the Stream* (1977). Herrmann, Bernstein (*The Shootist,* 1976), and others had contributed a few. But until *Star Wars* and *Close Encounters,* big science fiction films hadn't been made for years—sci-fi was considered a dead genre. After 1977, it was a genre that bore Williams' imprint.

SPOTTING

Close Encounters was released at 135 minutes, and re-edited to 132 minutes in the 1980 special edition, which is used here. The score is approximately 61 1/4 minutes long, plus the source music and all the communication cues. The spotting is very sparse during the early part of the film. The last 27 minutes of music (almost half of the score) doesn't begin until the arrival of the first spaceship at the spaceport (cue #39). The placement of music often defers to the sound effects, with music either withheld until after the effects make their statement, or fading out so that sound effects can take over.

In the notes below, Williams' cue titles have

been retained as much as possible, with occasional clarifying titles in brackets.

#1. Main Title (1:30) Music starts on the "Richard Dreyfuss" card, not at the very beginning of the titles, continues with a single high note which sustains softly under the sound effects of the winds, and goes out under the dialogue in the desert.

#2. Navy Planes/Lost Squadron (3:45) Music starts as the men run toward the airship, and fades out on the cut to air control.

#3. Phonograph Source Music—"The Square Song" (Joe Raposo; :59) Source music starts as the phonograph suddenly turns on after the toy monkey begins clapping its cymbals, and fades out after Barry is downstairs.

#4. Eleven Commandments [TV Movie Source Music] (:35) Music starts as one of Roy's sons swings the TV set around toward the camera, and goes out as the power shuts down.

#5. Car Radio Source Music (:08) Music starts during the electrical disturbance as Roy is checking his map, and goes out a few seconds later.

#6. Trucking [The First Sighting] (1:35) Music starts sporadically as Roy listens to the excited cross-talk on his CB, and goes out abruptly as his truck screeches to a stop.

#7. The First Encounter (:20) Music starts on the last second of the shot of Jillian and Barry on the road with their backs to camera, and goes out as the spaceships approach.

#8. Radio Source Music—"Love Song of the Waterfall" (Bob Nolan, Bernard Barnes, and Carol Wing; :24) Music starts in progress on the cut to the tollbooth, and goes out with the sound effects of the spaceships as they pass through.

#9. The Next Encounter [Chase Spaceships] (:35) Music starts on the high shot of the tollbooth as the police cars go through, and goes out on the shot of the ships against the sky.

#10. Mountain Visions [Waiting/Gobi Desert] (2:55) Music starts as Ronnie begins, "I remember when we used to come to places like this just to look at each other . . ." and fades out on the shot of the newspaper.

#11. Shaving Cream Mountain (:23) Music starts as Roy contemplates the mound of shaving cream in his hand, and fades out as Ronnie says, ". . . I want you to spray it on half of your face . . ."

#12. Indian Chant (2:00) Vocal chanting (sometimes visual on screen) starts after the cut to Dharmsala, India, and goes out as the tape recorder is stopped. This chant consists of the same pitches as the "communication motif," but in a slightly different form.

#13. Introducing the Communication Motif Lacombe explains the Kodaly hand signs to a group of scientists, leading to a complete statement of the "communication motif."

#14. Dirt Mountain (:15) Music starts as Roy stares at the mountain shaped out of dirt, and goes out as he says, "I know this sounds crazy . . ."

#15. The Second Sighting (1:30) Music starts as Roy touches Barry's dirt mountain, and goes out under the sound effects of the wind and helicopter.

#16. Communication Motif (:12) The motif starts in progress on the cut to the satellite dish, and goes out on the cut to dialogue. Although later integrated into the score, the motif is sounded by a synthesizer as part of the sound effects.

#17. Communication Motif The motif (sounded by a synthesizer) starts during the dialogue in the research center at Goldstone Radio Telescope, and goes out on the final, "Excuse me."

#18. Communication Motif Lacombe plays the motif on screen on a keyboard in the research center.

#19. Communication Motif Barry plays the motif on screen on a toy metal xyophone.

#20. The Storm (1:35) Music starts on the clouds just before the move in to a close-up of Barry looking out the window, and goes out as Jillian closes the door.

#21. The Fireplace (:30) Music starts as Jillian grabs Barry to move him away from the fireplace, and goes out as the chimney flue slams shut.

#22. Visual Phonograph Source Music— "Chances Are" (Al Stillman and Robert Allen, sung by Johnny Mathis; :50) Source music starts in progress, overlapping cue #21, and goes out on the sound effect of the grate exploding.

#23. Barry Kidnapped (1:45) Music overlaps the source music, starting as the screw begins to turn open on the grate, and goes out when the sound effects subside as all the appliances stop shaking.

#24. Warehouse Scene (2:30) Music starts on the cut to the vans, and goes out with an accent just before the cut to Ronnie and her family at the dinner table.

#25. Forming the Mountain (1:15) Music starts as the camera moves in on the clay mountain Roy is sculpting, and fades out on Ronnie waking up.

#26. Forming the Mountain (Part 2) (:30) Music starts on the cut to a close-up of the clay mountain, and slowly fades out on the time lapse to the next morning, as Roy sleeps.

#27. Visual TV Cartoon Source Music— "Duck Dodgers in the 24 1/2th Century" (Carl Stalling; 1:38) Music segues from cue #26 after the time lapse to the next morning, and goes out on the cut to Ronnie and kids.

#27A. Visual Music Box Source Music— "When You Wish Upon a Star" (Ned Washington and Leigh Harline; :23) Music starts in progress as Roy bumps a small Pinocchio music box while cleaning up his UFO clippings. At this point the music box effect plays simultaneously with cue #27 as the cartoon music continues. It winds down to a stop as Roy pulls the top off of his clay mountain.

#28. TV Soap Opera Source Music— "Theme from Days of Our Lives" (T. Boyce, C. Albertine and B. Hart; :20) Source music starts in progress on the cut to Roy after Ronnie has driven off with the kids.

#29. TV Soap Opera Source Music #2 (:13)

#30. TV Soap Opera Source Music #3 (:13)

#31. TV Jingle Source Music—"Here Comes the King" (Steve Karmen; :24) The Budweiser jingle plays during the commercial.

#32. Television Reveals {The Mountain on TV} (1:30) Music starts as Roy sees the mountain on TV, and goes out on the cut to Roy reading a map in his car.

#33. Across the Fields {They Drive} (1:10) Music starts on the cut to Roy and Jillian in the car after they meet, and comes to a sustained note as their car stops.

#34. The Mountain (3:25) Music segues from cue #33 on the cut to a 2-shot as the camera moves in on them, and goes out as David (Bob Balaban) says, "We have very little time."

#35. Who Are You People (1:35) Music starts on the cut to Army vehicles after

Roy says, "Who the hell are you people?" and goes out on the cut to David and Lacombe with officer.

#36. The Escape (1:35) Music starts on the cut back to David and Lacombe after Roy and Jillian take off their gas masks, and fades out under the sound of the helicopter.

#37. Climbing the Mountain (3:45) Music starts on the cut to the three running after, "Tell them we're gonna dust," and comes to a sustained note as Roy and Jillian stop at the top of the mountain and look down.

#38. Mountain Spaceport (:40) Segues from cue #37 as they look out at the spaceport, and goes out under the loudspeaker dialogue, "One, two, three—testing."

#39. The Light Show [Spaceships Arrive] (2:50) Music starts as the ships approach, and fades out as the supervisor says, "Go ahead," and they prepare to send signals.

#40. Communication Motif Played repeatedly on a synthesizer as the spaceship arrives, and answered by the spaceship.

#41. The Approach (4:00) Music starts as the large cloud moves toward the spaceport, and goes out as Roy descends to the spaceport grounds.

#42. Communication Motif The motif begins immediately after the last note of cue #41.

#43. Arrival of the Mother Ship (1:50) Music starts as a man in white uniform bumps into Roy as he looks up at the mother ship, and fades out under a voice coming from the loudspeaker saying, "All departments at operational during this phase, signify by beeping twice."

#44. The Conversation (3:11) A musical dialogue between the spaceport and the mother ship begins immediately, retard-

ing to end softly just before the mother ship begins to open.

#45. The Pilots Return (3:35) Music begins just after the mother ship begins to open, and fades out as Lacombe says to Roy, ". . . What do you want?"

#46. The Visitors/Mother Ship/End Titles (14:30) Music starts as the ship opens again, and continues with overlapping cues through the end of the film and the end credits.

THEMES

Close Encounters is alternately thematic and textural. The two main themes are actually short motifs. Depending on the orchestration and dynamics, they can stand out as themes or function unobtrusively as part of the texture when a nonthematic approach is best, and in this way they help unify the score.

The "mountain motif," a smooth, lyrical motif, is used to play the powerful spiritual attraction and mystery of the mountain, the spaceships, and the space visitors. It is heard clearly for the first time accompanying Roy as he says, "This means something," while Roy is looking at the dirt mountain.

The "tension motif" is used to create varying degrees of dissonance, to suggest excitement, and to reflect apprehension and anxiety. It is first heard near the very end of cue #6, in short, plucked-sounding notes. Its first clear use is in cue #15, as Roy and the others stare at the spaceships.

A "high sustained string texture" is another musical idea used repeatedly (especially early in the film) to heighten the sense that something is going to happen. Even though it doesn't have a melodic line, the texture itself is as much a thematic idea as the motifs. This material is first used at the very beginning of cue #1.

A fourth thematic idea, the "Baroque action theme," is used for several of the action sequences, beginning with the last part of cue #24, on the

Bars 17 through 24 of cue #34 (The Mountain) of John Williams' score for *Close Encounters of the Third Kind* (1977) contain two of the score's main motifs. The "mountain motif" begins in bar 19, as Roy and Jillian see the mountain. Williams adds the "tension motif" in bar 21 played by the woodwinds while the strings sustain the preceding phrase.

Close Encounters of the Third Kind (John Williams)

Copyright © 1977 Columbia Pictures Industries, Inc.

second cut after the officer says, ". . . of every living Christian soul."

The "communication motif," largely functioning as visual source music, is used by the scientists and space vistors to communicate with one another. It is first heard in cue #13, as Lacombe explains the Kodaly hand signs to a group of scientists.

The pop song "When You Wish upon a Star" (from Walt Disney's *Pinocchio*) has been interpolated several times into the score, first played by a Pinocchio music box, and toward the end of the film integrated into the score several times.

Other significant moments played by the "mountain motif" include: cue #15, on the close 2-shot of a gray-haired couple and through the shot of the spaceships; on the clay mountain at the beginning of cue #26, using the same sound and feeling without using the exact motif; cue #32, as Roy sees the mountain on television; at the beginning of cue #34, on the move-in to Jillian and Roy, and then a fuller version as the mountain is revealed (accompanied by the "tension motif"); the end of cue #36, beginning on the shot of Lacombe as he watches them escape and the shot of them running (also accompanied by the "tension motif"); played quietly just before the end of cue #38, on the shot of the mountain spaceport; cue #43, as the ship comes in to land (suggested by the violins, but not used exactly) and a full orchestral version as the ship lands (heard again with the "tension motif"); cue #46, on the cut to the scientists after the space visitor returns Lacombe's hand signals, and again during the End Titles, beginning on Dreyfuss' credit.

Other significant moments played by the "tension motif" include: cue #32, used during the first part of the cue, while the TV reveals the mountain, in a smooth, flowing fashion played first by the strings and subsequently by the woodwinds, and later as Roy drives played as a series of short notes; cue #33, in which the motif is suggested at the beginning of the cue, is played smoothly and elongated as Roy breaks through the fence, and then is further developed as they drive; cue #34, with development as Roy and Jillian walk up the hill, and

then softly along with the "mountain motif" as the mountain is revealed, continuing through their drive past the dead cattle; the second half of cue #37, in which the motif is developed beginning on the cut back to the three climbing the mountain after the helicopter takes off, as Roy says, "Larry—come on"; and cue #46, after Roy has looked around inside the ship, as he breathes heavily.

Other significant moments played by the "high sustained string texture" include: cue #7, overlapping the whistling of "She'll Be Coming 'Round the Mountain"; and the beginning of cue #10, used in a less dissonant version until the cut to the Gobi Desert, at which point the notes in the high cluster change to a more dissonant, tension-producing sound.

Other significant moments played by the "Baroque action theme" include the beginning of cue #35.

Other significant moments played within the score by the "communication motif" include: on Jillian in cue #43, played by the cellos after the full shot of the mother ship; near the beginning of cue #46, played by the cellos on the shot of the ship just after the space visitor has been revealed and before they come out of the ship; again in cue #46, as Lacombe gives hand signals to the visitor; later in cue #46, as the ship lifts off just prior to the End Titles; and finally, during the last moments of cue #46, performed with voices.

Other significant moments played by "When You Wish upon a Star" include: cue #46, as Dreyfus is led toward the ship; later in cue #46, after he has looked around the ship's interior (played by the French horns); and during the End Titles.

PLAYING THE DRAMA

Williams plays *Close Encounters* in a very traditional way, accenting significant moments and cuts, and shifting the emotional quality and texture of the music with the flow of the drama. The harmonic language, however, incorporates many twentieth-century devices, which makes the score sound much more current than, for example, *Dark Victory*.

The "mountain motif" and the "tension motif" recur regularly and as needed, frequently playing simultaneously, and are well developed throughout the score. (Cue #33 is an easily heard example of the development of the "tension motif.")

Surges and accents occur within the flow of the score as needed for emphasis. The following moments are good examples of strong accents used by Williams for emphasis:

Cue #1
on the cut to the desert

Cue #2
on opening the door of the airplane
on the photograph in the cockpit
on the calendar in the cockpit

Cue #20
on the unusual light coming through the keyhole

Cue #39
on the last small light to enter the spaceport area before they begin to send signals

SOURCE MUSIC

The most important source music in *Close Encounters* is the five-note "communication motif," which is used many times as a plot device. Even Barry picks it out on his toy metal xylophone (cue #19). Source music is also used more than once to demonstrate the disruption of electric power caused by the spaceships (examples of this include the children's song in cue #3, the country song at the toll booth in cue #8, and Johnny Mathis singing "Chances Are" in cue #22). The music accompanying the cartoon in cue #40 is appropriate for the

cartoon, but actually adds emotional power to the end of this sequence when Roy is staring at the dirt mountain. Although costly to license, using the Budweiser jingle instead of a newly-created jingle for that cue gives the scene an added touch of reality. Listen for the man whistling "She'll Be Coming 'Round the Mountain" on-screen during cue #6. This is considered to be visual source music (it most likely was post-recorded). By playing *against* the scene and the score, the whistling adds another mysterious element to the drama.

TEMPO AND PULSE

The "Baroque action theme" gives those scenes it plays added drive, and some of the more dissonant, modern-sounding cues have a strong rhythmic push. The "tension motif" is used for drive when necessary, and more lyrically elsewhere.

The Untouchables   1987
Music by Ennio Morricone.
Directed by Brian De Palma. Kevin Costner, Sean Connery, Robert De Niro, Charles Martin Smith, Andy Garcia.

SYNOPSIS

During Prohibition in Chicago in 1930, Eliot Ness (Kevin Costner) is assigned by the Treasury Department "to inaugurate a special program to deal with the flow of illegal liquor and the violence which it creates." After a false start, he and his team of three other crime fighters raid a storehouse of bootleg liquor, their first step toward the indictment and conviction of Al Capone (Robert De Niro). Ultimately,

The "Untouchables," left to right: George Stone (Andy Garcia), Jim Malone (Sean Connery), Eliot Ness (Kevin Costner), and Oscar Wallace (Charles Martin Smith). Ennio Morricone's score for *The Untouchables* (1987) combines a traditional musical approach and sound with the occasional addition of contemporary drumming which gives added edge to the Main Title and some of the action sequences.
Photo courtesy of Paramount Pictures
Copyright © 1987 by Paramount Pictures. All Rights Reserved.

by capturing Capone's accountant and obtaining his ledgers for Capone's business operations, they are able to bring him to court on charges of federal income tax evasion, but not without personal sacrifice and loss of life.

STYLE AND CONCEPT

Although Morricone's score does not play off of the 1930s period at all, he basically takes a very traditional approach in this score; the scenes with Eliot Ness and his family have a warm, romantic setting; the tragic moments sound rich, somber, and reminiscent of Nino Rota's tragic/romantic main theme for *Romeo and Juliet* (1968); and the heroic and triumphant moments are played appropriately by the brass, supported by strings.

The strongest conceptual element in the score is the use of simple, powerful after-beat drumming as an important instrumental color for the more aggressive tension music in the score. Used this way, the drums add a contemporary element and edge to this period picture without making the music seem too anachronistic. By 1987 the blending of synthesizers and drum machines with orchestra was not unusual; the exceptionally exposed use of drums in this context (with no contemporary keyboards or other rhythm sounds) made Morricone's score stand out at that time. Using this idea for the Main Titles also helped in this regard, giving it immediate exposure.

SPOTTING

The Untouchables is 119 minutes long and contains approximately 50:18 minutes of score, plus two source cues (an additional 2:28)—which is about average for a film like this. The spotting is effective and well balanced, utilizing natural sounds in several key dramatic moments. Scenes played without music include Ness' first warehouse break-in, his confrontation with Capone in Capone's hotel lobby, and Nitti's murder of Malone. There are several short cues, including cue #9, which plays the aftermath of Capone's vicious murder of one of his men with a baseball bat. Even though it is only :18 long, it is quite effective because it plays immediately after such a strong moment. Cue #12 is even shorter, playing the action as Ness and his men turn and run down the street to begin their trip to the Canadian border. This cue, however, is less dramatically effective than cue #9, sounding much more like a gratuitous bridge.

The titles are taken from the cue sheet, as are the cue numbers in parenthesis. There is no M4 indicated on the cue sheet, and other numbers are also skipped.

#1. The Strength of the Righteous Man (Main Title; M1) (2:28) Music starts

on "Paramount Pictures Presents," and goes out with a final accent on the cut to the overhead shot of Al Capone (Robert De Niro) being shaved.

#2. **"Mood Indigo" (M2)** (Duke Ellington, Irving Mills, and Barney Bigard; 1:32) Music starts on the cut to the street after the above scene with Capone, and goes out on the bomb exploding.

#3. **Ness and His Family—Part I (M3)** (1:36) Music starts as a hand tears a page from the wall calendar, and plays through the scene with Ness and his wife Catherine (Patricia Clarkson). Music goes out on the cut to the Police Chief (Richard Bradford) introducing Ness at the press conference.

#4. **False Alarm (M5)** (1:07) Music fades in on the cut to Ness' point of view as he sees a man standing on the street, and goes out as Scoop, the reporter, turns around and says, "Mr. Ness."

#5. **Ness Meets Malone (M6)** (1:18) Music starts on the dissolve to Ness walking down the stairs of the bridge after the break-in, and goes out as he throws his wife's note in the river, just before Jim Malone (Sean Connery) says, "Now, what do you think you're doing?"

#6. **Al Capone—Part II (M7)** (1:35) Music starts just before the cut to the newspapers landing on the red carpet, and fades out to the two-shot of the two cops.

#7. **A Mother's Plea (M8)** (:50) Music starts after, "It was my little girl that got killed by that bomb," and goes out on the cut to Ness standing on the street corner.

#8. **Victorious (M11)** (2:07) Music starts as Oscar Wallace (Charles Martin Smith) looks at the gun in his hands, continues through the raid, and goes out on the cut to Ness, Malone, Oscar, and George Stone (Andy Garcia) sitting at the table.

#9. **Murderous (M12)** (:18) Music starts on Capone after he has murdered one of his men with a baseball bat, and goes out on the cut to Ness.

#10. **Goodnights (M13)** (1:16) Music starts just after the above cut at the end of M12, as Ness' wife and daughter begin to pray off-screen, and goes out as Ness holds up a newspaper for Oscar to see.

#11. **Nitti Harasses Ness (M14)** (:55) Music fades in on the cut to Ness walking with a gift under his arm, and goes out as the camera pans to his daughter.

#12. **Waiting for What? (M16)** (:11) Music starts after Ness says, "Well, what are we doin' standing here, then?" and goes out on the cut to Oscar looking at the ledger.

#13. **Montana Intro (M17)** (:28) Music starts during the long pan to men on horseback, and goes out as Ness says, "A convoy of five to ten trucks. . ."

#14. **Waiting at the Border (M18)** (2:28) Music starts after Malone says, ". . . and standing in the rain," just before the dissolve to the bridge, and goes out as Ness and his men approach the horses.

#15. **The Untouchables (M19)** (3:02) Music starts while the gang exchanges money for liquor barrels, as Ness says, "Malone, you and I will take the . . . ," continues through the raid, and goes out after Oscar knocks out one of the gang.

#16. **Surprise Attack (M20)** (:40) Music starts on the cut to the cabin just after M19, continues through Ness stalking another gang member, and goes out as Ness bursts into the cabin, shouting, "all right . . ."

#17. **Dead Man's Bluff (M21)** (:30) Music starts as Malone sees the dead man on the porch, and goes out as Malone shoots him.

#18. **Ness and His Family—Part II (M22)** (1:11) Music starts on the cut to the baby as Ness and his wife discuss his name, and goes out on the cut to the district attorney speaking to the reporters.

#19. In the Elevator (M23) (1:05) Music starts as Nitti moves into frame, dressed as a cop assigned to run the elevator, and goes out as Nitti shoots the witness.

#20. Four Friends (M24) (2:46) Music starts almost immediately after the end of M23, just after Oscar is shot, as Ness and Malone react to the gunshots. Music continues as they find Oscar dead in the elevator, and goes out on the cut to Ness walking toward Capone's hotel.

#21. Payne and Bowtie (M25-A) (:13) Music starts on the cut to Capone's accountant reading the newspaper, and goes out on the cut to the chief shooting pool.

#22. Al Capone—Part I (M26) (:21) Music starts on the cut to the opera house staircase, and goes out as Capone turns to speak to the reporters.

#23. The Man with the Matches (M27) (2:44) Music starts on the cut to Malone's apartment building, continues as Capone's man stalks Malone, and goes out as Malone pulls the shotgun from his phonograph.

#24. "Vesti la Giubba" (no M number; by Leoncavallo, from the opera *I Pagliacci*) (:56) Source music starts as Malone crawls across the floor before the cut to the opera, and goes out on the cut to Ness' car stopping outside Malone's building.

#25. Malone's Death (M30) (2:12) Music starts on the cut to Malone's blood as Ness calls out, and goes out as Capone and the opera singer clink glasses.

#26. Machine Gun Lullaby—Part I (M31) (5:16) Music starts during the cut to the close-up of the railroad station clock reading 11:56, continues as Ness pulls the baby carriage up the steps, and goes out as he shoots the man with the bandaged nose.

#27. Machine Gun Lullaby—Part II (M32) (1:55) Music fades in a few seconds after the above cue, on the cut after the man who has been shot crashes through the glass door, continues through the gunfight, and goes out as the accountant yells, "What are you doing?"

#28. Kill Bowtie (M33) (:25) Music starts as the gangster holding a gun on the accountant falls after Stone shoots him, and goes out on the cut to the courtroom.

#29. Courthouse Chase (M34) (1:36) Music starts after Ness strikes the match, as he sees Malone's address written on the inside of the matchbook, continues through the chase to the courthouse roof, and goes out as Ness rolls off the roof.

#30. On the Rooftops (M35) (2:32) Music starts just after Ness shoots Nitti, continues through the chase, and goes out on the cut to Nitti after Ness uncocks his gun.

#31. Nitti's Fall (M36) (:20) Music starts a moment after Nitti says to Ness, "Now you think about that when I beat the rap," and goes out as Nitti crashes onto the car below.

#32. He's in the Car (M37) (:10) Music starts just before the cut to Nitti after Ness says, "He's in the car," and goes out on the cut to the judge's chambers.

#33. Swap Juries (M38) (:15) Music starts on the cut to Ness smiling after Capone's attorney says, ". . . and enter a plea of 'Guilty,'" and goes out as Capone struggles to free himself from being restrained.

#34. Here Endeth the Lesson (M38-A) (:23) Music starts on Ness after he says, "Here endeth the lesson," and goes out on the cut to him looking at newspaper clippings.

#35. **Death Theme (M39)** (2:40) Music starts on the close-up of the photograph of "The Untouchables," continues as Ness and Stone say goodbye, and fades out as Ness walks away before the cut to the street.

#36. **The Untouchables (End Title) (M40)** (3:54) Music starts after Scoop says, "What will you do then?" continues through the end titles, and goes out just before the end of the title crawl.

The two family scenes with Ness are spotted from the beginning of the scene, not from any specific dramatic moment within the scene (cues #3 and #18). By spotting this way, these cues become a part of the ambiance of the scenes themselves, but cannot point up a significant moment in the drama by entering at any particular moment. On the other hand, the music for cue #4 doesn't start on the cut to the street at the beginning of the stakeout, but waits for a more specific dramatic motivation—the moment when Ness sees the man standing on the street. This spotting allows the music to create a dramatic emphasis just by entering the scene.

Several cues sound as though they were re-printed from another part of the score and added to the film in dubbing. In some films this is done to add a new cue where none was spotted. Since Morricone creates cues that are designed to be played for more than one scene (with several cue numbers and routines), it is possible that he intended these cues to play just as they are dubbed on the soundtrack. For example, cue #10 may be a re-print of the family theme—it seems to simply fade out in the middle of a musical phrase at the appropriate place in the picture. Similarly, cue #33 (:15) also sounds like it was added during dubbing. This technique is not at all unusual, and doesn't necessarily detract in any way from the score, but music editors generally splice ("intercut") sections of cues together to create a new cue that sounds as though it was recorded just like the spliced version. The effectiveness of this technique depends entirely on how successfully the reprinted music works with the scene, and, to a lesser extent, how well it is edited and/or mixed on the soundtrack.

THEMES

The score for *The Untouchables* is primarily melodic, and is developed from five basic themes: the "Untouchables theme" (heard for the first time in cue #8, as Ness and his men go to raid the storehouse); the "action theme" (heard for the first time throughout the Main Title); the "Capone theme" (heard in its basic form in the Main Title accompanied by the "action theme," and in a more chromatic version in cue #6, as Capone is brought his breakfast); the "family theme" (heard for the first time in cue #3); and the "death theme" (heard for the first time in cue #5). Another piece of material, the "tension theme" (heard first in cue #4) is primarily high sustained strings, but often has the "Capone theme" playing against it.

Other significant moments played by the "Untouchables theme" include the ride to the bridge and the gunfighting in cue #15; cue #34, which plays the end of the courtroom scene; and the end credits (cue #36).

Other significant moments played by the "action theme" include the second half of cue #11, after Ness realizes that Nitti's warning is serious and he turns to rush into his house; the end of cue #23, as Nitti moves in on Malone to kill him; cue #28, which plays on the shot of the accountant after the gangster holding him has been killed; cue #29, after Nitti shoots the cop; and cue #30, throughout the chase (with the "Capone theme" occasionally added).

Other significant moments played by the "Capone theme" include Capone's accountant ready to leave town (cue #21), and Capone at the opera house (cue #22).

The "tension theme," often used along with a version of the "Capone theme," can be heard in cue

The first four bars of an ensemble statement of Ennio Morricone's "Untouchables theme" for *The Untouchables* (1987). The orchestration is in the composer's hand; here the woodwinds are playing a fast figuration in counterpoint to the high violin melody. This orchestration of the theme is used for the big upbeat moments, including the walk to the post office in cue #8 and the ride to the bridge in cue #15.

The Untouchables (Ennio Morricone)

Copyright © 1987 by Famous Music Corporation

#4; cue #11; cue #19; at the beginning of cue #23, as Nitti moves toward Malone's apartment; and at the beginning of cue #29, as Ness sees Malone's address written on Nitti's matchbook.

Other significant moments played by the "family theme" include Ness and his family as their daughter prays and goes to bed in cue #10, and cue #18, as Ness and his wife discuss their baby's name and Ness' job.

Other significant moments played by the "death theme" include Ness on the bridge after his first (unsuccessful) raid, played here by a solo alto sax accompanied by strings in order to suggest a more personal downbeat, meditative attitude rather than the suggestion of loss of life; Ness' visit with the dead girl's mother (cue # 7); Oscar's death (cue #20); Malone's death (cue #25); and cue #35, which plays Ness' thoughts about his friends and their experiences, and his goodbye to Stone (with the theme played by the alto sax again).

PLAYING THE DRAMA

Morricone plays the drama with strength in *The Untouchables,* but largely with an overview approach, without hitting a lot of nuances within each scene. Most of the cues are dubbed with a full, rich sound, and some are scored to end loud for dramatic effect (such as cue #11, on the pan over to Ness' daughter, and cue #28, leading to the cut to the courtroom scene).

Cue #25, which plays Malone's death, is a good example of Morricone's score playing *through* the drama, without catching any of the action or emphasizing anything specifically with the music.

Cue #15 demonstrates how Morricone plays the drama when he is acknowledging particular moments in the action. Although the score plays through much of the drama, notice the shifts in emphasis from the bold, heroic treatment of the "Untouchables theme" as Ness and his men ride toward the bridge, to other material as the scene develops on the bridge. Key dramatic moments are played with changes in the musical material and dynamics.

Cue #11 contains a clear shift in dramatic emphasis and material, from the tension material with a suggestion of the "Capone" theme to the "action theme." Similarly, in cue #29, the "tension theme" shifts to the "action theme" after Nitti shoots the cop.

The harmonica-like sound stating the "Capone theme" on Nitti opening his matchbook with Malone's address on it near the start of cue #23, as Nitti stalks Malone for the kill, is a good example of Morricone pointing to a specific dramatic moment in the film through the entrance of a theme at that precise instant.

Cue # 4 is a red herring, building suspense up to the moment that Scoop turns around with his camera in his hand. Although the high, sustained strings play the greatest role in developing the tension, the soft melody that plays with the strings is a shortened version of the "Capone theme," which also contributes to the overall effect. The first half of cue #11 is based on the same material, as Nitti (sitting in his car) warns Ness.

The use of music and sound effects during the stake-out and shoot-out in the train station is highly stylized. Cue #26 begins with a children's tune played on a celesta-like keyboard, which is then joined bit by bit by the orchestra playing in another key. This gives a strange, surrealistic tone to the scene. The use of sound effects is very selective throughout this sequence. Important sounds are emphasized, including significant footsteps, shots, and the sounds of the baby carriage going up and down the steps. Others are left out completely, including the mother shouting "My baby" as the carriage rolls down the steps. Announcements of incoming and outgoing trains are omitted, as is the usual crowd noise, or "walla," normally added to a train station scene. The result is a very clean and dramatically powerful soundtrack in which every sound is important and is heard clearly.

Ennio Morricone goes over a passage of his score for *The Untouchables* with director Brian De Palma during one of the scoring sessions.
Photo courtesy of Paramount Pictures
Copyright © 1987 by Paramount Pictures. All Rights Reserved.

TEMPO AND PULSE

The "action theme" and the "Untouchables theme" have a strong rhythmic pulse, and add drive to the score, as does the drum-oriented setting of "Capone's theme" in cue #6. Overall, the score doesn't have a lot of drive to it, although the rhythm of the Main Title does a lot for the film by establishing energy as an important *dramatic* element in this story.

Steady rhythmic drumming occurs in the following cues: the Main Title; cue #6 (the "Capone theme"); the end of cue #23, as Nitti moves in on Malone (the "action theme"); and portions of the chase in cue #30.

SOURCE MUSIC

The visual source cue at the opera (cue # 24) is the only source cue in the score.

If the volume levels of "Mood Indigo" (#2) were adjusted for perspective, thereby giving the music an imaginary distance from an unseen radio, then it would be a source cue. However, it has been treated as score—mixed at one uniform level regardless of the perspective, with no visible source.

Although "Vesti la Giubba" from Leoncavallo's *I Pagliacci* (cue #24) is played as visual source music at the opera, it continues at the same level through the cut to Malone in his apartment and back again to Capone at the opera. This source music begins :07 prior to the cut to the opera, a device sometimes used for source music (and sound effects).

Reviews

I think that the composer has been unjustly left behind in the scheme of assessing the various elements of filmmaking.

Jon Burlingame,
syndicated television columnist

I think it's still an overlooked art.

Randall D. Larson, film music author

THE CRITICS

Critics should be aware. It's so obvious that great classic films would be much less without those scores.

Tony Thomas, film music author

Newspaper and magazine film reviews rarely mention the music at all. In the Hollywood trade papers, a short wrap-up sentence—"Tech credits are pro"—may sum up the contribution of such major elements as the score, the cinematography, the editing, the sound and music editing, the mixing, the costumes, and the art direction. Occasionally the score is singled out as a significant element, but rarely with any detail or analysis.

"I've never understood the ignorance of the reviewers, who are supposed to know something about picture making, not realizing the contribution of the music," says author Tony Thomas. "Most people are unqualified to discuss music anyway. They can say they liked it, it was effective, etc., it was terrific. But most people can't discuss music on any kind of an intellectual level. . . . But how can you have *Gone with the Wind* without that score? It's one of the pillars of Tara. It's not great music, but it fits, it's perfect for it."

Historically, film composers have always felt overlooked. In 1941, Aaron Copland suggested that *music* critics become more involved in film music.

In his book, *Our New Music,* he said, "Why shouldn't the music critic cover important film premieres? True, the audience that goes to films doesn't think about the music and possibly shouldn't think about the music. Nevertheless, a large part of music heard by the American public is heard in the film theater. Unconsciously, the cultural level of music is certain to be raised if better music is written for films. This will come about more quickly, I think, if producers and directors know that scores are being heard and criticized."

Similar observations continued. In 1945, composer George Antheil also called for a greater attention to movie music. "I sometimes wonder greatly at music critics. They take infinite pains with the molding of public taste, at least insofar as the concert hall and the symphonic radio program is concerned, but they absolutely ignore the most important thing of all, the background movie score."

Thirty years after these notes, Bernard Herrmann continued to sound the same chord. "My only real complaint is that film music is not reviewed in the press, though it reaches the greatest audience in the world. A film score will live longer than any other kind of music. I predict the twenty-first and twenty-second centuries may not be interested in our art but will be interested in, and study, our cinema. Wouldn't you like to see a movie that was made in 1860?"

Was Copland suggesting a separate film music review in local newspapers and national magazines like *People* and *Time?* Fortunately, we now have several specialized journals that do review the music of new films and soundtrack albums on a regular basis (including *Soundtrack!, CinemaScore,* and *Film Score Monthly*).

There are not many people who write about films who are really educated in music. So it's hard for them, of course, to find the right terms to describe the music.
Mattias Büdinger, film music journalist

A good film music reviewer should have an awareness and understanding of both music and drama and their interaction, and the ability to discuss this interaction perceptively. To be accessible, a reviewer must use dramatic terms, not musical terms. This would be the same language recommended for a composer-director dialogue in discussing a new score, addressing the same principles previously outlined for evaluating a score.

One difficulty all moviegoers face in evaluating the score is the challenge of ignoring an offensive or bad film. Music critic Lawrence Morton said, "Film criticism has not yet reached the point where it can discern the merits of a score in the context of a poor picture, although it frequently does this much for photography and acting and scenic designing." That was written in 1949, yet the problem is no less challenging now. He added, "The majority of film scores are barely worth discussion." But he pointed out that this has always been true of all art, which would include any consideration of the films as well.

Leonard Maltin, author and television commentator on films and video for "Entertainment Tonight," is more aware of the music than most critics, whether the films are good or not so good. In his popular annual reference book, *Leonard Maltin's Movie and Video Guide,* he mentions an outstanding score when he feels it is appropriate, just as he evaluates the films themselves. So you will find Maltin citing scores like Rózsa's score for *Spellbound* and Herrmann's score for *The 7th Voyage of Sinbad* as major contributors to the artistic success of these films.

THE REVIEWS AND FILM MUSIC CRITICISM

During the past 50 years there have been several journals appealing primarily to professionals working in the film industry, and film and film music students and fans, that have regularly printed film music reviews. These include *Film Music Notes* (during the forties and fifties) and *Films in Review.*

First published in October, 1941, *Film Music Notes* began with an unusually conciliatory attitude that did nothing for the cause of sensible criticism. A few years later, when many readers protested this policy, the editors apologized for their misjudgment and promised to be honest and forthright in the future. From then on their reviews became much more analytical and objective.

The following is Celeste Hautbois' March, 1946 review of Miklós Rózsa's score for *Spellbound,* which I have annotated below.

The score for this picture could win the Academy Award. Seldom has music been called on to contribute as much to a picture as in this production, and Mr. Rózsa solved the problems magnificently.[1] Among the best sequences (from a musical point of view) are the scenes in which Constance gives in to her womanly heart. The dubbing was done very skillfully and allowed the music to sound like a full orchestra and not like in many other pictures like a choking chamber group.[2] The skiing sequence showed [an] originality and imagination in movie scoring only too rare in other productions.[3] One of the finest bits of characterization was a scene where the entire musical structure contained one long sustained note. This note increased and decreased in intensity and showed that one single note can express more than a complex musical structure.[4]

Mr. Rózsa's harmonic idiom is sweet and romantic, which is fine for all lyric scenes, but in the stark and dramatic moments of this picture the harmony could have been as bold and striking as his rhythmic and orchestral and contrapuntal ideas. It is too bad that he was obviously avoiding a more advanced harmonic idiom.[5] Having heard some of Mr. Rózsa's concert music, I know that he is capable of more interest than he showed in those sequences mentioned.[6] The overemployment of high divided strings gives certain moments a tinge of cheapness unworthy of the score and the picture. The color of woodwinds and brass was almost invariably suffocated in a mist of strings and harp glissandos. I think that all that richness should have been reserved for the emotional peaks. This way the only way to top the full and rich orchestration for a climax was to turn on the volume control. This seems to me an admission of faulty handling of the orchestral and harmonic forces. . . .[7] All these faults are, however, vastly overshadowed by the merits of the score—one of the best.

1. The score is very important to this film, and therefore the musical solutions are important. The film *needs* this score.
2. Relating the quality of the dubbing to the overall effect is vital in much critical evaluation, and very well taken here; the music he wrote for these sequences would not have been as effective with a poor (softer) dub. I have never noticed this factor mentioned in other reviews.
3. Hautbois justifiably admires originality when it serves the film well.
4. The use of a solitary sustained note relying on instrumental color and dynamics, while not usually a sufficiently interesting musical device for the concert hall, can be perfect for playing the drama. Since she realizes how important it is for the music to get inside the film and play the drama, she admires this effect.
5. Ideally, the harmonic vocabulary used to score a film, and its various scenes, will perfectly suit the nature of the film itself, its characters and dramatic situations. This was not necessarily so in the scores of the thirties, forties, and fifties, a factor which causes many of those scores to sound generic rather than specific.
6. This implies Rózsa was either disinclined to use more advanced harmonic techniques, or was restrained by his sensitivity to the less sophisticated tastes of the filmmakers. In any event, she is suggesting that he write up to his ability.
7. This entire passage continues to refer to the occasional lack of dramatic *specificity*. She suggests playing the drama with the perfect

orchestral texture for each moment, always with an eye on the overall structure of the score. Not easy, but definitely the ultimate goal.

Ms. Hautbois wasn't always as complimentary as the above review might suggest. Here is her review of Max Steiner's score for the 1946 film *My Reputation,* starring Barbara Stanwyck and George Brent, which Leonard Maltin calls a "well-mounted Warner Bros. soaper" in his *Movie and Video Guide.*

The score is one of Max Steiner's less successful efforts. It is indeed painful to see this composer, who only a few years ago was deservedly on the top, go down under the strain of overwork and further diluting his watery product by a fanatic desire to be commercial. This picture score has sunk to the level of circus music, the kind you hear when the horses come in. Most of it which is, as usual, too long, sounds like the stuff which accompanies the weekly announcements about a late show on Saturday night. The picture, affording many fine opportunities for dramatic and highly effective sequences, is scored in an entirely inadequate manner. Mr. Steiner has developed a certain passion for "Christmas effects" consisting of bells, harp, vibraphone, and pizzicato strings. He uses it without discrimination, and some of the more dramatic and intense scenes are scored in an almost frivolous manner. The music definitely succeeds in making it impossible for the audience to be gripped by the story, always reminding one that it is only a picture anyway. *My Reputation* adds nothing to Mr. Steiner's ! !

Her chief complaint here is that Steiner doesn't provide the dramatic support that this film requires. This is precisely the way film scores should be reviewed—that is, as music for the film. If it fails on this level, then no matter how brilliant the music is apart from the film, it is a failure as a film score.

In Lawrence Morton's review of the music for *The Red Pony,* which appeared in the *Film Music Notes* February, 1949 special issue, Morton explains the above premise in terms of Aaron Copland's outstanding score.

There is no dearth of film scores which perform admirably but which fail to satisfy our demands for music of high quality. There are, on the other hand, occasional scores which possess purely musical virtues in abundance but which scorn their functional obligations. Most rare are those which satisfy at once the practical demands of the film medium and the rigorous requirements of musical art. These scores, though infrequent, have fully demonstrated that there is nothing wrong with film music that a good score can't correct.

　　Such a score is the one that Aaron Copland has written for *The Red Pony.* . . . This score . . . demonstrates that while imitators have been able to appropriate for themselves a few Copland trademarks, there are still personal qualities in the music which are the composer's exclusive property and not negotiable on the creative market. It demonstrates too that he has untapped resources of inventiveness which keep him far ahead of his most talented imitators. It is this inventiveness that generates the ever increasing body of commentary on his work. . . . *The Red Pony* is in all ways a memorable score. It has all the technical-industrial slickness of the Hollywood product; and Copland has achieved this without any sacrifice of artistic integrity. His sense of cinema is now as highly developed as his musical skill, and the special problems of the medium have become as easy to solve as a modulation to the subdominant. . . ."

In Hautbois' 1946 review of Korngold's score for *Devotion,* she suggests that the music does not always seem to be connecting with the film on a psychological level—the single most important criterion for evaluating a film score.

The action of the picture takes place about the middle of the nineteenth century. The romantic composers, poets, and painters were creating music, poetry, and paintings of unheard-of emotional intensity. Mr. Korngold's score, however, does not convey that atmosphere convincingly. There is a lot of music in this picture and ample opportunity to display invention, feeling, even a bit of sentimentality. As it actually happens, there is mostly sentimentality and little else. Mr. Korngold writes with care and brilliance. He shows superb command of all phases of music in general and picture music in particular. But *what* he says is much inferior to *how* he says it. There are only too many points when the apparently deep and mature emotions being portrayed on the screen are accompanied by music suggesting adolescent sentimentality and superficiality, in utter contrast to the story contents. When the music suggested happy and playful moods it was very convincing and genuine. The eerie sequences were good and showed imagination. The orchestrations were probably Mr. Korngold's or by a very capable orchestrator {Hugo Friedhofer}. There was an unusual amount of continuity to the score and the catching of cues {hitting the action/phrasing the drama} was never in conflict with the natural development of the musical material at hand. From the orchestral viewpoint, the almost continuous use of harp glissandi gave a cheap and slick tinge to the score which might have been more convincing if clothed in more sensitive and lean orchestration. The sound recording was good, but the general volume of the music in relation to the dialogue might have been a little lower.

THE REVIEWS—A SAMPLING

The ideal film score is one which, while at all times maintaining its own integrity of line, manages at the same time to coalesce with all the other filmic elements involved; sometimes as a frame, at other times as a sort of connective tissue, and in still other (although naturally rarer) instances, as the chief actor in the drama.

Hugo Friedhofer, composer

Reviews that focus on film music can be helpful in directing your attention to the different aspects of a score that contribute to a film's strength or weakness. Following is a sampling of review excerpts organized according to the particular characteristic of the music that the critic has emphasized. The elements referenced in these reviews are some of the same ones discussed in Chapter Four, "What to Listen For."

These reviews are excerpted primarily from the motion picture trade papers (*The Hollywood Reporter* and *Daily Variety*) and from film and film music journals (*Films in Review, Soundtrack!, CinemaScore, Movie Music,* and *Film Music Notes*). Some of the scores are reviewed in the context of their films, while others are reviewed on the basis of the original soundtrack album. Those reviewed as an album are marked with an asterisk. The reviewers of the soundtrack albums have usually heard the score in context also, and write their reviews accordingly.

Emotional Strength

Awakenings (Randy Newman, 1990; Reprise Records)

■ *Awakenings* is music from the heart; a purely emotional response to the film for which it was conceived. It is neither sentimental nor hackneyed, as the film tends to be in its treatment of the unusual events surrounding the use of a seemingly miracle drug on patients in a hospital suffering from Parkinson's disease.

—*Movie Music,* Spring 1991, p. 8, reviewed by Graham Butler

■ The film tries to maintain a balancing act between clinical fact and Hollywood button-pushing, and on the occasions that manipulation takes obvious hold, the music undoubtedly plays a damning role. Within the bonds of his brief, Newman has actually turned out a sensitive and poignant musical depiction,

even if its sole aim is to reinforce what is already on-screen.
—*Soundtrack!* Vol.10, No. 38,
June 1991, pp. 18–19

Edward Scissorhands (Danny Elfman, 1990; MCA Records)

■ ... Never has [Elfman] so eloquently demonstrated his capacity to write such tragically beautiful music. Not only are the themes tender and lyrical, but the sheer expression of the writing is the fullest possible realization of the power of an orchestral/choral combination—many of the cues on this album are quite the equal of anything Williams or Horner have produced in this field, and several are incandescently beautiful.... This is still larger-than-life music, of course—Elfman's love of all things fantastical continues to imbue his work with an operatic sensibility—but what makes this effort so substantially superior is the number of levels on which it succeeds.... The basic approach to the score can best be summarized as a gentle nursery rhyme expanded to epic proportions....
—*Soundtrack!* Vol. 10, No. 38, June 1991, pp. 19–20, reviewed by Rob Allison

The Robe (Alfred Newman, 1953)

■ ... *The Robe* is a landmark score from Hollywood's late Golden Age, and is probably Newman's masterpiece. Certainly it ranks with his later *The Diary of Anne Frank* [1959] as some of the most powerful and emotionally moving music to come out of Hollywood in the fifties.
—*Soundtrack!* Vol. 9, No. 33, March 1990, p. 16, reviewed by Ross Care

■ *The Robe* features Alfred Newman at his most inspired. The likelihood of hearing music of this quality in a modern film is next to nil.
—*Soundtrack!* Vol. 7, No.27, September 1988, p. 16, reviewed by Doug Raynes

RoboCop (Basil Poledouris 1987; Varèse Sarabande Records)

■ Basil Poledouris underlines all the explosive hi-tech, and the poignant humanity, quite effectively in his best score since he gained fame with *Conan the Barbarian* [1982]. Like *Conan*, *RoboCop* presents itself as an epic of grandiose violence, but with a human focus. The same with Poledouris' music.... The penultimate word for the *RoboCop* score is *intensity*, and it rarely lets up in its driving determination to march where ever it wants to go.... Like the film, it's not to be missed.
—*Soundtrack!* Vol. 6, No. 24, December 1987, p. 16, reviewed by Steven J. Lehti

Form and Concept

Body Heat (John Barry, 1981)

■ John Barry's *Body Heat* is the sexiest film score since Alex North's classic *Long Hot Summer* [1958]. It is also Barry at the peak of his creativity. Rarely has film music been so much a part of the film's fabric as in *Body Heat*. This updating of *Double Indemnity* [1944] needed a sensuous undercurrent to permeate the picture and this was accomplished by Barry's music.
—*Soundtrack!* Vol. 2, No. 8, December 1983, p. 27, reviewed by Thom Santiago

Empire of the Sun (John Williams, 1987; Warner Bros. Records)

■ On film, the score suffers from inspecificity; most cues seem to have little to do with each other, so that when one motif finally gains dominance over the rest, it becomes the only really affecting one in the score. That is the wordless boys' chorus which represents the wonder of flight as envisioned by young Jim.... *Empire of the Sun* is an imperfect film, score, and album: its lows are

low, but its peaks are very high, and that's why I recommend them all.
—*Soundtrack!* Vol. 7, No. 25, March 1988, p. 13, reviewed by Guy Tucker

The Fall of the Roman Empire (Dimitri Tiomkin, 1964)

■ Tiomkin's conception of what the Roman music may have been like borders on the juvenile, and much of his music for *Fall* could easily have come from his scores for *The Guns of Navarone* [1961] or *The Alamo* [1960] (maybe some of it did).
—*Films in Review* April, 1964, Vol. XV, No. 4, pp. 233–34, "The Sound Track," reviewed by Page Cook

The Greatest Story Ever Told (Alfred Newman, 1956)

■ Alfred Newman's score, which, though marred by two regrettable lapses I will speak of later, is the most esthetic and subtly integrated of all Biblical film scores. Although Newman's basic style is richly and even extravagantly toned, his style in *Story* is spare. He uses Handel's "Hallelujah!" chorus from the *Messiah,* with full chorus and orchestra. The effect is one of vulgar theatricality wholly alien to the rest of *Story's* score. I have been told that Newman wrote a "Hallelujah!" chorus of his own, and that Stevens made him substitute the Handel. If so, Stevens damaged his picture. Using Handel to ring down the curtain for the intermission was banal, but using it *again*—as the finale accompanying the Resurrection and Ascension—is inexcusable. [Stevens *did* insist on both uses.]
—*Films in Review,* April 1965, Vol. XVI, No. 4, pp. 244–45, "The Sound Track," reviewed by Page Cook

Johnny Belinda (Max Steiner, 1948)

■ The music is again evidence of the long-indulged-in single-track expression of Max Steiner—the same sweet stuff. For Bette Davis' kerchief-ripping it usually fits fine, but in *Johnny Belinda* simplicity has a hard time trudging the distracting motion of the score's pretty melodies.
—*Film Music Notes,* January–February 1949, Vol. VIII, No. 3, p. 20, reviewed by Gene Forrell

*License to Kill (Michael Kamen, 1989; MCA Records)

■ What is most striking about this score is *not* relying on an excessive pop sound in the action themes.... Kamen apparently takes Bond very seriously, providing music which captures 007's lethal and near reckless manner, with powerful orchestration very much in the style of his riveting score for *Die Hard* [1988], rather than the pop style of *Lethal Weapon* [1987].... As action scores go, *License to Kill* is top-notch.
—*Soundtrack!* Vol. 8, No. 31, September 1989, p.11, reviewed by Andrew MacLean

A Man Called Horse (Leonard Rosenman, 1970)

■ It remains one of the most striking examples of combining avant-garde techniques and primitive musical material.
—*Film Score,* p. 234, Tony Thomas

Originality

*Aliens (James Horner, 1986; That's Entertainment Records)

■ There simply isn't any real originality or emotional depth to this music. None of the characters are provided with a musical identity, hence the score never reaches beyond being an exciting accompaniment to the action.... It's very easy to sit through this score and pick out references to every major science-fiction film of the past ten years. Goldsmith's jerky rhythms in the "Docking" sequence of *Capricorn One* [1978] are in-

voked in the opening section of "Futile Escape." "Bishop's Countdown" uses the same crashing full orchestral chords so familiar from Williams' *Star Wars*.
—*Soundtrack!* Vol. 5, No. 20,
December 1986, p. 17,
reviewed by David J. Rimmer

The Silence of the Lambs (Howard Shore, 1991; MCA Records)
■ This is the first great score of the 1990s. Howard Shore ... has created a powerful and demanding score for Jonathan Demme's terrifying thriller. Written for a very large string section, with relatively little brass, woodwind, and percussion, Shore's score fearlessly captures a wide range of emotions; at times distressing, tense, hesitant, and ultimately overwhelming. . . . Overall, an original and perceptive score that reaches deeply into the human psyche.
—*Movie Music* Spring 1991, pp. 8–9, reviewed by Graham Butler

Melody

Born on the Fourth of July (John Williams, 1989; MCA Records)
■ It's not a bad or particularly sentimental film, yet Williams' score often makes it feel mawkish. I heard the album first, and was impressed by its striking, heartfelt music; in the theater I discovered that for the most part it's in the wrong movie. . . . "The Early Days" scores the town parade sequence, a bit of slow-motion Americana, for which the scoring is only tantalizingly overripe . . . and the theme really is lovely, another of those Williams tunes that doesn't come out in the wash, even though the movie subjects it to some pretty hard scrubbing, repeating it—especially its opening bars—ad nauseam. It ceases to have an effect after a while, yet this theme and the trumpet motif are pretty

much all the score has to offer, over and over again. . . .
—*Soundtrack!* Vol. 9, No. 33, March 1990, p. 19, reviewed by Guy Tucker

Edward Scissorhands (Danny Elfman, 1990; MCA Records)
■ A veritable delight from start to finish, Elfman charms the captive listener with a collection of the most sumptuous themes to be heard in quite some time.
—*Movie Music,* Spring 1991, p. 13, reviewed by Graham Butler

The Great Escape (Elmer Bernstein, 1963)
■ From Paul Brickhill's true story of a remarkable mass breakout by Allied POWs during World War II, producer-director John Sturges has fashioned a motion picture that entertains, captivates, thrills, and stirs. . . . Elmer Bernstein's rich, expressive score is consistently helpful. His martial, Prussianistic theme is particularly stirring and memorable.
—*Daily Variety* [© Daily Variety Ltd. Reprinted by permission.]

Sleeping With the Enemy (Jerry Goldsmith, 1991; Epic Records)
■ Seldom has Goldsmith relied so heavily on one theme to carry an entire score, but in this instance it works perfectly. With each new play the music becomes more rewarding, offering as it does so many of Goldsmith's beautifully delicate nuances.
—*Movie Music,* Spring 1991, p. 12, reviewed by Kevin McGann

Musical Independence

Joan of Arc (Hugo Friedhofer, 1948)
■ The high craftsmanship behind Hugo Friedhofer's score for *Joan of Arc* is apparent throughout the film. In all its technical aspects, the score justifies Friedhofer's top-flight Hollywood reputation. . . . The score, though it accompanies and complements the

picture, has a vital musical logic of its own. The score has considerably more distinction than the picture . . .
—*Film Music Notes,*
January–February 1949,
Vol. VIII, No. 3, p. 19

*Not Without My Daughter (Jerry Goldsmith, 1991; Intrada Records; in Europe: Silva Screen Film Records)
■ *Not Without My Daughter* presents itself as something of a rarity in the career of Jerry Goldsmith. The score is so unremarkable that while playing it you can virtually forget that you are actually listening to anything. Not that it's a bad score; far from it. It works well in the film, but lacks even a single point of musical interest away from it.
—*Movie Music,* Spring 1991, p. 10,
reviewed by Graham Butler

Sincerity

The Last Starfighter (Craig Safan, 1984)
■ The score has no empty, pompous big-orchestra blatherings, and its strength is its humanity.
—*Soundtrack!* 1984

The Use of Orchestration and Color

Dr. Jekyll and Mr. Hyde (Franz Waxman, 1941)
■ . . . The musical score shows appropriate feeling for creating dramatic intent, and Mr.

Waxman has used again some of those remarkable sound effects with which we are beginning to associate him and which add so materially in establishing mood and interest. . . .
—*Film Music Notes,* Vol. I, No. 1,
October 1941

Extreme Prejudice (Jerry Goldsmith, 1987; Intrada Records)
■ Like his previous score *Hoosiers,* this one incorporates a masterful blend of orchestra and electronics in the true Goldsmithian spirit. . . . With each cue it does not seem that Goldsmith can top himself and just minutes later he does. . . .
—*Soundtrack!* Vol.6, No.22, June 1987,
pp. 18–19, reviewed by Roger Feigelson

Spotting and the Use of Silence

The Fall of the Roman Empire (Dimitri Tiomkin, 1964)
■ The main trouble with this music is Tiomkin's relentless "overscoring." He embellishes from the first scene to the last—occasionally pleasantly, but rarely meaningfully.
—*Films in Review,* April 1964, Vol. XV,
No. 4, pp. 233–34, "The Sound
Track," reviewed by Page Cook

The Silents and Other Special Films

■ ■ ■

SILENT FILMS

Watch a film run in silence, and then watch it again with eyes and ears. The music sets the mood for what your eye sees; it guides your emotions; it is the emotional framework for visual pictures.

D. W. Griffith, director

The Orchestras

When the Lumière brothers demonstrated their films in 1895 in Paris, a piano accompanied the silent action on screen. The lonely pianist pounding out popular and semiclassical music for silent movies remains one of the most vivid images in the history of entertainment. A pianist watching the screen and catching each changing mood was a neighborhood fixture during the days of the silents. Most theaters around the country were small nickelodeons and cinemas, and in these moviehouses the pianist prevailed.

The resultant sound wasn't always pleasant. A 1920 article in *The Musician* explained problems that had existed from the beginning. "The instrument is generally old, out of tune, strings dusty, and incapable of producing the correct vibrations. The stool has no back and the pianist plays for hours with the muscles of her back becoming constantly more strained. The light, both night and day, is poor and inadequate, forcing the pianist either to play by memory, ear, or incorrectly by notes which she strives to make out."

By 1909, an editorial in *Moving Picture World* begged for mercy and suggested that theater managers either tune the pianos or burn them. "Better still, we think, is our advice, wherever practical, to engage a small orchestra of strings, with the addition of the piano and the sound effects. Of course, this costs money, but we think that the outlay would recoup itself."

The size of the ensembles accompanying silent movies ranged from a piano or several instruments (perhaps a violin and piano) in the smallest theaters, to medium-sized groups of 10 to 20, and on to larger groups of 20 to as many as 80 musicians at the first class theaters and deluxe motion picture palaces.

Joseph Gershenson, who later became music director at Universal Studios, never forgot the experience of accompanying silent films in the twenties. "I worked in little theaters, with just violin and piano. When I played the silent movies in the small theaters, they had a big machine with pulleys. If you wanted a rooster crow, you'd pull one button. If you wanted an auto horn, you'd pull another. And the pianist used to do that. These things were all set up. It was an old Wurlitzer machine, a big machine, attached to a piano. A knock at the door, or a telephone bell, another lever. The pianist would have cue sheets for it." Men were employed to create sound effects behind the screen also, creating door slams, gunshots, and a variety of other sounds to help create the illusion of reality.

A typical instrumentation for a small orchestra might be 6 violins, 2 violas, 2 cellos, 1 bass, flute, oboe, clarinet, 2 horns, 2 trumpets, 1 trombone, drums, and piano. "At the Coliseum [Theater] I think the orchestra had 14 musicians," says Gershenson. "At the Palace, 18. Of course, the Palace was only vaudeville, no pictures." The Rialto and Rivoli Theaters in New York City each had 45-piece orchestras. Hugo Riesenfeld, music director of these theaters, estimated that in 1922 there were 500 theaters around the country with full orchestras.

The International Theatre in Los Angeles in 1910.
Photo courtesy of the American Museum of the Moving Image (Astoria, N.Y.)

Mechanical Instruments and Theater Organs

During the teens, several instrument manufacturers developed mechanical instruments designed and equipped to accompany silent movies. They were outfitted with an enormous selection of instrumental sounds, plus every kind of popular sound effect, including crackling fire, gunshots and cannon blasts, and traffic and automobile claxon horns. Some of them assumed gargantuan proportions, culminating in the biggest Fotoplayer, made by the American Photo Player Company. It was 21 feet long, 5 feet wide, and approximately 5 feet tall.

These machines were not nearly as prevalent as theater organs, which also could be as gigantic as they were versatile. The theater organist had to carry the performance as a solo for long stretches in order to give the orchestra musicians a chance to rest. They were also required to perform as a feature attraction during the stage show. Good players were so much in demand that in 1921 a school specifically for theater organists was established in Chicago, with two more opening in New York and one in Boston. The famous ones like Jesse Crawford and his wife, Helen, commanded top salaries—in fact, the Crawfords were invited out to Hollywood from New York to play one of the local theaters for a reported salary of $1,000 a week, an offer they refused.

The Silent-Movie Musician

The typical moviehouse ran four shows (including the stage show presented in between the movies), beginning at noon and ending at midnight. Their schedules were brutal. In her excellent book *Music for Silent Films 1894–1929*, Gillian B. Anderson cites an article in *The American Organist* describing their workday:

> The schedule started . . . with two hours and ten minutes of solo organ. A five-minute break was followed by two hours of orchestra with organ. A fifteen-minute break was followed by organ alone for two hours. A thirty-minute break was followed by three hours of orchestra and organ, followed by one and a half hours of organ alone. Additionally, during the orchestral periods, the organ frequently gave the instrumentalists a fifteen- to thirty-minute break.
>
> This schedule was followed regardless of what was on the screen, so it was common for the orchestra to stop in the middle of a film and for the organ to take up alone.

In Russia, the great composer Dmitri Shostakovitch didn't find it any easier when he worked in a movie house as a young man. In a letter, his wife recalled how it was in 1924.

> Down in front of the screen sat Mitya, his back soaked with perspiration, his near-sighted eyes in their horn-rimmed glasses peering upwards to follow the story, his fingers pounding away on the raucous upright piano. Late at night he trudged home in a thin coat and summer cap, with no warm gloves or galoshes, and arrived exhausted around one o'clock in the morning. . . .

The Music and Cue Sheets

During the earliest days of silent movies, the pianists played absolutely anything that came to mind, with no regard for what was happening on the screen. For a short while nobody seemed to care. But with the increasing sophistication of the films and the audiences, the musicians began to consider what music to play to best accompany the films.

Their first choices were the familiar popular and semiclassical pieces of the day. Then the classics were added to the repertoire. As a 1909 *Motion Picture World* review of *A Fool's Revenge* points out, ". . . a pleasant variation from the eternal ragtime was a refined deliverance of classical music, corresponding to the character of the picture, including Schumann's *Träumerei* and Beethoven's *Moonlight Sonata*. The first time, indeed, we have ever heard Beethoven in a five-cent theater."

On their own, musicians didn't have the opportunity to see the films before the show, and often didn't know what to play. This meant that they were usually guessing about mood, timing, tempo, and scene changes—an astonishing situation. With so little preparation, the gaffes could be ludicrous. Even as late as 1921 a group in Britain accompanying the epic film *The Queen of Sheba* selected the pop tune "Thanks for the Buggy Ride" to score the dramatic chariot race.

There was an ingenious solution to this problem. In 1909, the Edison and Vitagraph film companies began distributing lists of instrumental music that could be used as appropriate accompaniment for their films. Standard compositions and popular tunes that were available at music stores were selected for each scene. The need for this service was so great that musicians quickly responded to these cue sheets. Even if they didn't use the recommended pieces, they now had a much better idea of what would work for the various sequences. Over the next few years, the practice of distributing specially prepared "cue sheets" for each film that was shipped became common, and was equally useful for pianists and orchestra leaders.

Max Winkler, a clerk working for the Carl

Fischer Music Company in 1912, was a major figure in the further development and application of this idea. "One day after I had gone home from work I could not fall asleep. The hundreds and thousands of titles, the mountains of music that Fischer's had stored and catalogued, kept going through my mind. There was music, surely, to fit *any* given situation in *any* picture. If we could only think of a way to let all these orchestra leaders and pianists and organists know what we had! If we could use our knowledge and experience not when it was too late, but much earlier, before they ever had to sit down and play, we would be able to sell them music not by the ton but by the trainload.

"That thought suddenly electrified me. It was not a problem of getting the music. We had the music. . . . It was a problem of promoting, timing, and organization. I pulled back the blanket, turned on the light, and went over to my table, took a sheet of paper, and began writing feverishly. . . ."

The sample cue sheet he created stimulated interest at Universal, where he was asked to prepare similar cue sheets for all their productions. After a while he began to run out of ideas. "In desperation, we turned to crime. We began to dismember the great masters. We began to murder the works of Beethoven, Mozart, Grieg, J. S. Bach, Verdi, Bizet, Tchaikovsky, and Wagner—everything that wasn't protected by copyright from outright pilfering.

"The immortal chorales of J. S. Bach became an 'Adagio Lamentoso' for sad scenes. Extracts from great symphonies were hacked down to emerge again as 'Sinister Misterioso' by Beethoven, or 'Weird Moderato' by Tchaikovsky. Wagner's and Mendelssohn's wedding marches were used for marriages, fights betwen husbands and wives, and divorce scenes: we just had them played out of tune, a treatment known in the profession as 'souring up the aisle.' If they were to be used for happy endings, we jazzed them up mercilessly. Finales from famous overtures, with the 'William Tell' and 'Orpheus' the favorites, became gallops. Meyerbeer's 'Coronation March' was slowed down to a majestic pomposo to give proper background to the inhabitants of Sing Sing's deathhouse. The 'Blue Danube' was watered down to a minuet by a cruel change in tempo."

If you were a pianist and owned the suggested music, this system worked fine. If not, the cue sheets might be less helpful. Realizing musicians needed a comprehensive resource, Sam Fox published *The Sam Fox Moving Picture Music Volumes* by J. S. Zamecnik in 1913. Two collections that followed became especially popular: Giuseppe Becce's *Kinothek,* published in Berlin in 1919, and Erno Rapée's book *Motion Picture Moods for Pianists and Organists, a Rapid Reference Collection of Selected Pieces Adapted to Fifty-Two Moods and Situations,* published in 1924. In Rapée's book, the music was in sections for quick reference, and included categories like "Aëroplane," "Battle," "Chase," "Fire-Fighting," "Grotesque," "Humorous," "Mysterioso," "Orgies," "Passion," "Religioso," and "Sadness." Typical musical selections included the well-known "Funeral March" by Chopin, "Rondo Capriccioso" by Mendelssohn, "Marche Héroïque" by Schubert, folklike songs like "Home Sweet Home" and "Drink to Me Only with Thine Eyes," and, for orgies, the fourth movement from "l'Arlésienne Suite" by Bizet.

In the twenties, cue sheets were commonly distributed to the theaters along with the films. "It was up to every individual leader to set his music up," Joseph Gershenson explains. "If he didn't have that particular composition, he'd substitute a similar type." In the smaller theaters there was no rehearsal. "You did it. If it didn't work, you'd change it at the next show."

Abraham H. Lass, who played at the Eagle Theater in Brooklyn from 1923 to 1926, found that the cue sheet system wasn't foolproof. "Like most of the neighborhood movie pianists, I never pre-viewed any of the pictures. Some motion picture producers supplied cue sheets for each picture. These cue sheets provided appropriate music for every scene. But I rarely got to see them. They were usually lost in transit or mislaid by the management. So I was thrown entirely on my own musical resources and perforce became an 'instant composer'. . . ."

★ This Filmusic Guide is issued in compliance to the request of Theatre Owners of America and Chambers of Commerce.

WARNER BROS. present

"DON JUAN"

STARRING

JOHN BARRYMORE

Projection time 1 hour 49 minutes—based on speed of 11 minutes per 1000 ft. (10 reels)

This Form Cue Sheet issued exclusively by the TAX-FREE MUSIC CO., 1674 BROADWAY, N. Y. The descriptive section gives the musician an idea of each scene, before arrival of film, enabling him to select from his library the proper compositions which match the scenes accurately, thus conveying the full value of the picture to the audience, resulting in satisfaction to the patrons and exhibitors and continued contracts for film exchange. We are constantly receiving letters from musicians throughout the world praising and preferring this form cue sheet above all others.

TAX FREE (and additional TAXABLE)

"DESCRIPTIVE FILMUSIC GUIDE"

Country of Origin, U. S. A.—Copyright 1926 by Michael Hoffman

CUE	Appearing on Film	Time Min.	Descriptive Action of Each Scene	Tempo of Action & Music Required	TAX-FREE MUSICAL SUGGESTIONS	TAXABLE MUSICAL SUGGESTIONS
	At screening of titles	3	Grandioso opening	4|4 Maestoso	Regal Splendor (Luz)	Pomposo (Borch)
T	Not long will you suffer	1	Romantic	4|4 Andte. romance	Don Juan Andante (Mozart) Pub. Ascher	Don Juan Andante (Mozart) Fischer Co.
S	Trumpet calls (as he leaves)		Trumpet calls	Trumpets	Trumpet call	Trumpet calls
S	Street scene and soldiery	1	Spanish gallantry	4|4 Maestoso	Pomp and Pageantry (Schertzinger)	Carmen March (Bizet) Fischer Co.
S	Lover scales wall	1	Sentimental	3|4 Moderato	Appasionato (Carrabotta)	Reverie (Conterno)
S	Don returns on horse	3	Mysterious-foreboding	4|4 Mystical	Villains Den (Damaur)	Plotting Foe (Kilenyi)
S	Hunchback and laborers	3	Heavy dramatic	4|4 Trem. dramatic	Preludio (Cordova)	Affizione (Gabriel Marie)
S	Don orders wife to leave	1	Pathetic	3|4 Andante	Good Bye (Tosti) Ascher Co.	Good Bye (Tosti) Fischer Co.
T	In the years that followed	3½	Nymph dances—hilarity	2|4 Allegro	Don Juan Allegro (Mozart) Ascher Co.	Don Juan Allegro (Mozart) Fischer Co.
T	Is not one member	4	Heavy tragedy	4|4 Tragic Trem.	The Vow (Francheschi)	Silvio Pellico (Zerco)
T	THE STORY (Watch trumpet calls)	1	Pompous procession	4|4 Maestoso Pomp	Nobility (Rosey)	Aida March (Verdi) Fischer Co.
S	They stop to pray	⅙	Sacred	4|4 Religioso	Holy! Holy! (Dykes) Ascher Co.	Holy! Holy! (Dykes) Fischer Co.
S	After prayers	1½	Sentimental	3|4 Moderato	Ivano (Amadei)	Alysia (Frey)
T	Giano dear	2	Processional scenes	4|4 Pomposo	Spanish Soldiery (de Smetsky)	March Norma (Bellini)
T	Don Juan's home	3½	Sentimental ladies	6|8 Moderato	Pompeian Serenade (Strollo)	Castle in Spain (Miramontes)
T	Don Juan De Marana	3½	Love scene	4|4 Romance	Carmen Flower Song (Rosey-Bizet) Rosey Co.	Carmen Flower Song (Bizet) Fischer Co.
T	You must hasten (1st woman leaves)	2	Suspense and sentiment	4|4 Moderato	Non e Ver (Mattei) Photo-Play Music Co.	Non e Ver (Mattei) Fischer Co.
S	Duke Vargoni arrives	2½	Villainous	4|4 Dramatic	Ferocity (Carrozzini)	Despair (Berge)
T	From the Borgia	2	Neutral	3|4 Moderato	Serenade Italienne (Shebek)	Barcarolle Italienne (Czibulka)
T	The glory of the Borgia	3	Palace—Pomp	4|4 Maestoso	Marcia Pomposa (Egener)	Grandioso (Finck)
S	Don Juan arrives on horse	2	Romeo effect	3|4 Aria	Aria Romeo Juliet (Gounod) Ascher Co.	Aria Romeo Juliet (Gounod) Fischer Co.
T	We shall see	2	Intrigue	4|4 Mysterioso	The Plotters (Carrozzini)	Enigma (Borch)
T	My apologies for the wretch	3½	Rather sentimental	2|4 Moderato	Serenade (Leoncavallo) Ascher Co.	Madriola (Samuels)
T	None so dreaded	4	Weird—mystical	4|4 Mystical	Fiendish Eyes (Hoffman)	Gruesome Mysterioso 31 (Borch)
S	Don spills wine on flowers	3	Gruesome — foreboding	4|4 Mystical	Agony (Kempinski)	Sinister Tension (Vely)
T	To-night you saved	3	ROMANTIC THEME	4|4 ROMANCE	LOVE SONG from Bocaccio THEME Ascher Co.	LOVE SONG from Bocaccio THEME Fischer Co.
T	You promised to reward me	2	Slow dramatic	4|4 Moderato	Dovce Recontre (Gabriel Marie) Ascher Co.	Dilemma (Savino)
T	For three days	2	ROMANTIC	4|4 ROMANCE	THEME	THEME
T	Before midnight Rome was	4	Heavy dramatic	OVERTURE	Titus Overture (Mozart) Ascher Co.	Titus Overture (Mozart) Fischer Co.
S	Lady Borgia arrives with mask	2½	Neutral	3|4 Moderato	Dame Cavalieri (Frontini)	La Serenata (Braga)
T	Rome is laughing	2	Tumult	2|4 Agitato	Eccitamento (Retlaw)	Allegro Scherzando (Frey)
T	If you betray	2½	ROMANTIC	4|4 ROMANCE	THEME	THEME
T	Rome celebrated (Several sets of church bells, chime)	3	Dancing—Hilarity	2|4 Allegro	Nottambuli (Cuscina)	Sherzo Primo (Conterno)
T	Close the window you fool (Bell chimes continue)	2½	Weird dramatic	2|4 Dram. trem	Ondes Mystereuse (Francheschi)	Flick and Flock (Patou)
S	Woman falls dead (Chimes continue)	4½	Pathetic	3|4 ANDANTE	Intermezzo (once) and Siciliana (once) from Cavalleria Rusticana (Mascagni) Ascher Co.	Intermezzo (once) and Siciliana (once) from Cavalleria Rusticana (Mascagni)
S	Don drinks & throws cup away	2	Spanish fest., etc.	3|8 Allegro	Spanish Dance No. 1 (Moszkowski) Ascher Co	Spanish Dance No. 1 (Moszkowski) Fischer Co.
S	Adriana goes up stairs	2	Slow dramatic	2|4 Slow dram	Solitudine (Muli)	Recitative and Soliloquy (Savino)
S	Don appears with swords	1½	Threatening	2|4 Hy. dram	Maggiolata (Culotta)	Finale Dramatic (Noyes)
T	You must believe me	4	Exciting duel	2|4 Agitato	Tumult (Verdi) Sonnemann Co	Heavy Agitato (Noyes)
T	Arrest him for the murder	1	Slow dramatic	3|4 And. dram	La Bas (Francheschi)	Romeo's Farewell (Baron)
T	When the gates of St. Angelo	3	Gruesome—dungeon	4|4 Mystical	Greed (Kempinski)	Prowling Schemers (Carbonara)
T	Your quarters, rash Spaniard	2	Solemn	3|4 Andante	Cuore in Pena (Gracchino)	Desolation (Conterno)
T	It will amuse us	2	Weird & gruesome	4|4 Heavy trem	Wind and Mermaids (Humperdinck) Ascher Co.	Dramatic Mysterioso (Savino)
S	Water flows into cell	3	Tumult & escape	4|4 Furioso	Etna (Francheschi)	Disaster (Savino)
S	Neri's room (Adriana tied)	2½	Fiendish—witch	4|4 Weird	Looms of Fate (St. Saens) Sonnemann Co.	Weird Nature (Kilenyi)
S	Neri pulls bell	3½	Furious excitement, fights, horses, etc.	4|4 Furioso	L'Abine (Francheschi)	Bold Riders (Carbonara)
T	Ahead of us, beloved	1	ROMANTIC	4|4 ROMANCE	THEME	THEME
S	Moon scene is warning for Chord until THE END.					

NOTE: All tax free music is tax free as of January 1st 1927.

Musicians may procure all tax-free music at less than store prices, direct from Tax Free Filmusic Co., 1674 Broadway, N. Y. This is in conformity with Warner Brothers policy to serve exhibitors and their musicians in the best way possible. Mail your orders to TAX FREE FILMUSIC CO.

TAX FREE MEANS that by using tax-free publications, the theare owner is relieved of paying the music tax to the Society of Authors, Composers and Publishers.

If you have not the compositions suggested in this last column you may easily substitute accurate music by following the DESCRIPTIVE ACTION OF EACH SCENE and TEMPO.

This 1926 cue sheet for the full-length silent feature *Don Juan* gives the pianist and/or conductor a visual guide for each change of musical mood, the duration of the cue, the emotional nature and tempo of the cue, and two suggested published compositions to perform or use as a role model, one copyrighted (including arrangments of Mozart, Bizet, and others) and another not copyrighted.

Courtesy of the Academy of Motion Picture Arts and Sciences

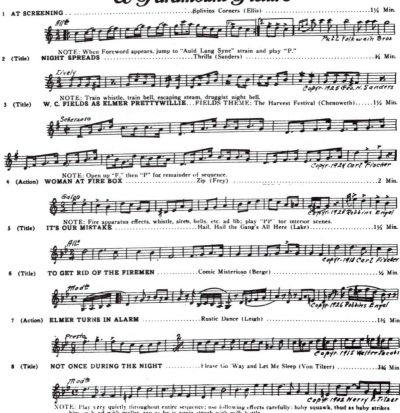

This late 1920s cue sheet is really a compilation score, and gives enough single-staff music for each cue so that the music director can easily understand the nature of the recommended music. If these pieces weren't already in the music director's library, he would order them or replace them with similar music. This cue sheet also suggests appropriate sound effects.

Courtesy of the Academy of Motion Picture Arts and Sciences

The fact that the smaller neighborhood houses changed pictures five or six times a week made empathetic musical accompaniment even more difficult. A major feature might play for several months in a deluxe theater, but in the bigger standard theaters the films changed twice a week. This didn't allow any time to establish a routine before a new film was shown.

Compiled Scores

D. W. Griffith, the director who was responsible for developing many cinematic techniques in order to create an overwhelming emotional experience for the audience, saw the value of preparing a complete score specifically designed and shaped to the needs of his films. When he finished shooting *Birth of a Nation* (1915) he began to create a full-length score in collaboration with composer-music director Joseph Carl Breil. Griffith had studied music and composition, and had specific ideas about how to score his film. In the manner of the cue sheet "scores" of the day, he used mostly pre-existing music, supplemented by some of Breil's original composition. Classics by Wagner, Tchaikovsky, Beethoven, and Liszt were interwoven, as were popular tunes like "Dixie" and other Civil War songs.

The enormous success of both the film and its accompanying score established the nature of film scoring at that time. Full orchestral accompaniments became standard for any theater that could afford the musicians. Griffith also collaborated with Breil on *Intolerance* (1916) and continued to use compiled scores into the twenties.

Compiling a score like this was an extremely demanding task. Things got so tense while Griffith and Breil were working on the *Birth of a Nation* score, that at one point Griffith exclaimed, "If I ever kill anyone, it won't be an actor but a musician."

Hugo Riesenfeld, who was music director of both the Rialto and Rivoli Theaters in New York, put together scores for all the films that played these theaters. His library of available music included 6,000 orchestral scores, and thousands of piano works. T. Scott Buhrman, writing in *The American Organist* in 1920, visited Riesenfeld in order to watch him prepare the score for a forthcoming movie.

> Mr. Riesenfeld had already seen the picture once, of course, so he began his search for music of a certain well-defined type. Piece after piece (only a little of each, of course) was played on the piano as this or that conductor would pick out one as a suggestion, and all that could be gotten out of Mr. Riesenfeld was "No," "Not that," "No, that won't do," "Oh, no, not that"—and all the while the cameras [i.e., projectors] were waiting to click their first inch of the film, not a picture as yet having gone to the screen; the [music] director had his head stuck deep in a folio of possibly two hundred selections of a given type, every one of which he glanced through in his search for the "right" one. Finally it was found; and what a relief. "Slower; oh, not so fast," then "Ah, that's it, that's it," and the ready amanuensis jotted down a few abbreviations to show that when the picture was ready to begin the music would be this piece, and that so much of it would be used. A mark was put lightly on the score. All that work for about sixty seconds' worth of music! . . .
>
> After little snatches of the film are thus projected and music fitted intimately with the moods of each, with proper record made of each separate bit of film and the music corresponding with it, Mr. Riesenfeld takes the music under his wing and spends laborious hours over it, marking, timing, cutting, trimming, fitting, and preparing it to time rightly with the film. . . .

Original themes were interpolated in these compiled scores, and some were very successful. "Charmaine," written by Erno Rapée and Lew Pollack for *What Price Glory?* (1926), sold over a million copies of sheet music, as did "Diane," written by the same songwriters for *Seventh Heaven* (1927).

Original Scores

The most frequently cited example of an early original score is the Camile Saint-Saëns 1908 score for *L'Assassinat du Duc de Guise*. Although written by a famous composer, it didn't start a trend, nor did American Walter Cleveland Simon's original score for *Arrah Na Pough* (1911). But in 1916, Thomas Dixon commissioned Victor Herbert to create an original score for his film *The Fall of a Nation*.

Herbert saw the potential in original film scores. "For the first time in the history of American pictorial drama a complete accompanying score will be played that has never been heard anywhere else. When listening to music that marks the flight of cavalry you will not say, 'Oh, that is "The Ride of the Valkyries,"' nor in scenes of stress and storm will you be regaled by the strains of 'In the Hall of the Mountain King.' In brief, the musical program will not be a mosaic or patchwork of bits of Wagner, Grieg, Beethoven, Schumann, Mendelssohn, Gounod, Verdi, Liszt, Bizet, Berlioz, and other writers. It will be strictly new. Hundreds of music lovers have told me their pleasure in picture presentations was often to a large extent spoiled by patchwork music. When the orchestra played, they heard bits of *Faust* or *Tannhäuser, Carmen,* or *Traviata*; the hearing of that music flashed pictures from those operas on the minds of the spectators, and attention was distracted from the characters in the story. . . ."

When *The Fall of a Nation* premiered at the Liberty Theater in New York on June 6, 1916, *Musical America* was enthusiastic about Herbert's score. "He has not merely written an orchestral accompaniment with a series of 'motifs.' His score is interesting and worthwhile from a purely musical standpoint. . . . Mr. Herbert's stimulating score clearly indicates the marked advance that music is making in the domain of the photoplay and should prove encouraging to composers who have not yet tried their hand at this type of work."

In spite of this success, original scores didn't flourish until the mid-twenties, when a number of outstanding works were commissioned, including *The Thief of Bagdad* (1924, Mortimer Wilson), *Potemkin* (1925, Edmund Meisel), and *La Passion de Jeanne D'Arc* (1928, Victor Alix).

The results were often thrilling. In 1928, Herman G. Weinberg, writing for the *New York Herald Tribune,* recalled the initial impact of Meisel's score for *Potemkin*.

> For the New York presentation of *Potemkin* at the Biltmore the original accompanying score by Dr. Edmund Meisel, of Berlin, was used. . . . The score is as powerful, as vital, as galvanic and electrifying as the film. It is written in the extreme modern vein, cacophonies run riot, harmonies grate, crackle, jar; there are abrupt changes and shifts in the rhythm; tremendous chords crashing down, dizzy flights of runs, snatches of half-forgotten melodies, fragments, a short interpolation of jazz on a piano, and a melody in the central portion of the film when the people of Odessa stand on the steps waving to the sailors on the cruiser Potemkin and others go out on fishing boats with provisions for them—that is one of the loveliest I have ever heard. It sings! It soars and endears itself to the heart. It is full of gratitude and the love of man for man. It is one of the warmest, tenderest passages that has found its way into the cinema-music repertoire.

Synchronizing the Music

To facilitate sync, the preparation of these scores and cue sheets included detailed notes on the timing of each sequence. Griffith and Breil also included specific metronome markings for each selection. To ensure perfect sync, though, Riesenfeld actually *cut the film* to suit his needs. As a 1920 article in *The American Organist* explained, after timing the scenes and selecting each individual piece of music, having the music orchestrated and prepared as necessary ". . . the film itself is taken in hand for revision. Projection machines can be made to run at variable speeds to suit the occasion, and these speeds can be arbitrarily set by a projector without interfering in any way with the picture; I doubt if any but a very skilled man would be able to detect the many changes Mr. Riesenfeld must get from his operators. Many times the titles and joints in the film are deleted to just the right amount to make the film time exactly with the music, while at other times, the speed accomplishes the result. Thus

In this scene from the 1922 film *Shackles of Gold*, the on-screen pianist is playing for dinner guests. The accompanying pianist in the theater would play an appropriate dance tune as if the music were coming from the party.
Photo courtesy of the American Museum of the Moving Image (Astoria, N.Y.)

after the music is first fitted to the picture, the picture is then fitted exactly to the music."

The filmmakers must have been shocked to see their films carved up like this. Variable speed projectors caused other problems as well. "There was always the hazard . . . that we were not running in those days at a standard speed of 90 feet a minute," Hugo Friedhofer says. "If the projectionist happened to have a heavy date, let's say (I'm not kidding), all of a sudden the film would be speeded up on you and you'd have to watch the conductor very carefully because he'd cut you off in the middle of a phrase or in the middle of a sixteenth note."

In neighborhood theaters, the accompaniment could get quite loose, with cues ignored and difficult changes missed. "Sure," Joseph Gershenson said, these things happened, "but no one cared. It was a haphazard operation."

Music on the Set

There was a time when the appearance of a violinist and a pianist on the set in a studio provoked

laughter. *Their presence elicited ridicule, but not now.*

New York Times, *June 24, 1923*

Sometimes the actors would ask you to play certain tunes.

Joseph Gershenson,
silent movie musician/music director

There is disagreement as to exactly when musicians began performing mood music for actors during shooting. This practice had become commonplace by the twenties. "I asked Mr. DeMille if we might have music during our scenes," Geraldine Farrar said, "as I was so accustomed to orchestral accompaniment for certain tempi and phrasings, I felt I could better pantomime the rhythm of the effects. A little piano was hastily wheeled on the set and the talented Melville Ellis . . . inspired all my scenes with his impromptu playing. I believe this started the habit for music 'off-stage' for all later aspirants to emotional appeal. At any rate, from that time on I always had a musician at my elbow whose soulful throbs did more to start my tears than all the glycerine drops or onions more frequently employed by less responsive orbs."

Griffith didn't care for music on the set, claiming it would be distracting. "Under the spell of the music, I might be deeply moved by the scene, but later, when I ran it on the screen in silence, find it cold and flat. . . ." Blanche Sweet recalled that "most of the music was between takes, for relaxation, a kind of morale booster. It pepped up everybody. . . . Griffith never used any music while he was filming that I remember. He always said that he would never employ actors who could not feel the role enough to weep at rehearsals. . . ." Nevertheless, he employed Ralph Berliner's 30-piece Palm Court Orchestra for the battle sequence in *The Ten Commandments* (1923), and had Ruth Dickey on the set with a 10-piece band. Other directors, including Abel Gance, the great French director of *Napoleon* (1927), thought it a good idea. "I always had music on the set [organ, violin, cello] not only to give the mood, but to keep everyone quiet. You can capture their attention more easily by the use of music. In the scene where the young Napoleon lies on the cannon . . . he had to cry in that scene. He couldn't, until the musicians played Beethoven's *Moonlight Sonata.*"

The actors and actresses generally responded well to music while they worked. Writing about Betty Compson, director Adrian Brunel said that when they filmed *Woman to Woman* in 1923, "She was incapable of registering emotion without the aid of a 3-piece orchestra (piano, cello, violin). Throughout most of the scenes in *Woman to Woman* this orchestra would churn out 'Mighty Like a Rose' and Miss Compson would then perform and cry real tears (glycerine not being required). . . ."

Colleen Moore adds, "We always had mood music on the sets. I had a three-piece orchestra that played continually, not only to put us in the mood, but to amuse us between scenes, since I was making comedies and needed to keep in high spirits. . . ."

Although the practice died with the coming of sound, *Film Music Notes* documented the use of music to set the mood as late as 1944. "Jean Arthur . . . is one of the few remaining believers in music for creating moods. During the filming of the picture [*The Impatient Years*] a utility man played recordings for her from her private collection. She ordered serious symphonic music as a mood maker for comedy scenes, and jive as a conditioner for serious scenes."

Ruth Dickey, on the left with her violin, led a 10-piece ensemble during exterior scenes in the biblical prologue to Cecil B. DeMille's 1923 film *The Ten Commandments*. She and her musicians were reported to have contributed significantly to the overall morale of the cast and crew during the weeks of location shooting on remote sand dunes. Her orchestra also played for dancing at night for the 2500 or so actors and crew. *Photo courtesy of the American Museum of the Moving Image (Astoria, N.Y.)*

Contemporary Performances

Composers in Europe have been commissioned by European television stations in recent years to create new scores to silents like *The Passion of Joan of Arc* (France, 1928, score by Jo Van den Booren); *The Curious Adventure of Mr. West in Bolshevik Land* (USSR, 1924, score by Benedict Mason); *Nosferatu* (Germany, 1922, score by Richard McLaughlin); and *Greed* (1924), *The Big Parade* (1925), *Ben-Hur* (1926), *Intolerance* (1916), and *The Thief of Bagdad* (1924), all with original scores by Carl Davis.

There are now live orchestral performances ac-

companying silent films all over the world. Live performances in Los Angeles have included the first West Coast showing of Chaplin's *City Lights* with Carl Davis conducting his score with the Los Angeles Chamber Orchestra; *Lucky Star* (directed by Frank Borzage in 1929) with a new score by British composer Adrian Johnston, performed at UCLA in 1991 as a benefit screening for UCLA's film preservation work; and *Sunrise* (1927) with a new original score by David Newman, performed as a benefit in January, 1992. Carmine Coppola, Francis Ford Coppola's father, created a score for Gance's *Napoleon* in 1981.

No location was too unlikely for music on the set. The strains of the violin, harmonium (a small portable organ), and cello set the mood for the actors in this action scene from *Little French Girl* (1925).
Photo courtesy of the American Museum of the Moving Image (Astoria, N.Y.)

Perhaps the most active composer in this field is Carl Davis, who has composed new scores for over a dozen silents. "With silent films the music has to do everything. It has to do effects, dialogue, create the mood. It's the only sound. I did a silent film called *The Big Parade.* We know that in silent days they had a lot of people in the major cinemas making battle noises behind the screen. We tried not to do that. We tried to make it in the orchestra as part of the music. It's like writing an opera or a ballet, everything must be in the score.

"Except for *Napoleon,* I've done the most performances of *Ben-Hur.* I've conducted it in London, Liverpool, New York, Melbourne, Brisbane, Barcelona, and Luxembourg. I recorded the video version in London with the London Philharmonic, and I recorded the album with the Liverpool Philharmonic.

"The important part of *Ben-Hur* is the New Testament. That had to be presented in a very serious and good way, so I tried to model that on Bruckner. . . . The only thing I borrowed from the 1925 score was the rhythmic pattern for the race,

which was unusual. . . . The use of leitmotifs is very important in silent films. You evolve themes and interweave them as characters, situations, or ideas come up in the films. Even in comedies it's useful."

Gillian Anderson (who works in the Music Division of the Library of Congress) is the most active *re-creator* of period scores for silents. She has conducted all over the world, performing many authentic original scores to screenings of classic silent films. "I got started in it because I was basically bored with what I was doing, which was eighteenth-century music that was performed in this country. I wanted something greasy and sentimental by comparison. . . . So I got into nineteenth-century American and film music at that time. The common thread in all this is that I like music that has an interaction with something else—some other discipline. And I also like music that works with something that moves.

"The first one I did was *The Passion of Joan of Arc* in 1979 or '80 [original score by Léo Pouget and Victor Alix]. . . . I just made up my mind after seeing it that I was going to synchronize it. I was going to learn how to do it. It was probably the *worst* one for me to have started with, because it has the fewest cues, and the hardest to decide. So I had to look at her burn to death over and over and over again. We had four strings, piano and organ, and a choir. Subsequently I've done it with . . . percussion, harp, and lots of strings also."

Anderson has since re-created and synchronized performances of *Intolerance, Way Down East, The Thief of Bagdad, Wings, Carmen,* and the 1904 *Parsifal.* She conducted the world premiere screening of the re-created Breil score for *Intolerance* in New York City; the European premiere in Portanona, Italy; and the South American premiere in Rio. She has performed the score she most admires, Mortimer Wilson's score for *Thief of Bagdad,* with the Columbus, Virginia, San Diego, and Puerto Rican Symphonies.

She has also re-created the score for *Yankee Clipper* using the cue sheet. This experience led her to a great admiration for the orchestrator-arrangers who often worked from piano scores. "The arrangers were *fabulous.* I'm very keen on recognizing the contribution that American arrangers have made to American music."

Silent movie music, once discarded with disinterest, has been carefully preserved and catalogued at a number of institutions around the world, including the Library of Congress; the Museum of Modern Art in New York; the Fédération Internationale des Archives du Film in Brussels, Belgium; the Arthur Kleiner Collection at the University of Minnesota; and at the Society for the Preservation of Film Music in Los Angeles.

Silents are also being documented on laser disc. In 1991 a special laser disc edition of *Birth of a Nation* was released by Lumivision. The original Breil score is re-created from the 1915 and 1921 orchestral parts, piano scores and cue sheets. Also, MGM/UA Home Video Silent Classics Series reissued King Vidor's *The Crowd* (1928) and Victor Seastrom's *The Wind* (1927, released in 1928) as a laser set. The scores are by Carl Davis. There are a number of others available as well.

Conductor Gillian Anderson re-creates a silent film score, using a live orchestra to accompany the picture.
Photo: H. Bellamy

ANIMATION

Animation relies very heavily on music for storytelling.

Jerry Goldsmith

The term "Mickey-Mousing" in film scoring came from hitting all the action in cartoons. Mickey took a sneaky step, and the music accented his foot hitting the floor. Elmer Fudd got hit on the head, and the music accented the moment. Even in more life-like animated storytelling, like *Pinocchio* (1940) or *Beauty and the Beast* (1991), composers often hit a little more with their scoring than they would in a live action movie.

"For example," says Buddy Baker, "in the Main Title for *The Fox and the Hound* (1981), when the little fox struck at the lady, I caught that, because there was no sound effect for it, and it looked cute.

Well, if you did the same thing in live action, it would be Mickey-Mousing. I wouldn't necessarily have caught that motion if it had been a live fox."

Unlike live action features, an animated picture like *The Fox and the Hound* or *Snow White and the Seven Dwarfs* (1937) calls for almost continuous music throughout the film. "Keeping your continuity without getting monotonous is the big problem," Baker points out. He learned to vary the size and texture of the instrumentation from cue to cue. "I may end up with four or five different instrumental combinations. A big orchestra thing, then relief with guitar and harmonica (if it's a country-type thing). You can't keep going full-bore with a big orchestra all the time. It's like eating too much candy—it can make you not feel too good."

When Henry Mancini scored *The Great Mouse Detective* (1986), he wanted to avoid hitting all the action, but found it was necessary sometimes. "It was a challenge to get themes that played themselves behind the action, and yet get some recognition to the audience that you knew that there were other things going on up on that screen. So, within the framework of the melodies, somehow, if something happened on the screen, I would serve both masters."

Pacing is different, too, as Jerry Goldsmith discovered when he scored *The Secret of Nimh* (1982). "In animation, the length of scenes is much shorter than in live action, because every frame is drawn, or every other frame at least. Things just can't take as long, so it's more difficult to get a flowing line in the music. One can be broader, dramatically, because of the fact that it is all abstract."

Alan Silvestri, who scored *Who Framed Roger Rabbit* (1988), found the actual motion of the characters was different from live action. "Animation is a tremendous force on the screen. Animated characters move differently, their emotional pace is far, far quicker than humans." He consequently adapted his scoring to this faster flow. J.A.C. Redford learned this the hard way. When he was scoring *Oliver & Company* (1988), the filmmakers "didn't want it to be cartoony." But when he scored it like a live-action feature, the results were disappointing. "The tempos in the music needed to be faster; there needed to be

more of the kinds of leaps and color changes associated with animated pictures. So we went back and redid those cues, and it really helped the picture."

Walt Disney loved music, and reinforced the relationship between music and animation by developing the Silly Symphony cartoon shorts in the late twenties. At first, the scores constantly quoted familiar tunes. *Plane Crazy,* an early Mickey Mouse cartoon, used tunes such as "Yankee Doodle," "Dixie," "Auld Lang Syne," and "Rock-a-Bye Baby." Continual repetition quickly killed the effectiveness of these musical references, though.

By the time *Snow White* was in development, music was as important to his films as any other element, and he wanted to use it in a sophisticated way. He was always personally involved in nurturing the development of the songs, which are prerecorded (as is the dialogue) so the animators can draw the mouth motions accurately as the characters sing the lyrics. Frank Churchill ("Who's Afraid of the Big Bad Wolf") and lyricist Larry Morey were assigned to the film. In his book *Behind the Scenes,* Rudy Behlmer describes the development process.

> Innumerable song possibilities were discussed, developed, and eventually discarded because they did not come up to Disney's expectations. Disney was always on hand to dictate the content of each song, to say what had to be expressed at each point, to listen and then have things modified or redone when needed, and to correct lyrics and put in new words. Since the musical sequences, which constituted a large percentage of the film, could not be animated until the tunes were recorded, most of the numbers were recorded in 1936. The background score was done after the picture was finished and edited.

Disney was looking for a more organic way to use songs in the film. During a story conference, he said, "We still haven't hit it in any of these songs. . . . It's still that influence from the musicals they have been doing for years. Really, we should set a new pattern—a new way to use music—weave it into the story so somebody doesn't just burst into song." This has become an ideal throughout the years, both on the stage and on the screen, and with *Snow White*'s success, this goal seemed more attainable.

Meanwhile, composers for cartoon shorts stuck to the old practice of quoting numerous tunes, but managed to develop characteristic styles even while doing so.

Carl Stalling, while in charge of Warner Bros. cartoons from 1936 until 1958, scored the great Bugs Bunny shorts, as well as Daffy Duck, Porky Pig, and others. Excerpts from his scores for these cartoons are available on a CD entitled "The Carl Stalling Project: Music from Warner Bros. Cartoons." Randall D. Larson reviewed the CD in 1991 for *Soundtrack!* "This remarkable collection of cartoon music at first seems little more than a curiousity until, after a good listening or two, one realizes what a treasure-chest of marvelous music this is. After virtually inventing the process of scoring for animation at the Disney Studios, Carl Stalling moved to Warner Bros., where he was in charge of all music for the studio's cartoon shorts from 1936 until 1958, writing an incredible amound and variety of music, all types and nearly wall-to-wall preponderance, on hundreds of cartoons from Bugs Bunny to Daffy Duck, Porky Pig to Tweety. . . . Not only has his work gone virtually unrecognized, but cartoon music as a whole has been routinely unappreciated. This new collection of original soundtrack recordings will do much to rectify this."

Scott Bradley, who scored the MGM cartoons, including the Tom and Jerry series, was also very innovative and helped establish an appropriate and surprisingly sophisticated style.

COMEDIES

"I really don't like comedy scores. To me the old-fashioned comedy scores sound like cartoons, with little jokes for solo instruments and the music trying to duplicate what is happening on the screen, which is ridiculous. Music can create funny effects, but not by trying to sound funny. . . . The biggest mistake is to play comedy music against funny dialogue. . . . Comedy plays itself. You don't have to make comments about comedy. If somebody would say something funny, in old times, or make what they call a *take-um,* a silly face with the eyes rolling, the music would come to show you that it was funny, as if you didn't know."

Bronislau Kaper, composer

"In *The Pink Panther* . . . the theme itself was the backdrop and the canvas without caring about what they were doing. I very rarely pay attention to comedy in any of Blake's pictures."

Henry Mancini, composer

"John Landis was the director of *Animal House.* And, at that point in time, it was John Landis' idea—the idea of approaching comedy scoring with playing the music fairly straight and let the comedy take care of itself. Let the music support the straight aspect of it. . . . Certainly, in *Airplane!*, I definitely made reference by style to very old film scoring. A lot of that. It was serious. It was meant to be serious, but sort of great, big serious. . . . If I just made the music funny, then it's funny on funny—so what do you need the music for?"

Elmer Bernstein, composer

"If a scene in a movie is funny, I would almost prefer to leave it unscored unless, of course, it is some kind of slapstick or burlesque where music can provide it a balletic sense, tempo."

John Williams, composer

DOCUMENTARIES

It is particularly significant that the so-called documentary films, including those sponsored by the government, have all paid special attention to the quality and appeal of the musical score.

Sigmund Spaeth,
American music historian (1942)

Documentaries have always offered great potential for composers. During the forties they were being made for the government and also for theatrical distribution. Many concert hall composers scored them, including Morton Gould, Robert Russell Bennett, Oscar Levant, Paul Creston, Gail Kubik, Mark Blitzstein, and others. Virgil Thomson scored three: *The Plow That Broke the Plains* (1936), *The River* (1937), and *Louisiana Story* (1948).

Frederick W. Sternfeld, writing in *Film Music Notes* in 1948, commented on a basic difference in the point of view of documentary filmmakers.

The makers of documentaries have faith in the twentieth-century composers. Flaherty, Lorentz, Rodakiewicz, Van Dyke, all realize that a contemporary film requires a contemporary score. Instead of commissioning paste-and-scissors jobs on Chopin, Tchaikovsky, et al., they have offered opportunities to our foremost composers. They have done so neither with the pretense of altruism nor with despotic arrogance, but with a singleness of purpose that demands the contemporary musician because his idiom fits the job. The time-honored general formula that allows full rein to a master craftsman, once chosen, is the one largely responsible for the superior musical scores of the documentaries. Here the composer is not cramped by a director who seeks to appeal to the lowest common denominator, nor is he checked by an overly conservative and unimaginative studio music department. He decides of his own will when and how to use his art, and music critics and teachers will testify to the successful results of such collaboration. So, too, will the audiences, although they may not articulate their reactions.

During the fifties, Disney produced a number of outstanding live-action nature studies, many of which were scored by Disney staff composer Oliver Wallace.

Theatrical distribution is difficult, but fine documentaries continue to be produced and scored, often offering excellent opportunities for composers. Those outside the Hollywood mainstream are especially attracted to them, though several of the films made for the Imax projection system have been scored by established Hollywood composers like Bill Conti. Many outstanding scores have been written for television documentaries such as those produced for the National Geographic series and the Jacques Cousteau series.

HORROR FILMS

I write novels for a living, and when RKO was looking for producers, someone told them I had written horrible novels. They mistook the word horrible *for* horror *and I got the job.*

Val Lewton, producer

In scoring horror pictures, the main element is that of creating atmosphere—the apprehensive mood, which keeps the viewer on the edge of his seat....

Hans J. Salter, composer

Tony Thomas' fascinating *Film Score: The Art & Craft of Movie Music* includes a section by Hans J. Salter in which he discusses his work in this genre at Universal Studios.

The Universal horror pictures were a great challenge to me, as they would have been to any composer, because it was apparent when we looked at these things in their naked form that music would have to play a great part in their effectiveness. To be candid about it, a lot of these films were really not good—the scenes were disjointed, there was little cohesion, and they were not even scary. You had to create the horror with the music, to create the tension that was otherwise not there on the screen. It was such an obvious challenge that I became more and more interested in doing this kind of film.... They were so much in need of music, and for reasons that I have never been able to fully explain, I was able to devise a technique in dealing with them. I became known as "The Master of Terror and Suspense," and people could never understand how a nice, mild-mannered fellow from Vienna could become a specialist in such material. Neither could I, except to say that perhaps I had a certain affinity with fantasy stories. . . . Whenever other studios set out to make horror pictures, they usually showed the composers some of ours to give them an idea of what it was all about. . . .

We thought little about the horror pictures when we were scoring them, but time has given them a kind of distinction. It seems to me that those horror items of that era may survive better than most of the other films made at the time. It's a valid piece of Americana, and it is a unique body of work, with a certain style that cannot be duplicated.

Franz Waxman and Boris Karloff during the production of *Bride of Frankenstein* (1935). Waxman's score was unusual in its use of symphonic music for this genre, and various cues from *Bride* were used many times thereafter for other Universal horror films and serials.
Photo courtesy of Marc Wanamaker/Bison Archives

MUSICALS

Effective use of film music is not limited to pictures of a dramatic nature. It is in musicals that film music has had its greatest use and development. In these pictures music is an integral part of the story.
      Nathaniel Shilkret, music director

Right now it is impossible to cross the lobby of the Roosevelt Hotel without wading waist-deep through song-writers. In Hollywood's cafés they get into your hair.
      Jerry Hoffman, Photoplay, September 1929

After the popular success of *The Jazz Singer* in 1927, many songwriters caught the first train to Hollywood, and with good reason. Virtually every film released in 1928 had at least one interpolated song. By 1930, though, audiences had heard enough, and were no longer interested in having the story stop while someone sang an often unrelated song on-screen. Musicals were passé.

Then, in 1932, Rouben Mamoulian directed *Love Me Tonight,* one of the great screen musicals.

In that one film, he demonstrated how entertaining and dramatically effective it could be to listen to a song being sung while the plot actually continued to develop. There are several terrific examples in this Maurice Chevalier–Jeanette MacDonald vehicle, one of the best being the Rodgers and Hart song, "Isn't It Romantic?" Miles Kreuger, musical theater authority and founder of the Institute of the American Musical, points out that it is also the most complicated number.

"'Isn't It Romantic?' begins in the tailor's shop, and Bert Roach, the brother of Hal Roach, is a customer in Maurice Chevalier's shop," he says. "The two of them begin to sing the song. Bert Roach continues to sing the song as he comes out and walks past a taxicab. Ralph Sedan is sitting there at the curb in his cab and overhears it, and he begins to sing it. Tyler Brooke gets into the cab as a cus-

When the introduction of sound, Hollywood began filming songs and musicals. They were in, they were out, and then, with Busby Berkeley's staging of the musical numbers in *42nd Street* in 1933, musicals became more popular than ever. That same year, Berkeley staged the production numbers in *Footlight Parade*, in which a dancing/singing James Cagney starred with Joan Blondell, Ruby Keeler, and Dick Powell. Cagney was featured in "Shanghai Lil." The staging for "By a Waterfall" is classic Berkeley. Both songs are by Harry Warren (music) and Al Dubin (lyrics).

then take up the tune with a gypsy violin. And then, in the distance, there just happens to be a castle, and there just happens to be a lovelorn princess, Jeanette MacDonald, who overhears the distant sound of the gypsies playing and singing, and she starts to sing it. In that one musical number—think of all the sets involved: there was the tailor shop, the sidewalk, the taxicab, the train, the countryside, and the castle. That's six different sets. One song has linked two people who have not yet met each other in the story, that are destined to become the lovers of the story.

"Now, if there is a better use of a song in a film, I can't think of one. It's brilliant because not only is 'Isn't It Romantic?' a splendid song by Rodgers and Hart, but that use of the song could never have been done on a stage. It *requires* film. Now, *that* is a positive use, to me, of film within the medium of the musical. And that's *1932*."

In those days we didn't wait for a New York show to become a hit before putting it on the screen. We were content to write original stories with original musical scores, and embellish them with unusually daring and spectacular musical numbers—and the audiences loved them.

Busby Berkeley, director

In my opinion, no picture except an operetta should have more than four songs, but these four should be sung often. Even a musical comedy shouldn't have more than four, or at the most, five, songs, of which two are almost certain to become hits.

Irving Berlin, songwriter (1930)

tomer. He hears Ralph Sedan sing the song, and he begins to sing the song. He gets on a train, where he's trying to write some poetry, but it happens for some curious reason to be a troop train occupied largely by soldiers, and they hear him singing this song, and they start to sing it. Now there's a cut, and now they're marching and 'Isn't It Romantic?' is being sung as a military march. Meanwhile, this troupe of marching soldiers singing 'Isn't It Romantic?' are overheard by a campsite of gypsies, who

The following year, in 1933, Busby Berkeley staged the production numbers for a seemingly innocuous backstage musical, *42nd Street*. Differing from Mamoulian, Berkeley took the opposite approach, setting up elaborate and dazzling production numbers that deliberately stopped the story cold. He was so imaginative that it worked—his staging was far more interesting than the plot, and audiences loved it. He did two more films in 1933, *Gold Diggers of 1933,* and *Footlight Parade,* starring James Cagney. Musicals were back, and remained in fashion for the next 20 years.

Both types of song usage had value, but in general, the *musicals* sought to integrate the songs into the plot, whereas there were many films made that were vehicles for songs relatively unrelated to the story development (including some of Berkeley's subsequent films) and many more featuring bands and nightclub singers. The success of both the organic songs (often written specifically for the movie) and the nonorganic songs depended on the talents of the songwriters, most of whom had come to California from New York.

The Songwriters

The Hollywood songwriters of the thirties and forties were well established before coming out to the Coast. They had written hit Broadway shows, nightclub revues, and pop songs. There were many songwriters working in Hollywood during those years, but none more illustrious than Harold Arlen, Irving Berlin, George Gershwin, Jerome Kern, Cole Porter, Richard Rodgers, and Harry Warren. They were as influential in the evolution of film songs as Max Steiner and his colleagues had been for the art of film scoring. They collaborated with some of the greatest lyricists, including Ira Gershwin, Dorothy Fields, Oscar Hammerstein II, Lorenz Hart, E. Y. "Yip" Harburg, and Johnny Mercer. The lyricists, of course, contributed tremendously to the successful organic integration of songs into films. (See the Bibliography for a selected listing of books on Hollywood musicals and songwriters.)

NEWSREELS

A primitive form of newsreel—a filmed documentation of current events—began shortly after the development of motion pictures, well before the turn of the century. Pathé began producing them in 1910, and by the end of the twenties, companies like Fox Movietone and others were also distributing newsreels, which were run as a regular feature at moviehouses. Television ultimately doomed them to obsolescence during the fifties.

They all used music which sounded "canned," because it was, in fact, canned music, having been recorded as library music to be used as needed. "After I became head of the music department at Universal," Joseph Gershenson recalled, "I'd select certain compositions that would be suitable for newsreels, like marches. And once a year I would go to New York, and we had a deal with [James C.] Peterillo [head of the musicians union]. He would let me record a lot of music, and that [music] they could use in newsreels."

Over the years, the lives and music of many illustrious songwriters have been used as the basis for biographical musicals—a sub-genre of the bio-pic. Robert Alda stars as George Gershwin in the 1945 Warner Bros. film *Rhapsody in Blue*. Band leader Paul Whiteman commissioned and conducted the title composition at its premiere in New York in 1924. That premiere performance is re-created in the film performed by Whiteman and his band, with Oscar Levant playing the piano solo on the soundtrack.

Not all newsreel music was cut together from a prerecorded library, though. In 1935, the MARCH OF TIME series began, a prestigious newsreel associated with *Time* magazine, which used specially created music. In 1943, Jack Schaindlin was director of music for the series. "The task of fitting music to the MARCH OF TIME is not a simple one. In fact, it is, perhaps, the most complex task that any musical director has to face, for a knowledge of music is only a small part of the job, representing about one-tenth of what the musical director has to know.

"It is an accepted practice in Hollywood to give the composer three to six weeks and often longer to score a motion picture. This seemingly reasonable amount of time enables the musical director and his staff to give proper thought and care to the selections and musical treatments. Not being quite as fortunate, I sometimes have to prepare a score for a picture in two or three days.

"The MARCH OF TIME being a 'news' subject necessitates the watching of news events, and very often Mr. Louis de Rochemont, the producer of MARCH OF TIME, has to issue an order to change the subject matter two or three days before the deadline."

Some of these newsreels are available on videocassette.

SERIALS

During the thirties, serials like *Flash Gordon, Buck Rogers, Dick Tracy, The Green Hornet, Superman,* and many others were produced to run as a special added attraction along with the regular full-length features. They were designed to be shown episode by episode, one two-reeler each week, each ending in a cliffhanger that left some doubt as to the survival of the hero. Typically, serials consisted of 12 to 15 "chapters." Some original music was written for them, but a lot of the music that found its way onto these soundtracks came from existing material already recorded and used in other films.

Through the end of 1938, the American Federation of Musicians allowed the studios to reuse any music in their library without rerecording it. They could simply print another copy of a cue and cut it in where they wanted it, ready for dubbing. Beginning in January of 1939, however, they were required by the union either to record new music for all their films, or to rerecord the existing music for each new usage. Frequently the newly recorded versions were so poor they would then reprint the original anyway, a practice that was later adopted for episodic television scoring.

Flash Gordon (1936) was the most expensive serial ever made, and featured a new piece of music by Clifford Vaughan for the Main Title. The rest of the score consisted of cues from *The Invisible Man* (Hans Roemheld, 1933), Karl Hajos' *Werewolf of London* (1935), Roemheld's 1934 score for *The Black Cat,* and other science fiction and horror films in the Universal library.

Portions of Waxman's score for *Bride of Frankenstein* (1935) were dubbed onto the soundtrack of *Flash Gordon's Trip to Mars* (1938). Hans Roemheld's 1936 score for *Dracula's Daughter* was also used on that soundtrack.

The last serial produced was Columbia's *Blazing the Overland Trail* in 1956.

Serials, cartoons, musicals, and many other genre films, like Westerns, film noir, war films, crime melodramas, and so on, evolved during the days of the powerful Hollywood studios. From the thirties through the mid-fifties, the studio system flourished. With year-to-year contracts and strong backup from the music departments, the art and craft of film music developed and matured.

PART THREE

HOLLYWOOD

■ ■ ■

The Studio System

∎ ∎ ∎

People now . . . say that everything was so terrible in those days—that's foolish. Either we were all terribly indiscriminate or it was a hell of a lot better than people ever imagined. I believe that's the way it was.

David Raksin, composer

Looking back, I sometimes think I was much overworked and perhaps a bit too timid to stand up for my rights. I've worked Christmas; I've worked the Fourth of July—in fact, I've worked when two of my children were being born and I should have been there in case anything went wrong.

Alfred Newman, composer

THE STUDIOS

From the moment Al Jolson immortalized the line "You ain't heard nothin' yet!" and then sang "Toot, Toot, Tootsie" in *The Jazz Singer* (1927), it was easy to see the business and entertainment potential for music in film. By the end of 1927 Hollywood began cramming songs into both musicals and dramatic films. The possibilities for music in this new medium seemed unlimited. Darryl Zanuck (then a screenwriter at Warner Bros.) observed, "Harry Warner didn't give a damn what the characters were saying on the screen, and I have to say that I didn't bother about it much, either. We all thought Harry had a point when he said, 'Do you realize what this means? From now on we can give every small town in America, and every moviehouse, its own 110-piece orchestra.'"

By the beginning of 1929, it was obvious that on-screen sound was a big attraction, and music was the best way to exploit this new medium. "Every songwriter who could play one chord was hired by Hollywood," said Oscar Levant. "I went out to play my original part in the film version of *Burlesque* and stayed on to write songs for several movies at RKO Studios."

When MGM's *The Broadway Melody* opened in February, 1929, it became a big hit. Photoplay's review was ecstatic:

> *The Broadway Melody* is going to sing merrily across the screens of the country, entertaining millions and making new friends for the talking pictures. For *The Broadway Melody* is sparkling, smart, and entertaining—a credit to its makers and a joy to the fans . . .
>
> The crafty directorial hand of Harry Beaumont has tickled, teased, and whipped it into a fast, funny, sad little story, alive in turn with titters and tears. . . .

Broadway Melody became the movie to imitate. Backstage musicals were in, and so were hundreds of musicians.

In the early days of sound, all the elements had to be recorded live on the set while the picture was being shot. Live (or "set") recording was necessary at first even on songs and more complex musical numbers. The orchestra would be assembled at the side of the set, and would accompany the songs and dances as they were being shot—the same process music editor Ralph Ives has described (in Chapter 3) as prevalent when he began working in films at the Fleischer Animation Studios in 1934.

This could create enormous artistic and technical problems. A proper balance had to be achieved between the voices and the orchestra. Microphones were hidden in flowers and other props as necessary (just as in *Singin' in the Rain*), so the vocalists were required to stay close to the hidden mic. And the performances by the singers and the orchestra had to be excellent—simultaneously. If the singer made a mistake, both the singer and the orchestra had to record the whole number over again.

As trying as this was, it created a bonanza for the recording musicians. Violinist Louis Kaufman recalls the time an actress on one of these early sessions was having a particularly hard time getting her part right. In fact, it took her *six hours.* "She was supposed to look down, and then look up, and say 'Do you really, Dick?' We didn't mind, because we were cleaning up on that." And cleaning up they were—musicians were paid by the hour, with double time after midnight (not an unusual hour to be shooting a sound film in those days—it was quieter than the daytime hours).

Six hours, then, is no exaggeration—it took forever to record and shoot simultaneously. As the problems were overcome—and technical advances were rapid—it became possible to record the music *before* the scenes involving vocalists and dancers were photographed. Hollywood began to use the technique of prerecording as soon as the necessary technology was available. As Kaufman notes, "They learned the hard way that it cost too darn much money [to record live]."

Hollywood had its economic ups and downs during the early thirties, due in part to the Depression and in part to the unpredictable evolution of the talkies. Theater attendance fell dramatically in 1930, and again in 1931. Although it took longer for the studios to feel the results of the country's economic hardships, it became evident that even the movies were not Depression-proof. Furthermore, by the time the studios had whipped up dozens of full-length musicals, audiences were no longer interested in the genre—another severe blow to the business. Only MGM seemed to be avoiding hardship. They continued to earn substantial, though scaled-down, profits.

Hollywood, like Rocky Balboa, never seems to go down for the count. As the dust settled and the industry stabilized, eight major studios emerged: Columbia, MGM, Paramount, RKO, Twentieth Century Pictures (later merging with Fox to become Twentieth Century–Fox), United Artists, Universal, and Warner Bros. Each studio had a personality of its own, dictated by the strengths, weaknesses, and personal inclinations of its leader, and there were differences in their approaches to moviemaking. Warner Bros., for example, developed gangster films with James Cagney and the backstage musical extravaganzas staged by Busby Berkeley, while Universal developed the horror film, beginning in 1931 with *Dracula* and *Frankenstein*.

There were many similarities in the major studios' approaches to running their businesses and making movies, and the first composers and other music personnel who came out to Hollywood as the talkies developed worked by and large within the Hollywood studio system.

First of all, music directors were needed to administer the business matters, conduct the orchestras as needed, and build and run the departments; Leo Forbstein had been hired by Warner Bros. in the late twenties, Max Steiner was at RKO in 1930, and the other studios were each developing their own music departments. Arthur Lange was invited to join MGM in 1929 to create the MGM music department. He arrived with his business associate, Ernst Klapholz.

Lange was dismayed. "We had no music and we had to make a music department. It was still just bungalows. It was terrible. It was one little room with a piano in it. I came out here on the premise that I was to be musical director, and Ernie was to be the business head of the music department. We didn't have an office. All they gave us was a little two-by-four building that had a room with a desk in it and a piano. It was like the old piano rooms that they had in publishing houses."

"They took one of the bungalows and started to tear it apart," Klapholz remembered, "and Broones [titular executive-in-charge] had one big office with a secretary, Arthur had an office, and I had an office. Then I requested the second and the third and the fourth and the fifth bungalows, so the whole music department was located in bungalows outside. Each pair of songwriters had a bungalow. [Herb] Brown [1896–1964] and [Arthur] Freed [1894–1973] had a bungalow, then [Roy] Turk [1892–1934] and [Fred E.] Ahlert [1892–1953] had a bungalow. I told them what I needed. They'd say, 'How much [money] do they want?' I said, 'So-and-so much.' 'Okay.' There was no argument about it."

"We had the full run of the thing," Lange explains. "Nobody told us what to do."

"When they heard something new, they'd say, 'My God, it's genius!' Klapholz adds.

I loved the studio, I loved the way it smelled, I was crazy about Indians in the lunchroom, and Romans making phone calls, and the highly charged and technically dazzling music making on the recording stage. Most of all, I loved being a part of it, a part of a peculiar fraternity, belittled and superior at the same time, envied for all the wrong reasons and commiserated with for the stuff we all took in our stride. . . .

André Previn, composer

Most of the musicians working in the Hollywood studio system seemed to enjoy it. In 1975, reflecting on the general attitude in the workplace during the early forties, music editor June Edgerton said, "The whole world had a different spirit then. Everyone was in there to really do their job. Now everyone gripes if they have to do a little bit extra or something. But then you thought nothing of it. It was your job, and you wanted to do it to the best of your ability. There was much more spirit than I find now. Now, some of these young kids who come in, say, 'Oh, that's too heavy; I can't lift that,' or, 'You mean I have to walk all the way over *there*?' And I don't blame it on the young people. It's just a general feeling [of the times]."

The system had a lot to offer the aspiring film composer. "I must say that I was a great beneficiary of that system, coming here as a young man [in 1950]," says Elmer Bernstein. "I had never done films, I had done radio. My office at Columbia Pictures, my first employer, was right next to George Duning and Arthur Morton, who were under contract to Columbia at that time. And I have to tell you, the atmosphere was amazing. They helped teach me about mechanical things that I didn't know, about how film worked. It was an era in which we went to each other's recordings, and it's amazing to think about that. A David Raksin recording or a Bernard Herrmann recording or a Miklós Rózsa recording was an *event*. And we all

Some of the 20th Century-Fox music staff in the early fifties included (left to right) Franz Waxman, Alfred Newman (head of music), Bernard Herrmann, Ken Darby (who worked closely with Newman on large-scale projects such as *How the West Was Won* and *The Greatest Story Ever Told*), Vinton Vernon (scoring stage music mixer), Alex North, and Hugo Friedhofer.
Photo courtesy of the USC-Cinema-Television Library and Archives of Performing Arts and Martha Newman Ragland

went, and we were very interested in what each of us were doing.

"The studios helped, actually, to create what was basically a community of composers. I'm not saying that we necessarily loved everything each of us did—don't get the wrong idea—we were competitors, and we got upset, hurt, angry, if somebody else got some job we wanted, or we didn't get to do something we thought we could do better than the person who got it. But there was a sense of community—we really cared about each other. And we communicated."

David Raksin concurs. "It was an atmosphere of mutual encouragement, and there was comparatively little envy, less than one might have expected. It is amazing and wonderful that in a profession in which there are so many more competent people than jobs, in which so many suffer the humiliation

of having to sit around and see their talents wasted, so many of the composers are good friends and admirers of the work of others. That speaks well of our profession."

If you became part of the system, working either under contract to one studio for a period of time, or freelancing among them on a job-by-job basis, you became part of this community Bernstein and Raksin describe. Many would often stay at one studio for years—even decades—developing an increasingly deep sense of loyalty for their own studio. Hans J. Salter started at Universal in 1938 and stayed on for thirty years. John Hammell worked in the mailroom at Paramount in 1934, became a music editor in 1938, and continued there until he retired 45 years later. "Of course, you didn't go to other studios in those days," Hammell explains. "You were in there for life in your studios—they were family institutions. There were weeks sometimes that we sat around and never turned a wheel at Paramount. No work coming through." Still, the checks kept coming, work or no work. Usually, though, they had more work than they could handle. "We prided ourselves on saving that company money—and they had a responsibility with us."

The composers, orchestrators, and arrangers came and went as they pleased. At Paramount they weren't required to work on the lot, but they each had an office in the music building to use when necessary. "They'd come in during the day and pick up music and maybe run some reels and talk with the necessary people," says John Hammell. "Some to the cutting room, some of them, and then go on and work at home. Many, many were the days, though, that we'd walk through that library and they'd be all working in those rooms.

"A permanent room was usually assigned to one person. It was their room; a grand piano, and in those day, of course, no tape equipment or anything like that. But a good desk, and it was home to many men through the years. We'd have big meetings on the musicals in those rooms, and the producers, directors, composers, orchestrators would all be in there for various reasons. Songs would be played and approved. Oh, the songs that were played in those rooms."

Fellow music editor Bill Stinson, starting as a mailboy for Paramount in 1940, eventually became so indispensable to the studio over the years as executive in charge of music that they never could really replace him, so they kept coaxing him out of retirement to help them out. "Beautiful studio," he reminisced in 1986. "It's been my home and I love it. It's a very music-oriented studio. . . . I had many chances to leave there and I just never would. I just said, 'This is my home.'"

Paramount music editors (from left to right) John Hammell, Bill Stinson, June Edgerton, and Steve Cillag [*Chillog*] in the early fifties. Every studio developed a staff of music editors who were assigned on specific projects and also helped each out when deadlines became impossible.
Photo courtesy of Paramount Pictures

Herbert Stothart listens in the control booth in January, 1943, during the scoring of *Thousands Cheer*, a musical starring Mickey Rooney, Judy Garland, Gene Kelly and many others. Stothart scored many films for MGM during the thirties and forties—dramas such as *Madame Curie* (1943), and many musicals, including *The Wizard of Oz* (1939), featuring songs by Harold Arlen and E. Y. Harburg. On his right is recording mixer Mike McLaughlin. In the days before multitrack and stereophonic recording, the console had only a few round-knob faders for balancing the music.
Photo courtesy of Marc Wanamaker/Bison Archives

This family feeling wasn't exclusive to Paramount. Walt Disney Studios was a smaller studio, a factor that was even more conducive to promoting the family environment. Disney himself seemed more accessible than the heads of the other studios. "I saw him just about every day," says composer Buddy Baker. "I parked my car about two cars from his. . . . It was probably the most family-oriented lot of them all, because it was smaller, and we had to work so closely together with the animators and writers, it gave music people a chance to be closer than you would ordinarily to the creative end, from a writing standpoint."

When Miklós Rózsa first came to Metro-Goldwyn-Mayer in 1948, he had some misgivings. MGM was, of course, much bigger than Disney, or even Paramount, and was dominated by Louis B. Mayer. "I had heard much bad and little good about MGM before I arrived there: that its immense and relentless conveyor-belt-style productivity

When John Green (then known as "Johnny" Green) was executive in charge of music at MGM, his staff meetings were a weekly event. Present on May 7, 1951 (from left to right) are Rudy Kopp (a music editor who temp-tracked films with recordings), Adolph Deutsch (whose scores include *The Maltese Falcon* in 1941), Georgie Stoll (assistant conductor), Charles Wolcott (a specialist in vocal arranging and an assistant to Green), John Green, David Raksin, Bronislau Kaper, Alberto Columbo (a composer and assistant to Green), and David Rose (who composed "Holiday for Strings" and "The Stripper", and whose film scores include *The Princess and the Pirate* [1944] and, beginning in 1974, the television series "Little House on the Prairie").
Photo courtesy of Marc Wanamaker/Bison Archives

depended on a constant ingestion of new creative talent, but that artists counted for little or nothing apart from their ability to deliver the goods. Well, I can only report that, in my early days, at least, I saw little or nothing of this. I was treated in all quarters with the greatest kindness and consideration."

Director George Sidney describes the aura surrounding the studio. "It was the Emerald City, a kingdom of magic, a world within a world. Everything was there—food, dentistry, all your physical problems attended to. There was any kind of per-

son you needed—someone to fix your watch, to fix your toenails, to teach you to speak French, to duel, to sing, to dance, to speak English, to speak American. . . . There were always specialists at MGM at that time."

But times change, and by the end of the fifties the studio system of the golden years would never be the same again. Sadly, even the attitudes were different, reflecting a more impersonal, business-is-everything point of view. Miklós Rózsa remembers the spring of 1962: ". . . It was obvious that my contract with MGM wasn't going to be renewed; the studio proposed they give me *Sodom and Gomorrah* and terminate it immediately, as there was nothing more for me to do there. I was glad to go; it wasn't the MGM of the old days. I left without a word of thanks or a goodbye from anybody."

CLASS DISTINCTIONS

The first thing I learned upon coming to Hollywood was that class distinctions here were bigger than in India.

Bronislau Kaper, composer

There were several clear-cut and socially accepted distinctions that were part of the Hollywood system. The first was that the departments were encouraged to be separate entities, and to have a sense of their social status within the hierarchy. Each department had its own table in the studio commissary, and that helped to delineate class distinctions. The music department (both staff and any visiting musicians) sat at the "music table" during lunch. There was a "writers' table," a "sound table," and so on. This discouraged the intermingling of so-called "crafts" people with the writers, directors, producers, and executives. It also helped to insulate the stars from the employees.

The second distinction was made *within* the music department itself. Although some of the music heads, like Alfred Newman at Fox, socialized after hours with the musicians, music editors, and others, John Hammell remembers that the music editors at Paramount would not be invited to certain functions. And very often, in order to keep the intermingling of classes to a minimum, the music director would become intermediary to those working under him in his department. In that way, the music directors (who were executives) communicated with the studio executives (including the head office) and the filmmakers, and then passed the word on to their staffs.

Nevertheless, the Hollywood community feeling and the accompanying perks were there, for those on the lower as well as the upper levels—as long as you were part of the system. If you came in from the outside, things were not always quite so warm or friendly. Newcomers could find the going rough. Alex North scored two movies for Elia Kazan during his first year in Hollywood. He felt some resistance to him, as a stranger in Hollywood. "I had a tough time here. It was a 'closed shop,' and if it hadn't been for Elia Kazan who pushed for me to do *Streetcar*, I wouldn't be out here. . . . I was lucky to first work for Ray Heindorf at Warner Bros. He was a marvelous, innate musician. He made me feel very much at home in Hollywood, as opposed to other composers and studio heads who felt I was some guy coming from some attic in New York suddenly doing major films. I did feel very much out of place. The only one besides Heindorf who befriended me was Hugo Friedhofer." Soon North was accepted as a member of the Hollywood community and himself became an insider.

STUDIO CONTRACTS

We signed the usual seven-year contract. It sounded big, but every year they could either pick it up or not, you know. Those things are things of the past; you were really slaves. But I loved it because I could learn a lot about pictures.

Herb Spencer, orchestrator

By the end of 1930, Paramount Pictures had a surprisingly large music staff. *Étude* magazine described their music department: "Its music director Nathaniel Finston, who got his start in pictures as a silent movie conductor in New York and Chicago, headed a staff comprising 4 conductors, 5 arrangers, 12 composers and lyricists, 5 librarians, and 2 'executives.' There were 25 musicians in the contract orchestra, 75 outside players employed on a weekly basis, plus 10 people in miscellaneous occupations."

In 1930, films were not being scored yet, but musicals were everywhere, and the use of songs interpolated into dramatic films was exploding. During the thirties, as the use of music became a more and more important aspect of motion picture production, the Hollywood music departments evolved into extremely efficient operations, able to handle any amount of work required.

Their first job was to sign a staff of composers, arrangers, orchestrators, and others to contracts with their studios. Leo Forbstein, head of music at Warner Bros., was able to sign both Max Steiner and Erich Wolfgang Korngold, who became perhaps the two most highly regarded composers scoring films. Victor Young signed with Paramount at the end of 1935, and composer/conductor Alfred Newman became music director at Fox in 1940.

Before moving to Warners, Max Steiner had worked for RKO-Radio for about five years, during which time he had scored 111 pictures for them. When he asked for a salary increase in 1936, he was told that the studio would make a decision over the weekend. They did—and replaced Steiner with Nathaniel Shilkret as general music director. Steiner read about it in Monday's *Variety*.

Korngold didn't want to sign with a studio. "So far," he said in 1940, "I have successfully resisted the temptations of an all-year contract because, in my opinion, that would force me into factory-like mass production. I have refused to compose music for a picture in two or three weeks or in an even shorter period. I have limited myself to compositions for just two major pictures a year."

When he finally signed with Warner Bros., he included a list of stipulations that were very unusual in Hollywood, including the guarantee that he would score no more than two films a year, he could refuse an assignment, he would get longer than the "usual four to six weeks" to compose, he would receive credit on his own title card, he would receive credit in paid advertisements when the director was mentioned, and he would retain sole ownership of the copyrights.

Sometimes I had a year-to-year contract, sometimes two years straight. I once even had three years straight. It was fabulous.

Bronislau Kaper, composer

Herb Spencer's contract with MGM in 1942 was a seven-year contract, with yearly options, for $1,000 a week. In December of 1946, when John

Columbia Pictures Music director Morris Stoloff (on the left) watches a portion of *Lost Horizon* (1937) with composer Tiomkin. The phone on the desk was used to communicate with the projectionist. Although Tiomkin had been scoring films for several years, *Lost Horizon* was his first major motion picture. He never signed a staff contract with a studio, preferring to remain independent throughout his career.
Photo courtesy of Marc Wanamaker/Bison Archives

Green's yearly option came up, he too was making $1,000 a week, and the option would have increased his salary to $1,250. The studio wouldn't renew at that higher price, which would have set a precedent, so Green left, though he would return later as executive in charge of music.

Not all studio contracts were so lucrative. At Universal in the fifties, Joseph Gershenson was the music director, and the staff composers were getting about $300 a week, not at all comparable to the MGM contracts. In 1946, 16-year-old André Previn was offered a job at MGM. "Within a month of my first visit, I was offered a contract. . . . I was given an all-inclusive weekly salary of $125, for which I did everything but park cars. I loved it, and was grateful for the chance, as well I should have been."

We were captives, but for the most part happy and well-paid captives.

Miklós Rózsa, composer

All studio contracts allowed the studio to "lend" the person under contract to another studio on "loan-out," for which the lending studio would be paid a fee, often much higher than the person's weekly salary. When MGM had a disagreement with Clark Gable, they loaned him out to Columbia, for whom he made *It Happened One Night* (1934). Gable returned to MGM with an Oscar for his efforts.

Composers also went to work for other studios on a loan-out basis, under the same financial terms. But you never knew when or why you'd be sent off the lot. "All my loan-outs were very strange," says Kaper. "Suddenly they wanted me to do *Jet Pilot*, for no reason at all. . . . I must have done a picture before at MGM, where either the word 'jet' or the word 'pilot' was in the title. They said, 'Kaper is good for anything that has to do with jet, or with pilot.'"

Many composers weren't on contract, though. Actually, a 1949 survey concluded that no more than 25 composers were on contract at the studios, out of a total of 40 or 50 who worked exclusively in film music (many of whom also worked as arrangers and orchestrators as well).

Like Korngold, some chose not to sign with a studio, including the high-profile Dimitri Tiomkin. Elmer Bernstein was offered a contract after composing his first film score in 1950, for *Saturday's Hero,* and also decided not to sign. "I turned the contract down at that time simply because I felt that while it was nice to have that kind of security, I realized that there were seven people ahead of me [already signed to the studio], and that I'd be doing B pictures for the next 20 years. And I had another career at that time as a concert pianist."

Sometimes the staff composers weren't really captives at all, and could have the best of both worlds. Miklós Rózsa says that at the same time he had a contract with Universal for a specified number of pictures, he also had a contract with Hal Wallis at Paramount. When he signed with MGM in 1948, he, like Korngold, insisted on certain prerequisites to his signing. "I decided to accept, but felt I had to lay down certain conditions. Nobody was to add a note to any of my pictures, nor was I to be asked to add anything to anybody else's. I was not to be required to attend the studio if I had no work to do at the time. I was to do my composing in the privacy of my own home. My teaching job at the University of Southern California was not to be called in question. . . . Another part of my agreement . . . allowed me first refusal on MGM's most prestigious films; furthermore, I could request any film that took my fancy. . . . When the time came for renewal of my contract, I said I would be glad to continue, but it was important that I have three months off, unpaid, each summer. . . . Finally they agreed."

The front office apparently never did really understand what he was all about. After a great success with Jascha Heifetz's premiere of his violin concerto, said Rózsa, "I fondly imagined that MGM would be happy to bask in my reflected glory. On the contrary, one of the executives called up John Green and complained that he had read in the trade papers . . . that I had written a concerto for Heifetz. How was this possible when I was under

contract to MGM? He had to be told that the piece was written in my own time, in the three unpaid summer months. The executive grudgingly accepted this, but said that I ought to have been spending my holidays writing themes for future films."

THE ORCHESTRAS

At the end of the year, you'd get an awfully big check—six thousand, seven thousand—it was wonderful.

Mike Rubin, musician

If Rózsa felt unappreciated when his services were no longer required in 1962 by MGM, his contract nevertheless outlasted not only those of most of his colleagues in Hollywood, but also the musicians who played in the studio contract orchestras. When the musicians went on strike in mid-February, 1958, hoping to receive reuse residuals when the films they scored were shown on television, they never again recorded as members of a specific studio's orchestra. No lengthy goodbyes there, either. The composers weren't on strike, so the scores were written, management recorded them in Europe, and business went on more or less as usual. When the strike was over on September 3, contract orchestras were extinct.

But for over twenty years, every studio had its own orchestra. Fox, MGM, and Warner Bros. each had 50-piece orchestras on staff. The slightly smaller studios—Columbia, Paramount, and RKO—had 45 musicians in each orchestra. In 1950 Universal had 36. These salaried players were required as a result of the American Federation of Musicians labor agreement signed by the studios.

The basic contract called for 52 weeks of paid work per year (by comparison, the actors only got paid for 40 weeks), plus an additional two weeks' pay for vacation. The musicians were required to work an average of 10 hours a week. Anything more than that was considered to be overtime. All the extra hours were paid for at the end of the year, when the studios would add up all the overtime. Mike Rubin, who joined Fox's orchestra playing string bass in 1948, thought it was a great system, especially when you received all that extra money all at once. "After the end of the year, the swimming pools came up, the cars, and all of that."

Whereas some of the studios tried to stay within the 10-hours-a-week budget, Fox was never concerned with that. At a time when Hollywood was averaging between 500 and 600 scores per year, it couldn't have been easy for the studios to limit their recording time that much, but often the studios tried to do so. "In fact," Mike Rubin, says, "we were the only people that really went way over, at Fox.

Gilbert Kurland conducts Franz Waxman's score for the Universal horror film *Bride of Frankenstein* (1935). Waxman is standing in front of the podium facing Kurland, and director James Whale is seated to Kurland's left. Composed two years after Max Steiner's adventurous score for *King Kong*, Waxman suggested new possibilities for future film music with his dramatic scoring for Whale's classic horror film.
Photo courtesy of Marc Wanamaker/Bison Archives

"Sometimes we'd have a week off, but we still got the check every week. I think in the fifties the salary was something like $185 a week. But then, with the doubles {extra payment for playing two or more instruments} and everything. . . . And everybody got overscale. Al [Newman] was very generous. I know that the harpist always got a double check—even in those days. And all the first-chair men. We loved to go to work."

The contracts were restrictive, however, and did not allow staff musicians to work for an outside studio if they had already worked their 10 hours with their own studio orchestra. Exceptions were made for a few musicians, such as violinist Louis Kaufman. "For some time I had a personal contract with Newman {as his concertmaster}. I did have the freedom to play for other conductors, but I gave him first choice. Then, once contracts came in, I kept the same arrangement. He was very nice about letting me play freelance as long as I gave him first preference."

As far back as 1934, Kaufman remembers that the studio orchestras were surprisingly good. "They were not just hack musicians. Generally speaking, the quality of the musicianship and instrumental playing, even during the early days, was on a very high level. . . . They were disciplined, and there were very few that were just ignoramuses who would come in at the wrong place. They were a pretty highly selected group. Naturally, uneven. But on the whole, starting with the very early efforts, if one listens to them carefully, the quality is rather superior."

Sometimes we'd do fifty takes.
Herb Spencer, orchestrator

Although the studios eventually got budget-conscious and curtailed lavish spending on their recording sessions, things started out in the grand Hollywood manner. "In those days, the studio was ablaze day and night," Arthur Lange said of his first years at MGM in the early thirties. "Night recordings—all night. And money didn't count at all. Expenses didn't mean a thing."

According to John Hammell, things didn't seem to have changed too much by the end of the decade. "The recording time, when I started at Paramount in 1938, was unbelievable. Night and day. I remember the trucks backing into that scoring stage building at Paramount with the food—they had to feed at midnight if they went beyond it. And the food was *unbelievable* that they would bring in. Hot dinners—everything! The same group of players would stay right through till the end, too."

At best, this kind of situation encouraged the quest for excellence. Herb Spencer started at MGM in 1942. "In the old days, at MGM, if it didn't fit [sync with the picture], they'd do it over again. Look, when you have the orchestra under salary, you could work on Sunday. We'd do anything over again that wasn't right, because we were getting paid anyhow. We'd do it until we got it right. We didn't hurry through the recording at all."

It must be said that Newman's budgets at Fox were astronomical by comparison to budgets at some of the other studios. Stinson points out that Newman's annual budget was probably around a million dollars, while Paramount gave Stinson something like $150,000.

Still, money isn't everything. It's what you do with it that makes the difference, and Alfred Newman had a very special quality as music director/conductor at Twentieth Century-Fox. Stinson was unqualifiedly enthusiastic: as he recalled, "I think that everyone would say that 'Pappy' Newman at Fox had the best orchestra." The Fox orchestra had a reputation for producing a recognizable sound—the famous "Newman sound"—which referred primarily to the sound of the string section. Many symphony orchestras develop their own special sound under the guidance of their conductors, and the quality and texture of the strings has a lot to do with the overall effect. "He realized the emotional possibilities of strings," Kaufman notes, "and it got to be that, as likely as not, a lot of pictures ended up by being almost fiddle solos."

"He was a wizard," Raksin adds. "He was the

In 1936, Gladys Swarthout sings along with the Paramount Pictures orchestra during the recording of one of the songs from *Champagne Waltz*. Composer Victor Young is standing facing her.
Photo courtesy of Marc Wanamaker/Bison Archives

best conductor that they've ever had out here, and they've had some very good ones. Al was really a marvel."

Players and composers alike admired Newman, but there were the inevitable creative differences from time to time. "Sometimes," says David Raksin, who was on staff at Fox during the early fifties, "when he was conducting my scores at Fox, we'd fight a lot, because I have a different approach than the one he had. I'm no less sentimental than he was, I think, except that my whole idea was to compose something which was itself expressive, and then play it with reticence. But sometimes Al would exaggerate things, and I'd say, 'God damn it, Al, don't gypsy it up!'"

Composer Fred Steiner (no relation to Max)

points out that it was not unusual for Newman to take three hours or so to record a piece of music for one film sequence, whether it was his own music, or a colleague's score.

THE MUSIC DEPARTMENTS

Behind all this were the music departments, and it was the men in charge of these departments who set the tone for each individual, and ultimately for the entire industry. Some were practicing musicians—conductors, composers, arrangers, orchestrators—

In 1935, Louis De Francesco, a music director at Fox, looks at the conductor parts for a completed score. Prepared from the orchestrations by the music library, these conductor parts were two- or three-line reductions of the full orchestral score, and were used by conductors during scoring.
Photo courtesy of Marc Wanamaker/Bison Archives

In 1947, Columbia Pictures Music head Morris Stoloff (seated) and composer Hugo Friedhofer discuss the score for *The Swordsman* (1948), a historical drama starring Larry Parks and Ellen Drew. Friedhofer had just won the Oscar for his music for *The Best Years of Our Lives*, a score in which he used a harmonic language suggested by the works of Aaron Copland. Although the caption circulated with this photo said, "Oscar winners collaborate," Stoloff functioned as the music executive for the studio, not as a collaborator.
Photo courtesy of Marc Wanamaker/Bison Archives

while others were basically administrators who took care of the mountain of business details, gave the composers their film assignments, and supervised the results. When Elmer Bernstein arrived in Hollywood in 1950, he found a distinguished group of music executives in charge—Alfred Newman (Fox), John Green (MGM), Ray Heindorf (Warner Bros.), and Morris Stoloff (Columbia). "All accomplished musicians," says Bernstein. "If something went wrong with the score, they took the heat, and they gave you guidance."

Some of the early music heads were strictly administrators, but most of them conducted also. At Fox, for example, Louis De Francesco was head of music for a while in the thirties. He conducted, but tried to avoid working on Wednesday nights, when his interests were elsewhere. If they scored on a Wednesday night, he would do his best to get off

Composers like Alfred Newman not only handled all the day-to-day administration chores and spotted and conducted films, but scored films also. "Al, remember, was a dynamo," says David Raksin, who worked closely with him for a period of time. "You know, one of those small men who simply exuded energy. . . . He was always inundated with too many things to do. He had to be the musical director of a studio and he also had to score pictures. So the result was that we all helped out in one way or another. I orchestrated for him and I co-composed for him, usually sequences based on his material."

Ray Heindorf, who was music head at Warner Bros. from 1947 to 1959, was highly respected by everyone. When Bronislau Kaper composed the music for *Auntie Mame* (1958), Heindorf was still music director there. "He was one of those heads of the department who are not only administrators, but a full-blooded musician; and probably one of the greatest in the motion picture business."

Fred Astaire was one of the many illustrious musical artists who worked with Alfred Newman during his long career. Newman, who was the most sought-after conductor on Broadway before coming to Hollywood in 1930, was music director and/or conductor for many screen musicals. Astaire and Newman are shown here in 1955 during the production of *Daddy Long Legs*.
Photo from the USC-Cinema-Television Library and Archives of Performing Arts, courtesy of Martha Newman Ragland

Ray Heindorf, who arranged many of the songs for the lavish Busby Berkeley production numbers in *Footlight Parade* (1933), *Gold Diggers of 1933*, *Gold Diggers of 1935*, and others, gets an earful from Jack Carson during the scoring of *It's a Great Feeling* (1949) while co-stars Dennis Morgan and Doris Day stand by. Heindorf served with distinction as music director at Warner Bros. from the late forties through the fifties.
Photo courtesy of Tina Morrow

the podium and out of there as quickly as possible. As music editor George Adams used to tell it, one Wednesday night he was conducting a cue, and he hit the last chord about five to seven seconds too soon. Rather than stop and do another take, he just held the note. Then, when the streamer came in, he cut off the orchestra and he said, "Exactly right on the nose. We make-a no more. I go to the wrestling match."

Boris Morros, who was at Paramount for a short while in the late thirties, championed "modern composers," and encouraged Igor Stravinsky and Arnold Schoenberg to compose scores for Paramount films. Although these men never did score a film, the management allowed Morros to bring in symphonic composers such as George Antheil. Upon the resignation of Morros in 1939, however, they replaced him with a more conservative music executive, Louis Lipstone.

Boris Morros was head of the Paramount music department in the late-thirties. During his tenure at the studio he urged Paramount executives to commission distinguished concert composers to score films for Paramount. He tried to interest Igor Stravinsky, but the great Russian composer, then living in Los Angeles, reportedly wanted $100,000 to score a picture—a sky-high fee at that time.
Photo courtesy of Marc Wanamaker/Bison Archives

Joseph Gershenson was head of music at Universal Pictures during the fifties, while Henry Mancini was a staff composer there. Gershenson conducted most films that they did in those days, no matter who composed the music. In fact, he frequently conducted even before he became department head, when Charles Previn (André's uncle) was head of music. "Charlie was a nice man and a fine musician, a good conductor," Gershenson said. "And when I came to Universal to do musical shorts, he . . . conducted the first musical. Where it used to take me about three hours, it took him about eight hours, and we went way over budget. That's when I went to his secretary and said, 'Do you think Charlie would mind if I would conduct?' She said, 'Ask him.' So I went to Charlie and said, 'Charlie, look—here is my budget. I'm used to this kind of crap. Do you mind if I conduct?' He said, 'Oh, no. Of course not.'"

Gershenson never wanted to compete with his staff, and never composed any music for the Universal films. He supervised. "The way I worked with these composers—they'd come into my office and play the cues on the piano for me. And I liked them or didn't like them. And if I didn't like something, most of the boys squawked. But Hank [Mancini] would never do that. . . . He'd pick it up, and come back an hour later. He'd sit down and play something else. I never criticized the music itself, just the dramatic application." (Gershenson was, in fact, a champion of the gifted up-and-coming composers.) In order to be completely responsible for the final product, he went to all dubbing sessions also.

Let me say that many times I felt like quitting the business. . . . They would make a suggestion that would tear your heart out, you know, and in some cases actually leave out something that would happen to be the melody.

Leo Shuken, orchestrator

Leo Shuken, who was one of the great Hollywood orchestrators, also composed a bit. "There was a particular head of one of the major music departments who was certainly not understanding—for example, he came on the scoring stage and I happened to have written a piece for a very brutal murder, and he came in right at the point when the orchestra was rehearsing a section which contained a dissonant chord, and in front of the whole orchestra he said, "Why don't you throw those God damn harmony books away?"

So the composer's relationship with a music director was not always idyllic. Some of the music directors had a very conservative attitude about the type of music that would be most appropriate for their studio's films. This could create real problems, especially in that the music director was often presenting his own personal bias to the filmmakers. When Miklós Rózsa worked with director Billy Wilder on *Five Graves to Cairo* for Paramount Pictures in 1943, he had a typical run-in with the head of music (Louis Lipstone). "As it turned out, both Billy and [producer] Charles Brackett liked the score, but the studio's musical director was not so sure. Their chief composer was Victor Young, a kind and charming man whom I liked very much, but who wrote in the Broadway-cum-Rachmaninoff idiom which was then the accepted Hollywood style. My own music was not like this at all, and despite Wilder's and Brackett's praises, the musical director became very perturbed. He once asked me why I had so many dissonances in my music. 'What dissonances?' I asked. 'Well, in one spot the violins are playing a G natural and the violas a G sharp. Why don't you make it a G natural in the violas as well—just for *my* sake?' When I refused he became furious—one thing you don't do in Hollywood is disagree with an executive. However, Billy Wilder came to my aid and told him that he wasn't in the *Kaffeehaus* where he once played his violin and that he'd better stay in his office in the future and leave the composing to me. This was all very embarassing, but the man finally left in a rage and let us finish the picture in peace."

The following year Rózsa scored *Double Indemnity* (1944) for Wilder, again for Paramount. Nothing had changed. "Enter now the figure of the musical director [still Lipstone] who, when the time of the recording came, made no secret of the fact that he disliked the music intensely. Wilder finally turned to him and snapped, 'You may be surprised to hear that I *love* it. OK?' At this point the musical director disappeared and we didn't see him at the sessions again. Later I was summoned to his office where, in the presence of his assistant, he reprimanded me for writing 'Carnegie Hall' music which had no place in a film. This I took as a compliment, but he assured me that it wasn't intended as such. He suggested I should listen to Herbert Stothart's recent score to *Madame Curie* to learn how to write properly for the movies, and when I pointed out that that film was basically a love story, he described my title music to *Double Indemnity* as being more appropriate to *The Battle of Russia*. He was convinced that when the artistic director of the studio, Buddy de Sylva, heard the score it would be thrown out and all of us would suffer. Soon after this lecture the film was previewed in Long Beach, and Buddy de Sylva [head of production] called the man over as he tried to make a hasty exit afterward. He walked over like Louis XVI going to the guillotine, expecting heads to roll. De Sylva, however, began praising the music to the skies, saying that it was exactly the sort of dissonant, hard-hitting score the film needed. The only criticism he had to make was that there wasn't enough of it. By this time the musical director was grinning from ear to ear and put his arm around de Sylva, saying, 'I always find you the right guy for the job, Buddy—don't I?' Well that, it seemed, was the Hollywood way. . . . From then on I had to dance less and less to the tunes of musical directors and studio executives."

Rózsa has a very strong opinion about the influence of the powerful studio music heads during those years, which offers an interesting contrast to the plaudits extended to most of them. "As can be seen in situations like this, the producers and directors themselves were hardly ever to blame. The trouble stemmed from the heads of the music departments, men from jazz bands and theater pits who hadn't the faintest notion of music as an adjunct to drama, and always wanted to 'play it safe' (literally). They were the arbiters of musical taste in Hollywood, and since they employed hacks when real composers were available they caused the ruin of many potentially good films."

This was not true of all music executives at that time. As we have seen, many were excellent musicians and composers themselves, including John Green at MGM, Alfred Newman at Fox, and Ray Heindorf at Warner Bros. One of the truly outstanding and most deservedly well loved of all the music directors was Stanley Wilson, head of music at Universal during the seventies. In an era when music executives no longer supervised contract composers and orchestrators, Wilson made his mark in a different way. What made him so unusual was his sincere interest in finding and sponsoring young, promising talent. Some department heads had offered this kind of support to composers during the previous decades; Alfred Newman recognized Alex North's brilliance, his brother Lionel had favored Jerry Goldsmith and John Williams early on in their careers, Joseph Gershenson had taken Henry Mancini and others under his wing at Universal. But never had the development of film music talent become an art form in itself.

Sandy De Crescent was the orchestra contractor at Universal when Wilson became head of music. She was responsible for preparing budgets for the scoring sessions, hiring the orchestras, and handling all of the administrative details involved with the actual recording. "Stanley Wilson was the most wonderful, nurturing kind of person. He started a lot of young composers. Dave Grusin, Quincy Jones, Oliver Nelson, Lalo Schifrin, Billy Goldenberg—he was like the big daddy. There was never a kinder person than Stan.

"He found talent through their tapes, and the recommendations of other people. And Stanley was always looking and always wanting to help people. There are so few people like that today, you know.

"When Stanley Wilson died, I don't think I have ever, ever seen an outpouring of grief as there was for this man. . . . The nature of the business has changed so dramatically—I don't think that could ever happen again."

THE ASSIGNMENTS

When the studios retained a staff of composers, the producers could call the heads of the music departments and request a particular composer. If he was available, that was that. In practice, the music heads often simply assigned a composer to a given film. "Don't forget that at this time, we did many movies," says Bronislau Kaper. "I was sometimes assigned to two movies ahead of time."

There was a catch, though. Each studio had one or two composers who were their favorites, and they got all the juicy assignments. The other staff composers got the leftovers. "For instance," Kaper explains, ". . . Herb Stothart . . . was God at MGM, because he was blond, had blue eyes, and in the eyes of the executives, he was a showman. He was the greatest. They said, 'Maybe he doesn't know music that well, but he is a showman. . . .' He was the number one composer with tremendous influence. Full of intrigue. When he wanted a movie, he got it." When Miklós Rózsa joined the MGM staff in 1948, he became that studio's new favorite.

It wasn't always so easy to get the most popular composers, though. As we have seen, Korngold was particularly recalcitrant, not wanting to work under less than ideal circumstances, nor too often. Inasmuch as Hollywood patented the fine art of saying no when you mean yes, the filmmakers often took this as a sign of encouragement. Imagine, then, how excited Hal Wallis and Henry Blanke must have been when they read the following, contained in a note written by Korngold:

> Robin Hood is no picture for me. I have no relation to it and therefore cannot produce any music for it. I am a musician of the heart, of passions and psychology; I am not a musical illustrator for a ninety-percent-action picture. Being a conscientious person, I cannot take the responsibility for a job which, as I already know, would leave me artistically completely dissatisfied and which, therefore, I would have to drop even after several weeks of work on it. . . . Please do not try to make me change my mind; my resolve is unshakable.

Within 24 hours, Warner Bros.' head of music Leo Forbstein, representing the filmmakers and the studio, visited Korngold, hoping to dissipate his resolve. In his book *Behind the Scenes* Rudy Behlmer explains what happened: "When Forbstein said that Korngold could work on a weekly basis and could leave the project at the end of any given week, in which case someone else might finish the score, Korngold agreed. What prompted him to change his mind was hearing that Chancellor Schushnigg of Austria had had his ill-fated meeting with Hitler at Berchtesgaden. Shortly afterward Korngold's property in Vienna was confiscated."

Korngold's score for *The Adventures of Robin Hood* was highly regarded at the time of its first release, and continues to be one of the most celebrated scores in the history of film music. (See Chapter 6 for more on this score.)

As a matter of course, most of the men took the jobs they were assigned. But there were propitious exceptions. David Raksin got his first big break because the first choice composers weren't interested. He was on staff at Fox at the time the film was ready to score. "It was a detective story. It was also in trouble. And Al [Newman] decided he didn't want to do it because he'd heard it was a 'trouble' picture. You know how that is, you don't want to get tarred with that brush. And then Al decided that since it was a detective story he'd give it to Bennie Herrmann, who said, 'Well, if it's not good enough for Newman, it's not good enough for Herrmann.' You know him. And so, I was the next detective story composer in line, so Al assigned me to it, and I saw *Laura* as something else."

WORKING WITH THE FILMMAKERS

Once given the assignment, it was typical for the composer to report to the head of the music department, rather than the producer or director. However, there were exceptions. For decades, Cecil B. DeMille was one of the most colorful and powerful of all filmmakers. Although he produced and directed during the silents and through the days of the studio system, he set the tone for the most autocratic of the filmmakers who would follow. John Hammell was a music editor at Paramount when DeMille was there, and remembers how he worked with Paramount's star composer, Victor Young, and others.

"He told them all, 'I know two tunes. One is "Going Home" and the other is "Yankee Doodle."' He said, 'The closer you stay to those, the better off you'll be.'

"DeMille would come in, and the first thing he demanded was that the orchestra see his picture. He said it's absurd to ask an orchestra to play a picture if they hadn't seen it. And they used to bring them in to projection room 9, and they would see the picture, weeks before they recorded.

"The spotting of the music was something that no one else did in Hollywood like DeMille. We'd be called in maybe two o'clock in the afternoon. Now we're going to spot the music, the sound effects, the trailer people, everybody, for a big DeMille picture. And the first thing he'd do, he'd get up in front of all the people and talk for at least an hour, about what this picture is. *Unbelievable*. You couldn't get out—no talking, no nothing. And then he'd start reel by reel, and it went *way* into the night without dinner or anything. When he started spotting the music, it would be discussed *forever* —where it would start, what type of music it would be. Really unbelievable."

When Young had finished some cues, he would be called to the studio to demonstrate the music. "And poor Victor—he and Ray Turner would try to play a two-piano version of the score for DeMille. And then, one night, they would bring the whole orchestra in, and the score would be played for him. And he'd say, I like this, I don't like that, I don't like—oh, terrible language—'That's the damndest thing I've ever heard,' and so on.

"There were terrible sessions in that room in the music building downstairs. They would play what he had written up till that point. And then, mind you, DeMille would start throwing things out— now the staff orchestrators and copyists were brought in at night to rewrite. I remember one sequence—the split sequence in *Reap the Wild Wind* [1942]—I don't know how many times Victor rewrote it, and to his credit I never heard that man say an unpleasant word to anyone. His composure was unbelievable. He must have rewritten that sequence five or six times—maybe eight or ten times. It was music for the squid under the sea. DeMille kept saying, 'That's not from the bowels of the earth. I want more low music,' and he'd try again. That music stretched clear across the file cabinets in the library—up one side and back up the other side. That's why the hours were so terrible.

"And then, oh my God, when the scoring sessions started, that was unbelievable—they went *forever*. On *Ten Commandments* [1956], for example, with Elmer Bernstein, I would say they were there three or four weeks. Rewriting and rewriting and trying and failing or succeeding. DeMille's secretaries took down *every word* that he said. So on the scoring stage he could turn to the secretary and say, 'What did I say on such and such a day about that sequence?' He would turn to a secretary and scream in her ears, if he heard something he didn't like. While he was jingling the coins in his pocket, you knew he was happy."

THE SCHEDULES

We need time—time to create.
Franz Waxman, composer

The schedules imposed by the studios could be impossible. With so many films being released every year, there was an absolutely mountainous amount of music generated by the studios day after day, week after week. During the golden days, composers frequently were asked to score a film in significantly less than four weeks. Here is what several composers say about the schedules at that time.

For us, time was the fulcrum upon which careers and destinies balanced and seesawed. . . . It was work and more work: 140-hour weeks, last-minute tournaments of skill and endurance in which we slept only when we keeled over from fatigue.
David Raksin

I wrote the 3 hours and 45 minutes of original music for Gone with the Wind *plus the score for another film and supervised the recording of both, all within the space of four weeks. . . . I did it by getting exactly 15 hours of sleep during those four weeks and working steadily the rest of the time. You can't be a Beethoven under those conditions.*
Max Steiner

[He also had medical aid; a doctor came in frequently to administer benzedrine.]

I often wonder what could be achieved if we were given enough time to work on a film score.
Alfred Newman

Now and then composers would do what they could to increase their writing time. In 1958, when Franz Waxman made arrangments with director Fred Zinnemann and producer Henry Blanke to score *The Nun's Story*, he wrote a letter to the filmmakers in which he stated his case for allowing more time to create his score for their film:

As far as my *official* starting date is concerned, I always find it rather strange that the production company is reluctant to give a composer sufficient time ahead of the actual writing of the score in order to digest and prepare the musical material. Babies are not born overnight. There is a natural process of pregancy which takes care of the growth of the sperm. And so it is with music or anything completely creative, for that matter. First comes the idea, then the time, however short or long, in which one becomes pregnant with many developments of this idea, keeping one and discarding another. This takes some time. After all, everyone else connected with this picture has now been thoroughly drenched in it, has watched its growth from the first pages of the screenplay through the watching of dailies now, and has had time to give it adequate thought. How, then, can a composer, if he is to do a decent job of creating, see a film one day and start writing it the next morning at nine o'clock?

Not even the great geniuses of the past have been able to create that fast. True, it took Rossini 29 days to write the music for *The Barber of Seville*. But then his other virtuosity as one of the great cooks of his time probably helped sustain himself. On the other hand, it took Brahms seven years to write the *Requiem*. I am neither a good cook nor will I take seven years to write the score for *The Nun's Story*, but for heaven's sake, let me have a few days of contemplation and relaxed thinking. As a matter of fact, the time before I start writing is always the most crucial and difficult for me because I try to think through the entire score in order to give it form and shape and not write one sequence after another haphazardly. So, I thought if I were to arrive during the first week of July, I would have ample time for "digestion."

His letter was effective; Zinnemann and the others involved did agree on his early start. Other composers weren't always so lucky, but some composers jumped into the pressure cooker on their own. Victor Young was under contract with Paramount Pictures, who naturally had him doing as much as possible. But, according to Bill Stinson, as good as he was, "Victor had one failing: Victor always did too much. He'd do eight or nine pictures a year for Paramount. . . . But he also might be doing two out at Republic and one at Columbia at the same time he was doing one of ours. So he was pretty sloppy. . . . He'd wind up short or long and we'd have to doctor the film before we sent it to the dubbing stage. . . . Almost every sequence that Victor ever conducted was either short or long. But the melody was so great that you overlooked it."

Some filmmakers were unhappy about the unrealistically demanding schedules, but few of those were able to make a difference. In a 1961 memo to Henry Weinstein at Fox, David O. Selznick complained about the studio methods:

Music supervisor Lou Forbes and Max Steiner take a break during the scoring of *Gone With the Wind* (1939). Steiner received medical assistance in order to meet his deadlines on *GWTW*, which included the composing of nearly four hours of music for the landmark historical epic. American television schedules have made these time pressures commonplace. Many television miniseries have been scored in three to four weeks; as an example, Bill Conti was given three weeks to compose the four hours of underscoring in *North and South* (1985), another Civil War drama.
Photo courtesy of Marc Wanamaker/Bison Archives

In my opinion one of the great mistakes that is made by the big studios is that they don't even bother thinking about the underscoring until after the picture is finished. Obviously, this means a hasty and bad job. This is another reason why the scores of the better independent pictures are so much better than the scores of the big studios . . . . At Twentieth the situation and the danger is aggravated because of its policy of hasty editing and hasty releasing . . . .

COLLABORATIONS

One reason why we put in the incredible hours we did was to make sure that we were not compelled by the pressure of time to produce shoddy work.
David Raksin, *composer*

How were these horrendous deadlines accomplished during the studio days? The answer is simple— collaboration in one form or another.

In most cases, one or more orchestrators took the composer's sketches of the score and orchestrated the music for full orchestra. This might involve no additional musical material whatsoever— just a straight transcription onto full-size orchestral music paper. But with difficult schedules, the orchestrator could add a great deal to the basic music sketch, thereby relieving the composer of much of the detailed work that goes into finishing a score. This system hasn't changed over the years.

If there was even less time, then a totally collaborative approach would be taken, in which case two or more men actually *composed* the music. Then the sketches they had written would be turned over to orchestrators for completion. Several studios worked this way when necessary.

Just before Newman came to Fox in 1940, Raksin had already been part of a team of composers at that studio who collaborated on a number of films. There were two others besides Raksin—Cyril Mockridge and David Buttolph, both staff composers at Fox at the time. And they worked out an amazingly efficient way of scoring those films. "It was assembly-line stuff. We'd see the picture on Monday and Thursday we'd record it. They were pictures of no particular consequence, like *Who Is Hope Schuyler?*; *Through Different Eyes, The Postman Didn't Ring, The Magnificent Dope, Just Off Broadway, Whispering Ghosts, Manila Calling.*

"We'd get together on Monday and we'd see the picture. By noon we would have gone through it and allocated all the cues. A different cutter [music editor] was assigned to each reel; and then

sometimes a guy would have reel one and four, and another guy would have two and five, three and six. So we'd tell them where the music went. There was no time to feel out the situation, to do any real thinking or let the problem sink in at all; you had to come up with something immediately.

"We'd sit there with [music director Lou] Silvers, and then Cy Mockridge, Dave Buttolph, and I would go and confer about what kind of thematic material was needed. And we'd go to our little studios and write a couple of love themes, and a couple of this and a couple of that, and whatever the hell it was, and we'd get together after lunch and play the stuff for one another. With a lot of very, very honorable, decent feeling, we would choose which ones. Nobody ever seemed to get miffed— this would work, this would work, I don't think I can use that, we'll use this, and everything like that, and then they'd be photostatted (in those days we didn't have Xeroxes). Everybody would get a set.

"By that time the cutters had stuff and we would take the reels in order. Perhaps Cy would take reel one, Dave would take reel two, and I'd take reel three—generally there were about nine reels. And we'd start working at the studio, writing sequences based on the material. Whenever something came up in any reel that you were involved with which included some other guy's theme, you'd use his theme where it was appropriate and yours where that was appropriate. If you had to write additional material and you thought you'd written something worth doing, which might be useful to the other guys, you'd say, 'Fellas, I've just come across a place where I need this extra theme. Is this going to work for you later on?' and we'd go home and start writing.

"We'd write Monday night. Tuesday we'd come in with stuff, which they would photostat again and give to the orchestrators, and we'd do 30 minutes, 35, 40, 45 minutes, and then Thursday and Friday we recorded—sometimes just Thursday. And we did a lot of pictures that way. The [screen] credit on those films was "Lou Silvers." I don't think any of us ever got credit, although they were very good composers, and especially Buttolph, who was also a marvelous conductor. We used to have a standard joke about him: 'He had a bad week last week—he only did three pictures.'

Then, when Newman took over Fox, he asked Raksin to join his staff. "I worked a lot for Al, because Al was always overworked. They wouldn't take no for an answer from him, and he couldn't do that, he was head of the department. So he would give me five reels out of a ten-reel picture, and Buttolph would sometimes do a few reels. . . . We used Al's material, but we composed—he didn't sketch the cues. Remember, I'd orchestrated for him a lot. Eddie Powell and I used to orchestrate for Al, and so I knew his stuff very well. He would start the film, and then he would keep writing. But he'd just give us certain reels, and we'd do them."

Newman's score for *The Blue Bird* is a good example, but by no means unusual. A 1940 newspaper article stated the challenge: "It might be of interest to musicians that Mr. Newman composed the background music for *The Blue Bird* in just 10 days, working night and day . . . and that he was simultaneously employed on musical scores—actual composition, not just arrangement—for *The Hunchback of Notre Dame* at RKO, *The Broadway Melody* at Metro, and three other pictures at Fox, including *Grapes of Wrath*."

Newman, of course, had help, including Raksin, who worked with him on *Blue Bird*. ". . . It nearly killed me," Raksin remembers. "I did a lot of work in his movies. He'd give me some of his early sketches—he would show us what was going on—but even they were very sparse. They would contain a melody, and sometimes a few bass notes. But it was all there, if you knew what he was doing. . . . We would actually harmonize them ourselves. . . . We were working day and night. Sometimes this went for weeks without a let-up at all

I don't ordinarily go around telling people how much I wrote in Newman's pictures—but only *some* of them. On the music, a lot of it says 'Alfred Newman, thematic material, comp. and dev. David Raksin.' I never got cue sheet credit. But I got a lot of [screen] credits there."

There were no thoughts about writing for posterity. We [at Universal] were just trying to keep up with the frantic pace of one picture after the other. . . . It was like a factory, where you had to turn out, say, so many dozens of red socks and so many dozens of green socks.

Hans J. Salter, composer

Universal Studios had a similar arrangement for collaborations when Henry Mancini worked there in the fifties, during the first years of his film career. "Joe Gershenson would call in Herman Stein and me to look at a picture. Herman and I would decide where the music would go and discuss it with Joe—or with the producer, if he came around. Usually, though, the producer was off in another part of the factory making his next picture. Directors rarely showed up at our screenings. They were out in the hills of the back lot, shooting another chase. . . .

"After we saw the picture, Joe would say, 'Hank, you take half, and Herman, you take half.' Which half didn't matter.

I would get my five reels and Herman his five. If the love theme fell in his half of the picture, he'd write it. And if he used it in the first half of the picture, I would use it in the second half and vice versa. The theme, whichever of us wrote it, would be just a melody line, which we would then arrange and give to David Tamkin for orchestration.

"We certainly didn't produce great music by this process. It was Universal's style. . . . We did our best, but we couldn't afford to fool around with lofty aesthetic aspirations, and what we turned—or churned—out deserves to be referred to bluntly as what it was: mostly crap. "When several of us worked on a score, Joe Gershenson was given the [screen] credit as musical director, which was all right with us. But when Joe assigned us a score for a picture of our own, he would always make sure we got full credit." By the sixties, with the demise of the studio orchestras and the breakdown of the studio system, most composers, arrangers, and orchestrators were freelancing—taking their assignments on a film-by-film basis.

Freelancing

■ ■ ■

No matter how well you did the job, the producers rarely made any comment. Perhaps they were afraid that if they paid us a compliment, we would ask for a raise.

Hans J. Salter, composer

Many film composers don't know what or when their next assignment will be, and the stress can be debilitating. Since the sixties, that's the way it has been. Composers are hired for a specific project. If it's a television series, they may be signed for a season, either to score the entire season's shows or perhaps to score only one show out of every two or three that goes on the air (especially if the schedules are extremely tight and there is a lot of music). If they establish a good working relationship with a director, they may find themselves working with that director on many of his or her films. Mancini has scored most of Blake Edwards' films since his television series "Peter Gunn" and *Breakfast at*

Tiffany's (1961); John Williams scores most of Spielberg's films; Angelo Badalamenti has worked consistently on projects directed by David Lynch, including his offbeat television series "Twin Peaks"; director Tim Burton has worked on a number of films with Danny Elfman.

For the great majority of composers, though, it takes a resilient personality to deal with the anxiety that goes with the lifestyle of a freelance artist—a lifestyle that is tough on families and frequently destructive to a composer's self-esteem. Because of this, a strong ego is absolutely necessary in this field. Even so, maintaining a solid self-image can be as demanding as the work itself.

STATUS AND SELF-IMAGE

When Miklós Rózsa was working with director Mervyn LeRoy on *Quo Vadis* (1951), he was asked by MGM to do some scoring on *The Miniver Story* (1950) in London. LeRoy had been unapproachable until then—simply too busy to meet with Rózsa to discuss the music or hear any of the themes. "Just before I was about to leave for London a message came from LeRoy to the effect that he could spare me a little time," Rózsa recounts in his autobiography. "I hurried to the stage with all my music, ordered a piano, and found him directing a scene with Bob Taylor. At the end of the scene he came over to me at my piano. He said that he understood that I was going to London the next day—would I pick up some cigars for him? We would talk about the music on my return. This was our first and last discussion about music."

Practically speaking, status is not a social issue—it is an artistic one. The more seriously a composer's potential contribution is taken, the more opportunity there is for a fruitful collaborative relationship. After Richard Rodney Bennett was nominated for an Academy Award for his score for *Far from the Madding Crowd* (1967), he said, "I think one of the reasons *Madding Crowd* came out well was because I felt I was valued. They cared about me being there."

> *The music is cheap—it's the name that's expensive.*
> Igor Stravinsky, composer

> *I'm very realistic about myself and my talent. I know I'm not Beethoven or Brahms—I have a certain kind of talent, but I never pretend to do things I cannot. I know many pretenders in this town.*
> Bronislau Kaper, composer

> *I'm more than just a composer: I'm a film composer.*
> Philippe Sarde, composer

A strong self-image is vital to success in this field. The great Erich Wolfgang Korngold (his

French composer Maurice Jarre conducts his score for the MGM film *Grand Prix* (1966) directed by John Frankenheimer and starring James Garner, Eva Marie Saint, Yves Montand, and Toshiro Mifune. Ever since the end of staff orchestras in 1957, Hollywood studio orchestras have been assembled by a music contractor, who usually engages all of the composer's available personal choices and supplements those musicians as needed.
Photo courtesy of Marc Wanamaker/Bison Archives

father named him after Mozart) set a good example. There is a legendary story about Korngold and his colleague Max Steiner, both of whom had come from middle Europe. David Raksin was told this story by Korngold's son, George. In this version of the story, as Raksin recounts, "George, his father and Mrs. Korngold went to a movie in Westwood with music by Max Steiner, and as they were coming out, Mrs. Korngold said, 'Erich, I noticed a strange thing. In the time you've been at Warners, Maxie's music has been getting better and yours has been declining. How do you explain that?' He said, 'Simple. I'm copying him and he's copying me!'"

Raksin points out, though, that humor will

help, but you've got to be tough. "You're trying to survive. There you are, and you're doing what you're doing, and the only way to sustain yourself in the face of ignorance is to have some sense of arrogance. I used to say to Alex North, 'That's your problem, kiddo, you're not arrogant enough.' Well, he became arrogant enough later."

What makes this assumed air of arrogance difficult is that most composers retain a very realistic attitude about their work. Dimitri Tiomkin did his best to promote himself whenever possible as the greatest composer ever—a combination of George Gershwin, Carl Sandberg's entire folk-song anthology, and Tchaikovsky, with any other composers added as needed. He asked for—and got—top dollar, and was the highest paid composer in Hollywood for years. And yet, in a moment of thoughtful candor in his 1959 autobiography, *Please Don't Hate Me,* he was comfortably self-appraising. "I take as detached a view of myself as I can. I could never have been a Beethoven, Chopin, or Wagner. Anyway, the age of musical titans seems to be past. If I had devoted myself seriously to composition in the concert field I think I might have been as good as Rachmaninoff. . . . I've gone over to the technology of motion pictures, music for the masses, music for the machine in an age of machines.

"When I say I write music only for money, it isn't entirely true. Music for movies gives me many opportunities to compose in as fine a style as I am capable of. . . ."

TYPECASTING

Typecasting can be one of a freelancing composer's biggest problems. "Part of Hollywood," John Williams explains, "is the tendency to pigeonhole people—actors, writers, and composers and all the rest—and I have been burdened with that sort of thing in my life, from time to time. In the sixties I did a lot of comedies. For years, the only calls I got were to do comedies. And then disaster films. . . ."

André Previn had a similar experience. "It isn't just actors who get typed to a specific mold. Composers suffer the same fate. I had done some successful musicals; therefore, I was the one to get for a musical. Then I did four of Billy Wilder's comedies in a row and I became the comedy expert. After I did *Elmer Gantry* [1960], every script that was tough and uncompromising came my way. Producers love pigeonholing everybody; it makes assigning and casting so much easier."

This can be exasperating, as Jerry Goldsmith has found: "Producers and directors continue to approach me with science-fiction films because I have been successful in writing for them." In 1992 he broke away from this typecasting, scoring *Mr. Baseball, Forever Young, Dennis the Menace* (1993), and other comedies and romantic films.

After *Rocky* (1976), Bill Conti not only scored most of the sequels, but also many of the other films that had the same kind of story and ending (*Karate Kid, Karate Kid II, Karate Kid III, Victory,* and on and on).

Elmer Bernstein has had at least three separate periods in his career, the victim of serial typecasting: "There was a period when I was considered to be a jazz composer and everyone wanted me to do jazz pictures; and there was a period when I was considered to be a Western composer, after *The Magnificent Seven,* where everybody wanted me to do Westerns. [And then] . . . comedy."

In order to turn this situation around, he walked away from the assignment to score *Ghostbusters II,* feeling that after *Animal House, Airplane!, Meatballs, Ghostbusters,* and many other comedies, he had to take some responsibility himself for his own image. He deliberately looked around for personal dramas, and subsequently has scored a variety of films including *My Left Foot, The Grifters, Cape Fear,* and *The Babe.*

Like Bernstein, Hans Zimmer looks for projects that will keep him diversified and interested. "I'm very consciously controlling it. I did *Days of Thunder* with cars going round and round and round, and while I was doing it, I realized I wasn't any good at it. Which was a bit of a rude awakening. But there you go. So now I just won't take those sort of things any more. I would hate to be stuck in the action picture thing. One car chase after the other. Because I think there are basically two car chases you can write, and that's it.

"I get scripts constantly, and if I get an idea on something, that's the one I want to go with. . . . Just to try out that idea, because I think it would make something happen with the picture. And having directors who have enough confidence to let you get away with it."

GETTING THE JOB

Most of the film composers who have already worked in the field have representation, just like actors, directors, writers, and producers. Most have agents, though in a few cases they may have either personal managers or lawyers representing them. Getting an agent before you get a few good credits is virtually impossible. There are only a few experienced, reputable film music agencies and representatives, while at the same time more and more musicians come to Hollywood every day with the hope of scoring films.

It is the agent's responsibility to submit the composers for assignments, and to keep all of the agency's clients working more or less simultaneously. If there were as many legitimate jobs as there are composers, this system would work. In reality, of course, there are many more composers than films.

To increase the odds of success, the composers usually promote themselves, making calls, meeting people, and sending out demo tapes of their music. For instance, Dimitri Tiomkin sent Alfred Hitchcock a telegram on November 18, 1965, in which he told Hitchcock that he had heard that no composer was set for *Torn Curtain,* and that he would love to work again with him. Although a good try, Tiomkin nevertheless failed to get the job.

In 1956, when Aaron Copland learned of the plans to make *The Old Man and the Sea,* he wrote a letter directly to the director, Fred Zinnemann, telling him he wanted to score the picture:

Dear Mr. Zinnemann:
Ever since I read in the paper that you were going to do "The Old Man and the Sea" I thought of dropping you a note. The story lends itself so wonderfully to musical treatment—or so it seems to me, that I can't resist the temptation of telling you how much I would enjoy working on such a film, especially with you at the directorial helm.

I wouldn't have dared write you this letter except for the fact that we both happen to be agented by the William Morris office, and when I told them of my interest they urged me to tell you of it personally.

I very well remember our single meeting in New York and still regret we weren't able to work together at that time. Perhaps we shall be luckier this time. At any rate, I wanted you to know of my interest.
         Sincerely,
         Aaron Copland

He received a quick reply from Zinnemann:

Dear Mr. Copland:
Needless to say, I was delighted to hear of your interest in The Old Man and the Sea. As you know, I too, have wanted to work with you for a very long time.

I must tell you in confidence that discussions have been under way with several musicians, relative to this project. No commitments have been made as yet. It would be quite difficult to bring your name into this situation at the present time. However, I would like to assure you that I will be most happy to bring up your name, very emphatically, if our present discussions should not materialize. As you probably know, Leland Hayward is the producer of the picture.

My only regret is that I did not realize until now that you are interested in The Old Man and the Sea.
         Very best regards
         Sincerely,
         Fred Zinnemann

Zinnemann and Hayward had already asked Richard Rodgers to score the film, and were in fact waiting for his reply. But when he couldn't spare the time, they then tried Trude Rittman, a folk music specialist with whom they had been conferring about adapting Cuban folk music for the score. She did some research on Cuban music before turning down the project, and coincidentally, recommending Aaron Copland for the job. Ultimately, though, Dimitri Tiomkin was hired and won an Oscar for his score for *The Old Man and The Sea*.

On July 31, 1963, studio executive Joseph H. Hazen sent a telegram to producer Hal Wallis, in which he discussed possible composers for *Becket*. He was very candid about his reactions: he felt that Alex North was a brilliant composer, but on the cold side; believed that Franz Waxman would give an inspired score with greater warmth; asked whether Wallis had considered Maurice Jarre (citing his score for *Lawrence of Arabia*) or Alfred Newman. Eventually, Laurence Rosenthal, who had done the incidental music for the theatrical production, was signed to do the score.

Hazen's comments are illustrative of typical behind-the-scenes dialogue. The filmmakers get many suggestions from production associates (like Hazen) and agents as to who they recommend and who is available, but they also frequently have their own ideas as to who they want for the job. And many times they may have someone in mind with whom they have already established a successful working relationship, or who has scored a recent film that they admire.

TIME PRESSURES

Seemingly only a composer knows that it takes time to write music.

                                        Miklós Rózsa, composer

Just as time pressures could be exhausting during the studio contract days, short schedules prevailed

when the composers began freelancing. In 1966, Alfred Newman explained how it was after the demise of the staff jobs: "Composers in America are usually contracted for ten weeks, but very rarely are we given the opportunity to utilize the full term to write a score. I would off-hand guess that generally six weeks, and in some cases eight weeks, would be the maximum time allotted us to complete the score. Very often some composers are asked to do it in four weeks, which is quite ridiculous. These shorter times do not apply to a film which contains two or two and one-half hours of music. However, there have been occasions when it's been tried. In my opinion, there has never been ample time for one to do one's very best work."

The standard ten-week contract (for nonstaff freelance composers) rarely guaranteed anybody a specific amount of time. It only specified the composer's obligations to the studio and, in most cases, allowed the studio to forestall the final payment to the composer until the film had been dubbed. The *Los Angeles Times* reported in 1952 that most of Dimitri Tiomkin's scores were delivered in 38 days, including the recording. But the typically outspoken Tiomkin, who often did big pictures with a lot of music, had this to say in 1961 (transcribed by the newspaper columnist with his Russian syntax intact):

Four weeks was all I was allowed to write the *Alamo* [1960] score. For *Guns of Navarone* [1961] it is five weeks. "This old fellow Tiomkin will do it," they say to me. "Your experience will enable you to do it."

Yes, my experience allows me to do it—working day and night. It is ruining my health and my heart. Five weeks I have to do *Navarone*, the complete score for a 2-hr.-and-47-minute film. Every picture it is the same. Impossible. How can you create—yet they expect from you big symphonic score.

They took two years to make *Navarone*, six months to edit it, so some exhibitor wants it all of a sudden now and I have five weeks to score it.

In the nineties, there are more and more rush jobs, even on important feature films. Frequently the editing gets behind schedule, while the release date remains the same, or even advances. Rózsa is the voice of reason for all composers when he speaks out against these incredible pressures: "The demands made upon composers and musicians in the film industry are of a kind that stagger belief. . . . While directors, writers, actors, and set designers may have worked on a film for half a year, it is not uncommon for a composer to be called in and asked to provide a score in a matter of weeks."

THE FILMMAKERS

I've spent my entire career combatting ignorance.
Bernard Herrmann, composer

We film composers like to sit around and swap stories about producers, and of course we exaggerate. Mostly they are men with no musical education, and it is therefore difficult to communicate with them.

Hans J. Salter, composer

While it is enjoyable and productive for me often to work closely with some of them, by the same token I feel that I can do better when left alone by some of the others.

John Williams, composer

Once the composer gets the job, perhaps no factor excercises as powerful an effect on film music as his or her relationship with the filmmakers. Whether the composer complies with the filmmakers' inspired or outrageous wishes, engages in an open and free exchange of ideas as one of the collaborators in the filmmaking process, or blatantly ignores or defies the filmmakers, the music is a result of this relationship.

Since the 1960s, the power of the director has increased over the years. The director now controls the music—where it goes, how it is used, what kind of music it is—much as producers did from the thirties through the fifties. Directors are participating more and more in the scoring process. They want to determine the nature and the course of the music for their films before they hire a composer. "In general," orchestra contractor Sandy De Crescent points out, "the director seems to have everything to say about everything. Including the score."

The ideal working relationship between a composer and a director is one of true collaborative give-and-take developed in an atmosphere of mutual trust. When a director tries to actually *become* the composer and enlist the composer as a sort of musical secretary, the results can be less than satisfying. This is especially so when the filmmaker is neither knowledgeable about nor sensitive to the possibilities of music in motion pictures.

Composers don't always waffle to the whims of the filmmakers, but the pressures can get very intense. Like Rózsa and Herrmann, Dimitri Tiomkin often held his ground, fighting for what he thought was best for the film. In a 1966 interview by Curtis Lee Hanson for *Cinema*, Tiomkin had this to say in explaining his attitudes about the most appropriate climate for composing film music:

In my field, it is normal to desire dictatorship. You *must* go your individual way to be an artist. The best work was done when I was left alone. Why? Because nobody can say to the creative artist, "Be Charlie Chaplin or Marlon Brando." When they let me alone, sometimes I do little things which are not important, but occasionally they are important. For the picture *High Noon* [1952], no one told me I should have a song in the picture with the lyrics coming through the dialogue. But the very progressive and wonderful producer Mr. [Stanley] Kramer permitted me to do it. Most producers would not go along with this type of experiment. They would say, "That's too much. Why do we need lyrics when we have dialogue?" But Kramer said, "Let him do it."

Many times when I was working with Capra, he permitted me to do different things. Sometimes a producer is a great help. I worked on *The*

Alamo [1960]. We needed a song directly before the soldiers made the final raid, and the audience knew, and the writer knew, and we all knew that the defenders would die. They could not stand against so many enemies. We needed a song for a kind of last goodbye. Paul Webster, the lyric man, and I went to the location in San Antonio. Duke Wayne was the producer and director. I knew him for many years, and I admire his talent and sense of motion pictures. So we played our music. Many different things. He liked lots of them. But for this one particular song he said, "No, I don't feel that." I could not defend the song, because I too felt that something was not absolutely right. We were meeting there at three o'clock in the morning because they had night shooting. And Duke Wayne said, "We need a serious song. A song that says it is time to die, time to leave." He talked about an apple tree. He said that when his wife was expecting a baby, he was feeling like that. And as he told about these things, I began to see a whole song. I got together with Webster the next day and in one day we wrote "The Green Leaves of Summer"; and it was right. Sometimes creative men can be a great help. . . .

Tiomkin's description of the work process is particularly illuminating because there are instances when the composer believes it essential to fight for his ideas when they are contrary to those of the filmmakers, and yet there are other times when the composer can greatly benefit from a collaborative approach with the filmmakers.

Outside of the most powerful heads of the music departments, very few composers have had the authority to work autonomously. In 1973, Bernard Herrmann claimed it was essential for him—"Otherwise I refuse to do the music for the film. The reason for insisting upon this is that all directors—other than Orson Welles, a man of great musical culture—are just babes in the woods. If you were to follow the taste of most directors, the music would be awful. They really have no taste at all. I'm overstating a bit, of course; there are exceptions. I once did a film, *The Devil and Daniel*

Webster [aka *All That Money Can Buy*, 1941], with a wonderful director, William Dieterle. He was a man of great musical culture. Hitchcock is very sensitive; he leaves me alone! (Fortunately, because if Hitchcock were left by himself, he would play 'In a Monastery Garden' behind all his pictures!). It depends on the composer, and I'm not making a rule about it. But for myself, personally, I'd rather not do a film than have to take what a director says. I'd rather skip it, for I find it's impossible to work that way. . . ."

This attitude requires solid self-confidence, coupled with a certain nonchalance about any possible affect on future job offers. But then, it takes guts to be as consistently outspoken as Herrmann, who had no tolerance at all for anything less than artistic excellence. "I can't understand how a producer of a sophisticated film will pander in the score to the lowest common denominator," he said once, thereby immediately alienating himself from most of his future potential employers.

There is sometimes a complete disregard for the dramatic values a composer can bring to a film. This can be both aggravating and emotionally painful for the composer. The disenchantment caused by a lack of regard and understanding between the composer and the filmmaker can push the composer to the breaking point. André Previn, who worked in Hollywood from the late forties to the late sixties, came home one day after one meeting too many (this last one with producer Arthur Jacobs), and realized he just couldn't take it any longer. "After a while, I found it just impossible to work with people who knew so little about music and who still had the right in the film hierarchy to say something about it. After the Jacobs incident, I got so angry and upset that when I got home I had three drinks, one after the other; and I thought to myself that here I am getting drunk because I just talked music with a man who is an absolute musical illiterate. . . . He wasn't *the* reason that I quit Hollywood, but he was the straw that broke the camel's back."

A different kind of challenge for a composer is working with a filmmaker like Cecil B. DeMille, as

Elmer Bernstein did on *The Ten Commandments* (1956). This film was Bernstein's first major motion picture, after a dozen or so less prominent films, and he was still learning.

"Here was a case of a producer who knew exactly what he wanted. Knew *exactly,* and could state it. But what he would do was listen to every piece of music you had written, on the piano, and accept or reject it at that point, before the recording.

"It was difficult, but—it was fascinating. Not only did he know what he wanted, but he had a whole philosophy of what motion picture scoring was for. It's a philosophy I don't happen to agree with, but I must say it worked perfectly well for his pictures. That philosophy was the use of music as a storytelling device; by that I mean that in a very doctrinaire way each screen character has a theme, and whenever that character is on-screen, that music plays. Very Wagnerian. . . .

"He spotted that my music behind the great exodus scene in *The Ten Commandments* was too slow and what he wanted was usually right—for his films. I must say I learned a great lesson from him on that. The original piece was rather slow and ponderous: Moses leading his people forth and all that. But that's what it looked like to me on the screen. He took great exception to that. He hated it. And I said to him, 'If we do something that's rousing and fast, won't it look wrong?' He said, 'No, trust me, it will work.' He was absolutely right about it. The great lesson I learned was that music can appear to speed action up and it's a lesson I put to very good use in *The Magnificent Seven*. But DeMille was, of course, very experienced in music. . . ." (See Chapter 6 for a discussion of Bernstein's score for *The Magnificent Seven*.)

Most filmmakers are neither as experienced nor as aware of their musical tastes as DeMille. Filmmakers, in fact, often tend to be afraid of the music, and therefore can be overly cautious in using it. This affects both the *style* of music, its *degree of dramatic involvement,* and, of course, the *volume* at which the music is mixed onto the soundtrack. In 1946, John Green commented about this: "Despite the notable strides that have been made toward raising the composition of film music to art-form level in the short thirty-five years of its existence, it is still forced to live and breathe in an environment of fear. Those who commission it are afraid of it."

Over the years, Sandy De Crescent has had the opportunity to observe dozens of directors every year while functioning as orchestra contractor for the films produced at Universal Pictures, plus many others as well. She sees that there are those who are still fearful. "They shouldn't be afraid of music, but I think a lot of people are. I've been with directors who are absolutely afraid of music. It's only what's familiar to them, and if they don't understand it, it scares them."

She believes that one explanation for this fear of music is the expanding list of musical choices now available to the director. "It could be that we have so many more styles of music today than in the thirties and forties, where everything was sort of more traditional. There were just so many ways you scored a film. Of course, there were the greats and the not-so-greats, but I don't think there were so many different styles and ways of scoring films, and now with synths, and the use of records, and on and on. Maybe that's part of it."

When the composer and filmmaker are working toward the same end, and are communicating well, the relationship can be both powerful and fruitful. After a very successful preview of *A Double Life* in 1947, Rózsa was surprised to learn that the executives were not entirely satisfied with the score. "The next day the front office complained that the title music was 'too modernistic' and ordered it be changed. I rushed over to [director George] Cukor's bungalow, where he was reading the enthusiastic comments the public had made on their [preview] cards, and told him what had happened. Cukor grabbed me and shouted 'If you change one note, I'll kill you!' I was glad to send a message back to the front office politely suggesting that they jump in the lake, Toluca being the closest. The picture went out with the score as written, and for it I received my second Oscar. Sometimes it pays to be stubborn."

PART FOUR

SHOW BUSINESS

■ ■ ■

The Oscars

■ ■ ■

My father was a barber and I lived over a store in Brooklyn. . . . Winning an award like this seemed an impossible dream. It was an overwhelming feeling that night when my name was announced. I remembered the days over that store and said to myself, "This can't be happening to Al Kasha!"

Al Kasha, songwriter

The Academy of Motion Picture Arts and Sciences was organized in 1926 under the leadership of Louis B. Mayer. One of the stated purposes was to honor distinguished achievements each year. The first Awards ceremony was a banquet held on May 19, 1929. However, the first music awards were given at the seventh annual Awards banquet, for achievements during 1934. The first winners were: Best Song, "The Continental," music by Con Conrad, lyric by Herb Magdison, and Best Scoring, *One Night of Love,* Columbia Pictures Corporation Music Department.

From 1934 to 1937, the studio music executives selected achievements for consideration, and a special committee then selected the five nominees. Starting in 1937, the music executives each selected a work, and all these selections were considered nominees. That's why for a few years there were so many nominations for the music awards. The music award winners were given gold plaques until the 18th Annual Awards for achievements during the calendar year 1945. From then on they have been given the familiar Oscar statuette, which is 10-carat gold plated and is 13½ inches high.

As national interest in the Oscars grew, a portion of the ceremony was broadcast on radio. In 1953, thanks to the urging of composer John Green, the Academy first televised the awards show with Green as the show's producer. Since then, the annual network television fee has continued to increase and is the chief source of revenue for the organization.

Academy membership is by invitation only. To be invited by the Music Branch, you must have three major credits and/or have achieved distinction in the motion picture industry. Nominees and win-

Ginger Rogers presented Miklós Rózsa with his Oscar for Best Scoring of a Dramatic or Comedy Picture (*Spellbound*) for the year 1945, during the 18th Annual Academy Awards. There were a total of 21 nominations in this category that year, including Rózsa's *The Lost Weekend*, the Chopin bio-pic *A Song to Remember* (submitted by Stoloff to the Academy as a split credit for Rózsa and Stoloff), Alfred Newman's *The Keys of the Kingdom*, Victor Young's *Love Letters*, and Franz Waxman's *Objective, Burma!*
Photo courtesy of the Academy of Motion Picture Arts and Sciences

ners are not automatically invited—they are, however, automatically considered. There are approximately 5,400 members, 5,000 of whom have voting privileges. Within the organization there are 12 branches, each of which is solely responsible for nominating the achievements within that branch. The Editors Branch votes for the five editing nominations, the Directors Branch is responsible for the directing nominations, and the Music Branch (consisting of between 230 to 250 composers, arrangers, orchestrators, and music editors) votes for the five nominations in each music category. The

entire membership receives ballots with the nominations listed, and they vote for the winners. The exceptions to this rule are the Best Foreign Picture, Best Short Films, and Best Documentaries.

As the *Guinness Book of Movie Facts and Feats* reports, "The largest number of films qualifying for consideration for an Academy Award was 264 for the 47th Awards in 1974. During the 1980s the figure . . . fluctuated around the 250 mark, representing a little less than half the films released annually in the USA. To qualify, a film has to have played publicly in Los Angeles for at least a week prior to the end of the calendar year."

In 1986, Alex North became the first composer to receive a special honorary Oscar, given by the Board of Governors for lifetime achievement.

The Music Branch can give three awards: Original Score, Original Song, and Original Song Score. Here's how the Academy defines the three music awards, quoted directly from its rules book:

Original Score. An original score is a substantial body of music in the form of dramatic underscoring originating with the submitting composer(s).

Original Song. An original song consists of words and music, both of which are original. There must be a substantive rendition (not necessarily visual) of both lyric and melody (clearly audible, intelligible and recognizably performed as a song) in the film.

Original Song Score. An original song score consists of not fewer than five original songs by the same writer or team of writers used either as voice-overs on the sound track or visually performed. Each of these songs must be substantively rendered and must be clearly audible, intelligible, and recognizably performed as a song. The score's chief emphasis must be the dramatic usage of these five or more songs. What is simply an arbitrary goup of songs unessential to the story line of the film will not be considered a valid song score. The adapter (if any) may be eligible together with the writer(s) of the songs if his or her contribution is substantial and includes alterations of the song score material.

The key elements here are: (1) the works are original and specifically created for the picture; (2) the scores must be significant enough in duration and effect to warrant being considered an achievement; (3) the songs must be audible.

This, in brief, is how the process of choosing the Oscars works:

- As with other branches, the Music Branch selects five nominees (three if there are fewer than 20 eligible achievements in a category), choosing from categorized eligibility lists enclosed with the ballots. (At times in the past a preliminary vote has created a list of 10 achievements to be considered, from which five nominations are chosen.)
- The nominated music achievements (along with all other nominated achievements) are then screened twice each at the Academy Theater for all members.
- The entire membership receives a list of nominees in all categories and votes for one choice in each category. These ballots are sent directly to Price Waterhouse, the accounting firm responsible for tabulation and secrecy. This vote results in the selection of the Oscar winners.
- The Music Branch executive committee is appointed by the three elected co-chairmen of the branch. According to Arthur Hamilton, "The executive committee are the orderlies of the Music Branch. It is the executive committee's job to learn the rules, to make the rules, to modify the rules, and then to make them clear enough to the music community—the studios, the independent producers, and the agents, and the composers and lyricists in the field—so that they understand them. And then to administer those rules, to circulate them and then make people abide by them."

THE RULES AND THE CRITERIA FOR VOTING

Somehow they don't go for the offbeat in music. It's always the tune which is played loudest and longest which tends to get it.
  Richard Rodney Bennett, composer

Some day the [Academy] judges will be instructed to choose pictures for their music and pay no attention to their general popularity.
  Isabel Morse Jones,
Los Angeles Times *Music Editor (1944)*

During the mid-seventies the Music Branch developed and refined the Music Branch rules with the hope that members would be required to *see* the films before they voted. This may seem like an obvious goal, but with the exception of the Best Foreign Language Film Award, the Shorts, and the Documentaries, there is no such requirement.

They were also hopeful that selection of the outstanding music achievements would be considered solely on the basis of the music's contribution to the film regardless of any independent impact the music might have as a bestselling song or album, or its association with a top-grossing film.

For a while, viewing the films was mandatory in order to vote. Although viewing the submitted (or nominated) films is no longer required, the branch rules have retained much of the philosophy inherent in those reforms. In its annual "Notes on Voting," the Music Branch makes some valid points about each of these three awards, in an attempt to clarify for the branch members what the achievement actually is in each category, and what it is not.

Original Score—what it isn't: an Original Score *isn't* a group of songs or production numbers, nor is it necessarily concerned with any music you might *see* being performed on the screen. An Original Score is *not* "source music," i.e., music spilling from radios, being performed in nightclubs, discos, concert halls, videos, and the like. It is *not* additional music "tracked" in from old records or other pre-existing sources.

What it is: an Original Score *is* the instrumental music created expressly for the film which underscores the action and supports its dramatic needs. To be "best," a score must make a substantial contribution, be of high musical quality, and satisfy the emotional needs of the story. A great score is one that provides dramatic power, humor, thematic beauty, emotional impact, and/or any other musical attribute of significance to the film. (The score must always be considered an entity unto itself, *to be judged independently of any songs or production numbers*).

Original Song—what it isn't: an Original Song *isn't* simply a hit record or the video made of that record. The artist or group performing the song is *not* to be considered, as this is an award for *writing* (not performing) music and lyrics. Commerical popularity, per se, is one factor that should *never* be considered in determing this award. A song may win other industry awards for popularity. The Oscar, on the other hand, is an award given for excellence in *writing songs specifically for the film medium.*

What it is: an Original Song *is* a composition of music and words written expressly for a particular motion picture. To be "best," a song must make a significant contribution to the film and the story being told.

Original Song Score—what it isn't: an Original Song Score *isn't* a hit soundtrack album. Nor is it a "score" in the sense of an orchestral score—even though the word "score" appears in the category title.

What it is: an Original Song Score *is* a group of five or more songs (music and lyrics) all of which are *essentially and integrally linked to the plot of the movie.* (Such classic film musicals as *Gigi* or *Seven Brides for Seven Brothers* provide a reference for this.) Whether or not the songs are visually performed on the screen, it is their relationship to the story line that defines this group of songs as a special category. To be "best," a song score must be judged by the same criteria as Original Song, with the added requirement that the

body of songs be sufficiently cohesive as to provide the film with essential dramatic and/or character development. (*This category only appears on the ballot when there have been a sufficient number of eligible submissions.*)

CRISIS CONTROL

It's interesting to look at these rules and criteria in terms of the various problems that seem to come up every year. The Music Branch executive committee (a group of 30-some branch members appointed by the co-chairmen) is responsible for all decisions regarding eligibility and the interpretation of the rules. Throughout the history of the branch, it seems as though the rules have been modified continually to prevent a crisis from recurring. "Always," says Arthur Hamilton, longtime member of the executive committee. "That's how we do it. The rules committee plays catch-up football from the year before. And I don't think it could be done any other way. Listen, you know something, I think our laws are the same way in this country."

Here is a behind-the-scenes inside look at the sort of problems that invariably arise.

Original Score

Music from the Score Previously Used in Another Film

If a significant theme or body of musical material has been previously used in another picture, then a score would not meet the rulebook definition of being "a substantial body of music in the form of dramatic underscoring originating with the submitting composer(s)." This requires a judgment call by the executive committee, because many scores use "Jingle Bells," pre-existing and newly created pop songs, classical music as source (or even as a cue), and so on. It's a question of emphasis.

The most controversial of these decisions affected Nino Rota's great (and popular) score for *The Godfather* in 1972. Bill Stinson was head of music at Paramount at the time. "Nino Rota, who wrote the score for *The Godfather,* wrote what was later known as 'The Love Theme from Godfather.' And we submitted the score as Best Original Score. And one day I received a call from [then Music Branch chairman] John Green, who said that he had received a telegram from a group of anonymous Italian composers, stating that the theme from *The Godfather* had previously been composed for an Italian picture, and therefore they couldn't understand how, under the Academy regulations, it would qualify for Best Original Score. And John Green called me and asked me if I knew this to be a fact, and I said that no, I did not. So far as I knew, this theme was original, [and] I had a signed contract from Rota stating that the music was original with him. Well, Green said that it had caused quite a disturbance, because the picture was such a huge success, and the score seemed certainly destined to win for best score. I said I would look into it.

"The next morning I called Nino Rota in Rome. I posed the question, 'Has the love theme from *The Godfather* been used ever, in prior motion pictures?' And he said, 'Yes, I used it once in a picture for Italian television. But,' he said, 'it's my theme, and it's original with me . . . .' I had to call Green, and I told him that by his own admission, yes, he had used the theme previously. But I pointed out to Johnny that the theme had occurred for seven minutes in a score that was more than an hour long, and it occurred in only three places in the picture, for a period of seven minutes. And by my calculation, based on original scores, the score was substantially original, based on total running time of original music. Even if we disqualified that particular piece of music, the score was still original. Johnny took that to the committee, and they came back to me and said that the word 'substantially' did not necessarily mean quantitatively, it meant qualitatively, and that we had done such an outstanding job of exploiting 'The Love Theme from Godfather' that it was the most memorable piece of

music from the picture, and therefore they were going to disqualify it. I told them that it was unfair, that nobody had ever brought in the word 'qualitatively' before. This was the first I had ever heard of it. So finally they relented, and John explained the situation to the Music Branch at large. I sent hand-delivered telegrams to every Music Branch member explaining our position. And the next day they balloted, and voted our score out. So we were not nominated."

Original Score or Adaptation?

During the many years when the Academy gave an Award for Best Adaptation, this classification was often difficult to define on a picture-by-picture basis. Bronislau Kaper faced this problem while serving for years on the executive committee. "There are many, many situations where you have to check a picture. A movie might be a combination of adaptation and original music. The composer can say, 'I want to present this movie as an adaptation,' or he can say, 'I think this is an original score mostly.' Now we have to go to the cue sheet [a log listing each cue and the music in it] and find out the relation in minutes of what is adaptation, what is original. And if it's very close, we, the executive committee, have to decide, by running the movie, what is the *thrust,* the important thing. Sometimes you might have 25 minutes of adaptation, and 28 of original, but the original score does not play the important part, really. You leave the movie with the feeling that you heard an adaptation of, let's say, 'God Bless America.'"

The *Godfather* classification was complicated by the fact that the seven minutes of the "Love Theme," regardless of its emotional impact, wasn't substantial enough to consider the entire score an adaptation, because quantitatively it contained so much original music. The use of Christmas standards during the appropriate scenes in the same picture wouldn't of itself qualify a score as an adaptation either—as is so often the case, they were really incidental to the score itself.

Original Song

There have been a number of problems in this category also.

Inaudible or Unintelligible Lyric

Sometimes the lyrics are inaudible on the soundtrack. This has become more and more common with the inclusion of songs and licensed records used as source music. Often these songs play for 10 or 20 seconds and are virtually inaudible on the soundtrack, but appear on the soundtrack album as full cuts. In February, 1992, *The Hollywood Reporter* ran a center story about the songs from *Jungle Fever* on the front page with the headline, "Motown fumes as Wonder ruled ineligible for Oscar." The subheading clarified the problem. "*Jungle Fever* songs are 'not clearly audible.'" Motown Records called the decision a "slap in the face" because two of Stevie Wonder's songs were not on the ballots. There were other heated responses from Motown ("They totally screwed him over on that") and a succinct reply from Bob Werden, representing the Academy: "The rules speak for themselves . . . . It's a subjective thing. The Music Branch didn't think it was intelligible in the film."

No Lyric on the Soundtrack

"Freddy's Dead," a hit tune by Curtis Mayfield for *Superfly* (1972), was actually voted one of the 10 preselected songs to be listed on the ballot for nomination selection. When the executive committee subsequently learned that the lyrics were not sung in the film—only the instrumental version of the theme was on the film's soundtrack—the song was disqualified and taken off the ballot.

A classic controversy centered around Dimitri Tiomkin's theme for *The High and the Mighty* (1954), which was not sung on the soundtrack when the film was first released. Tiomkin, always aggressive in promoting his works, ultimately was effective in getting the song on the ballot. An article in *The Film Daily* in early 1955 explains:

After some backing and filling, the proper committee of the Motion Picture Academy on the Coast has just ruled that Dimitri Tiomkin's title theme song for *The High and the Mighty* is eligible for an Oscar nomination . . . . It's a rather intriguing situation . . . . The question of eligibility of the song arose over the fact that the lyrics were not actually heard in the picture, although the song was hummed and whistled frequently by John Wayne and others . . . . Now a sequence in which the words are sung by a chorus has been put back in the release prints of the picture and everything is OK.

Tiomkin expressed his own position via a UP news release. "I really don't care that much about winning, but I just like to see fair play. The music branch of the Academy insisted the song was theme. It was not theme! It was written as song, and the Ned Washington lyrics originally were in the picture. But the director had a good shot of an airplane in the sky so they cut out the lyrics."

The current Academy rules preclude changing the print or prints of a released picture in order to qualify in this way.

Not Created Specifically for the Film

The branch often hears rumors about songs that were written for other purposes prior to the film, sometimes many years earlier. These rumors are frequently true, though rarely verifiable in time for the Awards process deadlines. The executive committee inquires, but unless there is proof, little can be done to regulate this clear violation of the rules.

Original Song Score

The most typical classification question in this category is whether five or more songs actually constitute the chief thrust and intention of the film's score, highlighting the film's dramatic moments and developing the drama as it unfolds. Because this particular approach to scoring has become rare, the category Original Song Score has not been on the ballots for some years now. There simply haven't been enough valid submissions to warrant an award (more than four are required). For this reason, *Beauty and the Beast* was not on the ballot as a Song Score in 1991; it was, however, considered an Original Score because of its underscoring (as opposed to the songs). The last award given in this category went to Prince for *Purple Rain* in 1984.

CREDITS AND COLLABORATORS

Bronislau Kaper remembered many cases where the committee questioned the official credit on a film. "Sometimes we get a credit, and it says, 'Musical score by this-and-this-and-this,' and no other credits. And we *know* that the name of this man tells us that this man cannot even whistle a melody. He couldn't have written the score. So suddenly we become the FBI. And we say that we know that there must have been another man, so he can get credit, too."

"Becoming the FBI" is unpleasant at best, but has led to some candid admissions of collaboration. Charles Chaplin was questioned about his credit for *Limelight* (1952) when the film's first Los Angeles run qualified it for Awards consideration in 1972. "I was surprised at the way that worked out nicely," says Arthur Hamilton. "There was a lot of discussion about that inside the executive committee, and people were asked to come in and talk to us about that, and send letters. A lot of investigative time was spent. And such a strong case was made that Chaplin had indeed not done it all by himself, that I think if he hadn't acceded to their request, he would have been disqualified." He did accede, and split the credit with Raymond Rasch and Larry Russell.

The Color Purple (1985) has probably been the most publicized case of confusing credits. "What a challenge that was," Hamilton says. "That was a mess. Initially we came in, and looked at *The Color Purple,* and we all groaned and said, What have we got here, we've got *nineteen* composers on the cue sheets? And they were all declared. Quincy Jones

was very fair. Everybody's name went on the cue sheet, they got the performance money for the cues.

"We had talked to so many of the guys who actually wrote the music. The big thing was the *number* of them. So we asked Quincy to come in . . . . We asked him to look at those cues very, very carefully and to narrow down the number, hoping we could narrow it down to three. But instead he narrowed it down to twelve, I think." So there were twelve nominees, including Jones, for *The Color Purple.*

With the committee's concern that this situation might repeat itself, they immediately set to work and modified the rules. "We had a terrible time trying to explain to each other in the executive committee what we meant by 'there shouldn't be a committee of writers.' But how do you put that into language even that *we* could deal with? I was sitting there one day, and I said, "We have a right to look at composition for a film in the following way: it's the Indianapolis race, and if a car starts with a driver in it, he has to go all 260 laps. He can't drive 40 laps, and get out, and another guy gets in the same car and drives 20, and gets out . . . . You can't do that. It's the guy who can drive 260 laps who gets an Oscar. It's for the *whole* job. That's what we're doing. Otherwise you're going to give a guy a statuette for doing six minutes of film work." I think that's unfair, and that's not what the Academy Award's about. And that image, somehow, made all of us clear our throats and say, Hey, yes, that's really what we're talking about. Now that we have this new rule, if *The Color Purple* were submitted again, we would bounce it all the way to Anaheim. It would be ineligible."

ADAPTATIONS

Traditionally, the designated music director has received the *screen credit* for the adaptation of a musical, and therefore is the person eligible for nominations and awards for the scoring of film musicals. Very often the music director not only conducted all the recording sessions, but truly supervised all the arranging, orchestrating, and underscoring for these films. These men were, in fact, largely responsible for the taste and artistry reflected on the soundtrack.

Usually, though, the incredibly talented arrangers and orchestrators who worked on these shows were, in reality, the adaptors. The following excerpt from Frank Verity's article in the May 1964 *Films in Review* raises concerns about this inequity.

Charles Previn, Universal's General Music Director, received the Oscar for *One Hundred Men and a Girl* (1937), the scoring of which was done by several composers on the studio's musical staff.

A change in 1938 in the Academy's classification of Best Score from a departmental to an individual achievement did not prevent musical directors, rather than composers, from receiving Awards. Alfred Newman won an Oscar for *Alexander's Ragtime Band* (1938), for which he composed, adapted, arranged, or orchestrated nary a note. Newman conducted the orchestra, but the scoring was done by no fewer than eight arrangers, the most contributory being Herbert Spencer, Gene Rose, and Edward Powell. Another Oscar went to Newman for *Mother Wore Tights* (1947), which Newman conducted, but to which he made no creative contribution. Again eight arrangers were responsible for the scoring, the most prominent being David Buttolph, Gene Rose, and Herbert Spencer.

The 1944 Award for Scoring a Musical Picture (*Cover Girl*) went to both Carmen Dragon and Morris Stoloff, although Stoloff's sole contribution was conducting the orchestra. Stoloff also received Oscars for *The Jolson Story* (1946), which was scored by several composers who were at Columbia at the time, and for *Song Without End* (1960), which he conducted but which was scored by Harry Sukman. Sukman did, however, *share* the Award!

The 1948 Award for Scoring a Musical Picture, won by Johnny Green and Roger Edens for *Easter Parade,* should have gone to Conrad

Salinger and Edens, Green's function being limited to conducting. For *An American in Paris* (1951), this time in collaboration with Saul Chaplin, Green collected a second Oscar, which belonged to Conrad Salinger and Chaplin, who were the actual scorers.

Lennie Hayton, whose contribution to *On the Town* (1949) consisted of conducting the orchestra, shared the Academy Award with Roger Edens, although the true scorers were Edens and Conrad Salinger.

Even though Jay Blackton only conducted the production numbers for *Oklahoma!* (1955), he shared the Oscars with arranger Robert Russell Bennett and adapter Adolph Deutsch.

LAWSUITS

Whenever anyone is declared ineligible, lawyers circle the playing field. Time and again the Music Branch has received threats of lawsuits, usually written on the letterhead of one of the major studios or production companies. "There is a lot of pressure," Hamilton acknowledges. "But what we've tried to do throughout the years is be very, very careful to become familiar with the rules and how they are applied in each individual circumstance, and once we're sure that this is following the rule or not following the rule as we understand it, if lawyers get involved, we just tell the Academy to talk to their lawyers . . . . A couple of attorneys have tried to send me letters, and I just smile and give it to the Academy counsel."

When Warner Bros. threatened to sue over the disqualification of Leonard Rosenman's adaptation score for *Barry Lyndon* in 1975 for reasons of *quality* (one of the few years this was possible), the Branch rescinded its decision, feeling in part that the new rules prevailing at that time could not be totally supported in such a dispute, as they had not been completely refined through practical experience. Motown and others have also applied the threat of legal pressure, but with less favorable re-sults. The branch does not accede to threats, but al-ways looks at the facts thoroughly before final adjudication.

STUDIO POWER PLAYS

During the thirties, forties, and fifties, the studios exercised tremendous control and influence over the voting. Music editor Robert Tracy commented about the voting in 1949, stating that when the front office sent out word that the studio employ-ees were to vote for a specific film in a category, that's what you did. He explained that the studios even policed the ballots before sending them on to the Academy, just to be sure that they had voted correctly. Apparently MGM was notorious for this.

For years, each studio was given complete au-thority to select the film score or song of its choice for consideration in each category. In 1944, *Los Angeles Times* music editor Isabel Morse Jones outlined the weakness of this system. "That limits the whole idea. The judges therefore have only to consider Al Newman's *Bernadette* music . . . . Max Steiner's *Casablanca*; Aaron Copland's *North Star* . . . . Vic-tor Young's *For Whom the Bell Tolls*; Waxman's *Destination Tokyo*; Roy Webb's *Fallen Sparrow*; Rózsa's *Sahara*; and Alexander Tansman's *Flesh and Fantasy.* I have heard nothing said of Albert Coates' and Herbert Stothart's scoring of *Song of Russia,* nor anything of a perfect scoring for the Eu-ropean picture *Jeannie,* with its Scotch rightness and its Viennese waltzes played by the London Phil-harmonic." Since each studio got only one choice, the major studios usually overlooked low-budget films and those that were less successful at the box office.

Even the extinction of studio contracts did not eliminate studio loyalties to any extent. Business was business. Bronislau Kaper had a song in a film he did at Fox in 1968. It got on the preliminary list of 10, and was a big hit as performed by Claudine

Longet, a major artist at that time. "But at the same time," says Kaper, "the studio had a movie called *Star!* And there was a song in it by Sammy Cahn and Jimmy Van Heusen . . . . Now, the stu-dio did not promote my song . . . . I talked to Lionel [Newman, the head of music] and I said, 'What's happening?' And he said, 'Listen, your movie is a two-million-dollar flop. *Star!* is a six-million-dollar flop, so we have to help the six-million-dollar flop. So we are not going to work on your song. We're going to work and vote for the other one.' So the other one was nominated, be-cause when you have a big studio going after a song, and all feel a loyalty to the studio, they vote for what's supposed to be voted for . . . . The branch is a limited group, so every vote counts."

WHO VOTES

Surprisingly, not every eligible member of the Academy votes. Commenting on the final balloting in a letter to the editor of *Films in Review* in 1961, Gene Ringgold said: "Basically, its voting system is a good one, but those eligible to vote do not always do their own voting. I know one musical composer who claims he rarely attends movies, and is unfa-miliar with some of them, and who marks his ballot in the musical categories and then hands it to anyone present to vote the other categories. I know two Academy members who voted for a per-formance neither had seen!" In reality, a large number of members vote without having seen all the films.

The most blatant instance of ballot-stuffing concerned an Oscar-winning lyricist—a since de-ceased member of the Music Branch who used to visit the widows of recently deceased branch mem-bers, pick up the unclaimed ballots, mark them, and send them in for counting. Since the ballots are not signed, neither Price Waterhouse nor the execu-tive committee ever knew about this.

PROMOTION AND
ADVERTISING

Advertising got so out of hand in 1961 that the Academy Board of Governors (composed of two members from each branch at that time, and later augmented to three) published a statement at the front of the 1961 rules book admonishing against "vulgar solicitations." This cautionary attitude still prevails as a matter of record, and though the language has varied over the years, in 1992 it read as follows:

> This year, as in the past, you may be importuned by advertisements, promotional gifts, dinner invitations, and other lobbying tactics in an attempt to solicit your vote.
>
> Though the crude solicitations that occasionally surfaced in earlier years seem to be a thing of the past, we would ask each individual Academy member to be on guard against inappropriate attempts to influence your vote, and to register your displeasure with anyone who might make such an attempt.
>
> The more emphatically that all of us can convey to the industry and the wider public that excellence in filmmaking is the ONLY factor we consider in casting our Academy Award votes, the more reason the world will have to respect our judgment.

Nevertheless, advertising and promotion continue to play a sometimes vital role in the selection process. *The Hollywood Reporter* and *Daily Variety* actually count on this revenue during the Awards season just as a retailer banks on Christmas. The fine line between normal business practices and excessive promotion has been difficult to define over the years, but there was a time when it wasn't unusual to have private cocktail parties and dinners served before or after special screenings for the Music Branch. These have been discontinued. Gifts were sometimes sent directly to members' homes, and parties and other social events were geared to-

ward the promotion of films and specific achievements like a song or score. Records, cassettes, CDs, and videocassettes are still sent out for branch members to consider during the voting season.

In 1963, Sammy Cahn and Dimitri Tiomkin were embroiled in a heated public debate. Cahn spoke out in John G. Houser's column "What's the Score?" which appeared in the *Daily Variety* on March 15.

"The reason I've become so avidly competitive this year is that Tiomkin has made it a fight for life," explained Mr. Cahn. "Have you noticed what he's been doing with the ads and interviews and cocktail parties?

"The feud between Tiomkin and me began the year he wrote the theme music for *The High and the Mighty.* During the first previews someone arbitrarily took the lyrics out of the picture. That made it ineligible as the best song, because Academy rules state a song must play in the Los Angeles area for one week during the Academy Award year. But that didn't end the matter for Tiomkin. He had them put the lyrics back in just one print that ran locally for a week, although all the other prints were without lyrics [contrary to the 1955 *Film Daily* article previously quoted]. That's when the feud began.

"It would have been better if he had just gracefully accepted the fact that my song for the year—'Three Coins in a [sic] Fountain'—was better, and let it go at that.

"Tiomkin has stimulated a virus that has infected every branch of the music industry. I never needed a press agent before. I can blow my own horn better than anyone I ever met. But I can't help it if he's lowered the barriers of good taste. It used to be that everybody tried to play the game on a level of elegance, but no more. If we don't win this year it won't be because we didn't fight a valiant battle according to the new rules."

Mr. Cahn said all the composers and song writers are vying so strongly for Oscars because if his song is given an Academy Award, it more than likely becomes a standard (or classic). "That's great for a music writer's ego if his song takes on an air of immortality of sorts," said Mr. Cahn. "Also, the Academy Award is the most priceless of all the awards in the entertainment business. The day after you win an Oscar your phone never stops ringing. It's a wonderful honor."

THE AWARDS SHOW

Ten times I have been music director and conductor of the Awards show. Having been present at several of the shows prior to my first time on the podium, and having been appalled at the number of missed cues, endless repetition of the same meaningless fanfare, no real connection between the music in the pit and the achievements being honored, I am the one who dreamed up the actually simple device by which the right music for the specific achievement hits instantaneously with the last syllable of the announcement of the winner—and this despite the fact that the conductor and his players have absolutely no advance inkling of any kind as to who the winner will be.

John Green, composer

The world's most vivid impression of the Academy is the Academy Awards television presentation. This is so even though the Academy is very active in a variety of educational and historical projects, and makes available the world's foremost library of motion picture reference materials. "The Academy's biggest money-making operation is the Academy Awards show," says Bill Conti, frequent music director for the show. "They sell it to the networks, who in turn sell airtime at whatever those rates are. In order to keep costs down, the show's music directorship has, until recently, been an honorary assignment, performed without a fee. It was an honor to be chosen to do your industry's Academy Award show."

Franz Waxman was the first music director, in 1944. Other well-known, distinguished film conductors have included John Green (10 times), Alfred Newman (3 times), André Previn (3 times),

Henry Mancini (5 times), Elmer Bernstein (twice), John Williams (twice), David Rose, Marvin Hamlisch, and Quincy Jones.

In 1992, Conti served as the show's music director for the eighth time. After William Friedkin, who was producing the show in 1977, asked him to do the show the first time, he did some telephone research. "I spoke with Johnny Williams, who had done the show before, Mancini, Elmer Bernstein, and started gathering an understanding of the show, and the people that you're going to need. You're going to need the official librarian of the Academy Awards show—Jean Woodbury, [orchestrator] Al Woodbury's widow, who has done the show at least 44 times. You're going to need a roomful of copyists, you'll need your orchestra contractor, you'll need orchestrators (at times it's been up to ten or twelve; I got it down this past year to four or five)."

The producer plans the show for months in advance, usually beginning concept meetings before Christmas with the writers, the director, the choreographer, and the music director. Still, none of the creative plans can begin to be realized until the morning of the nominations in February.

The week before the show is grueling. Here's a typical rundown:

Tuesday: Rehearse all music to be prerecorded on Wednesday. This includes all music for the film clips, and also certain aspects of the production numbers. In 1992, the orchestral accompaniment for "Belle" was prerecorded, and segued directly into a live accompaniment for Jerry Orbach's vocal on "Be Our Guest." The choreographer is there to be sure all the dance tempos are perfect.

Wednesday: Record all music to be prerecorded.

Thursday: Mix down all the prerecorded music.

Thursday night: A three-hour sound check in the hall. "That's the first time when we're going to have the bodies at the place," Conti says. "And there are reasons for the sound check other than just on-the-air stuff. One engineer's outside in a truck, and he is the master feed, and he will go to the guy that's working the sound in the house, and the sound mixer who's working the monitor mixes on the stage. So there's three engineers. Well, if someone's singing on stage, they have speakers so they can hear everybody. Monitor mix, house mix, on-the-air mix. And then we split off the feed to accommodate when necessary. They want to hear more drums on the stage, then maybe they get more kick and snare, stuff like that. In the house, depending on the quality of the engineer, he might just get a stereo feed from my guy in the truck."

Friday: Rehearsal to read the rest of the music. This includes the overture, music for the arrivals, all the play-ons and play-offs (remember, there are approximately 150 play-ons just to cover every possible winner).

"Madonna called a Friday evening rehearsal because she was nervous. So that meant 16 singers, 52 musicians, sound people, and from 10 to 12 at night we rehearsed Madonna. But her 'deal' was we've gotta do it good, and she's a rehearsal freak. So, how can you object to that? So we rehearsed a lot with Madonna. Only to have the elevator not go up right, the microphone not come out right."

Saturday: Rehearsal for the stars. "Who is singing live? Well, one year we had Harry Connick, Jr., Madonna, Reba McIntyre—we did five numbers, and they were all live. We like our vocalists to sing live, so we need to rehearse. The first time I met Reba was the day of the Saturday rehearsal. I got her key for the Meryl Streep tune over the phone, 'cause she's on the road. You don't get singers who say, 'Well, I'll drop by the house on Friday.' Diana Ross sang 'Over the Rainbow' once—she was in the Bahamas. I got her key over the phone, did the chart [arrangement], but she never heard the chart till she got there.

"Now, Billy Crystal the past three years has always started with an opening tune. And the opening tunes are parodies of the nominated songs. So the rehearsal was set, and all of a sudden we find out they can't get clearance. The charts are done, it's been copied, it's ready. They didn't get clearance to make fun of a couple of tunes. They sent the parody lyrics to the publisher and the publisher said, 'You can't do that.' So they changed the tunes, and that meant now we're gonna pop another rehearsal, 'cause we've gotta rehearse it. We're

gonna rehearse it off stage. Meanwhile the people have moved into the Dorothy Chandler from Monday the week before. Sets, camera. We're still not on the site (only the Thursday night sound check).

"Now you're into Sunday to slip in Billy Crystal to rehearse. Now, Sunday night, the guy's gonna want to do a run-through of the show. So you're back down at the hall where you're going to do the show, to do a run-through, checking that everything works."

Monday morning: "We start at ten or eleven in the morning, we do a dress rehearsal. The dress rehearsal has to stop by three-ish so that we can actually eat, change into tuxedos, and be on the air at six. Now, some things will happen that haven't happened before. Billy Crystal has only done the tune in the studio, so he wants to work out the moment on stage. And before we begin that, any act that didn't get to town until Monday morning and didn't have a chance to rehearse. We run some of these things as best as we can, and fight our way through a rehearsal. We're in our seats at 5:30, and wait for the countdown."

With all of that careful planning and rehearsing, there can be, and frequently are, glitches. "Madonna began rehearsing from the time that she had agreed to do the *Dick Tracy* number 'Sooner or Later.' And she didn't want to do it the way she had done it in the movie, she wanted to do it differently, so I met with her for about a month, a couple of times a week, and got together, worked on the number, with her choreographer, me setting up the chart, her running it, then I assigned a drummer and a piano player to her to begin rehearsing on a daily basis, when we got about two weeks from the show.

"She was coming up on an elevator from the back of the stage and—lots of music, lots of music, strike an attitude, walk forward—a mechanical microphone would come out of the floor. *Mechanical* rather than a man, because we could not fit a man in the pit. So instead, they put an apparatus in at the cost of around $16,000, to have the microphone come up. And then it came up crooked.

"The night of the show, of course, the microphone *did not* come up. And the camera came in tight on her, and an AD {assistant director} ran out and handed her a hand-held mic. A pretty unnerving thing, to have rehearsed it and then have some failure like that, which we thought was mechanical. Six months later we found out it was not at all mechanical—the man who was supposed to hit the button did not hit the button. So she did the whole song holding her mic."

There have been even more nervewracking moments during the broadcasts. "There was a night with Ann-Margret when the curtain never came up on the opening production number. Ann-Margret was dancing and her husband, Roger Smith, had asked to just tape it during the dress rehearsal to see it in the booth. And they did tape it, and they did look at it. So, 'We're on the air in 3—2—1.' Tympani roll, 'Ladies and gentlemen,' and the curtain raises six inches and jams. I can see Ann's ankles. I've begun the music. So we crossed over to the videotape they had rolled in the dress rehearsal, and Marty Pasetta going, 'Bill, listen, listen, listen real close, listen, listen.' I knew where they were. I put the orchestra in the same place. On television, people were watching Ann-Margret do the thing. The people in the house were watching her *ankles,* with stage hands pulling, yelling—they're back-timing because they *know* that this is off in four minutes minus. And they're saying, 'We'll cut the thing down if we have to.' And they eventually got it to raise, but people watching on the air never knew what happened."

It's amazing that Conti and the other Academy Awards music directors have managed to coordinate all this while conducting a live show. In order to make it work, they're rigged up with a headset that includes a small microphone suspended in front. Through one ear they hear the director giving instructions. Through the other ear they hear the show itself (which they can't really hear from the live source at all while they are in the pit). And they have three footpedals used to determine who hears their own voice: one sends the music director's comments to the director; another sends his comments to the recording engineer; and the third al-

lows him to talk to the orchestra musicians, who all have on a one-sided headset in order to hear him. They also hear clicks and/or singers through their headsets, if necessary.

A time-honored technique makes it relatively easy to play the proper music within seconds of the announcement of each winner. The musicians have a page or two of music for each Award category, each with five short excerpts representing the five nominated films. When the winner is announced, they know from the winning film and the winning nominees which of the five pieces to play, and are ready almost instantly as the conductor gives the downbeat.

With all this equipment around, there's just that much more to malfunction. "I've had my video go out" Conti explains. "I've had my audio go out"

John Williams gives his acceptance speech for his Oscar-winning score for *Star Wars* (1977). The other nominees were *Julia* (Georges Delerue), *Mohammad—Messenger of God* (Maurice Jarre), *The Spy Who Loved Me* (Marvin Hamlisch), and another score by Williams, *Close Encounters of the Third Kind.*
Photo courtesy of the Academy of Motion Picture Arts and Sciences

"I'm not hearing *anything*. I'm in the pit, and I hear the show only through my headphones. The house monitors are such that they're going out to the audience—we don't really hear those. So they say, 'The winner is—' and you hear static. Two years ago, I turned around to the first row of people, and said, 'Who won?' They told me who won, and I yelled it out to the musicians, and we played. And no one ever knew any different. So sometimes we have technical difficulties. I'll use the footpedal to talk to engineering. I'll tell them, 'I just lost the sound.' I've had AD's standing beside me with a walkie-talkie while they get it fixed. Everything that can happen *has* happened. 1992 was my eighth show. And you think, Well, I know how to do this show. But you get just as caught up in 'Oh, my God'—as the first time."

Songs and Soundtrack Records

■ ■ ■

SONGS

Hollywood is going gaga thinking of titles for new theme songs. . . . Writing of theme songs is becoming one of Hollywood's greatest industries. Every picture has its theme melody, and songs are turned out at the various studios about as rapidly as newborn flivvers. Tunes are growing scarce, with about everything in use from Handel's "Messiah" to "London Bridge Is Falling Down". . . . It is now a question as to which has absorbed which. Is the motion picture industry a subsidiary of the music publishing business—or have film producers gone into the business of making songs?

Photoplay *(1929)*

The minute you put a song over the titles or in any part of the picture, you're unconsciously trying to play on the viewer's pocketbook—you're trying to get him to listen, to go out and buy.

Henry Mancini, composer

The business prospects of a film can be greatly enhanced by a hit song associated with the film. Since the decision to use songs in a film is typically business-oriented, restraint has more often than not been obviated by the huge profit potential of multimillion unit sales. Songs and records are merchandizing, exactly like Teenage Mutant Ninja Turtle masks, Batman toys, and dinosaurs.

Few film composers are sympathetic to the gratuitous use of songs in films, even though they themselves may benefit from their success. Most do support the artistically valid use of songs when appropriate. The artistic criteria for using a song in a film is no different than that for developing a proper score: the music and the lyric both should be relevant emotionally and dramatically to the characters and the story, and enhance and augment the drama. There have been examples of this throughout the years, but fewer by far in the eighties and nineties, except in the occasional (often animated) musical like *Beauty and the Beast* (1991) and *Aladdin* (1992). Filmmakers frequently insert one or more songs onto the soundtrack, and composers rarely have the authority to argue successfully against this practice.

In the sixties and seventies there was a greater tendency to seek a consensus of opinion. During those years, Henry Mancini, who has enjoyed many successful songs developed from his film themes, had a persuasive voice in final decisions on whether or not to use a song in his scores. "In *Two for the Road* [1967], we had a song that had no place in the picture, so we agreed not to use it. *Sunflower* [1970] also had a title theme with words. It was originally planned to be used at the beginning, but it proved distracting so it was used in an instrumental form only. In *Days of Wine and Roses* [1962], a title song worked just fine, as in *Dear Heart* [1964]. . . . It's simply a matter of whether the song fits with the story and mood, or whether you're doing it for pure exploitation."

One of Mancini's most popular songs came from his score for *Breakfast at Tiffany's* (1961), and it was perfectly suited to the film. It's not always easy to totally integrate a song into the dramatic context, but that's when film songs work best. Mancini always designs his song usage carefully. "'Moon River' was one of the toughest I have ever had to write. It took me a month to think it through. What kind of a song would this girl sing? What kind of melody was required? Should it be a jazz-flavored ballad? Would it be a blues? One night at home, I was relaxing after dinner. I went out to my studio off the garage, sat down at the piano, and all of a sudden I played the first three notes of a tune. It sounded attractive. I built the melody in a range of an octave and one. It was simple and . . . it came quickly. It had taken me one month and half an hour to write that melody."

When a song works in a film, the emotional power is tremendous and demonstrates that songs can be as valid and effective as any other form of dramatic scoring. Consider Simon and Garfunkel singing "The Sounds of Silence" and "Mrs. Robinson" in *The Graduate (1967),* and the Bee Gees singing "Staying Alive" in *Saturday Night Fever* (1977).

Adapting a Theme from the Film

I didn't—and still don't—think of myself as a songwriter. Most of the songs in my career have been written as instrumental themes for scores and had lyrics added later. I write themes that can be used in different ways, and developed in the course of the scores.

Henry Mancini, composer

Almost all the film composer-songwriters of the sixties and seventies used their main themes as the basis for their film songs. The philosophy was that the themes were scoring the film and had to serve the film in a variety of ways. Therefore, themes should be written first. Mancini's theme for *Days of Wine and Roses* is an extraordinarily good example of the theme of the film preceding the lyric. Johnny Mandel's theme for *The Sandpiper* (1965) is another. With Paul Francis Webster's lyric, it became "The Shadow of Your Smile." And Michel Legrand wrote most of his film songs in this way, including

"The Windmills of Your Mind" for *The Thomas Crown Affair* (lyrics by Alan and Marilyn Bergman, 1968). Sometimes, as was true with Burt Bacharach and Hal David, there was more give-and-take, with segments of lyrics coming before the melody. They collaborated more like traditional songwriters.

In either case, songs derived from themes have an excellent chance of being organic to the score and to the film, since they are derived from the score itself. A variation of this technique uses a song melody as a main theme for the dramatic score. Max Steiner's use of "As Time Goes By" in *Casablanca* is a prototypical example of this. Steiner was originally unenthusiastic about using this already established pop song and claimed he didn't like the tune, didn't think it appropriate for Bogart and Bergman, and would have preferred to write his own theme. Hal Wallis, who produced the film, actually agreed to let him write his own tune, even though the title of the song had already been mentioned by the characters in the film. This would have necessitated reshooting several of Ingrid Bergman's scenes, which, as it turned out, was impossible, because she had already cut her hair for her role in *For Whom the Bell Tolls*. So Steiner used "As Time Goes By," which quickly became a standard and an example of the successful integration of a song theme in a dramatic score.

Buying the Title of a Hit Tune

My first picture . . . was originally called Fashions for Sale. *At that time [1940], "Ma, He's Makin' Eyes at Me" was a very popular song. So I suggested we buy the song title and the song, and use it.*
                    Joseph Gershenson, producer/composer

In general, this has been the least common way of using songs in films. Bio-pics have used existing song titles—*With a Song in My Heart* (1952, about the singer Jane Froman) and *Three Little Words* (1950, about the songwriters Bert Kalmar and Harry Ruby), for instance. Fictional films about musical comedy and vaudeville artists have often used a standard song title, such as *I'll Get By*

(1950). Films that use well-known musical artists have been named after an existing song (usually featured in the film)—*Stormy Weather* (1943), for example. Similarly, The Beatles' film *Let It Be* (1970) featured the title song and other songs created for the album of the same name. More recently, *Honeysuckle Rose* (1980) starring Willie Nelson was named after the standard, but the film was later retitled *On the Road Again* after Nelson's song from the film became a major hit.

When Joseph Gershenson was producing films at Universal, he realized that using an established song title would help to presell his films. He suggested this to the front office. "They thought it was a great idea. And the exhibitors liked it. So I made a deal with Mills Music, and I bought ten of their songs for $10,000. That was to use the titles and unlimited usage [of the songs] in the pictures, which was quite a deal. . . . So hit song titles like 'She's Nobody's Sweetheart Now,' 'Margie,' and 'Where'd You Get That Girl' became film titles."

Songs Written to Fit the Title

All Hollywood needs to start a cycle is one smashing success.
                    The Citizen News *(May 1945)*

A successful title song can have enormous impact at the box office today, but the follow-the-leader producers are already hard at work trying to kill the goose that lays the golden eggs. . . . Let's use a little judgment and restraint, please! before I am asked to write a title song for The Rise and Fall of the Roman Empire!
                    Dimitri Tiomkin, composer (1958)

Although the term "title song" is often used to refer to any important song in a film, strictly speaking, a title song must be known by the title of the film. "Fame," "The Rose," and "The Way We Were" are all outstanding title songs, capturing the essence of the film and the chief characters, and commenting about the dramatic themes of their films. Their integral relationship to the films is unquestionable.

Tex Ritter, who performed the title song on the soundtrack of *High Noon* (1952), stands between Dimitri Tiomkin (on the left, who composed both the melody and the score) and lyricist Ned Washington. Some film composers regret the growing awareness of the value of a hit film song among Hollywood producers and executives, since the desire for a hit has often taken precedence over artistic considerations. Nevertheless, worldwide record sales and radio and television performances of successful film songs generate tremendous income not only for the publishers (who are almost always owned by the production company), but for the writers as well.
Photo courtesy of Marc Wanamaker/Bison Archives

Title songs became a mania in the fifties after the overwhelming success of the Dimitri Tiomkin–Ned Washington title song for *High Noon* in 1952. After their hit, Hollywood filmmakers didn't care if the title made any sense or not as a song. Paramount music executive Bill Stinson saw a growing interest in title songs during those years. "There

were titles of pictures which were so inappropriate for title songs," says Stinson, "but most producers wouldn't take that for an answer. I learned right away that songs should be a title song, because it's a built-in promo. One play and your picture is on the air. Yes, every producer wanted one. I had a picture called *Love in a Goldfish Bowl* [1961]. Now you wouldn't think of a title song there, would you? Of course you wouldn't. But every writer in Hollywood thought of a title song and I was deluged by 'Love in a Goldfish Bowl.'"

Elmer Bernstein has observed that *High Noon* really was a turning point in the use of songs, because it was so successful commercially. "It led to a tremendous problem for film composers. The studios very quickly could see that it was an advantage to have a song in the film that could be exploited. It was a form of advertising. You get the name of the picture on the radio all the time if you have a title song. Well, the producers never are slow to grasp at anything that will make them an extra dollar, no matter how destructive it might be to their own business in the long run. They began to request composers to have title songs in every film. . . . There was a sense that what David [Raksin] had done in *Laura* was germaine to the film. In fact, seemed almost inseparable from the film . . . . But when *High Noon* came along, with the lyrics in the film, with the title of the picture in the lyric of the song, this was something that the producers couldn't resist. And it created a tremendous conflict among brothers and sisters in this business in the sense that the composers became very vocal, and said, 'I write my own music, and if I write a score I'm not going to be given a song and have somebody say that I have to base the music of the film on the song, because it's the tail wagging the dog.'"

Since *High Noon* opened in 1952, title songs have dominated the industry more than once. Their appeal has sometimes been irresistible to songwriters. "We produced a picture in 1958 called *I Married a Monster from Outer Space,*" says Stinson. "And when the picture came on the production schedule, I called Ed Wolpin in New York and I said, 'My

God, thanks. Here's one picture we will not have to worry about a title song.' And I forgot all about it. Within two weeks, in one of the columns of the Hollywood trade papers, there was an article about an entertainer in a La Cienega nightclub who had written a song titled 'I Married a Monster from Outer Space.' Our legal department called me and told me that I would have to get in touch with this man, and tell him he had no right to use the title of our picture as the title of his song, and would I please follow through with it. So after a number of phone calls, I located the guy, and I said to him, 'We object to your use of our title as the title of a song, and we don't want it used.' Several days went by, and the same column wrote a story, a little blurb, that said the man who had written a title song called 'I Married a Monster from Outer Space,' was changing the title of that song, at Paramount's request, and that he had changed it to 'I Nearly Married a Monster from Outer Space.'"

There have been many successful and outstanding title songs throughout the years, but in the more contemporary films the song has to be just right or it may sound like a parody. "The ultimate is to have a great title song that fits," says Gary LeMel, president of music at Warner Bros. "It's very difficult because a title song in the main title would be too corny, too on-the-nose, and almost never would work. We made it work in *Ghostbusters* [1984] by having it come in with the logo, and there had been so much pre-hype that it worked. But it rarely works, and usually the song ends up in the end title. If there's a spot in the body of the film where it really would work, like a montage sequence or something, then that's even better. . . .'"

Interpolated Songs

"Raindrops Keep Fallin' on My Head" from *Butch Cassidy and the Sundance Kid* is an interpolated song. The song adds a momentary diversion to *Butch Cassidy,* but basically puts the story on hold while the song has a chance to sell itself. It was de-signed to make people feel good and that in itself was to be an emotional contribution during the bicycling montage it accompanied.

Bacharach and David were hired to write a new song for that montage. During the eighties, however, filmmakers began to audition demo tapes as a matter of course from publishers, songwriters, and agents whenever songs were needed. This practice wasn't new; there had been isolated examples prior to then, especially on the Elvis Presley films in the sixties. Bill Stinson was the head music executive during the time that Hal Wallis produced the Presley movies for Paramount. "After the scripts had been sent to New York, the songwriters back there would have maybe six different versions of a song for a specific thing . . . indicated in the script. New York would send . . . 200 records. Wallis and I would go over these records well in advance of Elvis coming to the studio, and we would select the score that was to be done. When Elvis would arrive we would have our meeting with Elvis, the Colonel [Elvis's manager, Tom Parker], a lot of hangers-on (there were always hangers-on). Wallis was always in control and command, and he would say, "This is what we're going to do here," so on and so on, right on down the line. Elvis knew he had to do what Wallis wanted. He never really fought Wallis. Once in a great while he'd say, 'Couldn't we do this?' Because he would have heard the song, too, and Wallis would bend when he had to."

In the eighties and nineties there has been much greater collaboration between the music supervisor and the director. Others may be significantly involved in the selection process as well, including the film editor, the music editor, and possibly, though not necessarily, the composer of the score. Music editor Bob Badami was part of the scouting expedition looking for the right songs for *Beverly Hills Cop* (1984) and *Top Gun* (1986). "There was a song search, almost a cattle call, in a way. They were showing the film to a number of writers and rock-and-roll people. For example, on *Top Gun* we got well over one hundred cassettes and just started wading through them. The producers, Jerry Bruckheimer and Don Simpson, the director, Tony Scott, composer Harold Faltermeyer and myself, and a representative of the record company. We knew where we needed songs, and Harold, because he had a good background in records, had a great deal of input as to whether the song was good."

Ghostbusters II, Twins, and *Earth Girls* each had more than 60 songs submitted. Small fees were paid to some of the submittors to defray the costs of making these demos.

Licensing Existing Songs

Any copyrighted song must be licensed for use in a film, with permission being granted by the copyright owner(s) for a negotiated fee. Depending primarily on the popularity of the song and the status of the songwriter(s), these fees can vary from $500 to $50,000 or more. If the songwriter is a prestigious performing artist, this, too, would influence the licensing fee.

It always surprises people to learn that "Happy Birthday" is protected by copyright and must be licensed every time it is sung or played in a film. It was adapted from an 1893 children's song called "Good-Morning to All" written by Mildred J. Hill and her sister Patty Smith Hill, who were schoolteachers in the midwest. Adding the birthday lyrics a few years later, they copyrighted their song as "Happy Birthday" in 1935. "They used to control the copyright themselves," says music supervisor Terri Fricon, "and we used to have to deal directly with them. Actually, those two little old ladies used to be pretty tough to deal with." Now the licensing is supervised by Warner-Chappell Music Group, a division of Time Warner, and the procedure is the same as with any other song. Directors are still astonished when a music supervisor explains to them that the going rate is around $12,000 to $13,000 for perpetual rights worldwide for a TV and home-video buyout. If the song is important enough to the film, the fee is paid. "A lot of people will use a substitute like, 'For He's a Jolly Good Fellow,' or something," says

Fricon. "Not too long ago a scene had been shot with 'Happy Birthday' sung, and as it turned out they ended up cutting the scene because they didn't want to spend the money."

Master-use licenses for a recording can range from as little as $10,000 to more than $50,000, depending on the artist, the song he or she is performing, and the use in the film. That fee is in addition to the fee paid for permission to use the *song* in the film. The scoring budget for a typical studio release might be about $500,000 (as was the case for *The War of the Roses*), but on big-budget films and films that need to license a lot of songs and master recordings, the budgets can go higher. In almost every case, the production company is hoping for major returns on this investment through the sale of rights to the original soundtrack album and future record sales.

When George Lucas was planning *American Graffiti* (1973), he knew the authentic rock 'n' roll of the early sixties was absolutely necessary to make it work. When Universal began to pressure him to trim down his wish list of popular songs to a half dozen, he refused, and set about creating a final list of songs to be licensed that would fit his $90,000 budget.

On his list were eight songs by Elvis which would have been much too expensive. Out they went. Finally, with the help of the Beach Boys, who licensed two of their songs inexpensively to their friend as a favor, Lucas had made enough affordable deals to create a final song list that included "The Great Pretender," "Smoke Gets in Your Eyes," "Get a Job," "I Only Have Eyes for You," and "See You in September." These songs were an important creative contribution to *Graffiti.*

On *Mermaids* (1990) the song budget was drafted at $150,000; it eventually tripled to $450,000 as more and more songs were added over time. They started with six songs and ended up with eighteen. On one song, "Be My Baby," they offered $40,000, but the copyright holder wouldn't license the song for less than $200,000. They passed. "Oklahoma!", which was sung *a cappella* on screen, was quoted at $18,000, and paid for.

SOUNDTRACK ALBUMS

Early Soundtrack Albums

Judging from the letters that many of the composers are receiving constantly, people have gone to see the same movie three, four, and five times in order to listen to the music scores. There are thousands of letters in the files of the various music departments in the Hollywood studios from people asking for copies or recordings of the themes from motion picture scores.

Franz Waxman, composer (1945)

Walt Disney's *Snow White and the Seven Dwarfs* was the first 78 rpm album from a movie, released in December, 1937. The word "soundtrack" didn't appear anywhere on the album. *Snow White* and the next one to be released, *The Wizard of Oz,* both featured songs from the films, not the score. Victor Young conducted the *Oz* album, and Judy Garland was the only star represented from the film. An album of the songs from *Gulliver's Travels* followed shortly thereafter.

In 1942, Victor issued a three-disc "Recordrama" of *The Jungle Book* featuring Miklós Rózsa's score and narration by one of the film's stars, Sabu. Since record companies hadn't been interested in releasing music from films until then, RCA Victor's involvement was surprising. Rózsa was thrilled that *The Jungle Book* was the first American album. "They thought that as Prokofiev's 'Peter and the Wolf' was so good with its narration, here, too, the music should be linked by a recital of the story, and Sabu would be a natural choice as narrator. I agreed, and Anthony Gibbs put together a text derived partly from Kipling, partly from the picture . . . We recorded the *Jungle Book Suite* in New York, and I was thrilled to be conducting Toscanini's great orchestra, the NBC. . . . It did very well. . . . About 42,000 albums were sold, which was a very large number at that time. . . ."

More movie music was released in the United States over the next seven years, but none of the original dramatic scores was released directly from the film soundtrack. Rudy Behlmer recites the chronology of these releases. "Victor Young's music from *For Whom the Bell Tolls* (1943), Alfred Newman's *The Song of Bernadette* (1943), Rózsa's *Spellbound* (1945), Dimitri Tiomkin's *Duel in the Sun* (1946), David Raksin's *Forever Amber* (1947), Newman's *Captain from Castile* (1947), and Young's *Golden Earrings* (1947) were all produced specifically for records and not taken directly from the soundtrack. The first original dramatic score from an American feature film to be transferred to record from the film studio music tracks was Rózsa's *Madame Bovary* (1949) for MGM Records."

Jesse Kaye worked as soundtrack record producer for MGM, the company that originated the phrase "original soundtrack." The first MGM original soundtrack album was released in 1947 from the Jerome Kern bio-pic *Till the Clouds Roll By.* MGM, and then Decca, began releasing scores to important new films as a matter of course, a practice that MGM continued until 1953. In 1951, MGM recorded its first major musical on tape. Throughout those years, Kaye was responsible for putting together, programming, and remixing all the MGM soundtracks.

Over at Paramount, Bill Stinson saw the value of soundtrack albums and encouraged the studio to make individual deals with various companies to release their scores. "I came in [in 1958] on the beginnings of what was really the start of the general thinking [in the industry] that there should be music exploitation and soundtrack albums for all of our pictures. And all of the studios were thinking similarly. . . . I became very involved with that aspect of the business.

"I really feel in a sense that I invented the soundtrack album. There were just a few before me. But when I got into music, into my own department, it seemed to me that one of the most important things I could do, apart from supplying the right score for the picture—that was number one, I never lost sight of that—was to get a soundtrack album. And with the soundtrack album, to get a single record to exploit the picture. . . . The company loved me because I could do that."

Stinson managed to sell two separate albums of the *Romeo and Juliet* soundtrack in 1968 (featuring Nino Rota's music), and they were both bestselling hits. "The score and the album from Capitol probably meant somewhere between three and four million dollars to Paramount and Famous Music [Paramount's publishing company] in combination. I'm talking about the mechanical income, the performance income to Famous, and the royalty income to Paramount from the record."

The Graduate soundtrack by Simon and Garfunkel had been a big seller, and then *Easy Rider*, in 1969, was enormously successful, starting a genre of soundtracks using compilations of rock

songs. Other landmark albums include Isaac Hayes' *Shaft* in 1971, *Rocky* in 1976, *Saturday Night Fever* in 1977 (riding the crest of the disco wave), *Star Wars* in 1977 (heralding the revival of interest in symphonic scores on records), and *Chariots of Fire* in 1981 (stimulating interest in electronic pop).

Song-Oriented Soundtrack Albums

People who go to movies are usually the same people who buy records.

James G. Robinson,
owner, Morgan Creek Productions

The album of Robin Hood *has generated so many pieces of fan mail for me, and I've had so many wonderful experiences meeting people who were enthusiastic about the score.... over 3 million records have been sold.... I've enjoyed more success with that score than most composers have had in a lifetime.*

Michael Kamen, composer

Song-oriented soundtrack albums remain the key element in the business. James G. Robinson, owner of Morgan Creek Productions, was responsible for inserting the pop song "(Everything I Do) I Do It for You" over the end credits of *Robin Hood: Prince of Thieves,* even though the contrast in style, attitude, and instrumentation coupled with a pop-rock vocal created a jarringly anachronistic effect. It didn't matter. The soundtrack album sold more than 2 million copies during its first 90 days of release, based largely on the success of the Bryan Adams single. Similarly, there is almost none of Elmer Bernstein's dramatic orchestral score on the *Ghostbusters* album, but you'll hear a lot of songs you never knew were in the film, in addition to the catchy hit title song by Ray Parker, Jr.

Filmmakers had recognized the value of appealing to the pop market for years. By the mid-seventies, culminating with the sale of 20 million units of *Saturday Night Fever,* the youth market became the target audience. That same year, after the first screening of the rough cut of *Star Wars* for

Italian director Franco Zeffirelli created a popular film version of *Romeo and Juliet* (1968) at a time when there was a general reaction in Hollywood against expressing sentimentality and making truly romantic films. 15-year old Olivia Hussey (shown here with the director during filming) and 17-year old Leonard Whiting played the ill-fated lovers. Nino Rota's score was released on two different best-selling soundtrack albums, one with portions of the dialogue track accompanied by his score, and another featuring the score without dialogue. *Copyright © 1968 by Paramount Pictures. All Rights Reserved.*

several Fox executives, Alan Livingston (then in charge of Fox Records) asked Ashley Boone (head of marketing) to convince George Lucas to release a disco version of the score. "I don't think I even answered him," Boone reported. He knew Livingston was serious, though. As it turned out, Meco Monardo *did* release a disco version, performed by a 75-piece orchestra, which danced its way to the top of the charts on October 1.

Song-oriented albums have been released for many contemporary films such as *Beverly Hills Cop I* and *II, Ghostbusters II, Do the Right Thing,* and *New Jack City.* However, soundtrack albums for films with one strong song are featuring the dramatic score with one or two tracks of that song. *Ghost,* by Maurice Jarre, with two tracks of Alex North's "Unchained Melody," is a good example of this. *Home Alone* features John Williams' instrumental score, along with two of his own songs composed for the film (with lyrics by Leslie Bricusse) and several other pop and traditional standards.

Original Dramatic Scores on Record

Another interesting development is the intention of recording companies to wax scores from motion pictures. This should go a long way toward perpetuating film music and letting the composer assume his rightful place in the Hollywood hierarchy.

Franz Waxman, composer (1944)

Soundtracks are more than just background music or marketing tools these days. They are a forum for contemporary classical musical composition, taken seriously as a music form unto itself.

Robert Townson,
Varèse Sarabande Records (1993)

Until 1942, with the release of *Jungle Book* by Miklós Rózsa, there were no scores released on records. Selznick couldn't convince his friend David Sarnoff, then head of RCA Records, to release an album of Max Steiner's music from *Gone with the Wind*—he believed nobody would be interested in just the music.

Now, of course, there is a growing market for original soundtrack recordings of scores. In part this is fueled by the tremendous potential profits of a huge hit. The *Star Trek* series, the *Star Wars* trilogy, almost all the John Williams and Jerry Goldsmith scores, fantasies like Danny Elfman's *Edward Scissorhands* (1990)—more and more soundtracks containing scores are being released, including interesting electronic scores like Thomas Newman's *The Player* (1992) and Christopher Young's *Bat*21* (1988). Scores for successful comedies are often released as instrumental albums, if that's the score's emphasis. *Kindergarten Cop* (1990) by Randy Edelman is a good example of this kind of album. Many of the contemporary comedies feature song scoring and source songs, however—you won't find any underscoring on the hit album from *Wayne's World* (1992).

There are also more and more CD reissues of older scores, soundtracks like *The Egyptian* (Alfred Newman and Bernard Herrmann, 1954, conducted by Alfred Newman, Varèse Sarabande VSD-5258), *The Nun's Story* (Franz Waxman, 1959, conducted by Franz Waxman, Stanyan STZ-114), *The Time Machine* (Russell Garcia, 1960, conducted by Russell Garcia, GNP Crescendo GNPD-8008), and a three-volume collector's edition limited-release set from Bay Cities Records featuring Jerry Fielding's music from *Straw Dogs, The Mechanic, The Nightcomers,* and many others.

Interest in newly performed and recorded versions of classic scores continues to grow. Bay Cities has released the World Premiere recording of Korngold's complete score for *The Private Lives of Elizabeth and Essex* (1939, Munich Symphony Orchestra conducted by Carl Davis, Bay Cities BCD 3026). Varèse Sarabande has released a number of rerecordings, including a new release on CD of Elmer Bernstein's Film Music Collection performance of *The Ghost and Mrs. Muir* (Bernard Herrmann, 1947, conducted by Elmer Bernstein, VCD 47254). Silva Screen has produced new versions of the classic *The Big Country* and *Lawrence of Arabia* scores.

The first of the great rerecordings were the legendary Charles Gerhardt RCA Victor Classic Film

Music Series. The National Philharmonic Orchestra of London was conducted by Gerhardt, and the recordings were produced by George Korngold, the composer's son. Those who were film music fans in the early seventies all mention the tremendous influence those LPs had on them. In the liner notes to one of the albums, "The Spectacular World of Classic Film Scores," Gerhardt explained how the series came to be.

> My policy from the outset was to restore neglected symphonic film scores to . . . musical status. . . . I wanted to go back to the days before the advent of the soundtrack LP and systematically explore the substance of the great movie scores of the late thirties and forties in direct relation to the picture, as dramatic entities. . . . I determined to re-create these scores or selections from them in the original orchestrations, and this could be done only by going back to the ultimate sources—the composers and their music as they originally wrote it. . . .
>
> Although in the interests of good "attention-getting" we gave each volume in the series the title of a well-known picture, when selecting the contents I was always concerned with the quality of the music, not with that of the film. Times without number great music has been written for average films.

Sometimes the original orchestrations existed, or the original instrumental parts. But there were times when only a piano-conductor version of the score existed, with some indications of orchestration, in which case the full orchestrations had to be re-created from the piano-conductor parts. *King Kong* (1933) was done that way. In several cases, including Waxman's *Bride of Frankenstein* (1935), Rózsa's *Four Feathers* (1939), and Tiomkin's *Guns of Navarone* (1961), the entire score had to be painstakingly re-created by transcribing the score bit by bit from the existing film soundtrack. In some of the individual tracks for the series, such as *Casablanca: Classic Film Scores for Humphrey*

Bogart, two or more cues have often been joined together to create longer pieces for the recordings.

The 12-album series was remixed for CDs by Grover Helsley in Dolby Surround Stereo for the RCA Victor label, distributed by BMG Classics. Helsley remembers when the first LP in the series was released in 1972. "They put it out and it hit the charts! Who could believe that a 1930-whatever score for a motion picture that had long since been forgotten would *ever* made the charts? I honestly don't know how it happened. I don't think anybody does. Maybe the public was just hungry for orchestras again. And there it suddenly was. And that was a very impressive recording. It was well recorded, and it was an incredible emotional experience to put this thing on and hear that huge orchestra."

Specialty Soundtrack Labels

It's like a clock's ticking. There's a lot of stuff that's not being preserved, or getting misplaced.

Robert Townson,
Varèse Sarabande Records

Big labels with money to spend on licensing the soundtracks from current film releases tend to favor the new, potentially bestselling projects—companies like Epic, Warner Bros., and MCA Records are aggressive in that market. But there are a number of labels that specialize in the production and release of soundtrack albums, either exclusively or as an important aspect of their catalog. They usually favor the reissuing of soundtracks from older films and/or the rerecording of classic film scores.

Nick Redman (formerly with Bay Cities Records) finds that market research is illuminating. "We've figured out that there are probably about 2,000 hard-core buyers in the world that will pretty much buy anything with the word 'soundtrack' on it. Which is fine for the reissues, and it's fine for albums that don't carry new-use payments to the American Federation of Musicians. Once you start going into the areas where you *do* have to start making those payments, or new recordings such as

Elizabeth and Essex, you've got to go beyond those 2,000 people. You've really got to get closer to 10,000 people, and there's an awful chasm between 2 and 10. It really is difficult to get to 10,000. This is where, as an independent label, you really struggle." Bay Cities closed their doors in 1993; some of their releases will continue to be distributed by Varèse Sarabande. (Redman is now producing original soundtrack recordings of classic film scores for 20th Century Fox.)

Following are some of these specialty soundtrack labels and their addresses:

Creazioni Artistiche Musicali (C.A.M.)
Via Virgilio
8-00193 Roma, Italy
(396) 687-4220

Concentrates primarily on Italian and French films. "CAM's Soundtrack Encyclopedia" includes reissues from its vast catalog, including scores by Georges Delerue, Nino Rota, and Ennio Morricone.

GNP Crescendo Records
8400 Sunset Boulevard
Los Angeles, CA 90069
(213) 656-2614

Gene Norman, president of Crescendo, and his son Neil Norman have well-rounded, eclectic tastes, but Neil does lean toward sci-fi, fantasy, and horror movie soundtracks.

Intrada Records
1488 Vallejo Street
San Francisco, CA 94109
(415) 776-1333

Douglass Fake began Intrada in 1985 as a soundtrack label, specializing in orchestral scores. You can also order from them a variety of soundtrack albums released internationally by a number of companies.

Prometheus Records
c/o Luc Van de Ven
Astridlaan 171
2800 Mechelen
Belgium

Founded by Luc Van de Ven in order to release neglected French film scores, Prometheus has expanded to include other scores as well. Van de Ven publishes the outstanding film music journal *Soundtrack!*.

Silva Screen
c/o One World Records
1250 West NW Highway
Suite 505
Palatine, IL 60067

In 1984 Reynold D'Silva and James Fitzpatrick began working on their soundtrack projects, and in 1986 they formed Silva Screen to import records like the CD release of *The Godfather* by Nino Rota. They produce newly performed versions of older scores also.

Varèse Sarabande
13006 Saticoy Street
North Hollywood, CA 91605
(818) 764-1172

Product includes new releases, "as well as rerecordings of older scores," says Robert Townson, "but we also maintain a very active reissue series of what I think are some of the classic scores."

Facts and Figures

Music Budgets
The music budget for a movie can reach $1 million. The composer alone can earn $40,000 to $400,000 for a film. Interscope paid more than $100,000 each to KISS, Faith No More, and Slaughter for recorded versions of new songs for their soundtrack for *Bill & Ted's Bogus Journey.*

Fees to license use of a master on soundtrack
"We got $175,000 for a Rod Stewart record for the end title for *Legal Eagles.* The range can go from a high of $300,000 to a low of $3,500. It depends on how badly the producer or director wants that song and who the artist is—and how popular the song has become. A proven hit sets

the time or mood of the period and it's instantaneous nostalgia of the moment."

Michael Kapp,
president of Warner Special Products

Advances for Soundtrack Album Rights

Record companies pay an advance of anywhere from $30,000 to $1 million for soundtrack rights. "Speaking very generally," says Jeffrey Ainis, who researched the subject for *The Hollywood Reporter,* "for a $5 million film the advance may be around $150,000; for a $10 million film, around $200,000; and for a big-budget film, perhaps $400,000."

Examples

■ Giant Records, for *New Jack City*: $100,000+
■ Qwest Records, for *Boyz N the Hood*: in the $250,000 to $500,000 range.
■ Epic, for *Dances With Wolves*: $700,000
■ Epic, for *City of Joy*: $400,000

Record Sales

"Generally speaking, sources estimate that the orchestral soundtrack to a quality low-profile film may sell 9,000–10,000 units, with 2,500 in France and 1,000 in the U.K. An orchestral soundtrack that sells 50,000 units is considered to have done well."

Jeffrey Ainis (*The Hollywood Reporter,* August, 1989)

A major hit soundtrack album can sell millions of albums. By way of comparison, Bruce Springstein's "Born to Run," "Live 1975-1985," and "Tunnel of Love" albums each sold 3 million in the U.S. His 1980 album "The River," sold 2 million, and his monster hit "Born in the U.S.A." sold 12 million albums in the States. The biggest selling soundtrack album, *Saturday Night Fever,* sold 20 million units worldwide.

Examples (not final figures)

■ *The Big Easy,* 300,000 units
■ *Boyz N the Hood,* 900,000+ units
■ *The Commitments,* 2 million+ units
■ *Dirty Dancing,* 3 million+ units
■ *Doctor Zhivago,* 2 million+ units
■ *Ghost,* 1 million+ units
■ *Jungle Fever,* 1 million units
■ *La Bamba,* 2 million+ units
■ *The Mission,* 500,000 units
■ *New Jack City* 2 million+ units
■ *Saturday Night Fever,* 20 million units
■ *Working Girl,* 500,000 units

The Charts

During the first week of December 1991, there were nine soundtrack albums on Billboard Magazine's Top 200 albums. Among them were *Robin Hood: Prince of Thieves, Pretty Woman, The Commitments, House Party II,* and *Beauty and the Beast.*

Over the years, a number of soundtracks have done well on the charts. However, only four *Original Scores* (in LP format) without songs on the albums reached Number 1 on charts through June 30, 1990 (** = Grammy). They are:

Doctor Zhivago** (Maurice Jarre; was on the charts for 115 weeks beginning in 1966. MGM 6)

Exodus** (Ernest Gold; reached No. 1 for 14 weeks; was on the charts for 55 weeks in 1961 and 1962. RCA 1058)

Chariots of Fire (Vangelis; reached No. 1 for 4 weeks; was on the charts for 20 weeks in 1982. Polydor 6335)

Around the World in 80 Days (Victor Young; was on the charts for 10 weeks in 1957. Decca 79046)

The following are the other songless original scores that have been in the Top 40 on the charts (** = Grammy), listed in descending order based on their highest position on the charts:

Cleopatra (Alex North,1963); *Lawrence of Arabia* (Maurice Jarre, 1963); *Love Story* (Francis Lai, 1971); *The Man with the Golden Arm* (Elmer

Bernstein/Shorty Rogers & His Giants, 1956); *Never On Sunday* (Manos Hadjidakis, 1961); *Romeo & Juliet* (Nino Rota, 1969 and 1970); *Star Wars*** (John Williams, 1977); *The Empire Strikes Back*** (John Williams, 1980); *The Good, the Bad and the Ugly* (Ennio Morricone, 1968); *Hatari!* (Henry Mancini, 1962 and 1963); *How the West Was Won* (Alfred Newman, 1963); *Rome Adventure* (Max Steiner, 1962); *Ben-Hur* (Miklós Rózsa, 1960 and 1961); *Picnic* (George Duning, 1956); *The Alamo* (Dimitri Tiomkin, 1960 and 1961); *The Pink Panther* (Henry Mancini, 1964 and 1965); *A Man and a Woman* (Francis Lai, 1967); *Children of Sanchez* (Chuck Mangione, 1978); *Mutiny on the Bounty* (Bronislau Kaper, 1963); *Mondo Cane* (Riz Ortolani and Nino Oliviero, 1963); *Giant* (Dimitri Tiomkin, 1956); *Close Encounters of the Third Kind*** (John Williams, 1978); *The Apartment* (Adolph Deutsch, 1961); *Return of the Jedi* (John Williams, 1983); *The Godfather*** (Nino Rota, 1972); *Born on the Fourth of July* (John Williams, 1990); *E.T. The Extra-Terrestrial*** (John Williams, 1982); *El Cid* (Miklós Rózsa, 1962); *Experiment in Terror* (Henry Mancini, 1961); *Gone with the Wind* (Max Steiner, 1967); *Jaws*** (John Williams, 1975); *The Lord of the Rings* (Leonard Rosenman, 1979); *Out of Africa*** (John Barry, 1986); *Rain Man* (Hanz Zimmer, 1989); *Tom Jones*** (John Addison, 1964); *Walk on the Wild Side* (Elmer Bernstein, 1962).

PART FIVE

A SHORT CHRONOLOGY

■ ■ ■

Decade by Decade

■ ■ ■

THE TWENTIES

If I were an actor with a squeaky voice I would worry.
Welford Beaton (in The Film Spectator, *1927)*

1925

"Warners will enter a policy of talking pictures. Our researchers show that this is practical and will bring to audiences in every corner of the world the music of the greatest symphony orchestras and the voices of the most popular stars of the operatic, vaudeville, and theatrical fields."

Hal Wallis (then publicity chief,
Warner Bros.)

1926

■ August 6 marks the premiere of the John Barrymore film *Don Juan* (Warner Bros.), with a fully synchronized score by William Axt and David Mendoza, using the Vitaphone disc process.

"At the New York premiere of the Vitaphone, films and records of the New York Philharmonic Orchestra, as well as of Martinelli, Elman, Zimbalist, Bauer, Anna Case and Marion Talley were presented with astonishing success."

Photoplay (October)

"The executives of Warner Brothers, the Bell Telephone Company, and the Western Electric Company believe that the Vitaphone will revolutionize the presentation of motion pictures. It will bring famous singers and orchestras to the smallest theaters. Exhibitors will be able to get an accompaniment to their feature pictures played by the most famous orchestras. . . . Perhaps, back in their minds, these experts believe that the Vitaphone eventually will make possible a genuine talking picture. However, no definite plans have been made along this line. So far they are confining their activities to an invention which bids fair to transform the exhibition of pictures."

Photoplay (October)

1927

- The October 6 premiere of *The Jazz Singer* (Warner Bros.) in New York features six songs sung by Al Jolson.

"*The Jazz Singer* definitely establishes the fact that talking pictures are imminent. Everyone in Hollywood can rise up and declare that they are not and it will not alter the fact."

Welford Beaton (The Film Spectator)

"Al Jolson with Vitaphone noises. Jolson is no movie actor. Without his Broadway reputation, he wouldn't rate as a minor player. The only interest in the picture is his six songs. The story is a fairly good tearjerker about a Jewish boy who prefers jazz to the songs of his race. In the end, he returns to the fold and sings Kol Nidre on the Day of Atonement. It's the best scene in the film."

Photoplay review of
The Jazz Singer (December)

- Warner Bros. releases an all-talking Vitaphone two-reeler, *Solomon's Children,* in December.

1928

- In July, Warner Bros. releases the Vitaphone process *Lights of New York,* the first all-talking feature from Hollywood.
- In autumn, Warner Bros. completes the conversion of its facilities to sound.

"There were some people who didn't like it. Sam Goldwyn, for example, thought it was only a passing fancy, that people, when they get in a theater, want to relax and think, and they don't want somebody talking to them. . . . [When I heard my first talkie] it was a relief to me that I didn't have to put the music to it. So I was kind of happy about the whole thing, not knowing that talking

pictures would soon put us out of business. Most of the theaters that had silent pictures and vaudeville acts soon did away with the acts when the talking pictures came in. The musicians really didn't realize what was going to happen to them."

Joseph Gershenson,
silent film accompanist,
and later, music director at Universal

1929

"*Don't dare to miss* The Broadway Melody. *It is a Double A, triple-distilled picture entertainment.*"

Photoplay review (April)

THE THIRTIES

It was hard work in those days to write music to the measure of film, to make tunes and chords fit the action on the screen and not have the snarling dissonance for the villain's entrance fall upon the heroine's innocent lips. . . . In the old days . . . the composer had to run the picture over and over again, timing scenes and action with a stopwatch. As I look back, it seems a nightmare of sweating out endless hours in the projection room.

Dimitri Tiomkin, composer

1930

- Virtually all films being made are now sound films.
- *Sunny Side Up* is released with Janet Gaynor and Charles Farrell.

". . . The first original all-talking, singing, dancing musical comedy written especially for the screen. Words and music are by De Sylva, Brown, and Henderson, authors of such stage musical comedy successes as 'Good News,' 'Manhattan Mary,' 'Three Cheers,' 'Hold Everything,' and 'Follow Through,' so you know what kind of music to expect when you hear *Sunny Side Up!*"

Photoplay review (January)

- Theater admissions and profits for the studios reach record levels.

"Hollywood was having a boom in music. . . . A great deal of music was needed, and anyone who could think of a tune and put a few notes together might be hired to concoct motion picture scores. Stray violinists and piccolo players were placed under contract as composers."

Dimitri Tiomkin, composer

1931

"By this time Hollywood was beginning to feel the slump, and RKO decided they didn't want any music in their dramatic pictures. This was motivated not only by the economic factor, but because they had decided you could not have background music unless you showed the source. In other words, you had to have an orchestra on view, or a phonograph or performers, so that people would not wonder where the music was coming from. . . ."

Max Steiner, composer

■ Virtually no musicals are being made.

1932

■ *Love Me Tonight* is released, directed by Rouben Mamoulian.

"What a picture! First you have Chevalier (and last, you have Chevalier, and all through this riot of entertainment you have Chevalier)—zat Maurice who captures you with his risqué songs, his magnetic smile, and his rakish straw hat. And, adding her beauty and lovely voice, you have that delightful Jeanette MacDonald. And those two ridiculous Charlies—Ruggles and Butterworth. And C. Aubrey Smith, who plays a doughty old duke and puts over a solo as inimitably as Maurice. Then there is Myrna Loy. And others equally good. The story? About a lowly tailor who woos a princess. The music? Woven through the whole picture like a brilliant symphony, accented with some of the catchiest tunes of the season. You'll surely be humming 'Isn't It Romantic?' or we miss our guess."

Photoplay review of *Love Me Tonight*
(October)

1933

■ *42nd Street* is released.

"Ruby Keeler's début as a picture personality—and, make no mistake about it, a new star is born. As the country girl who comes to Broadway and steps in at the last minute for a musical queen, she makes good in a big way. Almost an out-and-out musical, with one number at least sufficient to stop any show. Excellent performances by Warner Baxter, Guy Kibbee, George Brent, Bebe Daniels, and Ginger Rogers."

Photoplay review of *42nd Street* (March)

"*King Kong* was the film that saved RKO from failure. But when it was finished, the producers were skeptical about what kind of public reception they could expect. They thought that the gorilla looked unreal and that the animation was rather primitive. They told me that they were worried about it, but that they had spent so much money making the film there was nothing left over for the music score—and would I use some available tracks. I explained that we had nothing suitable. But the man who was most responsible for the picture, producer Merian C. Cooper, took me aside and said, 'Maxie, go ahead and score the picture to the best of your ability and don't worry about the cost because I will pay for the orchestra or any extra charges.' His confidence in the film was certainly justified. . . . It was made for music. It was the kind of film that allowed you to do anything and everything, from weird chords and dissonances to pretty melodies."

Max Steiner, composer

"Music had a way of being thrown in and dubbed finally along with sound effects. I remember being on the scoring stage at one time during a nightclub scene, and there was music in the background, the orchestra was on the stage, and in front was a whole line of sound effects men, tinkling glasses and pouring liquids out of bottles—I'll tell you it was wild, but one learned!"

Hugo Friedhofer, composer/orchestrator

1935

- *Bride of Frankenstein,* featuring Franz Waxman's innovative score, is released.
- Max Steiner scores *The Garden of Allah* for David O. Selznick, the first film using the "push-pull track."

"This [push-pull track] was far superior to the old system, producing about the same difference in sound as between mono and stereo. It allowed for a wider range, with lots of bass and lots of highs. On the opening night at Grauman's Chinese Theatre in Hollywood, people were amazed at the sound that came from the screen."

Max Steiner, composer

"Even in those days, when we made a lot of money, we had no prestige. We were considered just songwriters. George Gershwin, too. He'd be invited to a party and be expected to sit down and play like a hired entertainer. George liked to play, but he resented being expected to."

Harold Arlen, songwriter

1938

- *The Adventures of Robin Hood* is released with Erich Wolfgang Korngold's classic score.

THE FORTIES

In those days the studios were locked *in personnel—nobody ever got in. To become an editor, an editor had to die. That was the only way. There was no moving around. That wasn't until after the war. The first one that did it was Hal Wallis at Paramount; he brought Warren Loew in from Warner Bros.—his cutter. Unheard of. So if you were an assistant, the only way you could ever hope to get anywhere was that your cutter would die, or leave or something."*

John Hammell, music editor and executive (Paramount)

1941

- The first two films Bernard Herrmann scored are released—*Citizen Kane* and *All That Money Can Buy.*

1943

"Only as short a time ago as *Fantasia* the music for the better films was generally adapted from the classics or semiclassics. In that way the public, willy-nilly, absorbed much good music as background. 'But times have changed,' says Louis Lipstone, Music Director of Paramount. 'The music is of growing importance. It is written to fit the mood and situation, expertly synchronized, and enhances the value of the whole production.'"

Film Music Notes (February)

"The war films were all scored with tracks given to the Army by the studios. They gave transfers of their entire libraries to the Army and the other services. So that we had five or six vaults full of film music that we scored Army pictures with."

John Hammell, music editor and executive

1944

- David Raksin's score for *Laura* is a big success. With Johnny Mercer's lyrics added to the theme after the film's release, the song becomes a major hit.

"Films of an inspirational or religious character promise to figure most importantly on studio production schedules for 1944. The trend toward this type of picture is no doubt traceable to the phenomenal reader interest in Lloyd C. Douglas' novel *The Robe,* Franz Werfel's *The Song of Bernadette,* and other recent bestsellers and the industry acceptance of the tradition that during wartime there is a more general tolerance toward things spiritual. All major studios will produce at least one picture in this category during the year. Metro-Goldwyn-Mayer will make no less than four, in addition to the company's proposed remake of the spectacular story of early Christianity, *Quo Vadis.*"

Film Music Notes (February)

1945

"Music for the movies is becoming simpler and more melodic."

Alexandre Tansman, *Citizen News* (May)

■ Laurence Oliver's *Henry V* is released with a score by William Walton.

"They had a number of men in the music department, three or four of them. They were called *scorers*. A scorer would sit down in a projection room with the motion picture, and take [the sequences] down in detail, and using a stopwatch, he would time the action of the sequence which was to be composed prior to recording. . . . The old scorers frequently made mistakes in timing because of the inadequacy of the system."

Bill Stinson,
music editor and executive (Paramount)

"Paramount had more supervisors than they did music people. You looked at the picure with them. They did the timing with the clock. (The music editors didn't do the timing.). . . . They gave you the instructions. You had to show the music to them; they also functioned on the scoring stage in the booth."

Leo Shuken, orchestrator

1946

■ *The Best Years of Our Lives* is released with Hugo Friedhofer's score.

1947

"In the final analysis, it is on the music director that responsibility falls for the end result and the intrinsic importance of music in a picture. This importance may be little if the music is merely a backdop to the action, but even in such instances its impact must be properly judged and proportioned and it must be timed for complete effectiveness. And it is the judgment of the music director which must maintain the delicate balance between Bach and box office."

Morris Stoloff, music director
(*Los Angeles Times,* March)

1949

■ *The Red Pony* and *The Heiress* both are released with critically acclaimed scores by Aaron Copland.

"The main complaint about film music as written today in Hollywood is that so much of it is cut and dried, rigidly governed by conventions that have grown up with surprising rapidity in the short period of twenty-odd years since the talkies began."

Aaron Copland, *New York Times*

THE FIFTIES

I remember the studios fighting television all the way. And that was another scary thing that was happening, and it did not bode well at first for the security that we had as composers before.

Elmer Bernstein, composer

■ In the fifties, Hollywood introduced a variety of innovations hoping to lure the public from their television sets. 3-D, Cinerama, Cinema-Scope, and stereo sound were all offered as a way of making moviegoing more of an event.

1950

"In 1950 we didn't want to use the big orchestras; we were, for instance, trying to find ways of treating the love scenes without using strings—that sort of thing."

John Addison, composer (England)

■ Paramount records a score on 35mm magnetic film stock for the first time—Victor Young's music for *September Affair.*

1951

■ Elia Kazan's *Streetcar Named Desire* is released by Fox, with Alex North's landmark score integrating jazz materials with orchestra.

1952

■ *High Noon* is released, using the title song (featuring a vocal by Tex Ritter) throughout the movie.

1953

"I remember one horrible day in 1953 when Fox Studios laid off something like 2,500 people in one day, because of the changing styles. . . . Another thing that happened in 1953—it was the period of the witch hunts, of the Un-American Activities Committee. And there was a period in there when they didn't care about how good your music was, they were very interested in who your friends *weren't*. And that had an effect on many careers. Because that kind of atmosphere inculcates fear. Art does not flourish in an atmosphere of fear.

"So it was a chaotic period at that point. Suddenly composers that had been under contract to studios for very, very long periods of time either were unemployable because of their political opinion, or had to start functioning as independents because the studios couldn't retain composers on contracts."

Elmer Bernstein, composer

1954

■ MGM's first CinemaScope production, *Knights of the Round Table,* is released with a score by Miklós Rózsa—their first film with stereophonic sound.

1955

"I would say that the big difference in the middle fifties was that you found yourself much more with the popular idiom rather than a symphonic idiom."

Leo Shuken, orchestrator

"*The Man with the Golden Arm,* using a highly jazz-oriented score for the film, . . . sold 100,000 LPs, which in that day was unheard of. And once again the response was, 'Oh, pop music—that's wonderful.' I began to regret it, because it did open the door to a particular concept of once

again scoring a film in such a way that it will make records that sell, rather than what it does for the film. Apparently from about 1955 to 1957 the time was right, but *Man with the Golden Arm* in 1955 and 'Peter Gunn' in 1958 opened the floodgates to the concept of—get the pop stuff in the score, let's get it out there, and let's make money on the records. And it is true, it was very seductive. In one case, I was involved with a film where the records made more money than the movie.

"This trend was, I think, absolutely ruinous for the art of film music."

Elmer Bernstein, composer (1992)

1957

"We live in strange belief that noisiness and loudness is giving kick to audience!"

Dimitri Tiomkin, composer

1958

■ The "Peter Gunn" television series debuts with an extremely popular jazz-oriented theme and scores by Henry Mancini.

"I think one of the reasons the 'Peter Gunn' music caught the ear was its sparseness—the economy of the scoring. Up until then, economy had not been a major factor in filmmaking in California. It had been a super-rich industry, it was a mentality geared to abundance. . . .

"If it can be said that I had any influence, I think it was this—using good musicians to give personality to the music and having those musicians well recorded."

Henry Mancini, composer

"February 19th, I believe, of '58, the musicians called a strike. It was over television . . . residual payment of musicians. They struck and they didn't resume services to us until September 3, 1958, so we went damn near a year. . . . When the strike was over, September 3, 1958, there were no longer to be contract orchestras anywhere in the industry."

Bill Stinson, music editor and executive

1959

- The staff orchestras are gone, but vestiges of the contract system remain at the studios for a few years. Alfred Newman is still music director at Fox. His salary is $104,000. He has the following staff:

Edward B. Powell, Herbert Spencer, Emil Newman, and Lionel Newman, orchestrators

Cyril Mockridge, composer

Guest composers David Raksin, Hugo Friedhofer, Franz Waxman, Leigh Harline, Daniele Amfitheatroff, Alex North, and Bernard Herrmann

THE SIXTIES

In the sixties, what had become an art was being forgotten or badly abused.

Elmer Bernstein, composer

The movies were a lot more interesting then. I tend to be a sucker for movies of that period. I mean, a film like Hud, *which has very little music in it, and it's just Elmer Bernstein and a few guitars. It's just a very simple score, but really effective.*

Richard Kraft, composers' agent

1960

- Alfred Newman resigns as music director of Fox.

"We now need a lot of new talent in film composing because it will bring with it originality."

Dimitri Tiomkin, composer

"Universal, with Stanley Wilson as music director, signed on a talent pool—I don't know if it's ever been done since then (not that I know of, and certainly not before then, except at MGM, when they had all those people under contract). Some awfully good music came out of those years. This was 1960. It was Elmer Bernstein, John Williams, Jerry Goldsmith, Lalo Schifrin, Mortie

Stevens, Jack Marshall; and then people like Connie Salinger, who were there all the time. It was the *most* fantastic thing, because, I mean, Johnny Williams in those years was doing 'Bachelor Father,' if you can imagine that. They were under contract on a one-year basis; in some cases it went on for a few years. One guy would be doing a 'Wagon Train' one week, and another guy would be doing 'The Virginian'; 'The Deputy'—a lot of pretty crappy shows, but they were very successful. The budgets were broader then than they are now. So that was quite a time to be there. It was wonderful. It was like a family, very different from today. Much more of a close-knit group. If there was any backstabbing going on, I sure wasn't aware of it."

Sandy De Crescent, orchestra contractor

- Alfred Hitchcock's *Psycho* is released with Bernard Herrmann's score.

1962

- *To Kill a Mockingbird* is released with Elmer Bernstein's score.
- John Barry's theme for James Bond, used in the first Bond film, *Dr. No,* launches a series of his lush, jazzy Bond scores.

1964

"I think some film composers are destroying the taste of good movie music in America. They're doing things in pictures which aren't normal or healthy. It's a degeneration of music and it has no aesthetic value."

Dimitri Tiomkin, composer

1966

- Sergio Leone's *The Good, the Bad and the Ugly* is released with a score by Ennio Morricone.

"The leading composers in the world are in the picture business, but there are no pictures for them."

Dimitri Tiomkin, composer

1967

"Music today in pictures doesn't exist. It is destroyed. . . . Film music today is in bad shape, but then, everything is in bad shape. Today must be good lawyer or dentist to be in studio. . . . Today the tragedy of my colleagues is that there are new guys who can't write music."

Dimitri Tiomkin, composer

■ Simon and Garfunkel's song score for *The Graduate* is a big hit.

1968

■ Nino Rota's lyrical, romantic orchestral score for Franco Zeffirelli's *Romeo and Juliet* becomes a top-selling soundtrack album.

1969

■ *Easy Rider* is released, with a hit album based on the compilation of rock songs on the soundtrack, inaugurating a record-oriented trend.

THE SEVENTIES

I don't think that the musical developments of the past ten years are a passing phenomenon, but I am unhappy to the extent that everything has to be "with it," everyone has to follow the leader.

John Green, composer (1970)

1970

"If I were starting now I'd have no career in films."

Bernard Herrmann, composer

1971

"Motion picture Main Titles had always been a great source of pop songs. *High Noon* comes to mind. But again, that had all gone away, and *Shaft* brought that back. Suddenly we were getting hit songs out of films again. Along came Isaac Hayes and brought songs to the forefront again."

Grover Helsley, music recording engineer

1972

■ The first of the RCA Victor Classic Film Scores series of twelve LPs is issued. "The Sea Hawk" album, conducted by Charles Gerhardt and produced by George W. Korngold, hits the charts.

"A recent and thoroughly reprehensible fiasco occured when Bronislau Kaper's score for *The Salzburg Connection* was replaced by rock ruckus because the director felt Kaper's music 'irrelevant for today's sound. . . .'

"William Wyler has confessed that if a director allows a violin on today's soundtrack, he is considered something of a senile relic."

Page Cook (*Films in Review*)

1976

"[George] Lucas wanted the [*Star Wars*] sound and music recorded in Dolby Stereo, an innovation in the mid-1970s. Fox opposed the idea, arguing that the equipment was not reliable and theater owners were reluctant to invest in it."

Dale Pollock, author

1977

■ *Star Wars* is released, breaking all records. The double-record album of the John Williams score becomes the highest-selling orchestral soundtrack to date.

"After *Star Wars*, everybody wanted *Star Wars*. I did a picture just shortly after that called *Can't Stop the Music*. It was rock-and-roll. I remember the executive music supervisor coming to me and saying, 'I want *Star Wars*!' And I went, 'Wait a minute. You've got five- or six-man rock-and-roll—how are we going to get *Star Wars* out of that!' The Main Title was big orchestra, though.

"Suddenly music was important again. Music had kind of slipped away during the Beatles era. Music had become unimportant in films. Things were starting to get real expensive. Orchestras had gotten to the point where you really couldn't afford to use them much any more. And synthesized scores at that time weren't very good. . . . Then, suddenly, it was orchestras again, and the importance was brought back."

Grover Helsley, music recording engineer

■ The *Saturday Night Fever* soundtrack album, featuring songs and performances by the Bee Gees, sells 20 million worldwide.

1978

"Today, you have to work with people you wouldn't be too happy to have lunch with."

Bronislau Kaper, composer

THE EIGHTIES

We're in a period now, in the last 10 years, which has been antisentimental. Which is one of the reasons I think Stand by Me *[1986] is now a hit, because finally the people went, "Come on, give me a break. I want some sentiment."*

Marvin Hamlisch, composer (1986)

1983

"I think that the composer, because of the success of the Williams scores, is in a somewhat better position now than he has been in for some time. The attitudes appear to be a little bit looser, less doctrinaire on the part of the producers. There was one time a feeling, you know, that they wanted either a rock score or a commercial score. You hear much less of that now, in spite of the fact that certain types of scores have taken off. There have been, let's say, two great influences: one is *Star Wars,* and the other side is *Saturday Night Fever.* Each has inaugurated a trend. *Fever's* influence was to get producers interested in buying old pop records and using them as a score to a film: pictures like *Car Wash,* to a certain degree even *Animal House,* which I was involved with.

Making a score out of what are essentially pop records. . . ."

Elmer Bernstein, composer

1985

■ Jan Hammer's rock-and song-oriented electronic scores for the hit television series "Miami Vice" become the basis for the number one album of the year on Billboard's charts, riding the No. 1 spot for 11 weeks nonconsecutively. This is not an instrumental album, but television and film scores are greatly influenced by the use of songs in the series, and by Hammer's scores.

1987

"I do think more people are aware of film music now than they were 20 or 30 years ago. The major change seems to be in the desire of producers to have a viable record album and to do what they can to have that type of score written as opposed to the traditional score."

Jerry Goldsmith, composer

"I would say a few years ago it was interesting. There were a number of scores being written by people that were all over the map, and one year you'd have a great symphonic score, the next something else. The first few synth scores were exciting because they were new and no one had approached a movie that way before. *Thief* [1981] and *Midnight Express* [1978] were so different— it's like, 'Oh, my God, you can just hold the note for a minute, and it creates suspense.' And now it's like, 'It's on TV every night and it doesn't mean anything.'"

Richard Kraft, composers' agent (1991)

1989

■ Disney releases *The Little Mermaid,* with a song score by Alan Menken (music) and Howard Ashman (lyrics). Both the film and the score are well integrated into the film, and very popular, a hopeful sign for the future evolution of film musicals.

THE NINETIES

By today's standards, To Kill a Mockingbird [1962] could not happen. A producer would step in and say, "That's too busy! Where's the theme?"

We've gotten so much more conservative. Action scores used to be so brash—look at Korngold's greatest scores, Alfred Newman's wonderful stuff and my favorite, Max Steiner—and now they've become so nondescript.

Danny Elfman, composer (1993)

PART SIX

PERSONAL PROFILES

■ ■ ■

How They Get Started

■   ■   ■

The first thing a film composer better be is a good dramatist, and I think the only way to develop a sense of what's appropriate is to have a lot of experience in drama.

Elmer Bernstein, composer

My inspiration as a composer comes from being a film fan. My training comes from watching and listening to films.

Randy Edelman, composer

Film composers love films. British composer Richard Rodney Bennett is typical. "I go to the pictures much more often than I go to the theater, and with more excitement. . . . If there is a project going on which I think sounds marvelous, I can't wait to see it."

However as Ernest Gold points out, the love of film is not enough. "If you like the work so well that despite the fact that I will guarantee failure you would still rather work in that particular field than anything else, I would say go to it and you have a great chance to succeed. But if you go into it because you think it'll either make you famous or rich, forget it."

Coupled with the love of the medium and the work, good film composers typically have an intuitive theatrical instinct. Sometimes their background is musical comedy (Alfred Newman, John Morris) or music drama (Erich Wolfgang Korngold, Max Steiner). Film composers have different kinds of backgrounds, but there is clearly one common denominator. "I'm constantly asked about what it takes to be a film composer," Henry Mancini says, "and I reply, 'A sense of drama.'"

People often ask how someone gets to be a film composer. There is, of course, no single answer. As composers' agent Richard Kraft says, "No one has ever gotten their first film through an agent. It is because they met the editor at a party, they went to school with the director, they slipped a tape to the producer, they got their music in a temp track that the filmmakers fell in love with. Or they are famous for something other than scoring movies that makes them unique; Ry Cooder is the best slide guitar composer, so they went to him."

There are as many variations on breaking into the business as there are composers. Here are eleven of them, told by composers who have become active since the mid-eighties—stories that suggest an intriguing blend of talent and luck.

Randy Edelman had done a lot of television scoring, including the "MacGyver" television series, and he had scored *Executive Action,* a 1974 feature starring Burt Lancaster and Robert Ryan. By the time the eighties were on the way out, though, so were his high hopes.

"Then I got a little movie called *Feds* [1988]. I didn't think I was ever going to get a film. I had literally given up. I got this film—I still don't know to this day why the guy let me do the film. It's not that I couldn't do it—of course I could—but it was like, Why?

"And it turns out that it was executive-produced by Ivan Reitman. Even though Ivan probably never even heard my score. He wasn't even involved. But these people liked me, and it came out great. And even though the film wasn't successful, Ivan was making a movie called *Twins.*"

There was extra music to be written for *Twins* (1988) in addition to Georges Delerue's score, so Reitman called Edelman in and he and Delerue each have cues on the soundtrack.

"Then I did *Ghostbusters II* [1989], and I think what you need to get started, really, in this field in this town is—you have to get with a director who is powerful, who takes you under his wing. Tim Burton did it with Danny Elfman, Robert Zemeckis did it with Alan Silvestri [*Romancing the Stone,* 1984]—you know. You need the Blake Edwards–Henry Mancini thing. And you know what? That's the only way to get started in a big way. Now, if you don't get started that way, it doesn't mean that

you can't do stuff. If you ask me how I got started—Bill Murray hired me [for *Quick Change,* 1990] because Ivan had hired me."

Ironically, Edelman considers his greatest strength to be his dramatic writing, even though he has now established himself with contemporary comedy. To prove the point, he made a special effort to get the assignment for Alan Parker's *Come See the Paradise* (1990), a story involving the Japanese internment camps during World War II. His action films include *Dragon: The Bruce Lee Story* (1993).

Danny Elfman, who has been associated with director Tim Burton on many films, including *Beetlejuice* (1988), *Batman* (1989), *Edward Scissorhands* (1990), and *Batman Returns* (1992), had grown up interested in modern symphonic music and the classic film scores.

"The composers I loved growing up were Prokofiev, Stravinsky, Shostakovich, Ravel, and Bartók. My knowledge of classical music is very much limited to these composers. The fact is, I may very well be quoting Mahler and Wagner, but [laughs] through Herrmann or Korngold or Rózsa or Franz Waxman. It's second-hand knowledge; my knowledge of film music is considerably better than my knowledge of classical music.

"By the time I was 15, I could listen to movies and say, 'That's a Goldsmith score, that's a Korngold score, that's an Alfred Newman score.'"

That's around the time he began playing music. "Somewhere in high school I picked up violin, because I knew I was graduating, and I just wanted to take a small instrument up, and take it with me. And I literally flipped a coin between the flute and the fiddle, and it was a fiddle. I could go home and I could pick up anything really quick, but I wasn't learning to read music. I was memorizing everything. I ended up getting hired into a troupe called the Grand Magic Circus that my brother was performing with, as a conga drummer. And I toured France and Belgium, even though I'd only been playing for three months. It was very avant-garde, and they did not care about technique.

"I was 18, and I spent a year in West Africa. And my brother, Richard, came back and started what became The Mystic Knights of the Oingo Boingo—the predecessor to Oingo Boingo, the rock band. It was really musical street-theater. What I started doing was picking up all kinds of instruments. Suddenly, in 1978, I was in a rock band.

"Tim [Burton] and Paul [Reubens, aka "Pee Wee Herman"] came to me. Tim was a fan of the band—he used to come to Oingo Boingo concerts. And Paul Reubens heard a film I did back in '78, for my brother, called *Forbidden Zone.* Although it wasn't a legitimate score, it was a strange little film score for an *extremely* low-budget movie.

"I didn't know why they wanted to call me in. I think they were really just interviewing nontraditional composers, and my name came up. And in meeting them, we kind of hit it off. But I still wasn't convinced that I had any right to do it. When I found out they were actually interested in me, that's where I started to get cold feet. My manager came in and said, 'Look, try it. What have you got to lose?' Well, ruining this young Mr. Burton's first film, how about that? I wrestled with it, and I finally decided, what the hell. I'll give it a whack, and if I fail dismally, at least I'll know that I tried."

The Tim Burton–Danny Elfman teaming has been very successful, and they do have an afinity for each other's vision, the most important factor in a meaningful collaboration. One of the most interesting films they have worked on together is *Edward Scissorhands,* in which the tone of the film and the texture of the score augment each other perfectly.

James Newton Howard had an orchestral and classical background; he majored in piano in college. Then, as is often the case in a career in music, one thing led to another. "I got into rock-and-roll as a session keyboardist, and later, as a producer and arranger for quite a few years. Probably the most significant thing that happened to me during that period of time was joining Elton John's band in 1975 for about two years. It was the first time he had a synthesist. Because of the orchestral nature of a lot of his work, that was a really good opportunity for somebody like me to come in there and make the most of it.

"He actually gave me my first opportunity to work with orchestra, which is something I'd always wanted to do. I worked with the London Symphony on the 'Blue Moods' album. And then he let me do the strings on a couple of singles—'Don't Go Breaking My Heart,' and 'Sorry Seems To Be the Hardest Word.' It was a very important thing for me, because it gave me the confidence, and reinforced what I suspected, which is that it was something I really would love to do.

"The Elton association brought me to a lot of people's attention, so my career was improved significantly, and then I just started doing a lot more work on all levels. After I left the band, I eventually started producing records. My managers at the time were always pushing me into the direction of doing a film, which I was terrified of doing because of the technology involved. I just didn't have the confidence. But I took a film in 1985 called *Head Office,* which was a farce—it was like the *Airplane!* of the business world, with Danny DeVito. It was a synth score, and from day one I felt like I'd finally found what I was supposed to be doing."

Howard has gone on to do a variety of scores, including those featuring contemporary keyboard writing (*Pretty Woman,* 1990; *Grand Canyon,* 1991) and more orchestral works (*Prince of Tides,* 1991; *Falling Down,* 1993; and *The Fugitive,* 1993).

Mark Isham is a jazz trumpet player. Back in 1982, he hadn't given a thought to the possibility of scoring films.

"I didn't come at this having studied anything about film scoring, or even having studied film composers. I loved movies, and I respected good-sounding music that I heard in films, but I didn't know anything about it, I didn't know who the guys were that did it, I didn't buy their records.

"I'd just been writing a lot of music, hopefully

looking for record deals, and I got offered this chance to score *Never Cry Wolf*. [Director] Carroll Ballard just happened to hear some music I had written for synthesizer and Chinese flute. It was a record demo. The Chinese flute player and I were trying to get a record deal with ECM Records. We didn't, but Carroll managed to hear this through a friend of a friend. The flute player had a friend who was doing the poster art for Carroll. And it just happened to be playing at this guy's apartment when Carroll came over to see the test of the poster. It was totally by chance. I was living in London and he actually tracked me down. There was no promotional activity here going on whatsoever. . . . It was sort of a revelation to me that this could be a profession.

"I'd never written for orchestra, so it never even occurred to me to write an orchestral score. I was a synthesizer-based composer with a jazz background. So I just went into it like that, and Carroll seemed to say, Well, OK, why not? Because he just liked the sound of the way I put synthesizers together. And it *did* work. But it was definitely off-the-wall. It was not the normal thing anybody would have thought of doing.

"Exactly about the same time I started doing that film was when Windham Hill approached me. I actually made those two projects back-to-back, that film and my first Windham Hill record came out actually in the same month. And I was living in England at the time, when they both came out, and all of a sudden I realized, Wait a minute, I've got my first solo record and my first Hollywood picture coming out in America—maybe I should go home to America and get a job."

And he did, including *The Moderns* (1988), *Reversal of Fortune* (1990), *Little Man Tate* (1991), *A River Runs Through It* (1992), and *Of Mice and Men* (1992)—some favoring synths and others more orchestral.

Michael Kamen also has rock-and-roll roots. "I backed into film composing. I had been an oboe player. I started a rock 'n' roll band, like everybody else did in the sixties, in New York. I toured the

country for about seven years, and then gave up rock-and-roll to write a ballet score—a very neoclassical piece based on Rodin sculpture. "Then I became music director for David Bowie, which gave me my first taste of stadium rock 'n' roll. And for the next several years I wrote many ballet scores for companies in New York and Europe. . . . And then I started working with Pink Floyd."

While producing Pink Floyd, he was brought in to produce the music for the film version of "The Wall," their landmark LP. He was an arranger on the album, and then continued with them for the next three or four years. "That led to [director Terry] Gilliam, through Ray Cooper. I brought Ray in as a percussionist. Ray is a wonderful musician, and perhaps the smartest guy I know in terms of designing film scores. Ray was an actor in *Brazil*, and helped Terry to produce the film. He, in fact, put us together."

When *Brazil* was released in 1985, it attracted a lot of attention, and so did the score, in which Kamen interpolates the 1939 pop song "Brazil." On *Lethal Weapon* (1987) Kamen collaborated with guitarist Eric Clapton; by the time *Die Hard* (1988) came around, he was well established, and he has done the sequels to both *Lethal Weapon* (with Clapton and David Sanborn) and *Die Hard*. *Robin Hood: Prince of Thieves* (1991) offered him a showcase for his orchestral writing, along with the hit song "(Everything I Do) I Do It for You," written with Clapton and Bryan Adams, who performed it. He returned to the action genre with *Last Action Hero* (1993).

David Newman is one of Alfred Newman's sons. He studied violin at the University of Southern California, and then earned his living as a performing musician.

"I first did a couple of industrial films. And I did recording work and television work for eight years in studio orchestras. I played from about '77 to about '84—I just decided I wanted to do it.

"I did some theater conducting, and did some things around, but I certainly wasn't doing what I wanted to do. I studied conducting at USC, and I studied privately for years and years with William Kettering. I was going three times a week to see Bill, and doing ear training. I knew all the repertoire because [my brother] Tommy [Newman] and I had played in orchestras all our lives. We were in orchestras four nights a week, and by the time we were 14 or 15, we'd gone through everything.

"I was working with somebody else at the time, and we did a demo—a big orchestra 15-minute demo piece. And we did a really great demo. And then it got us a few things, and then we split up, and then I did a film called *Critters* (1986), and then I slowly started scoring films." His other films have included *The War of the Roses* (1989), *Other People's Money* (1991), and *Hoffa* (1992).

Randy Newman, who is a cousin of David and Thomas Newman, is well known for his engaging, sometimes offbeat songs like "I Love L.A.," "Short People," "Sail Away," and "I Love To See You Smile," from *Parenthood* (1989). Sung by Newman in his uniquely personal way, these songs have helped establish him as a major recording artist. He grew up surrounded by music, including the film music of his uncles Alfred Newman and Lionel Newman.

"I was offered films, and I would turn them down. I finally did one in 1970—I did *Cold Turkey* for Norman Lear. It always scared me a great deal, I think because my uncles never seemed confident about their abilities. I'd hear Al say, "Ah, this is no good, it's no good." When I was a little kid, to see something like that, you think, Jesus, he's the greatest. What could I do? It looked real big and real hard, and *still,* the sound of an orchestra tuning up, before I'm going to do something—it isn't a sound that I love, it's a sound that makes me *real* nervous. Once I get up on the stand, I'm all right.

"With *Ragtime* (1981), [director Milos] Forman was a fan of mine, and knew I had an interest in the period, and I had a tremendous interest in the book, so I did it. On *Cold Turkey,* I was hesitant about making a very specific sketch for Arthur Morton, I was still sort of scared. I figured, well,

maybe he'll know how to voice the brass and strings. But by then [on *Ragtime*] I was more sure that I could think of the sounds myself. It takes practice. You do it all the time, you get a little better at it."

In addition to *The Natural* (1984), Newman wrote two of 1990's most satisfying scores: the nostalgic *Avalon,* for director Barry Levinson, and Penny Marshall's heartbreaking *Awakenings,* starring Robert De Niro and Robin Williams.

Rachel Portman has a classical music background. She began piano lessons at 8 years old, violin at 10, organ at about 13, and started composing at 15. "I think the most valuable thing in the world you can have is a classical training, because then *everything* is accessible to you," she says. She found the way to film scoring through her interest in the theater while she was studying at Oxford University.

"Because I was one of the only people writing music for theater at Oxford, I was doing most of the shows there. So, naturally, when there was a film made there, I was the one that was asked to do it. And then I was entirely smitten with the idea. The film was called *Privileged,* which was directed by Mike Hoffman, who has since gone on direct *Some Girls* [1989] and *Soapdish* [1991]. He was a student, too. It was entirely a student thing, only it was released worldwide as a film theatrically. . . .

"So when I left, I got my first break from [producer] David Puttnam, via [director] Alan Parker, who I met, oddly, giving a talk about *Midnight Express.* And he was the only person I had ever met in the film business. . . . A couple of weeks later I sent him a cassette of this little film I had done the music for, and he sent it on to Puttnam, who had a film called *Experience Preferred . . . But Not Essential* [1983]. And I stepped into it and did a very late rewrite. And that was my first professional job. And from then on I just did films—films for television. And I was really lucky, I never had to sort of crawl around the outside to get into it. I did a lot of drama for television, and gradually, bit by bit, film work came in—sort of in bits and bobs."

British director Beeban Kidron was another factor contributing to Portman's increasing involvement in film scoring. In the late eighties Kidron asked Portman to write the music for a three-hour BBC television production entitled *Oranges Are Not the Only Fruit*. "It won a lot of awards—it was a brilliant thing. And then I did *Antonia and Jane* [1991] with her, and then *Used People* [1992], and the film I'm working on now, *Great Moments in Aviation History*."

Marc Shaiman simply followed his dream. In his understated way, he describes himself as "lucky."

"I started as a vocal arranger for cabaret acts in New York. And then I was extremely lucky—charmed—because I was a fanatical Bette Midler fan and all I ever wanted to do was somehow get into show business and somehow meet with Bette Midler. And I was just extremely lucky that the first person that I met in New York when I was 17 was a girl who lived across the hall who was one of her backup singers. They needed a musical director for their own group. They wanted to branch out on their own—the Harlettes, that is—and because of my studying of Bette Midler records and then the kind of music that Bette Midler turned me on to—swing music and Hollywood musical–type things—I just knew the kind of vocal arrangements they wanted. And I lived across the hall. So I became their musical director, and by the time I was 18, less than a year later, I was on the road with Bette Midler when she asked them to come back on the road with her.

"I worked a lot on 'Saturday Night Live' over the years, doing special musical material for that show. And through that I began an association with a lot of people, but especially Billy Crystal. And so Billy Crystal and Bette Midler's film careers really started taking off just about the same time. With Bette, suddenly in the movie *Big Business* [1988], she had a scene where she sang, both yodeling with a steel band in the streets of New York, and then, as a reveal of her character, singing a song while

milking a cow. So she brought me in at the very last minute, and I did this little arrangement for her, and co-wrote the song—wrote her special lyrics for an old traditional country and western song. An old yodeling song.

"And through that, I met Jim Abrahams, the director on that film, and Michael Peyser, producer, and I just could sense that these were nice people, and I didn't need to be intimidated. They weren't like Louis B. Mayer, you know, your image of the Hollywood producer-types. They were really nice. And so I just blurted out, 'How does a person get to score movies? Can I audition?' And I think they were charmed by my audacity and naïveté, and they actually sent me some reels, and I did a piano, bass, and drums demo. And did some music for the film. I didn't know *anything* about synchronization.

"I came out here and rented a house, started to get to work on that. And although that ended not so well, and I thought it was the end of the world, I was also then working with Bette on *Beaches* [1988] as a music supervisor. And that became very successful and all the songs I chose for her made up the record, which became very successful.

"And then at the same time, I had met Rob Reiner through Billy Crystal, working on some HBO specials, and I met with Rob about the music for *When Harry Met Sally* . . . [1989], and he gave me that job, which was just the greatest job a person could get—basically, getting paid for my record collection. I know all those songs backward and forward, and I tried to get a couple of ones in there that weren't so on the nose. Rob really knew what he wanted. And then, of course, that became another blessed event, because I always wanted to be Nelson Riddle [who had arranged many of Sinatra's great records], and didn't really have an artist to work with, to do that kind of orchestration and arrangement for. And then all of a sudden there was this guy, Harry Connick, Jr."

When the cost of licensing a master recording by Ella Fitzgerald or Frank Sinatra became unworkable, Connick and Shaiman cut their own record, which launched both their careers. Reiner asked Shaiman to score *Misery* (1990) next, followed by

Billy Crystal's *City Slickers* (1991), and Shaiman has being going full speed ever since. Other films include *The Addams Family* (1991), *A Few Good Men* (1992), and *Sleepless in Seattle* (1993).

Shirley Walker arranged, orchestrated, and conducted (and sometimes composed) for other composers throughout the eighties, being associated in one or more of these capacities on such diverse high-profile projects as *Apocalypse Now* (1979), *The Black Stallion* (1979), and *Batman* (1989). She also paid her dues by doing three low-budget theatrical films during that time. When the Chevy Chase film *Memoirs of an Invisible Man* (1992) was released with her score, she says, "That's the first one that's been out in a theater for more than two days, or a week."

She credits her first small-budget films with being very useful, though. "It helps you get over whatever nerves you might have about yourself as a composer, which aren't going to come up until you're on projects like that. So it helps you to see, Where is it that I tend to freeze if I do it all, and how do I get myself to get that first note on the piece of paper? It helps you deal with all of those things.

"It has the potential for you to be meeting people in the business, and people in the business to hear about you. So that's always a potential plus with things like that. And then, it gives you the confidence to see how you're representing yourself as one of the characters in the industry. Either coming off, or failing. Like, How visible am I? How flesh-and-blood am I capable of being? How dynamic can I possibly be? Can I maintain the attention span of these incredibly neurotic people for more than ten minutes at a time? So that's the value of all those other projects. Sharpening those skills that you need. There's absolutely no other place to practice them."

Hans Zimmer, like Elfman and Kamen, also came from rock-and-roll. "I was in bands in England. I never made music school or anything. I grew up pretty much everywhere in Europe. I was born in Germany, grew up in Germany and Switzerland, and finally England. And I started doing commercials. I was basically a synthesizer programmer. I used to program synths for people. And then I started writing a bit of my own. People let me do 30-second things for commercials. It was a pretty good training ground. And there was a film composer with the same commercials company, Stanley Myers. And Stanley, basically, took me on as an apprentice. I did a load of films with him. Stanley hated writing car chases, so I got to do all the car chases. But he would do all the orchestral stuff, because he really knew his way around. He really taught me everything I know about this stuff. . . . And he was very good.

"I would go to spotting sessions with Stanley. I would play my cues for the director, and Stanley would play his cues, because that's part of the learning curve. When the director turns around and throws up, that's part of it. He would just totally let me run riot. And then when the director hated it, Stanley would come and gently fix it.

"The first movie I did all by myself was a thing called *World Apart* [1988], which Barry Levinson's wife saw about nine times. Barry never saw it, I don't think. She bought the CD, the record, and the tape. Wherever he went, there was either CD or records. And then they started temping with it. And then Barry came over to England to meet me. And I was working on something, and he came down to the studio and saw the Fairlight [sampler-synthesizer]. And he couldn't believe what that thing could do. This wasn't what he was used to. He was used to somebody playing something on the piano, and then he would wait four weeks and they would have the orchestra. So he thought it was all very exciting."

Levinson happened to be working on a film called *Rain Man.* And he called Zimmer in London. "When you're in Europe there is that myth—*Hollywood.* And somebody from Hollywood phones you up. And you go, Whoa—I'll do anything! I'll do *anything!* Get me to Hollywood. And then you get here, and it's the most frightening place on earth. Because *they* all seem to know what they're doing. It took me three years to work out that— they *don't* know what they're doing. *Nobody* knows what they're doing. You're just flying by the seat of your pants. And that's the fun part of it. And the more courageous the people are you work with, the better the result is going to be."

When *Rain Man* opened in 1988, Zimmer's score became one of the role models of the year, and he was on his way. He likes diversity, and first-rate films like *Driving Miss Daisy* (1989), *Green Card* (1990), *Thelma and Louise* (1991), and *The Power of One* (1992) have offered him that opportunity.

The Composers and Their Credits

■ ■ ■

In the late forties, the Department of State asked the National Film Music Council to conduct research on film music in the United States. In 1949 they reported that the following composers worked *exclusively* in films: Daniele Amfitheatrof, David Buttolph, Robert Emmett Dolan, Adolph Deutsch, George Duning, Hugo Friedhofer, Johnny Green, Frederick Hollander, Leigh Harline, Werner Heymann, Bronislau Kaper, Michel Michelet, Cyril Mockridge, Alfred Newman, David Raksin, Miklós Rózsa, Max Steiner, Dimitri Tiomkin, Franz Waxman, Roy Webb, and Victor Young.

Many other composers worked now and then in the motion picture industry, including the following list of composers the Council mentions as having an "international reputation": George Antheil, Mario Castelnuovo-Tedesco, Aaron Copland, Bernard Herrmann, Erich Wolfgang Korngold, Darius Milhaud, Alexander Tansman, Ernest Toch, Richard Hageman, and Louis Gruenberg.

The Film Music Council pointed out that there were also dozens of arrangers, orchestrators, conductors, and musicians employed both regularly and on a part-time basis.

In the fifties there were only a few dozen film composers—an amazingly small number, considering the amount of work to be done. That number has grown to many hundreds, even though far fewer films are being produced. In 1992, *The Hollywood Reporter* listed almost 500 composers with several television and/or film credits. Many have not made the move from television to features, and most never will—the sheer number of available job applicants makes this unlikely.

The absence of women from the lists above is not an oversight—in the forties there were only a few scoring films in Hollywood. Elizabeth Firestone (daughter of Harvey S. F. Firestone, the tire magnate) became the first woman to score a Hollywood film when she composed the music for *Once More, My Darling* in 1949. She also scored *That Man from Tangier* (1953). Ann Ronell had already scored *The Story of G.I. Joe* (1945), but shared the credit with Louis Appelbaum and Louis Forbes. Other scores of hers included *One Touch of Venus* (1948 adaptation of the Kurt Weill–Ogden Nash score) and *Love Happy* (1949), starring the Marx Brothers. Elisabeth Lutyens worked on a number of films, including *World Without End* (1954) and *Dr. Terror's House of Horrors* (1964).

Although there have been excellent opportunities for women as film editors and music editors, until recently female composers have been given little encouragement as film composers. Several songwriter-performers have written songs for films, including Carole King (*Murphy's Romance*, 1985) and Carly Simon (*Working Girl*, 1988). Betty Comden, Sylvia Fine, Dorothy Fields, and later, Dory Previn, Marilyn Bergman, Ayn Robbins, and others have had great success writing lyrics and songs for films, but Shirley Walker became the first woman to score a major American feature when she contributed all the music for John Carpenter's *Memoirs of an Invisible Man,* released in 1992. Jill Fraser and Laura Karpman each have scored several motion pictures, and a number of women, including Nan Schwartz Mishkin and Angela Morely, have scored many television projects. British composer Rachel Portman has scored a number of films, including the 1992 film *Used People* and *The Joy Luck Club* (1993), and Anne Dudley has scored several films, including *The Crying Game* in 1992.

If Wagner had lived in this century, he would have been the number one film composer.

Max Steiner, composer

Throughout the history of Hollywood, the composers selected for films have reflected the current taste of the filmmakers and executives. Obviously, in order to achieve any career continuity, a composer needs to attract filmmakers who like his music. Over the years, in turn, the composers themselves have also been influential to some extent in shaping the tastes of filmmakers. Major commercial successes, including hit songs and bestselling albums, often have had a temporary effect on the selection of composers.

The first group of composers who dominated and influenced film music during the thirties and forties came either from Europe (**Erich Wolfgang Korngold**, Czechoslovakia; **Miklós Rózsa**, Hungary; **Max Steiner**, Vienna; **Dimitri Tiomkin**, Russia; **Franz Waxman**, Germany); or from New York (**Bernard Herrmann, Alfred Newman**) or Chicago (**Victor Young**). The native Americans got their training in pit orchestras and, in the case of Herrmann, radio. On the other hand, the Europeans came up through the concert halls, operetta (Steiner), and opera (Korngold). Their background influenced the kind of music they wrote, although this was most certainly a reflection also of the musical tastes of the studio executives and the filmmakers. Others who contributed a great deal to the film music of the thirties and forties include **Bronislau Kaper** and **Roy Webb.**

Two other composers significantly expanded the established musical vocabulary during the forties: **David Raksin** and **Hugo Friedhofer.** Just as Rózsa's *Spellbound* extended the psychological approach to scoring, Raksin's *Laura* and Friedhofer's *Best Years of Our Lives* offered new harmonic choices and fresh ways to play the drama.

The next generation of composers didn't arrive until the fifties—**Alex North, Leonard Rosenman, Elmer Bernstein,** and **Henry Mancini,** who achieved prominence later in the decade. Their music was characterized by their interest in American influences of all sorts (folk music, jazz, Aaron Copland's symphonic Americana) and a desire to expand the stylistic possibilities. In Italy, **Nino Rota** had been creating unique scores (including those for the Fellini films), but his work didn't have any immediate influence on mainstream Hollywood. His compatriot, **Ennio Morricone,** gained international fame with his scores for Sergio Leone's "spaghetti" Westerns in the mid-sixties.

In the sixties, composers continued to explore different stylistic approaches, encouraged by the successful use of jazz materials in North's *Streetcar Named Desire* (1951), Bernstein's *Man with a Golden Arm* (1955), and Mancini's enormously popular theme and music for the "Peter Gunn" television series (1958). **Jerry Goldsmith,** coming from radio as Herrmann had, made a strong impression with *Freud* (1963), *Lilies of the Field* (1963), and *Planet of the Apes* (1968). And British composer **John Barry** exploded onto the international scene, first with his James Bond scores, and then, at the end of the decade, with the pop-oriented *Midnight Cowboy* (1969). Two composers from France became prominent, **Maurice Jarre,** with his score for *Lawrence of Arabia* in 1962, and **Georges Delerue,** who scored *Jules and Jim* and other Truffaut pictures at the beginning of the decade, and internationally successful films like *A Man for All Seasons* (1966) and *Anne of the Thousand Days* (1969) as the decade drew to a close.

In the late sixties, two rock-oriented scores opened the floodgates for the wave of similar songs and scores that would follow: *The Graduate,* Simon and Garfunkel's 1967 folk-rock song-score, and *Easy Rider,* a nonscored film using a compilation of rock-and-roll records for music. This 1969 release basically redefined the function of music for films during the first years of the seventies, when the music choice of many filmmakers became record-oriented rock, folk, and pop music of various kinds.

In the early seventies, the songwriters often became the scorers, an experiment that was seldom totally successful, and far too often a disaster. Scores were not delivered on deadline, timings were out-of-sync, and so on. When it worked, it worked—Isaac Hayes' score for *Shaft* in 1971 is an example—and these new approaches became

mainstream scoring techniques, using idiomatic pop, rhythm and blues, and rock rhythms and colors. Song-scoring reached its commercial peak in 1977 with the release of *Saturday Night Fever,* which rocketed its way into the Guiness Book of Records with its soundtrack sales. Along the way, there were also lush pop-oriented scores based on song themes, like **Michel Legrand**'s *Summer of '42* (1971) and **Marvin Hamlisch**'s *The Way We Were* (1973). At the same time that **Bill Conti**'s 1976 score for *Rocky* stimulated a universal response with its pop flavor, symphonic orchestral scoring slowly began to make a comeback, beginning with scores by **John Williams** for *The Poseidon Adventure* (1972), *The Towering Inferno* (1974), and *Jaws* (1975). The release of *Star Wars* and *Close Encounters* in 1977 brought full symphonic scoring back into vogue.

Chariots of Fire (1981), with its electronic/acoustic theme by Vangelis, interested filmmakers in the commercial possibilities of electronic music written and performed from an acoustic (nonelectronic) point of view. Even though most of the score has an acoustic sound, the electronic percussion driving the main theme inspired dozens of imitations. Dramatic scores using electronic instruments became more prevalent, such as Maurice Jarre's electronic score for *Witness* (1985) and **Thomas Newman**'s score for *Reckless* (1984). For several years it looked as though everyone who ever thought of writing music for the movies was going to get one chance to do so, typically creating and recording generic pop electronic music in their garage or a spare bedroom. There were plenty of orchestral scores, of course, from Williams, Goldsmith (who increased his emphasis on blending electronic elements into his orchestral scores), **David Shire** (*Return to Oz,* 1985) and newer composers like **James Horner** (*Star Trek II,* 1982) and **Basil Poledouris** (*Conan the Barbarian,* 1982).

Each succeeding generation of composers seems to be coming closer and closer on the heels of the preceding group. Five or six years can now be called a "generation." As you look at the names of the composers and their credits, be aware that many have careers that continue for decades, even though their good fortunes may rise and fall with the current fashion. There are only a few film titles listed for each of them, just enough to help identify the composers with their music. These entries are not in any way to be considered as filmographies—only a point of reference. In 1939 alone, Alfred Newman was represented by nine scores, including *Gunga Din, Wuthering Heights, Young Mr. Lincoln, Beau Geste, Drums Along the Mohawk,* and *The Hunchback of Notre Dame.*

The following books and journals include much more information on individual composers and their filmographies (check the Bibliography for details):

> *American Film Music* by William Darby and Jack Du Bois (includes filmographies only of those generally considered to be "major" composers)
>
> *Film Composers Guide* by Steven C. Smith
>
> *Film Composers in America* by Clifford McCarty (through 1952)
>
> *Film Music: From Violins to Video* by James Limbacher (includes filmographies through 1972, but with many errors and omissions)
>
> *Keeping Score* (Limbacher's two-volume supplementary work which continues from 1972 through 1979 [Vol. I], and 1980 through 1988 [Vol. II with H. Stephen Wright])
>
> *Film Score* by Tony Thomas (includes complete filmographies of 25 composers)
>
> *Soundtrack!* (a film music quarterly, includes many filmographies)

Most composers have contributed to a great variety of films during their careers, including both distinguished motion pictures and likely candidates for the Golden Turkey Award. Composers tend to work in a variety of genres as well. Nino Rota not only scored Fellini's *La Dolce Vita* and *8½,* but also Francis Ford Coppola's *The Godfather.* All three are classics. On the other hand, not all composers represented here have had such good luck. These pages have been designed as a reference section, so you'll find some undistinguished genre films scored by obscure composers mixed in with the classics. These scores are not necessarily recommended; the intention is to provide you with a good cross-section of composers, each with some sample film credits. To identify the composer of a particular film, look up the film title in the Filmography (pages 323–76).

You will see an occasional entry called "first film." This may be the very first feature film scored, but often indicates one or more of the composer's early works (sometimes a composer scores three or four films released in his or her first year or two in the field, and sometimes composers begin with collaborations or adaptations). The time span between these early films and the next film listed does not imply that the composer didn't score any films during the intervening years. The credits of composers from other countries may include an early film that received attention in the United States. A lot of composers have started with extensive work in television (Bruce Broughton, Charles Fox, Patrick Williams, and Lee Holdridge, for instance) so their first film credits may have been preceded by years of work in that field. Many composers continue working in both mediums.

Some split credits have been indicated, but this does not mean that the composers actually collaborated, or even necessarily met one another. The 1987 Oscar-winning score for *The Last Emperor* was composed by three individuals, each of whom independently created his own portion of the score. The soundtrack of *The Last of the Mohicans* (1992) includes music by Trevor Jones, Randy Edelman, and Daniel Langois, even though they didn't collaborate.

Some representative songs and musicals have also been listed, when appropriate, and they, too, are meant to illustrate the scope of a composer's work. The birth dates, death dates, and places of birth represent the most accurate information available at this time.

In addition to the alphabetical list of film titles with composer credits in the Appendix, the composers are also listed in the Index.

adapt. = adapted
add. = additional music
arr. = arranged
m.d. = music director (supervisor/
         conductor; may have adapted)
ms = television miniseries
orch. = orchestration
o.s. = original score
* = Oscar or Emmy nomination
** = Oscar or Emmy

Richard Addinsell

Born January 13, 1904, London, England
Died November 15, 1977
1939   Goodbye, Mr. Chips
1941   Dangerous Moonlight (aka Suicide
         Squadron)
1945   Blithe Spirit
1951   A Christmas Carol
1965   Life at the Top

Addinsell's score for *Dangerous Moonlight* included his "Warsaw Concerto," which became a very popular concert piece.

John Addison

Born March 16, 1920, Chobham, England
1950   Seven Days to Noon
1960   The Entertainer
1963   Tom Jones**
1966   Torn Curtain
1970   Start the Revolution Without Me
1972   Sleuth*
1977   A Bridge Too Far
TV: Centennial** (1980 ms)
         "Murder, She Wrote" (series theme)

Bob Alcivar

Born July 8, 1938, Chicago, Ill.
1972   Butterflies Are Free
1982   One from the Heart (orch./arr./add.)

Jeff Alexander

Born July 2, 1910, Seattle, Wash.
Died December 23, 1989
1957   Jailhouse Rock
1969   Support Your Local Sheriff!

William Alwyn

Born November 7, 1905, Northampton, England
Died September 12, 1985
1947   Odd Man Out
1953   The Master of Ballantrae
1955   Bedevilled

Daniele Amfitheatrof

Born October 29, 1901, St. Petersburg, Russia
Died June 7, 1983
1943   Lassie Come Home
1944   Days of Glory
1946   The Virginian
1946   Song of the South* (w/ Paul Smith)
1951   The Desert Fox
1954   The Naked Jungle
1965   Major Dundee

David Amram

Born 1933
1961   Splendor in the Grass
1962   The Manchurian Candidate

George Antheil

Born June 8, 1900, Trenton, N.J.
Died February 12, 1959
1937   The Plainsman
1946   Specter of the Rose
1949   Knock on Any Door
1955   Not as a Stranger
1957   The Pride and the Passion
Autobiography: *Bad Boy of Music*

Malcolm Arnold

Born October 21, 1921, Northampton, England
1953   The Captain's Paradise
1957   The Belles of St. Trinian's
1957   The Bridge on the River Kwai**
1958   The Inn of the Sixth Happiness

Georges Auric
Born February 15, 1899, Lodève, France
Died July 23, 1983
1931   À Nous la Liberté
1946   Beauty and the Beast
1949   Passport to Pimlico
1951   The Lavender Hill Mob
1952   Moulin Rouge
1953   Roman Holiday
1958   Bonjour Tristesse
1961   The Innocents (w/ Kenneth V. Jones)
1968   Thérèse and Isabelle

William Axt
Born April 19, 1882, New York, N.Y.
Died February 13, 1959
1925   The Big Parade (silent film)
1926   Ben-Hur (silent film)
1926   Don Juan (silent film)
1933   Dinner at Eight
1934   The Thin Man

Burt Bacharach
Born May 12, 1929, Kansas City, Mo.
1966   Alfie (incl. "Alfie"*)
1969   Butch Cassidy and the Sundance Kid**
          (incl. "Raindrops Keep Falling on
          My Head"**)
1981   Arthur (incl. "Best That You Can Do"**)
1982   Night Shift (incl. "That's What Friends
          Are For")
Theater: "Promises, Promises"

Angelo Badalamenti
Born March 22, 1937, New York, N.Y.
1986   Blue Velvet
1987   Nightmare on Elm Street III
1990   Wild at Heart
1992   Twin Peaks—Fire Walk with Me
TV: 1990 "Twin Peaks" (series)

Buddy Baker
Born January 4, 1918, Springfield, Mo.
1975   The Apple Dumpling Gang
1981   The Fox and the Hound

Comp./arr./cond. orig. Mickey Mouse Club music.

Richard Band
Born December 28, 1958, Los Angeles, Calif.
1985   Re-Animator
1989   Puppet Master

Brian Banks
Born October 21, 1955, Los Angeles, Calif.
1988   Young Guns (w/ Anthony Marinelli)
1990   Internal Affairs (w/ Marinelli and Mike
          Figgis)

John Barry
Born November 3, 1933, York, England
First film: Wild for Kicks (1959)
1962   Dr. No (James Bond theme only)
1963   From Russia with Love
1965   Thunderball
1966   Born Free**
1967   You Only Live Twice
1968   The Lion in Winter**
1969   On Her Majesty's Secret Service
1969   Midnight Cowboy
1971   Mary, Queen of Scots*
1977   The Deep
1979   Hanover Street
1980   Somewhere in Time
1981   Body Heat
1985   Out of Africa**
1990   Dances With Wolves**
1992   Chaplin
1993   Indecent Proposal

Though John Barry's roots include jazz and classical music, some of his early scores for the more popular films leaned heavily toward jazz, including his first smash hit—the first James Bond movie, *Dr. No*. It started with a friend saying, "We need a theme—real quick." After recording his now-famous theme, he heard nothing more until he saw the film and heard his theme used throughout the picture, even though he got no credit. It didn't matter—he went on to do most of the Bond films. He is equally well known for

John Barry
Photo: Gay Wallin

Because my father had theaters, I always wanted to write film music. It wasn't a secondhand thing because I wanted to do something else and this came along. I'd always wanted to do it, from a very, very early age.

his lush scores for films such as *Out of Africa* and *Dances With Wolves*, period dramas such as *The Lion in Winter*, and the scores to contemporary films including *Midnight Cowboy* and *Body Heat*.

George Bassman
Born February 7, 1914, New York, N.Y.
1946   The Postman Always Rings Twice
1962   Ride the High Country

Sir Arnold Bax
Born November 8, 1883, London, England
Died October 3, 1953
1948   Oliver Twist

Les Baxter
Born March 14, 1922, Mexia, Texas
1960   House of Usher
1961   The Pit and The Pendulum
1964   Black Sabbath (U.S. version)

David Bell
Born April 17, 1954, Middletown, Ohio
1992   The Lounge People
1992   There Goes the Neighborhood

Arthur Benjamin
Born September 19, 1893, Sydney, Australia
Died April 9, 1960
1934   The Man Who Knew Too Much
1935   The Scarlet Pimpernel

Richard Rodney Bennett
Born March 29, 1936, Broadstairs, England
1967   Far from the Madding Crowd*
1971   Nicholas and Alexandra*
1974   Murder on the Orient Express*
1977   Equus
1979   Yanks

Charles Bernstein
Born February 28, 1943, Minneapolis, Minn.
1979   Love at First Bite
1984   A Nightmare on Elm Street
TV: Sadat (1983 ms)

Elmer Bernstein
Born April 4, 1922, New York, N.Y.
First films: Saturday's Hero (1951)
              Boots Malone (1952)
1955   The Man with the Golden Arm*
1956   The Ten Commandments
1960   The Magnificent Seven*
1961   The Comancheros
1962   Walk on the Wild Side
1962   To Kill a Mockingbird*
1962   Birdman of Alcatraz
1963   The Great Escape
1966   Hawaii*
1967   Thoroughly Modern Millie**
1969   True Grit

1976	The Shootist
1978	Animal House
1979	The Great Santini
1980	Airplane!
1983	Trading Places*
1984	Ghostbusters
1989	My Left Foot
1990	The Grifters
1991	Rambling Rose
1991	Cape Fear (adapt. Herrmann's music)
1992	The Babe
1993	The Age of Innocence
Theater:	"How Now, Dow Jones?"

At first, Bernstein [Bern-steen] wanted to be a concert pianist. While in the service, he scored dozens of dramatic radio programs for the Armed Forces Radio Service. This led to scoring a project for Norman Corwin, which in turn led to his first film assignment in 1950.

Elmer Bernstein
Photo: Gay Wallin

In 1956, he was doing incidental music for *The Ten Commandments*. When Victor Young became too ill to score the film, Bernstein was asked to take on the job. Since then he has contributed greatly to the history of film music, most especially in bringing fresh approaches to film scoring, often using a distinctly American musical language. His score for *The Man with the Golden Arm* (1955) helped break down Hollywood's resistance to the use of jazz and other idiomatic writing. *The Magnificent Seven* (1960) became synonymous with western Americana. His score for *To Kill a Mockingbird* (1962) helped popularize an intimate, more personalized use of music in films.

In 1970, he became President of the Composers and Lyricists Guild of America, and served as an eloquent spokesperson for all film composers and lyricists in their long-lived attempt to retain the ownership rights to their film works.

At various periods in his career he has been known as the King of Jazz (due to the success of *Man with the Golden Arm*), the King of Westerns (due to the success of *The Magnificent Seven*), and the King of Comedy (due to the success of *Animal House* in 1978 and *Airplane!* in 1980). He refuses to be typecast, though, and his films in the nineties showcase his versatility.

Leonard Bernstein
Born August 25, 1918, Lawrence, Mass.
Died October 14, 1990

1954	On the Waterfront*
Theater:	"West Side Story," which was adapted for film in 1961
Book:	*The Joy of Music*

Although he scored only one film, Bernstein's (Bern-styne) score for *On the Waterfront* is admired and studied.

Peter Bernstein
Born April 10, 1951, New York, N.Y.

1983	National Lampoon's Class Reunion
1985	My Science Project

Peter Bernstein is Elmer Bernstein's son.

Terence Blanchard
Born March 13, 1962, New Orleans, La.

1991	Jungle Fever
1992	Malcolm X

Perry Botkin, Jr.
Born April 16, 1933, New York, N.Y.
1971   Bless the Beasts and Children
1984   Silent Night, Deadly Night

Bruce Broughton
Born March 8, 1945, Los Angeles, Calif.
First film: The Prodigal (1984)
1985   Silverado*
1985   Young Sherlock Holmes
1986   The Boy Who Could Fly
1990   The Rescuers Down Under
1992   Honey, I Blew Up the Kid
1993   Homeward Bound: The Incredible Journey
1993   So I Married an Axe Murderer
1993   Tombstone
TV: The Blue and the Gray* (1982 ms)
        The First Olympics** (1984 ms)
        "Tiny Tunes" (m.d., animated series)

Ralph Burns
Born June 29, 1922, Newton, Mass.
1972   Cabaret** (adapt.)
1979   All That Jazz** (adapt.)
1982   Annie* (adapt.)
1985   A Chorus Line (adapt.)
Song: "Early Autumn"

Carter Burwell
Born November 18, 1955, New York, N.Y.
1987   Raising Arizona
1991   Barton Fink
1992   Waterland
1993   This Boy's Life
1993   Kalifornia
1993   A Dangerous Woman

Artie Butler
Born December 2, 1942, Brooklyn, N.Y.
1972   What's Up, Doc?
1975   At Long Last Love (adapt.)
1982   Grease 2 (adapt.)

David Buttolph
Born August 3, 1902, New York, N.Y.
1942   My Favorite Blonde
1942   Wake Island

1943   Guadalcanal Diary
1944   Till We Meet Again
1945   The House on 92nd Street
1948   June Bride
1950   Pretty Baby
1951   Fort Worth
1953   House of Wax
1953   The Beast from 20,000 Fathoms
1959   The Horse Soldiers

John Cacavas
Born August 13, 1930, Aberdeen, S. Dak.
1975   Airport 1974
1977   Airport '77
TV: The Gangster Chronicles (1981 ms)
        A Death in California (1985)

Mario Castelnuovo-Tedesco
Born April 3, 1895, Florence, Italy
Died March 16, 1968
1945   And Then There Were None
1948   The Loves of Carmen
    Teacher of many film composers—incl. John
Williams, Jerry Goldsmith, Henry Mancini, Jerry
Fielding

Gary Chang
Born February 22, 1953, Minneapolis, Minn.
1985   The Breakfast Club
1989   Miami Blues
1992   Under Siege

Charles Chaplin
Born April 16, 1889, Walworth, England
Died December 25, 1977
1931   City Lights (w/ Arthur Johnston)
1936   Modern Times (w/ David Raksin)
1940   The Great Dictator* (w/ Meredith
        Willson)
1952   Limelight** (w/ Raymond Rasch, Larry
        Russell)

Tom Chase
Born January 10, 1949, Los Angeles, Calif.
1987   And God Created Woman
        (w/ Steve Rucker)

1988	976-Evil (w/ Steve Rucker)
1992	Little Nemo (w/ Steve Rucker)

Jay Chattaway
Born July 8, 1946, Monongahela, Pa.

1984	Missing in Action
1985	Stephen King's Silver Bullet

Paul Chihara
Born July 9, 1938, Seattle, Wash.

1977	I Never Promised You a Rose Garden
1986	The Morning After
1988	Crossing Delancey

Frank Churchill
Born October 20, 1901
Died May 14, 1942

1938	Snow White and the Seven Dwarfs* (w/ Harline and P. Smith)
1941	Dumbo** (w/ Oliver Wallace)
1942	Bambi* (w/ Edward Plumb)

Alessandro Cicognini
Born January 25, 1906, Italy

1949	The Bicycle Thief
1953	Indiscretion of an American Wife

Stanley Clarke
Born June 30, 1951, Philadelphia, Pa.

1991	Boyz N the Hood
1993	What's Love Got To Do with It

Alf Clausen
Born March 28, 1941, Minneapolis, Minn.

1987	Number One with a Bullet
TV:	"Moonlighting" (series episodes)
	"The Simpsons" (series episodes)

Robert Cobert
Born October 26, 1924, New York, N.Y.

1976	Burnt Offerings
1993	Me and the Kid
TV:	The Winds of War (1983 ms)
	War and Remembrance (1988 ms)

Anthony Collins
Born September 3, 1893, Hastings, England
Died December 11, 1963

1940	Irene* (adapt.)
1940	No, No, Nanette (adapt.)
1941	Sunny*
1952	Trent's Last Case

Michel Colombier
Born May 23, 1939, Lyons, France

1985	White Nights
1986	Ruthless People
1992	Diary of a Hitman
1993	The Program

Bill Conti
Born April 13, 1942, Providence, R.I.
First film: Harry and Tonto (1974)

1976	Rocky (*song)
1976	Next Stop, Greenwich Village
1978	An Unmarried Woman
1979	Rocky II
1980	Private Benjamin
1981	For Your Eyes Only
1981	Victory
1982	Rocky III
1983	The Right Stuff**
1984	The Karate Kid
1985	Gotcha!
1986	The Karate Kid II
1987	Broadcast News
1988	Betrayed
1988	Cohen and Tate
1989	Lean on Me
1989	The Karate Kid III
1990	Rocky V
1993	The Adventures of Huck Finn
TV:	"Dynasty" (series theme)
	North and South, Book II**(ms)

Bill Conti has become most well known for his scores for *Rocky I, II, III,* and *V*. Establishing a close association with *Rocky* director John Avildsen, Conti went on to score other Avildsen films, including the Karate Kid trilogy. His theme from *Rocky* ("Gonna Fly Now") was a role model for years after the film's release. He has also created popular television themes, and scored both *North and South* miniseries in the mid-eighties.

Michael Convertino

1986	Children of a Lesser God
1988	Bull Durham
1992	The Waterdance

Ry Cooder

Born March 15, 1947, Los Angeles, Calif.

1980	The Long Riders
1984	Paris, Texas
1986	Crossroads
1993	Geronimo: An American Legend

Aaron Copland
Photo: Alexander Courage

Stewart Copeland

Born July 16, 1952, Alexandria, Va.

1983	Rumble Fish
1987	Wall Street
1988	Talk Radio
1988	She's Having a Baby
1993	Airborne

Aaron Copland

Born November 14, 1900, Brooklyn, N.Y.
Died December 2, 1990

1939	Of Mice and Men*
1940	Our Town*
1949	The Red Pony
1949	The Heiress**
Books:	*Our New Music*
	What to Listen for in Music

Copland brought his interest in American folk music to films, just as he had done so definitively in ballets such as *Appalachian Spring* (1944, Pulitzer Prize), *Billy the Kid* (1938), and *Rodeo* (1942). His style and musical approach have become an enduring role model for expressing the wide-open spaces of the West.

Carmine Coppola

Born June 11, 1910, New York, N.Y.
Died April 26, 1991

1974	The Godfather, Part II** (w/ Nino Rota)
1979	The Black Stallion
1979	Apocalypse Now
1980	Napoleon (1927 silent film)
1990	The Godfather, Part III (adapt.)

Carmine Coppola was director Francis Ford Coppola's father. They worked together on *Apocalypse Now*, *Godfather II*, and *Godfather III*.

John Corigliano

Born February 16, 1938, New York, N.Y.

1980	Altered States
1985	Revolution

Mainly a concert and operatic composer, Corigliano hit the top of the classical charts in 1991 with his Symphony No. 1.

Alexander (Sandy) Courage

Born December 10, 1919, Philadelphia, Pa.

1957	The Left Hand of God
1971	Fiddler on the Roof (arr./orch.)
1987	Superman IV: The Quest for Peace (adapt.)
TV:	the original "Star Trek" series theme

Mason Daring

Born September 21, 1949, New York, N.Y.

1988	Eight Men Out
1992	Passion Fish

Carl Davis

Born October 28, 1936, Brooklyn, N.Y.

1981   The French Lieutenant's Woman

Silent films: new scores for many silents, including The Big Parade, Greed, Ben-Hur, Intolerance, The Thief of Bagdad.

John Debney

Born August 18, 1956, Burbank, Calif.

1990	Jetsons: The Movie
1993	Gunmen
1993	Hocus Pocus

Georges Delerue

Born March 12, 1925, Roubaix, France
Died March 20, 1992

First internationally known film:
Hiroshima, Mon Amour (1959, w/ Giovanni Fusco)

1960	Shoot the Piano Player
1961	Jules and Jim
1966	A Man for All Seasons
1969	Anne of the Thousand Days*
1970	Women in Love
1971	The Conformist
1973	Day for Night
1973	The Day of the Dolphin*
1977	Julia*
1979	A Little Romance**
1981	True Confessions
1983	The Black Stallion Returns
1983	Silkwood
1985	Agnes of God*
1985	Casanova (silent film)
1986	Salvador
1986	Platoon
1988	Biloxi Blues
1989	Steel Magnolias

Delerue scored eleven films directed by Francois Truffaut, including *Shoot the Piano Player* and *Jules and Jim*. In 1973 he scored that director's *Day for Night*; though he came to Los Angeles in the seventies, he continued to score French films in addition to his Hollywood projects. His heartfelt, classically-oriented music was assertive (*Salvador*), sweeping (*Black Stallion Returns*), and sensitive (*Agnes of God*) as needed.

Georges Delerue
Photo: Gay Wallin

With films, one should not use language that is too complex—the trick is to be simple without being trivial. . . . It has helped develop me as a composer. I have had to be flexible and versatile and find other colorations in musical language. It is a really important field for a composer.

Manuel de Sica
Born February 24, 1949, Rome, Italy
1971   The Garden of the Finzi-Continis

Adolph Deutsch
Born October 20, 1897, England
Died January 1, 1980
1940   They Drive by Night
1941   The Maltese Falcon
1942   George Washington Slept Here
1943   Action in the North Atlantic
1944   The Mask of Dimitrios
1949   Intruder in the Dust
1949   Take Me Out to the Ballgame
1950   Annie Get Your Gun** (adapt.)
1951   Showboat* (adapt.)
1953   The Band Wagon* (adapt.)
1954   Seven Brides for Seven Brothers** (adapt.)
1956   Oklahoma!** (adapt.)
1957   Funny Face (adapt.)
1959   Some Like It Hot
1960   The Apartment

Frank De Vol
Born September 20, 1911, Moundsville, W.Va.
1955   The Big Knife
1959   Pillow Talk
1967   Guess Who's Coming to Dinner?
1974   The Longest Yard

Barry DeVorzon
Born July 31, 1934, New York, N.Y.
1975   Hard Times
1979   The Warriors
1990   Exorcist III

James Di Pasquale
Born April 7, 1941, Chicago, Ill.
1976   Fast Break
1986   One Crazy Summer

Robert Emmett Dolan
Born August 3, 1906, Hartford, Conn.
Died September 26, 1972
1942   Holiday Inn* (adapt.)
1944   Going My Way

1944   Lady in the Dark* (adapt.)
1945   The Bells of St. Mary's
1949   The Great Gatsby
1957   The Three Faces of Eve
Book: *Music in Modern Media*

Klaus Doldinger
Born May 12, 1936, Berlin, Germany
1981   Das Boot
1984   The NeverEnding Story
           (w/ Giorgio Moroder)

Pino Donaggio
Born November 24, 1941, Venice, Italy
1974   Don't Look Now
1976   Carrie
1980   Dressed to Kill
1984   Body Double

Steve Dorff
Born April 21, 1949, New York, N.Y.
1978   Every Which Way but Loose

Patrick Doyle
Born April 6, 1953, Uddingston, Scotland
1989   Henry V
1991   Dead Again
1992   Indochine
1993   Much Ado About Nothing
1993   Into the West

Carmen Dragon
Born July 28, 1914, Antioch, Calif.
Died March 28, 1984
1943   Cover Girl** (adapt.)
1956   Invasion of the Body Snatchers

Anne Dudley
Born May 7, 1956, Chatham, Kent, England
1989   Say Anything . . .
1992   The Crying Game

George Duning
Born February 25, 1908, Richmond, Ind.
1947   Johnny O'Clock
1949   Jolson Sings Again

1953	From Here to Eternity*
1955	Picnic*
1957	3:10 to Yuma
1958	Houseboat
1958	Bell, Book and Candle
1963	Toys in the Attic
1966	Any Wednesday
1970	Then Came Bronson
1983	Beyond Witch Mountain

Paul Dunlap
Born July 19, 1919, Springfield, Ohio

1957	I Was a Teenage Werewolf
1957	I Was a Teenage Frankenstein

John du Prez
Born December 14, 1946, Sheffield, England

1988	A Fish Called Wanda
1990	Teenage Mutant Ninja Turtles
1991	Teenage Mutant Ninja Turtles II: The Secret of the Ooze
1993	Teenage Mutant Ninja Turtles III

Bob Dylan
Born May 24, 1941, Duluth, Minn.

1973	Pat Garrett and Billy the Kid

Randy Edelman
Born June 10, 1947, Patterson, N.J.

1988	Feds
1988	Twins (co-comp.)
1989	Ghostbusters II
1990	Come See the Paradise
1990	Kindergarten Cop
1992	My Cousin Vinny
1992	Beethoven
1992	The Distinguished Gentleman
1992	The Last of the Mohicans (co-comp.)
1993	Dragon: The Bruce Lee Story
1993	Gettysburg

Cliff Eidelman
Born December 5, 1964, Los Angeles, Calif.

1989	Triumph of the Spirit
1990	Crazy People
1991	Star Trek VI

1992	Christopher Columbus: The Discovery
1992	Leap of Faith
1993	The Meteor Man

Hanns Eisler
Born July 6, 1898, Leipzig, Germany
Died September 6, 1962

1943	Hangmen Also Die*
1944	None but the Lonely Heart*

Danny Elfman
Born May 29, 1953, Los Angeles, Calif.

1985	Pee Wee's Big Adventure
1988	Beetlejuice
1989	Batman
1990	Darkman
1990	Dick Tracy
1990	Edward Scissorhands

Danny Elfman
Photo: Dennis Keeley

1992   Batman Returns
1993   Sommersby
1993   The Nightmare before Christmas

Edward Kennedy "Duke" Ellington
Born April 29, 1899, Washington, D.C.
Died May 24, 1974
1959   Anatomy of a Murder
1961   Paris Blues*

Jack Elliott
Born August 6, 1927, Hartford, Conn.
1970   Where's Poppa?
1978   Oh, God!
1979   Just You and Me, Kid
1979   The Jerk
1990   Sibling Rivalry

Harold Faltermeyer
Born October 5, 1952, Munich, Germany
1984   Beverly Hills Cop
1985   Fletch
1986   Top Gun
1987   Beverly Hills Cop II

Robert Farnon
Born July 24, 1917, Toronto, Canada
1951   Captain Horatio Hornblower

George Fenton
Born October 19, 1950, London, England
1982   Gandhi* (w/ Ravi Shankar)
1987   Cry Freedom* (w/ Jonas Gwangwa)
1988   Dangerous Liaisons*
1990   Memphis Belle
1991   Final Analysis
1991   The Fisher King*
1992   Hero
1993   Groundhog Day

Allyn Ferguson
Born October 18, 1924, San Jose, Calif.
1971   Support Your Local Gunfighter
1979   Avalanche Express

Jerry Fielding
Photo courtesy of Camille Fielding

Brad Fiedel
Born March 10, 1951, New York, N.Y.
1984   The Terminator
1987   The Big Easy
1988   The Accused
1991   Terminator 2
1992   Straight Talk
1993   Striking Distance

Jerry Fielding
Born June 17, 1922, Pittsburgh, Pa.
Died February 17, 1980
First films: Advise and Consent (1962)
            The Nun and the Sergeant (1962)
1964   McHale's Navy
1969   The Wild Bunch*
1971   Johnny Got His Gun
1971   Straw Dogs*
1972   The Nightcomers
1972   The Mechanic
1973   Scorpio

1974	The Gambler
1975	The Killer Elite
1976	The Bad News Bears (adapt.)
1976	The Outlaw Josey Wales*
1976	The Enforcer
1977	The Gauntlet
1978	Gray Lady Down

Jerry Fielding began his career as an arranger, writing for Tommy Dorsey and other dance bands. His career was progressing well when, in 1953, he was blacklisted as a result of the Un-American Activities Committee's hearings. He worked for almost 10 years in Las Vegas before returning to a television job in L.A. His dynamic score for *The Wild Bunch* was the first of several films he scored for Sam Peckinpah, including *Straw Dogs* and *The Killer Elite*. He worked with Clint Eastwood on four films, including *The Outlaw Josey Wales*. He was an extraordinary individual who defined his values and expressed his opinions with great passion and sincerity. As Sandy De Crescent says, "If he said something to you, you never had to weigh it—I mean, that was it. It was so."

Robert Folk
Born March 5, 1949, New York, N.Y.

1984	Police Academy (and Police Academy sequels II through VI)
1990	The NeverEnding Story II
1991	Toy Soldiers

David Foster
Born November 1, 1949, Victoria, B.C., Canada

1985	St. Elmo's Fire
1987	The Secret of My Success

Charles Fox
Born October 30, 1940, New York, N.Y.

1969	Goodbye, Columbus
1975	The Other Side of the Mountain
1978	Foul Play
1980	Nine to Five
1988	Short Circuit II
1989	The Gods Must Be Crazy II

David Michael Frank
Born December 21, 1948, Baltimore, Md.

1988	Above the Law
1988	Call Me
1991	Out for Justice

Benjamin Frankel
Born January 31, 1906, London, England
Died February 12, 1973

1945	The Seventh Veil
1952	The Importance of Being Earnest
1952	The Man in the White Suit

Jill Fraser
Born October 11, 1952, Cincinnati, Ohio

1982	Personal Best (w/ Jack Nitzsche)
1989	Cutting Class

Gerald Fried
Born February 13, 1928, New York, N.Y.

1957	Paths of Glory
1968	What Ever Happened to Aunt Alice?
1975	Birds Do It, Bees Do It*
TV:	I Will Fight No More Forever (1975 docudrama)
	Roots** (w/ Quincy Jones, 1977 ms)
	Roots: The Next Generations (1979 ms)

Hugo Friedhofer
Born May 3, 1902, San Francisco, Calif.
Died May 17, 1981
First films: Sunny Side Up (1929, arr.)

1938	The Adventures of Marco Polo
1944	The Lodger
1945	Brewster's Millions
1946	The Bandit of Sherwood Forest
1946	Gilda
1946	The Best Years of Our Lives**
1947	Body and Soul
1947	The Bishop's Wife*
1948	A Song Is Born
1948	Joan of Arc*
1950	Broken Arrow
1951	Ace in the Hole
1954	Vera Cruz
1955	The Rains of Ranchipur

1957	Boy on a Dolphin*
1958	The Young Lions*
1958	The Barbarian and the Geisha
1960	One-Eyed Jacks
1971	Von Richtofen and Brown

Friedhofer began studying cello at 13 (inspired by his father, who was a cellist). By 1925 he was playing cello in silent movie theaters. As his interest in arranging and writing music increased, he began studying and doing arrangements for the theater orchestra. He

Hugo Friedhofer
Photo: Alexander Courage

There are so many factors to consider: the tempo of the film, the pacing, the lighting, the editing, the way the dialogue is delivered, and the moods established by all these things. If a composer is to be good at his craft, he should know a lot more than just composition. He must be conscious of everything that is going on.

came to Hollywood in July 1929 to write the arrangements for *Sunny Side Up.* He stayed at Fox for 5 years, arranging and orchestrating.

He moved to Warner Bros. in 1936, and orchestrated other people's scores for the next 11 years. He orchestrated over 50 of Max Steiner's scores, beginning with *Charge of the Light Brigade.* Over the years he orchestrated 15 of Korngold's 18 scores, plus scores by Newman and others. The only complete score he actually composed during that time was *The Adventures of Marco Polo* in 1937, on loan-out to Samuel Goldwyn.

In 1943 Alfred Newman offered him a contract to compose at Fox, and he gladly accepted. His 1946 score for *The Best Years of Our Lives* was a landmark score. In speaking of his stylistic tendencies, Friedhofer said, "I am happy to admit that Copland has been an influence on my work, especially with the score for *Best Years.* . . . His influence helped me weed out the run-of-the-mine schmaltz and aim to do more straighforward and simple, even folklike scoring." Friedhofer was and is greatly admired by his colleagues. His film score, *Private Parts,* was released in 1972, and his last film, *Die, Sister, Die!,* in 1978.

Those who know his music have great admiration for him. David Raksin has said, "I think he has a better understanding of film music than any composer I know. He is the most learned of us all, the best schooled, and often the most subtle."

Dominic Frontiere
Born June 17, 1931, New Haven, Conn.
| 1968 | Hang 'em High |
| 1980 | The Stunt Man |

Peter Gabriel
Born February 13, 1950, England
| 1988 | The Last Temptation of Christ |

Douglas Gamley
Born September 13, 1924, Melbourne, Australia
1958	Another Time, Another Place
1972	Tales from the Crypt
1975	The Land That Time Forgot

Russell Garcia

Born April 12, 1916, Oakland, Calif.

1960   The Time Machine

Herschel Burke Gilbert

Born April 20, 1918, Milwaukee, Wis.

1950   The Jackie Robinson Story
1952   The Thief*
1953   The Moon Is Blue*
1954   Riot in Cell Block 11

Philip Glass

Born January 31, 1937, Baltimore, Md.

1983   Koyaanisqatsi
1988   Powaqqatsi
1992   Candyman
1992   A Brief History of Time

Albert Glasser

Born January 25, 1916, Chicago, Ill.

1949   I Shot Jesse James
1957   The Amazing Colossal Man

Patrick Gleeson

Born November 9, 1934, Seattle, Wash.

1979   Apocalypse Now (perf./arr.)
1981   The Howling: The Freaks

Ernest Gold

Born July 13, 1921, Vienna, Austria

1959   On the Beach*
1960   Exodus**
1961   Judgment at Nuremberg
1963   It's a Mad, Mad, Mad, Mad World*
1969   The Secret of Santa Vittoria*

Billy Goldenberg

Born February 10, 1936, New York, N.Y.

1971   Red Sky at Morning
1988   18 Again
TV: Queen of the Stardust Ballroom* (1975)
        Helter Skelter* (1976)
        King** (1978 ms)

Elliot Goldenthal

Born May 2, 1954, Brooklyn, N.Y.

1989   Drugstore Cowboy
1992   Alien 3
1993   Demolition Man

Jerry Goldsmith

Born February 10, 1929, Los Angeles, Calif.

First Film: Black Patch (1957)

1962   Lonely Are the Brave
1963   Freud*
1963   Lilies of the Field
1965   A Patch of Blue*
1966   The Blue Max
1966   The Sand Pebbles*
1968   Planet of the Apes*
1970   Patton*
1973   Papillon*
1974   Chinatown*
1975   The Wind and the Lion*
1976   The Omen**
1977   Islands in the Stream
1978   Damien: Omen II
1978   The Boys from Brazil*
1979   Alien
1979   Star Trek: The Motion Picture*
1982   Poltergeist*
1982   First Blood
1983   Twilight Zone: The Movie
1983   Under Fire*
1984   Gremlins
1985   Rambo: First Blood Part II
1986   Hoosiers*
1989   Star Trek V: The Final Frontier
1990   Total Recall
1991   Sleeping with the Enemy
1992   Medicine Man
1992   Basic Instinct
1992   Forever Young
1993   Dennis the Menace
1993   Malice
TV: "The Man from U.N.C.L.E."
            (1964, series themes)
        "The Waltons" (1971, series theme)
        QB VII** (1974 ms)

Jerry Goldsmith
Photo: Alexander Courage

Some people might imagine a composer as a quiet, romantic figure, dreaming up beautiful chords and melodies, but to me every assignment is a scramble and a crunch. Each assignment becomes an agonizing experience. Where shall I begin? What notes shall I play? What combination of sounds will be at once so melodic and original and attention-grabbing that the audience will be hooked?

Goldsmith started at CBS at 21, not as a composer but as a script typist hoping to break into the music business. His visits to the music department led to his scoring radio programs, and in 1955, he was offered a contract at $150 a week to compose scores for television—2 or 3 hours of music every week. By 1957 he had scored his first feature film.

Since then, Goldsmith has created an enormous body of distinguished work, displaying great artistry and versatility. Though well known for his suspense and action thrillers like *Alien*, *Poltergeist*, and the *Omen* trilogy, he also created the theme for the folksy "Waltons" television series, and the scores for the romantic *Islands in the Stream*, the off-the-wall *Flim Flam Man*, and the heartwarming basketball-themed *Hoosiers*.

Joel Goldsmith
Born November 19, 1957, Los Angeles, Calif.
1983   The Man with Two Brains
        Joel Goldsmith is Jerry Goldsmith's son.

William Goldstein
Born February 25, 1942, N.J.
1976   The Bingo Long Traveling-All Stars and
        Motor Kings

Miles Goodman
Born August 27, 1949, Los Angeles, Calif.
1984   Footloose (adapt.)
1986   About Last Night
1986   Little Shop of Horrors (adapt.)
1988   Dirty Rotten Scoundrels
1991   What About Bob?
1991   He Said, She Said
1993   Sister Act 2: Back in the Habit

Ron Goodwin
Born February 17, 1925, Plymouth, Devon, England
1960   Village of the Damned
1965   Those Magnificent Men in Their Flying
        Machines
1972   Frenzy

Michael Gore
Born March 5, 1951, New York, N.Y.
1980   Fame**
1983   Terms of Endearment*
1986   Pretty in Pink
1991   Defending Your Life
1991   The Butcher's Wife
1993   Mr. Wonderful

John Green
Born October 10, 1908, New York, N.Y.
Died May 15, 1989
Head of MGM Music 1949-1958
1947   Fiesta*
1948   Easter Parade** (m.d.)
1951   The Great Caruso*
1951   An American in Paris** (m.d.)
1954   Brigadoon (m.d.)
1956   High Society*

John [Johnny] Green
Photo: Alexander Courage

1957	Raintree County*
1961	West Side Story* (adapt. w/ Saul Chaplin, Irwin Kostal, Sid Ramin)
1963	Bye Bye Birdie* (m.d.)
1968	Oliver!** (m.d.)
1969	They Shoot Horses, Don't They?* (adapt. w/ Al Woodbury)
Songs:	"Body and Soul"
	"I Cover the Waterfront"

Ferde Grofé
Born March 27, 1892, New York, N.Y.
Died April 3, 1972
1950   Rocketship X-M
1950   The Return of Jesse James

Charles Gross
Born May 13, 1934, Cambridge, Mass.
1979   Heartland
1984   Country
1988   Punchline
1989   Turner and Hooch

1990   Air America
TV: The Burning Bed (1984)

Louis Gruenberg
Born 1884, Brest-Litovsk, Russia
Died June 6, 1964
1941   So Ends Our Night*
1949   All the King's Men

Dave Grusin
Born June 26, 1934, Littleton, Colo.
First films: Divorce American Style (1967)
              The Graduate (1967, underscoring only)
1968   The Heart Is a Lonely Hunter

Dave Grusin

I like films that mean something . . . I like films that make a statement. I feel I'm spending my time more in an adult profession if the movie is an adult movie.

1975	The Yakuza
1976	Murder by Death
1978	Heaven Can Wait*
1979	The Champ*
1980	My Bodyguard
1981	On Golden Pond*
1982	Tootsie
1986	Lucas
1988	The Milagro Beanfield War**
1988	Clara's Heart
1989	The Fabulous Baker Boys*
1990	Havana
1991	For the Boys
1993	The Firm

Dave Grusin has become associated with scores that are either hip (*Tootsie* is a good example) or lush (*On Golden Pond*). While he does do these types of scores beautifully, his range is considerably greater than that. The classical *Heart Is a Lonely Hunter* and the chamber sound of *My Bodyguard* clearly demonstrate his ability to get inside a film with an appropriate musical language. His theme for *Heaven Can Wait*, blending a 1920s-style saxophone melody with a contemporary point of view, is perfectly suited for Warren Beatty's saxophone-playing character. He is especially good at using the appropriate ethnic flavor in his scores; good examples include *The Milagro Beanfield War*, *Clara's Heart*, *Havana*, and *The Yakuza*. A popular recording artist for his own successful independent jazz label, Grusin is co-owner of GRP Records.

Jay Gruska
Born April 23, 1952, New York, N.Y.

1989	Sing
1992	Mo' Money

Manos Hadjidakis
Born 1925, Athens, Greece

1960	Never on Sunday

Richard Hageman
Born July 9, 1882, Leeuwarden, Holland
Died March 6, 1966

1938	If I Were King*

1940	The Long Voyage Home*
1947	Mourning Becomes Electra
1948	Fort Apache
1949	She Wore a Yellow Ribbon

Marvin Hamlisch
Born June 2, 1944, New York, N.Y.
First films: The Swimmer (1968)
            Take the Money and Run (1969)

1971	Bananas
1973	The Way We Were** (incl. title song**)
1973	The Sting** (adapt.)
1977	The Spy Who Loved Me
1979	Ice Castles
1982	Sophie's Choice*
1987	Three Men and a Baby
1991	Frankie and Johnny

Herbie Hancock
Born April 12, 1940, Chicago, Ill.

1984	A Soldier's Story
1986	'Round Midnight**
1988	Colors

Leigh Harline
Born March 26, 1907, Salt Lake City, Utah
Died December 10, 1969

1938	Snow White and the Seven Dwarfs*
	(w/ Churchill and Smith)
1940	Pinocchio** (w/ Paul Smith)
1942	The Pride of the Yankees*
1943	They Got Me Covered
1943	Johnny Come Lately
1946	Nocturne
1948	Mr. Blandings Builds His Dream House
1948	The Boy with Green Hair
1949	It Happens Every Spring
1954	Black Widow
1958	Ten North Frederick

W. Franke Harling
Born January 18, 1887, London, England
Died November 22, 1958

1932	Broken Lullaby
1941	Penny Serenade

Richard Hartley
Born July 28, 1944, Holmfirth, England
1975   The Rocky Horror Picture Show

Marvin Hatley
Born April 3, 1905, Reed, Okla.
Died August 26, 1986
1937   Way Out West*
1937   Topper
1938   Swiss Miss
1938   Blockheads*
1940   A Chump at Oxford
1940   Saps at Sea

Fumio Hayasaka
Born August 19, 1914, Minagi, Japan
Died October 15, 1955
1950   Rashomon
1952   Ikiru
1953   Ugetsu
1954   The Seven Samurai

Isaac Hayes
Born August 20, 1942
1971   Shaft*

Neal Hefti
Born October 29, 1922, Hastings, Nebr.
1965   Sex and the Single Girl
1966   Barefoot in the Park
1968   The Odd Couple
TV: "The Odd Couple" (theme and series)
         "Batman" (theme and series)

Ray Heindorf
Born August 25, 1908, Haverstraw, N.Y.
Died February 3, 1980
Head of Warner Bros. music 1948-1959
1933   42nd Street (arr.)
1933   Footlight Parade (arr.)
1935   Gold Diggers of 1935 (arr.)
1942   Yankee Doodle Dandy** (arr.)
1943   This Is the Army** (arr.)
1945   Rhapsody in Blue (arr.)
1946   Night and Day (arr.)
1962   The Music Man** (adapt.)
1968   Finian's Rainbow (adapt.)

Bernard Herrmann
Born June 30, 1911, New York, N.Y.
Died December 24, 1975
1941   Citizen Kane*
1941   All That Money Can Buy**
         (aka The Devil and Daniel Webster)
1942   The Magnificent Ambersons
1945   Hangover Square
1947   The Ghost and Mrs. Muir
1951   The Day the Earth Stood Still
1953   Beneath the 12-Mile Reef
1954   The Egyptian (w/ Alfred Newman)
1955   The Trouble with Harry
1955   The Kentuckian
1956   The Man Who Knew Too Much
1956   The Man in the Gray Flannel Suit
1958   Vertigo
1958   The 7th Voyage of Sinbad
1959   North by Northwest
1960   Psycho
1962   Cape Fear
1963   Jason and the Argonauts

Bernard Herrmann conducting *Citizen Kane* in 1940.

1964	Marnie
1966	Fahrenheit 451
1973	Sisters
1976	Obsession*
1976	Taxi Driver*
TV:	"The Twilight Zone" episodes

1933	Staff conductor for CBS Radio in NYC.
1938	Worked with Orson Welles and Mercury Theater group at CBS.
1940	Began first film score: *Citizen Kane*.
1955	First Hitchcock film released: *The Trouble with Harry*; continued scoring Hitchcock's films through *Marnie* in 1964.
1972	Scored *Sisters* for Brian De Palma.
1976	Died the night he finished recording his score for Martin Scorsese's *Taxi Driver*.

Herrmann is among the most influential of all film composers. He had a very direct, frequently gruff manner. As an example, he would often say to a producer after a screening, "Why do you show me this garbage?" It is said that when Miklós Rózsa once said Herrmann was his own worst enemy, another composer replied, "Not while I'm alive!" However, those who knew him well were able to see past his irascible nature, and many composers and filmmakers had the greatest admiration for his music.

"He was really a master at that art of creating something that hits you the first time you hear it, and yet it is interesting enough to return to over and over again, so it's there for the students, it's there for the person who has only seen *Psycho* once and will always remember the score." Steven C. Smith, Bernard Herrmann's biographer.

Werner R. Heymann
Born February 14, 1896, Königsberg, Germany
Died April 8, 1950

1939	Ninotchka
1940	One Million B.C.
1942	To Be or Not To Be
1944	Knickerbocker Holiday* (adapt.)
1945	It's in the Bag

Michael Hoenig
Born January 4, 1952, Hamburg, Germany

1983	Koyaanisqatsi (w/ Philip Glass)
1988	The Blob
1989	I, Madman

Lee Holdridge
Born March 3, 1944, Port-au-Prince, Haiti

1973	Jonathan Livingston Seagull (w/ Neil Diamond)
1978	The Other Side of the Mountain: Part 2
1983	Mr. Mom
1984	Splash
1985	16 Days to Glory
1987	Born in East L.A.
1988	Big Business
1989	Old Gringo
TV:	"Moonlighting" (theme, 1985)
	"Beauty and the Beast" (theme, 1987)

Frederick Hollander
Born October 18, 1896, England
Died January 19, 1976

1935	Shanghai
1941	Here Comes Mr. Jordan
1942	The Man Who Came to Dinner
1942	The Talk of the Town*
1945	Christmas in Connecticut
1950	Born Yesterday
1955	We're No Angels

Arthur Honegger
Born March 10, 1892, Le Havre, France
Died November 27, 1955

1934	Les Misérables
1935	Crime and Punishment
1936	Mayerling
1938	Pygmalion

Kenyon Hopkins
Born 1912
Died April 7, 1983

1956	Baby Doll
1957	Twelve Angry Men
1969	Downhill Racer

James Horner
Born August 14, 1953, Los Angeles, Calif.
First Films: Up from the Depths (1979)
The Lady in Red (1979)

James Horner
Photo: Gay Wallin

1993   The Man Without a Face
1993   The Pelican Brief

Horner is quite versatile, though he is known primarily for large-scale works such as *Star Trek II* and *III*, and *Glory*. To sample other facets of his scoring, try *Brainstorm*, an excellent mix of textures; *Field of Dreams*, with its largely understated electronic sound; and *Testament*, with an intimate chamber-music approach.

Richard Horowitz
Born January 6, 1949, Buffalo, N.Y.
1990   The Sheltering Sky

James Newton Howard

1982   Star Trek II: The Wrath of Khan
1982   48HRS.
1983   Brainstorm
1983   Testament
1983   Gorky Park
1984   Star Trek III: The Search for Spock
1985   Cocoon
1986   Aliens*
1986   An American Tail
1987   Batteries Not Included
1988   Cocoon: The Return
1989   Field of Dreams*
1989   Glory
1990   Another 48 HRS.
1990   Class Action
1991   An American Tail II
1992   Patriot Games
1992   Sneakers
1993   Searching for Bobby Fischer

James Newton Howard
Born June 9, 1951, Los Angeles, Calif.
First films: Head Office (1986)
                    8 Million Ways to Die (1986)
1989   Tap
1990   Pretty Woman
1991   The Man in the Moon
1991   Grand Canyon
1993   Falling Down
1993   Dave
1993   The Fugitive

Alan Howarth
Born August 6, 1948, South River, N.J.
1981   Escape from New York
                (w/ John Carpenter)
                (Halloween sequels II through V
                w/ Carpenter)

Dick Hyman
Born March 8, 1927, New York, N.Y.
1983   Zelig
1983   Broadway Danny Rose
1985   The Purple Rose of Cairo
1987   Radio Days
1987   Moonstruck

Shinichiro Ikebe
Born September 15, 1943, Ibaraki, Japan
1980   Kagemusha: The Shadow Warrior
1990   Akira Kurosawa's Dreams

Jerrold Immel
Born September 9, 1936, Los Angeles, Calif.
1982   Megaforce
1982   Paradise

Mark Isham
Born September 7, 1951, New York, N.Y.
1983   Never Cry Wolf
1984   Mrs. Soffel
1988   The Moderns
1990   Reversal of Fortune
1991   Little Man Tate
1991   Billy Bathgate
1992   A Midnight Clear

Mark Isham

1992   Cool World
1992   A River Runs Through It*
1993   Made in America
1993   Short Cuts

Howard Jackson

1936   Mr. Deeds Goes to Town
1958   Cry Terror

Alaric Jans
Born January 27, 1949, St. Louis, Mo.
1987   House of Games
1988   Things Change

Werner Janssen
Born June 1, 1899, New York, N.Y.
Died September 19, 1990
1936   The General Died at Dawn
1938   Blockade*
1939   Eternally Yours*
1945   The Southerner*

Maurice Jarre

Born September 13, 1924, Lyons, France

1962	Sundays and Cybele*
1962	Lawrence of Arabia**
1965	Doctor Zhivago**
1970	Ryan's Daughter
1975	The Man Who Would Be King
1977	Mohammed, Messenger of God*
1983	The Year of Living Dangerously
1984	A Passage to India**
1985	Witness*
1985	Mad Max Beyond Thunderdome
1987	No Way Out
1987	Fatal Attraction

Maurice Jarre

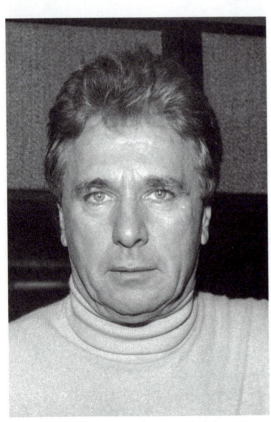

I think the best way to use music is when it's a complement of the film, instead of being an illustration.

1988	Gorillas in the Mist*
1989	Dead Poets Society
1990	Ghost
1993	Fearless
TV:	Jesus of Nazareth (1978 ms)
	Shogun** (1980 ms)

Jarre's first major breakthrough was the score for *Lawrence of Arabia* in 1962, which began a close association with David Lean, for whom he also scored *Doctor Zhivago* and *Ryan's Daughter*. These epic, lush-sounding scores created an image for Jarre that he dramatically expanded with his electronic music for director Peter Weir's *The Year of Living Dangerously* and *Witness*. Unlike many composers, he records all his electronic instruments simultaneously with a small group of musicians, rather than either prerecording, or performing the music himself. *Witness* was recorded in five days with five musicians.

Quincy Jones

Born March 14, 1933, Chicago, Ill.

1965	The Pawnbroker
1967	In Cold Blood*
1967	In the Heat of the Night
1978	The Wiz* (adapt.)

Trevor Jones

Born March 23, 1949, Cape Town, South Africa

1988	Mississippi Burning
1989	Sea of Love
1990	Arachnophobia
1992	The Last of the Mohicans (co-comp.)
1993	Cliffhanger

Michael Kamen

Born April 15, 1948, New York, N.Y.

1983	The Dead Zone
1985	Brazil
1987	Lethal Weapon (w/ Eric Clapton)
1987	Suspect
1988	Die Hard
1989	The Adventures of Baron Munchausen
1989	Lethal Weapon 2 (w/ Clapton and David Sanborn)
1990	Die Hard II

1991	Robin Hood: Prince of Thieves*
1992	Lethal Weapon 3 (w/ Clapton and Sanborn)
1993	Last Action Hero

Bronislau Kaper
Born February 5, 1902, Warsaw, Poland
Died April 25, 1983
Primary studio affiliation: MGM
First films: San Francisco (1936, title song only)
              The Captain Is a Lady (1940)

1941	The Chocolate Soldier* (adapt.)
1943	Bataan
1944	Gaslight
1945	Bewitched
1945	Our Vines Have Tender Grapes
1947	Green Dolphin Street (incl. title theme)
1951	The Red Badge of Courage
1952	Invitation (incl. title theme)
1953	Lili**
1958	Auntie Mame
1960	Butterfield 8
1962	Mutiny on the Bounty*
1965	Lord Jim
1968	Counterpoint; A Flea in Her Ear (last films)

Except for a few excursions ... I never tried to be typical American. How could I compete with the other foreigners, like Harry Warren?

An excellent pianist, Kaper began his career as a songwriter. He was discovered in Paris by Louis B. Mayer, who heard one of his current European hits and offered him a contract at MGM. Arriving there in 1936, he stayed 30 years. Because he wrote hit songs including "San Francisco" and "All God's Chillun Got Rhythm," and specialty numbers like "Cosi, Cosa," for the Marx brothers film *A Night at the Opera*, he remained typecast as a songwriter for four years before his first scoring assignment. Miles Davis immortalized his theme for *Green Dolphin Street*, and "Invitation" is played by jazz groups all over the world.

Sol Kaplan
Born 1913, Philadelphia, Pa. (deceased)

1942	Tales of Manhattan
1951	Rawhide
1953	Titanic
1965	The Spy Who Came in from the Cold
1972	Living Free

Dana Kaproff
Born April 24, 1954, Los Angeles, Calif.

1979	When a Stranger Calls
1988	Doin' Time on Planet Earth

Anton Karas
Born July 7, 1906, Vienna, Austria
Died January 10, 1985

1949	The Third Man

Fred Karlin
Born June 16, 1936, Chicago, Ill.

1968	The Stalking Moon
1969	The Sterile Cuckoo (incl. "Come Saturday Morning"*)
1970	Lovers and Other Strangers (incl. "For All We Know"**)
1973	Westworld
1976	Futureworld
1976	Leadbelly
1990	Strawberry Road
TV:	The Autobiography of Miss Jane Pittman** (1974)
Books:	*On the Track: A Guide to Contemporary Film Scoring* (with Rayburn Wright) *Listening to Movies*

Laura Karpman
Born March 1, 1959, Los Angeles, Calif.

1991	Johnny 99

Wojciech Kilar

1992	Bram Stoker's Dracula

David Kitay
Born October 23, 1961, Los Angeles, Calif.

1989	Look Who's Talking
1990	Boris and Natasha
1990	Look Who's Talking, Too
1993	Surf Ningas

Erich Wolfgang Korngold

Born May 29, 1897, Brno, Czechoslovakia
Died November 29, 1957
Primary studio affiliation: Warner Bros.
First film: A Midsummer Night's Dream (1935,
    adapt.)

1935	Captain Blood

Erich Wolfgang Korngold
Photo courtesy of ASCAP

When, in the projection room . . . I am watching the picture unroll, when I am sitting at the piano improvising or inventing themes and tunes, when I am facing the orchestra conducting my music, I have the feeling that I am giving my own and my best: symphonically dramatic music which fits the picture, its action, and its psychology, and which, nevertheless, will be able to hold its own in the concert hall.

1936	Give Us This Night
1936	The Green Pastures
1936	Anthony Adverse**
1937	The Prince and the Pauper
1937	Another Dawn
1938	The Adventures of Robin Hood**
1939	Juarez
1939	The Private Lives of Elizabeth and Essex*
1940	The Sea Hawk*
1941	The Sea Wolf
1942	Kings Row
1943	The Constant Nymph
1944	Between Two Worlds
1946	Devotion
1946	Of Human Bondage
1946	Deception
1947	Escape Me Never
1956	Magic Fire (adapt.)

Named after Mozart, Korngold was a child prodigy pianist-composer; he wrote his first ballet at 11. Puccini: "The boy has so much talent he could easily give us some and still have enough left for himself."

1934	To Hollywood.
1935– 1947	Scored 19 films; became the highest paid composer in Hollywood at that time.
1947	First heart attack. Retired from film scoring except for *Magic Fire* in 1956. Returned to Vienna to pursue his concert and operatic composing.

Korngold made a lasting impression on film music history. His symphonic-operatic way of scoring large-scale romantic dramas such as the Errol Flynn swashbuckler *The Sea Hawk* has become a definitive approach for this kind of film. His score for the more personal drama of *Kings Row* is equally beautiful and effective.

He scored only a film or two a year while in Hollywood, preferring to be very selective. He insisted on more time than usual to compose his scores. He was a passionate pianist, and Warners claimed he ruined eight of their pianos. Hugo Friedhofer orchestrated almost all of his scores. Friedhofer once said, "To be honest about it—we were all influenced by him."

"Erich Wolfgang Korngold was a master film composer," André Previn said in *No Minor Chords.* "His wonderful melodies, orchestrated in the most gorgeous Richard Strauss-oriented manner, are a joy to hear, even when the films are forgettable. *Robin Hood, The Sea Hawk,* and *Elizabeth and Essex* all display Korngold's musical extravertism, and for some reason, his unmistakably Viennese kind of sentiment helped Errol Flynn be a convincing English hero."

Joseph Kosma
Born October 22, 1905, Budapest, Hungary
Died August 7, 1969
1937   Grand Illusion
1944   Children of Paradise

Irwin Kostal
Born October 1, 1911, Chicago, Ill.
1961   West Side Story** (w/ Green, S.
            Chaplin, Ramin; adapt.)
1964   Mary Poppins* (adapt.)
1965   The Sound of Music** (adapt.)
1971   Bedknobs and Broomsticks* (adapt.)
1977   Pete's Dragon* (adapt.)

Francis Lai
Born April 26, 1932, Nice, France
1966   A Man and a Woman**
1970   Love Story**

John Lanchbery
Born May 15, 1923, England
1977   The Turning Point

Arthur Lange
Born April 16, 1889, Philadelphia, Pa.
Died December 7, 1956
1934   Stand Up and Cheer
1943   The Dancing Masters
1945   Along Came Jones
1952   The Pride of St. Louis

Bruce Langhorne
1971   The Hired Hand
1980   Melvin and Howard

William Lava
Born March 18, 1911, St. Paul, Minn.
Died February 20, 1971
1939   Dick Tracy's G-Men (serial)
1950   Colt .45

Bill Lee
Born July 23, 1928, Snow Hill, Ala.
1989   Do the Right Thing
1990   Mo' Better Blues

Michel Legrand
Born February 24, 1932, Paris, France
1964   The Umbrellas of Cherbourg*
1968   The Thomas Crown Affair*
            (incl. "Windmills of Your Mind"**)
1971   Summer of '42**
1974   The Three Musketeers
1983   Yentl**
1993   The Pickle
TV: Brian's Song** (1971)

Oscar Levant
Born December 27, 1906, Pittsburgh, Pa.
Died August 14, 1972
1937   Charlie Chan at the Opera (opera sequence)
1937   Nothing Sacred
1939   Made for Each Other
Autobiographical Books:
    A Smattering of Ignorance
    The Memoirs of an Amnesiac
    The Unimportance of Being Oscar
Film appearances include: An American in Paris, The
    Band Wagon, Rhapsody in Blue, and Humoresque

Sylvester Levay
Born May 16, 1945, Subotica, Hungary
1990   Navy Seals
1991   Hot Shots!

W. Michael Lewis
1981   Enter the Ninja (w/ Laurin Rinder)
1984   Ninja III—The Domination (w/ Rinder)

Michael J. Linn

Born July 27, 1952, Boston, Mass.

| 1985 | American Ninja |
| 1987 | Allan Quartermain and the Lost City of Gold |

Elisabeth Lutyens

Born July 9, 1906, London, England
Died April 14, 1983

1947	A String of Beads
1953	World Without End
1964	Paranoiac
1964	The Earth Dies Screaming

Henry Mancini

Born April 16, 1924, Cleveland, Ohio

First films: Lost in Alaska (partial, 1952)
           Back from the Front (1952, w/ Herman
           Stein)

1953	It Came from Outer Space (w/ Herman Stein and Irving Gertz)
1954	The Glenn Miller Story*
1958	Touch of Evil
1961	Breakfast at Tiffany's**
1962	Days of Wine and Roses
1964	The Pink Panther*
1967	Two for the Road
1967	Wait Until Dark
1970	Darling Lili
1974	That's Entertainment
1974	The White Dawn
1976	Silver Streak
1979	10*
1982	Victor/Victoria**
1985	Lifeforce
1987	The Glass Menagerie
1988	Without a Clue
1991	Switch
1993	Tom and Jerry: The Movie
1993	Son of the Pink Panther
TV:	"Peter Gunn" (1958 series)
	The Thorn Birds* (1983 ms)
Books:	*Did They Mention the Music?* (with Gene Lees)
	Sounds and Scores: A Practical Guide to Professional Orchestration

Henry Mancini
Photo: Gay Wallin

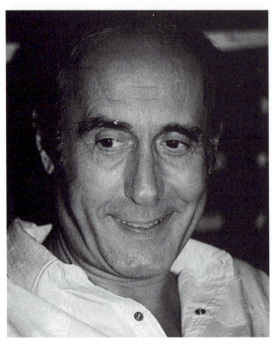

Ever since I was a kid, I've wanted to write picture music, like some kids dream of being another Mickey Mantle. I've always felt there was magic on a movie screen, seeing that bunch of light pouring out of the projector and creating images for you.

Henry Mancini started studying piccolo when he was eight, encouraged by his father. "If I didn't practice I got hit. That helped me get through the first couple of years, and then I got interested in playing the piano." In the early forties, he played the piano with the Tex Beneke band. In 1958, laid off after six years on staff at Universal, he stopped by the studio for a haircut, and coincidentally saw Blake Edwards, who was just working on a new TV show. "It was the score I wrote for the 'Peter Gunn' TV series that was the big break for me. That use of the jazz idiom, applied dramatically to the story, put music on everybody's mind as far as TV is concerned, and I say it modestly." When "Moon River" from Edwards' *Breakfast at Tiffany's* became an instant standard in 1961, Mancini's name became synonymous with exquisite melodies and creative orchestrations, often presented with a contemporary pop twist. The Blake Edwards-Henry Mancini collaboration has continued ever since, including the Pink Panther series, *10*, *Victor/Victoria*, and *Switch*. Although sometimes overlooked as a composer of heavier dramatic scores, he has done outstanding work in that genre, including *Wait Until Dark*, *The White Dawn*, and *Lifeforce*. In general, he has deliberately emphasized his pop-oriented material—both in songs and instrumental cuts—on his many soundtrack albums, to the exclusion of his dramatic scoring. In so doing, he has become a popular concert and television artist and a bestselling recording artist with a shelf-full of Grammys.

He is the author of two excellent books: *Sounds and Scores*, an extremely useful and popular orchestration text (with recorded examples); and his ingenuous and informative autobiography, *Did They Mention the Music?* (written with Gene Lees).

Johnny Mandel
Born November 23, 1935, New York, N.Y.
1958   I Want to Live*
1964   The Americanization of Emily
1965   The Sandpiper (incl. "Shadow of Your Smile"**)
1966   The Russians Are Coming! The Russians Are Coming!
1970   M*A*S*H (incl. "Suicide Is Painless")
1975   Escape to Witch Mountain
1979   Being There
1982   Deathtrap
1982   The Verdict

Harry Manfredini
Born August 25, 1943, Chicago, Ill.
1980   Friday the 13th (Friday the 13th II through VI sequels)
1982   Swamp Thing
1988   Friday the 13th Part VII—The New Blood (w/ Fred Mollin)
1993   My Boyfriend's Back

Hummie Mann
Born October 29, 1955, Montreal, Canada
1992   Year of the Comet
1993   Robin Hood: Men in Tights

Jim Manzie
Born May 24, 1956, Sydney, Australia
1990   Tales from the Dark Side: The Movie (co-comp.)

Anthony Marinelli
Born August 19, 1959, Burbank, Calif.
1988   Young Guns (w/ Brian Banks)
1990   Internal Affairs (w/ Mike Figgis and Banks)

Richard Markowitz
Born September 3, 1926, Los Angeles, Calif.
1961   The Hoodlum Priest
1965   The Wild Seed

Wynton Marsalis
Born October 18, 1961, New Orleans, La.
1990   Tune in Tomorrow

Cliff Martinez
Born February 2, 1954, New York, N.Y.
1989   sex, lies and videotape
1991   Kafka
1993   King of the Hill

Peter Matz
Born November 6, 1928, Pittsburgh, Pa.
1968   Bye Bye Braverman
1975   Funny Lady* (adapt.)

Billy May
Born November 10, 1916, Pittsburgh, Pa.
1963   Johnny Cool
1967   Tony Rome
1974   The Front Page

Brian May
Born July 28, 1934, Adelaide, Australia
1979   Mad Max
1981   Gallipoli
1982   The Road Warrior
1992   Dr. Giggles

Curtis Mayfield
Born June 2, 1942, Chicago, Ill.
1972   Superfly
1974   Claudine

Paul McCartney
Born June 18, 1942, Liverpool, England
1967   The Family Way
1973   Live and Let Die* (title song w/ Linda
         McCartney)
The following are all with the Beatles:
1964   Hard Day's Night
1965   Help!
1968   Yellow Submarine
1970   Let It Be** (Best Original Song Score)

David McHugh
Born May 29, 1941, Brooklyn, N.Y.
1984   Moscow on the Hudson
1988   Mystic Pizza

Gil Mellé
Born December 31, 1935, Jersey City, N.J.
1971   The Andromeda Strain
TV: Fatal Vision (1984)

Peter Melnick
Born July 24, 1958, New York, N.Y.
1989   Get Smart, Again!
1991   L.A. Story

Michael Melvoin
Born May 10, 1937, Milwaukee, Wis.
1979   Ashanti
1986   Armed and Dangerous (co-comp.)

Alan Menken
Born July 22, 1949, New York, N.Y.
1986   Little Shop of Horrors
1989   The Little Mermaid** (Oscars for Song
         {w/ Howard Ashman} and Score)
1991   Beauty and the Beast** (Oscars for Song
         {w/ Howard Ashman} and Score)
1992   Newsies
1992   Aladdin** (Oscars for Song {w/ Tim
         Rice} and Score)
1993   Life with Mikey
Theater: "Little Shop of Horrors"

Alan Menken
Photo: Bacharach

Michel Michelet
Born June 27, 1899, Kiev, Russia
1944   The Hairy Ape*
1949   The Man on the Eiffel Tower
1951   M

Darius Milhaud
Born September 4, 1892, Aix-en-Provence, France
Died June 26, 1974
1947   The Private Affairs of Bel Ami

Paul Misraki
Born 1908, Istanbul, Turkey
1956   And God Created Woman

Vic Mizzy
Born January 9, 1922, Brooklyn, N.Y.
1967	Don't Make Waves
1968	The Shakiest Gun in the West
TV:	"The Addams Family" (theme)

Cyril J. Mockridge
Born August 6, 1896, England
Died January 18, 1979
1943	The Ox-Bow Incident
1947	Miracle on 34th Street
1950	Cheaper by the Dozen
1953	How to Marry a Millionaire
1957	Desk Set
1957	Will Success Spoil Rock Hunter?
1962	The Man Who Shot Liberty Valance
1963	Donovan's Reef

Fred Mollin
Born February 10, 1953, Amityville, N.Y.
1988	Friday the 13th, Part VII (w/ Harry Manfredini)
1989	Friday the 13th, Part VIII

Dudley Moore
Born April 19, 1935, London, England
1967	Bedazzled
1982	Six Weeks

Actor Dudley Moore, who has starred in many films, including *Arthur* (1980), *Unfaithfully Yours* (1983), and *Blame It on the Bellboy* (1992), is a classical and jazz pianist.

Angela Morely
March 10, 1924, Leeds, Yorkshire, England
1974	The Little Prince* (adapt.)
1976	The Slipper and the Rose: The Story of Cinderella* (adapt.)
1978	Watership Down

Giorgio Moroder
Born April 26, 1940, Italy
1978	Midnight Express**
1980	American Gigolo
1982	Cat People
1983	Flashdance
1983	Scarface

Jerome Moross
Born August 1, 1913, Brooklyn, N.Y.
Died July 25, 1983
1958	The Big Country*
1960	The Adventures of Huckleberry Finn
1963	The Cardinal

Ennio Morricone
Born November 10, 1928, Rome, Italy
1964	A Fistful of Dollars
1965	For a Few Dollars More
1966	The Good, the Bad and the Ugly
1967	The Battle of Algiers

Ennio Morricone
Photo: Paul Van Hooff

Actually, people are little concerned with the musical element if they are watching a film, except when music is well mixed, or when it is particularly emphasized, as in Sergio Leone's films, for example, and a few others, where the music is really listened to.

1969	Once Upon a Time in the West
1977	Exorcist II: The Heretic
1977	1900
1978	Days of Heaven*
1984	Once Upon a Time in America
1986	The Mission*
1987	The Untouchables*
1989	Casualties of War
1992	City of Joy
1993	In the Line of Fire

"My first films were light comedies or costume movies that required simple musical scores that were easily created, a genre that I never completely abandoned even when I went on to much more important films with major director-writers." One of these director-writers was Sergio Leone, who created the "spaghetti Westerns." Morricone achieved international recognition with these scores, and many composers list his scores for *Once Upon a Time in the West*, along with *Once Upon a Time in America* among their favorites. He has a wonderful sense of color and theatricality, and has created many other outstanding scores, including *The Untouchables*, and two that he himself has singled out, *Exorcist II: The Heretic*, and *The Mission*.

John Morris
Born October 18, 1926, Elizabeth, N.J.

1968	The Producers
1973	Blazing Saddles
1974	Young Frankenstein
1975	The Adventure of Sherlock Holmes' Smarter Brother
1976	Silent Movie
1979	The In-Laws
1980	The Elephant Man*
1984	Johnny Dangerously
1984	The Woman in Red
1985	The Doctor and the Devils
1987	Dirty Dancing
1987	Ironweed
1987	Spaceballs
1990	Stella

Whenever I see anything on the screen in which somebody moves and nobody talks, it's a ballet to me. For instance, in Elephant Man, *all the drunken people come to torture him in his room at night. And I said, What I'm looking at is a ballet. Pure ballet. . . . So I scored it like a ballet.*

Beginning with *The Producers* in 1968, director Mel Brooks and John Morris have established an extremely successful working relationship. The key to Morris' comic touch is sincerity—he plays it straight, but always goes for the theatrical. When he's working within a genre, such as the gothic horror film (*Young Frankenstein*), musical comedy (*The Producers*), or Western (*Blazing Saddles*), he remains very free within the genre's parameters. He has an excellent sense of drama, which he applies equally well to serious films like *The Elephant Man*.

Lyn Murray
Born December 6, 1909, Pacific Palisades, Calif.
Died May 20, 1989

1955	The Bridges at Toko-Ri
1955	To Catch a Thief
1963	Come Fly with Me

Stanley Myers
Born October 6, 1930, Birmingham, England

1968	No Way to Treat a Lady
1974	The Apprenticeship of Duddy Kravitz
1985	My Beautiful Laundrette
1992	Sarafina! (score)

Mario Nascimbene
Born November 28, 1913, Milan, Italy

1954	The Barefoot Contessa
1957	A Farewell to Arms
1967	One Million Years B.C.
1969	When Dinosaurs Ruled the Earth

Oliver Nelson
Born June 4, 1932, St. Louis, Mo.
Died October 28, 1975

1973	Last Tango in Paris

Ira Newborn

Born December 26, 1949, New York, N.Y.

1984	Sixteen Candles
1986	Ferris Bueller's Day Off
1987	Dragnet
1987	Planes, Trains and Automobiles
1988	The Naked Gun: From the Files of Police Squad
1991	The Naked Gun 2½: The Smell of Fear

Alfred Newman

Born March 17, 1901, New Haven, Conn.
Died February 17, 1970
Primary studio affiliation: Fox
First film: Street Scene (1931)

1935	Les Miserables
1937	The Prisoner of Zenda*
1939	Gunga Din
1939	Wuthering Heights*
1939	Beau Geste
1939	The Hunchback of Notre Dame*
1940	The Grapes of Wrath
1941	How Green Was My Valley*
1941	Belle Starr
1943	The Song of Bernadette**
1944	Keys of the Kingdom
1945	Leave Her to Heaven
1946	The Razor's Edge
1947	Gentleman's Agreement
1947	Captain from Castile*
1948	The Snake Pit*
1949	A Letter to Three Wives
1949	Prince of Foxes
1950	The Gunfighter
1950	All About Eve*
1951	David and Bathsheba
1953	Call Me Madam** (adapt.)
1953	The Robe
1954	The Egyptian (w/ Bernard Herrmann)
1955	Love Is a Many Splendored Thing**
1959	The Diary of Anne Frank
1963	How the West Was Won*
1965	The Greatest Story Ever Told*
1970	Airport*

Alfred Newman
Photo courtesy of Martha Newman Ragland

The thing that changed my life was conducting the New York Philharmonic while I was in my teens. That's when I knew I wanted to be a conductor; not a performer, not a composer—but a conductor. I was always happiest as a conductor . . . I never wanted to compose . . . You see, composing is a very lonely life . . . while on the other hand, conducting is gregarious . . . There is fellowship and teamwork and the excitement of creating a beautiful performance.

A child prodigy, he began working in vaudeville at 13. At 17 he began conducting Broadway shows.

He worked with Al Jolson, Fred and Adele Astaire, and conducted Gershwin and Rodgers and Hart shows.

1930	Brought to Hollywood by Irving Berlin for 3 months' work on *Reaching for the*

cont'd.

Moon. Never returned to New York. Became music director of United Artists.

1931	Conducted *City Lights* for Charles Chaplin.
1934	Became general music director for Goldwyn and Zanuck at 20th Century Films.
1939	Became general music director of 20th Century-Fox.
1960	Resigned as Fox music director, and continued to work on a freelance basis until his death in 1970.

Alfred Newman was extremely popular throughout his career, and was generally acknowledged to be the finest conductor in Hollywood. Always interested in young talent, he helped many outstanding talents early in their careers, including David Raksin in the forties and Jerry Goldsmith in the late fifties.

His close-knit family has been musically active in Hollywood throughout the years, and includes brothers Lionel and Emil, sons David and Thomas, and nephew Randy.

David Newman
Born March 11, 1954, Los Angeles, Calif.
First film: Critters (1986)

1987	Throw Momma from the Train
1989	The War of the Roses
1990	The Freshman
1991	Other People's Money
1992	The Mighty Ducks
1992	Hoffa
1993	Coneheads
1993	Undercover Blues

David Newman is Alfred Newman's son.

Lionel Newman
Born January 4, 1916, New Haven, Conn.
Died February 3, 1989

1954	There's No Business Like Show Business*
1960	Let's Make Love*
1969	Hello, Dolly!** (adapt.)
Song:	"Again"

Lionel Newman was Alfred Newman's brother.

Randy Newman
Born November 28, 1943, Los Angeles, Calif.
First film: Cold Turkey (1971)

1981	Ragtime*
1984	The Natural*
1989	Parenthood
1990	Avalon
1990	Awakenings
TV:	"Cop Rock"** (pilot for series)

Randy Newman is Alfred Newman's nephew.

Randy Newman
Photo: Carl Studna-Songtalk

Thomas Newman

Born October 20, 1955, Los Angeles, Calif.

First films: Reckless (1984)

Revenge of the Nerds (1984)

1985	Desperately Seeking Susan
1985	The Man with One Red Shoe
1986	Gung Ho
1990	Men Don't Leave
1991	Fried Green Tomatoes
1992	The Player
1992	Scent of a Woman

Thomas Newman is Alfred Newman's son.

Lennie Niehaus

Born June 1, 1929, St. Louis, Mo.

1985	Pale Rider
1986	Heartbreak Ridge
1988	Bird
1990	White Hunter, Black Heart
1992	Unforgiven
1993	A Perfect World

Jack Nitzsche

Born April 22, 1937, Chicago, Ill.

1976	One Flew over the Cuckoo's Nest*
1981	Cutter's Way
1982	An Officer and a Gentleman*
1985	Jewel of the Nile
1986	Stand by Me
1990	The Last of the Finest
1990	The Hot Spot

Eric Nordgren

Born February 13, 1913, Sireköping, Sweden

Died March 6, 1992

1957	The Seventh Seal
1957	Wild Strawberries
1958	The Magician
1960	The Virgin Spring
1971	The Emigrants

Alex North

Born December 4, 1910, Chester, Pa.

Died September 8, 1991

First film: Death of a Salesman (1951)

1951	A Streetcar Named Desire*
1952	Viva Zapata!*
1955	Unchained (incl. "Unchained Melody")
1955	The Rose Tattoo*
1956	I'll Cry Tomorrow
1956	The Rainmaker
1960	Spartacus*
1961	The Misfits
1964	Cleopatra*
1965	The Agony and the Ecstasy*
1966	Who's Afraid of Virginia Woolf?*
1968	The Shoes of the Fisherman*
1981	Dragonslayer*
1984	Under the Volcano*
1985	Prizzi's Honor
1987	Good Morning, Vietnam
TV:	Rich Man, Poor Man** (1976 ms)

Alex North
Photo: Gay Wallin

I write best when I can empathize. When you can't do that, then you have to fall back on technique and write programmatic music.

North's parents were Russian. After using scholarships to study piano at the Curtis Institute of Music, and composition at Juilliard, he earned his living as a telegraph operator. In 1934, when he heard the Russians were looking for engineers, he took the opportunity to go to Russia as a telegraphic engineer, hoping to reduce economic pressures while studying there. He didn't have the telegraphic skills they needed, but they allowed him to study at the Conservatory for almost two years. Hearing a Duke Ellington record of "Mood Indigo" made him homesick, and he returned to the States in 1936.

In New York, he composed extensively for ballet and theater, including the incidental music for Elia Kazan's production of *Death of a Salesman*. When Kazan filmed *A Streetcar Named Desire* in 1951, he insisted North write the music. His score's emphasis on the New Orleans jazz indigenous to the story was very effective, and totally unique at the time. It brought him instant recognition in Hollywood, including Oscar nominations for both *Streetcar* and *Salesman,* also released in 1951.

Spartacus (1960) is one of the most well-known films he scored, its high profile assisted by the release in 1991 of a fully restored version. Like Rózsa, North enjoyed researching the music of the period, but he didn't try to write Roman-sounding music. "I decided here to conjure up the atmosphere of pre-Christian Rome . . . in terms of my own contemporary, modern style—simply because the theme of *Spartacus,* the struggle for freedom and human dignity, is every bit as relevant in today's world as it was then."

John Huston, who directed a number of films North scored, including *Prizzi's Honor,* said, "Alex is a past master at speaking to the unconscious. It is his genius to convey an emotion to the audience with its hardly being aware of the existence of a score."

Michael Nyman
Born March 23, 1944, London, England
1989   The Cook, the Thief, His Wife and
            Her Lover
1993   The Piano

Michael Oldfield
Born May 15, 1953
1984   The Killing Fields

Van Dyke Parks
Born January 3, 1943, Hattiesburg, Miss.
1988   Casual Sex?
1990   The Two Jakes

Don Peake
Born June 7, 1940, Los Angeles, Calif.
1991   The People Under the Stairs

Edward Plumb
Born June 6, 1907, Streator, Ill.
Died April 19, 1958
1942   Bambi* (w/ Frank Churchill)
1943   Saludos Amigos* (w/ Paul J. Smith)
1944   The Three Caballeros* (w/ Paul J. Smith)

Basil Poledouris
Born August 21, 1945, Kansas City, Mo.
First Film: Extreme Close-up (1973)
1980   The Blue Lagoon
1982   Conan the Barbarian
1987   RoboCop
1990   The Hunt for Red October
1991   White Fang
1992   Wind
1993   RoboCop 3
1993   Free Willy
TV: Lonesome Dove** (1989 ms)

Rachel Portman
Born December 11, 1960, Haslemere, England
1991   Life Is Sweet
1992   Used People
1993   Benny & Joon
1993   Ethan Frome
1993   The Joy Luck Club

Mike Post
September 29, 1944, Los Angeles, Calif.
1983   Running Brave
1984   Rhinestone (adapt.)

TV: "The Rockford Files" (theme, series)
         "Hill Street Blues" (theme, series)
         "L.A. Law" (theme, series)

Zbigniew Preisner
1991   At Play in the Fields of the Lord
1991   Europa, Europa
1992   Damage
1993   The Secret Garden

André Previn
Born April 6, 1929, Berlin, Germany
First Films: The Sun Comes Up (1949)
             Challenge to Lassie (1949)
1953   Kiss Me Kate* (m.d.)
1955   Bad Day at Black Rock
1957   Silk Stockings (m.d.)
1958   Gigi**
1959   Porgy and Bess** (m.d.)
1960   Elmer Gantry*
1962   The Four Horsemen of the Apocalypse
1964   My Fair Lady** (m.d.)
1966   The Fortune Cookie
Book: *No Minor Chords*

Charles Previn
Born January 11, 1888, Brooklyn, N.Y.
Died September 22, 1973
1936   My Man Godfrey
1941   Buck Privates* (adapt.)

Sergei Prokofiev
Born April 23, 1891, Sontsovka, Russia
Died March 5, 1953
1934   Lieutenant Kijé
1938   Alexander Nevsky
1945   Ivan the Terrible, Part I
1946   Ivan the Terrible, Part II

Prokofiev's *Alexander Nevsky* is often cited as dynamic concert-quality film music. His style is frequently used as a role model.

David Raksin
Born August 4, 1912, Philadelphia, Pa.
Primary studio affiliation: Fox (1940-1946)

First films: Modern Times (1936, arr. for
             Charlie Chaplin)
             Midnight Court (1937)
1944   Laura
1947   Forever Amber*
1947   The Secret Life of Walter Mitty
1948   Force of Evil
1952   The Bad and the Beautiful
1952   Carrie
1952   Pat and Mike

David Raksin

According to my friends, I talked about becoming a Hollywood composer when I was a boy. . . . My father became a conductor for silent films. I would go to films and hear the film scores, and some of them affected me very much, they were so brilliant. I always said, "If you can do that, I want to be there."

1958	Separate Tables
1959	Al Capone
1962	Two Weeks in Another Town
1964	Invitation to a Gunfighter
1966	The Redeemer
1968	Will Penny

"Before I came out to Hollywood, I played saxophone and clarinet, and arranged a lot and sang with the band. I've always had a certain improvisatory ability, you know. It's very important to have that freedom. And also, I was greatly affected by different kinds of music. . . . I wrote a lot of songs, and I wrote arrangements too. I was self-taught."

Raksin arrived in Hollywood in 1935 at the age of twenty-three, to work with Charlie Chaplin on Chaplin's music for *Modern Times*. Soon fired by Chaplin for being too argumentative, he was rehired at the urging of Alfred Newman, and they came to an understanding—Raksin would continue to be honest with Chaplin in an effort to create the best score possible. From 1936 to 1944 he arranged, orchestrated, and co-composed for countless projects (Newman had put him under contract to Fox in 1940). Then he got his big break—*Laura*—which became an enormous success. With words by Johnny Mercer, the title song quickly became a hit and then a standard.

Raksin, like Friedhofer and North, had a fresh musical approach, preferring the more American sounds to the traditional European style largely favored by Steiner and his colleagues. His score for *The Bad and the Beautiful,* with its uniquely angular yet flowing main theme, is another classic. He left Fox in 1946, preferring to freelance. While continuing to compose, he also has taught film scoring at USC and UCLA since the mid-fifties.

"David Raksin is another West Coast musician whose knowledge is encyclopedic," says André Previn. " . . . His sense of orchestral color was always unbeatable, his harmonic twists very clearly his own, and he thought nothing of setting himself some problems to make studio composing a little livelier. . . ."

Robert O. Ragland
Born July 3, 1931, Chicago, Ill.

1975	Seven Alone
1983	10 to Midnight
1989	Messenger of Death

J.A.C. Redford
Born July 14, 1953, Los Angeles, Calif.

1985	Trip to Bountiful
1986	Extremities
1988	Oliver & Company (score)
1992	Newsies (score)

Graeme Revell
Born October 23, 1955, Aukland, New Zealand

1989	Dead Calm
1992	The Hand That Rocks the Cradle
1993	Body of Evidence
1993	Hard Target

Nelson Riddle
Born June 1, 1921, Hackensack, N.J.
Died October 6, 1985

1959	A Hole in the Head
1960	Can-Can* (adapt.)
1967	How to Suceed in Business Without Really Trying (adapt.)
1969	Paint Your Wagon* (adapt.)
1974	The Great Gatsby** (adapt.)

Laurin Rinder
Born April 3, 1943, Los Angeles, Calif.

1981	Enter the Ninja (w/ W. Michael Lewis)
1984	Ninja III—The Domination (w/ Lewis)

Richard Robbins
Born December 4, 1940, South Weymouth, Mass.

1985	A Room with a View
1990	Mr. & Mrs. Bridge
1992	Howard's End
1993	The Remains of the Day

J. Peter Robinson
Born September 16, 1945, Fulmer, England

1988	Cocktail
1992	Encino Man
1992	Wayne's World—The Movie

Heinz Roemheld

Born May 1, 1901, Milwaukee, Wis.
Died February 11, 1985

1933	The Invisible Man
1934	The Black Cat
1941	The Strawberry Blonde*
1942	Yankee Doodle Dandy** (adapt.)
1944	Shine On, Harvest Moon
1948	The Fuller Brush Man
1950	The Good Humor Man
1952	Ruby Gentry

Alain Romans

Born 1907, Paris, France

1953	Mr. Hulot's Holiday
1956	My Uncle, Mr. Hulot

Leonard Rosenman

Born September 7, 1924, Brooklyn, N.Y.
First Film: East of Eden (1955)

1955	The Cobweb
1955	Rebel Without a Cause
1959	Pork Chop Hill
1960	The Rise and Fall of Legs Diamond
1966	Fantastic Voyage
1970	A Man Called Horse
1970	Beneath the Planet of the Apes
1975	Barry Lyndon** (adapt.)
1976	Birch Interval
1976	Bound for Glory** (adapt.)
1978	Lord of the Rings
1983	Cross Creek*
1986	Star Trek IV: The Voyage Home*
1990	RoboCop 2
TV:	Sybil (1976)
	Friendly Fire** (1979)

I think Mozart and Beethoven would have given their eyeteeth to write for films, because of the opportunity it gives to write something and hear it played the next day by 50 or 60 crack musicians. These are the optimum conditions in which to study orchestration, and to try out musical ideas.

Rosenman scored his first film after the star insisted he get the assignment. James Dean had been his piano student, and recommended him to director Elia Kazan. Rosenman quickly established himself in Hollywood with Dean's *East of Eden* and *Rebel Without a Cause*. A student of Ernst Bloch and Arnold Schoenberg, he has always balanced his career in Hollywood with that in the concert hall. His interest in using twentieth-century techniques helped open filmmakers' ears to the potential of more modern, dissonant musical approaches.

Laurence Rosenthal

Born November 4, 1926, Detroit, Mich.
First film: Yellowneck (1955)

1961	A Raisin in the Sun
1962	The Miracle Worker
1964	Becket*
1972	Man of La Mancha* (adapt.)
1975	Rooster Cogburn
1976	The Return of a Man Called Horse
1977	The Island of Dr. Moreau
1978	Who'll Stop the Rain
1981	Clash of the Titans
1983	Heart Like a Wheel
TV:	"Fantasy Island" (series theme)
	Who Will Love My Children?* (1983)
	Peter the Great** (1986 ms)
	Anastasia: The Mystery of Anna** (1987 ms)

I really feel that filmmaking is a collaborative effort. It's the very nature of film, and no composer can come in and say, "Look boys, just leave it to me—I know what this picture needs." Rapport and a genuine exchange between the collaborators on the film is essential.

Rosenthal started out composing incidental music for theatrical productions like *Raisin in the Sun, The Miracle Worker,* and *Becket.* In 1962, he scored Arthur Penn's film version of *The Miracle Worker.* The story of Helen Keller (who was blind, deaf, and mute) offered him a perfect vehicle in which music becomes another voice, and his score is a classic. His score for *The Return of a Man Called Horse* makes outstanding use of native American musical materials. He has become one of the foremost composers of television long forms, composing large-scale epic scores for miniseries including the eight-hour *Peter the Great* and *Mussolini: The Untold Story* (1985), and sensitive music for two-hour telefilms like *Who Will Love My Children?*

Nino Rota

Born December 3, 1911, Milan, Italy
Died April 10, 1979

1951	Anna
1954	La Strada
1956	War and Peace
1957	Fortunella
1960	La Dolce Vita
1962	Boccaccio '70
1963	8 1/2
1963	The Leopard
1965	Juliet of the Spirits
1968	Romeo and Juliet
1970	Fellini Satyricon
1971	The Clowns
1971	Waterloo
1972	Fellini's Roma
1972	The Godfather
1974	The Godfather, Part II* (w/ Carmine Coppola)
1978	Death on the Nile

Nino Rota
Photo courtesy of Nina Rota

Like Morricone, Nino Rota is another favorite of composers, especially his scores for the Fellini films, including *8 1/2, La Dolce Vita,* and *Juliet of the Spirits*. His music has an offbeat quality, sometimes with familiar musical forms treated in a personal, unconventional manner. He could be extremely lyrical, so much so that his themes for *Romeo and Juliet* and *The Godfather* became top-selling records internationally.

Bruce Rowland

Born May 9, 1942, Melbourne, Australia

1982	The Man from Snowy River
1983	Phar Lap
1988	Return to Snowy River

Miklós Rózsa

Born April 18, 1907, Budapest, Hungary
Primary studio affiliation: MGM (1949-1962)
First film: Knight Without Armour (1937)

1939	The Four Feathers
1940	The Thief of Bagdad*
1942	Jungle Book*
1944	Double Indemnity*
1945	A Song to Remember* (adapt.)
1945	The Lost Weekend*
1945	Spellbound**
1946	The Killers*
1947	The Red House
1947	A Double Life**
1949	Madame Bovary
1949	Adam's Rib
1951	Quo Vadis*
1952	Ivanhoe*
1953	Julius Caesar*
1956	Lust for Life
1959	Ben-Hur**
1961	El Cid*
1977	Providence
1979	Time After Time
1982	Dead Men Don't Wear Plaid

Autobiography: *Double Life*

Miklós Rózsa
Photo courtesy of Marc Wanamaker/ Bison Archives

As a young man, the satisfaction of having an income from music was the greatest joy I have ever experienced. However much I may modify my style in order to write effectively for films, the music of Hungary is stamped indelibly one way or another on virtually every bar I have ever put on paper.

Rózsa could read music before words. He studied Hungarian folk music, which became a lifelong passion.

1928	Signed a contract with music publishers Breitkopf and Härtel for his symphonic and chamber music.
1931	To Paris, where he achieved concert success.
1936	To London; Jacques Feyder heard his *Ballet Hungaria,* and asked him to score *Knight Without Armour.*

1940	To Hollywood to score *Thief of Bagdad* for Alexander Korda. Began scoring films needing exotic music.
1942	Excerpts from *Jungle Book* released as a 78 rpm album on RCA Victor—the first of its kind in the U.S.
1943	Contract with Paramount Studios, scoring *Double Indemnity* and *The Lost Weekend* while at that studio.
1945	Used theremin in *The Lost Weekend* and *Spellbound;* became known as a specialist in psychological drama.
	Appointed professor of film music at the University of Southern California; continued until 1965.
1946	Began series of hard-hitting, realistic films, starting with *The Killers*—his third film specialty.
1949	Signed long-term contract with MGM.
1951	With the release of *Quo Vadis,* he became known as a specialist in historical epics.
1962	MGM contract terminated; scored only four films from 1962–1970, and eight more through *Dead Men Don't Wear Plaid* (1982), his last film score.

Miklós Rózsa's film scores are a blend of intellect and heart. His ground-breaking psychological scores get inside the minds of the characters on the screens. After *The Red House,* he decided not to feature the theremin again, fearing he would become associated too closely with that sound: "I didn't want it to be the equivalent of Dorothy Lamour's sarong."

He was very happy to do the intense research he felt his epic films required. "This was the beginning of a long period of really interesting pictures which I feel brought out the best in me because I enjoyed my work so much. For that reason alone I am grateful to MGM."

Arthur B. Rubinstein
Born March 31, 1938, New York, N.Y.

1983	Blue Thunder
1983	WarGames

1985	Lost in America
1991	The Hard Way
1991	Another Stakeout

Steve Rucker
June 27, 1949, Los Angeles, Calif.

1987	And God Created Woman (w/ Tom Chase)
1988	976-Evil (w/ Tom Chase)
1992	Little Nemo (w/ Tom Chase)

William Russo
Born June 25, 1928, Chicago, Ill.

| 1985 | The Cosmic Eye |

Craig Safan
Born December 17, 1948, Los Angeles, Calif.

1984	The Last Starfighter
1985	Remo Williams: The Adventure Begins
1988	Stand and Deliver
1993	Money for Nothing

Ryuichi Sakamoto
Born January 17, 1952, Tokyo, Japan

| 1983 | Merry Christmas, Mr. Lawrence |
| 1987 | The Last Emperor** (w/ David Byrne and Cong Su) |

Hans J. Salter
Born January 14, 1896, Vienna, Austria

1942	The Ghost of Frankenstein
1944	Christmas Holiday
1945	Scarlet Street
1946	Magnificent Doll
1952	Bend of the River
1955	Wichita
1961	Bedtime Story
1966	Beau Geste

Philippe Sarde
Born June 21, 1945, Neuilly-sur-Seine, France

| 1982 | Quest for Fire |
| 1989 | The Bear |

Hans J. Salter
Photo courtesy of Tony Thomas

Masaru Sato
Born March 1, 1939, Tokyo, Japan

1957	The Lower Depths
1957	Throne of Blood
1961	Yojimbo
1962	Sanjuro
1965	Red Beard
1968	Godzilla vs. the Sea Monster

Paul Sawtell
Born February 3, 1906, Poland
Died August 1, 1970

1947	Dick Tracy Meets Gruesome
1958	The Fly (w/ Bert A. Shefter)
1959	A Dog of Flanders (w/ Shefter)
1961	Voyage to the Bottom of the Sea (w/ Shefter)

Walter Scharf

Born August 1, 1910, New York, N.Y.

1944	The Fighting Seabees*
1952	Hans Christian Andersen
1955	Artists and Models
1960	The Bellboy
1961	Pocketful of Miracles
1963	The Nutty Professor
1968	Funny Girl* (adapt.)
1969	If It's Tuesday, This Must Be Belgium
1972	Ben
1973	Walking Tall

Books: *Composed and Conducted by Walter Scharf*
The History of Film Scoring

Lalo Schifrin

Born June 21, 1932, Buenos Aires, Argentina
First film: Rhino! (1964)

1965	The Cincinnati Kid
1967	Cool Hand Luke*
1968	Bullitt
1971	THX-1138
1972	Dirty Harry
1973	Magnum Force
1975	The Four Musketeers
1979	The Amityville Horror*
1980	The Competition*
1983	Sudden Impact
1985	The Mean Season
1988	The Dead Pool
1993	The Beverly Hillbillies
TV:	"Mission: Impossible" (series themes)

Lalo Schifrin began as a jazz pianist/arranger, playing with Dizzy Gillespie's big band in the early sixties. His work for films and television has frequently been jazz-flavored, and his use of rhythmic jazz elements and percussion moving along under atonal-sounding winds and strings has been outstanding. He scored four of Clint Eastwood's Dirty Harry series, starting with the first one, *Dirty Harry.*

John Scott

Born November 1, 1930, Bristol, England

1984	Greystoke: The Legend of Tarzan
1986	The Whistle Blower
1988	The Deceivers

| 1988 | Shoot to Kill |
| 1989 | Winter People |

Tom Scott

Born May 19, 1948, Hollywood, Calif.

| 1980 | Stir Crazy |
| 1985 | The Sure Thing |

Marc Shaiman

Born October 22, 1959, Newark, N.J.

1989	When Harry Met Sally . . . (adapt.)
1990	Misery
1991	City Slickers
1991	The Addams Family
1992	Sister Act
1992	A Few Good Men
1993	Sleepless in Seattle
1993	Heart and Souls

Ravi Shankar

Born April 7, 1920, Benares, India

1956	Pather Panchali
1968	Charly
1982	Gandhi* (w/ George Fenton)

Bert A. Shefter

Born May 15, 1904, Poltava, Russia

1958	The Fly (w/ Paul Sawtell)
1959	A Dog of Flanders (w/ Sawtell)
1960	Five Guns to Tombstone (w/ Sawtell)
1961	Voyage to the Bottom of the Sea (w/ Sawtell)

Nathaniel Shilkret

Born December 25, 1895, New York, N.Y.
Died February 18, 1982

1936	Mary of Scotland
1936	Winterset
1937	The Toast of New York
1943	Air Raid Wardens

David Shire

Born July 3, 1937, Buffalo, N.Y.
First film: Skin Game (1971)

| 1974 | The Conversation |
| 1974 | The Taking of Pelham 1-2-3 |

1975	The Fortune (adapt.)		1984	Romancing the Stone
1975	The Hindenburg		1985	Back to the Future
1975	Farewell, My Lovely		1986	The Clan of the Cave Bear
1976	All the President's Men		1987	Outrageous Fortune
1977	Saturday Night Fever (adapt./add.)		1988	Who Framed Roger Rabbit
1979	Norma Rae (**Song)		1988	My Stepmother Is an Alien
1982	The World According to Garp		1989	Back to the Future Part II
1983	Max Dugan Returns		1990	Back to the Future Part III
1985	Return to Oz		1992	The Bodyguard
1986	Short Circuit		1993	Super Mario Bros.
1986	'night, Mother			
TV:	Promise**(1986)			
Theater:	"Baby" (1983)			

Shire's scores reflect an excellent command of a variety of musical materials. The big-band atonal jazz is exciting in *The Taking of Pelham 1-2-3*. His large-scale orchestral score for *Return to Oz* is notable, and he can have a light touch, as in the charming *Short Circuit* and the understated *All the President's Men* and *'night Mother*.

Howard Shore
Born October 18, 1946, Toronto, Canada

1984	Places in the Heart
1985	After Hours
1986	The Fly
1988	Big
1988	Dead Ringers
1991	The Silence of the Lambs
1992	Single White Female
1993	Philadelphia
1993	M. Butterfly
1993	Mrs. Doubtfire

Louis Silvers
Born September 6, 1889, New York, N.Y.
Died March 26, 1954

1920	Way Down East (co-comp./compiler)
1927	The Jazz Singer
1938	In Old Chicago* 1938
1939	Swanee River* (adapt.)
Song:	"April Showers"

Alan Silvestri
Born March 26, 1950, New York, N.Y.
First film: The Amazing Dobermans (1976)

Frank Skinner
Born December 31, 1898, Meredosia, Ill.
Died October 8, 1968

1939	Son of Frankenstein
1939	Destry Rides Again
1940	The Bank Dick
1942	Saboteur
1945	The Suspect
1947	The Egg and I
1950	Harvey
1954	Magnificent Obsession
1957	Man of a Thousand Faces
1964	Captain Newman, M. D.
1966	The Appaloosa
Book:	*Underscore*

Michael Small
Born May 30, 1939, New York, N.Y.
First film: Out of It (1969)

1971	Klute
1974	The Parallax View
1976	Marathon Man
1978	Comes a Horseman
1979	Going in Style
1981	The Postman Always Rings Twice
1983	The Star Chamber
1986	Brighton Beach Memoirs
1990	Mountains of the Moon

Paul J. Smith
Born October 30, 1906, Calumet, Mich.
Died January 25, 1985

1938	Snow White and the Seven Dwarfs*
	(w/ Frank Churchill and Leigh Harline)
1940	Pinocchio** (w/ Leigh Harline)

1943	Saludos Amigos* (w/ Edward Plumb)
1944	The Three Caballeros* (w/ Edward Plumb)
1950	Cinderella* (w/ Oliver Wallace)
1954	20,000 Leagues Under the Sea
1959	The Shaggy Dog

David Snell
Born September 10, 1897, Milwaukee, Wis.
Died March 27, 1967

1938	Love Finds Andy Hardy
1941	Ringside Maisie
1948	A Southern Yankee

Mark Snow
Born August 26, 1946, Brooklyn, N.Y.

1988	Ernest Saves Christmas
1993	High Risk

Tom Snow
Born October 25, 1947, Princeton, N.J.

1984	Footloose (w/ Miles Goodman; adapt)

Stephen Sondheim
Born March 22, 1930, New York, N.Y.

1974	Stavisky

Theatre: "A Little Night Music" adapted for film in
   1978

Herman Stein
Born August 19, 1915, Philadelphia, Pa.
Died October 27, 1985

1953	It Came from Outer Space (w/ Henry Mancini and Irving Gertz)
1954	Creature from the Black Lagoon (co-comp.)
1957	The Incredible Shrinking Man (w/ Gertz and Salter)

Ronald Stein
Born April 12, 1930, St. Louis, Mo.
Died August 15, 1988

1956	The Day the World Ended
1958	Attack of the 50 Foot Woman
1963	Dementia 13
1969	The Rain People

Max Steiner
Born May 10, 1888, Vienna, Austria
Died December 28, 1971
Primary studio affiliation: Warner Bros.
First film: Cimarron (1930)

1933	King Kong
1934	Of Human Bondage
1934	The Gay Divorcee (and other RKO musicals until 1937)
1935	The Informer**
1936	The Charge of the Light Brigade
1937	The Life of Emile Zola*
1938	Jezebel*
1939	Dodge City

Max Steiner
Photo courtesy of Albert Bender

*There is a tired old bromide in this business to the
effect that a good film score is one you don't hear.
What good is it if you don't notice it?*

1939	Dark Victory*
1939	Gone with the Wind*
1940	Dr. Ehrlich's Magic Bullet
1940	The Letter*
1942	They Died with Their Boots On*
1942	Now, Voyager**
1943	Casablanca*
1944	Since You Went Away**
1945	Rhapsody in Blue* (adapt.)
1946	The Big Sleep
1946	Night and Day* (adapt.)
1948	Key Largo
1948	Johnny Belinda*
1949	Adventures of Don Juan
1950	The Flame and the Arrow*
1952	The Miracle of Our Lady of Fatima*
1954	The Caine Mutiny*
1956	Helen of Troy
1959	A Summer Place
1962	Rome Adventure

A precocious child, Steiner at 14 wrote an operetta that ran a year. He conducted in London from 1906 to 1914.

1914	To New York in 1914 "with 32 dollars in my pocket."
1915	Arr/Orch/Cond'd for Broadway shows, including shows by Victor Herbert, Gershwin, and Kern.
1929	To Hollywood to conduct Rio Rita, arriving on Christmas day. Became head of RKO music department in 1930.
1933	Composed landmark score for King Kong. The large orchestra reportedly cost $50,000.
1936	Worked with David O. Selznick for a year.
1937	Signed with Warner Bros., where he stayed 16 years.
1953	Left Warners to freelance. Scored his last film in 1964.
	Steiner had serious vision problems in his later years.

Using a direct emotional approach, Steiner established the style of scoring dramatic films by accenting the action, hitting major dramatic points and shifts of emphasis. He used the leitmotiv technique—a theme or motif for each character and situation—which had been developed by Wagner for his dramatic operas. He scored 18 films starring Bette Davis, and 15 starring Errol Flynn.

"Max had a certain flair for dramatic characterization," Hugo Friedhofer said, "and it was big and important-sounding and he had a feeling for various kinds of exotic local color and whatnot as in the score for *King Kong*. . . . Jack Warner was really hooked on Max. . . . At one time it created a great deal of dissension amongst the music staff. The boys were all called in and a couple of Steiner's films were run for them and Leo Forbstein announced, 'Now, fellows, Jack Warner wants you to write as close to what Max is doing as you possibly can.'"

Leith Stevens
Born September 13, 1909, Mount Moriah, Mo.
Died July 23, 1970

1947	Night Song
1950	Destination Moon
1951	When Worlds Collide
1954	The Wild One
1959	The Five Pennies*
1967	Chuka

Herbert Stothart
Born September 11, 1885, Milwaukee, Wis.
Died February 1, 1949

1935	Naughty Marietta (adapt.)
1935	Mutiny on the Bounty*
1935	A Night at the Opera
1935	A Tale of Two Cities
1936	San Francisco
1937	The Good Earth
1939	The Wizard of Oz**
1942	Mrs. Miniver
1944	Madame Curie*
1944	The White Cliffs of Dover
1945	Thirty Seconds over Tokyo
1945	National Velvet
1945	They Were Expendable
Song:	"I Wanna Be Loved by You"

Taj Mahal [Henry Saint Clair Fredericks]
Born May 17, 1942, New York, N.Y.
1972   Sounder
1976   Sounder, Part 2

Toru Takemitsu
Born October 8, 1930, Japan
1964   Woman of the Dunes
1970   Dodes'Ka'Den
1985   Ran
1993   Rising Sun

Tangerine Dream
1981   Thief
1983   Risky Business

Tangerine Dream is a group from Germany that strongly influenced the use of electronic music in films when director Michael Mann's *Thief* was released with their music in 1981.

Mikis Theodorakis
Born July 29, 1926, Chois, Greece
1964   Zorba the Greek
1969   Z
1973   Serpico

Virgil Thomson
Born November 25, 1896, Kansas City, Mo.
Died September 30, 1989
1936   The Plow That Broke the Plains
1937   The River
1948   Louisiana Story
1958   The Goddess

Ken Thorne
Born January 26, 1924, Norfolk, England
1966   A Funny Thing Happened on the Way
          to the Forum** (adapt.)
1981   Superman II (adapt.)
1983   Superman III (adapt.)

Dimitri Tiomkin
Born May 10, 1894, St. Petersburg, Russia
Died November 11, 1979
First films: The Rogue Song (1930, ballet)
          Resurrection (1931, 1st score)
          Alice in Wonderland (1933)

1937   Lost Horizon*
1939   Mr. Smith Goes to Washington*
1941   Meet John Doe
1942   The Moon and Sixpence*
1943   Shadow of a Doubt
1946   Duel in the Sun
1948   Red River
1949   Champion*
1951   The Thing
1951   Strangers on a Train
1952   High Noon**
1952   The Big Sky

Dimitri Tiomkin
Photo courtesy of David Kraft

I'm a classicist by nature and if you examine my scores you will find fugues, rondos, and passacaglias. . . . I'm not in sympathy with the harsh, atonal music of today, it's enough to lacerate your ears. Perhaps that is why I have done well in films—it was music for the masses.

1954   Dial M for Murder
1954   The High and the Mighty**
1956   Giant*
1957   Gunfight at the O.K. Corral
1958   The Old Man and the Sea**
1959   Rio Bravo
1960   The Alamo*
1961   The Guns of Navarone*
1963   55 Days at Peking*
1964   The Fall of the Roman Empire*
1967   The War Wagon
Autobiography: *Please Don't Hate Me* (with
    Prosper Buranelli)

First worked as pianist for silent movies in St. Petersburg. A concert pianist, he moved to Berlin for three years, then to Paris as a duo-piano team with Michael Kariton. In 1925 they were booked for six months on the vaudeville circuit in the United States, making $1,000 a week. He married ballerina-choreographer Albertina Rasch. In 1928 he performed the European premiere of Gershwin's Concerto in F.

1929   To Hollywood, where Albertina was creating short ballets for films. Given the nickname "Dimi."
1937   His first big break was scoring Frank Capra's *Lost Horizon*. Then a broken arm ended his concert career.
1952   His unusual use of the title song for *High Noon* brought him great recognition, and started a trend.
1955   Gave famous acceptance speech to Academy upon receiving the Oscar, thanking many classical composers.
1968   When Albertina died, he moved to London, and remarried. The final film he scored, *Great Catherine*, was released in 1968.

Tiomkin was an outstanding concert pianist before coming to Hollywood. Without question the most flamboyant of all film composers, he believed in promotion and marketing, and for years was the highest paid composer in town. He had a commercial touch, and could write soft scores as well as his characteristically bombastic ones.

A 1960 newspaper columnist said he had a Russian accent that made Khrushchev sound like a native of Kansas. "They say I give a special flavor to a conference," Tiomkin wrote, "and no doubt I did. It went like this: 'Okay, good score we will have. I must tell the truth. Music will be good. I write fine orchestration for picture.'"

Jonathan Tunick
Born April 19, 1938, New York, N.Y.
1978   A Little Night Music** (adapt.)
1981   Endless Love
Has orchestrated Broadway shows, incl. "Sweeney Todd," "A Chorus Line," "A Little Night Music," and "Company."

Vangelis (Papathanassiou)
Born 1944, Athens, Greece
1981   Chariots of Fire**
1982   Blade Runner
1982   Missing
1984   Antarctica
1992   1492: Conquest of Paradise

Ralph Vaughan Williams
Born October 12, 1872, Down Ampney, England
Died August 26, 1958
1941   The Invaders (49th Parallel in U.K.)
1948   Scott of the Antarctic

Shirley Walker
Born April 10, 1945, Napa, Calif.
1979   The Black Stallion (w/ Carmine Coppola)
1990   Chicago Joe and the Showgirl (w/ Hans Zimmer)
1992   Memoirs of an Invisible Man
1992   Batman: Mask of the Phantasm

Bennie Wallace
Born November 18, 1946, Chattanooga, Tenn.
1989   Blaze
1992   White Men Can't Jump

Oliver Wallace
Born August 6, 1887, England
Died September 16, 1963
         Dumbo** (w/ Frank Churchill)

1950   Cinderella* (w/ Paul J. Smith)
1953   Peter Pan
1955   Lady and the Tramp
1957   Old Yeller

Sir William Walton
Born March 29, 1902, Oldham, Lancashire, England
Died March 8, 1983
1936   As You Like It
1941   Major Barbara
1945   Henry V*
1948   Hamlet*
1956   Richard III

Composers and film music aficionados often cite *Henry V* and *Hamlet* as outstanding and enduring film scores, both in the films and as independent concert pieces.

Wang Chung
1985   To Live and Die in L.A.
Wang Chung is a rock group.

Edward Ward
Born April 2, 1896, St. Louis, Mo.
Died September 26, 1971
1934   Great Expectations
1938   The Shopworn Angel
1941   Cheers for Miss Bishop
1943   Phantom of the Opera*
1948   The Babe Ruth Story
Song: "Who Takes Care of the Caretaker's
         Daughter?"

Franz Waxman
Born December 24, 1906, Königshutte, Germany
Died February 24, 1967
Primary studio affiliations: MGM/Warner Bros.
First film (other German films prior): Liliom (1934,
    French, co-comp.)
1935   Bride of Frankenstein
1937   Captains Courageous
1940   Rebecca*
1941   Dr. Jekyll and Mr. Hyde*
1941   Suspicion*

1942   Woman of the Year
1943   Air Force
1944   Mr. Skeffington
1945   Objective, Burma!*
1945   God Is My Co-Pilot
1945   To Have and Have Not
1946   Humoresque*
1947   The Two Mrs. Carrolls
1948   Sorry, Wrong Number
1950   Sunset Boulevard**
1951   A Place in the Sun**
1953   Botany Bay
1954   Prince Valiant
1954   The Silver Chalice*
1955   Mister Roberts
1957   The Spirit of St. Louis
1957   Peyton Place
1959   The Nun's Story*
1962   Taras Bulba*

Franz Waxman
Photo courtesy of John Waxman

The medium of film music is, under ideal conditions, the medium in which opportunity and outlet to a wide audience exist as never before. It is an art which has developed quickly, and it continues to develop. We need composers, producers, and critics who realize all this. There is always room for fresh musical ideas in writing for the screen.

Played piano in nightclubs as a teenager, then in a dance band, where he met composer Frederick Hollander.

Through Hollander, he met conductor Bruno Walter, who helped with his further education. In 1930, Hollander introduced him to producer Erich Pommer, and he was asked to arrange and orchestrate Hollander's score for *The Blue Angel*.

1934	Scored the French film *Liliom*. When he was accosted and beaten on the streets of Berlin, he moved to Paris with his bride. Then moved to Hollywood to be music director of Pommer's *Music in the Air,* with a Jerome Kern score.
1935	His score for *Bride of Frankenstein* was extraordinary for its time, and a significant role model. As a result of this score, he became music director for Universal.
1937	Given a seven-year contract at MGM.
1940	Loaned-out to David O. Selznick for *Rebecca,* directed by Hitchcock; this was a major break.
1943	Moved to Warner Bros. for five years (where Korngold and Steiner were on contract).
1947	Began to freelance, to be more selective. That same year he founded the Los Angeles Music Festival, which contributed an enormous vitality to the city's musical life. He conducted the concerts, giving Los Angeles premieres of outstanding contemporary works, and bringing in distinguished guest artists.
1966	His last film, *Lost Command,* was released.

Waxman had a fine blend of power and sensitive orchestration. He could write melodically, but as Bill Stinson (who worked with him many times as his music editor), said, "He had a sense of dramatics with his scoring. Now, when Franz would score a picture, he would put the dialogue in his ear and he would conduct to dialogue just to get the nuances in music that he needed."

Roy Webb

Born October 3, 1888, New York, N.Y.
Died December 10, 1982

First film (many prior with no credit): Alice Adams (1935)

1938	Bringing Up Baby
1940	Abe Lincoln in Illinois
1942	Cat People
1943	The Leopard Man
1944	The Master Race
1944	Murder, My Sweet
1944	The Seventh Cross
1945	The Enchanted Cottage*
1945	Back to Bataan
1945	Dick Tracy
1945	The Spiral Staircase
1945	The Body Snatcher
1946	Notorious
1947	Crossfire
1948	Blood on the Moon
1948	I Remember Mama
1949	Mighty Joe Young
1952	The Lusty Men
1955	Blood Alley
1955	Marty
1958	Teacher's Pet (last film)

I think you can hurt a motion picture a great deal by making audiences conscious of the music, unless you want them to be aware of it for a particular reason.

In 1914, Webb became one of the charter members of ASCAP, along with Victor Herbert and John Phillip Sousa, among others. Webb worked as a songwriter and Broadway orchestrator during the twenties in New York City. He went out to Hollywood briefly in 1929 to orchestrate *Rio Rita* for Max Steiner, and returned in 1933 as Steiner's assistant at RKO. He contributed scores to many of Val Lewton's horror films, including *Cat People, I Walked with a Zombie,* and *The Leopard Man.* He scored a broad range of genres throughout his career.

John Williams

Born February 8, 1932, Long Island, N.Y.

First films: Daddy-'O' (1959)
    I Passed for White (1960)

1966	How to Steal a Million

1967   A Guide for the Married Man
1967   Valley of the Dolls* (adapt.)
1969   The Reivers*
1971   Fiddler on the Roof** (adapt.)
1972   The Poseidon Adventure*
1972   Images*
1973   The Paper Chase
1974   The Towering Inferno*
1975   Jaws**
1977   Star Wars**
1977   Close Encounters of the Third Kind*
1978   Superman*
1979   Dracula
1980   The Empire Strikes Back*
1981   Raiders of the Lost Ark*
1982   E.T. The Extra-Terrestrial**
1983   Return of the Jedi*
1984   Indiana Jones and the Temple of Doom*
1984   The River*
1986   Spacecamp
1987   The Witches of Eastwick*
1987   Empire of the Sun*
1988   The Accidental Tourist*
1989   Indiana Jones and the Last Crusade*
1989   Born on the Fourth of July*
1990   Presumed Innocent
1990   Home Alone
1991   JFK*
1991   Hook
1992   Home Alone 2: Lost in New York
1993   Jurassic Park
1993   Schindler's List
TV: Jane Eyre** (1971)

Having considered a career as concert pianist, Williams started out in Hollywood as a studio pianist, and then composer. Through the sixties he scored mostly comedies, until *The Reivers,* in 1969. Steven Spielberg discovered Williams after hearing that soundtrack LP. "*The Reivers,*" Spielberg says, "is a fantastic score. It took flight, . . . had wings. It was American, a kind of cross between, I guess, Aaron Copland and Debussy. A very American score!" *Sugerland Express* (1974) was their first project together, a teaming which soon evolved into one of the great composer-director collaborations in film history. After *Sugardland,* Spielberg recommended him to his

John Williams
Photo courtesy of Columbia Pictures
© 1977 Columbia Pictures Industries, Inc.
All Rights Reserved.

friends George Lucas and Gary Kurtz for their new project—*Star Wars.*

Williams has spearheaded a tremendous revival in orchestral film scoring, beginning with his scores for *The Poseidon Adventure, The Towering Inferno, Jaws,* and then, in 1977, *Star Wars* and *Close Encounters.* His influence has been extraordinary. There are now many composers emulating the style he used for the *Star Wars* and Indiana Jones trilogies. Yet Williams is not limited to that approach; he can do it all. "John works on two levels," says author Tony Thomas. "The big Korngoldian stuff. . . . But he can do interior things, like *Accidental Tourist* and *Home Alone.* John is a master." From 1980 throuth 1993 he was conductor of the Boston Pops Orchestra.

Patrick Williams
Born April 23, 1939, Bonne Terre, Mo.
1969   Don't Drink the Water
1979   Breaking Away* (adapt.)
1984   Swing Shift
1984   All of Me
TV: "The Mary Tyler Moore Show" (series)

Stevie Wonder

Born May 13, 1950, Saginaw, Mich.

1978   The Secret Life of Plants
Song: "I Just Called to Say I Love You"**
            (from The Woman in Red, 1984)

Tsutomu Yamashita

Born March 10, 1947, Kyoto, Japan

1976   The Man Who Fell to Earth

Gabriel Yared

Born October 7, 1949, Beirut, Lebanon

1988   Clean and Sober
1990   Vincent and Theo
1992   The Lover

Christopher Young

Born April 28, 1957, Red Bank, N.J.

1985   Nightmare on Elm Street Part 2:
            Freddy's Revenge
1988   Bat-21
1988   Hellbound: Hellraiser II
1989   The Fly II
1992   Jennifer 8
1993   The Dark Half

Victor Young

Born August 8, 1900, Chicago, Ill.
Died November 10, 1956
Primary studio affiliation: Paramount
First films: Maid of Salem (1937)
                Wells Fargo (1937)
1939   Way Down South*
1939   Golden Boy*
1942   The Palm Beach Story
1943   For Whom the Bell Tolls*
1944   The Uninvited (incl. "Stella By Starlight"
            theme)
1945   Love Letters*
1946   To Each His Own
1948   The Night Has a Thousand Eyes
1948   The Paleface
1949   Sands of Iwo Jima
1949   My Foolish Heart
1952   The Quiet Man

Victor Young
Photo courtesy of the Academy of Motion Picture Arts and Sciences

Why would any trained musician let himself in for a career that calls for the exactitude of an Einstein, the diplomacy of a Churchill, and the patience of a martyr? Yet, after doing some 350 film scores, I can think of no other musical medium that offers as much challenge, excitement, and demand for creativity in putting music to work.

1953   Shane
1954   Three Coins in the Fountain
1956   Around the World in 80 Days**
            (posthumous Oscar)

As a child of six he loved to play "Yankee Doodle Dandy" holding the fiddle over his head. He was

cont'd.

seven when his mother died, and he moved to Warsaw, Poland, with his sister, living with his grandparents. He was required to polish the floor with his cushioned feet while he went through his scales. At the age of 17 he gave his concert debut with the Warsaw Philharmonic. He moved to Paris after World War I, and to New York in 1920; he played in Orchestra Hall in Chicago in 1921, and in vaudeville.

He then began to conduct and supervise vaudeville productions, eventually becoming assistant musical director of the Balaban and Katz theater chain, composing scores for silent movies as well. He subsequently developed an active and extremely successful career in radio and records. He played solo violin on the first recording of "Star Dust."

1935   To Hollywood, where he was under contract at Paramount.

1957   His last films were released posthumously.

Over the years many of his songs have become standards, including "Stella By Starlight," "When I Fall In Love," "Ghost of a Chance," and "My Foolish Heart."

"I probably worked with Victor on twenty pictures over the years, the first of which was *Love Letters*. Victor was a wonderful, wonderful man, with probably the most lyrical sense of any composer in Hollywood."

John Hammell, music editor/executive

"Overall, Victor Young was my hero. I've gone down his path."

Henry Mancini, composer

"He was an easygoing, wonderful personality, a wonderful musician. . . . All he wanted to do was get out of there and go to his card game."

June Edgerton, music editor

"He wrote music from his heart. He had so much melody within him. He may have been the best melody writer we ever had in Hollywood."

Bill Stinson, music editor/executive

Denny Zeitlin
Born April 10, 1938, Chicago, Ill.
1978   Invasion of the Body Snatchers

Hans Zimmer
Born September 12, 1957, Frankfurt, Germany
First Films: Moonlighting (1982, w/ Stanley Myers)
            Double Exposure (1987)
1988   Rain Man*
1989   Black Rain
1989   Driving Miss Daisy
1990   Green Card
1990   Pacific Heights
1991   Backdraft
1991   Thelma and Louise
1992   A League of Their Own
1992   Toys
1992   The Power of One
1993   Cool Runnings
1993   True Romance

Hans Zimmer
Photo: Bob Witkowski

Academy Award Original Score Nominees and Winners

■ ■ ■

The following is an alphabetical listing of the nominees and winners in the Original Score category through 1992. Space precludes listing the Original Song Score/Adaptations and the Original Song categories.

Alphabetical listing by composer has been included here because of the existing available reference material detailing chronological Academy Award nominees and winners. Note that certain music directors, including Morris Stoloff at Columbia and C. Bakeleinikoff at RKO, submitted their names to the Academy as a shared credit with the actual composers.

Winners are indicated with two asterisks [**].

ORIGINAL SCORE NOMINATIONS AND AWARDS BY COMPOSER

John Addison
  **Tom Jones   1963
  Sleuth   1972
Daniele Amfitheatrof
  Guest Wife   1945
Louis Applebaum
  The Story of G.I. Joe (w/ Ann Ronell) 1945
Malcolm Arnold
  The Bridge on the River Kwai   1957

Burt Bacharach
    **Butch Cassidy and the Sundance Kid 1969
Constantin Bakaleinikoff
    The Fallen Sparrow (w/ Roy Webb) 1943
    None but the Lonely Heart 1944
      (w/ Hanns Eisler)
Buddy Baker
    Napoleon and Samantha 1972
John Barry
    **Born Free 1966
    **The Lion in Winter 1968
    Mary, Queen of Scots 1971
    **Out of Africa 1985
    **Dances With Wolves 1990
Robert Russell Bennett
    Pacific Liner 1938
Richard Rodney Bennett
    Far from the Madding Crowd 1967
    Nicholas and Alexandra 1971
    Murder on the Orient Express 1974
Elmer Bernstein
    The Man with the Golden Arm 1955
    The Magnificent Seven 1960
    Summer and Smoke 1961
    To Kill a Mockingbird 1962
    Hawaii 1966
    **Thoroughly Modern Millie 1967
    Trading Places 1983
Leonard Bernstein
    On the Waterfront 1954
Chris Boardman
    The Color Purple 1985
      (w/ 11 others)
Phil Boutelje
    Hi Diddle Diddle 1943
Leslie Bricusse
    Doctor Dolittle 1967
Bruce Broughton
    Silverado 1985
Dale Butts
    Flame of the Barbary Coast 1945
      (w/ Morton Scott)
David Byrne
    **The Last Emperor 1987
      (w/ Sakamoto and Su)

Jorje Calandrelli
    The Color Purple (w/ 11 others) 1985
John Cameron
    A Touch of Class 1973
Gerard Carbonara
    The Kansan 1943
Charles Chaplin
    **Limelight (w/ Rasch and Russell) 1972
Frank Churchill
    Snow White and the Seven Dwarfs 1937
      (w/ Harline and Smith
    Bambi (w/ Edward H. Plumb) 1942
Anthony Collins
    Nurse Edith Cavell 1939
Alberto Colombo
    Portia on Trial 1937
Bill Conti
    **The Right Stuff 1983
Aaron Copland
    Of Mice and Men 1939
    Our Town 1940
    The North Star 1943
    **The Heiress 1949
Carmine Coppola
    **The Godfather, Part II (w/ Nino Rota) 1974
Frank Cordell
    Cromwell 1970
John Corigliano
    Altered States 1980
Andrae Crouch
    The Color Purple (w/ 11 others) 1985
Ken Darby
    How the West Was Won 1963
      (w/ Alfred Newman)
Georges Delerue
    Anne of the Thousand Days 1969
    The Day of the Dolphins 1973
    Julia 1977
    **A Little Romance 1979
    Agnes of God 1985
Jacques Demy
    The Umbrellas of Cherbourg 1965
      (w/ Michel Legrand)
Frank DeVol
    Pillow Talk 1959

Hush . . . Hush, Sweet Charlotte	1964		Ernest Gold	
Robert Emmett Dolan			On the Beach	1959
The Bells of St. Mary's	1945		**Exodus	1960
George Duning			It's a Mad, Mad, Mad, Mad World	1963
No Sad Songs for Me	1950		The Secret of Santa Vittoria	1969
From Here to Eternity (w/ Morris Stoloff)	1953		Jerry Goldsmith	
Picnic	1955		Freud	1962
Brian Easdale			A Patch of Blue	1965
**The Red Shoes	1948		The Sand Pebbles	1966
Hanns Eisler			Planet of the Apes	1968
Hangmen Also Die	1943		Patton	1970
None but the Lonely Heart	1944		Papillon	1973
(w/ C.Bakaleinikoff)			Chinatown	1974
George Fenton			The Wind and the Lion	1975
Gandhi (w/ Ravi Shankar)	1982		**The Omen	1976
Cry Freedom (w/ Jonas Gwangwa)	1987		The Boys from Brazil	1978
Dangerous Liaisons	1988		Star Trek—The Motion Picture	1979
The Fisher King	1991		Poltergeist	1982
Cy Feuer			Under Fire	1983
Mercy Island (w/ Walter Scharf)	1941		Hoosiers	1986
Jerry Fielding			Michael Gore	
The Wild Bunch	1969		**Fame	1980
Straw Dogs	1971		Terms of Endearment	1983
The Outlaw Josey Wales	1976		John Green	
Lou Forbes			Raintree County	1957
Brewster's Millions	1945		Louis Gruenberg	
This Is Cinerama	1953		The Fight for Life	1940
Gerald Fried			So Ends Our Night	1941
Birds Do It, Bees Do It	1975		Commandos Strike at Dawn	1943
Hugo Friedhofer			(w/ Morris Stoloff)	
Woman in the Window	1945		Dave Grusin	
(w/ Arthur Lange)			Heaven Can Wait	1978
**The Best Years of Our Lives	1946		The Champ	1979
The Bishop's Wife	1947		On Golden Pond	1981
Joan of Arc	1948		**The Milagro Beanfield War	1988
Above and Beyond	1953		The Fabulous Baker Boys	1989
Between Heaven and Hell	1956		Havana	1990
An Affair to Remember	1957		Joseph Gwangwa	
Boy on a Dolphin	1957		Cry Freedom (w/ George Fenton)	1987
The Young Lions	1958		Richard Hageman	
Herschel Burke Gilbert			If I Were King	1938
The Thief	1952		The Howards of Virginia	1940
Lud Gluskin			The Long Voyage Home	1940
The Man in the Iron Mask	1939		That Woman Is Mine	1941
(w/ Lucien Moraweck)			The Shanghai Gesture	1942

Karl Hajos
    The Man Who Walked Alone   1945
Marvin Hamlisch
    **The Way We Were   1973
    The Spy Who Loved Me   1977
    Sophie's Choice   1982
Herbie Hancock
    **'Round Midnight   1986
Leigh Harline
    Snow White and the Seven Dwarfs   1937
      (w/Churchill and Smith)
    **Pinocchio (w/ Smith and Washington)   1940
    The Pride of the Yankees   1942
    Johnny Come Lately   1943
W. Franke Harling
    Souls at Sea (w/ Milan Roder)   1937
    Three Russian Girls   1944
Marvin Hatley
    Way Out West   1937
    Blockheads   1938
Isaac Hayes
    Shaft   1971
Jack Hayes
    The Color Purple (w/ 11 others)   1985
Bernard Herrmann
    **All That Money Can Buy   1941
    Citizen Kane   1941
    Anna and the King of Siam   1946
    Obsession   1976
    Taxi Driver   1976
Jerry Hey
    The Color Purple (w/ 11 others)   1985
Werner Heymann
    One Million B. C.   1940
    That Uncertain Feeling   1941
    To Be or Not to Be   1942
Samuel Hoffenstein
    The Gay Divorcée (w/ K. Webb)   1934
Frederick Hollander
    The Talk of the Town (w/ Morris Stoloff) 1942
James Horner
    Aliens   1986
    Field of Dreams   1989
James Newton Howard
    The Prince of Tides   1991

Werner Janssen
    The General Died at Dawn   1936
    Blockade   1938
    Eternally Yours   1939
    Captain Kidd   1945
    Guest in the House   1945
    The Southerner   1945
Maurice Jarre
    **Lawrence of Arabia   1962
    **Doctor Zhivago   1965
    Mohammad—Messenger of God   1977
    **A Passage to India   1984
    Witness   1985
    Gorillas in the Mist   1988
    Ghost   1990
Quincy Jones
    In Cold Blood   1967
    The Color Purple (w/ 11 others)   1985
Gus Kahn
    **One Night of Love   1934
      (w/ Victor Schertzinger)
Bronislau Kaper
    **Lili   1953
    Mutiny on the Bounty   1962
Edward Kay
    King of the Zombies   1941
    Klondike Fury   1942
    G. I. Honeymoon   1945
Randy Kerber
    The Color Purple (w/ 11 others)   1985
Erich Wolfgang Korngold
    **Anthony Adverse   1936
    **The Adventures of Robin Hood   1938
Francis Lai
    **Love Story   1970
Arthur Lange
    Lady of Burlesque   1943
    Casanova Brown   1944
    The Woman in the Window   1945
      (w/ Hugo Friedhofer)
Michel Legrand
    The Umbrellas of Cherbourg   1965
      (w/ Jacques Demy)
    The Thomas Crown Affair   1968
    **Summer of '42   1971

Jeremy Lubbock		
The Color Purple (w/ 11 others)	1985	
Henry Mancini		
**Breakfast at Tiffany's	1961	
The Pink Panther	1964	
Sunflower	1970	
10	1979	
Muir Mathieson		
Genevieve	1954	
Toshiro Mayuzumi		
The Bible	1966	
Alan Menken		
**The Little Mermaid	1989	
**Beauty and the Beast	1991	
**Alladin	1992	
Michel Michelet		
The Hairy Ape (w/ Edward Paul)	1944	
Voice in the Wind	1944	
Lucien Moraweck		
The Man in the Iron Mask	1939	
(w/ Lud Gluskin)		
Giorgio Moroder		
**Midnight Express	1978	
Jerome Moross		
The Big Country	1958	
Ennio Morricone		
Days of Heaven	1978	
The Mission	1986	
The Untouchables	1987	
Bugsy	1991	
John Morris		
The Elephant Man	1980	
Alfred Newman		
The Hurricane	1937	
The Prisoner of Zenda	1937	
The Cowboy and the Lady	1938	
The Rains Came	1939	
Wuthering Heights	1939	
The Mark of Zorro	1940	
Ball of Fire	1941	
How Green Was My Valley	1941	
The Black Swan	1942	
**The Song of Bernadette	1943	
Wilson	1944	
The Keys of the Kingdom	1945	

Captain from Castile	1947
The Snake Pit	1948
All About Eve	1950
David and Bathsheba	1951
**Love Is a Many-Splendored Thing	1955
Anastasia	1956
The Diary of Anne Frank	1959
How the West Was Won (w/ Ken Darby)	1963
The Greatest Story Ever Told	1965
Airport	1970
Randy Newman	
Ragtime	1981
The Natural	1984
Avalon	1990
Jack Nitzsche	
One Flew over the Cuckoo's Nest	1975
An Officer and a Gentleman	1982
Alex North	
Death of a Salesman	1951
A Streetcar Named Desire	1951
Viva Zapata!	1952
The Rose Tatoo	1955
The Rainmaker	1956
Spartacus	1960
Cleopatra	1963
The Agony and the Ecstasy	1965
Who's Afraid of Virginia Woolf?	1966
The Shoes of a Fisherman	1968
Shanks	1974
Bite the Bullet	1975
Dragonslayer	1981
Under the Volcano	1984
[Honorary Oscar "in recognition of his brilliant artistry in the creation of memorable music for a host of distinguished motion pictures."]	1985
Edward Paul	
The Hairy Ape (w/ Michel Michelet)	1944
Edward H. Plumb	
Bambi (w/ Frank Churchill)	1942
Victory Through Air Power (w/ Smith and Wallace)	1943
Up in Mable's Room	1944
André Previn	
Elmer Gantry	1960

Charles Previn (as head, Universal music dept.)
  **One Hundred Men and a Girl   1937
David Raksin
  Forever Amber   1947
  Separate Tables   1958
Larry Rasch
  Limelight (w/ Chaplin and Russell)   1972
Frederic E. Rich
  Jack London   1944
Hugo Riesenfeld
  Make a Wish   1937
Milan Roder
  Souls at Sea (w/ W. Franke Harling)   1937
Ann Ronell
  The Story of G. I. Joe   1945
    (w/ Louis Applebaum)
David Rose
  The Princess and the Pirate   1944
Joel Rosenbaum
  The Color Purple (w/ 11 others)   1985
Leonard Rosenman
  Cross Creek   1983
  Star Trek IV: The Voyage Home   1986
Lawrence Rosenthal
  Becket   1964
Nino Rota
  **The Godfather, Part II   1974
    (w/ Carmine Coppola)
Miklós Rózsa
  The Thief of Bagdad   1940
  Lydia   1941
  Sundown   1941
  Jungle Book   1942
  Double Indemnity   1944
  Woman of the Town   1944
  The Lost Weekend   1945
  A Song to Remember (w/ Morris Stoloff)   1945
  **Spellbound   1945
  The Killers   1946
  **A Double Life   1947
  Quo Vadis   1951
  Ivanhoe   1952
  Julius Caesar   1953
  **Ben-Hur   1959
  El Cid   1961

Larry Russell
  **Limelight (w/ Chaplin and Rasch)   1972
Ryuichi Sakamoto
  **The Last Emperor (w/ Byrne and Su) 1987
Hans J. Salter
  The Amazing Mrs. Holliday   1943
    (w/ Frank Skinner)
  Christmas Holiday   1944
  This Love of Ours   1945
Philippe Sarde
  Tess   1980
Walter Scharf
  Mercy Island (w/ Cy Feuer)   1941
  In Old Oklahoma   1943
  The Fighting Seabees   1944
Victor Schertzinger
  **One Night of Love   1934
    (w/ Gus Kahn)
  Something to Sing About   1937
Lalo Schifrin
  Cool Hand Luke   1967
  The Fox   1968
  Voyage of the Damned   1976
  The Amityville Horror   1979
Morton Scott
  Flame of the Barbary Coast   1945
    (w/ Dale Butts)
Caiphus Semenya
  The Color Purple (w/ 11 others)   1985
Ravi Shankar
  Gandhi (w/ George Fenton)   1982
Richard M. Sherman
  **Mary Poppins (w/ Robert B. Sherman) 1964
Robert B. Sherman
  **Mary Poppins   1964
    (w/ Richard M. Sherman)
Nathaniel Shilkret
  Winterset   1936
Louis Silvers
  In Old Chicago [as head, Fox music dept.] 1937
  Suez   1938
Frank Skinner
  The House of Seven Gables   1940
  Back Street   1941
  Arabian Nights   1942

The Amazing Mrs. Holliday   1943
  (w/ Hans J. Salter)

Paul J. Smith
  Snow White and the Seven Dwarfs   1937
    (w/Churchill and Harline)
  **Pinocchio (w/ Harline and Washington) 1940
  Victory Through Air Power   1943
    (w/ Plumb and Wallace)
  Perri   1957

Fred Steiner
  The Color Purple (w/ 11 others)   1985

Max Steiner
  The Lost Patrol   1934
  **The Informer   1935
  The Charge of the Light Brigade   1936
  The Garden of Allah   1936
  The Life of Emile Zola   1937
  Dark Victory   1939
  Gone with the Wind   1939
  The Letter   1940
  Sergeant York   1941
  **Now, Voyager   1942
  Casablanca   1943
  The Adventures of Mark Twain   1944
  **Since You Went Away   1944
  Life with Father   1947
  Johnny Belinda   1948
  Beyond the Forest   1949
  The Flame and the Arrow   1950
  The Miracle of Our Lady of Fatima   1952
  The Caine Mutiny   1954
  Battle Cry   1955

Morris Stoloff
  Ladies in Retirement (w/ Ernst Toch) 1941
  The Talk of the Town   1942
    (w/ Frederick Hollander)
  Commandos Strike at Dawn   1943
    (w/ Louis Gruenberg)
  Address Unknown (w/ Ernst Toch)   1944
  A Song to Remember (w/ Miklós Rózsa) 1945
  From Here to Eternity   1953
    (w/ George Duning)
  Fanny (w/ Harry Sukman)   1961

Robert Stolz
  It Happened Tomorrow   1944

Herbert Stothart
  Mutiny on the Bounty   1935
  Maytime   1937
  Marie Antoinette   1938
  **The Wizard of Oz   1939
  Waterloo Bridge   1940
  Random Harvest   1942
  Madame Curie   1943
  Kismet   1944
  The Valley of Decision   1945

Cong Su
  **The Last Emperor   1987
    (w/ Sakamoto and Byrne)

Harry Sukman
  Fanny (w/ Morris Stoloff)   1961

Alexander Tansman
  Paris, Underground   1945

Rod Temperton
  The Color Purple (w/ 11 others)   1985

Max Terr
  The Gold Rush   1942

Dimitri Tiomkin
  Lost Horizon   1937
  The Corsican Brothers   1942
  The Moon and Sixpence   1943
  The Bridge of San Luis Rey   1944
  Champion   1949
  **High Noon   1952
  **The High and the Mighty   1954
  Giant   1956
  **The Old Man and the Sea   1958
  The Alamo   1960
  The Guns of Navarone   1961
  55 Days at Peking   1963
  The Fall of the Roman Empire   1964

Ernst Toch
  Peter Ibbetson   1935
  Ladies in Retirement (w/ Morris Stoloff) 1941
  Address Unknown (w/ Morris Stoloff) 1944

Vangelis
  Chariots of Fire   1981

Oliver G. Wallace
  Victory Through Air Power   1943
    (w/ Plumb and Smith)
  White Wilderness   1958

William Walton
   Henry V   1946
   Hamlet   1948
Edward Ward
   Cheers for Miss Bishop   1941
   Tanks a Million   1941
Ned Washington
   **Pinocchio (w/ Harline and Smith)   1940
Franz Waxman
   The Young at Heart   1938
   Rebecca   1940
   Dr. Jekyll and Mr. Hyde   1941
   Suspicion   1941
   Objective, Burma!   1945
   Humoresque   1946
   **Sunset Boulevard   1950
   **A Place in the Sun   1951
   The Silver Chalice   1954
   The Nun's Story   1959
   Taras Bulba   1962
Kenneth Webb
   The Gay Divorcée   1934
     (w/ Hoffenstein; RKO document credits
     Roy Webb)
Roy Webb
   Quality Street   1937
   My Favorite Wife   1940
   I Married a Witch   1942
   Joan of Paris   1942
   The Fallen Sparrow   1943
     (w/ C. Bakaleinikoff)
   The Fighting Seabees   1944
   The Enchanted Cottage   1945
John Williams
   The Reivers   1969
   Images   1972
   The Poseidon Adventure   1972
   Cinderella Liberty   1973
   The Towering Inferno   1974

   **Jaws   1975
   Close Encounters of the Third Kind   1977
   **Star Wars   1977
   Superman   1978
   The Empire Strikes Back   1980
   Raiders of the Lost Ark   1981
   **E.T. The Extra-Terrestrial   1982
   Return of the Jedi   1983
   Indiana Jones and the Temple of Doom   1984
   The River   1984
   Empire of the Sun   1987
   The Witches of Eastwick   1987
   The Accidental Tourist   1988
   Born on the Fourth of July   1989
   Indiana Jones and the Last Crusade   1989
   Home Alone   1990
   JFK   1991
Meredith Willson
   The Great Dictator   1940
   The Little Foxes   1941
Victor Young
   Army Girl   1938
   Breaking the Ice   1938
   Golden Boy   1939
   Gulliver's Travels   1939
   Man of Conquest   1939
   Arizona   1940
   Dark Command   1940
   Northwest Mounted Police   1940
   Hold Back the Dawn   1941
   Flying Tigers   1942
   Silver Queen   1942
   Take a Letter, Darling   1942
   For Whom the Bell Tolls   1943
   Love Letters   1945
   Samson and Delilah   1950
   **Around the World in 80 Days   1956
Hans Zimmer
   Rain Man   1988

Soundtrack Shops and Vendors

■ ■ ■

USA MAIL ORDER

Books Nippon
1123 Dominguez St., Suite K
Carson, CA 90746
Japanese animation soundtracks available.

Footlight Records
113 E. 12th Street, New York, NY 10003
(212) 533-1572
You can order by phone (no catalog available).

Harvard Square Records
PO Box 1975
Cambridge, MA 02238 (617) 868-3385
Imports, cut-outs, and other soundtracks. You can

order the following catalogs for $2 each: US in-print CDs and Cassettes, out of print LPs, out of print CDs, and Import CDs.

Intrada
1488 Vallejo Street
San Francisco, CA 94109 (415) 776-1333
This is Intrada Records, from whom you can order both Intrada CDs, and also many others. Free catalog available.

Koch International
177 Cantiague Rock Road
Westbury, NY 11590 (516) 938-8080
Distributes Chandos, Intrada, Mainstream, Silva America, and other labels.

One World Records
1250 West NW Highway, Suite 505
Palatine, IL 60067
(708) 934-0870
Distributes Silva Screen Records. Catalog available.

RTS
1982 N. Rainbow Boulevard, Suite 183
Las Vegas, NV 89108
LPs only. Prices high but may have the rare record you're looking for.

Screen Archives Entertainment
PO Box 34792
Washington, DC 20043
Catalog of CDs available.

Sound City 2000
PO Box 22149
Portland, OR 97222 (503) 654-2196
Distributes CDs from England, Japan, and Germany.

SoundTrack Album Retailers
PO Box 487
New Holland, PA 17557 (717) 656-0121
Free catalog available, with CDs and LPs.

West Point Records
24365 San Fernando Road
Newhall, CA 91321
LPs only. Over ten thousand records in stock. Catalog/newsletter available.

BRITISH MAIL ORDER

58 Dean Street Records
58 Dean Street
London W1V 5HH, England (071) 437-4500
CDs and LPs available.

Backtrack, Grammar School Records
The Old Grammar School, High St.
Rye, E. Sussex TN31 7JF, England
(0797) 222752
CDs and LPs. Free monthly catalogs available, one for soundtracks and one for original cast albums.

Derran Trax
99 High St.
Dudley, West Midlands DY1 1QP, England
(0384) 233191/2
CDs and LPs. Free catalog available.

Movie Boulevard
5 Cherry Tree Walk
Leeds LS2 7EB, England
(0532) 422888
A large selection of CDs, LPs, and cassettes, as well as books, magazines, 45s, and movie memorabilia. Catalog available for £1 or 4 international reply coupons (IRCs are sold at post offices).

Prior Arrangements
53 Rosedale Rd.
Romford, Essex RM1 4QR, England
(0708) 764835
CDs, LPs, and cassettes, both soundtracks and original cast.

The Record Album
8 Terminus Rd.
Brighton, Sussex BN1 3PD, England
(0273) 23853
LPs only, but "dedicated to the preservation of the LP format." Write for information, or send want list.

Screenthemes
22 Kensington Close
Totan, Beeston, Nottingham NG9 6GR, England
Specializes in TV themes and new CDs. Catalog available bimonthly for $5 from the US, £1, or 3 IRCs in Europe.

Soundtrack Deletions
1 B Woodstock Rd.
Strood, Rochester, Kent ME2 2DI, England
(0272) 711053
Write for information.

EUROPEAN MAIL ORDER

Chinatown Filmmusic
Wunstorfer Strasse 97
W-30453 Hannover, Germany
Write for info.

Ciné Musique
3 Rue François de Neufchâteau
75011, Paris, France 43 71 11 11.
CDs and LPs at their store or mail order. Free catalog available.

Cine City
PO Box 1710
1200 BS Hilversum, Holland (0)35 210234
CDs, LPs, and 45s, including Ennio Morricone albums. Also videotapes. Catalog available for $1 or 2 IRCs.

Cinema Soundtrack Club
Postfach 520151
Hamburg, Germany
Send for free catalog.

Cinesoundtrack Service
Chopinlaan 30
6865 EW Doorwerth
Holland
Write for info.

Soundtrack!
ATTN: Luc Van de Ven, Astridlaan 171
2800 Mechelen, Belgium.
Records released by various labels, including Van de Ven's Promethius label.

Tarantula Records
Hamburg, Postfach 11 02 82
20402 Hamburg, Germany
CDs and LPs. Large free catalog available.

This information has been provided by Lukas Kendall. Subscribe to his *Film Score Monthly* newsletter to receive the latest suggestions on where to find soundtrack recordings (Lukas Kendall, Box 1554, Amherst College, Amherst, MA 01002-5000 USA; summers and spring 1996 on: RFD 488, Vineyard Haven, MA 02568).

Filmography

∎ ∎ ∎

À Nous la Liberté	Georges Auric	1931
Abe Lincoln in Illinois	Roy Webb	1940
About Last Night	Miles Goodman	1986
Above the Law	David Michael Frank	1988
Accidental Tourist, The	John Williams	1988
Accused, The	Brad Fiedel	1988
Ace in the Hole	Hugo Friedhofer	1951
Action in the North Atlantic	Adolph Deutsch	1943
Adam's Rib	Miklós Rózsa	1949
Addams Family, The	Marc Shaiman	1991
Adventure of Sherlock Holmes' Smarter Brother, The	John Morris	1975

Adventures of Baron Munchausen, The	Michael Kamen	1989
Adventures of Don Juan	Max Steiner	1949
Adventures of Huck Finn, The	Bill Conti	1993
Adventures of Huckleberry Finn, The	Jerome Moross	1960
Adventures of Marco Polo, The	Hugo Friedhofer	1938
Adventures of Robin Hood, The	Erich Wolfgang Korngold	1938
Advise and Consent	Jerry Fielding	1962
African Queen, The	Allan Gray	1951
After Hours	Howard Shore	1985
Age of Innocence, The	Elmer Bernstein	1993
Agnes of God	Georges Delerue	1985
Agony and the Ecstasy, The	Alex North	1965
Air America	Charles Gross	1990
Air Force	Franz Waxman	1943
Air Raid Wardens	Nathaniel Shilkret	1943
Airborne	Stewart Copeland	1993
Airplane!	Elmer Bernstein	1980
Airport	Alfred Newman	1970
Airport 1974	John Cacavas	1975
Airport '77	John Cacavas	1977
Akira Kurosawa's Dreams	Shinchiro Ikebe	1990
Al Capone	David Raksin	1959
Aladdin	Alan Menken	1992
Alamo, The	Dimitri Tiomkin	1960
Alexander Nevsky	Sergei Prokofiev	1938
Alexander's Ragtime Band	Alfred Newman (md.)	1938
Alfie	Burt Bacharach	1966
Alice Adams	Roy Webb	1935
Alice in Wonderland	Dimitri Tiomkin	1933
Alien	Jerry Goldsmith	1979
Aliens	James Horner	1986

Alien 3	Elliot Goldenthal	1992
All About Eve	Alfred Newman	1950
All of Me	Patrick Williams	1984
All That Jazz	Ralph Burns (adapt.)	1979
All That Money Can Buy	Bernard Herrmann	1941
All the President's Men	David Shire	1976
Along Came Jones	Arthur Lange	1945
Altered States	John Corigliano	1980
Amazing Colossal Man, The	Albert Glasser	1957
Amazing Dobermans, The	Alan Silvestri	1976
American Gigolo	Giorgio Moroder	1980
American in Paris, An	John Green (adapt.)	1951
American Ninja	Michael J. Linn	1985
American Tail, An	James Horner	1986
American Tail II, An	James Horner	1991
Americanization of Emily, The	Johnny Mandel	1964
Amityville Horror, The	Lalo Schifrin	1979
Anatomy of a Murder	Duke Ellington	1959
And God Created Woman	Paul Misraki	1956
And God Created Woman	Tom Chase and Steve Rucker	1987
And Then There Were None	Mario Castelnuovo-Tedesco	1945
Andromeda Strain, The	Gil Mellé	1971
Animal House	Elmer Bernstein	1978
Anna	Nino Rota	1951
Anne of the Thousand Days	Georges Delerue	1969
Annie	Ralph Burns (adapt.)	1982
Annie Get Your Gun	Adolph Deutsch (adapt.)	1950
Another 48 HRS.	James Horner	1990
Another Dawn	Erich Wolfgang Korngold	1937
Another Time, Another Place	Douglas Gamley	1958
Antarctica	Vangelis	1984

Any Wednesday	George Duning	1966
Apartment, The	Adolph Deutsch	1960
Apocalypse Now	Carmine Coppola	1979
Apple Dumpling Gang, The	Buddy Baker	1975
Apprenticeship of Duddy Kravitz, The	Stanley Myers	1974
Arachnophobia	Trevor Jones	1990
Armed and Dangerous	James Di Pasquale/Michael Melvoin	1986
Around the World In 80 Days	Victor Young	1956
Arthur	Burt Bacharach	1981
Arthur 2: On the Rocks	Burt Bacharach	1988
Artists and Models	Walter Scharf	1955
As You Like It	William Walton	1936
Ashanti	Michael Melvoin	1979
At Long Last Love	Artie Butler (adapt.)	1975
At Play in the Fields of the Lord	Zbigniew Preisner	1991
Attack of the 50 Foot Woman	Ronald Stein	1958
Attack of the Killer Tomatoes	Gordon Goodwin/Paul Sundfor	1979
Auntie Mame	Bronislau Kaper	1958
Avalanche Express	Allyn Ferguson	1979
Avalon	Randy Newman	1990
Awakenings	Randy Newman	1990
Babe Ruth Story, The	Edward Ward	1948
Babe, The	Elmer Bernstein	1992
Baby Doll	Kenyon Hopkins	1956
Back Street	Frank Skinner	1941
Back to Bataan	Roy Webb	1945
Back to the Future	Alan Silvestri	1985
Back to the Future Part II	Alan Silvestri	1989
Back to the Future Part III	Alan Silvestri	1990
Backdraft	Hans Zimmer	1991
Bad and the Beautiful, The	David Raksin	1952

Bad Day at Black Rock	André Previn	1955
Bad Men of Tombstone	Roy Webb	1949
Bad News Bears, The	Jerry Fielding (adapt.)	1976
Bad Seed, The	Alex North	1956
Bambi	Frank Churchill/Edward Plumb	1942
Bananas	Marvin Hamlisch	1971
Band Wagon, The	Adolph Deutsch (adapt.)	1953
Bandit of Sherwood Forest, The	Hugo Friedhofer	1946
Bank Dick, The	Frank Skinner	1940
Barbarian and the Geisha, The	Hugo Friedhofer	1958
Barefoot Contessa, The	Mario Nascimbene	1954
Barefoot in the Park	Neal Hefti	1966
Barry Lyndon	Leonard Rosenman (adapt.)	1975
Barton Fink	Carter Burwell	1991
Basic Instinct	Jerry Goldsmith	1992
Bat-21	Christopher Young	1988
Bataan	Bronislau Kaper	1943
Batman	Danny Elfman	1989
Batman Returns	Danny Elfman	1992
Batman: Mask of the Phantasm	Shirley Walker	1993
Batteries Not Included	James Horner	1987
Battle of Algiers, The	Ennio Morricone	1967
Bear, The	Philippe Sarde	1989
Beast from 20,000 Fathoms, The	David Buttolph	1953
Beau Geste	Alfred Newman	1939
Beau Geste	Hans J. Salter	1966
Beauty and the Beast	Georges Auric	1946
Beauty and the Beast	Alan Menken	1991
Becket	Laurence Rosenthal	1964
Bedazzled	Dudley Moore	1967
Bedevilled	William Alwyn	1955

Bedtime Story	Hans J. Salter	1963
Beethoven	Randy Edelman	1992
Beetlejuice	Danny Elfman	1988
Being There	Johnny Mandel	1979
Bell, Book and Candle	George Duning	1958
Bellboy, The	Walter Scharf	1960
Belle Starr	Alfred Newman	1941
Belles of St. Trinian's, The	Malcolm Arnold	1957
Bells of St. Mary's, The	Robert Emmett Dolan	1945
Ben	Walter Scharf	1972
Ben-Hur	William Axt	1926
Ben-Hur	Miklós Rózsa	1959
Bend of the River	Hans J. Salter	1952
Beneath the 12-Mile Reef	Bernard Herrmann	1953
Beneath the Planet of the Apes	Leonard Rosenman	1970
Benny & Joon	Rachel Portman	1993
Best Years of Our Lives, The	Hugo Friedhofer	1946
Betrayed	Bill Conti	1988
Between Two Worlds	Erich Wolfgang Korngold	1944
Beverly Hillbillies, The	Lalo Schifrin	1993
Beverly Hills Cop	Harold Faltermeyer	1984
Beverly Hills Cop II	Harold Faltermeyer	1987
Bewitched	Bronislau Kaper	1945
Beyond Witch Mountain	George Duning	1983
Bicycle Thief, The	Alessandro Cicognini	1949
Big	Howard Shore	1988
Big Business	Lee Holdridge	1988
Big Country, The	Jerome Moross	1958
Big Easy, The	Brad Fiedel	1987
Big Knife, The	Frank De Vol	1955
Big Parade, The	William Axt	1925

Big Red One, The	Dana Kaproff	1980
Big Sky, The	Dimitri Tiomkin	1952
Big Sleep, The	Max Steiner	1946
Billy Bathgate	Mark Isham	1991
Biloxi Blues	Georges Delerue	1988
Bingo Long Traveling All-Stars and Motor Kings, The	William Goldstein	1976
Birch Interval	Leonard Rosenman	1976
Bird	Lennie Niehaus	1988
Birdman of Alcatraz	Elmer Bernstein	1962
Birds Do It, Bees Do It	Gerald Fried	1975
Bishop's Wife, The	Hugo Friedhofer	1947
Black Cat, The	Heinz Roemheld	1934
Black Patch	Jerry Goldsmith	1957
Black Rain	Hans Zimmer	1989
Black Stallion, The	Carmine Coppola	1979
Black Stallion Returns, The	Georges Delerue	1983
Black Widow	Leigh Harline	1954
Blade Runner	Vangelis	1982
Blaze	Bennie Wallace	1989
Blazing Saddles	John Morris	1973
Bless the Beasts and Children	Perry Botkin, Jr.	1971
Blithe Spirit	Richard Addinsell	1945
Blob, The	Michael Hoenig	1988
Blockade	Werner Janssen	1938
Blockheads	Marvin Hatley	1938
Blood Alley	Roy Webb	1955
Blood on the Moon	Roy Webb	1948
Blue Angel, The	Franz Waxman (arr./orch.)	1930
Blue Lagoon, The	Basil Poledouris	1980
Blue Max, The	Jerry Goldsmith	1966

Blue Thunder	Arthur B. Rubinstein	1983
Blue Velvet	Angelo Badalamenti	1986
Boccaccio '70	Nino Rota	1962
Body and Soul	Hugo Friedhofer	1947
Body Double	Pino Donaggio	1984
Body Heat	John Barry	1981
Body of Evidence	Graeme Revell	1993
Body Snatcher, The	Roy Webb	1945
Bodyguard, The	Alan Silvestri	1992
Bonjour Tristesse	Georges Auric	1958
Boots Malone	Elmer Bernstein	1952
Born Free	John Barry	1966
Born in East L.A.	Lee Holdridge	1987
Born on the Fourth of July	John Williams	1989
Born Yesterday	Frederick Hollander	1950
Botany Bay	Franz Waxman	1953
Bound for Glory	Leonard Rosenman (adapt.)	1976
Boy on a Dolphin	Hugo Friedhofer	1957
Boy Who Could Fly, The	Bruce Broughton	1986
Boy with Green Hair, The	Leigh Harline	1948
Boys from Brazil, The	Jerry Goldsmith	1978
Boyz N the Hood	Stanley Clarke	1991
Brainstorm	James Horner	1983
Bram Stoker's Dracula	Wojciech Kilar	1992
Brazil	Michael Kamen	1985
Breakfast at Tiffany's	Henry Mancini	1961
Breakfast Club, The	Gary Chang	1985
Breaking Away	Patrick Williams (adapt.)	1979
Brewster's Millions	Hugo Friedhofer	1945
Bride of Frankenstein	Franz Waxman	1935
Bridge on the River Kwai, The	Malcolm Arnold	1957

Bridge Too Far, A	John Addison	1977
Bridges at Toko-Ri, The	Lyn Murray	1955
Brief History of Time, A	Philip Glass	1992
Brigadoon	John Green (adapt.)	1954
Brighton Beach Memoirs	Michael Small	1986
Bringing Up Baby	Roy Webb	1938
Broadcast News	Bill Conti	1987
Broadway Danny Rose	Dick Hyman	1983
Broken Arrow	Hugo Friedhofer	1950
Buck Privates	Charles Previn (adapt.)	1941
Bull Durham	Michael Convertino	1988
Bullitt	Lalo Schifrin	1968
Burnt Offerings	Robert Cobert	1976
Butch Cassidy and the Sundance Kid	Burt Bacharach	1969
Butcher's Wife, The	Michael Gore	1991
Butterfield 8	Bronislau Kaper	1960
Butterflies Are Free	Bob Alcivar	1972
Bye Bye Birdie	John Green (adapt.)	1963
Bye Bye Braverman	Peter Matz	1968
Cabaret	Ralph Burns (adapt.)	1972
Caine Mutiny, The	Max Steiner	1954
Call Me	David Michael Frank	1988
Call Me Madam	Alfred Newman (adapt.)	1953
Can Can	Nelson Riddle (adapt.)	1960
Candyman	Philip Glass	1992
Cape Fear	Bernard Herrmann	1962
Cape Fear	Elmer Bernstein (adapt. Bernard Herrmann's music)	1991
Captain Blood	Erich Wolfgang Korngold	1935
Captain from Castile	Alfred Newman	1947
Captain Horatio Hornblower	Robert Farnon	1951

Captain Is a Lady, The	Bronislau Kaper	1940
Captain's Paradise, The	Malcolm Arnold	1953
Captains Courageous	Franz Waxman	1937
Cardinal, The	Jerome Moross	1963
Carrie	Pino Donaggio	1976
Casablanca	Max Steiner	1943
Casanova [silent film]	Georges Delerue	1985
Casual Sex?	Van Dyke Parks	1988
Casualties of War	Ennio Morricone	1989
Cat People	Roy Webb	1942
Cat People	Giorgio Moroder	1982
Champ, The	Dave Grusin	1979
Champion	Dimitri Tiomkin	1949
Chaplin	John Barry	1992
Charge of the Light Brigade, The	Max Steiner	1936
Chariots of Fire	Vangelis	1981
Charlie Chan at the Opera [opera sequence]	Oscar Levant	1937
Charly	Ravi Shankar	1968
Cheaper by the Dozen	Cyril J. Mockridge	1950
Chicago Joe and the Showgirl	Hans Zimmer/Shirley Walker	1990
Children of a Lesser God	Michael Convertino	1986
Children of Paradise	Joseph Kosma	1944
Chinatown	Jerry Goldsmith	1974
Chocolate Soldier, The	Bronislau Kaper (adapt.)	1941
Chorus Line, A	Ralph Burns (adapt.)	1985
Christmas Carol, A	Richard Addinsell	1951
Christmas Holiday	Hans J. Salter	1944
Christmas in Connecticut	Frederick Hollander	1945
Christopher Columbus: The Discovery	Cliff Eidelman	1992
Chump at Oxford, A	Marvin Hatley	1940
Cimarron	Max Steiner	1930

Cincinnati Kid, The	Lalo Schifrin	1965
Cinderella	Oliver Wallace/Paul J. Smith	1950
Citizen Kane	Bernard Herrmann	1941
City Lights	Charles Chaplin; Arthur Johnston (arr.)	1931
City of Joy	Ennio Morricone	1992
City Slickers	Marc Shaiman	1991
Clan of the Cave Bear, The	Alan Silvestri	1986
Clara's Heart	Dave Grusin	1988
Clash of the Titans	Laurence Rosenthal	1981
Class Action	James Horner	1990
Claudine	Curtis Mayfield	1974
Clean and Sober	Gabriel Yared	1988
Cleopatra	Alex North	1964
Cliffhanger	Trevor Jones	1993
Close Encounters of the Third Kind	John Williams	1977
Clowns, The	Nino Rota	1971
Cobweb, The	Leonard Rosenman	1955
Cocktail	J. Peter Robinson	1988
Cocoon	James Horner	1985
Cocoon: The Return	James Horner	1988
Cohen and Tate	Bill Conti	1988
Cold Turkey	Randy Newman	1971
Colors	Herbie Hancock	1988
Colt .45	William Lava	1950
Come Fly with Me	Lyn Murray	1963
Come See the Paradise	Randy Edelman	1990
Come September	Hans J. Salter	1961
Comes a Horseman	Michael Small	1978
Comancheros, The	Elmer Bernstein	1961
Competition, The	Lalo Schifrin	1980
Conan the Barbarian	Basil Poledouris	1982

Coneheads	David Newman	1993
Conformist, The	Georges Delerue	1971
Constant Nymph, The	Erich Wolfgang Korngold	1943
Conversation, The	David Shire	1974
Cook, the Thief, His Wife and Her Lover, The	Michael Nyman	1989
Cool Hand Luke	Lalo Schifrin	1967
Cool Runnings	Hans Zimmer	1993
Cool World	Mark Isham	1992
Corsican Brothers, The	Alfred Newman	1941
Cosmic Eye, The	William Russo	1985
Counterpoint	Bronislau Kaper	1968
Country	Charles Gross	1984
Cover Girl	Carmen Dragon (adapt.)	1943
Crazy People	Cliff Eidelman	1990
Creature from the Black Lagoon	Herman Stein (co-comp.)	1954
Crime and Punishment	Arthur Honegger	1935
Critters	David Newman	1986
Cross Creek	Leonard Rosenman	1983
Crossfire	Roy Webb	1947
Crossing Delancey	Paul Chihara	1988
Crossroads	Ry Cooder	1986
Cry Freedom	George Fenton/Jonas Gwangwa	1987
Crying Game, The	Anne Dudley	1992
Cutter's Way	Jack Nitzsche	1981
Cutting Class	Jill Fraser	1989
Cyrano de Bergerac	Jean-Claude Petit	1990
Daddy-O	John Williams	1959
Damage	Zbigniew Preisner	1992
Damien: Omen II	Jerry Goldsmith	1978
Dances With Wolves	John Barry	1990
Dancing Masters, The	Arthur Lange	1943

Dangerous Liaisons	George Fenton	1988
Dark Half, The	Christopher Young	1993
Dark Victory	Max Steiner	1939
Darkman	Danny Elfman	1990
Darling Lili	Henry Mancini	1970
Das Boot	Klaus Doldinger	1981
Dave	James Newton Howard	1993
David and Bathsheba	Alfred Newman	1951
Day for Night	Georges Delerue	1973
Day the Earth Stood Still, The	Bernard Herrmann	1951
Day the World Ended, The	Ronald Stein	1956
Days of Glory	Daniele Amfitheatrof	1944
Days of Heaven	Ennio Morricone	1978
Days of Wine and Roses	Henry Mancini	1962
Dead Again	Patrick Doyle	1991
Dead Calm	Graeme Revell	1989
Dead Men Don't Wear Plaid	Miklós Rózsa	1982
Dead Poets Society	Maurice Jarre	1989
Dead Pool, The	Lalo Schifrin	1988
Dead Ringers	Howard Shore	1988
Dead Zone, The	Michael Kamen	1983
Death of a Salesman	Alex North	1951
Death on the Nile	Nino Rota	1978
Deathtrap	Johnny Mandel	1982
Deceivers, The	John Scott	1988
Deception	Erich Wolfgang Korngold	1946
Deep, The	John Barry	1977
Defending Your Life	Michael Gore	1991
Demolition Man	Elliot Goldenthal	1993
Dennis the Menace	Jerry Goldsmith	1993
Desert Fox, The	Daniele Amfitheatrof	1951

Desk Set	Cyril J. Mockridge	1957
Desperately Seeking Susan	Thomas Newman	1985
Destination Moon	Leith Stevens	1950
Destry Rides Again	Frank Skinner	1939
Devils, The	Peter Maxwell Davies	1971
Devotion	Erich Wolfgang Korngold	1946
Dial M for Murder	Dimitri Tiomkin	1954
Diary of a Hitman	Michel Colombier	1992
Diary of Anne Frank, The	Alfred Newman	1959
Dick Tracy	Roy Webb	1945
Dick Tracy	Danny Elfman	1990
Dick Tracy Meets Gruesome	Paul Sawtell	1947
Die Hard	Michael Kamen	1988
Die Hard II	Michael Kamen	1990
Dinner at Eight	William Axt	1933
Dirty Harry	Lalo Schifrin	1972
Dirty Rotten Scoundrels	Miles Goodman	1988
Distinguished Gentleman, The	Randy Edelman	1992
Divorce American Style	Dave Grusin	1967
Do the Right Thing	Bill Lee	1989
Doctor and the Devils, The	John Morris	1985
Doctor Zhivago	Maurice Jarre	1965
Dodes'Ka'Den	Toru Takemitsu	1970
Dodge City	Max Steiner	1939
Dog of Flanders, A	Bert A. Shefter/Paul Sawtell	1959
Doin' Time on Planet Earth	Dana Kaproff	1988
Don Juan	William Axt	1926
Don't Drink the Water	Patrick Williams	1969
Don't Look Now	Pino Donaggio	1974
Don't Make Waves	Vic Mizzy	1967
Donovan's Reef	Cyril J. Mockridge	1963

Double Exposure	Hans Zimmer	1982
Double Indemnity	Miklós Rózsa	1944
Double Life, A	Miklós Rózsa	1947
Dr. Ehrlich's Magic Bullet	Max Steiner	1940
Dr. Giggles	Brian May	1992
Dr. Jekyll and Mr. Hyde	Franz Waxman	1941
Dr. No [James Bond Theme only]	John Barry	1962
Dr. Terror's House of Horrors	Elizabeth Lutyens	1965
Dracula	John Williams	1979
Dragon: The Bruce Lee Story	Randy Edelman	1993
Dragnet	Ira Newborn	1987
Dragonslayer	Alex North	1981
Drawing By Numbers	Michael Nyman	1987
Dressed to Kill	Pino Donaggio	1980
Driving Miss Daisy	Hans Zimmer	1989
Drugstore Cowboy	Elliot Goldenthal	1989
Duel in the Sun	Dimitri Tiomkin	1946
Dumbo	Frank Churchill/Oliver Wallace	1941
East of Eden	Leonard Rosenman	1955
Easter Parade	John Green (adapt.)	1948
Edward Scissorhands	Danny Elfman	1990
Egg and I, The	Frank Skinner	1947
Egyptian, The	Alfred Newman/Bernard Herrmann	1954
8 1/2	Nino Rota	1963
Eight Men Out	Mason Daring	1988
8 Million Ways to Die	James Newton Howard	1986
18 Again	Billy Goldenberg	1988
El Cid	Miklós Rózsa	1961
Elephant Man, The	John Morris	1980
Elmer Gantry	André Previn	1960
Empire of the Sun	John Williams	1987

Empire Strikes Back, The	John Williams	1980
Enchanted Cottage, The	Roy Webb	1945
Endless Love	Jonathan Tunick	1981
Enforcer, The	Jerry Fielding	1976
Enter the Ninja	Laurin Rinder/W. Michael Lewis	1981
Equus	Richard Rodney Bennett	1977
Ernest Saves Christmas	Mark Snow	1988
Escape from New York	Alan Howarth/John Carpenter	1981
Escape Me Never	Erich Wolfgang Korngold	1947
Escape to Witch Mountain	Johnny Mandel	1975
Eternally Yours	Werner Janssen	1939
E.T. The Extra-Terrestrial	John Williams	1982
Ethan Frome	Rachel Portman	1993
Europa, Europa	Zbigniew Preisner	1991
Every Which Way but Loose	Steve Dorff	1978
Exodus	Ernest Gold	1960
Exorcist II: The Heretic	Ennio Morricone	1977
Exorcist III, The	Barry DeVorzon	1990
Extreme Close-Up	Basil Poledouris	1973
Extremities	J.A.C. Redford	1986
Fabulous Baker Boys, The	Dave Grusin	1989
Fahrenheit 451	Bernard Herrmann	1966
Fall of the Roman Empire, The	Dimitri Tiomkin	1964
Fallen Sparrow, The	Roy Webb	1943
Falling Down	James Newton Howard	1992
Fame	Michael Gore	1980
Family Way, The	Paul McCartney	1967
Fantastic Voyage	Leonard Rosenman	1966
Far from the Madding Crowd	Richard Rodney Bennett	1967
Farewell to Arms, A	Mario Nascimbene	1957
Farewell, My Lovely	David Shire	1975

Fast Break	James Di Pasquale	1976
Fatal Attraction	Maurice Jarre	1987
Fearless	Maurice Jarre	1993
Feds	Randy Edelman	1988
Fellini Satyricon	Nino Rota	1970
Fellini's Roma	Nino Rota	1972
Ferris Bueller's Day Off	Ira Newborn	1986
Few Good Men, A	Marc Shaiman	1992
Fiddler on the Roof	John Williams (adapt.)	1971
Field, The	Elmer Bernstein	1990
Field of Dreams	James Horner	1989
Fiesta	John Green (adapt.)	1947
55 Days at Peking	Dimitri Tiomkin	1963
Fighting Seabees, The	Walter Scharf	1944
Final Analysis	George Fenton	1991
Finian's Rainbow	Ray Heindorf (adapt.)	1968
Firm, The	Dave Grusin	1993
First Blood	Jerry Goldsmith	1982
Fish Called Wanda, A	John du Prez	1988
Fisher King, The	George Fenton	1991
Fistful of Dollars, A	Ennio Morricone	1964
Five Guns to Tombstone	Bert A. Shefter/Paul Sawtell	1960
Five Pennies, The	Leith Stevens	1959
Flame and the Arrow, The	Max Steiner	1950
Flashdance	Giorgio Moroder	1983
Flatliners	James Newton Howard	1990
Flea in Her Ear, A	Bronislau Kaper	1968
Fletch	Harold Faltermeyer	1985
Flim Flam Man, The	Jerry Goldsmith	1967
Fly, The	Bert A. Shefter/Paul Sawtell	1958
Fly, The	Howard Shore	1986

Fly II, The	Christopher Young	1989
Footlight Parade	Ray Heindorf (arr.)	1933
Footloose	Tom Snow; Miles Goodman (adapt.)	1984
For a Few Dollars More	Ennio Morricone	1965
For the Boys	Dave Grusin	1991
For Love or Money	Bruce Broughton	1993
For Whom the Bell Tolls	Victor Young	1943
For Your Eyes Only	Bill Conti	1981
Force of Evil	David Raksin	1948
Forever Amber	David Raksin	1947
Forever Young	Jerry Goldsmith	1992
Fort Apache	Richard Hageman	1948
Fort Worth	David Buttolph	1951
Fortune, The	David Shire (adapt.)	1975
Fortune Cookie, The	André Previn	1966
Fortunella	Nino Rota	1957
48HRS.	James Horner	1982
42nd Street	Ray Heindorf (arr.)	1933
Foul Play	Charles Fox	1978
Four Feathers, The	Miklós Rózsa	1939
Four Horsemen of the Apocalypse	André Previn	1962
Four Musketeers, The	Lalo Schifrin	1975
1492: Conquest of Paradise	Vangelis	1992
Fox and the Hound, The	Buddy Baker	1981
Frankie and Johnny	Marvin Hamlisch	1991
Free Willy	Basil Poledouris	1993
French Connection, The	Don Ellis	1971
French Lieutenant's Woman, The	Carl Davis	1981
Frenzy	Ron Goodwin	1972
Freshman, The	David Newman	1990
Freud	Jerry Goldsmith	1963

Friday the 13th	Harry Manfredini	1980
Friday the 13th Part VII—The New Blood	Harry Manfredini/Fred Mollin	1988
Fried Green Tomatoes	Thomas Newman	1991
From Here to Eternity	George Duning	1953
From Russia with Love	John Barry	1963
Front Page, The	Billy May	1974
Fugitive, The	James Newton Howard	1993
Fuller Brush Man, The	Heinz Roemheld	1948
Funny Face	Adolph Deutsch (adapt.)	1957
Funny Girl	Walter Scharf (adapt.)	1968
Funny Lady	Peter Matz (adapt.)	1975
Funny Thing Happened on the Way to the Forum, A	Ken Thorne (adapt.)	1966
Futureworld	Fred Karlin	1976
Gallipoli	Brian May	1981
Gambler, The	Jerry Fielding	1974
Gandhi	George Fenton/Ravi Shankar	1982
Garden of the Finzi-Continis, The	Manuel de Sica	1971
Gaslight	Bronislau Kaper	1944
Gauntlet, The	Jerry Fielding	1977
General Died at Dawn, The	Werner Janssen	1936
Gentleman's Agreement	Alfred Newman	1947
George Washington Slept Here	Adolph Deutsch	1942
Gettysburg	Randy Edelman	1993
Ghost	Maurice Jarre	1990
Ghost and Mrs. Muir, The	Bernard Herrmann	1947
Ghost of Frankenstein, The	Hans J. Salter	1942
Ghostbusters	Elmer Bernstein	1984
Ghostbusters II	Randy Edelman	1989
Giant	Dimitri Tiomkin	1956
Gigi	André Previn (adapt.)	1958

Gilda	Hugo Friedhofer	1946
Give Us This Night	Erich Wolfgang Korngold	1936
Glass Menagerie, The	Henry Mancini	1987
Glenn Miller Story, The	Henry Mancini	1954
Glory	James Horner	1989
God Is My Co-Pilot	Franz Waxman	1945
Goddess, The	Virgil Thomson	1958
Godfather, The	Nino Rota	1972
Godfather, Part II, The	Nino Rota/Carmine Coppola	1974
Gods Must Be Crazy II, The	Charles Fox	1989
Godzilla	Akira Ifukube	1956
Godzilla vs. the Sea Monster	Masaru Sato	1968
Going in Style	Michael Small	1979
Going My Way	Robert Emmett Dolan	1944
Gold Diggers of 1935	Ray Heindorf (arr.)	1935
Golden Boy	Victor Young	1939
Gone with the Wind	Max Steiner	1939
Good Earth, The	Herbert Stothart	1937
Good Humor Man, The	Heinz Roemheld	1950
Good Morning, Vietnam	Alex North	1987
Good, the Bad and the Ugly, The	Ennio Morricone	1966
Goodbye, Columbus	Charles Fox	1969
Goodbye, Mr. Chips	Richard Addinsell	1939
Goodbye, Mr. Chips	John Williams (adapt.)	1969
Gorillas in the Mist	Maurice Jarre	1988
Gorky Park	James Horner	1983
Gotcha!	Bill Conti	1985
Graduate, The	Dave Grusin (add. music)	1967
Grand Canyon	James Newton Howard	1991
Grand Illusion	Joseph Kosma	1937
Grapes of Wrath, The	Alfred Newman	1940

Gray Lady Down	Jerry Fielding	1978
Grease 2	Artie Butler (adapt.)	1982
Great Caruso, The	John Green (adapt.)	1951
Great Dictator, The	Charles Chaplin/Meredith Willson	1940
Great Escape, The	Elmer Bernstein	1963
Great Expectations	Edward Ward	1934
Great Gatsby, The	Robert Emmett Dolan	1949
Great Gatsby, The	Nelson Riddle (adapt.)	1974
Great Santini, The	Elmer Bernstein	1979
Greatest Story Ever Told, The	Alfred Newman	1965
Green Dolphin Street	Bronislau Kaper	1947
Green Pastures, The	Erich Wolfgang Korngold	1936
Gremlins	Jerry Goldsmith	1984
Greystoke: The Legend of Tarzan	John Scott	1984
Grifters, The	Elmer Bernstein	1990
Groundhog Day	George Fenton	1993
Guadalcanal Diary	David Buttolph	1943
Guess Who's Coming to Dinner?	Frank De Vol	1967
Guide for the Married Man, A	John Williams	1967
Guilty as Sin	Howard Shore	1993
Gun in Betty Lou's Handbag, The	Richard Gibbs	1993
Gunfight at the O. K. Corral	Dimitri Tiomkin	1957
Gunfighter, The	Alfred Newman	1950
Gung Ho	Thomas Newman	1986
Gunga Din	Alfred Newman	1939
Guns of Navarone, The	Dimitri Tiomkin	1961
Hairy Ape, The	Michel Michelet	1944
Hamlet	William Walton	1948
Hand That Rocks the Cradle, The	Graeme Revell	1991
Hang 'em High	Dominic Frontiere	1968
Hangmen Also Die	Hanss Eisler	1943

Hangover Square	Bernard Herrmann	1945
Hanover Street	John Barry	1979
Hans Christian Anderson	Walter Scharf	1952
Hard Day's Night, A	The Beatles	1964
Hard Target	Graeme Revell	1993
Hard Times	Barry DeVorzon	1975
Hard Way, The	Arthur B. Rubinstein	1991
Harry and Tonto	Bill Conti	1974
Harvey	Frank Skinner	1950
Havana	Dave Grusin	1990
Hawaii	Elmer Bernstein	1966
He Said, She Said	Miles Goodman	1991
Head Office	James Newton Howard	1986
Heart and Souls	Marc Shaiman	1993
Heart Is a Lonely Hunter, The	Dave Grusin	1968
Heart Like a Wheel	Laurence Rosenthal	1983
Heartbreak Ridge	Lennie Niehaus	1986
Heartland	Charles Gross	1979
Heaven Can Wait	Dave Grusin	1978
Heiress, The	Aaron Copland	1949
Helen of Troy	Max Steiner	1956
Hellbound: Hellraiser II	Christopher Young	1988
Hello, Dolly!	Lionel Newman (adapt.)	1969
Help!	The Beatles	1965
Henry V	William Walton	1945
Henry V	Patrick Doyle	1989
Here Comes Mr. Jordan	Frederick Hollander	1941
High and the Mighty, The	Dimitri Tiomkin	1954
High Noon	Dimitri Tiomkin	1952
High Risk	Mark Show	1993
High Society	John Green (adapt.)	1956

Hindenberg, The	David Shire	1975
Hired Hand, The	Bruce Langhorne	1971
Hiroshima, Mon Amour	Georges Delerue/Giovanni Fusco	1959
Hocus Pocus	John Debney	1993
Hoffa	David Newman	1992
Hole in the Head, A	Nelson Riddle	1959
Holiday Inn	Robert Emmett Dolan (adapt.)	1942
Home Alone	John Williams	1990
Home Alone 2: Lost in New York	John Williams	1992
Homeward Bound: The Incredible Journey	Bruce Broughton	1993
Honey, I Blew Up the Kid	Bruce Broughton	1992
Honey, I Shrunk the Kids	James Horner	1989
Hoodlum Priest, The	Richard Markowitz	1961
Hook	John Williams	1991
Hoosiers	Jerry Goldsmith	1986
Horse Soldiers, The	David Buttolph	1959
Hot Shots!	Sylvester Levay	1992
Hot Spot, The	Jack Nitzsche	1990
House of Games	Alaric Jans	1987
House of Wax	David Buttolph	1953
House on 92nd Street, The	David Buttolph	1945
Houseboat	George Duning	1958
Housesitter	Miles Goodman	1992
How the West Was Won	Alfred Newman	1963
How to Marry a Millionaire	Cyril J. Mockridge	1953
How to Steal a Million	John Williams	1966
How to Succeed in Business Without Really Trying	Nelson Riddle	1967
Howard's End	Richard Robbins	1992
Howling VI: The Freaks	Patrick Gleason	1991
Humoresque	Franz Waxman	1946
Hunchback of Notre Dame, The	Alfred Newman	1939

Hunt for Red October, The	Basil Poledouris	1990
I Never Promised You a Rose Garden	Paul Chihara	1977
I Passed for White	John Williams	1960
I Remember Mama	Roy Webb	1948
I Shot Jesse James	Albert Glasser	1949
I Walked with a Zombie	Roy Webb	1943
I Want to Live	Johnny Mandel	1958
I Was a Teenage Frankenstein	Paul Dunlap	1957
I Was a Teenage Werewolf	Paul Dunlap	1957
I'll Cry Tomorrow	Alex North	1956
Ice Castles	Marvin Hamlisch	1979
If I Were King	Richard Hageman	1938
If It's Tuesday, This Must Be Belgium	Walter Scharf	1969
Ikiru	Fumio Hayasaka	1952
Images	John Williams	1972
Importance of Being Ernest, The	Benjamin Frankel	1952
In Cold Blood	Quincy Jones	1967
In Old Chicago	Louis Silvers	1938
In the Heat of the Night	Quincy Jones	1967
In the Line of Fire	Ennio Morricone	1993
In-Laws, The	John Morris	1979
Incredible Shrinking Man, The	Herman Stein/Irving Gertz/ Hans J. Salter	1957
Indecent Proposal	John Barry	1993
Indiana Jones and the Last Crusade	John Williams	1989
Indiana Jones and the Temple of Doom	John Williams	1984
Indiscretion of an American Wife	Alessandro Cicognini	1953
Indochine	Patrick Doyle	1992
Informer, The	Max Steiner	1935
Inn of the Sixth Happiness, The	Malcolm Arnold	1958
Innocents, The	Georges Auric/Kenneth V. Jones	1961

Internal Affairs	Brian Banks/Anthony Marinelli/Mike Figgis	1990
Into the West	Patrick Doyle	1993
Intruder in the Dust	Adolph Deutsch	1949
Invasion of the Body Snatchers	Carmen Dragon	1956
Invasion of the Body Snatchers	Denny Zeitlin	1978
Invisible Man, The	Heinz Roemheld	1933
Invitation	Bronislau Kaper	1952
Invitation to a Gunfighter	David Raksin	1964
Irene	Anthony Collins (adapt.)	1940
Ironweed	John Morris	1987
Island of Dr. Moreau, The	Laurence Rosenthal	1977
Islands in the Stream	Jerry Goldsmith	1977
It Came from Outer Space	Herman Stein/Henry Mancini/ Irving Gertz	1953
It Happens Every Spring	Leigh Harline	1949
It's a Mad, Mad, Mad, Mad World	Ernest Gold	1963
It's in the Bag	Werner R. Heymann	1945
Ivan the Terrible, Part I	Sergei Prokofiev	1945
Ivan the Terrible, Part II	Sergei Prokofiev	1946
Ivanhoe	Miklós Rózsa	1952
Jackie Robinson Story, The	Herschel Burke Gilbert	1950
Jailhouse Rock	Jeff Alexander	1957
Jason and the Argonauts	Bernard Herrmann	1963
Jaws	John Williams	1975
Jazz Singer, The	Louis Silvers	1927
Jennifer 8	Christopher Young	1992
Jerk, The	Jack Elliott	1979
Jetsons: The Movie	John Debney	1990
Jewel of the Nile, The	Jack Nitzsche	1985
Jezebel	Max Steiner	1938
JFK	John Williams	1991

Joan of Arc	Hugo Friedhofer	1948
Johnny Come Lately	Leigh Harline	1943
Johnny Cool	Billy May	1963
Johnny Dangerously	John Morris	1984
Johnny Got His Gun	Jerry Fielding	1971
Johnny 99	Laura Karpman	1991
Johnny O'Clock	George Duning	1947
Jolson Sings Again	George Duning	1949
Jonathan Livingston Seagull	Neil Diamond; Lee Holdridge (adapt.)	1973
Joy Luck Club, The	Rachel Portman	1993
Juarez	Erich Wolfgang Korngold	1939
Jules and Jim	Georges Delerue	1961
Julia	Georges Delerue	1977
Juliet of the Spirits	Nino Rota	1965
Julius Caesar	Miklós Rózsa	1953
June Bride	David Buttolph	1948
Jungle Book	Miklós Rózsa	1942
Jungle Fever	Terence Blanchard	1991
Jurassic Park	John Williams	1993
Just You and Me, Kid	Jack Elliott	1979
Kafka	Cliff Martinez	1991
Kagemusha: The Shadow Warrior	Shinchiro Ikebe	1980
Kalifornia	Carter Burwell	1993
Karate Kid, The	Bill Conti	1984
Karate Kid II, The	Bill Conti	1986
Karate Kid III, The	Bill Conti	1989
Kentuckian, The	Bernard Herrmann	1955
Key Largo	Max Steiner	1948
Keys of the Kingdom, The	Alfred Newman	1944
Kidnapped	Arthur Lange	1938

Killer Elite, The	Jerry Fielding	1975
Killers, The	Miklós Rózsa	1946
Killing Fields, The	Michael Oldfield	1984
Kindergarten Cop	Randy Edelman	1990
King Kong	Max Steiner	1933
King Kong	John Barry	1976
King of the Hill	Cliff Martinez	1993
Kings Row	Erich Wolfgang Korngold	1942
Kiss Me Kate	André Previn (adapt.)	1953
Klute	Michael Small	1971
Knickerbocker Holiday	Werner R. Heymann (adapt.)	1944
Knight Without Armour	Miklós Rózsa	1937
Knock on Any Door	George Antheil	1949
Koyaanisqatsi	Philip Glass	1983
L.A. Story	Peter R. Melnick	1991
La Dolce Vita	Nino Rota	1960
La Strada	Nino Rota	1954
Lady and the Tramp	Oliver Wallace	1955
Lady in Red, The	James Horner	1979
Lady in the Dark	Robert Emmett Dolan (adapt.)	1944
Land That Time Forgot, The	Douglas Gamley	1975
Lassie Come Home	Daniele Amfitheatrof	1943
Last Action Hero	Michael Kamen	1993
Last Emperor, The	Ryuichi Sakamoto/David Byrne/ Cong Su	1987
Last of the Finest, The	Jack Nitzsche	1990
Last of the Mohicans, The	Trevor Jones/Randy Edelman	1992
Last Starfighter, The	Craig Safan	1984
Last Tango in Paris	Oliver Nelson	1973
Last Temptation of Christ, The	Peter Gabriel	1988
Laura	David Raksin	1944

Lavender Hill Mob, The	Georges Auric	1951
Lawrence of Arabia	Maurice Jarre	1962
Leadbelly	Fred Karlin (adapt.)	1976
League of Their Own, A	Hans Zimmer	1992
Lean on Me	Bill Conti	1989
Leave Her to Heaven	Alfred Newman	1945
Left-Handed Gun, The	Alexander Courage	1957
Leopard Man, The	Roy Webb	1943
Leopard, The	Nino Rota	1963
Les Misérables	Arthur Honegger	1934
Les Miserables	Alfred Newman	1935
Let It Be	The Beatles	1970
Let's Make Love	Lionel Newman	1960
Lethal Weapon	Michael Kamen/Eric Clapton	1987
Lethal Weapon 2	Michael Kamen/Eric Clapton/ David Sanborn	1989
Lethal Weapon 3	Michael Kamen/Eric Clapton/ David Sanborn	1989
Letter to Three Wives, A	Alfred Newman	1949
Letter, The	Max Steiner	1940
Lieutenant Kije	Sergei Prokofiev	1934
Life at the Top	Richard Addinsell	1965
Life Is Sweet	Rachel Portman	1991
Life of Emile Zola, The	Max Steiner	1937
Life with Mikey	Alan Menken	1993
Lifeforce	Henry Mancini	1985
Lili	Bronislau Kaper	1953
Liliom	Franz Waxman (co-comp.)	1934
Lillies of the Field	Jerry Goldsmith	1963
Limelight	Charles Chaplin/Ray Rasch/ Larry Russell	1952
Lion in Winter, The	John Barry	1968
Little Man Tate	Mark Isham	1991

Little Mermaid, The	Alan Menken	1989
Little Nemo	Tom Chase/Steve Rucker	1992
Little Night Music, A	Jonathan Tunick (adapt.)	1978
Little Prince, The	Angela Morley (adapt.)	1974
Little Romance, A	Georges Delerue	1979
Little Shop of Horrors, The	Alan Menken; Miles Goodman (adapt.)	1986
Lodger, The	Hugo Friedhofer	1944
Lonely Are the Brave	Jerry Goldsmith	1962
Long Riders, The	Ry Cooder	1980
Long, Hot Summer, The	Alex North	1958
Look Who's Talking	David Kitay	1989
Look Who's Talking, Too	David Kitay	1990
Lord Jim	Bronislau Kaper	1965
Lord of the Rings	Leonard Rosenman	1978
Lost Command	Franz Waxman	1966
Lost Horizon	Dimitri Tiomkin	1937
Lost in America	Arthur B. Rubinstein	1985
Lost Weekend, The	Miklós Rózsa	1945
Louisiana Story	Virgil Thomson	1948
Love at First Bite	Charles Bernstein	1979
Love Finds Andy Hardy	David Snell	1938
Love Is a Many Splendored Thing	Alfred Newman	1955
Love Letters	Victor Young	1945
Love Story	Francis Lai	1970
Lover, The	Gabriel Yared	1992
Lovers and Other Strangers	Fred Karlin	1970
Loves of Carmen, The	Mario Castelnuovo-Tedesco	1948
Lower Depths, The	Masaru Sato	1957
Lucas	Dave Grusin	1986
Lust for Life	Miklós Rózsa	1956
Lusty Men, The	Roy Webb	1952

M	Michel Michelet	1951
M. Butterfly	Howard Shore	1993
Mad Max	Brian May	1979
Mad Max Beyond Thunderdome	Maurice Jarre	1985
Madame Bovary	Miklós Rózsa	1949
Madame Curie	Herbert Stothart	1944
Made for Each Other	Oscar Levant	1939
Made in America	Mark Isham	1993
Madwoman of Chaillot, The	Michael L. Lewis	1969
Magic Fire	Erich Wolfgang Korngold (adapt.)	1956
Magician, The	Eric Nordgren	1958
Magnificent Ambersons, The	Bernard Herrmann	1942
Magnificent Doll	Hans J. Salter	1946
Magnificent Obsession	Frank Skinner	1954
Magnificent Seven, The	Elmer Bernstein	1960
Magnum Force	Lalo Schifrin	1973
Maid of Salem	Victor Young	1937
Major Barbara	William Walton	1941
Major Dundee	Daniele Amfitheatrof	1965
Malcolm X	Terence Blanchard	1992
Malice	Jerry Goldsmith	1993
Maltese Falcon, The	Adolph Deutsch	1941
Man and a Woman, A	Francis Lai	1966
Man Called Horse, A	Leonard Rosenman	1970
Man for All Seasons, A	Georges Delerue	1966
Man from Snowy River, The	Bruce Rowland	1982
Man in the Gray Flannel Suit, The	Bernard Herrmann	1956
Man in the Moon, The	James Newton Howard	1991
Man in the White Suit, The	Benjamin Frankel	1952
Man of a Thousand Faces	Frank Skinner	1957
Man of La Mancha	Laurence Rosenthal (adapt.)	1972

Man on the Eiffel Tower, The	Michel Michelet	1949
Man Who Came to Dinner, The	Frederick Hollander	1942
Man Who Fell to Earth, The	Stomu Yamashita	1976
Man Who Knew Too Much, The	Arthur Benjamin	1934
Man Who Knew Too Much, The	Bernard Herrmann	1956
Man Who Shot Liberty Valance, The	Cyril J. Mockridge	1962
Man Who Would Be King, The	Maurice Jarre	1975
Man with One Red Shoe, The	Thomas Newman	1985
Man with the Golden Arm, The	Elmer Bernstein	1955
Man with Two Brains, The	Joel Goldsmith	1983
Man Without a Face, The	James Horner	1993
Manchurian Candidate, The	David Amram	1962
Marathon Man	Michael Small	1976
Marnie	Bernard Herrmann	1964
Marty	Roy Webb	1955
Mary of Scotland	Nathaniel Shilkret	1936
Mary Poppins	Irwin Kostal (adapt.)	1964
Mary, Queen of Scots	John Barry	1971
M*A*S*H	Johnny Mandel	1970
Mask of Dimitrios, The	Adolph Deutsch	1944
Master of Ballantrae, The	William Alwyn	1953
Master Race, The	Ron Webb	1944
Max Dugan Returns	David Shire	1983
Mayerling	Arthur Honegger	1936
McHale's Navy	Jerry Fielding	1964
Me and the Kid	Robert Cobert	1993
Mean Season, The	Lalo Schifrin	1985
Mechanic, The	Jerry Fielding	1972
Medicine Man	Jerry Goldsmith	1992
Meet John Doe	Dimitri Tiomkin	1941
Megaforce	Jerrold Immel	1982

Melvin and Howard	Bruce Langhorne	1980
Memoirs of an Invisible Man	Shirley Walker	1992
Memphis Belle	George Fenton	1990
Men Don't Leave	Thomas Newman	1990
Merry Christmas, Mr. Lawrence	Ryuichi Sakamoto	1983
Messenger of Death	Robert O. Ragland	1989
Meteor Man, The	Cliff Eidelman	1993
Miami Blues	Gary Chang	1989
Midnight Clear, A	Mark Isham	1992
Midnight Court	David Raksin	1937
Midnight Cowboy	John Barry	1969
Midnight Express	Giorgio Moroder	1978
Midnight Lace	Frank Skinner	1960
Midsummer Night's Dream, A	Erich Wolfgang Korngold (adapt.)	1935
Mighty Ducks, The	David Newman	1992
Mighty Joe Young	Roy Webb	1949
Milagro Beanfield War, The	Dave Grusin	1988
Miller's Crossing	Carter Burwell	1990
Miracle of Our Lady of Fatima, The	Max Steiner	1952
Miracle on 34th Street	Cyril J. Mockridge	1947
Miracle Worker, The	Laurence Rosenthal	1962
Misery	Marc Shaiman	1990
Misfits, The	Alex North	1961
Missing	Vangelis	1982
Missing in Action	Jay Chattaway	1984
Mission, The	Ennio Morricone	1986
Mississippi Burning	Trevor Jones	1988
Mister Roberts	Franz Waxman	1955
Mo' Better Blues	Bill Lee	1990
Modern Times	Charles Chaplin/David Raksin (arr.)	1936
Moderns, The	Mark Isham	1988

Mohammed, Messenger of God	Maurice Jarre	1977
Money for Nothing	Craig Safan	1993
Moon and Sixpence, The	Dimitri Tiomkin	1942
Moon Is Blue, The	Herschel Burke Gilbert	1953
Moonlighting	Hans Zimmer/Stanley Myers	1982
Moonstruck	Dick Hyman	1987
Morning After, The	Paul Chihara	1986
Moscow on the Hudson	David McHugh	1984
Moulin Rouge	Georges Auric	1952
Mountains of the Moon	Michael Small	1990
Mourning Becomes Electra	Richard Hageman	1947
Mr. & Mrs. Bridge	Richard Robbins	1990
Mr. & Mrs. Smith	Edward Ward	1941
Mr. Blandings Builds His Dream House	Leigh Harline	1948
Mr. Hulot's Holiday	Alain Romans	1953
Mr. Mom	Lee Holdridge	1983
Mr. Skeffington	Franz Waxman	1944
Mr. Smith Goes to Washington	Dimitri Tiomkin	1939
Mrs. Doubtfire	Howard Shore	1993
Mrs. Miniver	Herbert Stothart	1942
Mrs. Soffel	Mark Isham	1984
Much Ado About Nothing	Patrick Doyle	1993
Muppet Christmas Carol, The	Miles Goodman (score)	1992
Murder by Death	Dave Grusin	1976
Murder on the Orient Express	Richard Rodney Bennett	1974
Murder, My Sweet	Roy Webb	1944
Music in the Air	Franz Waxman (md.)	1934
Music Man, The	Ray Heindorf (adapt.)	1962
Mutiny on the Bounty	Herbert Stothart	1935
Mutiny on the Bounty	Bronislau Kaper	1962
My Beautiful Laundrette	Stanley Myers	1985

My Bodyguard	Dave Grusin	1980
My Boyfriend's Back	Harry Manfredini	1993
My Cousin Vinny	Randy Edelman	1992
My Fair Lady	André Previn (adapt.)	1964
My Favorite Blonde	David Buttolph	1942
My Left Foot	Elmer Bernstein	1989
My Man Godfrey	Charles Previn	1936
My Science Project	Peter Bernstein	1985
My Stepmother Is an Alien	Alan Silvestri	1988
My Uncle, Mr. Hulot	Alain Romans	1956
Mystic Pizza	David McHugh	1988
Naked Gun: From the Files of Police Squad	Ira Newborn	1988
Naked Gun 2 1/2: The Smell of Fear	Ira Newborn	1991
Naked Jungle, The	Daniele Amfitheatrof	1954
Name of the Rose, The	James Horner	1986
Napoleon [1927 silent film]	Carmine Coppola	1980
National Lampoon's Class Reunion	Peter Bernstein	1983
National Velvet	Herbert Stothart	1945
Natural, The	Randy Newman	1984
Naughty Marietta	Herbert Stothart (adapt.)	1935
Navy Seals	Sylvester Levay	1990
Never Cry Wolf	Mark Isham	1983
Never on Sunday	Manos Hadjidakis	1960
NeverEnding Story, The	Klaus Doldinger/Giorgio Moroder	1984
NeverEnding Story 2, The: The Next Chapter	Robert Folk	1990
Newsies	Alan Menken/J.A.C. Redford (score)	1992
Nicholas and Alexandra	Richard Rodney Bennett	1971
Night and Day	Max Steiner (adapt.)/Ray Heindorf (arr./orch.)	1946
Night at the Opera, A	Herbert Stothart	1935

Night Has a Thousand Eyes	Victor Young	1948
Night Shift	Burt Bacharach	1982
Night Song	Leith Stevens	1947
'night, Mother	David Shire	1988
Nightcomers, The	Jerry Fielding	1972
Nightmare Before Christmas, The	Danny Elfman	1993
Nightmare on Elm Street, A	Charles Bernstein	1984
Nightmare on Elm Street, A Part 2: Freddy's Revenge	Christopher Young	1985
Nightmare on Elm Street III, A: Dream Warriors	Angelo Badalamenti	1987
976—Evil	Tom Chase/Steve Rucker	1988
Nine to Five	Charles Fox	1980
1900	Ennio Morricone	1977
Ninja III—The Domination	Laurin Rinder/W. Michael Lewis	1984
Ninotchka	Werner R. Heymann	1939
No, No, Nanette	Anthony Collins (adapt.)	1940
No Way Out	Maurice Jarre	1987
No Way to Treat a Lady	Stanley Myers	1968
Nocturne	Leigh Harline	1946
None But the Lonely Heart	Hanss Eisler	1944
Norma Rae	David Shire	1979
North by Northwest	Bernard Herrmann	1959
Not as a Stranger	George Antheil	1955
Nothing Sacred	Oscar Levant	1937
Notorious	Roy Webb	1946
Now, Voyager	Max Steiner	1942
Number One with a Bullet	Alf Clausen	1987
Nun and the Sergeant, The	Jerry Fielding	1962
Nun's Story, The	Franz Waxman	1959
Nutty Professor, The	Walter Scharf	1963
Objective, Burma!	Franz Waxman	1945

Obsession	Bernard Herrmann	1976
Odd Couple, The	Neal Hefti	1968
Odd Man Out	William Alwyn	1947
Of Human Bondage	Max Steiner	1934
Of Human Bondage	Erich Wolfgang Korngold	1946
Of Mice and Men	Aaron Copland	1939
Of Mice and Men	Mark Isham	1992
Officer and a Gentleman, An	Jack Nitzsche	1982
Oh, God!	Jack Elliott	1978
Oklahoma!	Adolph Deutsch (adapt.)	1956
Old Gringo	Lee Holdridge	1989
Old Man and the Sea, The	Dimitri Tiomkin	1958
Old Yeller	Oliver Wallace	1957
Oliver & Company	J.A.C. Redford	1988
Oliver Twist	Sir Arnold Bax	1948
Oliver!	John Green (adapt.)	1968
Omen, The	Jerry Goldsmith	1976
On Golden Pond	Dave Grusin	1981
On Her Majesty's Secret Service	John Barry	1969
On the Beach	Ernest Gold	1959
On the Waterfront	Leonard Bernstein	1954
Once Upon a Time in America	Ennio Morricone	1984
Once Upon a Time in the West	Ennio Morricone	1969
One Flew over the Cuckoo's Nest	Jack Nitzsche	1976
One from the Heart	Bob Alcivar	1982
One Million B.C.	Werner R. Heymann	1940
One Million Years B.C.	Mario Nascimbene	1967
One-Eyed Jacks	Hugo Friedhofer	1960
Other People's Money	David Newman	1991
Other Side of the Mountain, The	Charles Fox	1975
Other Side of the Mountain: Part 2, The	Lee Holdridge	1978

Our Town	Aaron Copland	1940
Our Vines Have Tender Grapes	Bronislau Kaper	1945
Out for Justice	David Michael Frank	1991
Out of Africa	John Barry	1985
Out of It	Michael Small	1969
Outlaw Josey Wales, The	Jerry Fielding	1976
Outrageous Fortune	Alan Silvestri	1987
Ox-Bow Incident, The	Cyril J. Mockridge	1943
Pacific Heights	Hans Zimmer	1990
Paint Your Wagon	Nelson Riddle (adapt.)	1969
Pale Rider, The	Lennie Niehaus	1985
Paleface, The	Victor Young	1948
Palm Beach Story, The	Victor Young	1942
Panther Panchali	Ravi Shankar	1956
Paper Chase, The	John Williams	1973
Papillon	Jerry Goldsmith	1973
Parallax View, The	Michael Small	1974
Paranoiac	Elisabeth Lutyens	1964
Parenthood	Randy Newman	1989
Paris Blues	Duke Ellington	1961
Paris, Texas	Ry Cooder	1984
Passage to India, A	Maurice Jarre	1984
Passion Fish	Mason Daring	1992
Passport to Pimlico	Georges Auric	1949
Pat and Mike	David Raksin	1952
Pat Garrett and Billy the Kid	Bob Dylan	1973
Patch of Blue, A	Jerry Goldsmith	1965
Paths of Glory	Gerald Fried	1957
Patriot Games	James Horner	1992
Patton	Jerry Goldsmith	1970
Pawnbroker, The	Quincy Jones	1965

Pee Wee's Big Adventure	Danny Elfman	1985
People Under the Stairs, The	Don Peake	1991
Personal Best	Jill Fraser/Jack Nitzsche	1982
Peter Pan	Oliver Wallace	1953
Peyton Place	Franz Waxman	1957
Phantom of the Opera	Edward Ward	1943
Phar Lap	Bruce Rowland	1983
Piano, The	Michael Nyman	1993
Pickle, The	Michel Legrand	1993
Picnic	George Duning	1955
Pillow Talk	Frank De Vol	1959
Pink Panther, The	Henry Mancini	1964
Pinocchio	Leigh Harline/Paul J. Smith	1940
Place in the Sun, A	Franz Waxman	1951
Places in the Heart	Howard Shore	1984
Plainsman, The	George Antheil	1937
Planes, Trains and Automobiles	Ira Newborn	1987
Planet of the Apes	Jerry Goldsmith	1968
Platoon	Georges Delerue	1986
Playboys, The	Jean-Claude Petit	1992
Player, The	Thomas Newman	1992
Plow That Broke the Plains, The	Virgil Thomson	1936
Pocketful of Miracles	Walter Scharf	1961
Poetic Justice	Stanley Clarke	1993
Police Academy	Robert Folk	1984
Poltergeist	Jerry Goldsmith	1982
Porgy and Bess	André Previn (adapt.)	1959
Pork Chop Hill	Leonard Rosenman	1959
Poseidon Adventure, The	John Williams	1972
Postman Always Rings Twice, The	George Bassman	1946
Postman Always Rings Twice, The	Michael Small	1981

Powaqqatsi	Philip Glass	1988
Power of One, The	Hans Zimmer	1992
Presumed Innocent	John Williams	1990
Pretty Baby	David Buttolph	1950
Pretty in Pink	Michael Gore	1986
Pretty Woman	James Newton Howard	1990
Pride and the Passion, The	George Antheil	1957
Pride of St. Louis, The	Arthur Lange	1952
Pride of the Yankees, The	Leigh Harline	1942
Prince and the Pauper, The	Erich Wolfgang Korngold	1937
Prince of Foxes	Alfred Newman	1949
Prince Valiant	Franz Waxman	1954
Prisoner of Zenda, The	Alfred Newman	1937
Private Affairs of Bel Ami, The	Darius Milhaud	1947
Private Benjamin	Bill Conti	1980
Private Lives of Elizabeth and Essex, The	Erich Wolfgang Korngold	1939
Prizzi's Honor	Alex North	1985
Prodigal, The	Bruce Broughton	1984
Producers, The	John Morris	1968
Program, The	Michel Columbier	1993
Providence	Miklós Rózsa	1977
Psycho	Bernard Herrmann	1960
Punchline	Charles Gross	1988
Puppet Master	Richard Band	1989
Purple Rain	Michel Colombier	1984
Purple Rose of Cairo, The	Dick Hyman	1985
Pygmalion	Arthur Honegger	1938
Quest for Fire	Philippe Sarde	1982
Quick Change	Randy Edelman	1990
Quiet Man, The	Victor Young	1952
Quo Vadis	Miklós Rózsa	1951

Radio Days	Dick Hyman	1987
Radio Flyer	Hans Zimmer	1991
Ragtime	Randy Newman	1981
Raiders of the Lost Ark	John Williams	1981
Rain Man	Hans Zimmer	1988
Rainmaker, The	Alex North	1956
Rains of Ranchipur, The	Hugo Friedhofer	1955
Raintree County	John Green	1957
Raisin in the Sun, A	Laurence Rosenthal	1961
Raising Arizona	Carter Burwell	1987
Rambling Rose	Elmer Bernstein	1991
Rambo: First Blood Part II	Jerry Goldsmith	1985
Ran	Toru Takemitsu	1985
Rashomon	Fumio Hayasaka	1950
Rawhide	Sol Kaplan	1951
Razor's Edge, The	Alfred Newman	1946
Re-Animator	Richard Band	1985
Rebecca	Franz Waxman	1940
Rebel Without a Cause	Leonard Rosenman	1955
Reckless	Thomas Newman	1984
Red Badge of Courage, The	Bronislau Kaper	1951
Red Beard	Masaru Sato	1965
Red House, The	Miklós Rózsa	1947
Red Pony, The	Aaron Copland	1949
Red River	Dimitri Tiomkin	1948
Red Sky at Morning	Billy Goldenberg	1971
Redeemer, The	David Raksin	1966
Reivers, The	John Williams	1969
Remains of the Day, The	Richard Robbins	1993
Remo Williams: The Adventure Begins	Craig Safan	1985
Rescuers Down Under, The	Bruce Broughton	1990

Resurrection	Dimitri Tiomkin	1931
Return of a Man Called Horse, The	Laurence Rosenthal	1976
Return of Jesse James, The	Ferde Grofé	1950
Return of the Jedi	John Williams	1983
Return to Snowy River	Bruce Rowland	1988
Return to Oz	David Shire	1985
Revenge of the Nerds	Thomas Newman	1984
Reversal of Fortune	Mark Isham	1990
Revolution	John Corigliano	1985
Rhapsody in Blue	Max Steiner/Ray Heindorf (arr.)	1945
Rhinestone	Mike Post (adapt.)	1984
Rhino!	Lalo Schifrin	1984
Richard III	William Walton	1956
Right Stuff, The	Bill Conti	1983
Rio Bravo	Dimitri Tiomkin	1959
Riot in Cell Block 11	Herschel Burke Gilbert	1954
Rise and Fall of Legs Diamond, The	Leonard Rosenman	1960
Rising Sun	Toru Takemitsu	1993
Risky Business	Tangerine Dream	1983
River, The	Virgil Thomson	1937
River, The	John Williams	1984
River Runs Through It, A	Mark Isham	1992
Road Warrior, The	Brian May	1982
Robe, The	Alfred Newman	1953
Robin Hood: Men in Tights	Hummie Mann	1993
Robin Hood: Prince of Thieves	Michael Kamen	1991
RoboCop	Basil Poledouris	1987
RoboCop 2	Leonard Rosenman	1990
RoboCop 3	Basil Poledouris	1993
Rocketship X-M	Ferde Grofé	1950
Rocky	Bill Conti	1976

Rocky Horror Picture Show, The	Richard Hartley	1975
Rocky II	Bill Conti	1979
Rocky III	Bill Conti	1982
Rocky V	Bill Conti	1990
Roman Holiday	Georges Auric	1953
Romancing the Stone	Alan Silvestri	1984
Romeo and Juliet	Nino Rota	1968
Rookie, The	Lennie Niehaus	1990
Room with a View, A	Richard Robbins	1985
Rooster Cogburn	Laurence Rosenthal	1975
Rose Tattoo, The	Alex North	1955
'Round Midnight	Herbie Hancock	1986
Ruby Gentry	Heinz Roemheld	1952
Rumble Fish	Stewart Copeland	1983
Running Brave	Mike Post	1983
Russians Are Coming! The Russians Are Coming!, The	Johnny Mandel	1966
Ruthless People	Michel Colombier	1986
Ryan's Daughter	Maurice Jarre	1970
Saboteur	Frank Skinner	1942
Saludos Amigos	Paul J. Smith/Edward Plumb	1943
Salvador	Georges Delerue	1986
San Francisco	Herbert Stothart	1936
Sandlot, The	David Newman	1993
Sand Pebbles, The	Jerry Goldsmith	1966
Sandpiper, The	Johnny Mandel	1965
Sands of Iwo Jima	Victor Young	1949
Sanjuro	Masaru Sato	1962
Saps at Sea	Marvin Hatley	1940
Sarafina!	Stanley Myers (score)	1992
Saturday Night Fever	David Shire (adapt./add. music)	1977

Saturday's Hero	Elmer Bernstein	1951
Say Anything . . .	Anne Dudley	1989
Scarface	Giorgio Moroder	1983
Scarlet Pimpernel, The	Arthur Benjamin	1935
Scarlet Street	Hans J. Salter	1945
Scent of a Woman	Thomas Newman	1992
Scorpio	Jerry Fielding	1973
Scott of the Antarctic	Ralph Vaughan Williams	1948
Sea Hawk, The	Erich Wolfgang Korngold	1940
Sea of Love	Trevor Jones	1989
Searching for Bobby Fischer	James Horner	1993
Secret Garden, The	Zbigniew Preisner	1993
Secret Life of Plants, The	Stevie Wonder	1984
Secret Life of Walter Mitty, The	David Raksin	1947
Secret of My Success, The	David Foster	1988
Secret of Santa Vittoria, The	Ernest Gold	1969
Separate Tables	David Raksin	1958
Serpico	Mikis Theodorakis	1973
Seven Alone	Robert O. Ragland	1975
Seven Brides for Seven Brothers	Adolph Deutsch (adapt.)	1954
Seven Samurai, The	Fumio Hayasaka	1954
Seventh Cross, The	Roy Webb	1944
Seventh Seal, The	Eric Nordgren	1957
Seventh Veil, The	Benjamin Frankel	1945
7th Voyage of Sinbad, The	Bernard Herrmann	1958
Sex and the Single Girl	Neal Hefti	1965
sex, lies and videotape	Cliff Martinez	1989
Shadow of a Doubt	Dimitri Tiomkin	1943
Shaft	Isaac Hayes	1971
Shaggy Dog, The	Paul J. Smith	1959
Shakiest Gun in the West, The	Vic Mizzy	1968

Shane	Victor Young	1953
She Wore a Yellow Ribbon	Richard Hageman	1949
She's Having a Baby	Stewart Copeland	1988
Sheltering Sky, The	Richard Horowitz	1990
Shine On, Harvest Moon	Heinz Roemheld	1944
Shoes of the Fisherman, The	Alex North	1968
Shoot the Piano Player	Georges Delerue	1960
Shoot to Kill	John Scott	1988
Shootist, The	Elmer Bernstein	1976
Shopworn Angel, The	Edward Ward	1938
Short Circuit	David Shire	1986
Short Circuit II	Charles Fox	1988
Short Cuts	Mark Isham	1993
Showboat	Adolph Deutsch (adapt.)	1951
Sibling Rivalry	Jack Elliott	1990
Silence of the Lambs, The	Howard Shore	1991
Silent Movie	John Morris	1976
Silent Night, Deadly Night	Richard Band	1984
Silk Stockings	André Previn (adapt.)	1957
Silkwood	Georges Delerue	1983
Silver Chalice, The	Franz Waxman	1954
Silverado	Bruce Broughton	1985
Since You Went Away	Max Steiner	1944
Sing	Jay Gruska (adapt.)	1989
Single White Female	Howard Shore	1992
Sister Act	Marc Shaiman (adapt.)	1992
Sisters	Bernard Herrmann	1973
Six Weeks	Dudley Moore	1982
Sixteen Candles	Ira Newborn	1984
16 Days of Glory	Lee Holdridge	1985
Skin Game	David Shire	1973

Skull, The	Elisabeth Lutyens	1965
Sleeping with the Enemy	Jerry Goldsmith	1991
Sleepless in Seattle	Marc Shaiman	1993
Sleuth	John Addison	1972
Slipper and the Rose, The: The Story of Cinderella	Angela Morley (adapt.)	1976
Sliver	Howard Shore	1993
Snake Pit, The	Alfred Newman	1948
Sneakers	James Horner	1992
Snow White and the Seven Dwarfs	Frank Churchill/Leigh Harline/ Paul Smith	1938
So I Married an Axe Murderer	Bruce Broughton	1993
Soldier's Story, A	Herbie Hancock	1984
Some Like It Hot	Adolph Deutsch	1959
Sommersby	Danny Elfman	1993
Somewhere in Time	John Barry	1980
Son of Frankenstein	Frank Skinner	1939
Son of the Pink Panther	Henry Mancini	1993
Song Is Born, A	Hugo Friedhofer	1948
Song of Bernadette, The	Alfred Newman	1943
Song of the South	Daniele Amfitheatrof/Paul Smith	1946
Song to Remember, A	Miklós Rózsa (adapt.)	1945
Sophie's Choice	Marvin Hamlisch	1982
Sorry, Wrong Number	Franz Waxman	1948
Sound of Music, The	Irwin Kostal (adapt.)	1965
Sounder	Taj Mahal	1972
Sounder, Part 2	Taj Mahal	1976
Southern Yankee, A	David Snell	1948
Southerner, The	Werner Janssen	1945
Spaceballs	John Morris	1987
Spacecamp	John Williams	1986
Spartacus	Alex North	1960

Specter of the Rose, The	George Antheil	1946
Spellbound	Miklós Rózsa	1945
Spiral Staircase, The	Roy Webb	1945
Spirit of St. Louis, The	Franz Waxman	1957
Splash	Lee Holdridge	1984
Spy Who Came in from the Cold, The	Sol Kaplan	1965
Spy Who Loved Me, The	Marvin Hamlisch	1977
St. Elmo's Fire	David Foster	1985
Stand and Deliver	Craig Safan	1988
Stalking Moon, The	Fred Karlin	1968
Stand by Me	Jack Nitzsche	1986
Star Chamber, The	Michael Small	1983
Star Trek II: The Wrath of Khan	James Horner	1982
Star Trek III: The Search for Spock	James Horner	1984
Star Trek IV: The Voyage Home	Leonard Rosenman	1986
Star Trek V: The Final Frontier	Jerry Goldsmith	1989
Star Trek VI: The Undiscovered Country	Cliff Eidelman	1991
Star Trek: The Motion Picture	Jerry Goldsmith	1979
Star Wars	John Williams	1977
Start the Revolution Without Me	John Addison	1970
Stavisky	Stephen Sondheim	1974
Steel Magnolias	Georges Delerue	1989
Stella	John Morris	1990
Stephen King's Silver Bullet	Jay Chattaway	1985
Sterile Cuckoo, The	Fred Karlin	1969
Sting, The	Marvin Hamlisch (adapt. Scott Joplin's music)	1973
Stir Crazy	Tom Scott	1980
Straw Dogs	Jerry Fielding	1971
Strawberry Blonde, The	Heinz Roemheld	1941
Street Scene	Alfred Newman	1931

Streetcar Named Desire, A	Alex North	1951
Striking Distance	Brad Fiedel	1993
String of Beads, A	Elisabeth Lutyens	1949
Stunt Man, The	Dominic Frontiere	1980
Sudden Impact	Lalo Schifrin	1983
Sugerland Express, The	John Williams	1974
Summer of '42	Michel Legrand	1971
Sun Comes Up, The	André Previn	1949
Sundays and Cybele	Maurice Jarre	1962
Sunny	Anthony Collins	1941
Sunny Side Up	Hugo Friedhofer (arr.)	1929
Sunset Boulevard	Franz Waxman	1950
Superfly	Curtis Mayfield	1972
Superman	John Williams	1978
Superman II	Ken Thorne (adapt.)	1981
Superman III	Ken Thorne (adapt.)	1983
Superman IV: The Quest for Peace	Alexander Courage (adapt.)	1987
Super Mario Bros.	Alan Silvestri	1993
Support Your Local Sheriff!	Jeff Alexander	1969
Sure Thing, The	Tom Scott	1985
Surf Ninjas	David Kitay	1993
Suspect	Michael Kamen	1987
Suspicion	Franz Waxman	1941
Swamp Thing	Harry Manfredini	1982
Swimmer, The	Marvin Hamlisch	1968
Swing Shift	Patrick Williams	1984
Swiss Miss	Marvin Hatley	1938
Switch	Henry Mancini	1991
Take Me Out to the Ballgame	Adolph Deutsch	1949
Taking of Pelham 1-2-3, The	David Shire	1974
Tale of Two Cities, A	Herbert Stothart	1935

Tales from the Crypt	Douglas Gamley	1972
Tales from the Darkside: The Movie	Jim Manzie (co-comp.)	1990
Tales of Manhattan	Sol Kaplan	1942
Talk of the Town, The	Frederick Hollander	1942
Talk Radio	Stewart Copeland	1988
Tap	James Newton Howard	1989
Taras Bulba	Franz Waxman	1962
Taxi Driver	Bernard Herrmann	1976
Teacher's Pet	Roy Webb	1958
Teenage Mutant Ninja Turtles	John du Prez	1990
Teenage Mutant Ninja Turtles II: The Secret of the Ooze	John du Prez	1991
Teenage Mutant Turtles III	John du Prez	1993
10	Henry Mancini	1979
Ten Commandments, The	Elmer Bernstein	1956
Ten North Frederick	Leigh Harline	1958
10 to Midnight	Robert O. Ragland	1983
Terminator, The	Brad Fiedel	1984
Terminator 2: Judgment Day	Brad Fiedel	1991
Terms of Endearment	Michael Gore	1983
Testament	James Horner	1983
That's Entertainment	Henry Mancini	1974
Thelma and Louise	Hans Zimmer	1991
Then Came Bronson	George Duning	1970
There's No Business Like Show Business	Lionel Newman	1954
Therese and Isabelle	Georges Auric	1968
They Died With Their Boots On	Max Steiner	1942
They Drive by Night	Adolph Deutsch	1940
They Got Me Covered	Leigh Harline	1943
They Shoot Horses, Don't They?	John Green/Al Woodbury (adapt.)	1969

They Were Expendable	Herbert Stothart	1945
Thief	Tangerine Dream	1981
Thief of Bagdad, The	Miklós Rózsa	1940
Thief, The	Herschel Burke Gilbert	1952
Thin Man, The	William Axt	1934
Thing, The	Dimitri Tiomkin	1951
Things Change	Alaric Jans	1988
Third Man, The	Anton Karas	1949
Thirty Seconds Over Tokyo	Herbert Stothart	1945
This Boy's Life	Carter Burwell	1993
This Is the Army	Ray Heindorf (arr.)	1943
Thomas Crown Affair, The	Michel Legrand	1968
Thoroughly Modern Millie	Elmer Bernstein	1967
Those Magnificent Men in Their Flying Machines	Ron Goodwin	1965
Three Caballeros, The	Paul J. Smith/Edward Plumb	1944
Three Coins in a Fountain	Victor Young	1954
Three Faces of Eve, The	Robert Emmett Dolan	1957
Three Men and a Baby	Marvin Hamlisch	1987
Three Men and a Little Lady	Tom Snow	1990
Three Musketeers, The	Michel Legrand	1974
Three Musketeers, The	Michael Kamen	1993
3:10 to Yuma	George Duning	1957
Throne of Blood	Masaru Sato	1957
Throw Momma from the Train	David Newman	1987
Thunderball	John Barry	1965
THX-1138	Lalo Schifrin	1971
Tight Little Island	Ernest Irving	1949
Till We Meet Again	David Buttolph	1944
Time After Time	Miklós Rózsa	1979
Time Machine, The	Russell Garcia	1960
To Be or Not To Be	Werner R. Heymann	1942

To Catch a Thief	Lyn Murray	1955
To Each His Own	Victor Young	1946
To Have and Have Not	Franz Waxman	1945
To Kill a Mockingbird	Elmer Bernstein	1962
To Live and Die in L.A.	Wang Chung	1985
Toast of New York, The	Nathaniel Shilkret	1937
Tom and Jerry: The Movie	Henry Mancini	1992
Tom Jones	John Addison	1963
Tony Rome	Billy May	1967
Tootsie	Dave Grusin	1982
Top Gun	Harold Faltermeyer	1986
Topper	Marvin Hatley	1937
Torn Curtain	John Addison	1966
Total Recall	Jerry Goldsmith	1990
Touch of Evil	Henry Mancini	1958
Towering Inferno, The	John Williams	1974
Toy Soldiers	Robert Folk	1991
Toys	Hans Zimmer	1992
Toys in the Attic	George Duning	1963
Track of the Cat	Roy Webb	1954
Trading Places	Elmer Bernstein	1983
Trent's Last Case	Anthony Collins	1952
Trip to Bountiful	J.A.C. Redford	1985
Triumph of the Spirit	Cliff Eidelman	1989
Trouble with Harry, The	Bernard Herrmann	1955
True Confessions	Georges Delerue	1981
True Grit	Elmer Bernstein	1969
True Romance	Hans Zimmer	1993
Tune in Tomorrow	Wynton Marsalis	1990
Turner and Hooch	Charles Gross	1989
Turning Point, The	John Lanchbery	1977

20,000 Leagues Under the Sea	Paul J. Smith	1954
Twilight Zone: The Movie	Jerry Goldsmith	1983
Twin Peaks—Fire Walk with Me	Angelo Badalamenti	1992
Twins	Georges Delerue/Randy Edelman	1988
Two for the Road	Henry Mancini	1967
Two Jakes, The	Van Dyke Parks	1990
Two Mrs. Carrolls, The	Franz Waxman	1947
Two Weeks in Another Town	David Raksin	1962
Ugetsu	Fumio Hayasaka	1953
Umbrellas of Cherbourg, The	Michel Legrand	1964
Unchained	Alex North	1955
Under Fire	Jerry Goldsmith	1983
Under Siege	Gary Chang	1992
Under the Volcano	Alex North	1984
Undercover Blues	David Newman	1993
Unforgiven	Lennie Niehaus	1992
Uninvited, The	Victor Young	1944
Unmarried Woman, An	Bill Conti	1978
Untouchables, The	Ennio Morricone	1987
Up from the Depths	James Horner	1979
Up the Down Staircase	Fred Karlin	1967
Used People	Rachel Portman	1992
Valley of the Dolls	John Williams (adapt.)	1967
Vera Cruz	Hugo Friedhofer	1954
Verdict, The	Johnny Mandel	1982
Vertigo	Bernard Herrmann	1958
Victor/Victoria	Henry Mancini	1982
Victory	Bill Conti	1981
Village of the Damned	Ron Goodwin	1960
Vincent and Theo	Gabriel Yared	1990
Virgin Spring, The	Eric Nordgren	1960

Virginian, The	Daniele Amfitheatrof	1946
Viva Zapata!	Alex North	1952
Von Richtofen and Brown	Hugo Friedhofer	1971
Voyage to the Bottom of the Sea	Bert A. Shefter/Paul Sawtell	1961
Wait Until Dark	Henry Mancini	1967
Wake Island	David Buttolph	1942
Walk on the Wild Side	Elmer Bernstein	1962
Walking Tall	Walter Scharf	1973
Wall Street	Stewart Copeland	1987
War and Peace	Nino Rota	1956
War of the Roses, The	David Newman	1989
War Wagon, The	Dimitri Tiomkin	1967
WarGames	Arthur B. Rubinstein	1983
Warriors, The	Barry DeVorzon	1979
Waterdance, The	Michael Convertino	1992
Waterland	Carter Burwell	1992
Waterloo	Nino Rota	1971
Watership Down	Angela Morley	1978
Way Down South	Victor Young	1939
Way Out West	Marvin Hatley	1937
Way We Were, The	Marvin Hamlisch	1973
Wayne's World—The Movie	J. Peter Robinson	1992
Wells Fargo	Victor Young	1937
West Side Story	John Green/Saul Chaplin/Irwin Kostal/ Sid Ramin (adapt.)	1961
Westworld	Fred Karlin	1973
What About Bob?	Miles Goodman	1991
What Ever Happened to Aunt Alice?	Gerald Fried	1968
What's Love Got To Do with It	Stanley Clarke	1993
What's Up, Doc?	Artie Butler	1972
When a Stranger Calls	Dana Kaproff	1979

When Dinosaurs Ruled the Earth	Mario Nascimbene	1969
When Harry Met Sally . . .	Marc Shaiman (adapt.)	1989
When Worlds Collide	Leith Stevens	1951
Where's Poppa?	Jack Elliott	1970
Whistle Blower, The	John Scott	1986
White Cliffs of Dover, The	Herbert Stothart	1944
White Dawn, The	Henry Mancini	1974
White Fang	Basil Poledouris	1991
White Hunter, Black Heart	Lennie Niehaus	1990
White Men Can't Jump	Bennie Wallace	1992
White Nights	Michel Colombier	1985
White Tower, The	Roy Webb	1950
Who Framed Roger Rabbit	Alan Silvestri	1988
Who'll Stop the Rain	Laurence Rosenthal	1978
Who's Afraid of Virginia Woolf?	Alex North	1966
Wichita	Hans J. Salter	1955
Wild at Heart	Angelo Badalamenti	1990
Wild Bunch, The	Jerry Fielding	1969
Wild for Kicks	John Barry	1959
Wild One, The	Leith Stevens	1954
Wild Seed, The	Richard Markowitz	1965
Wild Strawberries	Eric Nordgren	1957
Will Penny	David Raksin	1968
Will Success Spoil Rock Hunter?	Cyril J. Mockridge	1957
Wind	Basil Poledouris	1992
Wind and the Lion, The	Jerry Goldsmith	1975
Winter People	John Scott	1989
Winterset	Nathaniel Shilkret	1936
Witches of Eastwick, The	John Williams	1987
Without a Clue	Henry Mancini	1988
Witness	Maurice Jarre	1985

Wiz, The	Quincy Jones (adapt.)	1978
Wizard of Oz, The	Herbert Stothart (score)	1939
Wolf Man, The	Charles Previn (co-comp.)	1941
Woman in Red, The	John Morris	1984
Woman of the Dunes	Toru Takemitsu	1964
Woman of the Year	Franz Waxman	1942
Women in Love	Georges Delerue	1970
World According to Garp, The	David Shire	1982
World Without End	Elisabeth Lutyens	1956
Wuthering Heights	Alfred Newman	1939
Yakuza, The	Dave Grusin	1975
Yankee Doodle Dandy	Heinz Roemheld (adapt.)/ Ray Heindorf (arr.)	1942
Yanks	Richard Rodney Bennett	1979
Year of Living Dangerously, The	Maurice Jarre	1983
Year of the Comet	Hummie Mann	1992
Yellowneck	Laurence Rosenthal	1955
Yellow Submarine	The Beatles	1968
Yentl	Michel Legrand	1983
Yojimbo	Masaru Sato	1961
You Only Live Twice	John Barry	1967
Young Frankenstein	John Morris	1974
Young Guns	Brian Banks/Anthony Marinelli	1988
Young Lions, The	Hugo Friedhofer	1958
Young Sherlock Holmes	Bruce Broughton	1985
Z	Mikis Theodorakis	1969
Zandy's Bride	Michael Franks	1974
Zelig	Dick Hyman	1983
Zorba the Greek	Mikis Theodorakis	1964

A Selective Annotated Bibliography

■ ■ ■

ACADEMY AWARDS

Osborne, Robert. *50 Golden Years of Oscar.* La Brea, California: ESE California, 1979.

———. *60 Years of the Oscar.* New York: Abbeville Press, 1989.

Wiley, Mason, and Damien Bona. *Inside Oscar.* New York: Ballantine Books, 1986.

A year-by-year account of the Academy Awards before, during, and after Oscar night. Entertaining and educative. Includes a complete listing of all nominations and awards.

ANALYSIS

Atkins, Irene Kahn. *Source Music in Motion Pictures.* East Brunswick, New Jersey: Fairleigh Dickinson University Press, 1983. Fred Baker and Ross Firestone, editors.

Bazelon, Irwin. *Knowing the Score: Notes on Film Music.* New York: Van Nostrand Reinhold Co., 1975.

The author has a very distinct attitude regarding concert music composers and Hollywood which is unnecessarily offputting. This attitude, emphasized again and again, is eventually softened by the author's use of many examples of film scores by non–concert music composers (some with jazz backgrounds, etc.).

Copland, Aaron. *Our New Music.* New York: McGraw-Hill Book Co., Whittlesey House, 1941.

Includes a section entitled "Music in the Films."

———. *What to Listen For in Music.* Revised edition, New York: McGraw-Hill, 1957. Reprinted, with a new introduction by William Schuman, 1988.

Eisler, Hanns. *Composing for the Films.* New York: Oxford University Press, 1947.

Gorbman, Claudia. *Unheard Melodies.* Bloomington & Indianapolis: BFI Publishing, 1987.

A scholarly examination of "narrative film music." Includes a detailed discussion of Max Steiner's score for *King Kong* (1933), and Maurice Jaubert's score for *Zéro de conduite* (early 1930s).

Kalinak, Kathryn Marie. *Music as Narrative Structure In Hollywood Film.* Ph.D. Thesis, University of Illinois at Urbana-Champaign, 1982.

Includes a detailed study of four scores: *Captain Blood* (Korngold), *The Informer* (Steiner), *The Magnificent Ambersons* (Herrmann), and *Laura* (Raksin). Written as a postgraduate thesis. Well researched, with an excellent list of bibliographic citations.

———. *Settling the Score: Music and the Classical Hollywood Film.* Madison, Wisconsin: The University of Wisconsin Press, 1992.

Prendergast, Roy M. *Film Music: A Neglected Art* New York: W. W. Norton & Co., 1977, 1992.

Organized primarily chronologically, with additional chapters on cartoons and animated films, aesthetics, and technique. Prendergast is a veteran music editor with practical as well as analytical insight.

Steiner, Fred. "Herrmann's 'Black and White' Music for Hitchcock's *Psycho,* " in *Filmmusic Notebook* Vol. 1, No. 1 (Fall 1974), pp. 28–36; Vol. 1, No. 2 (Winter 1974–75), pp. 26–46.

A detailed analysis of Herrmann's score for *Psycho.*

BIBLIOGRAPHIES

Marks, Martin. "Film Music: The Material, Literature and Present State of Research," in *MLA Notes 36 (1979),* pp. 282–325. Revised in *Journal of the University Film and Video.*

Sharples, Win, Jr. "A Selected and Annotated Bibliography of Books and Articles on Music in the Cinema," in *Cinema Journal* 17/2 (Spring 1978), pp. 36–67.

Wescott, Steven D. *A Comprehensive Bibliography of Music for Film and Television.* Detroit: Information Coordinators, 1985.

With entries through 1983. Library of Congress supplement issued in September 1986.

COMPOSER BIOGRAPHIES

Antheil, George. *Bad Boy of Music.* Hollywood: Samuel French, 1990 (© 1945).

Levant, Oscar. *The Memoirs of an Amnesiac.* Hollywood: Samuel French, 1969 (© 1965).

Mancini, Henry, with Gene Lees. *Did They Mention the Music?* Chicago: Contemporary Books, Inc., 1989.

Excellent, informal autobiography of this influential film composer.

Previn, André. *No Minor Chords: My Days in Hollywood.* New York: Doubleday, 1991.

Extremely winning account of Previn's Hollywood experiences, with dozens of engaging (and often enlightening) stories about the late forties to late sixties.

Rózsa, Miklós. *Double Life.* Tunbridge Wells, Kent: The Baton Press, 1982.

Rózsa's frank and compelling autobiography, with many references to his work on film scoring assignments. Although not gossipy in nature, it does give a feeling for what it was like to work in Hollywood from the mid-thirties to the mid-sixties.

Smith, Steven C. *A Heart at Fire's Center: The Life and Music of Bernard Herrmann.* Berkeley and Los Angeles: University of California Press, 1991.

Smith discusses both Herrmann the man and Herrmann the composer with insight and compassion. The available research resources have been supplemented with a great deal of new material derived from interviews with those close to the composer and his work. A definitive biography.

Tiomkin, Dimitri, and Prosper Buranelli. *Please Don't Hate Me.* New York: Doubleday and Company, Inc., 1959.

Colorful autobiography of Tiomkin, rich with anecdotes.

FILM HISTORY

Behlmer, Rudy. *Behind the Scenes.* Hollywood: Samuel French Trade, 1982, 1989.

Fascinating, with detailed information and stories regarding the making of sixteen motion pictures, including *Lost Horizon, The Adventures of Robin Hood, Casablanca, Laura, Singin' in the Rain, High Noon.* Behlmer knows film music, too, and provides behind-the-scenes insights.

_____. Selected, edited, and annotated by Behlmer. *Inside Warner Bros. (1935–1951).* New York: Simon & Schuster, Inc., 1985.

_____. *Memo from David O. Selznick.* New York: The Viking Press, 1972. Introduction by S. N. Behrman.

A sampling of the famous Selznick memos gleaned from his entire career, including behing-the-scenes intrigue during *A Star Is Born, Gone with the Wind,* and dozens of others.

Corey, Melinda, and George Ochoa. *The Man in Lincoln's Nose.* New York: Simon & Schuster Inc., 1990.

875 quotes on Hollywood and the movies, divided into 23 topics. Good first-person reading.

Eames, John Douglas. *The MGM Story.* New York: Crown Publishers Inc., 1975. Revised, New York: Portland House, 1990.

Additional text for 1982–1989 by Ronald Bergen. More than 1700 photos, plus notes about all MGM releases (both their own productions and those they picked up for distribution) year by year from 1924 to 1989.

Eastman, John. *Retakes: Behind the Scenes of 500 Classic Movies.* New York: Ballantine Books, 1989.

Goldner, Orville, and George E. Turner. *The Making of King Kong.* New York: A. S. Barnes, 1975.

Harmetz, Aljean. *The Making of The Wizard of Oz.* New York: Dell Publishing, 1989 (© 1977).

Hay, Peter. *MGM: When the Lion Roars.* Atlanta: Turner Publishing, Inc., 1991.

Includes 700 photos (150 in color) reproduced more faithfully than in *The MGM Story.* Historically rich with behind-the-scenes color and details. Chronicles the years from 1924 to 1959. No listing of the films.

Knight, Arthur. *The Liveliest Art: A Panoramic History of the Movies.* New York: Macmillan, 1957. Revised edition, 1978.

Maltin, Leonard. *Of Mice and Magic: A History of American Animated Cartoons.* New York: Plume, 1980. Revised edition 1987.

Maltin's definitive study of American cartoons, organized by studio, with great illustrations.

Norman, Barry. *The Story of Hollywood.* New York: New American Library, 1987.

Absolutely excellent history of Hollywood, told in a thorough but extremely engaging way. Plenty of first-person quotes make for great reading, and the photos are a bonus.

Oberfirst, Robert. *Al Jolson: You Ain't Heard Nothin' Yet.* San Diego, New York: A. S. Barnes & Company, Inc., 1980.

Pollack, Dale. *Skywalking: The Life and Films of George Lucas.* Hollywood: Samuel French, 1990 (© 1983)

Schatz, Thomas. *The Genius of the System.* New York: Pantheon Books, 1988.

> An outstanding history of Hollywood, focusing on the studios while maintaining a chronological frame of reference. Much of the book has been researched from primary archival materials originating from studio files.

Sherman, Eric. *Directing the Film: Directors on the Art of Directing.* Los Angeles: Acrobat Books, 1976.

FILM MUSIC HISTORY

Darby, William, & Jack Du Bois. *American Film Music: Major Composers, Techniques, Trends, 1915-1990.* Jefferson, North Carolina: McFarland & Company, Inc., 1990.

> Chapters on 14 major composers (including many single-line thematic quotes from their scores, and filmographies), plus silent movies, the studios, foreign composers, the '40s and '50s, the '60s and '70s, the '80s. Also, a very useful annotated bibliography.

Evans, Mark. *Soundtrack: The Music of the Movies.* New York: Da Capo Press, Inc., 1975.

> Organized chronologically, with additional chapters on functions of the film score and ethics and aesthetics, fable and folklore.

Huntley, John. *British Film Music.* London: Skelton Robinson, 1947. Reprinted New York: Arno Press, 1972. Foreword by Muir Mathieson.

London, Kurt, translated by Eric S. Bensinger. *Film Music.* London: Faber & Faber Ltd., 1936. Foreword by Constance Lambert.

> An early scholarly work on film music. Includes a fine group of chapters tracing the development of music for the silent films. The technical sections on sound and microphones are dated, but nevertheless give an interesting picture of the world of film music in the mid-thirties.

Larson, Randall D. *Musique Fantastique.* A Survey of Film Music in the Fantastic Cinema. New Jersey & London: The Scarecrow Press, Inc., 1985.

> An extensive survey of this genre, with biographical material on many lesser-known and relatively undocumented composers. Includes a filmography for the genre, and an extensive international checklist of recorded music.

McCarty, Clifford, editor. *Film Music 1.* New York & London: Garland Publishing, Inc., 1989.

> Eleven chapters on a variety of topics, including interviews with composer Bernard Herrmann and silent-movie organist Gaylord Carter, analysis of scores by Max Steiner (*The Informer,* by Kathryn Kalinak) and Miklós Rózsa (*Ben-Hur,* by Steven D. Wescott), music used in the *Flash Gordon* and *Buck Rogers* serials from 1936 to 1940 (by Richard H. Bush), and a fascinating essay by David Raksin recounting his early experiences as a film composer.

Palmer, Christopher. *The Composer in Hollywood.* New York and London: Marion Boyars Publishers, 1990.

> A knowledgeable musician's study of Hollywood music from 1930 to 1950, concentrating on Steiner, Korngold, Newman, Waxman, Tiomkin, Webb, Rózsa, Herrmann, North, Bernstein, and Rosenman.

Thomas, Tony. *Music for the Movies.* South Brunswick, New Jersey: A. S. Barnes and Co., 1973.

> Organized both chronologically and stylistically, Thomas' book is engaging, educative, and expert in his use of the composers' first-person quotes. Young, Green, Newman, Tiomkin, Waxman, Kaper, Rózsa, Steiner, Korngold, Herrmann, Friedhofer, Raksin, Antheil, Thomson, Copland, North, Bernstein, Mancini, Rosenman, Goldsmith, and Schifrin are profiled. Includes filmographies of the composers discussed, and great photos.

_____. *Film Score: The View from the Podium.* South Brunswick and New York: A. S. Barnes and Company, 1979.

This outstanding book contains chapters on 20 film composers; after a biographical sketch of each composer, the composer speaks to the reader, through either written remarks or interviews. Copland, Rózsa, Raksin, Waxman, Friedhofer, Steiner, Korngold, Tiomkin, Herrmann, Newman, Kaper, Salter, Bernstein, Mancini, Fred Steiner, Alwyn, Addison, Fielding, Goldsmith, and Rosenman are discussed. Many excerpts from *Film Score* have been included in *Listening to Movies.*

_____. *Film Score: The Art & Craft of Movie Music.* Burbank, California: Riverwood Press, 1991.

A new edition of the 1979 *Film Score,* with new chapters on Ernest Gold, Georges Delerue, Victor Young, Laurence Rosenthal, and John Williams. Includes some new photos, and expanded filmographies where relevant. Highly recommended.

Winkler, Max. "The Origins of Film Music," in *Films in Review,* December, 1951.

Winkler claimed to have been the first to devise the silent movie cue sheet. Whether or not he was first, he was on the cutting edge at that time, and his account is interesting from that vantage point.

FILMOGRAPHIES

Limbacher, James L. *Film Music: From Violins to Video.* New Jersey: The Scarecrow Press, Inc., 1974.

The first of three volumes of filmographies by Limbacher. The most comprehensive material available, but often cited by scholars like Fred Steiner and Clifford McCarty as being only about 80 percent accurate, due to both errors and omissions. It makes a very worthwhile supplement to the more accurate McCarty's *Film Composers in America.*

_____. *Keeping Score: Film Music 1972–1979.* New Jersey & London: The Scarecrow Press, Inc., 1981.

A continuation of *Film Music,* plus additional entries and corrections.

Limbacher, James L., and H. Stephen Wright. *Keeping Score: Film and Television Music, 1980–1988.* New Jersey & London: The Scarecrow Press, Inc., 1991.

A continuation of *Keeping Score,* "with additional coverage of 1921–1979."

McCarty, Clifford. *Film Composers in America: A Checklist of Their Work.* New York: Da Capo Press, 1953, 1972. Foreword by Lawrence Morton.

Carefully researched, comprehensive filmographies of 163 film composers through 1953. Includes many indications of the composite and collaborative scores, as well as occasional orchestration credits, which are otherwise difficult to trace without studying studio files (which McCarty has done). Indispensable for those interested in who scored which film. Look for his follow-up book, which will cover the years up to 1970, meticulously researched at the studios.

Smith, Steven C. *Film Composers Guide.* Beverly Hills: Lone Eagle, 1990.

Two extensive listings, one of living composers, one of "notable composers of the past." Filmography by title at the end. Revised occasionally.

MUSIC EDITING

Carlin, Dan, Sr. *Music in Film and Video Productions.* Boston & London: Focal Press, 1991.

A manual designed for the music supervisor as well as the editor. Both readable and useful.

Lustig, Milton. *Music Editing for Motion Pictures.* New York: Hastings House, 1980.

> A comprehensive how-to text on the various techniques and challenges of music editing. Filled with important details for the aspiring/working music editor, while at the same time providing helpful technical and historical background for the general reader.

MUSICALS

Altman, Rick. *The American Film Musical.* Bloomington and Indianapolis: Indiana University Press, 1989.

Altman, Rick, editor. *Genre: The Musical.* London, Boston, and Henley: Routledge & Kegan Paul, 1981

> An anthology of 13 essays (serious analytical writing) and an excellent annotated bibliography by Jane Feuer.

Astaire, Fred. *Steps in Time.* New York: Harper & Row, Publishers, 1959. Foreword by Ginger Rogers.

Casper, Joseph. *Vincente Minnelli and the Film Musical.* New York: A. S. Barnes, 1977.

> Includes a discussion of each aspect of his musicals: staging, music, dance, etc. Casper cites numerous scenes in detail throughout the book. Jane Feuer, in *The Hollywood Musical,* states that the research is based on secondary sources, and not too accurate.

Feuer, Jane. *The Hollywood Musical.* Bloomington: Indiana University Press, 1982.

> A thoughtful study of the Hollywood musical as an important film genre. Establishes and explains important aspects of musicals, including the significance of bringing live forms of entertainment onto the screen (backstage musicals), the use of jazz vs opera and the classics as a metaphor for "the war between elite and popular art." Excellent examples from film musicals cited throughout.

Green, Stanley. *Encyclopedia of the Musical Film.* New York: Oxford University Press, 1981.

———. *Hollywood Musicals Year by Year.* Milwaukee, Wisconsin: Hal Leonard Publishing Corporation, 1990.

Hirschhorn, Clive. *The Hollywood Musical.* Revised edition, New York: Portland House, 1991 (© 1981). Foreword by Gene Kelly.

> 1,399 films are discussed—every Hollywood musical from 1927 to 1990. Presented year by year, with songs listed for each film, synopses, and much background material. Hundreds of photos. Separate indexes for films, songs, composers and lyricists, performers, and other creative personnel.

Kimball, Robert, and Alfred Simon. *The Gershwins.* New York: Atheneum, 1973. Introduction by Richard Rodgers. Biographical Foreword by John S. Wilson.

> Rich with photos and quotes from personal letters of the Gershwins and others. Lyrics for all the songs.

Kobal, John. *Gotta Sing, Gotta Dance: A Pictorial History of Film Musicals.* London, New York: Hamlyn, 1971.

Kreuger, Miles, editor. *The Movie Musical from Vitaphone to 42nd Street.* New York: Dover Publications, Inc., 1975.

> An evocative collection of articles, photographs, film reviews, and advertisments from *Photoplay,* the monthly magazine which called itself "The National Guide to Motion Pictures." In his introduction, Kreuger has written a short history of early sound on film, and adds an introduction for each year (from 1926 through June 1933). All reviews of film song recordings released from October 1929 through October 1930 are included at the end of the book.

Minnelli, Vincente, with Hector Arce. *I Remember it Well.* Hollywood, California: Samuel French, 1974. Foreword by Alan Jay Lerner.

Mueller, John. *Astaire Dancing.* The Musical Films. New York: Wings Books, 1985.

> Lavish, with credits, educative photos, and documentation of every Astaire number, including

extraordinary background and behind-the-scenes material.

Pike, Bob, and Dave Martin. *The Genius of Busby Berkeley.* California: CFS Books, 1973.

> Primarily an extensive interview with Berkeley, and stills from his production numbers.

Stern, Lee Edward. *The Movie Musical.* New York: Pyramid Communications, Inc., 1974.

> A short history with separate chapters organized by decade. Readable and enjoyable, with nice photographs.

Taylor, John Russell, and Arthur Jackson. *The Hollywood Musical.* New York: McGraw-Hill Book Company, 1971.

> A fine book detailing the history of the Hollywood musical, throughout which Taylor states his artistic preferences. He includes separate chapters on the composers, the artists, and the filmmakers. The reference materials in the back are invaluable: the Selected Filmography lists credits for an impressive group of films; an index of names details information and film titles associated with the artists and creators of the Hollywood musicals; the index of songs includes approximately 2,750 song titles cross-referenced by the films in which they appear.

Thomas, Tony, and Jim Terry, with Busby Berkeley. *The Busby Berkeley Book.* Connecticut: New York Graphic Society Ltd., 1973. Foreword by Ruby Keeler.

> A biography followed by a film-by-film account of Berkeley's work, with credits and great photos.

PERIODICALS AND JOURNALS

Film music journals are labors of love, and sometimes go out of print without notice. They may be replaced with new publications, however, so it is a good idea to get on as many mailing lists as possible (by subscribing to several of these periodicals). Prices are subject to change. The following are recommended for additional reading and research.

The Cue Sheet c/o The Society for the
    Preservation of Film Music
PO Box 93536
Hollywood, CA 90093-0536
An excellent quarterly journal published by the Society for the Preservation of Film Music, with fine historical articles and photos, as well as information on current film music activities. Write for information regarding the society and journal.

Film Score Monthly
c/o Lukas Kendall
Box 1554
Amherst College
Amherst, MA 01002-5000
A monthly publication of The Soundtrack Club that is packed with news about other publications, film music concerts, current assignments, soundtrack album reviews, where to buy soundtrack albums, and letters from its readers. Kendall is particularly interested in making information about film music resources available, and provides lists of shops, mail order vendors, collectors, fan clubs and publications, and so on. Subscriptions are $15 a year in the U.S. and Canada (cash, check, money order); $20 per year elsewhere (American cash, international money/postal order). The editor is currently a student at Amherst College; during summers and after May 1996, write to RFD 488, Vineyard Haven, MA 02568.

From Silents to Satellite
c/o John Williams
1 Folly Square
Bridport, Dorset DT6 3PU, England
Published by the British film music publisher and journalist John Williams (not the composer) six times a year. Emphasis on British composers. Subscriptions are £13 for four issues or £20 for six issues (includes airmail postage to the U.S., Australia, and Canada).

The Hollywood Reporter
6715 Sunset Boulevard
Hollywood, CA 90028

This film and television trade paper publishes a special issue on film music twice a year (summer and winter). The issue is 75 cents in the U.S., and $1.25 elsewhere.

Movie Music
c/o Jonathan Axworthy
Membership Secretary
The Goldsmith Society
102 Horndean Road
Emsworth, Hants PO10 7TL, England

Excellent articles, interviews, news, and photos. Includes *Legend,* the Goldsmith Society journal. Published twice a year. Subscriptions are £7 in the UK (check or postal order); £9 in Europe (bank draft or international money/postal order); £12 in the U.S. and elsewhere (bank draft or international money/postal order).

Musica Sul Velluto,
Nieuwlandhof 114
1106 RM
Amsterdam, Holland

Five issues a year (in English) specializing in Ennio Morricone. Subscriptions are $20 a year in the U.S.; 30 Dutch guilders in Europe; 35 guilders elsewhere.

Music from the Movies
1 Folly Square
Bridport, Dorset, DT6 3PU, England

Published by the British film music journalist John Williams, who released the first issue in December, 1992. Many interviews, news about current and future soundtracks and CDs, CD reviews, etc. Very worthwhile. Williams has been active in publishing film music materials for years; it is a good idea to get on his mailing list so you will be informed of his forthcoming projects.

The New Zealand Film Music Bulletin
35 Jenken Street
Invercargill, New Zealand

A 20-page quarterly journal, published in February, May, August, and November. Subscriptions are $10 in the U.S.; £5 in the UK and Europe; $5 in New Zealand; and $10 in Australia.

The Score
c/o Society of Composers and Lyricists
400 S. Beverly Drive Suite 214
Beverly Hills, CA 90212

A fine quarterly newsletter which includes news and articles on technical and professional subjects. Contact SCL for information.

Soundtrack!
The Collector's Quarterly
c/o Luc Van de Ven
Astridlaan 171, 2800
Mechelen, Belgium

Excellent. Interesting articles, interviews with composers, and photos. Now includes CinemaScore. Published in March, June, September, and December. Back issues available also. Subscriptions are $15 a year (cash only, well-wrapped bills) in the U.S. and Canada; £10 for 6 issues (cash only) in the UK; and 500 Belgian francs (international postal order) in Europe and Japan.

The following are no longer published, but are available in some libraries (including the Academy of Motion Picture Arts and Sciences library); they contain interviews, reviews, and news, and have been cited a number of times in this book.

Filmmusic Notebook
Published during the mid-seventies by Elmer Bernstein, who transcribed some of his outstanding interviews with film composers, including David Raksin, Richard Rodney Bennett, John Addison, Leo Shuken, Jerry Goldsmith, Henry Mancini, Hugo Friedhofer, Bronislau Kaper, and John Green.

Film Music Notes
Published from 1941 through the forties and fifties.

REFERENCE

Ehrenstein, David, and Bill Reed. *Rock on Film*. New York: Delilah Books, 1982.

> A specialized resource that lists films by title, with the appropriate information for each.

Elsas, Diana, editor. *Factfile: Film Music*. Washington: American Film Institute, 1977.

> A well-rounded resource providing information on educational possibilities and various film music resources.

Halliwell, Leslie. *The Filmgoer's Companion*. New York: Avon Books, 1989 (seventh edition; © 1965).

> Film professionals and terms from A to Z.

Manvell, Roger, editor. *The International Encyclopedia of Film*. New York: Crown Publishers, Inc., 1972.

REVIEWS AND LISTS

Ebert, Roger. *Roger Ebert's Movie Home Companion*. Kansas City, Missouri: Andrews and McMeel, 1991 (1st edition © 1985).

> More than 1,000 reviews, plus some of Ebert's essays, and helpful resource listings. Revised frequently.

Halliwell, Leslie. *Halliwell's Film Guide*. John Walker, editor, eighth edition. Great Britain: Grafton Books (Collins Publishing Group) 1989 (1st edition 1977).

> Credits, plot synopses, Academy Award winners and nominations, critical evaluations, quotes from contemporary reviewers. The music credits for films requiring on-the-site research are not always accurate, but this is still a definitive film resource.

Hirschhorn, Clive. *The Columbia Story*. New York: Crown Publishers, 1990.

> Releases (including important films picked up for distribution) from 1922 through 1988.

Listed year by year, but with no credits listing as such, although directors and actors are mentioned in the synopses of each film. Over 1400 photos.

Kael, Pauline. *Kiss Kiss Bang Bang*. Boston: Little, Brown & Company, 1968.

> Reviews from 1985 to 1988.

————. *Movie Love*. New York: Plume, 1991.

> Reviews from 1988 to 1991.

————. *Hooked*. New York: E. P. Dutton, 1989.

Maltin, Leonard. *Leonard Maltin's Movie and Video Guide 1993*. New York: Signet, 1992.

> 19,000 films rated from **** to BOMB. TV films rated above average, average, or below average. Indicates films released on video. Directing and acting credits, plus synopses. Absolutely indispensable.

Variety Staff Writers. Derek Elley, consulting editor. *Variety Movie Guide*. New York: Prentice Hall, 1992. Foreword by Richard Attenborough.

> Sometimes-trimmed versions of more than 5000 film reviews as they first appeared in *Variety* from 1907 to 1991, presented in alphabetical order.

SCORING

Dolan, Robert Emmett. *Music in Modern Media*. New York: G. Schirmer, 1967.

> An excellent text and technical manual; covers some subjects rarely documented and of particular historical interest now, like microphone placement on the scoring stage.

Hagen, Earle. *Scoring For Films*. New York: Criterion Music Corp., 1971.

> A solid text especially strong in the traditional technical aspects of film scoring. Includes mu-

sical examples and a demonstration record. Paperback available from Imperial Creations, Box 66, New York, New York 10022.

―――――. *Advanced Scoring for Films.* Century City, California: E. D. J. Music Publishers, Inc., 1989.

Karlin, Fred, and Rayburn Wright. *On the Track: A Guide to Contemporary Film Scoring.* New York: Schirmer Books, 1990. Foreword by John Williams.

> Primarily a comprehensive textbook for those interested in scoring films. The many first-person accounts by composers, lyricists, producers, directors, editors, recording mixers, and businesspeople make this book accesible to the general reader also. Approximately 150 excerpts from a great variety of film scores.

Mancini, Henry. *Sounds and Scores: A Practical Guide to Professional Orchestration.* Greenwich, Connecticut: Northridge Music Inc., 1962, 1967, 1973.

> Examples of orchestral colors and effects, taken directly from Mancini's scores for "Peter Gunn" and "Mr. Lucky" television episodes and other scores, as recorded on RCA. Recorded examples are included with the book.

Manvell, Roger, and John Huntley. *The Technique of Film Music.* London: Focal Press, 1957. Revised edition by Richard Arnell and Peter Day. New York: Hastings House, 1975.

> Includes discussions of the scores for *Henry V, The Louisiana Story, The Best Years of Our Lives, Julius Caesar,* and *Odd Man Out.* Additional scores discussed in the 1975 edition.

Sabaneev, Leonid. *Music for the Films: A Handbook for Composers and Conductors.* Translated by S. W. Pring. London: Pitman, 1935. Reprinted New York: Arno Press, 1978.

Skinner, Frank. *Underscore.* New York: Criterion Music Corp., 1960 (© 1950).

> An early text by an accomplished craftsman.

Steiner, Max. "Scoring the Film," in Nancy Naumburg, editor, *We Make the Movies.* New York: W. W. Norton & Co., 1937. pp. 216–38.

SILENT FILMS

Anderson, Gillian B. *Music for Silent Films 1894–1929: A Guide.* Washington: Library of Congress, 1988. Foreword by Eileen Bowser.

> A beautifully produced catalogue of the silent film music contained in the Library of Congress Collection, the Museum of Modern Art, the George Eastman House, the New York Public Library, the Fédération Internationale des Archives du Film, and the Arthur Kleiner Collection. The 36-page introduction (including illustrations) offers a rich history and background.

Behlmer, Rudy. "Tumult, Battle and Blaze": Looking Back on the 1920s—and Since—with Gaylord Carter, the Dean of Theater Organists, in Clifford McCarty, *Film Music 1.* New York, Garland Publishing, Inc., 1989, pp. 19–59.

Brown, Karl. Edited and with an introduction by Kevin Brownlow. *Adventures with D. W. Griffith.* New York, Farrar, Straus and Giroux, 1973.

> Brown was assistant to Griffith's cameraman on all the major Griffith films until *Broken Blossoms.*

Brownlow, Kevin. *The Parade's Gone By . . .* New York: Knopf, 1968.

Gish, Lillian, with Ann Pinchot. *The Movies, Mr. Griffith, and Me.* San Francisco: Mercury House, 1969.

Hoffman, Charles. *Sounds for Silents.* New York: DBS Publications/Drama Book Specialists, 1970. Foreword by Lillian Gish.

> A short history of music in silent films, amply illustrated with both photographs and musical examples (including a short 33 1/3 rpm recording of Hoffman accompanying portions of several films at the Museum of Modern Art, 1968–69).

Koszarski, Richard. *An Evening's Entertainment: The Age of the Silent Feature Picture, 1915–1928.* New York: Charles Scribner's Sons, 1990. Volume 3 of the *History of the American Cinema* series, Charles Harpole, General Editor.

Outstanding background material on the development of silent films, with a number of references to the music which accompanied them.

Marks, Martin Miller. *Music and the Silent Film: Contexts and Case Studies, 1895-1924.* New York: Oxford University Press, 1994.

Scores discussed include *The Birth of a Nation* (a compiled score by Breil, 1915), Entr'acte (1924), and Camille Saint-Saens' score for *L'Assassinat du Duc de Guise* (1908).

Walker, Alexander. *The Shattered Silents: How the Talkies Came to Stay.* New York: William Morrow and Company, Inc., 1979.

Walker's emphasis on the transition years between silents and sound films (1926–1929) makes this book a particularly fascinating and valuable reference.

Wenden, D. J. *The Birth of the Movies.* New York: E. P. Dutton, 1975.

SONGWRITERS

Bergreen, Laurence. *As Thousands Cheer: The Life of Irving Berlin.* New York: Penguin Books, 1991.

Bordman, Gerald. *Jerome Kern: His Life and Music.* New York: Oxford University Press, 1980.

Hemming, Roy. *The Melody Lingers On: The Great Songwriters and Their Movie Musicals.* New York: Newmarket Press, 1986.

Chapters on Arlen, Berlin, Gershwin, Kern, McHugh, Porter, Rainger, Rodgers, Warren, and Whiting, plus another chapter on others. Photos, and film listings with credits and song titles.

Kimball, Robert, editor. *Cole.* New York: Holt, Rinehart & Winston, 1971. Biographical essay by Brendan Gill.

Photos, a listing of all Porter's songs. Lyrics, newspaper clippings, numerous first-person quotes.

Rosenberg, Deena. *Fascinating Rhythm: The Collaboration of George and Ira Gershwin.* New York: Dutton, 1991.

Thomas, Tony. *The Hollywood Musical: The Saga of Songwriter Harry Warren.* Secaucus, New Jersey: Citadel Press, 1975. Foreword by Bing Crosby.

Including the music and lyrics for 25 of Warren's songs. Excellent first-person quotes from Harry Warren and historical detail from Thomas. Nearly 300 photos.

SOUNDTRACK RECORDINGS

Harris, Steve. *Film and Television Composers: An International Discography, 1920–1989.* Jefferson, North Carolina and London: McFarland & Company, Inc., 1992.

Organized by composer, from Temple Abady to Hans Zimmer. "I have tried herein to list all the different productions with which the composers were involved ... Conventional phonograph records; United States pressings; full scores; and original soundtrack peformances."

————. *Film, Television and Stage Music on Phonograph Records.* Jefferson, North Carolina and London: McFarland & Company, Inc., 1988.

Osborne, Jerry. *The Official Price Guide to Movie/TV Soundtracks and Original Cast Albums.* Ruth Maupin, editor. New York: House of Collectibles, 1991.

Prices are considered unrealistically high by the collectors' market. Look for revised editions as time goes by.

Whitburn, Joel. *The Billboard Book of Top 40 Albums.* New York: Watson-Guptill Publications, 1991.

A chart guide to every album in the Top 40 since 1955.

THE WORKING ENVIRONMENT

Baker, Fred, and Ross Firestone, editors. *Movie People: At Work in the Business of Film.* New York: Douglas Book Corp., 1972.

Interview with Quincy Jones, pp. 147–70.

Faulkner, Robert R. *Hollywood Studio Musicians: Their Work and Careers in the Recording Industry.* Chicago: Aldine-Atherton, 1971. Reprinted Lanham, Maryland: University Press of America, 1985.

An inside look at the life and working conditions of Hollywood studio musicians.

————. *Music on Demand: Composers and Careers in the Hollywood Film Industry.* New Brunswick, New Jersey: Transaction Books, 1983.

Unique sociological study of the careers, attitudes, and observations of many top film and television composers of the seventies, with a great deal of direct quotation of the composers.

End Notes

■ ■ ■

The following abbreviations have been used:

AFI Oral history interviews taken by Irene Kahn Atkins for the American Film Institute Louis B. Mayer Library.
June Edgerton and George Adams, interviewed September 9, 1974 to April 17, 1975.
Hugo Friedhofer, interviewed in 1974.
Joseph Gershenson, interviewed March 4 to 15, 1976.
Bronislau Kaper, interviewed July 14 to October 14, 1975.

AMPAS Academy of Motion Picture Arts and Sciences Library.

AP André Previn, *No Minor Chords: My Days in Hollywood*, (New York: Doubleday, 1991).

K/W Fred Karlin and Rayburn Wright, *On the Track* (New York: Schirmer Books, 1990).

MR Miklós Rózsa, *Double Life* (Tunbridge Wells, Kent, England: The Baton Press, 1982).

SCN Soundtrack Collectors Newsletter.

SCS Stephen C. Smith, *A Heart at Fire's Center: The Life and Music of Bernard Herrmann* (University of California Press, 1991).

SMU Oral History interview of Bill Stinson for Southern Methodist University August 28, 1986 by Ronald L. Davis.

SPFM Elmer Bernstein speech to the Society for the Preservation of Film Music, March, 1992.

TT *Film Score: The View from the Podium* (South Brunswick and New York: A. S. Barnes and Company, 1979).

TT (rev.) *Film Score: The Art & Craft of Movie Music* (Burbank, CA: Riverwood Press, 1991. "Revised and expanded edition of *Film Score*").

USC University of Southern California Cinema-Television Library Archives.

YALE Oral History interviews by Irene Kahn Atkins for the Yale University American Heritage Oral History Series.
David Raksin, interviewed December 6, 1976 and February 15, 1977.
Bill Stinson, interviewed October 12 and 13, 1977.

All quotes not endnoted are from interviews with the author from September 1991 through April 1992 (except Portman, interviewed in February 1993).

PREFACE

xi "It is almost impossible to make movies": SCS, p. 295, from a quote in Kevin Thomas, "Film Composer Settles a Score," *L.A. Times*, February 4, 1968, p. 21.

CHAPTER I

3 "I agonized": Marshall Berges, "Carol and Jerry Goldsmith," *L.A. Times Home Magazine*, September 19, 1976.

3 "I always ask": David Kraft, "Alex North: The Master Speaks," *The Hollywood Reporter, January 22, 1988, p. S-57.*

3 In the late thirties: George Korngold, "The Sea Hawk," RCA Victor CD 60863-2-RG liner notes, p. 10 (reprinted from the original LP release).

3 "You can have": Wolfgang Breyer, "An Interview with John Barry," *Soundtrack!* Vol. 7, No. 25, March 1988, p. 30.

4 "It can get you in trouble": Shire to FK, 1985.

4 "If you have read": James Fitzpatrick, "An Interview with Maurice Jarre," *Soundtrack!* Vol. 3, No. 12, December 1984, p. 6.

5 "The film was so unusual": *Film Music Notes* Volume I, #1, October 1941.

6 "I try to find": Matthias Büdinger, "Carl Davis Unbound," *Soundtrack!* Vol. 9, No. 35, September 1990, p. 7.

6 "George made it": Dale Pollock, *Skywalking: The Life and Films of George Lucas*, (Hollywood, 1983), p. 180.

6 "All the time": Billy Wilder, "The Spirit of St. Louis," Varèse Sarabande CD VSD-5212 liner notes.

7 "We live now": "An Interview with John Scott," *Soundtrack!* Vol. 5, No. 18, June 1986, p. 5.

8 "I've changed my attitude": Steve Simak, "Another Pair of Blockbusters from Jerry Goldsmith," *CinemaScore* 11/12, Fall/Winter 1983, p. 5.

8 "David [Lean] did use": James Fitzpatrick, "A Conversation with Maurice Jarre," *Soundtrack!* Vol. 3, No. 12, December 1984, p. 8.

9 "I find an intelligent": David Kraft, "An Interview with Jerry Goldsmith," *Hollywood Reporter*, January 17, 1989.

9 "The hardest thing": Tony Thomas, *Music for the Movies*, (New Jersey, 1973), pp. 121–22.

9 "Before I have any meetings": AFI.

11 ". . . strictly spotted": John Wright, "John Williams Lecture," *SCN* Vol. 4, No. 15, October 1978, p. 17.

11 "Music can slow up": Thomas, pp. 121–22.

11 "If the film is working": Paul Seydor, "Interview with Jerry Fielding," *Filmmusic Notebook* Vol. III, No. 3, 1977, p. 45.

11 "Every time a producer": Art Buchwald, "Quiet! Tiomkin Talks," *Sacramento Bee*, July 9, 1961.

11 "The whole recognition": 1973 speech to Eastman College, cited in SCS, p. 360.

11 "Nothing is as loud": Thomas, p. 90.

12 "I was watching": John Wright, "Lecture by Jerry Goldsmith," *SCN* Vol. 4, No. 17, April 1979, p. 5.

12 "Economy is a strong factor": TT, p. 226.

12 "My idea had been": SCS, p. 322.

12 "I work completely": TT (rev.), p. 293.

12 "I think": Eric Sherman, *Directing the Film: Film Directors on Their Art* (California, 1976), p. 258.

12 "In general": Buchwald.

13 "There are all types": Mark Dery, "James Horner," *Keyboard*, July 1988.

13 "You're going to": Tony Crawley, *The Steven Spielberg Story* (New York, 1983), pp. 38–39.

13 "Anything I did": Randall D. Larson, "Jerry Goldsmith On *Poltergeist* and *Nimh*," *CinemaScore* 11/12, Fall/Winter 1983, p. 3.

14 "I look at": Charles Bernstein, "Danny Elfman—with Charles Bernstein," *The Score* Vol. IV, No. 2, Summer, 1989.

14 "We all talk": Jean-Pierre Pecqueriaux, "A Conversation with Philippe Sarde," *Soundtrack!* Vol. 4, No. 14, June 1985, p. 6.

14 "I didn't have a lot": Sue Gold, "Scoring at Home," *Mix Magazine*, October 1991.

14 "I remember": Elmer Bernstein, "A Conversation with Richard Rodney Bennett," *Filmmusic Notebook* Vol. II, No. 1, 1976, p. 20.

14 "I prefer directors": James Fitzpatrick, "An Interview with Maurice Jarre, *Soundtrack!* Vol. 3, No. 12, December 1984.

14 "When you're trying": YALE.

14 "Ron said something": Glenn Wooddell, June 22, 1989 interview for Music of the Cinema radio show.

14–15 "The critical thing": Randall D. Larson, "An Interview with Danny Elfman," *Soundtrack!* Vol. 9, No. 35, September 1990, p. 25.

15 Shortly after Dimitri: Dimitri Tiomkin and Prosper Buranelli, *Please Don't Hate Me* (New York, 1959), p. 220.

15 "When I was scoring": Wooddell

15 "something that is unobtrusive": Alfred Hitchcock, notes re: *Vertigo*, AMPAS Hitchcock Special Collection.

15 "Hitchcock . . . felt it": SCS, p. 237.

15 (1) ". . . The music": Fred Zinnemann, notes from a memo to Stuart Baird of the Ladd Company, June 9, 1982, AMPAS Zinnemann Special Collection.

16 "Both [Stanley] Kubrick:" Ronald Bohn, "A Conversation with Gerald Fried," *SCN* Vol. 4, No. 18, July 1979, p. 4.

CHAPTER 2

17 "I've heard some say": Berges.

17 "The task at hand": Paul Seydor, "Interview with Jerry Fielding," *Filmmusic Notebook* Vol. III, No. 3, 1977, p. 44.

17 "The biggest problem": Thomas, *Music for the Movies*, p. 191.

17–18 "The opening shots": MR, p. 128–9.

18 "Wanted to have": Glenn Wooddell, "Basil Poledouris," *Movie Music*, Spring 1991.

18 "The focus of the movie": Barry to FK, 1985.

19 "It was George Lucas": Tony Thomas, "A Conversation with John Williams," *The Cue Sheet* Vol. 8, No. 1, March, 1991.

20 ". . . for an instrument": Randall D. Larson, "An Interview with Gerald Fried," *Soundtrack!* Vol. 9, No. 35, September, 1990, p. 46.

20 "I wanted to write": Christopher Palmer, "Alex North," *Filmmusic Notebook* Vol. III, No. 1, 1977, p. 4.

20 "It's not a case": Thomas, p. 185.

21 "There was research": MR, p. 181

21 "I wanted to create": Miklós Rózsa, "More Music For Historical Films," *Film Music Notes* Vol. XII, No. II, November–December 1952, p. 13.

21 "It is not easy": MR, p. 147.

21 "In order to keep": AP, p. 90.

21 "On *Island in the Sun*": Christopher

Ritchie, "An Interview with Malcolm Arnold," *Soundtrack!* Vol. 7, No. 27, September 1988, p. 8.

21 "I have a vast library": Matthias Büdinger, "An Interview with John Scott," *Soundtrack!* Vol. 8, No. 29, March 1989, p. 6.

22 "If the picture": TT, p. 88.

24 "Because of the computer": Jeffrey Ainis, "Special Report: Film & TV Music," *The Hollywood Reporter*, January 22, 1988.

25 "He'd get up": Harry Haun, "Franz Waxman," *Films in Review*, Vol. XLII, No. 9/10, September/October, 1991, p. 326.

25–26 "Max always seemed to suffer": Elmer Bernstein, "Interview with Hugo Friedhofer," *Filmmusic Notebook*, Vol. 1, Fall 1974, pp. 16–17.

26 "I believe in strong themes": Thomas, pp. 75–76.

26 "Getting the theme": Rainer Pudill and Frank Inger, "Jerry Goldsmith Enjoys a Challenge," *Soundtrack!* Vol. 6, No. 23, September 1987, p. 15.

26 "I don't know how": Page Cook, "The Sound Track," *Films in Review* Vol. XL, No. 4, April 1989, p. 250.

27 "At some point": Todd Coleman, "Staying in Tune," *The Hollywood Reporter*, January 18, 1993, p. S-4.

27 "I try to add to the film": Irwin Bazelon, *Knowing the Score: Notes on Film Music* (New York, 1975), p. 212.

27 "I try for emotional penetration": Steve Simak, "Another Pair of Blockbusters from Jerry Goldsmith," *CinemaScore*, 11/12, Fall/Winter 1983, p. 5.

27 "Everything I do": Berges.

28 "In reality": Robert Bettens, "An Afternoon with Georges Delerue," *SCN* Vol. 5, No. 22, Summer 1980, p. 5.

28 "Almost every composer": Roger Feigelson, "An Interview with Laurence Rosenthal," *Soundtrack!* Vol. 7, No. 28, December 1988, p. 9.

28 "We like to think": Glenn Wooddell, June 1989 interview for Music from the Cinema radio show.

28 "Sometimes, when I'm working": YALE.

28 "I'm usually up": February 18, 1964 interview transcribed by Kaufman/Schwartz and Associates Public Relations, in AMPAS Special Collections.

29 "In my own case": Tony Thomas, "Interview with John Williams," *The Cue Sheet* Vol. 8, No. 1, March 1991.

29 "It seems almost incomprehensible": SCS, p. 186.

30 "I was trying to write it down": YALE.

33 "Orchestration is without doubt": *Film Music Notes* Vol. 4, No. 2, November 1944.

34 "I believe that the foremost principle": *Film Music Notes* Vol. 5, No. 1, September, 1945.

34 "What I try to create": TT, p. 215.

34 "There are instances": *Film Music Notes* Vol. 5, No. 1, September 1945.

35 "Since the middle": SCS, p. 78.

35 "Many sections were written": *Film Music Notes* Vol. 1, No. 1, October, 1941.

35 "The motion picture sound": TT, p. 144.

35 "To compose and to orchestrate": Giovanna Grassi, *The Hollywood Reporter*, January 17, 1989, p. S-6.

35 "Those people who feel": TT, p. 109.

35 "Don't let anyone mistake": AP, p. 89.

35 "Since he was a pianist": William H. Rosar, "Lost Horizon—An Account of the Composition of the Score," *Filmmusic Notebook* Vol. 4, No. 2, 1978, p. 43.

36 "There was a wonderful musician": Craig Stuart Garfinkle, "Interview with Arthur Morton," *The Score* Vol. VI, No. 1, Spring 1991.

36 Alfred Newman's sketches: Lawrence Morton, "Interview with Maurice De Packh," (June 20, 1950), *The Cue Sheet* Vol. 8, No. 3, September 1991.

36 "All of us": AP, p. 89.

36 "Victor Young would fill up": Elmer Bernstein, "Interview with Leo Shuken," *Filmmusic Notebook*, Spring 1975, p. 18.

36–37 "Young had a couple": SMU.

37 "In a score like *Hawaii*": Bazelon, p. 177.

37 "[Arthur Morton is] my closest friend":

John Wright, "Lecture by Jerry Goldsmith," *SCN* Vol. 4, No. 17, April 1979, p. 6.

37 "We sit down": Craig Stuart Garfinkle, "Interview with Jack Eskew," *The Score* Vol. VI, No. 1, Spring 1991.

37 "John generally makes a very good sketch": Carl Johnson, "Interview with Herb Spencer," *The Cue Sheet* Vol. 7, No. 3, July 1990.

40 "For years I'd heard about": David Kraft, "An Interview with Michael Kamen," *Soundtrack!* Vol. 7, No. 26, 1989, p. 27.

40 "The most important thing": Wolfgang Breyer, "An Interview with John Barry," *Soundtrack!* Vol. 7, No. 25, March 1988, p. 30.

40 "What bothers me a bit": Luc Van de Ven, "A Conversation with Georges Delerue, *Soundtrack!* Vol. 7, No. 27, September 1988, p. 31.

40 "Look at this": AP, p. 89.

CHAPTER 3

42 "I like working": Jacquet-Françillon, "An Interview with Basil Poledouris," *Soundtrack!* Vol. 8, No. 30, June 1989, p. 29.

42 "It's amazing": AFI.

42–43 Columbia Pictures did not reveal: MR, p. 123.

43 "We discovered that André's hands": MR, p. 157, footnote.

43–44 "Conrad Veidt": AFI.

44 "One can only marvel": Jack Hiemenz, "The Man Who Put Trumpets in 'Captain Blood,'" *Village Voice*, January 26, 1976.

44–45 "John Garfield": Oscar Levant, *The Memoirs of an Amnesiac* (Los Angeles, 1989; © 1965), pp. 182–83.

46 Dimitri Tiomkin claimed: Philip K. Scheuer, "His Melodies Linger On," *Los Angeles Times*, March 23, 1957.

46 Max Steiner used clicks: Max Steiner, *Notes to You*, (unpublished memoirs, p. 334, footnote).

47 "He hardly used": SCS, p. 180.

48 "The orchestra starts": Sidney Skolsky, "Flim-Flam," *Chicago Tribune*, 1935.

48 "In the recording": TT, p. 127.

51 "There isn't one score": David Kraft, "Interview with Jerry Goldsmith," *The Hollywood Reporter*, January 17, 1989.

51 "When we get to": Sherman, p. 257.

51 "Although I can't compose": Sherman, p. 257.

52 "If you fooled around": SCS, pp. 83–84.

52 "These players": AP, p. 87.

52 "A lot of the time": Jeff Silberman, "Hollywood Session Players: The Best Because They Have to Be," *The Hollywood Reporter*, January 22, 1988.

52 "They would casually glance": AP, pp. 87–88.

52 "The Hollywood studio": MR, p. 153.

52–53 "The pressure": Silberman.

53 "Alfred Newman was one": Bazelon, p. 194.

53 "Some great maestro": Dimitri Tiomkin and Prosper Buranelli, *Please Don't Hate Me* (New York, 1959), p. 205.

53 "I am no Prokofiev": Milton Z. Esterow, "Interview with Dimitri Tiomkin," *New York Times*, July 21, 1957.

53 "There is a famous story": AFI.

54 "He was tough:" Leslie Zador, "Newman/Darby Cantata Premieres at Bringham Young University," *The Cue Sheet* Vol. 4, No. 4, November 1987, p. 42.

56 "A film composer's immortality": Thomas, *Music for the Movies*, p. 139.

56 "Keep that God-damned music": TT, p. 108.

56 "Many a composer's heart": Henry Mancini with Gene Lees, *Did They Mention the Music?* (Chicago, 1989), p. 185.

56–57 "The tambourine scene": SMU.

57 "No, no, no! Louder!": YALE.

57–58 "Reel III In the marketplace": Hitchcock AMPAS Special Collection.

58 "Sometimes the music": TT, p. 37.

58–59 "For some time now": Rudy Behlmer, *Memo from David O. Selznick* (New York, 1972), p. 300.

59   "We must not forget": TT, p. 108.

59   "Do you know": Lawrence Thaw, Jr., "Stinkeroos Are Best, Hollywood Composer Says," *London American*, February 28, 1961.

59–60 "MGM had a fetish": AFI.

60   "They sit there": YALE.

60   "If there was thunder": AFI.

61   "Again and again": MR, p. 183.

61   "When it was a question": AFI.

62   "Changes after the preview": TT, p. 89.

62   "I have bad times": Margaret McManus, *Providence Sunday Journal TV Weekly*, September 15, 1957.

63   "You can imagine": TT, p. 30.

63   "There was a final sequence": Elmer Bernstein, "A Conversation with David Raksin," *Filmmusic Notebook* Vol. II, No. 3, 1976, p. 16.

63   "As to Bernie Herrmann": Behlmer, pp. 463–64.

64   "He realized": Harry Haun, "Franz Waxman," *Films in Review* Vol. XLII, No. 9/10, September/October 1991, p. 326.

CHAPTER 4

69   "One certainly couldn't": TT, p. 68.

69   "Almost half of the score": Rudy Behlmer, *Behind the Scenes* (Hollywood, 1989), p. 210.

69   "Quite often": Bergamino and Fenzi, p. 5.

69   "I attempted to treat": *Film Music Notes* Vol. 1, No. 1, October, 1941.

70   "You have to look at": Vincent Jacquet-Fançillon, "An Interview with Basil Poledouris," *Soundtrack!* Vol. 8, No. 30, March 1989, p. 31.

70   "He was a Post-Impressionist": MR, p. 167.

71   "Jazz, ragtime or blues": *Film Music Notes* Vol. XI, No. III, January-February 1952, p. 13.

71   "Victor Young's score": *Film Music Notes* Vol. XII, No. I, September–October 1952, p. 11.

71   "What interested me about Auntie Mame": TT, p. 123.

72   "Since the picture": *Film Music Notes* Vol. III, No. 3, December 1943.

72   "After I had been working:" David Raksin, "Holding a Nineteenth-Century Pedal at Twentieth Century Fox," in Clifford McCarty, ed., *Film Music 1*, p. 171.

72   "I've noticed that despite": TT, p. 228.

72   "The melody must be": Thomas, *Music for the Movies*, p. 190.

72   "I've always been really partial": John Capps, "A Conversation with Elmer Bernstein," *Soundtrack!* Vol. 2, No. 6, June 1983, pp. 14–15.

73   Max Steiner took this idea: Kathryn Kalinak, "The Informer," in McCarty, p. 128.

73   "The leitmotif technique is common": TT, p. 58.

73   "For myself, I try to make": TT, p. 215.

73   "Although I am not a great believer": *Film Music Notes* Vol. 1, No. 1, October, 1941.

73   "Overall, Victor Young was": AMPAS Mancini Special Collection.

74   "To me, tempo": Mancini with Lees, p. 181.

74   "I've got a [silent] picture": Rudy Behlmer, "Tumult, Battle and Blaze," in McCarty, p. 56.

75   "All of the big studios": Leslie Zador and Greg Rose, "Interview: Hugo Friedhofer," (Spring 1971), *The Cue Sheet*, Vol. 2, No. 3, August 1985, p. 26.

75   "The day will come": *Film Music Notes* Vol. 5, No. 6, February 1946.

75   "Warners always had": AFI.

75   "Many times there were instances": Zador and Rose, p. 26.

75   "Musically it was necessary": Dimitri Tiomkin, "Writing Symphonically for the Screen," *Music Journal*, January, 1959, p. 26.

75   "In *Citizen Kane*": *Film Music Notes* Vol. I, No. 1, October 1941.

77   "My basic approach": TT, p. 107.

77   "If the picture runs": *Film Music Notes* Vol. 5, No. 5, January 1946.

77 "Personally I like to": *New York Times*, 1949; cited in TT, p. 21.

77–78 "You've seen people": *Film Music Notes* Vol. IV, No. 7, April, 1945.

78 "I have received": TT, p. 122.

78 "I have, for example": TT, p. 202.

78 "Film music, even more than": David Kraft, "An Interview with Michael Kamen," *Soundtrack!* Vol. 7, No. 26, 1988, p. 27.

79 "I tend to walk on a film": Kraft, p. 27

79 "Yes, I overdo it sometimes": *Film Music Notes* Vol. 5, No. 7, March 1946, cited from *Hollywood Citizen-News*.

79 "When a scene is weak": *Film Music Notes*.

79 "*The Informer*": TT, p. 77–78.

79–80 "The root of our decision": Behlmer, *Memo from David O. Selznick*, p. 119.

80 "I wanted a very heavy": Randall D. Larson, *Musique Fantastique* (New Jersey, 1985), pp. 81–82.

80–81 "Steiner has a way": Harold Brown, "The Miracle of Our Lady of Fatima," *Film Music Notes* Vol. XII, No. I, September–October 1952, p. 4.

81 "This leitmotiv music": Isabel Morse Jones, (Music Editor, *Los Angeles Times*), *Film Music Notes* Vol. IV, No. 8, May 1945.

81 "Should music be synchronized": TT, p. 34.

82 "You do not try to force": YALE.

82 "The function of music": *Film Music Notes* Vol. IV, No. 1, October, 1944.

82 "Herrmann was the master": SCS, p. 344.

82 "I really do think": Elmer Bernstein, "A Conversation with Richard Rodney Bennett," *Filmmusic Notebook* Vol. II, No. 1, 1976, p. 23.

83 "Should adopt the tempo": TT, p. 34.

83 "As she spoke to Benny": SCS, p. 345.

83 "*Kong* is fascinating": YALE.

83 "What you actually saw": SCS, p. 239.

83–84 "Music in a film": Martin Van Wouw, *Musica Sul Velluto* #9 (Holland), September 1981, p. 9.

84 "I don't know who started": Thomas, p. 197.

CHAPTER 5

87 "What I object to": TT (rev.), p. 291.

87 "It was always my endeavor": TT, p. 107.

87 "I tried hard to write": Luc Van de Ven, "Michael Kamen and the Adventures of Baron Munchhausen," *Soundtrack!* Vol. 8, No. 29, March 1989, p. 30.

87–88 "The person watching": *Film Music Notes* Vol. 5, No. 6, February 1946.

88 "Of course, there should be": K/W, p. 166.

89 "The reason technical devices": TT, pp. 201–202.

89 "We try to do": Matthais Büdinger, "A Conversation with Henry Mancini," *Soundtrack!* Vol. 7, No. 27, September 1988, p. 7.

89 "On the other hand": *Cahiers du cinéma* February 8, 1966, in USC Alfred Newman Collection.

89–90 "Nearly every film-music": Jeffrey Embler, "The Sound Track," *Films in Review* Vol. IV, No. 2, February 1953, p. 88.

90 "I think film composers": Gordon Hendricks, "The Sound Track," *Films in Review* Vol. IV, No. 3, March 1953, p. 141.

90 "Like all prolific composers": *Daily Variety*, December 29, 1971.

91 Another film music: Jack Jacobs, "Alfred Newman," *Films in Review* August–September 1959, p. 409.

91 "Throughout his film career": SCS, p. 47.

91 "We movie composers": "Tales of Hoffman," *The Hollywood Reporter*, cited in *Film Music Notes* Vol. III, No. 6, March 1944.

91 "Good music can improve": TT, p. 173.

91 "No music has ever saved": Bazelon, p. 180.

91 "I know it is often said": TT (rev.), p. 94.

91 "If the picture is good": Thomas, p. 121.

91 "There have been some": Paramount press material October 22, 1935.

CHAPTER 6

93 "My father was on the verge": George Korngold, liner notes on Varèse Sarabande CD VCD 47202 "The Adventures of Robin Hood," performed by the Utah Symphony Orchestra.

100 "Max understood more": Tony Thomas, *Music for the Movies* (New Jersey, 1973), p. 116.

123 John Ford wanted to use: William R. Meyer, *The Making of the Great Westerns* (New York, 1979), p. 50.

123 "Ford always had live music": Rudy Behlmer, *Behind the Scenes* (Hollywood, 1989; © 1982), pp. 115–16.

123 "Of course, [Aaron] Copland's influence": AP, p. 92.

127 "They had very, very specific functions": EB to FK, 1986.

129 John Williams tried over 250: John Wright, *John Williams*, SCN/15 Vol. 4 No. 15, September 1978. From notes taken at a lecture Williams gave in London.

CHAPTER 7

146 "Why shouldn't the music critic": Aaron Copland, *Our New Music* (New York, 1941), cited in *Film Music Notes* Vol. VII, No. 5, May–June, 1948.

146 "I sometimes wonder": George Antheil, *Bad Boy of Music* (Hollywood, 1973; © 1945).

146 "My only real complaint": Page Cook, "The Sound Track," *Films in Review* Vol. XXI, No. 6, June–July 1970, p. 373.

146 "Film criticism has not yet": *Film Music Notes*, Vol. IX, No. 1, September–October 1949, p. 15.

147 "The score for this picture": Celeste Hautbois, *Film Music Notes* Vol. V, No. 5, January 1946.

148 "The score is one": Hautbois.

148 "There is no dearth": Lawrence Morton, *Film Music Notes*, February 1949, pp. 2–3.

148–149 "The action of the picture": Celeste Hautbois, *Film Music Notes* Vol. 5, No. 8, April 1946.

149 "The ideal film score": Thomas, p. 158.

Chapter 8

154 "Watch a film run": Lillian Gish with Ann Pinchot, *The Movies, Mr. Griffith, and Me* (San Francisco, 1988; © 1969), p. 152.

155 "The instrument is generally old": *The Musician*, June 1920, p. 7, cited in Richard Koszarski, *An Evening's Entertainment: The Age of the Silent Feature Picture 1915–1928* (New York, 1990), p. 45.

155 "Better still": "The Musical End," *Moving Picture World*, July 3, 1909, cited by Charles Hoffman in *Sounds for Silents* (New York, 1970).

155 "I worked in little theaters": AFI.

155 A typical instrumentation: Gillian B. Anderson, *Music for Silent Films 1894–1929* (Washington, D.C., 1988), pp. xviii–xix.

155 "At the Coliseum": AFI.

155 The Rialto and Rivoli: Anderson, p. xviii.

155 the biggest Fotoplayer: Roy M. Prendergast, *Film Music: A Neglected Art* (New York, 1977), p. 17.

156 "The schedule started": T. Scott Buhrman, "Photoplays DeLuxe," *The American Organist* Vol. 3, No. 9, 1920, p. 157–58, cited in Anderson, pp. xviii-xix.

156 "Down in front": D. J. Wenden, *The Birth of the Movies* (New York, 1975; © 1974), p. 39.

156 "... a pleasant variation": G. C. Pratt, *Spellbound in Darkness*, (Rochester, 1966), p. 364.

156 Even as late as 1921: Hunter Davies, *The Beatles, the Authorized Biography* (New York, 1968), p. 30, cited in Charles Hoffman, *Sounds for Silence*.

156–157 "One day after": Prendergast, p. 8.

157 "In desperation": Max Winkler, "The Origins of Film Music," cited in *Films in Review*, December 1951, p. 10.

157 "It was up to": AFI.

157 "Like most of the": Abraham H. Lass, "Piano-Player for the Silent Movies," liner notes for Asch Record AH 3856, cited in Koszarski, p. 43.

160 "If I ever kill": Gish with Pinchot, p. 152.

160 "Mr. Riesenfeld had already": Buhrman, "Photoplays DeLuxe," *The American Organist* Vol. 3, No. 5, 1920, pp. 171–73, cited in Anderson, pp. xxiii–xxiv.

161 "For the first time": Victor Herbert, *Musical America*, May 13, 1916, cited by Clifford McCarty in *Films in Review*, 1957, pp. 183–84.

161 "He has not merely written": *Musical America*, 1916.

161 "For the New York": Herman G. Weinberg, *New York Herald Tribune*, April 29, 1928, cited in Hoffman.

161 "The film itself": Buhrman, pp. 171–73, cited in Anderson, p. xxiv.

161–162 "There was always the hazard": Elmer Bernstein, "An Interview with Hugo Friedhofer," *Filmmusic Notebook* Vol. I, Fall 1974, p. 13.

162 "Sure," Joseph Gershenson: AFI.

162 "There was a time": "Real Inspiration," *New York Times*, June 24, 1923, cited in Koszarski, p. 131.

162 "Sometimes the actors": AFI.

162 "I asked Mr. DeMille": Geraldine Farrar, *Such Sweet Compulsion* (New York, 1928) p. 169, cited in Anderson, p. xlii.

162 "Under the spell": Cecil B. DeMille, *Autobiography* (New Jersey, 1959), cited in Hoffman.

162 "most of the music": Blanche Sweet to Hoffman, 1968.

162 he employed Ralph Berliner's: Charles Higham, *Cecil B. DeMille* (New York, 1973), p. 119, cited in Anderson, pp. xlii–xliii.

162–163 "I always had music": Kevin Brownlow, *Napoleon: Abel Gance's Classic Film* (New York, 1983), p. 73, cited in Anderson, p. xlii.

163 "She was incapable": Michael Balcon, A

Lifetime of Films (London, 1969), p. 36, cited in Wenden, *The Birth of the Movies*, p. 40.

163 "We always had": Colleen Moore to Hoffman, April 1969, cited in *Sounds for Silents*.

163 "Jean Arthur... is one": *Film Music Notes* Vol. IV, No. 2, November 1944.

164 "With silent films": Matthias Büdinger, "Carl Davis Unbound," *Soundtrack!* Vol. 9, No. 35, September 1990, pp. 5–6.

165 "Animation relies": Rainer Pudill and Frank Inger, "Jerry Goldsmith Enjoys a Challenge," *Soundtrack!* Vol. 6, No. 23, September 1987, p. 13.

166 "It was a challenge": Mancini to FK, 1986.

166 "In animation, the length": Randall D. Larson, "Jerry Goldsmith On *Poltergeist* and *Nimh*," *CinemaScore* 11/12, Fall/Winter 1983, p. 3.

166 "Animation is a tremendous": Steven C. Smith, "From Steamboat Willie to Roger Rabbit: Music & the Animated Film," *The Hollywood Reporter*, August 29, 1989.

166 "didn't want it to be cartoony": Smith.

166 At first, the scores: T.M.F. Steen, "The Sound Track," *Films in Review* February 1961, p. 116.

166 "Innumerable song possibilities": Rudy Behlmer, *Behind the Scenes* (Hollywood, 1989; © 1982), p. 55.

167 "This remarkable collection": Randall D. Larson, *Soundtrack!* Vol. 10/ No. 37, March 1991, p. 22.

167 "I really don't like": TT, p. 122.

167 "Comedy plays itself": AFI Oral History

167 "In *The Pink Panther*": Mancini to FK, 1986.

167 "John Landis was": Randal D. Larson, "Elmer Bernstein Interview," *CinemaScore* 13/14, Winter 1984/Summer 1985, p. 10.

167 "If a scene": John Caps, "Keeping in Touch With John Williams, *Soundtrack!* No. 1, March 1982, p. 5.

167 "It is particularly significant": *Film Music Notes* Vol. II, No. 1, October, 1942.

168 "The makers of documentaries": Frederick W. Sternfeld (Dartmouth College), *Film Music*

Notes Vol. VIII, No. I, September–October 1948, pp. 5–6.

168 "I write novels": Melinda Corey and George Ochoa, *The Man in Lincoln's Nose* (New York, 1990), p. 188.

168 "In scoring horror pictures": TT, p. 111.

168–169 "The Universal horror pictures": TT, p. 107.

169 "We thought little": TT, p. 111.

169 "Effective use of film music": Nathaniel Shilkret, "Some Predictions for the Future of Film Music," *Music Publishers' Journal*, January–February 1946, cited in *Film Music Notes* Vol. V, No. 8, April 1946.

169 "Right now it is impossible": Jerry Hoffman, *Photoplay*, September, 1929, cited in Miles Kreuger (ed.), *The Movie Musical from Vitaphone to 42nd Street* (New York, 1975).

170 "In those days we didn't wait": Bob Pike and Dave Martin, *The Genius of Busby Berkeley* (California, 1973), p. 15.

170 "In my opinion": *Photoplay*, June 1930, cited in Kreuger, p. 180.

171 "After I became head": AFI.

172 "The task of fitting": Jack Schaindlin, *Film Music Notes* Vol. II, No. 2, January 1943.

CHAPTER 9

175 People now": YALE.

175 "Looking back": Newspaper article by George Pratt in USC Alfred Newman Collection.

175 "Harry Warner didn't": Thomas Schatz, *The Genius of the System* (New York, 1988), pp. 58–59.

175 "Every songwriter": Oscar Levant, *The Memoirs of an Amnesiac* (Hollywood, 1989, © 1965), p. 97.

176 "*The Broadway Melody*": *Photoplay*, April 1929, cited in Kreuger, p. 20.

177 ". . . We had no music": "Reminicences of Composer Arthur Lange and His Business Partner Ernst Klapholz," 1954 interview by "Gary"; this and all following comments by Lange and Klapholz cited in *The Cue Sheet* Vol. 7, No. 4, December 1990, as edited by Jeannie G. Pool.

177 "I loved the studio": AP, p. 17.

177 "The whole world": AFI.

177 "I must say": SPFM.

178 "It was an atmosphere": Elmer Bernstein, "A Conversation with David Raksin (Part II), *Filmmusic Notebook* Vol. II, No. 3, 1976, p. 13.

179 "Beautiful studio": SMU.

179–180 "I had heard much bad": MR, p. 143.

180 "It was the Emerald City": Barry Norman, *The Story of Hollywood*, (New York, 1987), p. 45.

180 ". . . It was obvious": MR, p. 184.

180 "The first thing I learned": *Westways*, May 1978, p. 35.

181 "I had a tough time": David Kraft, "A Conversation with Alex North," *Soundtrack!* Vol. 4, No. 13, March 1985, pp. 4–5.

181 "We signed the usual": Carl Johnson, "Interview with Herb Spencer," *The Cue Sheet* Vol. 7, No. 3, July 1990, p. 86.

181 "Its music director Nathaniel Finston": Verna Arvey, "Present Day Musical Films and How They are Made Possible," *The Étude*, January, 1931, cited in Frederick Steiner's 1981 USC dissertation "The Making of an American Film Composer: A Study of Alfred Newman's Music in the First Decade of the Sound Era," p. 122.

181 Steiner read about: Harry Haun and George Raborn, "Max Steiner," *Films in Review*, May 1961, p. 343.

181 "So far": TT, p. 88.

181–182 When he finally signed: Kathryn Kalinak, "Music as a Narrative Structure in Hollywood Film," 1982 University of Illinois dissertation, p. 76.

182 "Sometimes I had": Elmer Bernstein, "A Conversation with Bronislau Kaper," *Filmmusic Notebook* Vol. IV, 1978, p. 22.

182 the staff composers were getting: AFI.

182 "Within a month": AP, p. 12.

182 "We were captives": MR, p. 12.

182 All studio contracts: Norman, p. 42.

182 "All my loan-outs": AFI.

182–183 Actually, a 1949 survey: *Film Music Notes* Vol. VIII, No. 4, March–April 1949. In 1949, the Department of State asked the National Film Music Council for information regarding music in motion pictures in the United States.

183 "I turned the contract": SPFM.

183 Miklós Rózsa says: MR, p. 141.

183 "I decided to accept": MR, p. 142.

183 "Another part of my agreement": MR, p. 144.

183 "When the time came": MR, p. 156.

183 "I fondly imagined": MR, p. 163.

183 by comparison, the actors: Norman, p. 71.

184 "Sometimes we'd do fifty takes": Johnson, p. 90.

184 "In those days": Lange/Klapholtz.

185 "In the old days": Johnson, p. 90.

185 Stinson points out: SMU.

185 "I think that everyone": SMU.

185 "He was a wizard": YALE.

185–186 Composer Fred Steiner: Steiner, p. 332.

186 "All accomplished musicians": SPFM.

187 As music editor: AFI.

187 "Al, remember": YALE.

187 "He was one": AFI.

188 "Charlie was a nice": AFI.

188 "Let me say that": Elmer Bernstein, "A Conversation with Leo Shuken," *Filmmusic Notebook*, Spring 1975, p. 19.

188–189 "There was a particular": Bernstein, p. 19.

189 "As it turned out": MR, pp. 119–20.

189 "Enter now the figure": MR, pp. 121–22.

189–190 "As can be seen in": MR, p. 142.

190 "Don't forget that": Elmer Bernstein, "A Conversation with Bronislau Kaper," *Filmmusic Notebook* Vol. IV, 1978, p. 23.

190 "For instance," Kaper explains: Bernstein, p. 21.

190–191 "Robin Hood is no picture": Behlmer, *Behind the Scenes*, p. 84.

191 "When Forbstein said": Behlmer, pp. 84–85.

192 "We need time": *Film Music Notes* Vol. V, No. 1, September 1945.

192 "For us, time was": TT, p. 47.

192 "I wrote the three hours": Mark Schubart, "Max Steiner Makes a Case for Hollywood Composers," August 2, 1943.

192 "I often wonder": Jack Jacobs, "Alfred Newman," *Films in Review*, August–September 1959, p. 408.

192–193 "As far as my *official*": 1948 letter by Waxman in AMPAS Zinnemann Special Collection.

193 "Victor had one failing": SMU.

193 "In my opinion": Behlmer, *Memo from David O. Selznick*, p. 458.

194 "One reason why": David Raksin, "Holding a Nineteenth Century Pedal at Twentieth Century Fox," in Clifford McCarty (ed.), *Film Music 1* (New York, 1989), p. 171.

194 "It was assembly..." through "*Manila Calling*": Raksin in *Film Music 1*, p. 175. Remainder of this long quote is Raksin to FK.

195 "It might be of interest": 1940 newspaper article by Frank Daugherty in USC Alfred Newman Collection.

195 "There were no thoughts": TT, 108.

195 "Joe Gershenson would call": Mancini with Lees, pp. 70–71.

195 "When several of us": Mancini, p. 75.

CHAPTER 10

196 "No matter how well": TT, p. 108.

197 "Just before I was": MR, p. 149.

197 "I think one": Elmer Bernstein, "A Conversation with Richard Rodney Bennett," *Filmmusic Notebook* Vol. II, No. 1, 1976, p. 21.

197 "The music is cheap": Evans, p. 75.

197 "I'm very realistic": *L.A. Magazine*, January, 1978.

197 "I'm more than": Jean-Pierre Pecqueriaux, "A Conversation with Philippe Sarde," *Soundtrack!* Vol. 4, No. 14, June 1985, p. 4.

198 "I take as detached a view": Tiomkin and Buranelli, p. 220.

198   "Part of Hollywood": Tony Thomas, "A Conversation with John Williams," *The Cue Sheet* Vol. 8, No. 1, March 1991, p. 13.

198   "It isn't just actors": AP, p. 90.

198   "Producers and directors": Pudill and Inger, p. 15.

198   "There was a period": Randall D. Larson, "Music for Ghostbusters: A Conversation with Elmer Bernstein," *CinemaScore* No. 13/14, Winter 1984/Summer 1985, p. 10.

199   "Dear Mr. Zinnemann": AMPAS Fred Zinnemann Special Collection.

199   "Dear Mr. Copland": AMPAS Fred Zinnemann Special Collection.

200   On July 31, 1963: AMPAS Hal Wallis Special Collection.

200   "Seemingly only a composer": TT, p. 36.

200   "Composers in America": *Cahiers du Cinéma*, February 8, 1966, in USC Alfred Newman Collection.

200   "Four weeks was all": unidentified 1961 newspaper article in USC Dimitri Tiomkin Collection.

200–201   "The demands made": TT, p. 36.

201   "I've spent my entire career": 1973 speech to Eastman College, cited in SCS, p. 364.

201   "We film composers": TT, p. 113.

201   "While it is enjoyable": John Caps, "Keeping in Touch with John Williams," *Soundtrack!* No. 1, March 1982, p. 5.

201–202   "In my field": Curtis Lee Hanson, "3 Screen Composers," *Cinema*, July 1966, p. 16.

202   "Otherwise I refuse": SCS.

202   "I can't understand": Thomas, *Music for the Movies*, p. 148.

202   "After a while": Leslie T. Zador, "Interview," *The Cue Sheet*, Vol. 3, No. 1, January 1986 (from 1971 conversation with Previn).

202–203   "Here was a case": John Caps, "A Conversation with Elmer Bernstein," *Soundtrack!* Vol. 2, No. 7, September 1983, p. 6.

203   "Despite the notable strides": *Hollywood Citizen-News*, 1946, cited in *Film Music Notes* Vol. V, No. 7, March 1946.

203   "The next day": MR, p. 139.

CHAPTER 11

207   "My father": Robert Osborne, *50 Golden Years of Oscar* (California, 1979). Best Song Oscar for "The Morning After" (with lyricist Joel Hirschhorn) from *The Poseidon Adventure*.

208   "The largest number": Patrick Robertson, *The Guiness Book of Movie Facts and Feats* (New York, 1991, © 1988), p. 224.

208   *"Original Score": Academy of Motion Picture Arts and Sciences 65th Annual Academy Awards Rules* (1992).

209   "Somehow they don't": Elmer Bernstein, "A Conversation with Richard Rodney Bennett," *Filmmusic Notebook* Vol. II, No. 1, 1976, p. 25.

209–210   "Original Score—what it isn't": *Notes on Voting*: For New Members of the Academy of Motion Picture Arts and Sciences (1992).

211   "Nino Rota, who wrote": YALE.

211   "There are many": AFI.

212   "After some backing": *The Film Daily*, January 10, 1955.

212   "I really don't care": Newspaper item by Aline Mosby (United Press Staff Writer), January 4, 1955, in USC Tiomkin Special Collection.

213   "Sometimes we get": AFI.

214   "Charles Previn, Universal's": Frank Verity, "The Sound Track," *Films in Review*, Vol. XV, No. 5, May 1964, pp. 295–300.

214   when the front office: AFI.

215   "That limits the whole idea:" Isabel Morse Jones (*Los Angeles Times* music editor) cited in *Film Music Notes* Vol. III, No. 5, February 1944.

215   "But at the same time": AFI.

215   "Basically, its voting": Gene Ringgold, *Film in Review*, May 1961, p. 370.

216   "This year, as in the past": *64th Annual Academy Awards Rules* (1991).

217   "Ten times I have been": Osborne.

CHAPTER 12

221   "Hollywood is going gaga": *Photoplay*, July 1929, cited in Kreuger, p. 21.

221 "Writing of theme songs": *Photoplay*, August 1929, cited in Kreuger, p. 47.

221 "It is now a question": Jerry Hoffman, "Westward the Course of Tin-Pan Alley," *Photoplay*, September 1929, cited in Kreguer, p. 56.

221 "The minute you put": TT, p. 171.

222 "In *Two for the Road*": TT, p. 171.

222 "'Moon River' was one": Mancini with Lees, p. 98.

222 "I didn't—and still don't": Mancini, p. 105.

223 Steiner was originally: Behlmer, *Behind the Scenes*, p. 174.

223 "My first picture": AFI.

223 "They thought it was": AFI.

223 "A successful title song": *The Hollywood Reporter*, September 25, 1958.

224 "There were titles of pictures": SMU.

224 "It led to a tremendous problem": SPFM.

224–225 "We produced a picture": YALE.

225 "The ultimate is": K/W, p. 538.

225 "After the scripts": SMU.

225–226 "There was a song search": K/W, p. 538.

226 On his list were eight: Dale Pollack, *Skywalking: The Life and Films of George Lucas* (Hollywood, 1990, © 1983), pp. 108–09.

226 On *Mermaids*: Todd Coleman, "How the 'Mermaids' Learned to Sing," *The Hollywood Reporter*, January 22, 1988.

227 "Judging from the letters": *Film Music Notes* Vol. V, No. 1, September 1945.

227 Rózsa was thrilled: David and Richard Kraft, "A Conversation with Miklós Rózsa," (Part 2), *Soundtrack!* Vol. 1, No. 4, December 1982, p. 22.

227 "They thought that as Prokofiev's": MR, pp. 111–12.

227 "It did very well": Kraft, p. 22.

227 "Victor Young's music": Rudy Behlmer, "A Conversation with Jesse Kaye," (December 15–21, 1988), *The Cue Sheet* Vol. 6, No. 3, July 1989, p. 100.

227 "I came in [in 1958]": YALE.

227 "I really feel in a sense": SMU.

228 "The score and the album": YALE.

228 Other landmark albums: Fred Bronson, *The Billboard Book of Number One Hits* (New York, Billboard Publications), p. 474.

228 "People who go to movies": *Los Angeles Times*, November 12, 1991.

228–229 after the first screening: Pollack, p. 180.

229 "Another interesting development": "Tales of Hoffman," *The Hollywood Reporter*, cited in *Film Music Notes* Vol. III, No. 6, March 1944.

229 "Soundtracks are more": Jeffrey Jolson-Colburn, "Soaring Scores," *The Hollywood Reporter*, January 18, 1993, p. S-36.

230 "My policy from the outset": Christopher Palmer, "A Talk with Charles Gerhardt," liner notes on "The Spectacular World of Classic Film Scores," RCA Victor CD 2792-2-RG.

231 The music budget: Eliot Tiegel, "Movie Soundtracks Have Become a Complex Minefield," *The Hollywood Reporter*, January 14, 1992, p. S-22.

231 Interscope paid: *Los Angeles Times*, November 12, 1991.

231 "We got $175,000": Tiegel, p. S-22.

232 "Speaking very generally": Jeffrey Ainis, "Soundtracks: Older But Wiser," *The Hollywood Reporter*, August 29, 1989, p. S-44.

232 Giant Records: Tiegel, p. S-22.

232 Qwest Records: Tiegel, p. S-22.

232 Epic, for: Industry insider, 1992.

232 "Generally speaking": Ainis, p. S-44.

232 Examples: *Los Angeles Times*, November 11, 1991, and other industry sources.

232 During the first week: Joel Whitburn, *The Billboard Book of Top 40 Albums* (New York, Billboard Books).

CHAPTER 13

237 "If I were an actor": Norman, p. 12.

237 "Warners will enter": April 1925 nation-

wide press release cited in Schatz, *The Genius of the System*, p. 59.

237 "At the New York premiere": "Bringing Sound to the Screen," *Photoplay*, October 1926, cited in Kreuger, pp. 2–3.

237 "The executives of Warner Brothers": *Photoplay*, October, 1926, cited in Kreuger, pp. 2–3.

238 "*The Jazz Singer* definitely": Norman, p. 12.

238 "Al Jolson with Vitaphone": "The Jazz Singer, *Photoplay*, October 1926, cited in Kreuger, p. 6.

238 In autumn, Warner Bros. completes: Schatz, p. 66.

238 "There were some people": AFI.

238 "Don't dare to miss": *Photoplay*, April 1929, cited in Kreuger, p. 20.

238 "It was hard work": Tiomkin and Buranelli, p. 170.

238 ". . . The first original": *Photoplay*, January, 1930, cited in Kreuger, p. 125.

238 Theatre admissions reached: Schatz, p. 69.

239 "Hollywood was having a boom": Tiomkin and Buranelli, p. 157.

239 "By this time Hollywood": TT, p. 76.

239 "What a picture!": *Photoplay*, October 1932, cited in Kreuger, p. 313.

239 "Ruby Keeler's début": *Photoplay*, March, 1933, cited in Kreuger, p. 125.

239 "*King Kong* was the film": Max Steiner, *Notes to You* (unpublished memoirs) cited in TT (rev.), p. 68.

239 "It was made for music": Steiner, cited in TT, p. 115.

239 "Music had a way": Elmer Bernstein, "An Interview with Hugo Friedhofer," *Filmmusic Notebook* Vol. I, Autumn 1974, pp. 13–14.

240 Max Steiner scores: TT, p. 78.

240 "This [push-pull track] was far superior": TT, p. 78.

240 "Even in those days": Edward Jablonski and William R. Sweigart, *Films in Review*, December 1962, p. 612.

240 "Only as short a time ago": *Film Music Notes*, Vol. II, No. 5, February 1943.

240 "Films of an inspirational": *Film Music Notes*, Vol. III, No. 5, February 1944.

241 "Music for the movies": Alexander Tansman, *Citizen News*, cited in *Film Music Notes* Vol. IV, No. 8, May 1945.

241 "They had a number of men": YALE.

241 "Paramount had more": Elmer Bernstein, "A Conversation with Leo Shuken," *Filmmusic Notebook* Vol. III, No. 3, Spring 1975, p. 19.

241 "In the final analysis": *Los Angeles Times*, March 2, 1947.

241 "The main complaint": *New York Times*, 1949, cited in TT, p. 11.

241 "I remember the studios": SPFM.

241 "In 1950 we didn't want": Elmer Bernstein, "A Conversation with John Addison," *Filmmusic Notebook*, Vol. III, No. 3, 1977, p. 20.

242 "I remember one horrible day": SPFM.

242 "I would say that": Bernstein, "A Conversation with Leo Shuken," *Filmmusic Notebook* Vol. I, Spring 1965, p. 21.

242 "*The Man with the Golden Arm*": SPFM, March 1992.

242 "We live in strange belief": Philip K. Scheuer, *Cue* Magazine, March 23, 1957.

242 "I think one of the reasons": Thomas, *Music for the Movies*, pp. 200–201.

242 "February 19th, I believe": SMU.

243 His salary is: Jack Jacobs, "Alfred Newman," *Films in Review*, August–September, 1959, p. 411.

243 "In the sixties": Elmer Bernstein, "A Conversation with David Raksin," *Filmmusic Notebook* Vol. II, No. 3, 1976, p. 14.

243 "We now need": John G. Houser, *Daily Variety*, July 20, 1960.

243 "I think some film composers": John G. Houser, *Los Angeles Herald-Examiner*, June 29, 1964.

243 "The leading composers": 1966 newspaper clipping, in USC Special Collections.

244 "Music today in pictures": Charles Champlin, "Tiomkin: Tovarich of Cinema," *Los Angeles Times*, February 19, 1967.

244 "I don't think that": Karen Monson, *Los Angeles Herald-Examiner*, March 23, 1970.

244 "If I were starting now": Thomas, *Music for the Movies*, p. 148.

244 "A recent and thoroughly": Page Cook, "The Sound Track," *Films in Review*, Vol. XXIII, No. 9, November 1972.

244 "[George] Lucas wanted": Pollock, p. 177.

245 "Today, you have to work": Elmer Bernstein, "A Conversation with Bronislau Kaper," *Filmmusic Notebook* Vol. IV, 1978, p. 21.

245 "We're in a period now": Hamlisch to FK, 1986.

245 "I think that the composer": John Caps, "A Conversation with Elmer Bernstein," *Soundtrack!* Vol. 2, No. 6, June 1983, p. 14.

245 "I do think more people": Pudill and Inger, p. 15.

246 "By today's standards": Frank Thompson, "Settling the Score," *The Hollywood Reporter* January 18, 1993, p. S-28.

CHAPTER 14

249 "The first thing a film composer": Bernstein to FK, 1986.

249 "I go to the pictures": Elmer Bernstein, "A Conversation with Richard Rodney Bennett," *Filmmusic Notebook* Vol. II, No. 1, 1976, p. 23.

249 "If you like the work": February 18, 1964 interview transcribed by Kaufman/Schwartz and Associates Public Relations, in AMPAS Special Collections.

249 "I'm constantly asked:" Thomas, *Music for the Movies*, p. 201.

249–250 "No one has ever gotten:" "Scoring a Job," Todd Coleman, *The Hollywood Reporter*, January 18, 1993, p. S-10.

250 "The composers I loved" through "... an Alfred Newman Score": Frank Thompson, "Settling the Score," *The Hollywood Reporter*, January 18, 1993, p. S-28.

CHAPTER 15

257 In the late forties: *Film Music Notes*, March/April, 1949.

258 Elizabeth Firestone: Mark Evans, *Soundtrack: The Music of the Movies* (New York, 1975), pp. 160–61.

258 "If Wagner had lived": Thomas, p. 122.

262 "We need a theme—real quick": K/W, p. 6.

263 "Because my father": K/W, p. 7.

268 "With films one should not use": TT (rev.), p. 151.

273 "There are so many factors": TT (rev.), p. 215.

273 "I am happy to admit": TT (rev.), p. 213.

275 "Some people might imagine": Berges.

275 "Each assignment": TT (rev.), p. 290.

276 "I like films:" Sumimaro Yagiyu, "A Conversation with Dave Grusin," *Soundtrack!* Vol. 7, No. 27, September 1988, p. 27.

282 "I think the best way": K/W, p. 132.

283 "Except for a few excursions": AFI.

284 "When, in the projection room": TT, p. 88.

284 Puccini: "The boy:" Thomas, *Music for the Movies*, p. 124.

284 "To be honest about it": Thomas, p. 125.

285 "Erich Wolfgang Korngold": AP, p. 92.

286 "Ever since I was a kid": *New York Sunday News*, April 5, 1964.

286 "I've always felt": AMPAS Special Collections biographical file.

286 "If I didn't practice": *New York Sunday News*, April 5, 1964.

286 "It was the score": *New York Sunday News*, April 5, 1964.

289 "Actually, people": Gianni Bergamino and Giuseppe Fenzi, "The Apologetics of Film Music—A Conversation with Ennio Morricone," *Soundtrack!* Vol. 9, No. 34, June 1990, pp. 5–6.

290 "My first films": Giovanna Grassi, *The Hollywood Reporter*, January 17, 1989, p. S-5.

290 "Whenever I see anything": K/W, pp. 156–57.

291 "The thing that changed": Ken Darby,

"Alfred Newman 1900–1970," in USC Alfred Newman Collection.

291 "I was always happiest": Tony Thomas, liner notes for Delos Records "Alfred Newman, The Composer vs. the Conductor."

293 "I write best": TT (rev.), p. 190.

294 "I decided here": TT (rev.), pp. 188–89.

294 "Alex is past master": TT (rev.), p. 193.

296 "David Raksin is another": AP, p. 96.

297 "I think Mozart": Thomas, *Music for the Movies*, p. 207.

297 "I really feel": K/W, p. 373.

299 "As a young man": MR, p. 27.

299 "However much I may": MR, p. 20.

299 "I didn't want it": Thomas, p. 95.

299 "This was the beginning": MR, p. 145.

303 "There is a tired old": TT (rev.), p. 72.

304 "with 32 dollars in my pocket": Thomas, p. 112.

304 "Max had a certain flair": Elmer Bernstein,

"A Conversation with Hugo Friedhofer," *Filmmusic Notebook* Vol. I, Fall 1974, p. 16.

304 "Jack Warner was really": Bernstein, p. 19.

305 "I'm a classicist": Thomas, p. 73.

306 A 1960 newspaper: Vernon Scott (UPI Hollywood Correspondent), *El Centro Imperial Valley Press*, May 4, 1960.

306 "They say I give": Tiomkin and Buranelli, p. 168.

307 "The medium of film music": TT (rev.), p. 43.

308 "He had a sense": SMU.

308 "I think you can hurt": Evans, p. 196.

309 "*The Reivers*": Crawley, p. 38.

310 "Why would any trained": TT (rev.), p. 162.

310 As child of six: *Film Music Notes*, Vol. 4, No. 9, June 1945.

311 "He was an easygoing": AFI.

311 "He wrote music": SMU.

Index

Films titles are listed in italics; photo page numbers are listed in bold type. The following abbreviations have been used as necessary: arr. (arranger); comp. (composer); dir. (director); E.T. (End Titles); exec. (executive); M.T. (Main Title); mus. (musician, music); music dir., mus. dir., or m.d. (music director); orch. (orchestrator, orchestration, orchestra); prod. (producer); pub. (publisher); rev. (review); th. (theme); and Univ. (Universal).

Abrahams, Jim (director), 254
Academy Awards
  adaptations, 212–14
  Awards ceremony, first, 207
  criteria for music awards, 208–10
  first music awards, 207
  Godfather score ineligible for Oscar, 211
  lawsuits, 214
  music awards defined, 208
  method for selecting winners, 209
  Music Branch exec. committee, 209–10
  Original Score listing, 312–19
  Original Song category, 212
  Original Song Score, 212–13
  promotion and advertising, 216–17
    studio "politics," 215
    voting (1949), 215
    who votes, 215
Academy Awards show, 217–20
  curtain doesn't rise, 219
  fanfares for winners, 217
  music directors, 217
Academy of Motion Picture Arts and Sciences, 207–8, 218
Accidental Tourist, The, 70, 309
Adagio for Strings (Barber), 68
Adams, Bryan (singer), 228, 252
Adams, George (music editor), 46
  Louis De Francesco to
    wrestling, 187
Adaptation, 68, 81
  Academy Music Branch definition, 211
  definition, 68
  Sister Act, 69
  The Sting, 69
Addams Family, The (1991), 255
  communicating with director, 33
  sincerity, 87
Addison, John (composer), 261
  explains clichés, 89
  Tom Jones, 78
  scoring in fifties, 241
Adventures of Baron Von Munchhausen, 87
Adventures of Robin Hood, The (1938), 81, 93–9
  Korngold worked from script, 3

Agents for composers, 199
Ahlert, Fred E. (songwriter), 177
Ainis, Jeffrey (journalist), 232
Airplane! 167, 198, 251, 264
Akst, Harry (songwriter), 111
Aladdin, 222
Alamo, *The* (1960)
  in *Fall of the Roman Empire* review, 151
  writing the song, 201
  time pressures, 200
Albertine, C. (songwriter), 132
Alda, Robert (actor), as Gershwin, 171
Aldrich, Robert (director)
  the director makes the movie, 12
  Gerald Fried worked with, 16
Alexander Nevsky, 87, 295
Alexander's Ragtime Band, 37
Alexander, Jeff (composer), 30, 259
Alice in Wonderland, clicks, 46
Alien, 9
  role model, 6
Aliens, review, 151
Alix, Victor (composer), 164
All About Eve (1950), source music, 69
All That Money Can Buy, 202
All the President's Men, 86, 302
Allen, Robert (songwriter), 132
Allison, Rob (reviewer), 150
"Also sprach Zarathustra," 27
Altman, Robert (director), *The Player*, 86
Alwyn, William (composer), 261
Amazing Colossal Man, The, (1957)
  hitting the action, 80
American Federation of Musicians, 172
  new-use payments, 230
American Graffiti, (1973)
  songs, 226
  source, 69
American Organist, The, 156, 161
American Tail, An, 13
American in Paris, An, 214
Anderson, Gillian (conductor/author), 156
  conducting, **165**
  silent film scores re-creation, 164
Animal House, 167, 198, 245, 264
Animation, 165–66
  The Fox and the Hounds, 165
  The Great Mouse Detective, 165
  Oliver & Company, 165
  Plane Crazy, 165
  prerecording, 166
  recording, 176
  The Secret of Nimh, 165
  Snow White and the Seven Dwarfs, 165
  use of songs, 167
  Who Framed Roger Rabbit, 165
Ann-Margret on Academy Awards show, 219
Anne of the Thousand Days, 259
Antheil, George (composer), 257, 261
  music critics, 146
  Paramount, 188
Anthony Adverse, 93
Antonia and Jane, 254
Apocalypse Now, 255
Appalachian Spring, 13, 267
Appelbaum, Louis (composer), 258
Arlen, Harold (songwriter), 171
  on Gershwin entertaining, 240
Armstrong, Louis, (jazz trumpeter), 42

Arnold, Malcolm (composer), 261
  research, 21
Around the World in 80 Days (1956), 70
  soundtrack album, 232
Arrau, Claudio (pianist), **43**
Arthur, Jean (actress), music on the set, 163
"As Time Goes By" (*Casablanca*), 69
ASCAP, 308
Ashman, Howard (lyricist), 245
Assignments, contract composers, 191
Astaire, Fred, with A. Newman (1955), **187**
At Long Last Love (1975) prerecording, 68
Audio sync pulse, 22
"Auld Lang Syne," 166
Auntie Mame, 187
  concept, 71
Auric, Georges (composer), 262
Avalon, 253

Babe, The, 60, 70, 198
Bacall, Lauren (actress), 69
Bach, Johann Sebastian (composer), 29
  "Concerto No. 1," 15
  role model for *Deathtrap*, 6
Bacharach, Burt (composer), 223, 262
  Butch Cassidy, 225
Back to the Future, role models, 6
Background score, definition, 68
Backstage musicals, 176
Bad and the Beautiful, The (1952), 14, 43
  Raksin demonstrates, 30
Bad Boy of Music (George Antheil), 261
Badalamenti, Angelo (composer), 262
  and David Lynch, 196
Badami, Bob (music editor), 225
  Edward Scissorhands spotting notes, 10
Baird, Stuart (film editor), 19
Baker, Buddy (composer), 260
  animation scoring, 165
  hitting the action, 165
  orchestration for animation, 166
  studio system, 179
Balaban, Bob (actor), 129, 132
Ballard, Carroll (director), 252
Barnes, Bernard (songwriter), 131
Barry Lyndon (1975), Oscar dispute, 214
Barry, John (composer), 29, 30, 259, 262–**63**
  Body Heat review, 150
  concept, 72
  orchestration, 40
  Out of Africa, 18
  reading script early, 3–4
Barrymore, John (actor), 237
Bartók, Béla (composer), 250
Bat 21 (1988), role models, 6
  album, 229
Batman, 24, 250, 255
  hitting the action, 80
  tempo and pulse, 74
Batman Returns, 24, 250
Battle of Russia, The, Lipstone cites, 189
Bax, Sir Arnold (composer), 263
"Be My Baby," 226
Beaches, 254
Beatles, The, 223
Beaton, Welford (journalist), 237
  talking pictures imminent, 238
Beatty, Warren (actor/director), 277
  Dick Tracy, 77

Beau Geste, 260
Beaumont, Harry (director), 176
Beauty and the Beast (1991), 165, 213, 223
  record album, 233
Becce, Giuseppe (silent films music), 157
Becket (1964), composer search, 200
Bee Gees, The, 222
Beethoven, Ludwig von, 19
  Fifth Symphony, 76
  Moonlight Sonata, 163
  in silent films, 156
  orchestration, 90
Beetlejuice, 250
Behind the Scenes (Behlmer), 123, 166, 191
Behlmer, Anna (sound effects mixer), 60
Behlmer, Rudy (author), 69, 165
  The Adventures of Robin Hood, 191
  early soundtrack albums, 227
  John Ford, 123
Bell Telephone Company, 237
Ben-Hur (1926), new score, 164
Ben-Hur (1956):
  research, 21
  spotting and sound effects, 78
  style, 70
Beneke, Tex, Mancini in band, 286
Benjamin, Arthur (composer), 263
Bennett, Richard Rodney (composer), 263
  composing, 27
  "funky flamenco," director request, 14
  loves films, 249
  Oscar winners, 209
Bennett, Robert Russell (arr.), 168, 214
Benny & June, 27
Bergman, Alan and Marilyn (lyricists)
  "The Windmills of Your Mind," 223
Bergman, Ingrid (actress), 82, 223
  Spellbound (1945), **104**
Bergman, Marilyn (lyricist), 258
Berkeley, Busby (director), 176
  musicals, 170
Berlin, Irving (songwriter), 171
  4 or 5 songs in musicals, 170
Berliner, Ralph (conductor), 162
Bernstein, Bill (music editor), 23
Bernstein, Elmer (composer), 89, 122, 217,
    243, 258–59, 263–**64**
  Cape Fear (1991) adaptation, 117
  comedy scoring, 167
  Film Music Collection, 229
  Five Days One Summer, 15–16
  function of score, 17
  film music in sixties, 243
  Ghostbusters, 228
  The Great Escape review, 152
  Herrmann's scoring procedure, 29
  High Noon significance, 224
  Hollywood in 1953, 242
  influence of *Star Wars* in 1983, 245
  The Magnificent Seven, 124
  melody, 72
  music a character, 82
  music execs in 1950, 186
  need sense of drama, 249
  no studio contract, 183
  orchestrators, 37
  originality, *Mockingbird* (1962), 89
  playing the drama, 78, 80
  scoring influenced by record sales, 242

Bernstein, Elmer (cont'd)
    studio system, 177–78
    television and Hollywood (fifties), 24
    tempo and pulse, 74
    Ten Commandments sessions, 192
    Trading Places role models, 6
    typecasting, 198
    working with Cecil B. DeMille, 202
Bernstein, Leonard (composer), 264
Best Years of Our Lives, The, 186, 258, 273
Beverly Hills Cop I and *II* CDs, 229
Big Business, 254
Big Country, The, rerecorded CD, 229
Big Easy, The, record sales, 232
Bigard, Barney (composer/clarinetist), 139
Bill & Ted's Bogus Journey, budget, 231
Billboard Magazine's Top 200 albums, 232
Billy the Kid (Copland), 260
Biographies, reference sources, 260
Birdman of Alcatraz, The, orchestration, 37
Birth of a Nation, The, compiled score, 160
Black Cat, The, 172
Black Stallion, The, 255
Blackton, Jay (music director), 214
Blanke, Henry (producer)
    Adventures of Robin Hood (1938), 190
Blazing Saddles, 290
Blazing the Overland Trail, 172
Bliss, Arthur (composer)
    "judge solely as music" 87–88
Blitzstein, Mark (composer), 168
Blondell, Joan (actress), 170
Blue Angel, The, Waxman orchestrated, 308
Blue Bird, The, collaborations, 195
Body Heat, 150
Bogart, Humphrey (actor), 69, 99
Bogdanovich, Peter (director), 68
Boone, Ashley (studio exec.), 229
Booren, Jo Van den (composer), 163
Booth representative, 49–50
Borzage, Danny (accordion player), 123
Borzage, Frank (director), 123, 163
Bow, Clara (actress), 48
Boyce, T. (composer), 132
Boyz N the Hood (1991)
    contemporary, 69
    record advance and sales, 232
Brackett, Charles (producer/writer), 18, 189
Bradford, Richard (actor), 139
Bradley, Scott (composer), 46
    cartoon scoring, 167
Brahms, Johannes, *Requiem*, 193
Brainstorm, 280
Brazil, 252
"Brazil" (song), 252
Breakfast at Tiffany's, 197
    "Moon River," 222, 286
Breil, Joseph Carl (composer), 160
    Birth of a Nation laster disc, 165
    Birth of a Nation with DeMille, 160
    Intolerance, 160
Brent, George (actor), 99, 148
Brickman, Paul (director), 7, 62
    demos, 30
    Men Don't Leave, 4, 32–33
    originality, 89
Bricusse, Leslie (lyricist), 229
Bride of Frankenstein (1935)
    score reused in serials, 172

scoring session, **184**
    Waxman, Franz, 308
Broadcast News, 37
Broadway Melody, The (1929), 176
    Alfred Newman's schedule, 195
    review, 238
Broderick, Matthew (actor), 68
Brokaw, Cary S. (prod.), *The Player*, 86
Broken Arrow, 123
Bronson, Charles (actor), 122, 125
Brooke, Tyler (actor), 169
Brooks, Mel (director), 53, 290
Broughton, Bruce (composer), 260, 265
Brown, Herb (songwriter), 177, 238
Brown, Royal S. (author, educator), 112
Browne, Harold (critic), 80
Bruckheimer, Jerry (producer), 225
Bruckner, Anton (composer)
    role model for Carl Davis, 164
Brunel, Adrian (director), 163
Brynner, Yul (actor), 122, 124
    The Magnificent Seven, **123**
Buchholz, Horst (actor), 122, 125
Buck Rogers serials, 172
Budgets, 231–32
    American Graffiti, 226
    Bill & Ted's Bogus Journey, 231
    Mermaids, 226
Budweiser jingle ("Here Comes the King"), 132
Bujold, Geneviéve (actress), 83
Buranelli, Prosper (author w/ Tiomkin), 306
Burlesque, 176
Burlingame, Jon (journalist), 67, 145
Burton, Richard (actor), 78
Burton, Tim (director), 250
    Edward Scissorhands, 10
"Bury Me Not on the Lone Prairie," 123
Butch Cassidy and the Sundance Kid (1969):
    interpolated song, 225
Butler, Graham (reviewer), 149, 152–53
Buttolph, David (composer), 214, 257, 265
    collaborations, 194
Büdinger, Mattias (journalist), 146
"By a Waterfall," 170
    (in *Footlight Parade*, 1933), **170**

Cahn, Sammy (lyricist)
    Tiomkin and Academy, 216
Camelot, 60
Can't Stop the Music, 244
Canned music, 171–72
    for war films, 240
Cape Fear (1962), 117, 198
Capitol Records
    Romeo and Juliet soundtrack album, 228
Capone, Al, 137
Capra, Frank (director), 201
Capricorn One, in *Aliens* review, 151
Captain Blood, 93
Car Wash, 245
Carbonara, Gerard (composer), 123
Care, Ross (reviewer), 150
Carl Fischer Music Company, 156
Carlin, Dan (music editor), **24**
Carmina Burana, role model, 6
Carpenter, John (director), 258
Carrie, film cut drastically, 63
Carroll, Leo G. (actor), 104, 119
Carter, Gaylord (silent film organist)
    tempo and pulse, 74

Cartoon music
    "Duck Dodgers" in *Close Encounters*, 132
    used in *Close Encounters*, 137
Cartoons, 47
    hitting the action, 79, 165
    Plane Crazy, 165
    use of familiar tunes, 166–67
Casablanca (see also "As Times Goes By," song),
        215
    "Classic Film Scores for Humphrey Bogart,"
        230
    source music, 69
Castelnuovo-Tedesco, Mario (composer), 257,
        265
Champagne Waltz scoring session, **185**
"Chances Are," 132, 137
Changes, 5, 51, 62
    after preview, 111
    Citizen Kane, 52
    during scoring sessions, 54
    film changes, 25
    Robin Hood: Prince of Thieves, 25
Chaplin, Charles (comp./filmmaker), 48, 265
    Limelight score collaborators, 213
    Raksin works with, 296
Chaplin, Saul (music director), 214
Charge of the Light Brigade (1936), 273
    role model for *Star Wars*, 6
Chariots of Fire, 259
    soundtrack album, 232
"Charmaine," 160
Charts, the: 232
    "Miami Vice," 245
    original scores, 232–33
Chase, Chevy (actor), 255
Chases
    Hans Zimmer doesn't enjoy, 198
Chekhov, Michael (actor), 105
Chevalier, Maurice (actor/singer), 169
    Love Me Tonight review, 239
Chihara, Paul (composer), 266
Chopin, Frédéric (composer), 43
Churchill, Frank (composer), 266
    Snow White, 166
Cicognini, Alessandro (composer), 266
Cillag, Steve (music editor), 46, **179**
Cimarron (1930), 28, 123
Cinema film journal, 201
CinemaScope, 241–42
CinemaScore film journal, 146
Cinerama, 241
Citizen Kane (1941), 278
    film and music changes, 52
    editorial changes, 5
    form, 75
    musical motifs, 73
    orchestration, 345
    musical style, 69
Citizen News, The, 223, 241
City of Joy, 71
    records advance, 232
City Slickers, 255
    dubbing, 57
Clan of the Cave Bear, role model, 6
Clapton, Eric (guitarist/composer), 252
    Lethal Weapon series, 19
Clara's Heart, 79, 277
    playing the drama, 79
Clarke, Stanley (composer), 266

Clarkson, Patricia (actress), 139
Class distinctions in Hollywood, 180
Classical music, 6, 19, 240
Cleopatra, 37
Clichés, 89–90
  Leonardo da Vinci review, 89
  use of strings, 90
Click tracks, 24, 47
  Star Trek—The Motion Picture M.T., 38
Clicks, 45–46
Clift, Montgomery (actor), 64
Clooney, Rosemary (singer), 57
Close Encounters of the Third Kind (1977), 74,
  129–37, 259
  spaceship, **129**
Coal Miner's Daughter, 70
Coates, Albert (composer), 215
Coburn, James (actor), 122, 125
Cold Turkey, 253
Collaborations, 192, 194–95
  The Blue Bird (1940), 195
  credits at Fox, 194
  at Universal, 195
  Universal Studios (fifties), 194
Colombier, Michel (composer), 266
Color Purple, The (1985)
  credits, 213
  on-screen source, 68
Columbia Pictures, 42
  music department, 177
  Stoloff, Morris (music director), **182**
Columbo, Alberto (composer)
  MGM staff meeting, **180**
Coma, role model, 6
Comden, Betty (songwriter), 258
Come See the Paradise, 250
  dubbing, 62
Comedies, 167
  Auntie Mame, 71
  form of scores, 92
Commitments, The, record album sales, 232
"Communication motif" (*Close Encounters*), 131
Competition, The, prerecording, 42
Compiled scores, 160
  Intolerance, 160
Composers (*see also Chapter 15 listing*
    beginning at 261)
  Addinsell, Richard, 261
  Addison, John, 78, 89, 241, 261
  Alcivar, Bob, 261
  Alexander, Jeff, 30, 261
  Alix, Victor, 164
  Alwyn, William, 261
  Amfitheatrof, Daniele, 64, 243, 257, 261
  Antheil, George, 146, 188, 257, 261
  Appelbaum, Louis, 258
  Arnold, Malcolm, 21, 261
  Auric, Georges 262
  Axt, William, 237, 262
  Bacharach, Burt, 262
  Bach, Johann Sebastian, 6, 15, 29
  Badalamenti, Angelo, 196, 262
  Baker, Buddy, 165–66, 262
  Band, Richard, 262
  Banks, Brian, 262
  Barber, Samuel, 68
  Barry, John, 3, 4, 18, 29, 40, 70, 72, 150,
    259, **263**, 263
  Bartók, Béla, 250

Bassman, George, 263
Bax, Sir Arnold, 263
Baxter, Les, 263
Beethoven, Ludwig von, 76, 156, 163
Bell, David, 263
Benjamin, Arthur, 263
Bennett, Richard Rodney, 14, 27, 249, 263
Bennett, Robert Russell, 168
Bernstein, Charles, 263
Bernstein, Elmer, 6, 15–16, 17, 29, 37, 77,
  80, 82, 89, 122–24, 152, 167,
  177–78, 183, 186, 192, 198, 202,
  217, 229, 241–43, 245, 249, 258–59,
  263–**64**
Bernstein, Leonard, 264
Bernstein, Peter, 264
Blanchard, Terence, 264
Bliss, Arthur, 87–88
Blitzstein, Mark, 168
Booren, Jo Van den, 163
Botkin, Jr., Perry, 265
Bradley, Scott, 46, 167
Breil, Joseph Carl, 165
Broughton, Bruce, 260, 265
Bruckner, Anton, 164
Burns, Ralph, 265
Burwell, Carter, 265
Butler, Artie, 265
Buttolph, David, 194, 257, 265
Cacavas, John, 265
Carbonara, Gerard, 123
Castelnuovo-Tedesco, Mario, 257, 265
Chang, Gary, 265
Chaplin, Charles, 48, 163, 265
Chase, Tom, 265
Chattaway, Jay, 266
Chihara, Paul, 266
Chopin, Frédéric, 43
Churchill, Frank, 266
Cicognini, Alessandro, 266
Clapton, Eric, 19
Clarke, Stanley, 266
Clausen, Alf, 266
Coates, Albert, 215
Cobert, Robert, 266
Collins, Anthony, 266
Colombier, Michel, 266
Columbo, Alberto, **180**
Conti, Bill, 37, 168, 193, 198, 259, 266
Convertino, Michael, 267
Cooder, Ry, 267
Copeland, Stewart, 267
Copland, Aaron 40, 71, 77, 124, 145–46,
  186, 199–200, 215, 241, 257, **267**, 273
Coppola, Carmine, 163, 267
Corigliano, John, 267
Courage, Alexander, 268
Creston, Paul, 168
Darby, Ken, w/ Fox music staff, **178**
Daring, Mason, 268
Davis, Carl, 6, 163–65, 229, 268
de Sica, Manuel, 269
De Vol, Frank, 269
Delerue, Georges, 28, 40, 68, 250, 259, **268**
Deutsch, Adolph, 36, **180**, 257, 269
DeVorzon, Barry, 269
Di Pasquale, James, 269
Dolan, Robert Emmett, 257, 269
Doldinger, Klaus, 269

Donaggio, Pino, 269
Dorff, Steve, 269
Doyle, Patrick, 269
Dragon, Carmen, 269
du Prez, John, 270
Dudley, Anne, 258, 269
Duning, George, 177, 257, 269
Dunlap, Paul, 270
Dylan, Bob, 270
Edelman, Randy, 7, 30, 37, 48, 51, 61–62,
  229, 249–50, 260, 270
Eidelman, Cliff, 268
Eisler, Hanns, 81, 268
Elfman, Danny, 8, 10, 14, 24, 30, 74,
  76–77, 79–80, 149, 151, 195, 227,
  244, 248, 249, **268**
Elgar, Edward, 6, 123
Ellington, Duke, 72, 294
Elliott, Jack, 271
Faltermeyer, Harold, 271
Farnon, Robert, 271
Fenton, George, 70, 271
Ferguson, Allyn, 271
Fiedel, Brad, 271
Fielding, Jerry, 11, 17, 26, 34, 73, 229,
  265, **271**
Firestone, Elizabeth, 258
Folk, Robert, 272
Foster, David, 272
Fox, Charles 260, 272
Frank, César, 70
Frank, David Michael, 272
Frankel, Benjamin, 272
Fraser, Jill, 258, 272
Fried, Gerald, 6, 20, 30, 272
Friedhofer, Hugo, 25, 36, 74, 90, 149,
  152, **178**, 186, 239, 243, 257–58,
  272–**73**
Frontiere, Dominic, 273
Gabriel, Peter, 273
Gamley, Douglas, 273
Garcia, Russell, 229, 273
Gershwin, George, 17, 238
Gilbert, Herschel Burke, 274
Glass, Philip, 274
Glasser, Albert, 80, 274
Gleeson, Patrick, 274
Gold, Ernest, 232, 249, 274
Goldenberg, Billy, 190, 274
Goldenthal, Elliot, 274
Goldsmith, Jerry, 6, 9, 12, 14, 17, 19, 26,
  27, 28, 37–39, 51, 72, 80, 87, 88,
  89, 91, 152, 153, 166, 190, 198,
  243, 250, 259, 265, **274–75**
Goldsmith, Joel, 275
Goldstein, William, 275
Goodman, Miles, 275
Goodwin, Ron, 275
Gore, Michael, 275
Gould, Morton, 168
Green, John, 43, **180**, 182, 186, 217, 244,
  257, **276**
Grofé, Ferde, 276
Gross, Charles, 276
Gruenberg, Louis, 257, 276
Grusin, Dave, 30, 79, 190, **276**
Gruska, Jay, 277
Hadjidakis, Manos, 277
Hageman, Richard, 123, 257, 277

Composers *(cont'd)*

Hajos, Karl, 172
Hamlisch, Marvin, 37, 68, 80, 217, 245, 259, 277
Hammer, Jan, 81, 245
Hancock, Herbie, 277
Hanson, Howard, 6
Harline, Leigh, 243, 257, 277
Harling, W. Franke, 123, 277
Hatley, Marvin, 278
Hayasaka, Fumio, 278
Hayes, Isaac, 228, 259, 278
Hefti, Neal, 30, 278
Heindorf, Ray, 111, 112, 115, 180, 184, 185, **186**, 188, 278
Herbert, Victor, 160
Herrmann, Bernard, **5**, 6, 11, 12, 15, 29, 34, 47, 52, 63, 69, 73, 75, 82–83, 88, 91, 116–22, 146, 177, **178**, 191, 201, 202, 229, 243, 244, 250, 257–58, 278–79
Heymann, Werner R., 257, 279
Hoenig, Michael, 279
Holdridge, Lee, 14, 15, 19, 20, 260, 279
Hollander, Frederick, 36, 257, 279
Holst, Gustav, 6
Honegger, Arthur, 279
Horner, James, 13, 37, 151, 259, 279–**80**
Horowitz, Richard, 280
Howard, James Newton, 13, 78, 87, 251, **280**–81
Howarth, Alan, 281
Hyman, Dick, 43, 281
Ikebe, Shinichiro, 281
Immel, Jerrold, 281
Isham, Mark, 87, 251, 252, **281**
Jackson, Howard, 281
Jans, Alaric, 281
Janssen, Werner, 281
Jarre, Maurice, 4, 8, **197**, 229, 232, 259, **282**
Johnston, Adrian, 163
Johnston, Arthur, 263
Jones, Quincy, 30, 34, 190, 217, 282
Jones, Trevor, 260, 282
Joplin, Scott, 68
Kamen, Michael, 18, 25, 30, 40, 77, 80, 87, 228, 252, 282
Kaper, Bronislau, 9, 11, 27, 33, 41, 43, 53, 59, 71, 74, 77, 90, 167, **180**, 182, 187, 190, 197, 213, 215, 244, 245, 257, 258, 283
Kaplan, Sol, 283
Kaproff, Dana, 283
Karas, Anton, 19, 283
Karlin, Fred, 34, 283
Karpman, Laura, 258
Kilar, Wojciech, 283
Kitay, David, 283
Korngold, Erich Wolfgang, 3, 19, 22, 43, 46, 55, 81, 93, 94, 96, 98, 148–49, 181–82, 197, 229, 249, 250, 257, 258, 273, **284**
Kosma, Joseph, 285
Kubik, Gail, 168
Lai, Francis, 285
Lanchbery, John, 285
Lange, Arthur, 177, 285
Langhorne, Bruce, 285
Langois, Daniel, 258

Lava, William, 285
Lee, Bill, 285
Legrand, Michel 222, 259, 285
Leipold, John, 123
Levant, Oscar, 168, 285
Levay, Sylvester, 285
Lewis, W. Michael, 285
Linn, Michael J., 286
Lizst, Franz, 70
Lutyens, Elisabeth, 258, 286
Mahler, Gustav, 250
Mancini, Henry, 21, 56, 74, 87, 89, 91, 167, 188, 190, 195, 197, 217, 221, 242, 249, 250, 258, **286–87**
Manfredini, Harry, 287
Manzie, Jim, 287
Marinelli, Anthony, 287
Markowitz, Richard, 287
Marsalis, Wynton, 287
Marshall, Jack, 243
Martinez, Cliff, 287
Mason, Benedict, 163
Matz, Peter, 287
May, Billy, 287
May, Brian, 287
Mayfield, Curtis, 287
McCartney, Paul, 288
McHugh, David, 288
McLaughlin, Richard, 163
Mellé, Gil, 288
Melnick, Peter, 288
Melvoin, Michael, 288
Mendelssohn, Felix, 6
Mendoza, David, 237
Menken, Alan, 245, **288**
Michelet, Michel, 257, 288
Milhaud, Darius, 257, 288
Misraki, Paul, 288
Mockridge, Cyril, 194, 243, 257
Mollin, Fred, 289
Moore, Dudley, 289
Morely, Angela, 258, 289
Moroder, Giorgio, 289
Moross, Jerome, 123, 289
Morricone, Ennio, 19, 30, 35, 70, 83, 89, 137–**44**, 229, 256, **289**
Morris, John, 26, 53, 249, 290
Murray, Lyn, 290
Myers, Stanley, 290
Nascimbene, Mario, 290
Nelson, Oliver, 190, 290
Newborn, Ira, 27, 291
Newman, Alfred, 27, 34, 36, 37, 48, 53–**54**, 55, 69, 70, 89, 90, 91, 149, 150, 151, 175, **178**, 184, 185, **187**, 190, 191, 192, 194, 195, 200, 215, 217, 227, 229, 246, 249, 250, 252, 253, 257, 258, 260, 273, **291–92**
Newman, David, 20, 27, 51, 163, 252, 253, 292
Newman, Lionel, 37, 253, 292
Newman, Randy, 12, 29, 72, 79, 86, **292**
Newman, Thomas, 4, **32**–33, 61–62, 86, 88, 227, 259, 293
Niehaus, Lennie, 26, 290
Nitzsche, Jack, 293
Nordgren, Eric, 293
North, Alex, 3, 20, 35, 37, 70, 71, 150,

178, 181, 190, 197, 208, 243, 258, 259, **293–94**
Nyman, Michael, 294
Oldfield, Michael, 294
Orff, Carl, 6
Parks, Van Dyke, 294
Peake, Don, 294
Plumb, Edward, 294
Poledouris, Basil, 6, 18, 41, 49, 55, 70, 150, 259, 294
Portman, Rachel, 27, 253–54, 258, 294
Post, Mike, 294
Pouget, Léo, 164
Preisner, Zbigniew, 295
Previn, André, 21, 30, 35, 40, 52, 124, 177, 198, 202, 217, 285, 295
Previn, Charles, 295
Prokofiev, Sergei, 50, 87, 227, 248, 295
Ragland, Robert O., 296
Raksin, David, 14, 27, 28, 30, 36, 37, 60, 72, 82, 83, 91, 175, 177, 178, **180**, 191, 192, 195, 197, 227, 243, 257, 258, 265, **295**
Rasch, Raymond, 265
Redford, J.A.C., 166, 296
Reich, Steve, 6
Revell, Graeme, 296
Riddle, Nelson, 296
Rinder, Laurin, 296
Robbins, Richard, 296
Robinson, J. Peter, 296
Roemheld, Heinz, 172, 294
Romans, Alain, 297
Ronell, Ann, 258
Rose, David, **180**, 217
Rosenman, Leonard, 258, 297
Rosenthal, Laurence, 28, 200, 297
Rota, Nino, 20, 34, 228, 231, 258–59, **298**
Rowland, Bruce, 298
Rózsa, Miklós, 17, 19, 21, 34, 70, 82, 89, 103–9, 146, 180, 182, 183, 189, 197, 201, 203, **208**, 227, 229, 230, 242, 257, 258, 279, 298–**99**
Rubinstein, Arthur B., 6, 299
Rucker, Steve, 300
Russell, Larry, 265
Russo, William, 300
Safan, Craig, 19, 153, 300
Sakamoto, Ryuichi, 300
Salter, Hans J., 35, 56, 59, 77, 87, 91, 168, 169, 195, 196, **300**
Sarde, Philippe, 14, 300
Sato, Masaru, 300
Sawtell, Paul, 300
Schaindlin, Jack, 172
Scharf, Walter, 301
Schifrin, Lalo, 34, 190, 243, 301
Schoenberg, Arnold, 188
Schumann, Robert, 156
Scott, John, 7, 301
Scott, Tom, 301
Shaiman, Marc, 33, 56, 69, 86, 254, 301
Shankar, Ravi, 71, 301
Shefter, Bert A., 301
Shilkret, Nathaniel, 301
Shire, David, 4, 86, 259, 301
Shore, Howard, 302
Shostakovitch, Dmitri, 155, 250
Shuken, Leo, 123

Composers *(cont'd)*
  Silvers, Louis, 302
  Silvestri, Alan, 6, 166, 250, 302
  Simon, Paul, 87
  Skinner, Frank, 302
  Small, Michael, 81, 302
  Smith, Paul J., 302
  Snell, David, 303
  Snow, Mark, 303
  Snow, Tom, 303
  Sondheim, Stephen, 303
  Stalling, Carl, 46, 167
  Stein, Herman, 303
  Stein, Ronald, 303
  Steiner, Fred, 185
  Steiner, Max, 6, 9, 11, 25, **28**, 34, 46, 52,
    69, 73, 79, 80, 81, 83, 89, 90, 91,
    99–104, 148, 151, 177, 181, 192,
    193, 197, 215, 229, 230, 239, 240,
    249, 257, 258, 273, **303–4**
  Stevens, Leith, 304
  Stevens, Mort, 243
  Stothart, Herbert, 215, 304
  Strauss, Richard, 6, 27, 94, 285
  Stravinsky, Igor, 6, 187, 197, 250
  Taj Mahal, 305
  Takemitsu, Toru, 305
  Tangerine Dream (group), 6, 305
  Tansman, Alexander, 215, 257
  Tchaikovsky, Peter Ilyitch, 50
  Theodorakis, Mikis, 305
  Thomson, Virgil, 168, 305
  Thorne, Ken, 305
  Tiomkin, Dimitri, 11, 12, 15, 35, 46, 53,
    59, 62, 75, 90, 151, 198, 99, 200,
    201, 224, 227, 230, 238, 239, 242,
    243, 244, 257, 258, **305**
  Toch, Ernest, 257
  Tunick, Jonathan, 306
  Vangelis, 232, 259, 306
  Vaughan Williams, Ralph, 306
  Vaughan, Clifford, 172
  Wagner, Richard, 248, 258
  Walker, Shirley, 78, 82, 86, 255, 258, 306
  Wallace, Bennie, 306
  Wallace, Oliver, 46, 168, 306
  Walton, Sir William, 307
  Ward, Edward, 307
  Waxman, Franz, 7, 25, 27, 34, 64, 69, 73,
    89–91, 110–16, 153, **178**, 192, 215,
    217, 227, 229, 230, 243, 248, 257,
    258, **307–8**
  Webb, Roy, 36, 215, 257–58, 308
  Weill, Kurt, 258
  Williams, John, 6, 11, 13, 19, 26, **29**, 30,
    37, 69, 73, 78, 80, 87 129, 130,
    134, 135, 150, 152, 167, 190, 196,
    198, 201, 217, 243, 259, 265, 308–9
  Williams, Patrick, 20, 260, 309
  Willson, Meredith, 265
  Wonder, Stevie, 310
  Yamashita, Tsutomu, 310
  Yared, Gabriel, 310
  Young, Christopher, 229, 310
  Young, Victor, 36, 64, 71, **185**, 191, 193,
    215, 227, 232, 257, 258, **310–11**
  Zeitlin, Denny, 311
  Zimmer, Hans, 5, 51, 63, 198, 255–56,
    309

Composers and Lyricists Guild of America, 264
Composers, women, 261
Composing, 17
  before film shot, 129
Compson, Betty (actress), 163
Computer, 22, 47, **53**
  programs, 24
Conan the Barbarian (1982)
  as role model, 6
  in *RoboCop* review, 150
Concept, 26
  Body Heat, 72
  Close Encounters of the Third Kind, 130
  definition, 18
  Die Hard, 18
  El Cid, 19
  ethnic/geographical influences, 19, 71
    Gandhi, 70
  from the characters, 19, 20, 33, 72
  from the harmony, 34, 74
  from the orchestration, 18, 19, 20, 34
  historic and period influences, 20
  instrument representing a character, 19
  Lethal Weapon films, 19
  The Mission, 19
  musical styles, 71
  The North Star, 72
  Old Gringo, 19–20
  Other People's Money, 20
  RoboCop, 18
  Romeo and Juliet, 20
  Spartacus, 20
  specific instruments, 71
  Spock's theme, 20
  Stand and Deliver, 19
  Star Wars, 19
  Swing Shift, 20
  Under Fire, 19
  The Untouchables, 138
Conducting, 53
  Jerry Goldsmith **49**
  John Green **43**
  Alfred Newman 48, 53–54
  Dimitri Tiomkin, **54**
Conducting aids 46–47
Conductor's score, 185
  Spellbound Main Title, 108
Connery, Sean (actor), 137
  The Untouchables, **138**
Connick, Jr., Harry (singer), 68, 218, 254
Conrad, Con (songwriter), 207
Conti, Bill (composer), 37, 259, 266
  Academy Awards show, 217
  Academy Awards show music dir., 217
  documentaries, 168
  North and South (1985) schedule, 193
  orchestration, 37
  typecasting, 198
"Continental, The," 207
Contract (staff) orchestras, 75
Cooder, Ry (composer), 267
  slide guitarist, 250
Cook, Page (reviewer), 151, 153, 244
Cooper, Ray (musician), 252
Copeland, Stewart (composer), 267
Copland, Aaron (comp.) 72, 215, 257, **267**
  as role model, 13, 124
  critics, 145–46
  ethnic concept for *North Star*, 72

film music in forties, 241
  harmony influences *Best Years*, 186
  influence on Friedhofer, 273
  Old Man and the Sea, 200
  orchestration, 40
  Red Pony review, 148
  spotting, 77
  Zinnemann re: *Old Man and the Sea*, 199
Copyright
  Doctor Zhivago temp track, 8
Corigliano, John (composer), 267
Costner, Kevin (actor), 58, 137
  The Untouchables, **138**
Count Basie band, 30
Courage, Alexander (composer), 268
Crawford, Jesse/Helen (organists), 155
Crawford, Joan (actress), 43
Crawley, Tony (author), 13
Creative process, 27
  Georges Delerue, 28
  Jerry Goldsmith, 27–28
  John Morris, 26
  Alfred Newman, 27
  Rachel Portman, 27
  David Raksin 27, 28
  Laurence Rosenthal, 28
Creazioni Artistiche Musicali (C.A.M.), 231
Creston, Paul (composer), 168
Crime in the Streets, 25
Critics, 145
  film, 146
  Hautbois, Celeste, 147
Critters, 253
Crosby, Bing (singer), 57
Crossroads, southern blues, 6
Cruise, Tom (actor), 75
Crying Game, The, 258
Crystal, Billy (actor), 216, 254
Csillag, Steve (music editor), 46, 178
Cue sheets, silent film
  Don Juan, 158
  It's the Old Army Game, 159
Cues reprinted for another scene, 141
Cukor, George (director), 43
  A Double Life, 203
Curtis Institute of Music, 294
Curtiz, Michael (director), 93

D'Silva, Reynold (record exec.), 231
Daddy Long Legs, **187**
Dailies, 4
Daily Variety, 152, 216
Dali, Salvidor, *Spellbound* sequences, 106
"Dance of the Seven Veils"
  Sunset Boulevard role model 6
Dances With Wolves (1990)
  dubbing, 58
  record rights advance, 232
Dangerous Liaisons, 70
Dangerous Moonlight, 261
Dante, Joe (director), temp tracks, 9
Darby, Ken (composer/arranger), **178**
Dark Passage, source music, 69
Dark Victory, 99–104, 111, 137
Darreg, Ivor (journalist)
  electronic music, 75
David, Hal (lyricist), 223
  Butch Cassidy, 225
Davis, Benny (songwriter), 112

Davis, Bette (actress), 44
Dark Victory, 99
Davis, Carl (composer), 268
silent film scores, 164
using role models, 6
Davis, Miles (jazz trumpeter), 283
Day for Night, 268
Day, Doris (actress/singer), 58, **187**
Days of Thunder, 198
Days of Wine and Roses (1962)
theme written before song, 222
title song, 222
De Crescent, Sandy (orch. contractor), 63
Jerry Fielding, 272
Universal in sixties, 243
Stanley Wilson, 190
working with filmmakers, 203
De Francesco, Louis (Fox music director), **186**
de Havilland, Olivia (actress), 93
De Niro, Robert (actor), 137, 139, 253
De Packh, Maurice (orchestrator), 36
De Palma, Brian (director), 11, 137
Herrmann's emotional subtext, 82
Obsession, 83
with Ennio Morricone, **144**
de Rochemont, Louis (producer), 172
de Sylva, Buddy (head of prod., Paramount)
Double Indemnity, 189
Deadlines, 25, 28
Deal of the Century, role models, 6
Dean, James (actor)
requests Rosenman, 297
"Dear Heart," title song, 222
Death of a Salesman (1951), 36
orchestration, 35
Deathtrap, Bach role model, 6
Deception, prerecording, 44
Deer Hunter, The, 60
Deitzel, Alfred (songwriter), 100
Delerue, Georges (composer), 259, **268**
creative process, 28
orchestration, 40
Platoon, 68
Twins, 250
Deliverance (1972)
playing through the action, 81
DeMille, Cecil B. (producer/director), 162, 203
how worked with composers, 191
The Ten Commandments, 162
Demme, Jonathan (director), 152
Demonstrating the score, 30
electronic demos, 30, 33, 48, 50
electronic music, 32
Elfman, Danny, 30
piano demos, 30
Raksin plays *The Bad and the Beautiful*, 30
Dennis, Sandy (actress), 34
Deputy, The, 243
Destination Tokyo, 215
Deutsch, Adolph (composer), 214, 257, 269
MGM staff meeting, **180**
sketches, 36
Development of music, 76–77, 88
Devil and Daniel Webster, The, 202
DeVito, Danny (actor), 20
Devotion, review, 148
Dexter, Brad (actor), 122, 125
Dialogue, 56, 62
Dialogue mixers, 59

Dialogue track, 46
"Diane," 160
Diary of Anne Frank, The (1959)
in *Robe* review, 150
Dick Tracy (1990), 172, 218
themes and development, 77
Dickey, Ruth (silent film musician)
music on the set, 162
The Ten Commandments (1923), **162**
Die Hard (1988), 18, 252
in *License to Kill* review, 151
Die Kathrin (Korngold opera), 93
Dieterle, William (director), 202
Digital metronome, 45, **47**
Digital time code, 22
Dillon, Melinda (actress), 129
Director's vision, 12, 16
Director, the, 12, 14, 19, 29, 33
and dailies, 4
and temp tracks, 7
auditioning scores, 32
communicating with, 7, 12–15, 30, 32–33, 62
controls the music, 201
cuts scene too short, 5
Danny Elfman and, 14
documentaries, 168
dubbing, 57–59, 61
ideal working relationship, 201
insists on "Hallelujah!" chorus, 151
miscommunication, 14
music notes, 57
must be satisfied, 12
not at Universal screenings, 195
on scoring stage, 51
strong and opinionated, 16
themes written before shooting, 4
too little communication, 14
vision, 16, 51
working with favorite composer, 197
works with composer before shooting, 4
Directors
Abrahams, Jim, 254
Aldrich, Robert, 16
Altman, Robert, 86
Attenborough, Richard, 70
Avildsen, John, 266
Ballard, Carroll, 252
Beatty, Warren, 76
Beaumont, Harry, 176
Berkeley, Busby, 170
Bogdanovich, Peter, 68
Borzage, Frank 123
Brickman, Paul, 4, 30, 32–33, 62, 89
Brooks, Mel, 53, 290
Brunel, Adrian, 163
Burton, Tim, 10, 251
Capra, Frank, 201
Carpenter, John, 258
Chaplin, Charles, 163
Coppola, Francis Ford, 163
Cukor, George, 43, 203
Curtiz, Michael, 93
Dante, Joe, 9
De Palma, Brian, 11, 82–83, 137, **144**
DeMille, Cecil B., 162, 163, 191, 202–3
Demme, Jonathan, 152
Dieterle, William, 202
Dixon, Thomas, 160

Donner, Richard, 19, 86
Dragoti, Stan, 15
Eastwood, Clint, 272
Edwards, Blake, 68, 167, 196
Fellini, Federico, 298
Ford, John, 71, 123
Forman, Milos, 253
Gance, Abel, 162, 163
Gilliam, Terry, 252
Griffith, D. W., 154, 160, 161, 162
Hitchcock, Alfred, 11, 12, 15, 77–78, 83, 104, 116, 199, 202
Hoffman, Mike, 253
Ron Howard, 14
Hughes, John, 68
Huston, John, 294
Jewison, Norman, 20
Kagen, Jeremy, 44
Kazan, Elia, 181
Keighley, William, 93
Kidron, Beeban, 254
Kramer, Stanley, 201
Kubrick, Stanley, 16
Landis, John, 167
Lear, Norman, 253
Leone, Sergio, 89, 259, 290
LeRoy, Mervyn, 197
Levinson, Barry, 75, 255
Lewin, Al, 60
Lucas, George, 19, 57, 309
Lynch, David, 196
McTiernan, John, 18
Mamoulian, Rouben, 169
Mann, Michael, 305
Marshall, Garry, 14
Marshall, Penny, 5, 253
Miller, George, **51**
Mulligan, Robert, 79, 88
Pakula, Alan J., 86
Parker, Alan, 62, 253
Peckinpah, Sam, 272
Penn, Arthur, 297
Pollack, Sidney, 18
Reiner, Rob, 68, 254
Reitman, Ivan, 250
Roach, Hal, 168
Schlesinger, John, 51
Scott, Tony, 226
Seastrom, Victor, 165
Sidney, George, 180
Spielberg, Steven, 11, 13–14, 28, 129, 197
Stevens, George, 64, 151
Sturges, John, 122, 152
Truffaut, Francois, 259, 266
Verhoeven, Paul, 18, **55**,
Vidor, King, 165
Wayne, John, 202
Weir, Peter, 4
Welles, Orson, **5**, 202
Whale, James, **184**
Wilder, Billy, 6, 7, 17, 18, 110, 189, 198
Wyler, William, 62, 244
Zeffirelli Franco, **228**
Zemeckis, Robert, 250
Zinnemann, Fred, 14–16, 192–3, 199
Dirty Dancing (1987)
dance source, 69
record sales, 232
Dirty Harry, 301

Dirty Rotten Scoundrels (1988)
    playing through the action, 81
Disco, 228
Disney films
    documentaries, 168
    The Fox and the Hound, 165
    Plane Crazy, 165
    Snow White and the Seven Dwarfs, 165
Disney Studios
    dubbing, machine room, 57
    first album from movie, 227
Disney, Walt, 166
    Snow White songs, 165
Dissonances, 189
"Dixie," 166
Do the Right Thing CD, 229
Doctor Zhivago (1965)
    record sales, 232
    soundtrack album, 232
    temp tracks, 8
Docudrama
    All the President's Men, 86
Documentaries, 166–67
    Jacques Cousteau series, 168
    National Geographic series, 168
    scored by concert hall composers, 168
Dodge City, 123
Dolan, Robert Emmett (comp.), 257, 269
Dolby Stereo, 56
    Star Wars, 244
Dolby Surround Stereo, 230
Don Juan, 235
    silent film cue sheet, 158
"Don't Go Breaking My Heart," 251
Donaggio, Pino (composer), 269
Donner, Richard (director), 19
    Ladyhawke generic rock score, 87
Double Indemnity (1944), 104, 189
    in *Body Heat* review, 150
Double Life (Miklós Rózsa), 21, 298
Double Life, A (1947), "too modern," 203
Douglas, Kirk (actor/producer), 25, 70
Douglas, Lloyd C., (author), 240
Doyle, Patrick (composer), 269
Dr. Jekyll and Mr. Hyde review, 153
Dr. No theme by John Barry, 263
Dr. Terror's House of Horrors, 258
Dracula, 177
Dracula's Daughter, 172
"Dragnet" theme, 27
Dragon: The Bruce Lee Story, 30, 250
Dragon, Carmen (composer), 269
Dragoti, Stan (director), role models, 15
Dramatic theme of a film, 18
Dramatic tone, 13
Dreyfuss, Richard (actor), 42, 129, 131
Driving Miss Daisy (1989), 256
    harmony, 74
Drugstore Cowboy (Cue 4M3), 23
Drums Along the Mohawk, 123, 260
Dubbing, 56–62
    Morricone re: Leone films, 289
    The Magnificent Seven (cue #37), 124
    Spellbound review, 147
Dubbing mixers, **60**
Dubbing session, **60**
Dubbing stage, 56
Dubbing stage console, 60
Dubbing stage machine room, 57

Duck Dodgers in the 24 1/2th Century, 132
Dudley, Anne (composer), 258, 269
Duel in the Sun (1946), 15, 123
    scoring session, **54**
Dummies, 57
Duning, George (composer), 257, 269
    at Columbia, 177
Dunworth, Charlie (music editor), 46
Dvořák, Antonin (composer)
    Star Wars role model, 6

E.T. The Extra-Terrestrial (1982)
    melody, 73
    role models used for, 6
    themes, 73
Early days of sound, 175–95
Early soundtrack albums
    Captain from Castile, 227
    Decca Records, 227
    Duel in the Sun, 227
    first from film soundtrack, 227
    For Whom the Bell Tolls, 227
    Forever Amber, 227
    Golden Earrings, 227
    Madame Bovary, 227
    MGM Records, 227
    "original soundtrack" first used, 227
    RCA Victor Records, 227
    Spellbound, 227
    The Song of Bernadette, 227
    Till the Clouds Roll By, 227
Earth Girls songs, 226
Earthquake, spotting/sound effects, 78
Easter Parade, 214
Eastwood, Clint (director), 272
Easy Rider, 259
Edelman, Randy, 48, 260, 270
    demos, 30
    electronic prerecording, 61
    a film fan, 249
    getting started, 250
    Kindergarten Cop album, 229
    The Last of the Mohicans, 81
    prerecording electronic tracks, 62
    temp scores, 7
Edens, Roger (arranger), 214
Edgerton, June (music editor), **179**
    attitudes during studio system, 177
    Victor Young, 311
Editing, film, 4, 7, 9, 51, 62
    changes, *Robin Hood: Prince of Thieves*, 25
    on-screen performances, 43
Editor, music (*see music editor*)
Editorial changes, *Citizen Kane*, 5
Edward Scissorhands (1990), 250, 251
    album, 229
    reviews, 150, 152
Edwards, Blake (director), 68, 167, 250
    asks Mancini to score "Peter Gunn," 286
Egyptian, The, soundtrack album, 229
Eisler, Hanns (composer), 81
El Cid (1961)
    concept, 19
    Rózsa's research, 21
    sound effects, 61
Electronic demonstrations, 48, 51
Electronic keyboards, 29, **32, 53**
Electronic music, 18, 75
    controller, 31

    demonstrating the score, 30, 32–33
    sampling, 31
    Synclavier, 31
    Tangerine Dream, 305
Electronic prerecording, 61
Electronic scoring, 259
    Witness, 282
    The Year of Living Dangerously, 282
Elephant Man, The, 290
Elfman, Danny, 14, 250, **270**
    and classical and film music, 250
    and Tim Burton, 196
    Batman, 24
    demos, 30
    developing the melody, 77
    developing the score, 76
    directors, 14
    Edward Scissorhands, 10
        album, 229
        review, 150, 152
    getting started, 250–51
    hitting the action, 79–80
    Max Steiner, 80
    rhythm of film, 74
    scores more conservative now, 246
    sync, 24
Elgar, Edward, English role model, 124
Ellington, Duke (composer), 139, 294, 271
Ellis, Melville (pianist), 162
Elmer Gantry, 198
Embler, Jeffrey (journalist), 89
    emotional depth, *Aliens* review, 152
Emotional strength
    cited in reviews, 149–51
Empire of the Sun, review, 150
Empire Strikes Back, The (1980), 81
    role models for, 6
Entertainer, The, 81
Eskew, Jack (orchestrator), 37
Ethnic influences, 72
Ethnic music, 4
    authentic, 72
Evaluating a score, 91
    Hugo Friedhofer, 149
    in bad films, 146
    psychological connection, 148
    serving the film, 86
    The Player, 86
    two vital aspects of, 85
    Franz Waxman, 91
    when music not "connected," 151
Executive Action, 250
Exodus soundtrack album, 232
Exorcist, The, 68
Exorcist II: The Heretic, 290
Experience Preferred . . ., 253
Extreme Prejudice, review, 153

Faith No More, fee, 231
Fake, Douglass (record exec.), 231
Faking it, (*see prerecording*), 42
Fall of the Roman Empire, The, review, 151
Fallen Sparrow, 215
Falling Down, 251
Faltermeyer, Harold (composer), 226, 271
Fame (1980), 223
    source music, 69
Famous Music Publishing Co.
    Romeo and Juliet soundtrack albums, 228

Fantasia, 240
Far from the Madding Crowd
    composer-filmmaker relationship, 197
Farrar, Geraldine (actress)
    music on the set, 162
Farrell, Charles (actor), 238
Feds, 250
Fees to license master record, 231
Feigelson, Roger (reviewer), 153
Fellini, Federico (director), 298
Fenton, George (composer), 271
    Gandhi, 71
Fernandez, Bobby (music mixer), 52, 55, 56,
    62, 70
Ferris Bueller's Day Off (1986)
    on-screen source music, 68
    use of sampling, 31
Few Good Men, A, 255
Fiddler on the Roof, 69
Fiedel, Brad (composer), 271
Field of Dreams, 280
Fielding, Jerry (composer), 29,265, **271–72**
    leitmotifs, 73
    "must serve the film," 17
    orchestration, 34
    procrastination, 26
    soundtrack CDs, 229
Fields, Dorothy (lyricist), 171, 258
Fifties, Bernstein describes, 242
Film Daily, The, 212, 216
Film editor, the, 9, 62
Film editors, 59
    Stuart Baird, 19
    Paul Hirsch, 12
Film music criticism, 146
    Film Music Notes, 147
Film Music Notes, 146, 147, 153, 163, 168, 240
Film noir, *Dark Passage*, 69
Film Score: The Art & Craft of Movie Music
    (Tony Thomas), 168
Film Score Monthly, 146
Film Spectator, The, 237, 238
Filmographies, reference sources, 260
Films in Review, 146, 151, 153, 214, 215, 244
Fine cut, 9
Fine, Sylvia (lyricist), 258
Finston, Nathaniel (Paramount m.d.), 181
Firebird Suite, The, role model, 6
Firestone, Elizabeth (composer), 258
First Blood, role model, 6
First screening, 4
Fitzgerald, Ella (jazz singer), 254
Fitzgerald, Geraldine (*Dark Victory*), **99**
Fitzpatrick, James (record exec.), 231
Five Days One Summer (1983)
    Zinnemann's notes, 15–16
Five Graves to Cairo, 189
Flash Gordon serials, 172
Flash Gordon's Trip to Mars, 172
Flashdance dance source, 69
Flatbed editing machine, 9
Fleischer Animation Studios, 47, 176
Flesh and Blood, playback, **55**
Flesh and Fantasy, 215
Flynn, Errol (actor), 99, 284–85
    The Adventures of Robin Hood, **93**
Folk music, *The Magnificent Seven*, 124
Fool's Revenge, A, review, 156
Footage counter, 9, 25, 56

Footlight Parade, **170**
Footloose dance source, 69
"For He's a Jolly Good Fellow," 226
For Whom the Bell Tolls, 215, 223
Forbes, Louis (music director), 258
    Gone With the Wind scoring, **193**
Forbidden Zone, 251
Forbstein, Leo (Warner Bros. music dir.), 177
    The Adventures of Robin Hood, 191
    Steiner and Jack Warner, 304
Force of Evil, 14
Ford, John (director), 79
    music on the set, 123
    The Quiet Man, 71
Forever Amber (1947), 37
    bad film, good music, 91
Forever Young, 198
Form, 76, 88
    and concept, 150
    and development, 88
Forman, Milos (director), 253
Fortune, The (1975)
    playing through the action, 81
Foster, David (composer), 272
Foster, Stephen, used in *Stagecoach*, 123
Four Feathers, rerecorded CD, 230
Fox and the Hound, The (1981)
    hitting the action, 165
Fox Movietone newsreels, 171
Fox, Charles (composer), 260, 272
Franck, César (composer), 70
Frankenstein, 177
Fraser, Jill (composer), 258, 272
"Freddy's Dead," 212
Freed, Arthur (producer/songwriter), 177
Freelancing, 196–203
    getting started, 249–56
    getting the job, 199–200
    schedules, 200
    television series, 196
    time pressures, 200
    typecasting, 198
Freeman, Morgan (actor), 74
Freud, 259
Fricon, Terri (music supervisor), 226
Fried, Gerald (composer), 30, 272
    Kubrick and Aldrich, 16
    Spock's theme, 20
Friedhofer, Hugo 69, 90, **178**, 243, 257,
    258, 272–**73**
    The Adventures of Robin Hood, 93
    and Alex North, 181
    Dark Victory, 99, 102
    Devotion review, 149
    ideal film score, 149
    Joan of Arc review, 152
    orchestration, 75
    The Outcasts of Poker Flat, 90
    procrastination, 25
    scoring in early thirties, 239
    silent film projectors, 161–62
    sketches, 36
    with Morris Stoloff (1947), **186**
Friedkin, William (director)
    Academy Awards show, 217
Froman, Jane (singer), 223
Fugitive, The, 251
Full coat (sound film), 45

Function of music, 11, 17
Funny Lady, 60

Gable, Clark (actor), 182
Gance, Abel (director), 163
    music on the set, 162
Gandhi, 70
Garcia, Andy (actor), 137, **138**, 139
Garcia, Russell (comp.)
    Time Machine CD, 229
Garden of Allah, The (1936)
    first push-pull track, 240
Garfield, John (actor), 34, 44, 90
Garland, Judy (singer/actress), 227
Garner, James (actor), *Grand Prix*, 197
Garr, Terri (actress), 129
Gaynor, Janet (actress), 238
Gellman, Harold (MGM librarian), 43
Genre scores
    originality, 89
    television, 8
Genres
    action/adventure, 93–99
    Biblical, 151
    comedy, 71, 167
    docudrama, 86
    film noir, 69
    historical epics, 21
    James Bond, 86
    jeopardy, 78
    parody (Mel Brooks), 290
    psychological drama, 105
    religious, 240
    science fiction, 130
    Westerns, 8, 13, 70, 78
    "Spaghetti Westerns," 83, 86
"Gentle Annie," 123
Gerhardt, Charles (conductor), 83
    rerecorded classic scores, 229, 230
Gershenson, Joseph (mus./Universal m.d.)
    accompanying films, 155
    buying existing songs, 223
    collaborations, 195
    composers' contracts, 182
    conducting, 188
    cue sheets for silent films, 157
    dubbing, 60, 61
    early sound, 238
    music on the set, 162
    newsreels, 171
    silent film performances, 162
Gershwin, George (composer), 171
    expected to entertain, 240
    The Lost Weekend, 17
Gershwin, Ira (lyricist), 171
"Get a Job," 226
Ghost (1990)
    record sales, 232
    "Unchained Melody," 229
Ghost and Mrs. Muir, The, orch., 35
    Elmer Bernstein's CD, 229
Ghostbusters (1984), 198
    title song, 225
Ghostbusters II (1989), 30, 198, 250
    CD, 229
    songs, 226
Gibbs, Anthony (writer), 227
Gibson, Mel (actor), 19
Gigi (1958)
    role model for original song score, 210

Gilliam, Terry (director), 252
Glass, Philip (composer), 274
Glasser, Albert (composer), 274
 hitting the action, 80
Glory, 13
Glover, Danny (actor), 19
GNP Crescendo Records, 231
Godfather, The (1972), 43, 60, 298
 orchestration, 34
 Nino Rota, 84
 soundtrack CD, 231
"Going Home," DeMille favorite, 191
Going in Style (1979)
 playing through the action, 81
Gold, Ernest (composer), 274
 creative process, 28
 Exodus album, 232
 love your work, 249
Gold Diggers of 1933, 170
Goldberg, Whoopi (actress), 69
Goldenberg, Billy (composer), 190, 274
Goldenthal, Elliot (composer), 23
Goldsmith, Jerry (composer), 19, 51,
  72, 243, 250, 259, 265,
  274–75
 and Steven Spielberg, 13
 animation, 165
 animation pacing, 166
 Arthur Morton (orchestrator), 37
 as role model, 13
 The 'burbs temp tracks, 9
 communicating with Spielberg, 14
 composing, 27
 concept, 3
 conducting, 49
 craft, 28
 creative process, 27, 28
 Extreme Prejudice review, 153
 good films, bad films, 91
 I Confess spotting, 12
 in *Aliens* review, 151
 Logan's Run, 3
 Not Without My Daughter review, 153
 playing the drama, 80
 Poltergeist, 13
 pop music, 87
 producers want record albums, 245
 recording, 229
 role model, 6
 Sleeping With the Enemy review, 152
 spotting, 12
 Star Trek orchestration, 39
 "structure," 88
 "suffering," 17
 temp tracks, 8, 9
 "theme," 26
 typecasting, 198
Goldwyn, Sam (producer), 54
 and early sound, 238
Gone With the Wind (1939), 90, 145
 scoring session, 193
 no album at first, 229
 Steiner's schedule, 192
Good films, bad films, 91
Goodman, Miles (composer), 275
 Dirty Rotten Scoundrels, 81
Goodmanson, Agnes (moviegoer), 67
Gould, Morton (composer), 168
Goulding, Edmund (director), 99, 101

Graduate, The (1967), 259
 songs, 87, 222
 soundtrack album, 228
Grand Canyon, 251
Grant, Cary (actor), 116
 North by Northwest, w/ Saint, 121
 on Mount Rushmore, 117
Grapes of Wrath, A. Newman's schedule, 195
Grauman's Chinese Theatre, 240
Great Escape, The, review, 152
Great Gatsby, The, source music, 69
Great Moments in Aviation History, 254
Great Mouse Detective, The, 166
"Great Pretender, The," 226
Greatest Story Ever Told, The, review, 151
Green Card, 256
Green Dolphin Street (1947), 283
 spotting and sound effects, 78
Green Hornet, The, serials, 172
"Green Leaves of Summer, The," 202
Green, Bud (songwriter), 100
Green, John (composer/music director) 14,
  217, 257, 275–76
 Academy Awards fanfares, 217
 film music in 1970, 244
 Godfather score Oscar dispute, 211
 MGM contract, 182
 MGM music department, 180
 MGM music director, 186, 190
 prerecording, 43
Griffith, D. W. (director), 160, 161
 music on the set, 162
Grifters, The, 198
Gruenberg, Louis (composer), 257
Grusin, Dave (composer), 30, 190, 276
 Clara's Heart, 79
 GRP Records, 277
 The Milagro Beanfield War, 84
Guffey, Cary (actor), 129
Gulliver's Travels, album, 227
Gunfighter, The, 123
Gunga Din, 260
Guns of Navarone, The (1961)
 in *Fall of the Roman Empire* rev., 151
 rerecorded CD, 230
 time pressures (1961), 200

Hageman, Richard (composer), 123, 257
Hajos, Karl (composer), serials, 172
Hamilton, Arthur (lyricist)
 Academy threatened by lawsuits, 214
 Chaplin's *Limelight* score, 213
 The Color Purple credits, 213
 Music Branch executive committee, 210
Hamilton, Murray (actor), 110
Hamlet (1948), 307
Hamlisch, Marvin (composer), 37, 217, 259,
  277
 antisentimental period in films, 245
 The Sting, 69, 81
Hammell, John (mus. ed./mus. exec.), 48,
  58, 64, 178–79
 Cecil B. DeMille, 191
 getting jobs in studios, 240
 Hollywood class distinctions, 181
 music for war films, 240
 scoring sessions in late thirties, 185
 timings, 25
 Victor Young, 311

Hammer, Jan (composer)
 "Miami Vice," 81, 245
Hammerstein II, Oscar (lyricist), 171
Hanging Tree, The, 123
Hanson, Curtis Lee (journalist), 201
"Happy Birthday," licensing, 226
"Harbor Lights," 123
Harburg, E. Y. "Yip" (lyricist), 171
Harlettes, The, and Marc Shaiman, 254
Harline, Leigh (composer), 132, 243, 257, 277
Harling, W. Franke (composer), 123, 277
Harmony, 74, 82
 and concept, 34
 in *The Adventures of Robin Hood*, 94
 in *Spellbound*, 105, 147
Harp glissandi, in *Devotion* review, 149
 in *Spellbound* review, 147
Hart, B., (songwriter), 132
Hart, Lorenz (lyricist), 169, 171
Hautbois, Celeste (film mus. critic), 77, 147
 Spellbound review, 148
Havana, 277
Hawaii orchestration, 37
Hayes, Isaac (composer/singer), 259, 278
 Shaft soundtrack album, 228
Hayes, Jack (orchestrator), 122
Hayton, Lennie (music director), 214
Hayward, Leland (producer), 199
Hazen, Joseph H. (studio exec.), 200
Head Office, 251
Headset, on scoring stage podium, 47
Heart at Fire's Center, A (Smith), 74, 83
Heart Is a Lonely Hunter, The, 277
Heaven Can Wait, 277
Hefti, Neal (composer), 30, 278
Heifetz, Jascha (violinist), 183
Heindorf, Ray (composer/music director),111,
  112, 113, 116
 and Alex North, 181
 Warner Bros. m.d., 186–87, 190, 278
 with Dennis Morgan and Doris Day, 187
Hello Dolly!, 37
 prerecording, 42
Helsley, Grover (music mixer), 56, 59, 230
 orchestras rediscovered, 245
 originality important, 89
 songs in seventies, 244
Henderson, Ray (songwriter), 238
Hendricks, Gordon (journalist), 90
Henreid, Paul (actor), 44
Henry V, 307
Herbert, Victor (composer)
 and ASCAP, 308
 The Fall of a Nation, 160
 The Fall of a Nation review, 161
"Here Comes the King" (Budweiser jingle), 132
Herrmann, Bernard (composer), 52, 88,
  117,177, 178, 243, 250, 257, 258,
  259, 278–79
 Citizen Kane, 5
 "combatting ignorance," 201
 creative process, 29
 critics, ideas about, 146
 editing changes, 63
 Egyptian, The CD, 229
 emotional subtext, 82
 form, 75
 The Ghost and Mrs. Muir CD, 229
 Hitchcock's *Vertigo* notes, 15

Herrmann, Bernard (cont'd)
    "If I were starting now," 244
    motifs, 73
    need to work autonomously, 202
    North by Northwest, 116–22
        use of themes, 121
    Obsession, 83
    orchestration, 34, 35
    own worst enemy, 279
    Psycho, 15, 83
    recording technology, 35
    role model, 6
    scoring Citizen Kane, **5**
    self-plagiarism, 91
    The 7th Voyage of Sinbad, 146
    spotting Sisters, 12
    style, 69
    timings, 47
    turned down Laura, 191
    Vertigo spotting, 11
    work methods, 29
Heyman, Edward (lyricist), 100
Heymann, Werner (composer), 257
Hiemenz, Jack (journalist), 44
"High and the Mighty, The," Oscar dispute, 216
High Noon (1952), 123
    lyrics under dialogue, 201
    title song, 224
    solo voice in score, 90
Hirsch, Paul (film editor), 12
Historical epics, 21
Historical research, 20. See also Research
Hitchcock, Alfred (director), 11–12, 78, 16, 202
    notes for Vertigo, 15
    Psycho, 83
    spotting, 12
    use of silence, 77
    Tiomkin and Torn Curtain, 199
Hitting the action, 79
Hoffa, 253
Hoffman, Dustin (actor), 75
Hoffman, Jerry (journalist), 169
Hoffman, Mike (director), 253
Holden, William (actor), 83
Holdridge, Lee (comp.), 15, 19, 260, 279
    communicating with director, 14
    Old Gringo, 20
Hollander, Frederick (comp.), 257, 279
    orchestration, 36
Hollywood Reporter, The, 212, 216, 232, 257
Holst, Gustav (composer), 6
Holzmann, Abe (composer), 113
Home Alone, 309
    role models, 50
Home Alone 2 form, 92
Home studio, **32**
Honegger, Arthur (composer), 279
Honeysuckle Rose, 223
Horner, James (composer), 29, 259, 279–**80**
    Aliens review, 151
    directors, 13
    Greig McRitchie's work with, 37
    orchestration, 37
    playing the drama, 80
Horror films, 168–69
Hot Spot, The, 70
House Party II, record album, 232

Houser, John G. (journalist), 216
How the West Was Won (1962), 123
    A. Newman as music director, 54
How composers get started, 249–56
How to listen, 84
Howard, James Newton (comp.), 280–81
    Garry Marshall and, 14
    getting started, 251
    Grand Canyon, 88
    Pretty Woman, 14
    The Man in the Moon, 79, **88**
    The Prince of Tides, 79
Howard, Ron (director)
    Splash, 14
Hud (1963), Bernstein's score, 243
Hughes, John (director), 68
    role models, 27
Hummers, 37
Humoresque (1946)
    prerecording, 44
Hunchback of Notre Dame, The, 260
    Newman's schedule, 195
Hunter, Ian (actor), 94
Hussey, Olivia (actress), **228**
Huston, John (director), 294
Hyman, Dick, (comp.), prerecording, 44

I Confess, spotting, 12
"I Love L.A.," 253
"I Love To See You Smile," 253
"I Only Have Eyes for You," 226
I Pagliacci, as source music, 140, 144
"I'll Get By," 223
Ikebe, Shinichiro (composer), 281
"I Married a Monster from Outer Space," 224–25
Impatient Years, The (1944)
    music on the set, 163
Importance of Being Oscar, The (Levant), 285
Impressionism, 130
"In a Monastery Garden," Hitchcock's favorite, 202
Indian Fighter, The, 25, 123
Indiana Jones series of films, tone, 99
Informer, The, hitting the action, 79
Instrumental color, 75. See also Orchestration
Intensity in RoboCop review, 150
International Theatre in Los Angeles, **155**
Interpolated songs, 225
Into the Night, 70
Intolerance, compiled score, 160
Intrada Records, 231
Invisible Man, The, 172
Invitation, 283
Isham, Mark (composer), **281**
    comfortable composers, 87
    getting started, 251–52
Island in the Sun, research, 21
Islands in the Stream, 130
"Isn't It Romantic?" 169, 170, 239
"It Had To Be You," 68
It Happened One Night, loan-out, 182
It's a Great Feeling, Ray Heindorf, **187**
It's the Old Army Game, cue sheet, 159
Iturbi, José (pianist), 42
Ivanhoe, Rózsa's research, 21
Ives, Ralph (music editor), 43, 47–48
    set recording at Fleischer, 176

Jackson, Howard (composer), 101
James Bond series, 259
    Dr. No theme, 263
    Licence to Kill review, 151
Janis, Elsie (songwriter), 101
Jarre, Maurice (composer), 4, 259, **282**
    communicating with director, 14
    Doctor Zhivago album, 232
    temp track, 8
    Ghost, 229
    Hazen comments, 200
    MGM scoring session (1966), 197
Jaws, 78, 130, 259
    motif, 26
    spotting, 11
Jazz
    Mancini, 286
    Taking of Pelham 1-2-3, The, 302
Jazz Singer, The (1927), 169, 175
    review, 238
Jeannie, 215
"Jeannie with the Light Brown Hair," 123
Jewison, Norman (director), 20
Jezebel, 99
Joan of Arc, review, 152
John, Elton (songwriter/performer), 251
Johnny Belinda, review, 151
Johnny Guitar, 123
Johnson, Ken (music editor), 24
Jolson, Al (singer/actor), 175, 238
Jones, Isabel Morse (music critic)
    Academy nominations, 215
    symphonic scoring/Mickey Mouse, 81
Jones, Quincy (comp.), 30, 190, 217, 282
    credits on The Color Purple, 213
    orchestration, 34
Jones, Trevor (composer), 260, 282
    The Last of the Mohicans, 81
Joplin, Scott (ragtime composer), 69
"Joy to the World," mus. development, 76
Jules and Jim, 259, 268
Juliet of the Spirits, 298
Jungle Book
    1942 album, 227, 229
Jungle Book Suite, 227
Jungle Fever
    record sales, 232
    songs ineligible for Oscar, 212
Just Off Broadway, 194

Kagen, Jeremy (director), 44
Kalmar, Bert (lyricist), 223
Kamen, Michael (composer), 19, 30, 282
    "real music," 87
    Die Hard, 18
    getting started, 252
    Lethal Weapon, 19
    License to Kill review, 151
    orchestrators, 40
    playing the drama, 78, 79, 80
    Robin Hood album sales, 228
    time pressures, 25
Kaper, Bronislau (composer), 257, 258, 283
    Academy Music Branch re: credits, 213
    before spotting, 9
    class distinctions, 180
    comedy scoring, 167
    concept, 71
    conducting, 53

Kaper, Bronislau (cont'd)
 dubbing, 59–60
 Ray Heindorf, 187
 loan-outs, 182
 MGM contracts, 182
 MGM music department, **180**
 orchestration, 33, 75
 prerecording, 42, 43
 realistic about talent, 197
 Salzburg Connection, 244
 silence, 11
 song not promoted at Fox, 215
 sound effects, 78
 "sounds like Franz," 27
 staff film assignments, 190
 The Red Badge of Courage, 90
 working in the late seventies, 245
Kapp, Michael (record exec.), 232
Karas, Anton (composer), 283
 The Third Man, 19
Karate Kid, The, 198
Karate Kid II, The, 37, 198
Karate Kid III, The, 198
Kariton, Michael (pianist), 306
Karlin, Fred (composer), 283
 Up the Down Staircase orch., 34
Karmen, Steve (composer), 132
Karpman, Laura (composer), 258, 283
Kasha, Al (songwriter), winning Oscar, 207
Kaufman, Louis (violinist), 54, 176
 Alfred Newman string sound, 185
 studio contracts, 184
Kaun, Bernhard (orchestrator), 35
Kaye, Jesse (record producer), 227
Kazan, Elia (director), 181
Keeler, Ruby (actress/dancer), 170
 42nd Street review, 239
Keighley, William (director), 93
Kentuckian, The, 123
Kern, Jerome (songwriter), 171
 Till the Clouds Roll By album, 227
Kessel, Barney (jazz guitarist), 20
Kettering, William (conductor), 253
Keyboardists (Mike Lang), **53**
Kidron, Beeban (director), 254
Kilar, Wojciech (composer), 283
Kindergarten Cop (1990), 60
 album, 229
King Kong (1933), 11, 28
 Friedhofer comments, 304
 psychological scoring, 83
 rerecorded CD, 230
 Steiner and producer, 239
King Richard the Lion-Heart, 94
King, Carole (songwriter), 258
King, Wayne (dance band leader), 100
Kings Row, 284
Kinothek, 157
KISS, license fee, 231
Klapholz, Ernst (MGM music exec.), 177
Klune, Ray (studio exec.), 58
Knights of the Round Table, 242
Kol Nidre, 238
Kopp, Rudy, (music editor), **180**
Korngold, Erich Wolfgang (composer), 44,
 249, 250, 257, 258, **284**
 The Adventures of Robin Hood, 3, 93–99,
 190–91
 and Max Steiner, 197

changes after the preview, 62
 Devotion review, 148–49
 dubbing, 56
 Friedhofer orchestrates, 273
 giving my best, 284
 heart attack, 284
 pianos ruined at Warner Bros., 284
 playing the drama, 98
 prerecording, 44
 Private Lives of Elizabeth and Essex CD, 229
 returned to Vienna, 284
 The Sea Hawk, 3
 Star Wars, 19
 "symphony music," 81
 themes, 98
 timings, 22, 47
 Warner Bros. contract, 182
 working from script, 3
Korngold, George (record prod.), 22, 93
Kraft, David (film music journalist), 89
Kraft, Richard (agent), 73, 89
 no agent when starting out, 249
 electronic demos, 32
 getting started, 250
 late '70s–mid-'80s, 245
 musical development in scores, 76
 "missed opportunities," in scores, 85
 role models, 5
 the sixties, 89, 243
 temp tracks, 8
Kreuger, Miles (author/president, Institute of
 the American Musical), 169
Kubik, Gail (composer), 168
Kubrick, Stanley (director), 27
 Gerald Fried and, 16
Kurland, Gilbert (conductor)
 conducting *Bride of Frankenstein*, **184**
Kurosawa, Akira (director)
 The Seven Samurai, 124
Kurtz, Gary (producer), 309

L'Assassinat du Duc de Guise, 160
L.A. Story, 60
La Bamba, record sales, 232
La Dolce Vita, 298
"La Marseillaise," 112
Ladyhawke (1985)
 score not connected to film, 87
Lancaster, Burt (actor), 250
Landau, Martin (actor), 118
Landis, John (director), comedies, 167
Lang, Mike (studio keyboardist), **53**
Lange, Arthur (comp./MGM m.d.), 285
 MGM, early thirties, 177, 184
Langois, Daniel (composer), 260
"Lara's Theme," 9
Larson, Randall D. (author), 80, 145
 themes, 88
Lass, Abraham H. (musician), 157
Last Action Hero, 252
Last Emperor, The, split credit, 260
Last of the Mohicans, The, (1992)
 playing against the action, 81
 split credit, 260
Last Starfighter, The, review, 153
Laura, 14, 27, 258, 296
 phrasing the drama, 82
Lawrence of Arabia (1962), 86, 200, 259, 282
 rerecorded CD, 229
 spotting, 86

Leader (film), 24
League of Their Own, A, editing, 5
Lean, David, *Zhivago* temp tracks, 8
Lear, Norman (director), 253
Lees, Gene (author/lyricist), 287
Legend, Goldsmith conducts, 49
Legrand, Michel (composer), 259, 285
 themes before lyrics, 222
Leigh, Janet (actress), 83
Leipold, John (composer), 123
Leitmotifs, 73
 in silent film scores, 164
 The Ten Commandments, 203
LeMel, Gary (Warners music president)
 title songs, 225
Leonard Maltin's Movie and Video Guide, 146,
 148
Leonardo da Vinci, clichés, 89
Leoncavallo, Rugero (opera comp.), 140, 144
Leone, Sergio (director), 83, 89, 259, 290
Let It Be, 223
Lethal Weapon (1987), 252
 concept, 19
 in *License to Kill* review, 151
 orchestration, 40
Lethal Weapon 2, concept, 19
Lethal Weapon 3, concept, 19
Letter, The, 99
Levant, Oscar (composer/pianist/actor), 168,
 285
 early sound days, 175, 176
 prerecording, 44
 Rhapsody in Blue, 171
Levinson, Barry (director), 253, 255
 Rain Man, 75
Lewin, Al (producer), 60
Lewton, Val (producer), 168
Librarian, music, 40, 49
License fees
 Legal Eagles, 231
 Rod Stewart record, 231
 to use master recording, 231
License to Kill review, 151
Licensing master recordings, 226
Lifeforce, 287
Lilies of the Field, 259
Limelight, 213
Lindbergh, Charles (aviator), 111
Lip-syncing "Twist and Shout," 68
Lipstone, Louis (Paramount m.d.), 18, 188
 and dissonances, 189
Liszt, Franz (composer), 70
Little Man Tate, 252
Little Mermaid, The, 245
Live (set) recording, 176
Livingston, Alan (record exec.), 229
Loan-outs, 182
Logan's Run, concept, 3
"London Bridge Is Falling Down," 221
London Symphony Orchestra (LSO), 41
Long cues, 53
Long Hot Summer (1958)
 in *Body Heat* review, 150
Longet, Claudine (singer), 215
Los Angeles Music Festival, 308
Los Angeles Times, 200, 209, 215
Lost Horizon (1937), 182, 306
 conducted by Steiner, 54
 orchestration, 35

Lost Weekend, The (1945), 18
  psychological drama, 105
  temp track, 17–18
Louisiana Story, 168
Love Happy, 258
Love in a Goldfish Bowl, title songs, 224
Love Me Tonight (1932), review, 239
"Love Song of the Waterfall," 131
"Love Theme from Godfather, The"
  Oscar dispute, 211
Lowe, Frederick (songwriter), 118
Lucas, George (director), 229, 309
  American Graffiti songs, 226
  dubbing, 57
  Star Wars, concept, 19
  role models, 6
Lumière brothers, 154
Lust for Life style, 70
Lutyens, Elisabeth (composer), 258, 286
Lyricists
  Ashman, Howard, 245
  Bergman, Alan and Marilyn, 223
  Bergman, Marilyn, 258
  Bricusse, Leslie, 229
  Cahn, Sammy, 215
  David, Hal, 223, 225
  Fields, Dorothy, 171, 258
  Fine, Sylvia, 258
  Gershwin, Ira, 171
  Hammerstein II, Oscar, 171
  Harburg, E. Y. "Yip," 171
  Magdison, Herb, 208
  Mercer, Johnny, 171
  Nash, Ogden, 258
  Previn, Dory, 258
  Robbins, Ayn, 258
  Washington, Ned, 224
  Webster, Paul Francis, 78, 201–2, 222

M*A*S*H, 37
"Ma, He's Makin' Eyes at Me," 223
MacDonald, Jeanette (actress/singer), 169–70, 239
MacLean, Andrew (reviewer), 151
Madame Curie (1943)
  Lipstone cites as role model, 189
Madonna (singer/actress)
  Academy Awards show, 218
Mag stripe, 45, 47
Magdison, Herb (lyricist), 207
Magnificent Ambersons, The (1942)
  orchestration, 35
Magnificent Dope, The, 194
Magnificent Seven, The, 122–29, 98, 264
  orchestration, 37
  the seven on horseback, **124**
  tempo and pulse, 74
Mahler, Gustav (composer), 250
Maltin, Leonard (author/film critic), 146
  My Reputation, 148
Mambo Kings, The, dance source, 69
Mamoulian, Rouben (director)
  Love Me Tonight, 169
  musicals, 169
Man Called Horse, A, review, 151
Man for All Seasons, A, 259
Man in the Moon, The (1990), 79
  form, 88
Man Who Knew Too Much, The (1956)
  Hitchcock's music notes, 57–58

Man with a Golden Arm, The, 259, 264
  record sales, 242
Mancini, Henry (composer), 217, 250, 258, 259, 265, **286**–87
  always wanted to write movie music, 286
  and Blake Edwards, 197
  animation scoring, 166
  composers need sense of drama, 249
  collaborations at Universal, 195
  comedy scoring, 167
  dubbing, 56
  good films, bad films, 91
  influence on film music, 242
  jazz, 287
  "Peter Gunn," 242, 287
  "Moon River," writing, 222
  music independent of score, 87
  music should be noticed, 84
  on "clichés," 89
  originality, 89
  research 21, 22
  songs for business reasons, 221
  source music, 68
  tempo, 74
  themes become songs, 222
  Universal staff composer, 188
  Victor Young, 73, 311
Mandel, Johnny (composer), 30, 37, 287
  Deathtrap, Bach as role model, 6
  The Sandpiper, 78
  theme, 222
Manila Calling, 194
Mann, Michael (director), 305
Mann, Paul (songwriter), 100
MARCH OF TIME newsreels, 172
"Margie," 223
Marsalis, Wynton (composer/jazz trumpeter), 287
Marshall, Garry (director), 14
Marshall, Jack (composer), 243
Marshall, Penny (director), 253
  Awakenings spotting, 12
  League of Their Own, A, 5
Marx Brothers (actors), 258
Mason, Benedict (composer), 163
Mason, James (actor), 116
Mathis, Johnny (singer), 132, 137
Max Steiner Society, 100
May, Brian (composer), 287
Mayer, Louis B., (studio mogul), 54, 179, 283
  organized Academy, 207
Mayfield, Curtis (songwriter/singer), 212
McCarthy, Joseph (senator), 112
McCartney, Paul (composer), 288
McCarty, Clifford (film music author), 100
McGann, Kevin (reviewer), 152
McHugh, David (composer), 288
McIntyre, Reba (country singer), 218
McLaglen, Victor (actor), 79
McLaughlin, Mike (music mixer), **179**
McLaughlin, Richard (composer), 163
McQueen, Steve (actor), 122, 125
  The Magnificent Seven, **123**
McRitchie, Greig (orchestrator), 29, 37, 50, 54, 55
  Jerry Fielding, 26
McTiernan, John (director), 18
Meatballs, 198
Mechanic, The, soundtrack CD, 229

Mechanical instruments, 155
Medicine Man, 70
Meisel, Edmund (comp.), *Potemkin,* 161
Mellé, Gil (composer), 288
Melody, 72, 82, 88
  in musical development, 76
Memoirs of an Amnesiac, The (Levant), 44, 285
Memoirs of an Invisible Man, 255, 258
Men Don't Leave (1990), 4
  demonstrating the score, 32
  dubbing, 62
Mendelssohn, Felix (composer), 6
Mendoza, David (composer), 237
Menken, Alan (composer), **288**
  Little Mermaid, The, 245
Mercer, Johnny (lyricist), 171
Merian C. (*King Kong* producer), 239
Mermaids, song budget, 226
Messiah, The, 151
MGM, 27, 43, 60
  Academy voting influenced by, 215
  Broadway Melody, 176
  CinemaScope, first production, 242
  first musical on tape, 227
  Doctor Zhivago temp track, 8
  dubbing, 59
  during Depression, 176
  orchestration, 36
  orchestrators, 35
  "original soundtrack" recordings, 227
  Rózsa's research, 299
  scoring sessions (forties), 185
  staff assignments, 190
  staff orchestra, 52
"Miami Vice," playing through the action, 81
Michelet, Michel (composer), 257
Mickey Mouse cartoon, 166
Mickey-Mousing, 79, 81, 165
MIDI, 31
Midler, Bette (singer/actress), 254
Midnight Cowboy, 259
Midnight Express, 253
Midsummer Night's Dream, A, 273
Mifune, Toshiro (actor), 197
Milagro Beanfield War, The, 277
Milhaud, Darius (composer), 257, 288
Milland, Ray (actor), 17,18
Miller, George (director), 51
Mills, Irving (songwriter/publisher), 139
Miniver Story, The, 197
Miracle of Our Lady of Fatima, The (1952)
  playing the drama, 80
Miracle Worker, The, 28, 297
Misery, 254
  communicating with director, 33
Mishkin, Nan Schwartz (composer), 258
Mission, The, (1986), 290
  concept, 19
  record sales, 232
Mixer, music, 49, 50, 52, 55–56, 59
Mixing
  premix music before dubbing, 61
Mockridge, Cyril (comp.), 243, 257, 289
Modern Times scoring session, 48
Moderns, The, 252
Monardo, Meco (record artist), 229
Montages, 5
Montand, Yves (actor), 197

"Mood Indigo," 139, 144
"Moon River," 286
   how written, 222
Moonlight Sonata, 163
Moore, Colleen (actress)
   music on the set, 163
Morely, Angela (comp./orch.), 258, 289
Morey, Larry (lyricist), 166
Morgan, Dennis (actor), **187**
Moroder, Giorgio (composer), 289
Moross, Jerome (composer), 289
Morricone Ennio (composer), 19, 30, 259, **289**–90
   dubbing in Leone films, 289
   ethnic influences in *The Mission*, 71
   orchestration, 35, 142
   originality, 89
   psychological scoring, 83
   soundtrack albums, 231
   style, 69
   The Untouchables (1987), 137–44
Morris, John (composer), 249, 290
   creative process, 26
   short cues, 53
   scores motion like ballet, 290
Morros, Boris (Paramount m.d.), **188**
Morse Jones, Isabel (*L.A. Times*), 209
Morton, Arthur (orchestrator),
   and Jerry Goldsmith, 37
   and Frederick Hollander, 36
   at Columbia, 177
   Cold Turkey, 253
   Star Trek orchestration, 39
Morton, Lawrence (music critic), 146
   Red Pony review, 148
Mosquito Coast, The, before shooting, 4
Motifs, 26, 73, 92, 93, 116
   Beethoven's Fifth, 76
   Close Encounters, 129, 131, 133–37
   Jaws, 26
   The Spirit of St. Louis M.T. sketch, 115
   "Twilight Zone," 26
Motion Picture Moods for Pianists . . ., 157
Motion Picture World, 156
Motives. See Motifs
Motown, 214
Motown Records, *Jungle Fever* songs, 212
Mount Rushmore action sequence, 117, 120, 121
Movie Music, 149, 152, 153
Moving Picture World, 154
Moviolas, 25
Mr. Baseball, 198
Mr. Mom, 15
Mulligan, Robert (director), 88
   Clara's Heart, 79
   The Man in the Moon, 79
Munich Symphony Orchestra, 229
Murphy's Romance, 258
Murray, Bill (actor), 250
Music in films
   function of, 9, 17, 18
   overlooked by critics, 145
Music contractor, 196
Music departments, 186–90
   20th Century Fox (fifties), **178**
   Columbia (fifties), 177, (1937), **182**
   MGM, (1929) 177, **180**
   Paramount Pictures (1930), 181

Twentieth Century-Fox (1959), 243
   Walt Disney Pictures, 179
Music director, the
   Academy Awards show, 217
   credits, 214
   finding talent, 190
   Morris Stoloff explains function, 241
Music directors
   Chaplin, Saul, 214
   Forbes, Louis, **193**, 258
   Gershenson, Joseph, 188, 190, 195
   Green, John, 186, 275–76
   Heindorf, Ray, 181, 186, **187**, 278
   Lange, Arthur, 184, 285
   Lipstone, Louis, 189
   Morros, Boris, **188**
   Newman, Alfred, 54–55, **178**, 181, 184, 185, 186, **187**, 195. *See also* Composers
   Newman, Lionel, 190, 292
   Previn, Charles, 188, 295
   Shilkret, Nathaniel, 301
   Silvers, Louis, 194, 302
   Stoloff, Morris, **182**, 186, 241
   Wilson, Stanley, 190, 243
Music editor, the, 9, 22, 23, **24**, 29, 45, 46, 48, 49
   Paramount staff in fifties, **179**
Music editors, 5, 63
   Adams, George, 46, 187
   Badami, Bob, 226
   Bernstein, Bill, 23
   Carlin, Dan, **24**
   Cillag, Steve, 46, **179**
   Dunworth, Charlie, 46
   Edgerton, June, 177, **179**
   Hammell, John, 25, 48, 64, **179**, 185
   Ives, Ralph, 43, 47, 176
   Johnson, Ken, 24
   Kopp, Rudy, **180**
   Stinson, Bill, 56, **179**
   Tracy, Robert, (music editor)
      Academy voting (1949), 215
   Treloggen, Abby, 45
Music for Eighteen Musicians, 6
Music for Silent Films (Anderson), 156
Music in Modern Media (Dolan), 269
Music Man, The, music tracks, 57
Music mixers, 49, 50, 52, 55–56, 59, 61
   McLaughlin, Mike, 179
   Steiner, Armin, **50**
   Vernon, Vinton, **178**
Music notes, 15, 58
Music on the set
   John Ford, 123
   The Ten Commandments, 163
   Woman to Woman, 163
Music supervisor, the, 24, 49
Music tracks, 57, 62
Music units, 45, 56–57, 61
Musical America, 161
Musical development, 75–77
   The Magnificent Seven, 128
Musical independence of scores, 87
   cited in reviews, 152
   Not Without My Daughter review, 153
Musical Instrument Digital Interface (MIDI), 31
Musical style
   changes during *The Quiet Man*, 71

Musical styles, 6
   ancient Greek, 20, 21, 70
   Belgian Congo, 72
   big-band atonal jazz, 302
   bluegrass banjo, 81
   blues, 6, 70, 71
   brass bands, 20
   Brazil (late-eighteenth-century), 19
   "Broadway cum-Rachmaninoff," 189
   chromaticism, 105
   classical, 19, 70
   contemporary Los Angeles Latino, 19
   country, 70
   Cuban folk, 200
   disco, 228
   electronic, 18, 75
   folk, 71
   forties, 20
   French troubadours, 21
   Gershwinesque, 17
   S. Grappelli jazz of the thirties, 81
   Impressionism, 130
   Indian, 21
   Indian sitar-and-tabla, 71
   jazz, 70, 71, 81, 259, 287, 301
   Johann Sebastian Bach, 6
   martial, 152
   medieval Spanish, 21
   Mendelssohn, 6
   Mexican folk, 84
   Mexico, 19
   mid 19th-century romanticism, 70
   Nicaragua, 19
   nineteenth-century (late), 19
   oriental, 19
   post-Impressionism, 70
   post-World War II, 19
   Prussianistic, 152
   quasi-religious, 13
   ragtime, 71
   rock-and-roll, 87, 259
   Roman, 21, 70
   romantic, 105, 130
   romantic symphonic, 70
   Russian folk song, 8
   southern blues, 6
   Spanish folk songs, 21
   symphonic, 70, 111
   symphonic scores for jeopardy films, 78
   Tiomkin's "Roman music," 151
   twelfth-century, 21
   vaudeville/dixieland jazz, 81
   Venuti-Lang jazz of the twenties, 81
   Vienna Opera House, 19
   waltz, 9
   West Indian, 21
   western Americana, 264
   World War II, 20
Musicals, 169–71
   adaptation, 69
   "backstage," 176
   Berkeley, Busby, 170
   Broadway Melody, The, 238
   "By a Waterfall," 170
   Cagney, James, **170**
   Footlight Parade, 170
   42nd Street, 170, 239
   Gold Diggers of 1933, 170
   Kreuger, Miles, 169–70

Musicals (cont'd)
 Little Mermaid, The, 245
 Love Me Tonight, 169, 239
 Mamoulian, Rouben, 169
 Rodgers and Hart, 169–70
 "Shanghai Lil," 170
 Shilkret, Nathaniel, 169
 Sunny Side Up, 238
Musician, The, 154
Musicians' strike, 183, 242
 Musicians, staff, salaries, 184
My Bodyguard, 277
My Left Foot, 198
My Reputation, music review, 148
Myers, Stanley (composer), 255, 290
Mystic Knights of the Oingo Boingo, The,
 251

Napoleon (1927), 162
Nash, Dick (studio trombonist), 52
Nash, Ogden (lyricist), 258
Nashville, 60
National Film Music Council
 film music research (1949), 257
National Philharmonic Orchestra, 230
Natural, The, 253
Nelson, Oliver (composer), 190, 290
Ness, Eliot (Treasury man), 137
Never Cry Wolf, 252
New Jack City, 87
 CD, 229
 contemporary, 69
 record advance, 232
 record sales, 232
New York Herald Tribune, 161
New York Philharmonic Orchestra, 237
New York Times, 162, 241
Newborn, Ira (composer), 291
 role models, 27
"Newman sound" at Fox, 185
Newman System, the, 46
Newman, Alfred (composer/music director),
 29, 37, 89, 178, 194, 215, 217, 249,
 250, 252, 253, 257, 258, 291–92
 Alexander's Ragtime Band Oscar, 214
 budgets, 185
 collaborations, 195
 composed while music director, 187
 conducting, 53, 54–55, 291
 creative process, 27
 The Egyptian CD, 229
 Fox music director, 181, 186, 190
 Hazen mentions for Becket, 200
 job for Friedhofer, 273
 Kaufman, Louis, 184
 Modern Times, 48
 Mother Wore Tights Oscar, 214
 music director, 181
 the Newman System, 46
 1939, 260
 orchestration, 34. 54
 Raksin and Chaplin, 296
 The Robe review, 150
 salary at Fox (1959), 243
 schedules, 175, 192
 scoring sessions, 185
 self-plagiarism, 91
 sketches, 36
 "something new," 89

Song of Bernadette album (1943), 227
 source music, 69
 time pressures (1966), 200
 turned down Laura, 191
 with Fred Astaire (1955), 187
 Wuthering Heights, 70
Newman, David (composer), 292
 Alfred Newman's creative process, 27
 getting started, 252–53
 Other People's Money concept, 20
 scoring sessions, 51
Newman, Emil (orchestrator), 243
Newman, Lionel (comp./orch./m.d.), 37, 50,
 68, 215, 243, 253, 292
Newman, Randy, 73, 292
 Awakenings: review, 149
 spotting, 12
 creative process, 29
 emotional scores, 86
 getting started, 253
 hitting the action, 79
 melody, 72
Newman, Thomas (comp.), 32, 253, 259, 293
 demonstrating the score, 32
 "effectiveness" of score, 86
 dubbing, 61, 62
 Men Don't Leave, 4, 32–33
 The Player: 86, 88
 album, 229
Newsreels
 Fox Movietone, 171–72
 MARCH OF TIME, 172
 Pathé, 171
 scoring schedules, 172
Niehaus, Lennie (composer), 293
 Jerry Fielding, 26
Night at the Opera, 283
'night, Mother, 302
Nightcomers, The, CD, 229
Nine Hours to Rama, research, 21
Nitzsche, Jack (composer), 293
No Minor Chords (André Previn), 285
Nolan, Bob (songwriter), 131
Norman, Gene (record exec.), 231
Norman, Neil (record exec.), 231
Norris, Chuck (actor), 84
North by Northwest (1959), 12, 116–22
 Main Title music, 117
 role model, 6
 spotting, 117
North Star, The (1943), 215
 ethnic, 72
North, Alex (composer), 36, 37, 90, 243,
 258, 259, 293–94
 concept, 71
 Duke Ellington record, 294
 Hazen comments on, 200
 honorary Oscar, 208
 John Huston praises, 294
 in Body Heat review, 150
 orchestration, 35
 Raksin tells not arrogant enough, 197
 Spartacus, 20, 70
 studio system, 181
 "Unchained Melody" (Ghost), 229
 with Fox music staff, 178
 working with script, 3
 write best when, 293
Not Without My Daughter, review, 153

Now, Voyager, 99
Nun's Story, The (1959)
 soundtrack album, 229
 Waxman letter re: schedule, 193
Nyman, Michael (composer), 294

Objective, Burma!, tempo and pulse, 74
Obsession (1976)
 Bujold and Herrmann, 83
 psychological subtext, 82
Of Mice and Men (1992), 252
Oingo Boingo, 251
Oklahoma!, 214, 226
Old Gringo (1989), 20
 concept, 19
Old Maid, The, 99
Old Man and the Sea, The (1958), 199
 form, 75
Oliver & Company, 166
Omen, The, 130
On Golden Pond, 277
"On the Road Again," 223
On the Town, 43, 214
On the Track (Karlin and Wright), 283
On the Waterfront, 264
On-screen performances, 42
Once More, My Darling, 258
Once Upon a Time in America, 290
Once Upon a Time in the West, 290
One Hundred Men and a Girl, 214
One Night of Love (1934)
 first scoring Oscar, 207
One Touch of Venus, 258
Oranges Are Not the Only Fruit, 254
Orbach, Jerry (singer/actor), 217
Orchestra contractor, 29, 40, 49, 63
Orchestration, 25–26, 33, 50, 51, 75, 82
 The Adventures of Robin Hood, E.T., 97
 animation, 166
 as musical development, 76
 at MGM, 36
 Beethoven, 90
 The Birdman of Alcatraz, 37
 Bride of Frankenstein, 230
 Close Encounters excerpt, 134–35
 concept, 18
 contract orchestras, 75
 Copland on, 40
 Dark Victory Main Title, 102
 Devotion review, 149
 Dr. Jekyll and Mr. Hyde review, 153
 economy of means, 242
 effect of recording on, 35
 Extreme Prejudice review, 153
 for:
  Bill Conti, 37
  Randy Edelman, 37
  Jerry Goldsmith, 37
  James Horner, 37
  Dimitri Tiomkin, 35
  John Williams, 37
  Victor Young, 36
 Four Feathers, 230
 Frederick Hollander, 36
 Hugo Friedhofer, 273
 from sketches, 36, 40
 Gerhardt rerecordings, 230
 The Guns of Navarone, 230
 Hawaii, 37
 Bernard Herrmann, 34, 75

Orchestration (cont'd)
High Noon, 90
in fifties, 242
in reviews, 153
instrumental color, 75
King Kong (1933), 230
Lost Horizon, 35
The Magnificent Seven, 36–37
My Reputation review, 148
Alfred Newman and, 34
odd instrumental combinations, 35
The Outcasts of Poker Flat, 90
A Place in the Sun, 90
Previn about Korngold, 285
The Red Badge of Courage, 90
Miklós Rózsa, 34
schedules, 35
similarity, 40
sketches, 36
smaller ensembles, 35
Spellbound, 105, 110, 147
The Spirit of St. Louis, 111
staff orchestras, 34, 35
Star Trek—The Motion Picture (M.T.), 39
Max Steiner, 34
subtlety, 90
symphonic, 35
television, 35
The Untouchables, 142
Orchestrator, the, 25, 40, 49–50
MGM, 35
to save time, 40
work method, 194
Orchestrators
Buttolph, David, 214
De Packh, Maurice, 36
Eskew, Jack, 37
Friedhofer, Hugo, 93, 97, 99, 102 149, 273
Hayes, Jack, 122
Heindorf, Ray, 278
Kaun, Bernhard, 35
Kostal, Irwin, 285
McRitchie, Greig, 29, 37, 50, 54, 55
Milan Roder, Milan, 93
Morely, Angela, 289
Morton, Arthur, 177
Newman, Emil, 243
Newman, Lionel, 243
Niehaus, Lennie, 26
Powell, Edward, 214, 243
Shuken, Leo, 36, 122, 123, 188–89, 241, 242
Spencer, Herbert, 37, 129, 182, 184, 185, 243
Strauss, Richard, 285
Tunick, Jonathan, 306
Woodbury, Al, 217
Orff, Carl (composer), role model, 6
Original score, Oscar definition, 68
Original scores on Top 40 charts, 232–33
Originality, 89, 130
and temp tracks, 7
Copland's Red Pony score, 148
Rain Man, 8
Silence of the Lambs review, 152
Spellbound review, 147
Oscars. See also Academy Awards
Original Score Nominees/Winners, 312–19
Other Love, The, prerecording, 43

Other People's Money, 20, 253
Our New Music (Aaron Copland), 146
Out of Africa (1985), 60
concept, 18
Outcasts of Poker Flat, The, woodwind, 90
Outland, role model, 6
Overlapping cues, 53, 105

Pacing, 4
Pakula, Alan J. (director)
All the President's Men, 86
Paramount Pictures, 36, 48
dubbing, 58, 59
music department (1930), 181
music director (1943), 189
replaced scores, 64
scoring session (1936), 185
scoring sessions (1938), 185
soundtrack albums, 227
35mm mag stock first used, 241
Parenthood, 253
Parker, Alan (director), 62, 250, 253
Parker, Colonel (Elvis' manager), 225
Parker, Jr., Ray (singer), 228
Parties, Gershwin expected to play, 240
Pasetta, Marty (director), 219
Patton, 130
electronic effect, 61
Peck, Gregory (actor), 82
Spellbound, 104, 106
Peckinpah, Sam (director), 272
Penn, Arthur (director), 297
Peter and the Wolf, 15, 227
"Peter Gunn" TV series, 197, 242, 259, 287
Peter the Great, 28
Peterillo, James C. (musicians union), 171
Peyser, Michael (producer), 254
Photoplay, 169, 176, 221, 237, 238, 239
Phrasing the drama, 81–83
The Magnificent Seven, 128
Pink Floyd, 252
Pink Panther series, 287
comedy scoring, 167
originality, 89
Pinocchio, 136, 165
Pinocchio music box, 132, 136
Place in the Sun, A (1951)
saxophone, 90
score partially replaced, 64
Plagiarism, 27
Plane Crazy, 166
Planet of the Apes (1968), 259
tempo and pulse, 74
Planets, The, role model, 6
Platoon, 68
Playbacks, 55, 56
Player, The (1992)
album, 229
electronic texture, 88
Playing the drama, 78, 79
The Adventures of Robin Hood, 98
Close Encounters, 136–37
Dark Victory, 103
economy of means, 242
inappropriately (My Reputation), 148
The Miracle of Our Lady of Fatima, 80
operatic approach, 94
The Spirit of St. Louis, 116
The Ten Commandments, 203

The Untouchables, 143
upbeat endings in forties, 110
Playing the psychological subtext, 82, 83
Playing through the action, 81
Playing through the drama
The Untouchables, 143
Please Don't Hate Me (Tiomkin/Buranelli), 198, 306
Plow That Broke the Plains, The, 168
Plumb, Edward (composer), 294
Poledouris, Basil (comp.), 50, 70, 259, 294
Conan as role model, 6
recording, 42
RoboCop, 18, 150
scoring session playback, 55
Pollack, Lew (composer), 160
Pollack, Sidney (director), 18
Pollock, Dale (author), 244
Poltergeist, 13
communication, 14
Porter, Cole (songwriter), 68, 118, 171
Portman, Rachel (composer), 258, 294
creative process, 27
getting started, 253–54
Portman, Richard (dialogue mixer), 60
Poseidon Adventure, The, 130, 259
symphonic score, 78
Post, Mike (composer), 294
Postman Didn't Ring, The, 194
Potemkin, 161
Pouget, Léo (composer), 164
Powell, Dick (actor/singer), 170
Powell, Edward (orch.), 195, 214, 243
Power of One, The, 256
Power, Tyrone (actor), 72
Pre-existing music, 68
Predubbing effects, 60
Preisner, Zbigniew (composer), 295
Prerecording, 42, 44, 68
Louis Armstrong, 42
Claudio Arrau, 43
At Long Last Love, 68
Faking it, 42
José Iturbi, 42, 43
Bronsilau Kaper, 44
on-screen songs, 68
Artur Rubinstein, 43
Presley, Elvis (singer/actor)
selecting songs for films, 225
Pretty in Pink, 68
Pretty Woman, 251
communicating with director, 14
record album, 232
Previews, 62, 111
Previn, André (composer), 30, 36, 118, 217, 295
Copland, 123–24
first MGM contract, 182
Korngold, 285
orchestras, 52
orchestration, 35, 40
prerecording, 43
Raksin, 296
Rózsa's research, 21
studio system, 177
typecasting, 198
uncle Charles Previn, 188
Westerns and Copland, 124
working with filmmakers, 202

Previn, Charles (Univ. m.d.), 188, 214, 295
Previn, Dory (lyricist), 258
Pride of the Marines, orchestration, 34
Prince, 213
Prince of Tides, The, 79, 251
Privileged, 253
Prizzi's Honor, 294
Procrastination, 25
Producer, the, 29–30, 58
  decisions, 16
Producers, The, 290
Production track, 68
Prokofiev, Sergie (comp.), 50, 53, 227, 250, 295
  Alexander Nevsky, 87
  Classical Symphony, 50
Prometheus Records, 231
Psycho, 11
  psychological subtext, 83
  shower scene, 15
Psycho II, role models, 6
Pulitzer Prize, 267
Punches (as conducting aid), 46
Purple Rain, 213
Push-pull track, quality of sound, 240

Queen of Sheba, The (1921)
  wrong tune for chariot race, 156
Quick Change, 250
Quiet Man, The, concept, 71
Quo Vadis, 43, 197, 240
  dubbing, 57
  Rózsa's research, 21
  style, 70
  style of musical performance, 52

Raab, Leonid (orchestrator), 110
Radio, 20
Radio Flyer, dubbing, 62
Ragtime, 253
Rain Man, 255
  and temp tracks, 8
  harmony, 75
  role model, 6
"Raindrops Keep Fallin' on My Head," 225
Rains, Claude (actor), 44,
Raksin, David 37, 177, 243, 257, 258, 265, **295**
  asked to score *Laura*, 191
  The Bad and the Beautiful, 296
  changes, 63
  changes theme, 27
  collaborations, 194–95
  communicating with director, 14
  community of composers, 178
  creative process, 27, 28
  demos *The Bad and the Beautiful*, 30
  dubbing, 60
  ethnic, 72
  Forever Amber, 91
    album (1947), 227
  Hugo Friedhofer, 273
  good films, bad films, 91
  King Kong, 83
  Korngold and Steiner story, 197
  Laura, 224, 296
  MGM music department, **180**
  Alfred Newman, as music director, 187
    conducting, 185
  phrasing the drama, 82

psychological drama, 105
schedules, 192, 194
sketches, 36
studio system, 175
  wanted to be film composer, 295
  working with Chaplin, 296
Rapée, Erno (composer), 157, 160
Raposo, Joe (composer), 131
Rasch, Albertina (Mrs. Tiomkin), 306
Rasch, Raymond (composer), 213
Rathbone, Basil (*Robin Hood*), **93**
Ravel, Maurice (composer), 250
Raynes, Doug (reviewer), 150
Razor's Edge, The, self-plagiarism, 91
RCA Victor, Gerhardt's rerecordings, 229–30
Reap the Wild Wind (1942)
  rewrites for DeMille, 192
Reckless, 259
Recording. *See also* Scoring sessions
  live while filming (set recording), 176
  scoring sessions, 48
Recording crew, 49, 50
Recording engineer (mixer), 49
Recording sessions. *See also* Scoring sessions
  Bride of Frankenstein, **184**
  Champagne Waltz, **185**
  Cecil B. DeMille at, 192
  Gone With the Wind, **193**
  MGM in early thirties, 184
  Paramount (1938), 185
  The Ten Commandments, 192
Recordings on soundtrack, 68
Recordist, 49
Recordrama, 227
Red Badge of Courage, The, banjo, 90
Red herring, 110
  The Untouchables, 143
Red House, The (1947), 299
  psychological drama, 105
Red Pony, The, 13
  orchestration, 40
  review, 148
Red River, 123
Redford, J.A.C. (comp.), animation, 166
Redford, Robert (actor), 18, 84
Redman, Nick (record producer)
  market research, 230
Reich, Steve (composer), role model, 6
Reiner, Rob (director), 68, 254
  Misery, 33
Reitman, Ivan (director), 250
Reivers, The (1969)
  Spielberg describes score, 309
Repetition in score, 76
Representation for composers, 199
Rerecording mixers, 56, 59–**60**
Research, 4, 20
  Ben-Hur, 21
  Cuban folk music, 199
  El Cid, 21
  Ivanhoe, 21
  Quo Vadis, 21
Return of a Man Called Horse, 297
Return of the Jedi, role models, 6
Return to Oz, 259, 302
Reubens, Paul (aka "Pee Wee Herman"), 251
Reversal of Fortune, 252
Reviews 145–53
  film music journals, 146

  not musically educated, 146
  Spellbound, 148
Reynolds, Burt (actor), 68
Rhapsody, prerecording, 43
Rhapsody in Blue, 171
Rhythm, 82
  as musical development, 76
Rhythmic drive
  Close Encounters "tension motif," 137
  The Magnificent Seven, 124, 129
  The Untouchables, drum machine, 138, 144
Richards, John (music mixer), 56
Rickman, Alan (actor), 18
Riddle, Nelson (arranger), 254
Riesenfeld, Hugo (comp./music director)
  cut the film to fit music, 161
  selecting music, 160
  silent films, 155
Rimmer, David J. (reviewer), 152
Ringgold, Gene (reviewer), 215
Rio Bravo, 123
Rise and Fall of the Roman Empire, 223
Risky Business, role models, 6
Ritter, Tex (singer)
  with Tiomkin and Washington, 224
Rittman, Trude (composer)
  The Old Man and the Sea, 199
River Runs Through It, A, 252
River, The, 168
Roach, Bert (actor), 169
Roach, Hal (director), 169
Robbins, Ayn (lyricist), 258
Robbins, Richard (composer), 296
Robe, The, 240
  review, 150
Robin Hood: Prince of Thieves, 94, 252
  record album, 232
  record sales, 228
  time pressures, 25
Robinson, James G. (record exec.), 228
RoboCop (1987)
  concept, 18
  review, 150
"Rock-a-Bye Baby," 166
Rocky, 198, 259
  soundtrack album, 228
Rocky V, 37
Rodeo, 267
Roder, Milan (orchestrator)
  The Adventures of Robin Hood, 93
Rodgers and Hart (songwriters), 169
Rodgers, Richard (songwriter), 171
  "Isn't It Romantic?" 169
Roemheld, Heinz (composer), 297
  serials, 172
Rogers, Ginger (actress/dancer)
  gives Oscar to Rózsa, **208**
Role Models, 5, 13
  The Adventures of Robin Hood, 94
  Alexander Nevsky (Prokofiev), 295
  "Also sprach Zarathustra," 27
  Appalachian Spring, 13
  "Bach Concerto No. 1," 15
  Bride of Frankenstein (1935), 308
  Anton Bruckner, 164
  classical music, 15, 19
  Aaron Copland, 123
  Stan Dragoti uses, 15

Role Models (cont'd)
  examples, 6
  Gershwinesque, 17
  "Going Home," 191
  Korngold's action films, 130
  Peter and the Wolf, 15
  "The Planets," 130
  Sergei Prokofiev, 50, 53
  The Red Pony, 13
  Star Wars, 19
  Tchaikovsky, 50, 53
  used in temp tracks, 7
  "Yankee Doodle," 191
Romancing the Stone, 250
Romantic Symphony (Hanson), role model, 6
Romanticism, 130
Romeo and Juliet, 138, 298
  concept, 20
  soundtrack albums, 228
Ronell, Ann (composer), 258
Rose and the Sword, The
  playback, 55
Rose, David (composer), 217
  MGM music department, 180
Rose, Gene (orchestrator), 214
Rose, The, 223
Rosenman, Leonard (composer), 258, 297
  James Dean requests, 297
  Man Called Horse, A, review, 151
  Mozart and Beethoven, 297
Rosenthal, Laurence (composer), 297
  creative process, 28
  filmmaking collaborative, 297
  hired for Becket, 200
  Miracle Worker, The, 297
  Return of a Man Called Horse, 297
Ross, Diana (singer/actress), 218
Rossini, Gioacchino (composer)
  Barber of Seville, The, 193
Rota, Nino (composer), 258, 259, 298
  The Godfather, 34, 298
    score ineligible for Oscar, 211
    soundtrack CD, 231
  Romeo and Juliet, 20, 298
  soundtrack albums, 228
  theme, 138
Rough cut, 4
Rózsa, Miklós (composer), 19, 89, 90, 116,
    215, 250, 257, 258, 298–99
  and Louis Lipstone, 189
  Ben-Hur, 70
  changes, 63
  A Double Life, 203
  dubbing, 58, 61
  Four Feathers, 230
  freedom with studio contract, 183
  Herrmann own worst enemy, 279
  Hungarian music, 299
  Jungle Book album, 227, 229
  Knights of the Round Table, 242
  The Lost Weekend, 17–18
  Mervyn LeRoy's cigars, 197
  MGM, contract, 183
    contract terminated, 180
    staff assignments, 190
    studio system, 180
  music directors, 189, 190
  orchestras, 52
  orchestration, 34–35

Paramount contract (1943), 299
phrasing the drama, 81, 83
prerecording, 43
psychological subtext, 82
Quo Vadis, 70
research, 21, 299
Spellbound, 104–10, 146
  Main Title, 108
  Oscar, Rózsa receives, 208
  review, 147
  studio system, 180, 182
  style, 70
  theremin, 299
  time pressures, 200
  violin concerto, 183
Rubin, Mike (musician/orch. contractor)
  orchestra wages, 183
  overtime, 184
Rubinstein, Arthur B. (composer), 299
  role models, 6
Rubinstein, Artur (pianist), 43
Ruby, Harry (songwriter), 223
Rush jobs, 200. See also Time pressures
Russell, Larry (composer), 213
Russell, Rosiland (actress), 71
Ryan, Robert (actor), 250

Saadia, dubbing, 60
Sabu (actor), Jungle Book album, 227
Safan, Craig (composer), 19, 300
  Last Starfighter review, 153
Sahara, 215
"Sail Away," 253
Saint, Eva Marie (actress), 116, 117, 121,
    197
  North by Northwest, on train, 121
    on Mount Rushmore, 117
Saint-Saëns, Camile (composer), 160
Sakamoto, Ryuichi (composer), 300
Salinger, Conrad (Connie) (orch.), 214, 243
Salome, 6
  Sunset Boulevard role model, 7
Salter, Hans J. (composer), 178, 300
  communication with filmmakers, 201
  dubbing, 56, 59
  good films, bad films, 91
  horror films, 168–69
  musical independence, 87
  not writing for posterity, 195
  orchestration, 35
  producers didn't comment, 196
  spotting, 77
Salzburg Connection, The (1972)
  Kaper's score replaced, 244
Sam Fox Moving Picture Music, 157
Sampling, 31, 51
  Ferris Bueller's Day Off, 31
  Synclavier, 31
San Francisco, spotting/sound effects, 78
Sanborn, David (saxophonist), 19, 252
Sandpiper, The, 222
  playing through the action, 81
  restrained, 78
Saratoga Trunk, spotting, 77
Sarde, Philippe (composer), 300
  "emotions," 14
  "I'm a film composer," 197
Sarnoff, David (record exec.), 229
Sato, Masaru (composer), 300

Saturday Night Fever, 245, 259
  album sales, 232
  dance source, 69
  soundtrack album, 228
  use of songs, 222
"Saturday Night Live," 254
Saturday's Hero, 183
Schaindlin, Jack (composer)
  MARCH OF TIME, 172
Scharf, Walter (composer), 301
Schedules, 25, 28, 35
  newsreels, 172
  Selznick re: Fox, 193
  Waxman letter to Zinnemann, 192
Schifrin, Lalo (composer), 190, 243, 301
  jazz, 301
  orchestration, 34
Schlesinger, John (director), 51
Schoenberg, Arnold (composer), 26
  Boris Morros wanted at studio, 188
Schumann, Clara (pianist), 43
Schumann, Robert (composer)
  Träumerei for silent films, 156
Science fiction films, 130
Score
  definition, 68
  style, 70
Scorers
  timing movies in forties, 241
Scores:
  electronic, 259
  replaced, 244
  synthesized in seventies, 245
Scores replaced, 64
Scoring sessions, 43, 47–54
  Bride of Frankenstein, 184
  Champagne Waltz, 185
  changes, 55
  Citizen Kane, Herrmann and Welles, 5
  Gone With the Wind, 193
  Maurice Jarre scores Grand Prix, 196
  Legend, 49
  Lost Horizon (1937), 54
  MGM in early thirties, 184
  Paramount (1938), 185
  playbacks, 55–56
  The Rose and the Sword playbacks, 55
  Armin Steiner at Fox console, 50
  The Ten Commandments, 192
  with Cecil B. DeMille, 192
Scoring stage, 25, 43, 45–47, 50–51
Scoring stage podium, 47
Scoring stage recording console, 50
Scott Joplin, prerecording, 44
Scott, John (composer), 301
  research, 21
  temp tracks, 7
Scott, Ridley (director), 51
Scott, Tom (composer), 301
Scott, Tony (director), 226
Screenings, first, 4
Script, reading the, 3–4
Sea Hawk, The, 3, 93, 284
Seastrom, Victor (director), 165
Secret of Nimh, The, 166
Sedan, Ralph (actor), 169
"See You in September," 226
Segue, 45
Self-esteem, composer's, 197–98

Self-plagiarism, 90–91
Selznick, David O. (producer), 15, 58–59, 63, 90, 104, 240
    Mickey Mouse scoring, 79
    schedules, 193
Sequencers, 24
Serials, 172
    cliffhanger, 172
Set (live) recording, 176
Seven Brides for Seven Brothers (1954)
    role model, original song score, 210
Seven Samurai, The, 124
Seventh Heaven, 160
Shackles of Gold (1922), **162**
"Shadow of Your Smile, The," 78, 287
Shaft, 259
    soundtrack album, 228
Shaiman, Marc (composer), 68, 301
    The Addams Family, 33, 87
    dubbing, 57
    getting started, 254
    Misery, 33
    Sister Act credit, 69
"Shall We Gather at the River," 123
Shane, 123
"Shanghai Lil," 170
Shankar, Ravi (musician/composer), 71, 301
"She'll Be Coming 'Round the Mountain," 137
"She's More to Be Pitied Than Censured," 123
"She's Nobody's Sweetheart Now," 223
Shefter, Bert A. (composer), 301
Shepherd, Cybill (actress), 68
Shilkret, Nathaniel (comp./m.d.), 301
    RKO music director, 181
    musicals, 169
Shire, David (composer) 259, 301
    All the President's Men, 86
    The Fortune, 81
    script, 4
    The Taking of Pelham 1-2-3, 302
Shoot the Piano Player, 268
Shootist, The, 130
Shore, Howard (composer), 302
    review of *Silence of the Lambs,* 152
Short Circuit, 302
Short cues, 53
"Short People," 253
Shostakovich, Dmitri (composer), 72, 250
    silent film accompanist, 156
Shuken, Leo (orchestrator), 122, 123
    felt like quitting, 188–89
    orchestration in fifties, 242
    supervisors in forties, 241
    Victor Young, 36
Sibelius, Jean (composer), orch., 90
Sidney, George (director)
    MGM studio system, 180
Silence, use of, 11, 77
    for emphasis, *Spellbound* (Cue 2), 106
    The Silence of the Lambs review, 152
Silent films, 154–65
    Alix, Victor, 164
    American Photo Player Company, 155
    Ben-Hur, 163, 164
    The Big Parade, 163–64
        laser disc, 165
    The Birth of a Nation, classical mus., 160
    Borzage, Frank, 163
    Breil, Joseph Carl, 160, 165

Carl Fischer Music Company, 157
Carmen, 165
City Lights, 163
Coliseum Theater orchestra, 155
compiled scores, 160
Compson, Betty, 163
contemporary live performances, 163
Crawford, Jesse and Helen, 155
The Crowd (King Vidor), 165
cue sheets, 156
    Don Juan, 158
    It's the Old Army Game, 159
    score, 165
The Curious Adventure of Mr. West in Bolshevik Land, 163
cutting the film to fit music, 161
Griffith, D. W., 154
Edison, 156
The Fall of a Nation, 160–61
film schedules, 157
A Fool's Revenge, 156
Fotoplayer, 155
Greed, 163
Herbert, Victor, 160
hit songs, 160
Intolerance, 160, 163, 165
L'Assassinat du Duc de Guise, 160
leitmotifs, 164
Lucky Star, 163
Mechanical instruments, 155
Meisel, Edmund, 161
metronome and timing markings, 161
Moore, Colleen, 163
Motion Picture Moods for Pianists . . ., 157
music on the set, 162–**63**, **164**
music played, 156
musicians, 156
musicians' schedules, 156
Napoleon, 162–63, 164
neighborhood performances, 162
nickelodeons, 155
Nosferatu, 163
on-screen pianist, **162**
orchestras, 154
organ, 156
original scores, 160
Palace Theater orchestra, 155
Parsifal, 165
The Passion of Joan of Arc, 163–64
pianists, 156
piano, 154
piano accompaniment, 155
piano quality, 155
Potemkin review, 161
The Queen of Sheba, 156
Rapée, Erno, 157
Rialto and Rivoli Theater orch's, 155
Hugo Riesenfeld selecting music, 160
Sam Fox Moving Picture Music, 157
school for theater organists, 155
Shackles of Gold, (1922), **162**
Simon, Walter Cleveland, 160
size of orchestras, 155
sound effects, 164
sound effects machine, 155
Sunrise, 163
synchronization, 161, 165
The Ten Commandments, **163**
theater organs, 155

The Thief of Bagdad, 161, 163, 165
    using classical standards, 157
    variable speed projectors, 161–62
The Wind, 165
Vitagraphy film company, 156
Way Down East, 165
Wings, 165
Winkler, Max, cue sheets, 156–57
Woman to Woman, 163
Yankee Clipper, 165
Zamecnik, J. S., 157
"Silent Night," musical development, 76
Silva Screen Records, 231
Silver, Joel (producer), 19
Silverado, 70
Silvers, Louis (comp./Fox m.d.), 302
    collaborations, 194
    ethnic, 72
Silvestri, Alan (composer), 250, 302
    animation pacing, 166
    role model, 6
Simon and Garfunkel (songwriters/singers), 259
    The Graduate, 87
        soundtrack album, 228
Simon, Carly (songwriter), 258
Simpson, Don (producer), 225
Sinatra, Frank (singer), 254
Sincerity, 87
    mentioned in reviews, 153
Singin' in the Rain, 176
    whistled in *North by Northwest,* 122
Sister Act, 69
Sisters, spotting, 12
Sixteen Candles, 68
Sketches, 29, 36, 38
    Bill Conti, 37
    Randy Edelman, 37
    Alfred Newman, 36
    Hugo Friedhofer, 36
    Jerry Goldsmith, 37
    Frederick Hollander, 36
    James Horner, 37
    David Raksin, 36
    The Spirit of St. Louis Main Title, 115
    Roy Webb, 36
    John Williams, 37
Skinner, Frank (composer), 302
Skolsky, Sidney (journalist), 48
Slaughter, fee for master recording, 231
Sleeping With the Enemy review, 152
Sleepless in Seattle, 255
Slug (film), 24
Small, Michael (composer), 302
    Going in Style, 81
Small-budget films, 255
Smattering of Ignorance, A (Levant), 285
Smith, C. Aubrey (actor), 239
Smith, Charles Martin (actor), 137, **138**, 139
    The Untouchables, **138**
Smith, Patricia (actress), 110
Smith, Paul J. (composer), 302
Smith, Roger (producer), 219
Smith, Steven C. (author), 74, 279
    Herrmann's self-plagiarism, 91
"Smoke Gets in Your Eyes," 226
SMPTE, 22, 24, 45
Snell, David (composer), 303

Snow White and the Seven Dwarfs (1937)
  first album from a movie, 227
  use of songs, 166
Snow, Mark (composer), 303
Snow, Tom (composer), 303
Soapdish, 253
Society of Motion Picture and Television
  Engineers, 22
Sodom and Gomorrah, 180
Solomon's Children, Vitaphone, 238
Some Girls, 253
Sondheim, Stephen (composer), 303
Song of Bernadette, The, 215, 240
Song of Love, prerecording, 43
Song of Russia, 215
Song to Remember, A, prerecording, 43
Song-scoring, 259
Songs, 221–26
  artistic criteria for Oscar, 222
  "As Time Goes By," (*Casablanca*), 69, 223
  Berlin, Irving, 170
  Beverly Hills Cop, 225
    CDs, 229
  buying hit tune title, 223
  "By a Waterfall," 170
  Do the Right Thing CD, 229
  early sound days, 221
  Earth Girls, 226
  "(Everything I Do) I Do It for You," 252
  "For He's a Jolly Good Fellow," 226
  for Presley films, 225
  for *The Alamo*, 201
  for *Top Gun*, 225
  "Freddy's Dead," 212
  "Gentle Annie," 123
  "Get a Job," 226
  Ghostbusters II, 226
    CD, 229
  "Going Home," DeMille's favorite, 191
  "Great Pretender, The," 226
  "Green Leaves of Summer, The," 202
  "Happy Birthday," licensing, 226
  "Harbor Lights," 123
  "Here Comes the King" (Budweiser), 132
  "High Noon," 224
  Home Alone CD, 229
  "I Love L.A.," 253
  "I Love To See You Smile," 253
  "I Married a Monster from Outer Space,"
    224–25
  "I Only Have Eyes for You," 226
  "I'll Get By," 223
  "In a Monastery Garden," Hitchcock's
    favorite, 202
  in early sound films, 175
  interpolated, 225
  "Isn't It Romantic?" 169–70, 239
  "It Had To Be You," 68
  "Jeannie with the Light Brown Hair," 123
  "Joy to the World," mus. development, 76
  Kol Nidre, 238
  "La Marseillaise," 112
  "Lara's Theme," 9
  licensing, 226
    "Happy Birthday," 226
    master recordings, 226, 254
  "London Bridge Is Falling Down," 221
  Love in a Goldfish Bowl, title songs, 224
  "Love Song of the Waterfall," 131

"Ma, He's Makin' Eyes at Me," 223
"Margie," 223
Mermaids budget, 226
"Mood Indigo," 139, 144
"Moon River," 286
  how written, 222
"Mrs. Robinson," 222
on-screen songs, 68
  prerecording, 68
"On the Road Again," 223
"Raindrops Keep Fallin' on My Head," 225
"Rock-a-Bye Baby," 166
Rodgers and Hart, 169–70
"Sail Away," 253
Saturday Night Fever, 259
"See You in September," 226
"Shanghai Lil," 170
"Shadow of Your Smile, The," 78, 287
"Shall We Gather at the River," 123
"She'll Be Coming 'Round the Mountain,"
  137
"She's More to Be Pitied Than Censured," 123
"She's Nobody's Sweetheart Now," 223
"Short People," 253
"Silent Night," musical development, 76
"Smoke Gets in Your Eyes," 226
"Sooner or Later," on Oscar show, 218
"Sorry Seems To Be the Hardest Word," 251
"Sounds of Silence, The," 222
"Square Song, The," 131
"Suicide Is Painless," 287
"Too Marvelous for Words," 69
"Toot, Toot, Tootsie," 175
Twins, 226, 250
"Twist and Shout," 68
Two for the Road, 222
"Unchained Melody" (*Ghost*), 229
use of "Isn't It Romantic?" 169
used gratuitously in films, 222
using existing song, 223
"Vesti la Giubba," 140, 144
"When You Wish Upon a Star," 132, 136
"Where'd You Get That Girl," 223
"Who's Afraid of the Big Bad Wolf?" 166
"Windmills of Your Mind, The," 223
"Yankee Doodle," 166
  DeMille favorite, 191
  Victor Young played as child, 310
Victor Young, 311
Songwriters, 171
  Ahlert, Fred E., 177
  Arlen, Harold, 171
  Bacharach, Burt, 223, 225
  Berlin, Irving, 170–71
  Brown, Herb, 177, 238
  Comden, Betty, 258
  Conrad, Con, 208
  De Sylva, Buddy, 238
  Freed, Arthur, 177
  Gershwin, George, 171
  Henderson, Ray, 238
  Hollywood (1929), 169
  Hollywood (1970s), 259
  Kalmar and Ruby, 223
  Kasha, Al, 207
  Kern, Jerome, 171
  King, Carole, 258
  Porter, Cole, 171
  Prince, 213

Rodgers, Richard, 171
Rodgers and Hart, 169–70
Simon, Carly, 258
Tierney, Harry, 112
Turk, Roy, 177
Van Heusen, Jimmy, 215
Warren, Harry, 171
Wonder, Stevie, 310
Sound
  early days, 47–48, 175
    contract composers, 239
    first 35mm mag stock, 241
    first all-talking feature, 238
    musicians, 238
    talking pictures imminent, 238
    Warner Bros., 237
    "If I were an actor . . ." 237
  first stereo film release, 242
Sound effects, 4, 47, 56–62, 116
  The Adventures of Robin Hood, 94
  and editorial changes, 5
  as story point, 78
  indicated in spotting notes, 10
  The Untouchables, 143
Sound effects editors, 5
Sound effects mixers, 60
Sound units in machine room, 57
Sounds and Scores (Henry Mancini), 287
"Sounds of Silence, The," 222
Soundtrack albums (titles), 227–33
  Around the World in 80 Days, 232
  Beauty and the Beast, 232
  Beverly Hills Cop I and *II*, 229
  The Big Country, rerecorded, 229
  Chariots of Fire (1981), 228, 232
  The Commitments, 232
  Do the Right Thing, 229
  Doctor Zhivago, 232
  Easy Rider (1969), 228
  The Egyptian, 229
  Exodus, 232
  Four Feathers, 230
  Ghost ("Unchained Melody"), 229
  Ghostbusters, 228
  Ghostbusters II, 229
  The Graduate (1967), 228
  Guns of Navarone, 230
  House Party II, 232
  King Kong, 230
  Lawrence of Arabia, rerecorded, 229
  New Jack City, 229
  Pretty Woman, 232
  Robin Hood: Prince of Thieves, 232
  Rocky (1976), 228
  Romeo and Juliet, 228
  Saturday Night Fever (1977), 228, 232
  Shaft (1971), 228
  Star Wars, 228
    disco version, 229
    sales, 244
  The Time Machine (1960), 229
Soundtrack albums (other)
  disco, 228
  early, 227–28
  Gerhardt series of classics, 230
  new-use payments, 230
  Paramount Pictures, 227
  re-recordings of classic scores, 229
  record advances, 232

Soundtrack albums (cont'd)
  record labels, 230–33
    Creazioni Artistiche Musicali (C.A.M.), 231
    GNP Crescendo Records, 231
    Intrada Records, 231
    Prometheus Records, 231
    Silva Screen, 231
    Varèse Sarabande, 231
  sales figures, 232
  scoring films to sell records, 242
  song-oriented, 228–29
  Bruce Springsteen sales, 232
  Bill Stinson takes to new level, 227
Soundtrack!, 146, 150, 151, 152, 153, 231
Source music, 67, 68. See also Spotting notes,
    Chapter 6
  The Adventures of Robin Hood, 99
  All About Eve, 69
  "As Time Goes By" (Casablanca), 69
  Close Encounters of the Third Kind, 137
    Budweiser jingle, 132, 137
    soap opera, 132
    whistling, 137
  dance-oriented, 69
  Dark Passage, 69
  documentaries, 99
  I Pagliacci, 140, 144
  The Magnificent Seven, 128
  North by Northwest, 122
  on-screen, 68, 99, 104, 114
  period flavor, 69
  phonograph, 69
  radio, 20
  Spellbound, 110
  The Spirit of St. Louis, 116
  synchronization, 99
  The Untouchables, 144
  used in score, 69
  "Vesti la Giubba," 144
Sousa, John Phillip (composer), 114
  and ASCAP, 308
Southern blues, 6
Spaeth, Sigmund (music historian)
  documentaries, 167
Spaghetti Westerns, 259
Spartacus (1960)
  North describes score, 294
  style, 70
"Spectacular World of Classic Film Scores,
  The," 230
Spellbound, 104–10, 146, 258
  conductor's score (Main Title), 108
  music review, 147
  orchestration, 34
  psychological subject, 82
  spotting, 86
Spencer, Herbert (orchestrator), 37, 129, 182,
    214, 243
  Close Encounters orch., 134, 135
  MGM contract, 182
  MGM scoring sessions, 185
  recording, 184
  studio contracts, 181
Spielberg, Steven (director), 129
  and John Williams, 13
  Poltergeist, with Jerry Goldsmith, 14
  spotting Jaws, 11
Spirit of St. Louis, The, 25, 110–16
Splash, communicating with director, 14

Spotting, 9–12, 77
  The Adventures of Robin Hood, 94–96
  All the President's Men, 86
  Close Encounters, 130–33
  Dark Victory, 100–101
  Cecil B. DeMille spotting, 191
  I Confess, too much music, 12
  in reviews, 153
  James Bond films, 86
  The Magnificent Seven, 124–27
  North by Northwest, 117–20
  overuse of music, 77
  Sergio Leone Westerns, 86
  short cues, 138
  silence, 77
  Spellbound, 86, 105–7
  The Spirit of St. Louis, 111–14
  Star Trek series, 86
  The Untouchables, 138–41
  use of silence, 12
Spotting notes, 9
Spotting session, 9
Sprocket-driven, 57
"Square Song, The," 131
Staff contracts, salaries, 182
Staff film assignments, 190–91
Staff orchestras, 34, 35
  A. F. of M. contract, 183
  musicians strike eliminates, 183, 242
  quality, 184
  salaries, 184
  sizes, 183
Stage manager, 49
Stagecoach, folk music, 123
Stalling, Carl (composer), 46, 132
  cartoon scoring CD, 167
Stand and Deliver, concept, 19
Stanwyck, Barbara (actress), 43, 148
Star Trek—The Motion Picture (sketch),
    38
Star Trek—The Motion Picture (orch.), 39
"Star Trek: The Next Generation" (th.), 39
Star Trek series, recordings, 229
  spotting, 86
Star Trek II, 13, 60, 259
  long cues, 53
Star Trek III, 13
  long cues, 53
"Star Trek" television series, 20
  Spock's theme, 20
Star Wars, 6, 19, 130, 245, 259
  dubbing, 57
  in Aliens review, 152
  symphonic scores, 78, 94
  tempo and pulse, 74
  tone, 99
Star Wars series
  recordings, 229
  spotting, 86
Star!, 215
Status of composers, 197
Staying Alive, 222
Stein, Herman (composer), 303
  collaborations with Mancini, 195
Stein, Ronald (composer), 303
Steiner, Armin (music mixer), 50, 56, 61
  "melodies," 88
Steiner, Fred (composer)
  A. Newman's scoring sessions, 185

Steiner, Max (composer), 28, 89, 103, 116,
    215, 249, 257–58, 303–304
  "As Time Goes By" (Casablanca), 69, 223
  changes, 52
  Charge of the Light Brigade, 6
  click track, 46
  conducted Lost Horizon, 54
  Dark Victory, 99–104
  Bette Davis films, 304
  first push-pull track, 240
  Errol Flynn films, 304
  Friedhofer orchestrates for, 273
  Gone With the Wind, scoring session, 193
    benzedrine to complete, 192
    no album when released, 229
  good films, bad films, 91
  hitting the action, 79
  Johnny Belinda review, 151
  King Kong, 230, 239
  leitmotifs, 73
  Korngold and, 197
  long scores, 12
  My Reputation review, 148
  Now, Voyager, 84
  obituary (self-plagiarism), 90
  operetta composed at 14, 304
  orchestration, 34
  playing the drama, 80
  procrastination, 25
  psychological scoring, 83
  RKO music director 177, 181
  schedules, 192
  self-plagiarism (obituary), 90
  signed with Warners, 181
  source music, 69
  spotting, 9, 11, 77
  "symphony music," 81
  "tired old bromide," 303
  vision problems, 304
  Jack Warner,and, 304
  where music coming from? 239
Steiner, Max, Society, 100
Stereo sound, first release on film, 242
Stern, Isaac, (violinist), 45
Sternfeld, Frederick W. (author), 168
Steven Spielberg Story, The, 13
Stevens, George (director), 64
Stevens, Leith (composer), 304
Stevens, Mort (composer), 243
Stewart, James (actor), 58, 110
  The Spirit of St. Louis, 111, 112
Stillman, Al, (lyricist), 132
Sting, The, adaptation, 69
  playing thorugh the action, 81
Stinson, Bill (music editor/exec.), 56, 179
  Godfather ineligible for Oscar, 211
  "I Married a Monster . . ." 224–25
  musicians strike (1958), 242
  A. Newman and Fox orchestra, 185
  "scorers" in forties 241
  songs for Elvis Presley films, 225
  soundtrack albums, 227
  title songs, 224
  Victor Young, 193, 311
    orchestrators, 36
  Waxman, 308
Stoll, Georgie,
Stoloff, Morris (Columbia music dir.), 207
  Columbia music director (1950), 186

Stoloff, Morris (cont'd)
  Hugo Friedhofer with, (1947), **186**
  MGM staff meeting, **180**
  music directors, 241
  Tiomkin with, **182**
Stone, Oliver (director)
  Adagio for Strings (*Platoon*), 68
Stopwatches used, 22, 24
Stormy Weather, 223
Story of G.I. Joe, The, 258
Stothart, Herbert (composer), 215, 304
  Kaper describes, 190
  Madame Curie cited as role model, 189
  MGM control booth, listens, 179
Strauss, Johann (composer), 101
Strauss, Richard (composer), 27, 36
  Korngold's orchestration, 285
  role model, 6, 94
  Sunset Boulevard role model, 7
Stravinsky, Igor (composer), 13, 250
  name is expensive, 197
  Boris Morros wants for score, 188
Straw Dogs (1971)
  procrastination, 26
  soundtrack CD, 229
Streamers, 46
Streep, Meryl (actress), 18
Streetcar Named Desire, A, 36, 181, 259
  concept, 71
  orchestration, 35
Strings
  clichés, 90
  disapproved in 1972, 244
  Spellbound review, 147
Studio contracts, 181–83
  musicians' salaries, 184
Studio musicians, 52
Studio system, 175–95
  budgets in forties, 185
  class distinctions, 180–81
  community of composers, 178
  contracts, 181–82
  Disney music department, 179
  Fox music department, 178
    staff orchestras, 184
  getting jobs, 240
  loan-outs, 182
  Mayer, Louis B., 179
  MGM music department, 180
  music departments, 186–90
  musicians' contracts, 184
  Paramount, 178–79
    music department, 179
  Miklós Rózsa, 180
  scorers, 241
  Selznick re: schedules, 193
Sturges, John (director), 122, 152
Style, 70–71
  analysis of, 70
Style and concept
  The Adventures of Robin Hood, 94
  Close Encounters of the Third Kind, 130
  Dark Victory, 100
  The Magnificent Seven, 124
  North by Northwest, 117
  Spellbound, 105
  The Spirit of St. Louis, 111
  The Untouchables, 138
Suez, ethnic role models, 72

Sugarland Express, The, 13, 309
"Suicide Is Painless," 287
Sukman, Harry (music director), 214
Summer of '42, 259
Sunflower, 222
Sunny Side Up, 238
Sunset Boulevard (1950)
  psychological subtext, 83
  role models, 6
  subtlety, 90
Superfly, 212
Superman, 172
Swanson, Gloria (actress), 6, 7
Swarthout, Glady (singer)
  with Paramount orchestra, **185**
Swayze, Patrick (actor), 71
Sweep-second clock, 46, **47**
Sweet, Blanche (actress)
  music on the set, 162
Swing Shift, concept, 20
Symphonic orchestral scoring, 130, 259
  jeopardy films, 78
Sync pulse, 45, 47
  audio, 22
Synchronization, 22, 24, 45, 47–48
  clicks, 45, 46
  the Newman System, 46
  punches, 46
  streamers, 46
Synclavier, 31
Synthesized scoring
  in seventies, 245
  Never Cry Wolf, 252
Synthesizers, 29, **53**
  in *The Untouchables*, 138
  Tangerine Dream, 305

Takemitsu, Toru (composer), 305
Talbot, Irvin (conductor), 48
Talkington, Paul (orch. contractor), **55**
Tamkin, David (orchestrator), 195
Tandy, Jessica (actress), 74
Tangerine Dream (elect. group), 305
  role models, 6
Tansman, Alexander (composer), 215, 257
  music simpler, 241
"Tara's Theme," 90
Taylor, Elizabeth (actress), 43, 64, 78
Taylor, Robert (actor), 197
Tchaikovsky, Peter Ilyitch, 50, 53
  in documentaries, 168
Television series
  freelancing, 196
  "Peter Gunn," 196
  scores, generic, 8
Temp tracks, 5, 7–9, 14, 62
  and spotting, 11
  as communication, 9
  Doctor Zhivago, 9
  The Lost Weekend, 17–18
  no role model, 89
Tempo and pulse
  The Adventures of Robin Hood, 99
  Batman, 74
  Close Encounters, 74, 137
  Dark Victory, 104
  The Magnificent Seven, 74, 129
  Objective, Burma!, 74
  That's my Wife, 74

  edited film, 74
  North by Northwest, soft music in, 122
  Planet of the Apes, 74
  Spellbound, 110
  The Spirit of St. Louis, 116
  Star Wars, 74
  The Ten Commandments, 203
  The Untouchables, 144
Ten Commandments, The (1923)
  music on the set, 162
Ten Commandments, The (1956), 264
  Bernstein and DeMille, 202
Tender Is the Night, changes, 63
Terminator II (1991)
  dubbing, 58
  sound effects, 58
Testament, 280
That Man from Tangier, 258
That's Life!, on-screen source, 68
That's My Wife, tempo and pulse, 74
Thaxton, Ford A. (record producer)
  The Addams Family, 87
  temp tracks, 7
Third Man, The, 19
Thelma and Louise, 256
Thematic unity, Herrmann, 116
"Theme from Days of Our Lives," 132
Themes, 8, 14, 26, 73, 77, 92, 93, 116
  The Adventures of Robin Hood, 97–98
  Born on the Fourth of July review, 152
  Close Encounters of the Third Kind, 133, 136
    "communication motif," 133
  Dark Victory, 103
  Edward Scissorhands review, 150, 152
  from instrumental colors, 34
  in reviews, 152
  Joan of Arc review, 152
  The Magnificent Seven, 127
  North by Northwest, 121
  repetition of, 152
  Sleeping With the Enemy review, 152
  Spellbound, 104, 107
  The Spirit of St. Louis, 114
  Max Steiner, 103
  The Untouchables, 141–43
  Franz Waxman, 114
  written before filming, 4
Theodorakis, Mikis (composer), 305
Theremin, 18, 34, 104, 105, 107
These Three, 91
They Died with Their Boots On, 123
They Made Me a Criminal (1939)
  Steiner self-plagiarism, 90
Thief of Bagdad, The (1924), 161
Thief of Bagdad, The (1940), 299
  orchestra, 52
Thomas Crown Affair, The, 223
Thomas, Tony (author), 145, 151, 168, 309
Thomson, Virgil (composer), 168, 305
  documentaries, 168
Thorne, Ken (composer), 305
Thousands Cheer (1943)
  Stothart listens in booth, 179
Three Coins in the Fountain (1954)
  Academy and Tiomkin, 216
Three Little Words, 223
3-D, 241
Through Different Eyes, 194
Tierney, Harry (songwriter), 112

Till the Clouds Roll By, 227
Time code, 22
Time Machine, The, CD, 229
Time pressures, 25, 28
    freelancing, 200
Time schedules, 192. *See also* Schedules
Timing notes, 22–23
Timing sheets, 26
Timings, 22–25
    "scorers" in forties, 241
Tiomkin, Dimitri (composer), 12, 35, 90,
    153, 257–58, **305**
    Sammy Cahn and Academy, 216
    Frank Capra and, 201
    changes, 62
    click track use, 46
    composing in thirties, 238
    conducting, 53, **54**
    contract composers, early, 239
    don't overuse title songs, 223
    dubbing, 59
    Duel in the Sun, 15
        album (1946), 227
    The Fall of the Roman Empire review, 151
    film music in sixties, 243
    form, 75
    The Guns of Navarone, 230
    The High and the Mighty theme, 212
    High Noon, 90
        "High Noon," 224
    Hitchcock re: *Torn Curtain*, 199
    movie business in sixties, 244
    music for the masses, 305
    need for new talent (1964), 243
    "noisiness and loudness," 242
    no staff contract, 182
    Old Man and the Sea, 200
    Russian accent, 306
    self-appraising, 198
    song for *The Alamo*, 202
    spotting, 11
    Morris Stoloff and, **182**
    time pressures, 200
    Ned Washington, Tex Ritter, and, **224**
    Westerns, 123
    working with filmmakers, 201
Title songs, 223
To Kill a Mockingbird, 246, 264
    orchestration, 37
    originality, 89
Toch, Ernest (composer), 257
Todd-AO Glen Glenn dubbing stage, **60**
Tom Jones, spotting and sound effects, 78
Tonal clusters, 130
Tone of film unclear, 18
"Too Marvelous for Words," 69
"Toot, Toot, Tootsie," 175
Tootsie, 277
Total Recall, role models, 6
Towering Inferno, The, 130, 259
    symphonic scores, 78
Townson, Robert (record exec.), 231
    preservation, 230
    scores taken seriously, 229
Tracy, Robert (music editor)
    Academy voting (1949), 215
Trading Places, 6
Treloggen, Abby (music editor), **45**
Tribute to a Bad Man, 123

Truffaut, Francois (dir.), 129, 259, 268
Tucker, Guy (reviewer), 152
Tunick, Jonathan (composer/orch.), 306
Turk, Roy (songwriter), 177
Turner, Ray (pianist) 191
Twentieth Century-Fox
    Armin Steiner, 50
    At Long Last Love, 68
    collaborations (1939), 194
    music department, **178**
        staff (1959), 243
    Alfred Newman, 185
    David Raksin, 72
    staff orchestra, 184
Twins (1988), 250
    songs, 226
"Twist and Shout," 68
Two for the Road, song, 222
Typecasting, 198–99

Un-American Activities Committee, 272
Under Fire, concept, 19
Underscore (Frank Skinner), 302
Underscoring, definition, 68
Union Forever, The, 123
Universal Pictures, 35
    collaborations (fifties), 195
    contracts, 182
    credits (fifties), 195
    dubbing, 60, 61
    Joseph Gershenson, 188
    horror films, 168–69
    Legend, 49
    newsreels, 171
    John Williams' writing studio, 29
    Stanley Wilson, 190, 243
University of Southern California, 252, 299
Untouchables, The, 137–44
Up the Down Staircase, orchestration, 34
Urei digital metronome, 45. *See also* Digital
    metronome
Used People, 27, 254, 258

Van de Ven, Luc (record exec./pub.), 231
Van Gogh, Vincent (artist), 70
Vangelis (composer), 259, 306
    Chariots of Fire album, 232
Varèse Sarabande Records, 112, 231
Variety, 181
Vaughan Williams, Ralph (composer), 306
Vaughan, Clifford (comp.), serials, 172
Vaughn, Robert (actor), 122, 125
Veidt, Conrad (actor), 43
Verhoeven, Paul (director), **55**
    RoboCop concept, 18
Verity, Frank (journalist)
    music director credits, 214
Vertigo (1958)
    Hitchcock's notes, 15
    spotting, 11
"Vesti la Giubba," 140, 144
Victory, 198
Videotape, used for composing, 22, 24
Vidor, King (director), 165
Virginia City, 123
"Virginian, The," TV series, 243
Visual effects, 4
Vitagraph film company, 156
Vitaphone
    Al Jolson, 238

Lights of New York, 238
Solomon's Children, 238
Vitaphone disc process, *Don Juan*, 237
Viva Zapata!, 36
Vocal dubbing (*see also* prerecording), 42

Wagner, Richard (composer), 70, 250
    film composer (Steiner), 258
"Wagon Train" TV series, 243
Wait Until Dark, 287
Waldman, Randy (composer), 52
Walker, Shirley (composer), 258, 306
    getting started, 255
    phrasing the drama, 82
    playing the drama, 78
    subtle scoring, 86
"Wall, The," Pink Floyd album, 252
Walla (as sound effect), 143
Wallace, Bennie (composer), 306
Wallace, Oliver (composer), 46, 306
    Disney documentaries, 168
Wallach, Eli (actor), 122, 124
    The Magnificent Seven, **127**
Wallin, Danny (music mixer), 56, **60**
Wallis, Hal (producer), 58, 200
    The Adventures of Robin Hood, 190
    "As Time Goes By," (Casablanca), 223
    early sound, 237
    songs for Elvis Presley films, 225
Walton, Sir William (composer), 307
War films
    canned music, 240
War of the Roses, The (1989), 253
    music budget, 226
Ward, Edward (composer), 307
Warner Bros., 12, 28, 44, 52
    The Adventures of Robin Hood, 93, 191
    composers contracted, 181
    contract orchestras, 75
    converts to sound, 238
    dubbing, 58, 59
        The Adventures of Robin Hood, 94
    early sound days, 175
    Jazz Singer review, 238
    Korngold's contract, 182
    My Reputation review, 148
    string section, 97
    threatens to sue Academy, 214
    Warner, Harry, early sound days, 175
Warner, Jack (studio mogul), 59
    spotting, 12
    Max Steiner and, 304
Warren, Harry (songwriter), 171
"Warsaw Concerto," 261
Washington, Ned (lyricist), 132
    "High Noon," 224
    Tiomkin, Tex Ritter, and, **224**
Waxman, Franz (composer), 6, 27, 89, 90,
    116, **178**, 215, 217, 229, 243, 250,
    257, 258, **307–8**
    Bride of Frankenstein, 230, 308
        Boris Karloff with Waxman, **169**
        scoring session, **184**
    changes, 64
    Dr. Jekyll and Mr. Hyde review, 153
    evaluating a score, 91
    Hazen comments for *Becket*, 200
    leitmotifs, 73
    letter to Zinnemann re: schedule, 192

Waxman, Franz *(cont'd)*
  Los Angeles Music Festival, 308
  meets Frederick Hollander, 308
  on film music, 307
  orchestration, 34
  A Place in the Sun, 90
  Rebecca (big break), 308
  requests for recordings, 227
  serials, music used in, 172
  source music, 69
  The Spirit of St. Louis, 110–16
    sketch, 115
    themes, 114
  "strong themes," 26
  Sunset Boulevard, 90
    role model, 7
  3 films at once, 25
  Zinnemann, letter to, re: schedule, 193
Waxman, John (film mus. preservation), 64
  father scored three films at once, 25
Way We Were, The, 37, 60, 223, 259
Wayne's World CD, 229
Wayne, John (actor/director)
  The Alamo, 201
  song for *The Alamo*, 202
Webb, Roy (composer), 111, 112, 113, 116,
  215, 257–58, 308
  changes, 52
  sketches, 36
  "you can hurt a film," 308
Webster, George (composer), 101
Webster, Paul Francis (lyricist), 78, 201
  "The Shadow of Your Smile," 222
Weill, Kurt (composer), 258
Weinberg, Herman G. (critic), 161
Weinstein, Henry (producer), 63
Weir, Peter (director), 4
Weiss, Stephen (songwriter), 100
Welles, Orson (director/actor), 202
  changes, 52
  scoring *Citizen Kane*, 5
Werden, Bob (Academy representative),
  212
Werewolf of London, 172
Western Electric Company, 237
Westerner, The, 123
Westerns, 8, 13, 25, 78, 123–24
  John Ford and folk music, 123
  Bernard Herrman, 123
  Alfred Newman, 123
  Miklós Rózsa, 123
  Silverado, 70
  spaghetti Westerns, 259
  Stagecoach (1939), 123
  Max Steiner, 123
  Dimitri Tiomkin, 123
  Franz Waxman, 123
  Victor Young, 123
Whale, James (director)
  at *Bride of Frankenstein* scoring, **184**
When Harry Met Sally . . . , 254
  source music, 68
"When You Wish Upon a Star," 132, 136
"Where'd You Get That Girl," 223
Whispering Ghosts, 194
White Christmas, music tracks, 56–57
White Dawn, The, 287
Whiteman, Paul (band leader)
  conducting in *Rhapsody in Blue*, 171

Whiting, Leonard (actor), 228
Who Framed Roger Rabbit, 166
Who Is Hope Schuyler? 194
"Who's Afraid of the Big Bad Wolf?" 166
Wild Bunch, The, 60, 272
Wild North, The (1952)
  spotting and sound effects, 78
Wilde, Cornel (actor), 43
Wilder, Billy) director, 198
  The Lost Weekend, 17, 18
  Rózsa and, 189
  Sunset Boulevard role model, 6, 7
Wilkinson, Scott (reviewer), 71
Williams, Billy Dee (actor), 44
Williams, John (composer), 29, 30, 37, 217,
  243, 259, 265, 308–9
  adaptation, 69
  Aliens review, 152
  as role model, 13
  Born on the Fourth of July review, 152
  Boston Pops Orchestra, 309
  Close Encounters, 129
    concept, 130
    orchestration, 134–35
    playing the drama, 136
  comedy scoring, 167
  creative process, 29
  Empire of the Sun review, 150
  Home Alone, 50
  Home Alone 2, 92
  Indiana Jones, 99
  influence on film composers, 309
  Jaws, motif, 26
    spotting, 11
  "jeopardy" films, 78
  melodies and form, 88
  George Miller with, **51**
  music independent of score, 87
  Alfred Newman's conducting, 53
  playing the drama, 80
  recordings, 229
  Reivers, The, 309
  role models, 6
  sound effects, 78
  Steven Spielberg and, 13, 196
  Star Wars, 19, 99, 309
    Oscar acceptance (1977), **219**
  tempo and pulse, 74
  themes, 73
  typecasting, 198
  work methods, 29
  working with filmmakers, 201
Williams, Patrick (composer), 260, 309
  Swing Shift, 20
Willis, Bruce (actor), 18
Wilson, Dooley (pianist), 69
Wilson, Mortimer (composer)
  Thief of Bagdad (1924), 161
Wilson, Stanley (Universal mus. dir.),
  190
  music department in sixties, 243
Wind and the Lion, The, 130
"Windmills of Your Mind, The," 223
Wing, Carol (songwriter/singer), 131
Winkler, Max, cue sheets, 156
Winters, Shelley (actress), 64
Wise, Robert (director)
  Citizen Kane changes, 52
Witches of Eastwick, 51

With a Song in My Heart, 223
Witness, 259
Wizard of Oz, The, record album, 227
Wolcott, Charles (vocal arranger)
  MGM staff meeting, **180**
Wolpin, Ed (studio exec.), 224
Woman to Woman, 163
Woman's Face, A, prerecording, 43
Wonder, Stevie (songwriter), 310
  Jungle Fever songs ineligible, 212
Woodbury, Al (orchestrator), 217
Woodbury, Jean (music librarian), 217
Woodstock, 60
Working Girl, record sales, 232
Working with filmmakers
  afraid of the music, 203
  John Barry and Sidney Pollack, 18
  Elmer Bernstein
    and Cecil B. DeMille, 192, 202–3
    and John Landis, 167
    and Fred Zinnemann, 15
  Breil and Griffith (*Birth of a Nation*), 160
  Churchill/Morey and Walt Disney, 166
  Sandy De Crescent, 203
  demonstrating the score, 30
  the director, 201
  documentaries, 168
  during playbacks, 55
  Randy Edelman and Alan Parker, 62
  "funky flamenco," 14
  film editing changes, 5
  Jerry Goldsmith, and Joe Dante, 9
    and Steven Spielberg, 13
  Bernard Herrmann
    and William Dieterle, 202
    and Hitchcock, 15, 83, 202
    and Orson Welles, 5, 202
  High Noon, 201
  Hitchcock's sound notes, 57
  Lee Holdridge, and Stan Dragoti, 15
    and Ron Howard, 14
  James Horner describes directors, 13
  Maurice Jarre, 14
  M. Kamen, on *Lethal Weapon* series, 19
  Bronislau Kaper and Al Lewin, 60
  Ennio Morricone and De Palma, **144**
  A. Newman and Charles Chaplin, 48
  David Newman and Norman Jewison, 20
  Randy Newman and Penny Marshall, 12
  Thomas Newman and Paul Brickman, 62
  Basil Poledouris and Paul Verhoeven, 18
  André Previn and Arthur Jacobs, 202
  David Raksin, 201
    Raksin and William Wyler, 63
  J.A.C. Redford (*Oliver & Company*), 166
  Miklós Rózsa, dubbing *El Cid*, 61
    Charles Brackett and, 17, 18
    Hitchcock and *Spellbound*, 104
  John Schlesinger at scoring, 51
  temp tracks, 7–9
  Dimitri Tiomkin, 201
    Frank Capra and, 201
    Stanley Kramer and, 201
    David O. Selznik and, 15
    John Wayne and, 202
  Franz Waxman and George Stevens, 64
    and Billy Wilder, 6
  John Williams
    Brian De Palma and, 11

Working with filmakers *(cont'd)*
  John Williams *(cont'd)*
    Alfred Hitchcock and, 11
    George Lucas and, 6, 19
    George Miller and, **51**
    Steven Spielberg and, 11, 13, 129
    Victor Young and DeMille, 191–92
    Hans Zimmer and Ridley Scott, 51
    working together, 32–33
World Apart, 255
World Without End, 258
Wright, Rayburn (composer/educator), 283
Wuthering Heights, 70, 260
Wyler, William (director), 63
  no violins acceptable in 1972, 244

Yakuza, The, 277
"Yankee Doodle," 166
  DeMille favorite, 191
Young Frankenstein (1974), 60, 290
  short cues, 53

Young Mr. Lincoln, 260
Young, Christopher (composer), 310
  Bat 21 CD, 229
  role models, 6
Young, Victor 116, 215, 257–58, **310–11**
  Around the World in 80 Days album, 232
  best melody writer, 311
  concept, 71
  June Edgerton describes, 311
  Golden Earrings album, 227
    John Hammell describes, 311
  played "Yankee Doodle," 310
  orchestration for, 36
  Rózsa describes, 189
  scoring session (Paramount, 1936), **185**
  sketches, 36
  songs, 311
  themes, 73
  timings always short or long, 193
  took too much work, 193
  vaudeville, 311

  violin, 311
  why work in film music? 310
  Wizard of Oz album, 227
  work with DeMille, 191

Zamecnik, J. S. (composer), 157
Zanuck, Darryl (writer/producer), 175
Zeffirelli, Franco (director), **228**
Zemeckis, Robert (director), 250
Zimbalist, Sam (producer), 57
Zimmer, Hans (composer), 5, **311**
  changes, 63
  electronic demos, 51
  getting started, 255
  harmony, 74, 75
  role model, 6
  typecasting, 198
Zinnemann, Fred (director), 192
  Five Days One Summer notes, 15–16
  Waxman's schedule, 193
Zither, 19